Mark Keown's New Testament introduction sorts through a myriad of New Testament issues and themes, giving readers a solid acquaintance with the views and ideas this text raises and the background to its construction. The options are presented and analyzed with care, making it a worthy guide to these crucial first five books of the New Testament.

—Darrell Bock
Executive Director for Cultural Engagement, Howard G. Hendricks Center for Christian Leadership and Cultural Engagement,
Senior Research Professor of New Testament Studies,
Dallas Theological Seminary

We are living at a time when students enter learning with questions: *Why? When? How? Show me!* Mark Keown's *Discovering the New Testament* (volume 1) is a detailed and text-based approach to the Bible. It is a book that allows students an excellent opportunity to ask their questions and have them answered.

—Sarah Harris
New Testament Lecturer,
Carey Baptist College

This lucid and illuminating *Introduction* is everything one would want in a book that aims to help us to read the New Testament. It gives a clear guide to historical setting, to methods of interpretation, and to key theological issues. It also shows us how the centre of the New Testament is Jesus Christ and how the New Testament needs to be read in the light of Christ. All those who read this *Introduction* will be grateful to Mark Keown for this accessible and engaging book.

—Paul Trebilco
Professor of New Testament, Department of Theology and Religion,
University of Otago

DISCOVERING
the NEW TESTAMENT

*An Introduction to Its Background,
Theology, and Themes*

DISCOVERING *the* NEW TESTAMENT

An Introduction to Its Background, Theology, and Themes

VOLUME I

———

THE GOSPELS & ACTS

MARK J. KEOWN

LEXHAM PRESS

Discovering the New Testament: An Introduction to Its Background, Theology, and Themes

Volume 1: The Gospels & Acts

Copyright 2018 Mark J. Keown

Lexham Press, 1313 Commercial St., Bellingham, WA 98225
LexhamPress.com

All rights reserved. You may use brief quotations from this resource in presentations, articles, and books. For all other uses, please write Lexham Press for permission. Email us at permissions@lexhampress.com.

Unless otherwise noted, Scripture quotations are from ESV® Bible (The Holy Bible, English Standard Version®), copyright 2001 by Crossway Bibles, a publishing ministry of Good News Publishers. Used by permission. All rights reserved.

Scripture quotations marked (HCSB) are from the Holman Christian Standard Bible®, Copyright © 1999, 2000, 2002, 2003, 2009 by Holman Bible Publishers. Used by permission. Holman Christian Standard Bible®, Holman CSB®, and HCSB® are federally registered trademarks of Holman Bible Publishers.

Scripture quotations marked (KJV) are from the King James Version. Public domain.

Scripture quotations marked (NET) are from the NET Bible ® copyright 1996-2006 by Biblical Studies Press, L.L.C. All rights reserved.

Scripture quotations marked (NIV) are from the Holy Bible, NEW INTERNATIONAL VERSION®. Copyright © 1973, 1978, 1984, 2011 by Biblica, Inc. Used by permission. All rights reserved worldwide.

Print ISBN 9781683592327
Digital ISBN 9781683592334

Lexham Editorial: Derek R. Brown, Karen Engle, Sarah Awa
Cover Design: Brittany Schrock
Typesetting: Abigail Stocker

CONTENTS

PREFACE	xiii
ABBREVIATIONS	xv

CHAPTER 1: General Introduction ... 1
   Christ the Center ... 1
   What is the New Testament? ... 2
   The New Testament as a Library of Books ... 2
   Dating New Testament Documents ... 4
   The Formation of the New Testament ... 5
   The New Testament in the Narrative of Scripture ... 9
   Reading the New Testament ... 10
   Questions to Consider ... 13

CHAPTER 2: The Jewish Context of the New Testament ... 14
   1. The Intertestamental Period (Second Temple Judaism) ... 14
   2. Geographic Features ... 15
   3. Population ... 16
   4. Socioeconomic Conditions ... 18
   5. Language ... 18
   6. Cultural Influences ... 19
   An Occupied Nation ... 20
   A Nation Under Roman Rule ... 25
   Judaism in New Testament Times ... 33
   The Literature of Judaism ... 41
   Important Jewish Parties and Features ... 43
   Other Features of Life in Israel ... 51

Questions to Consider	56

Chapter 3: The Greco-Roman Context of the New Testament — 57

Hellenism	57
The City	58
Social Institutions	60
Greek Religion	63
Roman Religion	70
The "Mystery" Religions	76
Paul and Greco-Roman Religion	77
Philosophy	80
Travel in the Roman World	86
Social Stratification	88
Patronage	92
Additional Features of Greco-Roman Society	96
Questions to Consider	98

Chapter 4: Understanding Critical Methodologies — 99

Key Terms	100
Textual Criticism	100
Historical Criticism	101
History of Religions (*Religionsgeschichte Schule*)	102
Source Criticism	103
Form Criticism	103
Redaction Criticism	104
Rhetorical Criticism	105
Narrative Criticism	106
The Quest for the Historical Jesus	107
Questions to Consider	109

Chapter 5: The Synoptic Gospels — 110

No Relationship	110
An Oral Ur-Gospel	112
An Aramaic Proto-Gospel	113
The Augustinian or Griesbach Hypothesis	114
Markan Priority, Q, and the Two- or Four-Source Hypothesis	115
Farrer or Farrer-Goulder Hypothesis	117

Wilke Hypothesis	118
Additional Possibilities	119
Conclusion	121
Questions to Consider	127
CHAPTER 6: Mark's Gospel	**128**
The Authorship of Mark's Gospel	128
The Date of Mark's Gospel	136
The Provenance of Mark's Gospel	139
The Setting for Mark's Gospel	140
The Audience of Mark's Gospel	141
The Sources for Mark's Gospel	142
Textual Issues of Mark's Gospel	143
The Context of Mark's Gospel	149
The Structure of Mark's Gospel	152
The Arrangement of Mark's Gospel	153
Theological Themes of Mark's Gospel	160
Questions to Consider	179
CHAPTER 7: Matthew's Gospel	**181**
Who Was Matthew?	186
The Date of Matthew's Gospel	189
The Provenance of Matthew's Gospel	193
The Structure of Matthew's Gospel	195
The Purpose of Matthew's Gospel	199
Similarities and Differences to Mark	200
Questions to Consider	214
CHAPTER 8: Luke's Gospel	**215**
The Authorship of Luke	216
The Provenance of Luke's Gospel	224
The Date of Luke's Gospel	225
The Recipients of Luke's Gospel	231
The Composition of Luke's Gospel	233
The Structure of Luke's Gospel	237
The Text of Luke	241
Key Emphases in Luke's Account	241
Questions to Consider	259

CHAPTER 9: John's Gospel	260
The Authorship of John	260
The Provenance of John's Gospel	270
The Date of John's Gospel	271
The Recipients of John's Gospel	272
The Text of John	274
The So-Called Johannine Community and Sources for John	275
The Relationship to the Synoptics	279
The Historicity of John	284
The Purpose of John	287
The Structure of John	288
Key Dimensions of John's Gospel	289
Conclusion	318
Questions to Consider	318
CHAPTER 10: The Acts of the Apostles	319
The Title	320
The Authorship of Acts	321
The Date of Acts	322
The Recipients of Acts	323
The Historicity of Acts	323
Emphases in Acts	330
The Text of Acts	332
Structure and Purpose of Acts	333
The First Church in Jerusalem	336
To the End of the Earth (Acts 13–28)	409
Questions to Consider	416
CHAPTER 11: The Kingdom of God	417
Terminology	416
Old Testament Antecedents	417
The Kingdom of God in Judaism	421
Jesus and the Kingdom of God	425
The Kingdom in the Redemptive Story	433
The Centrality of Christ to the Kingdom of God	434
The Subversive Nature of the Kingdom's Coming	435
The Centrality of the Kingdom in Jesus' Ministry	437
Dimensions of the Kingdom	438
Questions to Consider	457

Chapter 12: The Power of the Kingdom 460
    What Is a Miracle? 460
    Miracles in the Various Gospels 461
    Categories of Miracles 467
    Breakdown of Miracles in the Gospels 468
    Miracles of Healing, Deliverance, and Reanimation 469
    The Significance of the Miracles 485
    Conclusion 507
    Questions to Consider 510

Chapter 13: The Teaching of the Kingdom: Parables 511
    The Use of Parables Prior to Jesus 513
    Classification of Parables 513
    Characteristics of the Parables of Jesus 515
    Distribution of the Parables in the Gospels 518
    Allegory or Not? 522
    Additional Approaches to Parables 526
    The Triple Horizon of Parables 527
    The Purpose of the Parables 528
    The Genius of Parables 532
    Guidelines for Interpretation 534
    The Teaching of the Parables 538
    Parables and Theology 546
    Preaching and Parables Today 547
    Questions to Consider 548

Bibliography 549
Subject Index 565
Author Index 585
Ancient Texts Index 591

ILLUSTRATIONS

Figure 1: Map of Israel at the Time of Christ		17
Figure 2: The Roman Empire During the Reign of Augustus		24
Figure 3: Emperors in New Testament Times		25
Figure 4: Herod the Great's Family		29
Figure 5: Key Dates Concerning Rome		31
Figure 6: Roman and Greek Gods		71
Figure 7: Gospel Synopsis		111
Figure 8: Oral Ur-Gospel		113
Figure 9: Aramaic Proto-Gospel		114
Figure 10: Augustinian or Griesbach Hypothesis		115
Figure 11: Two-Source Hypothesis		116
Figure 12: Four-Source Hypothesis		117
Figure 13: Farrer Hypothesis		118
Figure 14: Wilke Hypothesis		119
Figure 15: Three-Source Hypothesis		120
Figure 16: Q + Papias Hypothesis		121
Figure 17: Greek Anthology Hypothesis		122
Figure 18: Eyewitness Hypothesis		125
Figure 19: Jesus' Ministry in Galilee		150
Figure 20: The Land of the Gospels		151
Figure 21: Diagrammatic Summary		154
Figure 22: The Seven Churches of Revelation		273
Figure 23: The Seven Outpourings in Acts		344
Figure 24: The Miracles of Jesus		466
Figure 25: The Parables of Jesus		522

PREFACE

This book has grown out of my teaching of New Testament Introduction courses at Laidlaw College in Auckland, New Zealand. Initially, what were notes for my courses have become this book, which is published in three parts. It is not a work that fully aligns with classic New Testament introductions or theology volumes but represents an approach to teaching the New Testament that incorporates elements of both, with a good degree of application to the contemporary church, particularly the dominant and popular evangelical and charismatic churches in New Zealand and some other European countries. As such, I have entitled it *Discovering the New Testament*. This first volume focuses on exploration of the Gospel and Acts. Subsequent volumes focus on discovering Paul (Vol. 2) and the other writings of the New Testament (Vol. 3).

In 1985 I became a devoted follower of Jesus. I was quickly directed to become an explorer, discovering God in and through the Bible. I fell in love with the New Testament. I had the privilege of studying the New Testament in ever greater depth as God led me on a journey of learning Greek, becoming a preacher and minister, writing a doctoral thesis, and as a New Testament lecturer. I have to say exploring the New Testament to discover what God has placed in its pages is one of the greatest things we can do. I encourage you to take up the challenge of being a lifelong explorer of the Bible.

This book is written from the perspective of historical-critical optimism and a hermeneutic of trust in the Scriptures as God's word. My hope in writing this material is that some are blessed and deepened in their faith and desire to serve our Savior and King, Jesus Christ our Lord. Shalom.

Mark J. Keown

ABBREVIATIONS

AB	Anchor Bible
ABD	Freedman, David Noel, Gary A. Herion, David F. Graf, John David Pleins, and Astrid B. Beck, eds. *The Anchor Yale Bible Dictionary*. New York: Doubleday, 1992.
AD	Anno Domini (Year of the Lord)
ANET	Pritchard, James Bennett, ed. *The Ancient Near Eastern Texts Relating to the Old Testament*. 3rd ed. with Supplement. Princeton: Princeton University Press, 1969.
ANZABS	Australia and New Zealand Association of Biblical Studies
AYB	Anchor Yale Bible
BC	Before Christ
BCNT	Black's New Testament Commentary
BDAG	Arndt, William, Frederick W. Danker, and Walter Bauer. *A Greek-English Lexicon of the New Testament and Other Early Christian Literature*. Chicago: University of Chicago Press, 2000.
BEB	Elwell, Walter A., and Barry J. Beitzel. *Baker Encyclopedia of the Bible*. Grand Rapids, MI: Baker Book House, 1988.
BECNT	Baker Exegetical Commentary on the New Testament
BJRL	*Bulletin of the John Rylands University Library of Manchester*

BT	*Bible Translator*
CBQ	*Catholic Biblical Quarterly*
Ch.	Chapter
CPNIVC	The College Press NIV Commentary
DBL Aramaic	Swanson, James. *Dictionary of Biblical Languages with Semantic Domains: Aramaic (Old Testament)*. Oak Harbor: Logos Research Systems, Inc., 1997.
DBL Greek	Swanson, James. *Dictionary of Biblical Languages with Semantic Domains: Greek (New Testament)*. Oak Harbor: Logos Research Systems, Inc., 1997.
DJG	Green, Joel B., Scot McKnight, and I. Howard Marshall, eds. *Dictionary of Jesus and the Gospels*. Downers Grove, IL: InterVarsity Press, 1992.
DJG (2)	Stanton, G. N., and N. Perrin. "Q." Edited by Joel B. Green, Jeannine K. Brown, and Nicholas Perrin. *Dictionary of Jesus and the Gospels, Second Edition*. Downers Grove, IL; Nottingham, England: IVP Academic; IVP, 2013.
DLNTD	Martin, Ralph P., and Peter H. Davids, eds. *Dictionary of the Later New Testament and Its Developments*. Downers Grove, IL: InterVarsity Press, 1997.
DNTB	Porter, Stanley E., and Craig A. Evans. *Dictionary of New Testament Background: A Compendium of Contemporary Biblical Scholarship*. Downers Grove, IL: InterVarsity Press, 2000.
DPL	Hawthorne, Gerald F., Ralph P. Martin, and Daniel G. Reid, eds. *Dictionary of Paul and His Letters*. Downers Grove, IL: InterVarsity Press, 1993.
EBC	The Expositors Bible Commentary
EDB	Freedman, David Noel, Allen C. Myers, and Astrid B. Beck. *Eerdmans Dictionary of the Bible*. Grand Rapids, MI: W.B. Eerdmans, 2000.
EDEJ	Collins, John J., and Daniel C. Harlow, eds. *The Eerdmans Dictionary of Early Judaism*. Grand Rapids, MI; Cambridge, U.K.: William B. Eerdmans Publishing Company, 2010.

EDNT	Balz, Horst Robert, and Gerhard Schneider. *Exegetical Dictionary of the New Testament*. Grand Rapids, MI: Eerdmans, 1990-93.
EEC	Evangelical Exegetical Commentary
esp.	especially
ExpTim	Expository Times
GNC	Good News Commentary
HIBD	Brand, Chad, Charles Draper, Archie England, Steve Bond, E. Ray Clendenen, Trent C. Butler, and Bill Latta, eds. *Holman Illustrated Bible Dictionary*. Nashville, TN: Holman Bible Publishers, 2003.
HNTC	Holman New Testament Commentary
HTR	*Harvard Theological Review*
HTS	*Harvard Theological Studies*
ICC	International Critical Commentary
ISBE	Bromiley, Geoffrey W., ed. *The International Standard Bible Encyclopedia, Revised*. Wm. B. Eerdmans, 1979-1988.
JBL	Journal of Biblical Literature
JSNT	*Journal for the Study of the New Testament*
LCL	The Loeb Classical Library
LSJ	Liddell, Henry George, Robert Scott, Henry Stuart Jones, and Roderick McKenzie. *A Greek-English Lexicon*. Oxford: Clarendon Press, 1996.
mod.	modern
mss	manuscripts
NA28	Aland, Kurt, Barbara Aland, Johannes Karavidopoulos, Carlo M. Martini, and Bruce M. Metzger. *Novum Testamentum Graece*. 28th Edition. Stuttgart: Deutsche Bibelgesellschaft, 2012.
NAC	New American Commentary
NBD	Wood, D. R. W., and I. Howard Marshall. *New Bible Dictionary*. Leicester, England; Downers Grove, IL: InterVarsity Press, 1996.
NCBC	New Century Bible Commentary
NICNT	New International Commentary on the New Testament
NIGTC	New International Greek Testament Commentary

NIVAC	The NIV Application Commentary
NovT	*Novum Testamentum*
NovTSup	Novum Testamentum Supplements
NTC	New Testament Commentary
ODCC	Cross, F. L., and Elizabeth A. Livingstone, eds. *The Oxford Dictionary of the Christian Church*. Oxford; New York: Oxford University Press, 2005.
par.	parallel
PBM	Paternoster Biblical Monographs
PCS	Pentecostal Commentary Series
PDBS	Patzia, Arthur G., and Anthony J. Petrotta. *Pocket Dictionary of Biblical Studies*. Downers Grove, IL: InterVarsity Press, 2002.
PDSNTG	DeMoss, Matthew S. *Pocket Dictionary for the Study of New Testament Greek*. Downers Grove, IL: InterVarsity Press, 2001.
PNTC	The Pillar New Testament Commentary.
PDTT	Grenz, Stanley, David Guretzki, and Cherith Fee Nordling. *Pocket Dictionary of Theological Terms*. Downers Grove, IL: InterVarsity Press, 1999.
SPCK	Society for Promoting Christian Knowledge
TBD	Elwell, Walter A., and Philip Wesley Comfort. *Tyndale Bible Dictionary*. Tyndale reference library. Wheaton, IL: Tyndale House Publishers, 2001.
TDNT	Kittel, Gerhard, Geoffrey W. Bromiley, and Gerhard Friedrich, eds. *Theological Dictionary of the New Testament*. Grand Rapids, MI: Eerdmans, 1964.
TNTC	Tyndale New Testament Commentaries
TynB	Tyndale Bulletin
UBCS	Understanding the Bible Commentary Series
v.	verse
vv.	verses
WBC	Word Biblical Commentary
WUNT	Wissenschaftliche Untersuchungen zum Neuen Testament

ZECNT	Zondervan Exegetical Commentary on the New Testament
ZNW	*Zeitschrift für die Neutestamentliche Wissenschaft*

GENERAL INTRODUCTION

CHRIST THE CENTER

The center of the Biblical narrative, God's story of salvation, is Christ. The story moves from God to creation, to fall, to Israel, with an ever-growing anticipation of a coming Messiah. The coming of Christ means we need to go back to the first parts of the story and reread them through the lens of his coming. We find that in so doing, some passages light up, clearly speaking of the Jesus who came (e.g., Ps 22; Isa 53; Dan 7:13–14). However, aside from a small remnant of disciples, Israel did not recognize this Jesus as Messiah because, although devoted readers of Scripture, they misread the sacred texts, most expecting a Davidic-warrior king who would smite the Romans and endorse Israel's supremacy, law, and story. The story then becomes dark and tragic for three days as this Messiah is killed as a fake and insurrectionist. The resurrection is the ultimate moment in the story, the climax of the narrative from which all else flows. He is risen! The letters of the New Testament then must also be read in the light of Christ, always pointing us to Christ and what he means for us, for the church, for life, and for everything! The Gospels then are central in that they take us directly to the account of Jesus' life. If we want to know Christ and the purposes of God, then the Gospels are the starting point. Acts and the letters that follow show us how the first followers understood this Christ. They show us how to live the "in Christ" life.

The purpose of this book is to do just that, enquiring into the richness of each part of the New Testament, its triune God, its message, the life it offers, and the wonderful hope it brings.

WHAT IS THE NEW TESTAMENT?

The word "testament" comes from the Latin *testamentum*, which translates the Greek *diathēkē*, meaning "covenant" or "contractual agreement." It refers to a legally binding agreement made with humanity by God through Jesus.[1] It calls to mind Jeremiah's vision of a "new covenant" in which God would write the law on the hearts of his people, they would know him, and their sins would be eradicated (Jer 31:31-34). In the New Testament, both Paul and Luke speak of "a new covenant in my blood" in regards to the Lord's Supper, and through Jesus' death, God has put this agreement in place. The early Christians recognized in the books of the New Testament those writings that faithfully represented this new covenant. Through these books God speaks, we respond, and we enter covenantal relationship with God.

THE NEW TESTAMENT AS A LIBRARY OF BOOKS

The New Testament is essentially a collection of writings that have become one book.[2] There are four categories, or genres, of writings in the New Testament: gospels, Acts, letters, and Revelation. The first four books of the New Testament are "gospels" (*euangelion*, "good news"), which narrate the story of Jesus (Matthew, Mark, Luke, John). These four portraits of Jesus, likely fashioned on the ancient *Bios* (biography) genre,[3] provide four windows into Jesus' life, ministry, and lasting impact.[4] The Synoptic

---

1. Further on "Testament," see K. L. Eades, "Testament," in *ISBE* 4:796-97.
2. It is also called the "Second" Testament in relation to the "First Testament."
3. On ancient Greek biographies (*Bios*), see R. A. Burridge, "Biography, Ancient," in *DNTB* 167-70.
4. Many other gospels have been discovered, some of which have become of interest to popular culture (e.g., the Gospel of Thomas, Gospel of Mary Magdalene, Gospel of Judas, Gospel of Peter, Gospel of Matthias, etc.). These are almost certainly second century ad and later gospels falsely written in the name of a famous early Christian (pseudonymous) reflecting gnostic thought. They are very unreliable witnesses to the historical Jesus and reflect more the theology of those who compiled them. See further, Richard J. Bauckham, "Gospels (Apocryphal)," in *DJG* 286-91, discussing the Gospel of Thomas (he dates it at the end of the first century), the Gospel of Peter (from before the middle of the second century), Papyrus Fragments of Unknown Gospels (*P. Oxy.* 840; *P. Egerton* 2; *Oxy P.* 1224; Fayyum Fragment; Strasbourg Coptic Fragment), Jewish Christian gospels (*Gospel of the Hebrews*; *Gospel of the Nazarenes*; *Gospel of the Ebionites*), the Gospel of the Egyptians, the *Secret Gospel of Mark*, birth and infancy gospels (*Protoevangelium of James*; *Infancy Narrative of Thomas*), Gospel of

Gospels—Matthew, Mark, and Luke—are all similar in structure and seem to share common material.[5] The Gospel of John, by comparison, has a distinctly more theological tone. Yet each of the four Gospels of the New Testament has the same basic portrayal of Jesus as an itinerant who preached and performed miracles; was arrested, tried, and sentenced to death; and was crucified, rose from the dead, and appeared to his followers.

After the Gospels comes the Acts of the Apostles, which is part two of the story told in Luke's Gospel. It is a first-century historical document narrating the story of the expansion of the church because of the mission and work of the Spirit through Christ's followers. The geographical, three-part shape of Acts is an explication of Acts 1:8: (1) the development of the Jerusalem church (Acts 1-8:4); (2) the missional expansion of the church into Judea, Samaria, and the beginning of its impact in the Gentile world, particularly by members of the Jerusalem church and especially Peter (Acts 8-12); (3) the extension of the faith to "the ends of the earth," primarily focusing on the ministries of Paul and others (Acts 13-28).

The remainder of the New Testament is made up of letters to churches and individuals.[6] These include letters written by the apostle Paul to various churches (Romans, 1 and 2 Corinthians, Ephesians, Galatians, Philippians, Colossians, 1 and 2 Thessalonians) and individual coworkers (1 and 2 Timothy, Titus, Philemon).[7] Hebrews, which some in the early church ascribed to Paul, lacks any name and so is written by an unknown author. It was written to Jewish Christians under pressure to return to Judaism.[8] James is a letter by Jesus' brother to Christian Jews in the diaspora.[9] There are two letters ascribed to the apostle Peter, written to churches

---

Nicodemus, and post-resurrection revelations. Others include the *Gospel of Truth*, the *Gospel of Philip*, the Coptic *Gospel of the Egyptians*, the *Gospel of Eve*, and the *Gospel of Mary Magdalene*.

5. Called Synoptic because they can be placed alongside one another in a Synopsis—i.e., viewed simultaneously because they contain common material (see Patzia and Petrotta, *PDBS* 110).

6. There is great debate about whether Paul wrote 1-2 Timothy and Titus and about whether Peter wrote 2 Peter. There is some debate over whether Paul wrote Ephesians, Colossians, and 2 Thessalonians.

7. Note in a number of these books there are coauthors/cosenders (e.g., 1 Cor 1:1, 2 Cor 1:1) or secretaries (e.g., Tertius [Rom 16:22]).

8. Most popular candidates as authors are Apollos and Barnabas, but this is speculation.

9. The "diaspora" refers to the significant number of Jews who were scattered in the gentile world beyond Israel.

in west Asia Minor (modern Turkey). In addition, we find three shorter letters written to churches and individuals that are associated with John (1, 2, and 3 John). There is also another letter supposedly written by another of Jesus' brothers, Jude.[10] Collectively, the non-Pauline letters of the New Testament are often called the General or Catholic Letters.

Finally, the book of Revelation is written as a letter but also contains prophecy. However, Revelation is likely an early example of Christian apocalyptic writing. Apocalyptic writings are found in the period 200 BC to AD 200, and they feature good versus evil, signs, war, apocalyptic woes of wrath, visions, symbolism, and imagery. They are notoriously difficult to interpret but are usually written to comfort God's suffering people giving hope of God's ultimate victory over the forces of darkness. Revelation addresses the people of God toward the end of the first century in seven of the churches of Asia Minor who are suffering under persecution. It speaks of the culmination of world events.[11]

DATING NEW TESTAMENT DOCUMENTS

The dating of the various books is a matter of great controversy and debate. However, we can generally date them as follows:

ca. 6–4 BC	The birth of Christ
AD 30/33	The death and resurrection of Jesus
AD 48–67	The letters of Paul
AD 55–75	The Gospel of Mark
AD 60s–80s	The Gospels of Matthew and Luke[12]
Late AD 60s–80s	The Gospel of John[13]
AD 60s–90s	The General Epistles and Revelation[14]

---

10. Hebrews, James, Peter's letters, John's letters and Jude are also called "Catholic Epistles" or "General Epistles."

11. Apocalyptic literature is a type of literature which is full of vivid symbolism, addresses a people in need of hope, has a strong sense of good and evil, judgment and reward, and speaks of the present and the future (see later Revelation). The word is drawn from the Greek *apocalypsis* indicating something unveiled (i.e., a vision of the hidden future).

12. Some date these later in the 80s; we will discuss this as we come to these books.

13. Most place John in the 80s but a case can be made for the 60s.

14. Some would argue James was written earlier; similarly, Hebrews.

THE FORMATION OF THE NEW TESTAMENT

Initially, Christians did not have their own Scriptures. The written documents they had were the Hebrew Scriptures, the Old Testament—particularly in Greek translation (the Septuagint or LXX), which was translated from Hebrew several centuries before Christ. This includes a wider range of texts than the Protestant Old Testament, including books such as Sirach, the Maccabees, and others from the Apocrypha. Today, these books are included in Catholic Bibles. We can see the influence of the LXX in that the New Testament, which was written mainly to gentile believers, is full of quotes, allusions, and echoes from the Greek Old Testament. It is believed that the teachings of Christ and the apostles were initially retained orally, along with fragments of written tradition. It was only as time passed after Christ's resurrection that the individual documents were formed into collections based on eyewitness testimony, particularly towards the time of the death of key figures such as Peter, Paul, and John.

A PERIOD OF ORAL AND FRAGMENTED WRITTEN TRANSMISSION

Most scholars agree that Paul's letters are the earliest New Testament documents. They typically date them to around AD 48-50, though some scholars argue James is earlier (46-48). Scholars are divided whether Galatians was written around 48 or in the mid-50s. If Galatians is dated later, 1 Thessalonians would be Paul's first letter, in AD 50. The earliest Gospel is almost certainly Mark, formed somewhere between AD 55-75, with most scholars placing it in the mid- to late 60s. This means a period of twenty to thirty years elapsed from the time of Jesus' death and resurrection to the writing of the first Gospel. It is believed that in this preliterary and pre-printing press time, in common with other cultures of the ancient world, Christians passed on their stories through oral tradition. Scholars also argue it is probable that some of the accounts were written down, perhaps in Aramaic, and then later translated into Greek. There have been attempts to prove that Mark was originally an Aramaic document. Certainly, this is possible with the number of Aramaic phrases that remain in the text (see Mark 7:34; 14:36; 15:34) and Aramaisms (Greek phrases which are dependent on Aramaic phraseology). However, there is no substantial evidence for this.

This early oral and fragmented written transmission leads some to argue against the authenticity and certitude of the accounts. This is especially true of form critics, who believe that little in the Gospels is reliable because the stories were augmented and mythologized over time in the early church.[15] However, oral and fragmented transmission does not necessarily mean the accounts are unreliable. Jesus, as a rabbinic teacher, would undoubtedly have taught the same stories and sayings repeatedly and expected his intimate group of followers to remember them. In addition, studies of oral transmission show an amazing accuracy in the passing on of material. Key people (apostles, prophets, priests, etc.) were charged with ensuring the accurate retelling of the stories. In recent times, the work of Richard Bauckham has shown that the Gospels demonstrate evidence of the use of eyewitnesses—that is, the evangelists gathered data directly from those who were there. This gives us great confidence that the stories were transmitted accurately as these eyewitnesses recalled them.[16]

THE WRITING OF THE ORIGINAL DOCUMENTS

The documents themselves each emerged from a distinct time and place. They were written by a person (or people) to a person or group with a specific intention in mind. The study of the initial authorship of the New Testament documents is quite technical, especially where the text itself does not tell us who wrote it. Even where there is a name attached to the document, the question of authorship can remain complex, as people note differences in style and theology that lead some scholars to suggest alternative authors. When we read the New Testament, we must be aware of the

---

15. Form Criticism is "an interpretive approach that seeks to uncover the oral tradition that is embedded in the written texts we now possess and to classify them into certain categories or 'forms' (German *Formgeschichte*, 'history of forms'). These literary forms (laments, hymns, etc.) are thought to have had a particular function in the *Sitz im Leben* ('setting in life') in which they originated ... In NT studies, form-critical scholars such as Martin Dibelius, Rudolf Bultmann and Vincent Taylor classified Jesus' sayings into categories such as paradigms, legends, parables, miracle stories and pronouncement stories. Form criticism is helpful in identifying the different forms of literature (see genre) and the typical elements of those forms (thus highlighting the different ways authors use those forms), but it is more speculative and less successful in establishing the life setting of the forms" (see "Form Criticism," in Patzia and Petrotta, *PDBS* 47).

16. See R. J. Bauckham, *Jesus and the Eyewitnesses: The Gospels as Eyewitness Testimony* (Grand Rapids, MI: Eerdmans, 2006). You can also see this in Luke 1:2, where Luke tells his readers that he consulted eyewitnesses in the compilation of his Gospel and his second work, Acts.

original context of the writing as we seek to interpret the text and apply its teaching to today. We must also remember that, while these accounts are inspired and so have a divine side to them, they are also human documents whereby the account of Jesus and the early church is shaped by the purposes of the writer. The Spirit worked in people as they wrote in very real, human language, concepts, and within a historical and social setting. So, for example, Luke sets out in his Gospel with the intention of bringing clarity to a Greek aristocrat, Theophilus (Luke 1:3; Acts 1:1). He organizes his material around the themes of salvation and mission, which results in a second part to the story that he presents in the book of Acts: the story of the expansion of this salvation and mission to the "ends of the earth," Rome.

THE FORMATION OF THE CANON

The process of bringing the documents together began early. The Gospels were apparently accepted as authoritative by the end of the second century. This process was catalyzed by early thinkers like Marcion, who rejected all but Luke and a selection of letters, and the gnostics,[17] who produced a range of spurious pseudonymous[18] gospels. By the end of the second century, the

---

17. On Gnosticism see Zachary G. Smith, "Gnosticism," *LBD*, which describes Gnosticism as "a variety of second-century ad religions whose participants believed that people could only be saved through revealed knowledge, or γνῶσις (*gnōsis*). Gnostics also held a negative view of the physical or material world. Early church fathers, such as Irenaeus, deemed Gnosticism heretical." The Nag Hammadi library has given insight into the diverse movement. Common beliefs include: (1) God is utterly transcendent and beyond human comprehension; (2) a dualistic view of reality, physical and spiritual, the world created by a lower deity, the demiurge. The human soul is divine, trapped in the material world of the body, which is hated. The soul is freed by knowledge and salvation; (3) gnosis through special revelation brings salvation and eventually, when all are released to the divine realm, the world will be destroyed; (4) highly complex myths. New Testament figures seen as gnostic in early church writings (esp. Irenaeus) include Simon Magus (Acts 8), Hymenaeus and Philetus (2 Tim 2:20), the Nicolaitans of Rev 2, and 1–3 John is seen by earlier scholars as a response to a proto-Gnosticism. See also Grenz, et al., *PDTT*, 56, which defines Gnosticism as "an early Greek religious movement of broad proportions that was particularly influential in the second-century church. Many biblical interpreters see in certain NT documents (such as 1 John) the attempt to answer or refute Gnostic teaching. ... Gnostics believed that devotees had gained a special kind of spiritual enlightenment, through which they had attained a secret or higher level of knowledge not accessible to the uninitiated. Gnostics also tended to emphasize the spiritual realm over the material, often claiming that the material realm is evil and hence to be escaped."

18. A pseudonymous document is falsely written in the name of another person to give it authority. Some believe 1–2 Timothy and Titus (the Pastoral Epistles) are pseudonymous works. While it was common for pseudonymous works to be written in the Jewish and Greco-Roman worlds, there is strong evidence that the early church rejected any work that was

unanimous voice of the church accepted the authority of the four Gospels. The Muratorian Canon, which most date to AD 170-200,[19] also includes Acts, Paul's letters, Jude, 1-2 John, and Revelation. It excludes Hebrews, James, 3 John, and 1-2 Peter. Surprisingly, it accepts the Wisdom of Solomon and the Apocalypse of Peter; however, the acceptance of these documents was not general. In the early fourth century, Eusebius, a church historian, notes that the Gospels, Acts, fourteen letters of Paul (including Hebrews), 1 John, 1 Peter, and perhaps Revelation were undisputed ("acknowledged"). He lists the following as disputed: James, Jude, 2 Peter, 2-3 John, the Acts of Paul, the Shepherd of Hermas, the Apocalypse of Peter, the Epistle of Barnabas, the Didache, perhaps Revelation, and the now-lost Gospel of the Hebrews. Among the writings rejected are the gospels of Peter, Thomas, and Matthias, along with the Acts of Andrew and John.[20]

It appears then that by the middle of the third century, the canon was forming, and various lists can be found among the church fathers that indicate which documents they viewed as canonical. By the fourth and fifth centuries, the church settled on the New Testament canon in the form of the twenty-seven books we have today.[21]

THE TEXT OF THE DOCUMENTS

When we read a Bible in our native tongue today, we are reading a translation or paraphrase of the original. There are various types of translation. Some seek to be literal to the text (e.g., NASB, ESV); others seek to be as literal as possible to the text while retaining a level of interpretation and quality of writing that makes the meaning more attainable to the reader

---

pseudonymous. See Thomas D. Lea and Hayne P. Griffin, 1, 2 *Timothy, Titus*, NAC 34 (Nashville: Broadman & Holman Publishers), 37-39; "Pseudonymity," in *HIBD* 1346-47.

19. On the Muratorian Canon or Fragment, see Benjamin Laird, "Muratorian Fragment," *LBD*. It is the oldest NT canon in existence. It was discovered by Ludovico Antonio Muratori in Milan and is a Latin manuscript from the seventh to eighth century. It contains and incomplete eighty-five-line description of the NT writings, including some content and background. While a few scholars date it in the fourth century, most date it ad 170-200. Others refute this, seeing it as fourth century. Luke and John are mentioned; references to Mark and Matthew are lost. Also important is that the writer sees Luke as a traveling companion of Paul and identifies thirteen Pauline letters including the Pastorals but notes two that were circulating that were spurious—to the Laodiceans and Alexandrians. It also notes that Revelation's authority was disputed.

20. H. Y. Gamble, "Canon (New Testament)," in *ABD* 1:856.

21. Gamble, "Canon," 1.852-58.

(e.g., NIV, NRSV, NKJV, NET BIBLE). Some versions are paraphrases that try to make the text easy to read; these are more prepared to take liberties with the original text (e.g., The Message, Living Bible, GNB). This does not rule out their use, as they have an important place in making the message of the Scriptures understood. However, those who wish to study the text closely and glean its original meaning need to use a more literal translation.

Originally all the documents were written in Koine ("common dialect") Greek.[22] Koine Greek was the dominant language across the Hellenized world—from the time of Alexander over three hundred years before Christ (the lingua franca) through and beyond the time of Christ. It was also the main language of the Roman Empire, with Latin used in an official capacity. The writing of the New Testament in Greek points to the dominance of Greek culture at the time. It also indicates the missiological nature of the documents—most of the writings of the New Testament date around the time at which the gospel was extending beyond Israel into the Greek world. They are borne out of their mission to enhance God's mission to the whole world.

THE NEW TESTAMENT IN THE NARRATIVE OF SCRIPTURE

As noted above, the New Testament can only really be read and understood with a good understanding of the Old Testament. The events of the New Testament continue God's work of salvation in history. The first part of the New Testament speaks of God's decisive act to save humanity and his world, the sending of his Son, Jesus. Through his life and ministry, he revealed God to the world. Through his death and resurrection, he saved those who would believe. His life also provides the essential shape of the human ideal: cruciform living—humility, service, selflessness, sacrifice, suffering, love, and even death. God now exercises his reign through Jesus. Jesus is the culmination of Israel's hopes and story—the great high priest, the ultimate sacrifice for sin, the temple, the place of Sabbath rest, the final and ultimate Word of God.

---

22. Introduced by the armies of Alexander the Great and common even among Jews in Israel at the time of Christ. See G. Hadjiantoniou, *Learning the Basics of New Testament Greek* (Chattanooga, TN: AMG Publishers, 1998), 3.

So, when considering Jesus, the Old Testament speaks of God's promise, and the New Testament proclaims the fulfillment of his word. This is reflected in Jesus' Jewish heritage and his lineage, which is traced through the Old Testament (Matt 1:1-16; Luke 3:23-38). The New Testament quotes an enormous number of Old Testament passages, often with notes of prophetic fulfillment of the Old Testament text in Jesus' life and ministry. There are also many more allusions and echoes[23] where the text of the Old Testament is not cited but the New Testament writer has an Old Testament text or passage in mind. The early church was initially Jewish, and the Old Testament presents the history of the Jewish nation and the culture and religion of Israel. Similarly, the God of the New Testament is the God of the Old Testament more fully revealed. Hence, becoming a competent student of the New Testament requires study of the Old Testament. Other Jewish writings from the period between the Old Testament and New Testament are also of great importance—the writings of the intertestamental period or, as it is more commonly described today, Second Temple Judaism.[24]

READING THE NEW TESTAMENT

Many people who read the Scriptures only do so in a simple way. They read the text from their own historical and cultural context, reflect on it devotionally, and apply it rather directly to their lives. Now, this is not all bad; God does want us to read his text and apply it. Many great Christians have lived this way, and many go on living like this today. However, as with all our Christian lives as we grow in maturity, we can go deeper in the way we read the Scriptures. We can become more adept with the word and to go and teach it to others as the Lord would want (e.g., Matt 28:18-20).[25] As God's workers, we want to handle well the word of truth (2 Tim 2:15).

---

23. Contemporary scholars use the three terms in relation to Old Testament passages mentioned in the New Testament: (1) citation (or quotation)—direct quotes; (2) allusion: an indirect, imprecise or passing reference where there is no direct quote, but an Old Testament passage is clearly in mind; (3) echo: sometimes a writer uses this interchangeably with allusion. At other times, it speaks of a use of the Old Testament that is faint or debated. This is the art of intertextuality, which explores those places where a text uses an earlier text (a subtext).

24. "Second Temple" refers to Israel after the reconstruction of the Jerusalem temple when the exiles returned from Babylon (521-516 bc). The period runs until the destruction of the temple in ad 70.

25. In the Great Commission in Matt 28:18-20 the disciples are told to "make disciples ... teaching them to observe all that I have commanded you." Clearly, for Matthew, this would

As such, we see that there is more to reading the Bible than reading it from our own perspective thousands of years later and directly applying it to our lives. Rather, we should adopt a much more nuanced method of interpretation. In the most basic terms, many today would endorse an approach like this:

1. **Read it in context**: The first step is to understand the text in its original context. That is, we don't just read it; we study it, and we seek to understand what it meant back when it was first written. This means working out what the author meant, what the words mean, what they meant to the first hearers, what was going on in the historical and social background of the text. The goal is to understand what the text meant when it was written to those who wrote it and read it. Care also needs to be taken not to interpret one part of Scripture against another without careful thought. All the New Testament has reference to the Old Testament, and especially where there is a quote, an allusion, or an echo to the Old Testament, we should read the relevant Old Testament passage and consider how it is used. John should be first interpreted against John's other writings (his letters and Revelation) and the obvious connections he makes, rather than reading John through the eyes of Paul. Similarly, Luke should be read in relation primarily to the author's other New Testament writing, Acts. We should not read Paul's theology into it. Nor should we read our church's religious traditions back in; rather, we should allow our traditions to come under the spotlight of Scripture. Matthew should not be read as if Paul wrote it, as if Matthew holds a Pauline theology. Rather, we read each author well. One way of understanding this is to ask, "What is the story behind a particular text?" That is, what is going on? How does it fit into the big story? Here the work of biblical scholars gives us a foundation for reading.

---

involve teaching them the Gospel of Matthew. We can broaden this out to the canon, which the whole church, led by the Spirit, agreed upon. See also 1 Tim 3:16–17; Rom 15:4.

2. **Draw the meaning from the text in context**: We should then seek the meaning that the text would have had for its first readers. The principles and lessons drawn from the story of the text are what is applied, not the text itself. Here the work of theologians is exceedingly helpful, as they seek to bring together meaning from the wide range of biblical texts and apply it.

3. **Reading our world**: When we apply the lessons and meaning of the text to today's world, we need to understand the world today just as deeply as we understand the text. We realize that the world today is hugely different from the worlds of the Old Testament and New Testament. We need to know the differences and our own situation. Here, sociological, worldview, and culture studies are important.

4. **Careful application**: Next, we apply what we have learned from the text to the world. In this way, we are careful not to make the Bible say what it does not say or falsely apply it and come up with strange results.

5. **A nonlinear process**: There is a constant movement between these four dimensions as we study the word. It is, as Grant Osborne suggests, a spiral—we move back and forth between these elements of interpretation.[26] Sometimes we start with the world and a question; at other times, we start with the text and a question. We all bring our own assumptions to the text based on our experience in life and faith, and these sometimes need sorting out. Being exposed to other perspectives on Scripture should not daunt us but excite us and make us more devoted to the search for God's truth in the text.

---

26. See Grant Osborne, *The Hermeneutical Spiral: A Comprehensive Introduction to Biblical Interpretation* (Downers Grove: IVP Academic, 2006). See also W. W. Klein, C. Blomberg, R. L. Hubbard, Jr., *Introduction to Biblical Interpretation* (Revised Edition; Nashville: Nelson, 1993, 2004); V. P. Long; T. Longman III, R. A. Muller, V. S. Poythress, M. Silva, *Foundations of Contemporary Interpretation: Six Volumes in One* (Leicester: IVP, 1996).

QUESTIONS TO CONSIDER

- How would you summarize the importance and message of the New Testament in one or two short sentences?

- How would you describe the relationship of the New Testament to the Old Testament?

- What questions does the concept of one story bring to your mind?

- How do you feel about the approach to Scripture mentioned here? What questions does it raise? Does it make sense?

THE JEWISH CONTEXT OF THE NEW TESTAMENT

CHAPTER 2

The New Testament accounts fall between 6 BC–AD 90 and primarily involve the region stretching from the north-eastern rim of the Mediterranean through to Rome. There is also the occasional mention of places to the east, including parts of Africa.

To accurately interpret the New Testament, it is helpful to understand its history, culture, religion, politics, and social world. In particular, it is helpful to examine the Jewish background to the New Testament as well as the wider context of the gentile world.

1. THE INTERTESTAMENTAL PERIOD (SECOND TEMPLE JUDAISM)

It is sometimes suggested that prophecy ended in Israel after Malachi (c. 433 BC), the last book in the Old Testament.[1] The time between Malachi leading up to the New Testament era has traditionally been called "the intertestamental period." Today, the more popular term for this period is called Second Temple Judaism, which stretched from the rebuilding of the Jerusalem temple after Israel's return from the Babylonian exile around 520 BC, to the time of Christ, and up to the destruction of the Second Temple in AD 70. Information on the intertestamental period is primarily

---

1. This is disputed as many consider the final form of Daniel to have been set in the Maccabean Period (see Jason M. Silverman, "Book of Daniel," *LBD*). Silverman argues that while Daniel was finally edited in this period, many of its stories are likely older.

derived from a set of important historical writings including Josephus, the Apocrypha, the Pseudepigrapha, and the Dead Sea Scrolls.

During the intertestamental period, Israel experienced a sequence of foreign rulers. Even when the nation returned to the land of Israel, it remained under the Medo-Persian Empire (550–331 BC). Israel next came under the rule of the Macedonian-Greek Empire, initially under Alexander the Great (331–323 BC). After Alexander's death, the kingdom was broken up and Israel found itself under Ptolemaic rule (323–198 BC) and later under Seleucid domination (198–167 BC). After this time of relative peace, the Maccabean revolt against the Seleucid Empire led to a period of Jewish self-governance, including the Jewish Hasmonean Dynasty (167–63 BC). Subsequently, the Roman Empire controlled Israel during the time of Christ and the New Testament writings. Both Jewish culture and theology were influenced by these experiences.

2. GEOGRAPHIC FEATURES

Israel is flanked on the west by the Great Sea (Mediterranean) and on the east by the Jordan River (in which Jesus was baptized), the Sea of Galilee, and the Dead Sea, beyond which are the rugged and arid lands of the Transjordan. To the north is Lebanon and to the south Egypt. At the time of Christ, Israel was divided up into three main areas:

1. **Galilee** (north of Samaria), where Jesus primarily ministered

2. **Samaria** (north of Judea, south of Galilee)

3. **Judea** (south), where Jerusalem is found

Another important and key geographical feature is the Sea of Galilee, where much of Jesus' ministry occurred. It is also known in the Bible as the "Sea of Chinnereth" (Num 34:11 ESV), "Sea of Chinneroth" (Josh 12:3 ESV), "Lake of Gennesaret" (Luke 5:1 ESV), and "Sea of Tiberias" (John 21:1 ESV). Today it is known as Yam Kinneret.[2] It is 21 kilometers (13 miles) long and 11 kilometers (5 miles) wide. Most of the towns in which Jesus ministered were on its western and northern shores (e.g., Capernaum, Bethsaida, and Magdala).

---

2. J. H. Paterson, "Galilee, Sea of," in *NBD* 395.

This part of Israel is dry and hot. The annual rainfall in Galilee is about 800 millimeters per year (31.5 inches). The annual rainfall is about 500 millimeters per year (20 inches) in Jerusalem, which is approximately equal to the driest places in Central Otago in New Zealand or Idaho in the United States. While there are variations in temperature, the region generally experiences mild winters and hot summers—as low as 7 degrees Celsius (44 degrees Fahrenheit) in Jerusalem in the winter, and up to 49 degrees Celsius (120 degrees Fahrenheit) in Jericho in the summer.

Israel varies in altitude from to 390 m (1,280 feet) below sea level at the Dead Sea to 1,020 m (3,346 feet) above sea level near Hebron, and subsequently, boasts a wide range of vegetation types.[3]

3. POPULATION

The Jewish historian Josephus estimated the population in Galilee at the time of Christ was between 200,000 and 300,000.[4] The population of Jerusalem was about 80,000,[5] but increased dramatically during the festivals. The overall Jewish worldwide population was approximately seven million, with more than five million living outside Israel in the diaspora (the dispersion). The Jewish population of Israel was around one- to one-and-a-half million, but the total population of Israel was around two million; only half of the population was Jewish. Most of the Jewish population lived in Judea, including Jesus and his disciples, in a pocket of Galilee in the north.

Jerusalem was the heart of the nation in every way. The city was not isolated from the world as people sometimes think, but quite cosmopolitan. It was the site of the Second Temple, one of the wonders of the world, making it the center of religious pilgrimage and festival. Jerusalem also boasted a hippodrome, a gymnasium, and theatres.

---

3. J. M. Houston, "Palestine," in *NBD* 856.
4. P. Riesner, "Galilee," in *DJG* 252.
5. See Philip J. King, "Jerusalem," in *ABD* 3:753.

FIGURE 1: MAP OF ISRAEL AT THE TIME OF CHRIST

4. SOCIOECONOMIC CONDITIONS

Socioeconomically, Israel's main revenue came from agriculture, fishing, trade, and commerce—in that order. From AD 10-70, the economy declined due to overpopulation, high taxation, natural disasters, and class struggles resulting in the rich growing richer and the poor growing poorer. There was substantial poverty. These conditions provide an illuminating backdrop to Jesus' many parables and teachings on wealth and poverty.

There were three main socioeconomic groups in Israel:

1. **The wealthy:** These tended to be land owners and those in political positions. This included the Herodian royal family, who owned around half the land, and the chief priests and their families. The priests derived income from the sacrifices and the temple treasury, as well as by exploiting the poor.

2. **The upper-lower class:** Like many modern third-world countries, there was no real middle class in Israel. However, there were tradesmen, artisans, and priests who serviced the nobility and lived above subsistence level. These two "upper" classes were a small minority, around 5-10 percent of the population.

3. **The poor:** The poor made up 90 percent of the population and, for the most part, they lived on the edge of poverty and often lost their land due to debts. They were burdened with taxation from Rome, the temple system, and the tithing structure.

5. LANGUAGE

There were four languages commonly used in Israel in this era. Aramaic had become the dominant language in the Persian period and remained the common language spoken by Jews. Greek had been introduced through Alexander the Great (331-323 BC) and leaders who followed and was the lingua franca of the Roman Empire. It was the common language among the educated in Israel and throughout the Mediterranean world. Hebrew was the official religious language of Judaism among scholars, used in worship and in temple activity. Latin was the official Roman language of the government and its citizens, but was rare among the general populace. Jesus likely spoke Aramaic, was familiar with Hebrew from his religious experience, and spoke Greek for business dealings (as a carpenter). It is unlikely he was familiar with Latin. Paul, however, may have been familiar with all four languages: He was a well-traveled Roman citizen who had been raised in the diaspora in a Hebrew home and trained in Jerusalem as a Pharisee.

6. CULTURAL INFLUENCES

Because of the impact of foreign powers and their cultures, Israel at the time of Christ was not monocultural. Apart from the obvious influences of Jewish culture, some of the influencing cultural and social factors included Hellenism (the influence of Greek culture) and the political dominance of Rome. In fact, although Paul's world was under Roman rule, it was a Greco-Roman world with a dominant Greek culture.

The first great influence was Hellenism. Philip II of Macedonia defeated the Greeks in 338 BC. His son, Alexander the Great, became emperor of Macedonia in 336 BC and there followed an amazing dissemination of Greek culture as his armies extended Macedonian rule. Alexander himself established thirty Greek cities. After his death in 323 BC, the Diadochi ("successors") split the kingdom in four—the Antigonids in Macedonia (Greece), the Ptolemies in Egypt, the Seleucids in Syria, and the Attalids in Pergamum in Asia Minor. The Ptolemies controlled Israel until 198 BC. This control was relinquished to the Seleucids, who governed Israel until the Maccabean revolt in 167 BC. Through Alexander's conquest and the subsequent domination of the eastern Mediterranean by his successors, the culture of Hellenism (Greek) tremendously impacted the region. This included language (Attic/Koine Greek), business models, education, and politics. Aramaic was the language of the people, while Koine Greek became the language of business, commerce, and politics.

A good example of the influence of Hellenism is Philo of Alexandria, Egypt, who wrote a wide range of books on Jewish ideas and law from a Greek perspective.[6] By the time of the New Testament, Hellenism had

---

6. On Philo, see G. E. Sterling, "Philo," in *DNTB* 789–793.

penetrated Israel's life for several hundred years. Greater cultural interaction and openness meant urban populations were more heavily influenced than rural. People responded to Hellenization in different ways. Some were indifferent. Some fused Jewish and Greek ideas (syncretism). Others responded with separatism (Essenes) or resistance (Zealots). The Roman era did not see a shift away from Hellenism. While the Romans vanquished the Greeks militarily, every aspect of Roman culture was highly influenced by the Greeks from as early as the eighth century BC. E. M. Yamauchi rightly posits, "There is hardly any aspect of higher culture that was not decisively influenced by the Greeks: art, architecture, literature, drama, medicine, philosophy, and religion were all deeply affected by the Greeks."[7] By the second century AD, all Romans were expected to know how to speak Greek. As evidenced by the New Testament written in Greek, the disciples were all Greek speakers, and as the Christian message spread, it engaged with Hellenistic culture.

The second major influence was Rome. The desire for political peace throughout the empire and the free flow of goods and taxes led to the establishment of the famed Roman roads and sea transport systems. Roman military bases were found throughout the empire. However, the short span of Roman rule (mid-first century BC), the Roman adoption of Hellenism, and Rome's approach to colonization through cooperative rather than merely coercive means meant that they did not influence culture as much as the Greeks. One example of Roman influence was its use of local tax collectors to gather taxes. Roman influence was greatest among the elite who received citizenship in and tended to favor cooperation with Rome. Latin was not spoken widely outside of Rome except among the elite.

AN OCCUPIED NATION

At the time of the New Testament, Israel had been an occupied country, at least in part, since the eighth century BC. Its location on the Fertile Crescent meant that anyone seeking to dominate the region had to take control of Israel as it provided a key trade and military link between Europe, Asia Minor, Mesopotamia, and Africa. Key historical events include:

---

7. E. M. Yamauchi, "Hellenism," in *DPL* 385.

1. **The *division* of north and south by Jeroboam:** After Solomon's death, long-term north-south hostility saw the north rebel and break away (930–913 BC; see 1 Kgs 12). At the time of the New Testament, this unresolved division was reflected primarily in the mutual hatred of Samaritans (identified with the Northern Kingdom) and Jews. The division also weakened the whole nation, making it more vulnerable to conquest. Israel's eschatological hopes also included the restoration of broken Israel (see Amos 9:11). The evangelization of Samaria in Acts 8 fulfills this hope in the new Christian community.

2. **The *conquest* and *exile* of the north by Assyria:** The northern region including Galilee and Samaria was invaded and conquered by Assyrian leaders Shalmanesar V and Sargon II. This conquest saw many from the northern tribes exiled to Assyria. The northern region was subsequently repopulated, leading to a syncretistic blend of Judaism and other religions. This did not help relationships with Jerusalem (722 BC; see 2 Kgs 17).

3. **The *conquest* and *exile* of the south:** Babylon invaded and conquered Judah and Benjamin in 587 BC, led by Nebuchadnezzar. Jerusalem and the temple were destroyed. Many of Israel's best were deported to Babylon for seventy years (see 2 Kgs 24–25).

4. **The *restoration* after the release of exiled Jews:** As predicted by Isaiah (Isa 44:28; 45:1), Cyrus the Great conquered Babylon and Babylon fell to the Medes and the Persians. The exiles were released, and the nation was rebuilt but remained under foreign rule (539–537 BC; see Ezra, Nehemiah, Haggai, and Zechariah).

5. **The conquest of Israel by Macedonia/Greece:** Led by Alexander the Great, Israel was taken by the expanding Macedonian Greek Empire (332–323 BC). This led to an

improved standard of living and administration, Hellenization, and the extension of Greek culture (see above).

6. ***Ptolemaic* rule (323-198 BC):** Greek rule continued from Egypt through the Ptolemies. This was a time of peace and freedom for Jews.[8] This period saw the development of "tax farmers," locals who took taxes for the Hellenistic authorities (i.e., tax collectors). Ptolemy III (246-222 BC) promoted scientific investigation, including the idea that the world was spherical.

7. ***Seleucid* control of Israel (198-143 BC):** Greek dominance shifted to Syria and the Seleucids. This period saw an increase in taxation and the promotion of Hellenism. Antiochus IV Epiphanes (175-164 BC), commonly described as "Epimanes" (madman) according to Polybius (*Hist.* 26.1), profaned the temple by erecting a statue of Zeus, enforced Hellenism, and advocated the violation of Jewish religious law. Many scholars see him as the "abomination of desolation" in Daniel (Dan 9:27; 11:31; 12:11). The figure mentioned in Mark 13:14 is fashioned after him. Antiochus IV Epiphanes' arrogant rule led to Jewish rebellion. Certain Jews called *Hasidim*, or "pious ones," stood up to this perceived syncretism, and conflict ensued.

8. **The *Maccabean* Revolt:** Antiochus' rule led to full-blown rebellion against Seleucid (Syrian) control (167-160 BC). After the desecration of the temple, Mattathias, an old priest, refused to sacrifice to Zeus, destroyed the pagan altar, and fled to the hills where he gathered an army (joined by the Hasidim) to fight the Syrians. Then the war began. Judas Maccabeus continued the attacks and by 164 BC had regained control of the temple. Hanukkah celebrates this Jewish liberation of Israel (see John 10:22). By 142 BC, Seleucid control was removed, leading to eighty years of independence, which was seen as "the golden age of Jewish nationalism."[9] This was the

---

8. Craig L. Blomberg, *Jesus and the Gospels: An Introduction and Survey* (Leicester: Apollos, 1997), 13.

9. Blomberg, *Jesus and the Gospels*, 17.

time of the Hasmonean Dynasty (c. 140–63 BC),[10] where Israel was ruled by a priestly royal aristocracy. This rebellion lies in the background of the anti-gentile sentiment and messianic hope in the New Testament (see Acts 22:3–21). It was a time when tremendous messianic hopes were kindled. The zeal for the Maccabean rebellion diminished over time. However, some of its hopes carried over to messianic figures in the time of Jesus and up to the Roman wars in the late 60s AD. During the Maccabean and Hasmonean Empire that arose from the Maccabean revolt, there was increased antagonism toward Samaritans. Ultimately, the Hasidim—the probable forerunners to the Pharisees—became critics of the Maccabees.

9. **Roman occupation and control:** In 63 BC, Pompey laid claim to Israel for Rome. By the time of Christ's ministry, Israel had been under Roman rule for around 100 years (see below). This rule was generally beneficent until the rebellions of the 60s and the destruction of the Temple in AD 70.

Apart from the brief Maccabean and Hasmonean period, by the time of the New Testament, Israel had been a divided nation for nearly 1,000 years and under foreign rule for some 600 years. Even in the time of the Jewish Hasmonean Dynasty, it resembled an aristocratic, Hellenistic regime that was sometimes hard to distinguish from the Seleucids. This long period of foreign rule was challenging to people who saw themselves as God's elect. The people of Israel yearned for freedom from oppression at the hands of these foreign powers. Some, like N. T. Wright, believe that Israel still considered itself in exile as it awaited its restoration.[11] This hope of God's redemption gives important background to Jesus and the New Testament.

---

10. On the Hasmoneans, see J. Sievers, "Hasmoneans," in *DNTB* 438–42. Herod the Great was installed as client king in 37 BC, and this marked the end of the Hasmonean period of influence.

11. See N. T. Wright, *Jesus and the Victory of God. Christian Origins and the Question of God* (London: SPCK, 1996), 576–77.

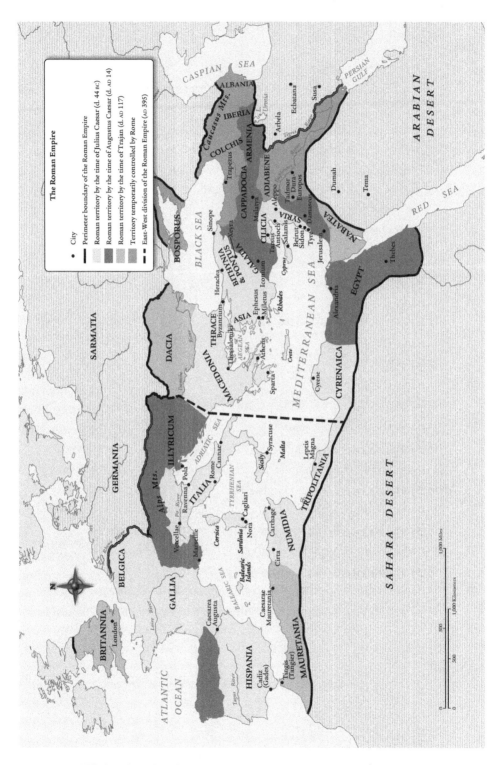

FIGURE 2: THE ROMAN EMPIRE DURING AUGUSTUS' REIGN

A NATION UNDER ROMAN RULE

The people of Judea had been under Roman rule since 63 BC. Thus, many Roman emperors are relevant to the study of the New Testament.

Dates	Name	Relationship to the New Testament
27 BC–AD 14	Augustus (Octavian)	Jesus and John the Baptist's births and childhood
AD 14–37	Tiberius	Jesus' youth, time as a carpenter, and ministry
AD 37–41	Gaius (Caligula)	Early parts of Acts
AD 41–54	Claudius	Acts—specifically a famine (Acts 11:28)—and the expulsion of Jews from Rome (Acts 18:2)
AD 54–68	Nero	Acts, Paul's writings from Roman prison, persecution, Hebrews, 1 Peter, and Revelation
AD 68–70	Jewish Civil War	Not directly mentioned, but Jerusalem's destruction predicted (Mark 13; Matt 24; Luke 21)
AD 69	Otho	Not mentioned (period of Jewish War)
AD 69	Vitellius	Not mentioned (period of Jewish War)
AD 69–79	Vespasian	The fall of Jerusalem led by Titus, Vespasian's general and next emperor (AD 66–70). Aside from predictions, not mentioned
AD 79–81	Titus	Not mentioned
AD 81–96	Domitian	Possibly Revelation
AD 96–98	Nerva	Post New Testament
AD 98–117	Trajan	Post New Testament

FIGURE 3: EMPERORS IN NEW TESTAMENT TIMES

GOVERNANCE OF ROMAN PROVINCES

As the above map shows, the Roman Empire at the time of Jesus was immense. To manage the empire, there were two kinds of provinces administered by governors of senatorial rank. The first type was public or consular provinces governed by proconsuls under the direct authority of the Roman Senate. Usually, these were the richer and more settled provinces such as Achaia in southern Greece created in 27 BC, the capital of which was Corinth, an important New Testament center. The second type of province, and of lesser status, was the imperial province. These provinces were governed by a legate, appointed by the emperor. Examples of imperial provinces include Galatia (Turkey) established in 25 BC (vital for understanding Galatians and sections of Acts), and Cappadocia (also Turkey) established in AD 18. These were mostly frontier provinces, such as Syria (at times including Israel), where legions were stationed to protect the empire.

There was another class of province called imperial procuratorial provinces, led by governors known as prefects (in Egypt) or procurators. These were non-senators of lower "equestrian" rank. A key example of this type of leader in the New Testament is Pontius Pilate, who figures prominently in Jesus' death. Such provinces were made up of smaller areas like Judea, which formed a part of the larger province. Judea was made a procuratorial province some ten to fourteen years after Jesus' birth in AD 6 and formed part of Syria, an imperial province. It was upgraded to a consular province by Hadrian in the early second century and called Syria Palaestina. These governors were financially astute, possessed judicial and military power, and had military troops. They tended to rule in a supervisory rather than an executive role, using local administration with minimal Roman officials. Hence, the Roman governor was ultimately responsible for the area, but a local council or client king administered the day-to-day running of the province. Herod was Israel's client king (followed by Herod's descendants) and was supported by Rome. These client kings were administered by the Sanhedrin, made up of seventy members plus the high priest. The Sanhedrin consisted of wealthy Jewish aristocrats who were mostly Sadducees and priests. The high priest, who was appointed by Rome in New Testament times, had leadership over the group. The Sanhedrin had a great degree of authority except it did not have the right to sentence someone to death (John 18:31). Through this medium, Rome tended to respect local laws and customs to ensure smooth government. Roman citizens came under Roman law.

Rome took Judea under Pompey in 66-63 BC. When Pompey captured Jerusalem, he cleansed the temple and reinstated the high priest, Hyrcanus. Syria, including Samaria, became a Roman imperial province. Judea, Galilee, Idumea (the region south of Judea, or Gaza), and Perea (the region east of the Jordan including parts of modern Israel, Syria, and Jordan) were left under Jewish rule but remained accountable to Rome. Julius Caesar appointed Antipater procurator of Judea. His son, Herod the Great—who had been governor of Galilee—won the title "King of the Jews" and reigned from 37-4 BC (see Matt 2:1; Luke 1:5), including the time of Jesus' birth in Bethlehem. Herod extended his territories and oversaw massive building projects. He rebuilt and enlarged Caesarea Maritima into a port city for the Romans boasting the largest human-built harbor in the Roman Empire. This port city served as the Roman provincial capital of Israel during the New Testament period; it was Philip's hometown and was where Paul was imprisoned (Acts 21, 23-26). Its aqueduct is still visible today. Herod also restored the Jerusalem temple on a lavish scale, including Greco-Roman architectural features (see John 2:20). He built Masada, a fortress in the desert overlooking the Dead Sea, where the Jews made their last stand against the Romans after the destruction of Jerusalem just forty years after Jesus died. Herod the Great loved Hellenistic and Roman culture and encouraged them. However, his people considered him to be cruel and ruthless. This is evidenced in the massacre of the children after Jesus' birth in Matthew 2.

After Herod's death, his kingdom was split into thirds. Herod Antipas was appointed tetrarch of Galilee and Perea (4 BC-AD 39)—governor of a fourth of the province. He was responsible for John the Baptist's imprisonment and death (cf. Matt 14:1-12; Luke 3:19, 20). Philip was appointed tetrarch of Trachonitis (southern Syria, east of Jordan) and Iturea (north of Galilee to Lebanon and parts of Syria), reigning from 4 BC-AD 34 (Luke 3:1).[12] Archelaus

---

12. Do not confuse Philip the Tetrarch with the Philip of Mark 6:17. The latter is Herod Philip, who is either unknown, or a conflation of Herod II (son of Herod the Great and Mariamne II) and Philip the Tetrarch.

was appointed ethnarch—governor of a province—of Judea, Idumea, and Samaria. He reigned from 4 BC–AD 6 (cf. Matt 2:22; Luke 3:1). Archelaus' rule ended in terrible riots. He was banished, and Judea came under the direct control of Roman governors. Another Herod of importance to the New Testament is Herod the Great's grandson, Agrippa I, son of Aristobulus IV and Berenice. Agrippa I was named ruler over Israel by the Roman emperor Caligula. Agrippa I is known as a persecutor of early Christians. He had James, the brother of John and son of Zebedee, put to death and had Peter arrested. Because of his cruelty and blasphemy, Agrippa was slain by an angel of the Lord (Acts 12). In AD 50, Agrippa's son, known as Agrippa II, was made the ruler of the king of Chalcis' territory. Later he was given Abilene (a plain in Syria), Trachonitis, Acra (fortress in Jerusalem), and important parts of Galilee and Perea. Agrippa II is mentioned in Acts 25:13–26:32, where he listened to Paul's defense in Caesarea Maritima. Paul subsequently appealed to Rome and was granted that request, even though Agrippa II was prepared to set him free (Acts 26:23).

SPECIAL JEWISH PRIVILEGES UNDER ROME

In line with their policy of tolerance to local religions, the Romans granted Jews special privileges. This included exemption from the worship of Roman gods and modified participation in the Imperial cult, due to their passionate Yahwistic monotheism and stubborn resistance to the point of death.[13] Rather than make sacrifices to Caesar, they made sacrifices and prayers "on behalf" of him. Jewish religious customs such as Sabbaths and dietary laws were sanctioned. Rome did this for pragmatic reasons: to maintain their hold on the nation and to ensure taxes came through. They also feared that the Jews, who were by that point dispersed, would join with the Parthians and cause an uprising. The Romans knew of the

---

13. For a summary of the Imperial cult, see M. Reasoner, "Imperial Cult," in *DLNTD*, 321–25. In the East, kings were often worshiped as divine (e.g., Hittites, Egypt) or deified after death (e.g., Cyrus the Great, Persia). In New Testament times, the Imperial cult was mainly deification of a deceased ruler or emperor (e.g., Julius Caesar, Augustus, Claudius). Sacrifices were performed to the spirit (genius) of living emperors. Jews and Christians rejected this, and their refusal to make such sacrifices became the basis for persecution. In the New Testament, hints of this can be found in Acts 12:20–23 concerning Agrippa I, and in Revelation 13 with the beast, which is patterned after the Imperial cult. Jews were given license not to take part in such sacrifices *to* an emperor; rather, they prayed and made sacrifices *for* him.

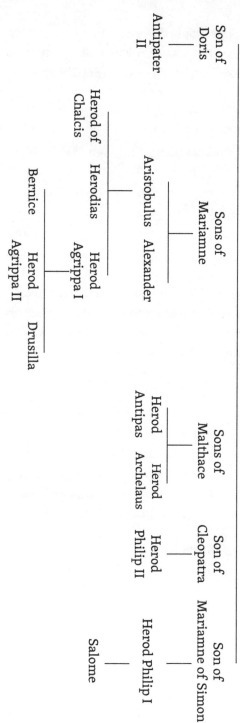

FIGURE 4: HEROD THE GREAT'S FAMILY

Jewish messianic prophecies suggesting another king would come to lead the Jews against them, so they kept a careful eye on any Jewish group or faction that strongly promoted this belief. The generally privileged position of the Jews within the empire resulted in intense anti-Semitism.

ROMAN EMPIRE UNITY

How did the Romans manage to hold together such a diverse and expansive empire? First, Rome's strong military enabled it to rule, and when necessary, use force. However, rule by force is not enough. Rome also granted favors to locals including Roman citizenship, particularly to those in power (to the elite, puppet kings, aristocrats, ruling priests, and other key leaders). This enabled Rome to elicit support from the power structures of conquered peoples and also rule *through* those people, who would want to retain their privileged position. Third, Rome allowed those in Roman territories to retain their traditions while maintaining a common culture based on language, trade, and travel. In particular, the Romans are famous for creating a network of roads throughout the empire. Many modern roads still follow the course of Roman roads. Finally, Rome had allowed the freedom of local religions, which helped avoid conflict with the religious and political power structures of the societies they encountered—many of whose religion and politics were fused and central to life. They would only intervene when religion impeded Rome's power or taxes, or if Jewish (and other) proselytism was gaining Roman citizens who then lost interest in their own religions. The Imperial cult was enforced, but this was as much a political measure as religious.

Date	Event
63 BC	Pompey captures Jerusalem
63 BC	Hyrcanus appointed ethnarch, reinstated high priest
55–43 BC	Antipater procurator of Judea
34 BC–4 BC	Herod the Great
4 BC–AD 6	Archelaus, ethnarch
AD 6	Judea made into a Roman province
AD 6–9	Quirinius governor of Syria
4 BC–AD 34	Philip, tetrarch
4 BC–AD 39	Herod Antipas, tetrarch
AD 26/27–36	Pontius Pilate governor of Judea
AD 41–44	Herod Agrippa I rules as "King of the Jews"
AD 44	Israel's rule returns to Roman governors
AD 66–70	Jewish War and siege of Jerusalem (AD 70)
AD 73	Masada (the last stand)
AD 132–135	Bar Kokhba revolt, Judea becomes a Roman colony

FIGURE 5: KEY DATES CONCERNING ROME

VARYING JEWISH ATTITUDES TOWARD ROMANS

The Jews held three predominant attitudes toward the Romans: pro-Roman, anti-Roman, and pragmatic.

1. **Pro-Roman:** These Jews benefited most from Roman rule, particularly the elite such as the Herodian rulers and the Sanhedrin. Many priests and Sadducees tended to cooperate with Rome for expediency to retain their position of privilege.

2. **Anti-Roman:** A few different groups in Judaism expressed anti-Roman sentiment, each in different ways. The Essenes, who were also disillusioned with the Jewish temple and priestly system, responded by withdrawing into the desert and forming an exclusive community. The Zealots worked for armed rebellion against the Romans, seeking an opportunity

to overthrow them. The Pharisees saw their first loyalty as absolute adherence to the Mosaic Law and traditions. At the time of the Roman wars, the Pharisees became swept up in Jewish nationalism, and some supported the Zealots. These groups had many reasons for opposing Rome. There was religious resentment whereby, intentionally or unintentionally, the Romans committed grievous offense against things the Jews held sacred. Economic resentment was caused by the huge tax burden placed on the Jews and especially the general populace. The various taxes took about as much as 40 percent of a person's income,[14] so the economic situation for the average Jewish non-Roman citizen was grim. Many faced poverty and some turned to violence. Many lost possessions and land in this environment. Finally, there were political grievances; the Romans were occupying the Jews' land! These grievances were done by the hands of Rome and the so-called *Pax Romana*,[15] a peace supported by a reign of blood. Combined, they led to intense resentment toward Rome and to the increased hope of a messiah to release the Jews from the bondage of gentile rule. One can see why Jesus' message of "good news to the poor" and egalitarianism was so widely received.

3. **Pragmatism:** Many of the *common people*, who were mostly poor and had little time to worry about who was in control, were focused on survival and making the best of their situations. While not happy to be under Roman gentile rule, which was offensive to them, their lives were largely spent trying to scrape together a living in a society where there was great inequality between rich and poor.

---

14. William Simmons, "Taxation," *LBD*.

15. On *Pax Romana*, the "peace of Rome," see J. E. Bowley, "Pax Romana," *DNTB* 770–75. It speaks of the peace established in the region by Caesar Augustus, which lasted for two-and-a-half centuries. It was a reality and ideal. A Roman cult, "Pax" gave religious support to this aspiration. It is especially applied to Augustus' reign, the so-called "Augustan Golden Age."

JUDAISM IN NEW TESTAMENT TIMES

No study of the Gospels and the New Testament can take lightly the central fact that Jesus was a Jew and that Christianity grew out of Judaism. Furthermore, the earliest period of the church was profoundly Jewish (Acts 1-8), as were the first missionaries. Hence, to understand the New Testament, it is essential to grasp Judaism at the time of Christ as fully as possible.

THEOLOGICAL FEATURES

1. **Monotheistic Yahwism:** Unlike most of the polytheistic nations around them, Jews at the time of Christ passionately believed in the one transcendent God. This belief in Yahweh and his utter holiness was at the heart of the Jewish worship system and is evidenced in the foundational creedal statement, the *Shema*: "Hear, O Israel: The LORD our God, the LORD is one. You shall love the LORD your God with all your heart and with all your soul and with all your might. And these words that I command you today shall be on your heart" (Deut 6:4-6). This was recited daily in Jewish worship. The essential oneness of God is confirmed in Jesus' teachings (Mark 12:29-30), Paul's writings (e.g., Rom 3:30; 1 Cor 8:4, 6; Gal 3:20; Eph 4:6), and elsewhere in the New Testament (Jas 2:19). Christian claims to Jesus' divinity and his encroachment on aspects associated with the divine, such as Sabbath and forgiveness, clash with their primarily numerical understanding of oneness.

2. **Nationalism or election:** Due to its astonishing heritage in the Exodus-Sinai event (Exod 19:5-6; 20:2), and the giving of the law and promise of land, Israel believed that it was the chosen race and never lost this sense of being the children and people of God. However, knowing they were chosen by God tended to foster a sense of racial superiority, which led to prophetic rebuke.

3. **Nomism:**[16] Nomism is the centrality of the law. This was the distinctive feature of Judaism, especially after the exile. The law included the torah and especially the Decalogue (the Ten Commandments), along with the oral law (*halakah*). The oral law, created by the Pharisees (and rejected by the Sadducees), was a set of laws that helped explicate the laws of the torah (Gen–Deut).[17]

4. **Covenant:** The concept of election and nomism centered on the covenant in which God had called Israel to be his people, and they were to respond by living according to the law of the covenant. The key covenants were the Abrahamic covenant (election) found in Genesis 15 and 17; the Mosaic covenant (law) found in Exodus 20; and the Davidic covenant (messianic hope) in 2 Samuel 7. The covenants are linked, each remaining in effect and building on the previous. Many Jews looked toward a "new covenant" that would see Israel restored (Jer 31:31).

5. **Eschatology (future hope):** Israel had an intense sense of corporate and individual eschatology. Corporately, the Jews saw themselves as the chosen people of God who awaited redemption on the "day of the Lord," when God would restore the nation, raise the dead, judge the nations, and triumph over evil. This would happen *at the end of time* (in marked contrast to Jesus' first coming *in the middle of time*). While there are hints of resurrection earlier in the Old Testament, a stronger expectation of individual resurrection developed during the intertestamental period—although this was denied by

---

16. From the Greek *nomos* meaning law (i.e., *nomism* is a focus on the law as central to Jewish life).

17. On Pharisaic oral law, see E. P. Sanders, "Law," in *ABD* 4:259–60. He notes that all Pharisees agreed on "traditions" which "altered or supplemented the written law." It is disputed whether they considered these traditions laws with traditionalists believing so, while some contemporary scholars (including Sanders) dispute this arguing that, while important, these traditions (*halakah*) are considered secondary to the torah. However, whether seen as equal or not, most agree that the Pharisees considered their observance important as a means of upholding torah.

the Sadducees (see Matt 22:23). This eschatological hope was increasingly pushed into the future after exile. There was a strong anticipation of a messiah, or alternatively named "deliverer," a man of great power whose coming was imminent. It was believed that God would intervene and remove the Roman Empire from Israel and establish his kingdom on earth.

6. **Angelology and demonology:** In Jewish literature from the intertestamental period, a considerable increase in interest in angelology and demonology developed as compared to the Old Testament where, while Satan and evil spirits are not absent (e.g., 1 Sam 16:14; Job 1:6–12; 2:1–7; 1 Chr 21:1; Zech 3:1–2), they are not prominent. Satan and demons are featured in the New Testament, although they are not as detailed as in Jewish apocalyptic literature. For New Testament writers, the real problem of the world is not merely demons, but human sin.

7. **Apocalyptic themes and literature:** In the intertestamental period, there was a considerable increase of interest in the coming of the kingdom, the messiah, separatism, and judgment.

8. **Missiological interest:** While it is debated whether Judaism had an active proselytizing approach, with the majority finding this uncommon (cf. Matt 23:15), Judaism was increasingly seen as a religious option for gentiles due to its monotheism and morality. Some God-fearing gentiles (cf. Cornelius) converted, were circumcised, and became full proselytes.[18] The Jewish vision was not of proactive evangelization of the gentiles, but God's intervention and the nations either coming to him or being destroyed. To come to Yahweh was to become a Jew. In the New Testament, Paul especially challenges this, believing people could come to Christ without becoming Jews by faith alone.

---

18. Zachary G. Smith, "Proselyte," *LBD*. Smith defines a proselyte as a "[r]eligious convert, especially to Judaism. One of the primary terms used to designate a gentile (non-Jewish) convert to Judaism." For further discussion, see the full article.

INSTITUTIONS OF JUDAISM

The Jerusalem Temple

In some Jewish traditions, the temple was supposedly built on the stone where God first created Adam, where Abraham bought Isaac for sacrifice (Mount Moriah) and where Jacob wrestled with an angel. David, a man of war, was not permitted to build the temple; his son Solomon oversaw construction of the first temple around 900 BC (1 Kgs 6–9).

This temple was destroyed by the Babylonians under Nebuchadnezzar in 586 BC (2 Kgs 25). The second temple, built by the returned exiles around 520–15 BC (Ezra 3:7–6:18), met great disappointment due to its inferior quality (Ezra 3:12). It was later enlarged and enhanced 500 years later by Herod the Great over the period 20/19 BC–AD 66—a project that was going on at the time of Jesus (see John 2:20). It was known as the Herodian temple and was one of the wonders of the ancient world. Its outer court was fourteen hectares (thirty-five acres). It had a fortress-like wall around it—one stone has been recorded to weigh 415 tons. It was built of white stone that melts when burned, thus explaining how it was razed to the ground by the Romans in AD 70. Material from the temple was used to build the Colosseum in Rome, and years later, some of that same material was used in building St. Peter's Basilica. Both Josephus and Mark 13:1 comment on its construction.

The temple was a spiritual symbol of God's presence with the Jews. God's glory dwelt there (e.g., 1 Kgs 8:11; 2 Chr 5:14; 7:1–3; Isa 4:5). However, God's glory had never filled the second temple, and so Israel yearned for God to do so.[19] In the New Testament, Jesus becomes God's temple into whom he pours his glory (John 1:14). Sacrifices and tithes were offered there. It was also the center of the Jewish festivals, and pilgrims flooded there regularly. Every Jewish male was expected to make at least one pilgrimage to the temple at Passover during his life. It also served as the economic hub of the Jews. It was a tourist attraction, and visitors needed everything from

---

19. See on the temple, Wright, *Jesus and the Victory of God*, 405–12. Write notes that the "Temple was, in Jesus' day, the central symbol of Judaism, the location of Israel's most characteristic praxis, the topic of some of her most vital stories, the answer to her deepest questions, the subject of some of her most beautiful songs" (p. 406). He notes three core aspects: God's presence, sacrifices, and its political significance. It was opposed as corrupt by the Essenes and endorsed by other key groups.

accommodations, to a suitable sacrifice to offer, to temple money to use when purchasing sacrifices. Builders and tradesmen were kept employed as they built the temple—and the markets flourished. The temple tax was a burden on the people, but they still paid it. This provides background to Jesus clearing the temple (John 2:13-25; Mark 11; and parr.). The temple was also the political center of the nation. The Sanhedrin met in a hall in the temple courts (see below). The Romans watched over the edifice from the Antonia Fortress. The temple was the central point of Judaism at the time of Christ. One can see why the claim that Jesus and his people are God's temple was so controversial. Moreover, Jesus' clearing of the temple was a challenge to Israel's religion, economy, and political system.

The Synagogue

The origins of the synagogue (in Greek *synagōgē*, or "gathering place") are obscure. It probably developed during the exile in Babylon as groups of Jews met to read the Scriptures, hear them preached, pray, and worship. In the New Testament, synagogues are found in every town and city in Israel and the diaspora (aside from Philippi, Acts 16:13, and Lystra).[20] There were hundreds of synagogues in Jerusalem alone. Originally, synagogues were established in homes, or homes were altered to accommodate the people. Whereas the temple was a priestly institution, the synagogue was a lay institution run by local elders. It was never in competition with the temple, where the Scriptures were read, prayers were offered, psalms were sung, and scribes would expound the torah. The people met at the synagogue on the Sabbath and two other days during the week. The synagogues were where the common people were educated; they were the schools of Judaism and what kept Judaism alive after the destruction of the temple in AD 70.

Sabbath and Feasts

The annual calendar was essential to Israel's self-understanding. Central to this is the Sabbath, Israel's day of stopping from work for rest and worship. It was instituted at creation (Gen 2:1-3), endorsed in the torah (Exod

---

20. No synagogue is mentioned of Lystra and Derbe in Acts 13, and the arrival of Jews in Lystra to persecute Paul seems to also indicate that there is no synagogue in the city (Acts 14:19, see also 16:1; 20:4; 2 Tim 3:11). Timothy was from the region, and his mother a Jewess, indicating some Jews were there (Acts 16:2-3).

20:8-11; Lev 23:3), and buttressed by a range of oral laws ensuring faithful observance. Each of the annual Mosaic feasts involved one or more key "convocation" Sabbaths. Each "new moon" involved a Sabbath rest (Num 10:10; 28:11-15), something Judaizers sought to enforce on new Christians (Col 2:16; Gal 4:10). The Sabbath principle extended to the Sabbatical Year of release and rest every seventh year (Exod 23:11; Lev 25:1-7; Deut 15:1). The year of Jubilee, when slaves were freed and debts canceled, occurred after seven Sabbaths of years in the fiftieth year (Lev 25:8-18).

"Israel's feasts served rather as divinely revealed expressions of the moral obligations of his people, as memorials of God's saving acts in the past, as sacraments of his sanctifying power in the present, and as types of his anticipated victory over sin in the forthcoming first and second advents of Jesus Christ."[21] Feasts speak of the importance of celebration, eating as symbolic of community, remembering, and worship of God.

The most well-recognized feasts are the three pilgrimage feasts, named for the expectation that all of Israel's men would travel to Jerusalem to celebrate them—Passover, the Feast of Weeks, and the Feast of Tabernacles (Lev 23).

Passover fell on Abib 14, also known as Nisan. Passover recalled the passing over of Israel's firstborn prior to the exodus (Exod 12:21-31). A lamb was sacrificed and eaten, anticipating Jesus, the Lamb of God (John 1:29). Passover is also recalled in Hebrews 11:28. Passover features in the Gospels with Jesus' family attending when he was twelve (Luke 2:41), later in his life (John 2:13, 23), and during the Passover at the time of his crucifixion (Matt 26:2, 17; Mark 14:1; Luke 22:1, 7; John 19:14). The feeding of the 5000 occurred just before Passover (John 6:4). Paul describes Jesus as the Passover Lamb (1 Cor 5:7). James was murdered and Peter arrested around the time of Passover and the Feast of Unleavened Bread (Acts 12:3-4).

Passover was held in conjunction with the week-long **Feast of Unleavened Bread**,[22] recalling Israel's hasty flight from Egypt leaving them no time to leaven the bread. All leaven is removed for the feast (Deut 16:4). While not technically a pilgrimage feast, the link to Passover meant many attended. The firstfruits were also waved, indicating the dedication of the

---

21. E. D. Isaacs and J. B. Payne, "Feasts," in *ISBE* 2:293.

22. There may have been variations of when the feast began as in Matthew 26:17; the first day of the feast is the preparation for Passover. See Donald A. Hagner, *Matthew 14-28*, WBC 33B (Dallas: Word, 1998), 764. See also Mark 14:12.

agricultural season (Exod 34:26; Lev 23:10-14). This also represents purity from sin (Lev 23:4-8). In the New Testament, the kingdom is likened to leaven that spreads through bread (Matt 13:33; Luke 13:21). Leaven is used of false teaching, which spreads and infects like yeast in bread (Matt 16:6, 11, 12; Mark 8:15; Luke 12:1). Unleavened bread is mentioned in relation to Jesus' death, which happened at Passover (Matt 26:17; Mark 14:1, 12; Luke 22:1, 7). Paul leaves Philippi's port Neapolis for Jerusalem with the collection after the feast (Acts 20:6). He warns of the dangers of immorality or false teaching infecting the church as yeast spreads through bread, urging the Corinthians to remove it as Israel removed yeast in preparation of the feast (1 Cor 5:6-8, see also Gal 5:9).

Seven weeks (seven times seven days, or forty-nine days) later is the second great pilgrimage feast (Deut 16:11), **Pentecost**. Pentecost is a term derived from the Greek for fifty (*pentēkostē*). It is also described as the "Feast of Harvest," the "Feast of Firstfruits," or the "Feast of Weeks." Pentecost celebrated the grain harvest, the offering of firstfruits covenant renewal, and the entry into the promised land (Lev 23:10). It was on the day of Pentecost, exactly fifty days after Passover, that the early believers were filled with the Holy Spirit (Acts 2:1-4). Pentecost also features in Paul's travel plans (Acts 20:16; 1 Cor 16:8).

Three feasts occur in autumn during the month of Tishri, or September-October. The first is the **Feast of Trumpets**, known to Jews today as "Rosh Hashanah." The focus was repentance, and it represented the beginning of the agricultural new year. Its name comes from the use of the trumpet, or *shofar*, to announce the beginning of the feast. The **Day of Atonement** came next on Tishri 10. It was a day of fasting, when the high priest would make fifteen sacrifices, pray for the people, enter the holy of holies to sprinkle blood on the altar, and release a scapegoat into the wilderness to make atonement for the nation's sins (Lev 16). The third autumn feast is the **Feast of Tabernacles**, also called the "Feast of Ingathering," or the "Feast of Booths." The Feast of Tabernacles occurred five days after the Day of Atonement on Tishri 15. This was the third of the pilgrimage feasts, and it recalled when Israel lived in tents during their wilderness wanderings. Jesus attended this feast in John 7:2, with subsequent events in John 7 and

8 occurring at the feast, and what follows in John 9–10:21 in Jerusalem.[23] Another festival is mentioned in John 5:1, "the feast of the Jews." Jesus traveled to Jerusalem for this feast, likely one of the pilgrimage feasts, (Passover, Weeks, or Tabernacles), but scholars are divided over which one.

During and after exile, because of God's deliverance at the time of Esther and the Maccabean revolt, three other feasts were introduced, none of which are pilgrimage gatherings. First, **Purim** or "the Feast of Lots," recalled Israel's salvation from Haman sometime during 473 BC.[24] Purim was characterized by celebration, not sacrifice. The second festival, **Hanukkah** or "the Festival of Lights or Dedication," recalled the Maccabean cleansing of the temple after its defilement by Antiochus IV Epiphanes in 164 BC. It was celebrated for eight days from Kislev 25, between November–December (see 1 Macc 4:52–59). The third was **Nicanor**, a general of Antiochus IV Epiphanes defeated by the Maccabees (161 BC). Nicanor was celebrated a day before Purim (Adar 13).[25]

For Jews, the annual calendar was critical. Early Christians were divided over whether to observe these festivals, with Judaizers and others seeing them as important (Gal 4:10; Col 2:16). Others, like Paul, were less concerned and saw them as optional (Rom 14:5; Col 2:23). Over time Christians developed their own calendar, especially Easter and Pentecost, indicating a shift from Sabbath to Sunday as the day of worship (Acts 20:7; 1 Cor 16:2; Rev 1:10). This day of worship recalled the day of Christ's resurrection, God's act of new creation (Matt 28:1; Mark 16:2; Luke 24:1; John 20:1, 19).

The Sanhedrin

This was a Jewish council (parliament) of aristocrats, mainly Sadducees and priests, and the chief priest—seventy-one members in all. They met in a hall adjoining the temple. The Sanhedrin had unlimited civil authority

---

23. The reference to living water relates to the daily march by priests with a golden pitcher of water from the pool of Siloam to the temple and the seventh day libation. Jesus' discourse on the light of the world occurred on an evening of the feast when youths lit four golden lamps with wicks from priests' discarded trousers and girdles while the Levitical musicians played and men danced. For detail, see George R. Beasley-Murray, *John*, WBC 36 (Dallas: Word, Incorporated, 2002), 113, 126–27.

24. King Ahasuerus is either King Artaxerxes II (404–359 BC), or, as is more likely, Xerxes I, son of Darius the Great, who reigned from 485–465 BC. See Mervin Breneman, *Ezra, Nehemiah, Esther*, NAC 10 (Nashville: Broadman & Holman Publishers, 1993), 303–304.

25. John T. Swan, "Feasts and Festivals of Israel," *LBD*.

over Judea, except it could not decide on political offenses and it could not enforce capital punishment in Jesus' time (cf. John 18:31).

Symbolism

Some of the key symbols of Jewish culture are the Sabbath, circumcision, festivals, prayers, feasts, and purity rituals. There was a strong emphasis on the external symbols of the faith in Jesus' time.

THE LITERATURE OF JUDAISM

Writings from the period of Second Temple Judaism and the time of Christ are important for understanding the first-century Jewish world.

THE JEWISH TARGUMS

The Jewish Targums were interpretative readings (paraphrases) of the Hebrew Bible in Aramaic. The term *targûm* (pl. *targûmîm*) is Aramaic for "translation." The Targums were used in synagogue worship. While some may be dated quite early, they tend to be dated in the Christian period.

THE SEPTUAGINT

The Septuagint is the Greek Old Testament translation. It is called the Septuagint (Latin for "seventy") because tradition says seventy-two scholars were commissioned to translate the Hebrew Old Testament and came up with word-for-word identical copies. The Septuagint is also called the LXX (Roman numeral 70). It was later revised and edited to meet the needs of non-Hebrew speakers. Within the different versions are different arrangements of the Hebrew text. The Septuagint also includes apocryphal books such as Tobit and Ecclesiasticus, which are in Catholic Old Testament canon (see next section). This is a vital piece of work; the Bible of the early church was the Septuagint, and most of the references in the New Testament to the Old Testament come from it.

THE APOCRYPHA

The term *apokrypha* means "hidden." The Apocrypha includes thirteen works from the old Greek codices of the Old Testament: Vaticanus, Sinaiticus, and Alexandrinus. None are found in the Hebrew Old Testament. These were written in the two centuries before Christ. These works were not accorded canonical status, as many Jews believed prophecy ended at Malachi (see Josephus, *Ag. Ap.* 1; *4 Ezra* 14; *B. Bat.* 14b–15c). All but one of these books found in the Catholic Bible are in the Septuagint. These include the Epistle of Jeremiah, Tobit, Judith, 3 Ezra (also named 1 Esdras and even III Esdras), Additions to Esther, The Prayer of Azariah and the Song of the Three Young Men, Susanna, Bel and the Dragon, 1 Baruch, Ben Sira (Sirach or Ecclesiasticus), 1 Maccabees, and 2 Maccabees. The latter two are important in giving historical background leading up to the time of Christ. These books are not referenced in the New Testament, indicating that they carried less importance for the early Christians than other Old Testament works.

THE PSEUDEPIGRAPHA

These are a range of books written under false names such as Moses, Adam, Ezra, and Abraham (i.e., they are pseudonymous).[26] There are sixty-five known books, including "last testaments" of dying leaders and Old Testament narratives expanded (e.g., the book of Jubilees and the Psalm of Solomon). Also included are many apocalyptic works, which are important to understanding Jewish eschatological expectations and are comparable to Revelation.

PHILO (C. 25 BC–AD 50)

Philo was a contemporary of Paul who was based in Alexandria, a center of philosophical and religious thought. He was an impressive Jewish theologian and philosopher who wrote extensively in a philosophical, theological, and missiological fashion. His writings reflect the influence of Hellenism on Jewish thought—especially Platonism—as he was motivated in part to communicate Judaism to Greek-thinking and -speaking peoples.

FLAVIUS JOSEPHUS (AD 37–C. 100)

Josephus was initially a rebel against Rome but surrendered and served the Romans. He wrote several important works, including *Jewish Antiquities*, the history of Israel; the *Jewish War*, an account of the Jewish rebellion against Rome; *Life*, his autobiography; and *Against Apion*, Josephus' defense of Judaism against a staunch critic, Apion. His writings are critical for

---

26. On pseudonymous works, see footnote 17.

providing insight into Jewish and Roman history in New Testament times. He references Christ in a disputed passage, the so-called *Testimonium Flavianum*, where Josephus mentions Christ's death and resurrection (Josephus, *Ant.* 18.63). He also mentions the Sanhedrin trying James, the brother of Jesus, and stoning him to death for breaking the law (Josephus, *Ant.* 20.200).

THE DEAD SEA SCROLLS

The Dead Sea Scrolls were found in 1947 in a cave at Qumran. They were written by a community of Essenes and stored in the desert. There are about 800 manuscripts that represent the library of the Essenes, a separatist apocalyptic Jewish sect. These scrolls give insight into the nature of the Old Testament texts and Judaism at that time. Ninety scrolls have been published dating from the second century BC. They include commentaries, copies of texts, documents on community life, and other works important to shed light on first-century Judaism.

IMPORTANT JEWISH PARTIES AND FEATURES

THE SADDUCEES

This group arose after the Maccabean Revolt (166–142 BC) but neither the specifics of their development nor the meaning of the term "Sadducees" is known. It is possible that they descended from the high priest Zadok and so saw themselves as the true priestly inheritors (2 Sam 8:17). Most chief priests were members of the Sadducees, as were "the nobles and the most eminent citizens" and "the leading men" (Josephus, *Ant.* 20.199, cf. *Ant.* 13.297). The power base of the party was in Jerusalem. Though the Sadducees were a minority within Israel, they wielded great power and were influential until their extinction in AD 70 with the destruction of the temple.

Theologically, the Sadducees believed the law was to be interpreted literally as it was written without any explanatory tradition. Thus, they rejected the authority of the Pharisees' oral law. In this sense, they have some likeness to modern fundamentalist conservatives. Because of their literalism, they believed the soul perished with the body and did not believe in the resurrection of the dead or the immortality of the soul as there is little reference to these in the torah.²⁷ This is why, when Jesus debates resurrection with them, he does so from the torah (Mark 12:24-27). Neither did they believe in any angelology, demons/devil, or lax approaches to the law. They rejected the belief in a messianic deliverer as this developed in the period after the Pentateuch, especially in the Prophets. Their chief concern was maintaining the temple worship cult. In this they can be likened to liberal Christians in their desire to retain traditional liturgical forms, while rejecting of the supernatural.

Politically, as noted above, they tended to be compromisers and collaborators with Roman oppressors. This meant they were liberal in the sense of being more open to Hellenistic lifestyle and values. Because of their theology and favorable position, they believed the chief priests should support Roman rule and cooperate with the Roman governors. Because of their cooperation with Romans and the oppressive tactics they used to manipulate the people for money and possessions, they were despised.

THE PHARISEES

The Pharisees' name derives from the Hebrew for "separate ones" and emphasizes their intense commitment to the law and its strict observance. This set them apart from pagans and other less-pious Jews. They believed they were the true holy ones (e.g., Phil 3:4-6). They believed that the path to God's liberation from foreign rule was committed law-observance. While some were priests, most were not aristocratic or priestly but were from the laity, the upper middle class. They were small in number and were active supporters of the synagogue. They were highly popular except among the upper classes. They joined and formed small "societies" in which they lived and studied. They likely originated before 135 BC from the Hasidim or "called-out ones."

The Pharisees, unlike the Sadducees, accepted the whole Old Testament as Scripture and were more open to new theological ideas found in the later writings. Some of these included the resurrection of the dead, the immortality of the soul, angelology, judgment, eternal reward and punishment, and the hope of a messiah.²⁸ They developed a system of oral tradition by

---

27. See Josephus, *Ant.* 18.16-17, cf. Matt 22:23-28; Acts 23:8.
28. See Josephus, *Ant.* 18.11-15; Acts 23:8.

which to interpret the law, or *halakah*. They identified 613 commandments in the torah Jews were required to observe—248 positive laws and 365 negative laws. They then set about interpreting these laws with thousands of others to ensure that the law was not broken. Their system was based on the traditions of famous rabbis. This *halakah* was an interpretation and commentary of the law. They developed traditions that taught this oral law was also given to Moses and was passed down through successive generations. In the second century AD, this oral law was written down as the *Mishnah*, and then modified and expanded. Scribes and lawyers studied these laws and applied the interpretations. This ongoing system of interpretation meant the Pharisees were the most flexible sect, as they constantly assessed the law with respect to their context. They were distinctive in that they believed the Mosaic laws regarding ritual purity were binding on all Jews, not just the priests. Hence, the many controversies between Jesus and the Pharisees concerning table fellowship, Sabbath keeping, and other areas the complex oral law had been developed make sense.

Politically they were conservative or quietest. They did not enjoy the Roman domination of Israel but did nothing about it. With their high view of the sovereignty of God, they believed Rome was God's judgment on the nation. However, toward the time of the rebellion against Rome, some were led to support the Zealots. The common people generally respected the Pharisees because of their strict observance of the law. Like all parties, there were "good" and "bad" Pharisees within the sect. From the Christian perspective, in the Gospels, the "good" included those like Nicodemus (John 3:1–8; 7:50; 19:39) and Joseph of Arimathea (Mark 15:43). These were devout men who sought to please God and became believers. The "bad" included those who succumbed to the dangers of legalism and put the "appearance" of observing a law before its purpose—to please God (see Matt 23:1–39; Luke 11:37–52). Like Nicodemus, Paul's story of redemption is one of a Pharisee finding Jesus and becoming a truly great Christian missionary. Some of the Judaizers he debated the law with in the Jerusalem Council were fellow Pharisees with a different perspective (Acts 15:5). Rabbinic Judaism that continued after Christianity, and is still established today, is basically Pharisaic.

THE ZEALOTS (OR NATIONALISTS)

While it is true the Zealots fully flowered in the years after Jesus' death, one can regard the whole country as ranged either with or against this party — and increasingly so, as the revolt against Rome in the 60s approached. Their central tenet was that no human being was their absolute lord, for God's rule is total — hence their virulent opposition to Rome, pagan gods, and Caesar as "Lord." They adhered literally to the first commandment, "You shall have no other gods before me" (Exod 20:3), and represented a revival of the Maccabean movement with its nationalism and desire to overthrow foreign oppressors. The movement's real home was Galilee, not Jerusalem — clearly something important, as this is Jesus' place of origin. The Zealots believed that to pay taxes to Rome or to even handle Roman coinage was treachery (hence, the question of paying taxes in Mark 12:13-17, i.e., is Jesus an insurrectionist?).[29] The Zealots enjoyed the support of the people and, because they represented a direct threat to Roman rule, they were punished severely when caught. They were often crucified. The Zealots first appeared in guerrilla bands that traversed Galilee under the leadership of Ezekias, whom Herod executed. Simon the Zealot, one of the disciples, probably came from this background (Mark 3:18).[30] It is also possible that Judas Iscariot's name indicates he was a member of the Assassins, Judas the Sicarii.[31] The nickname applied to James and John, "Boanerges" or "Sons of Thunder," may also indicate their zealot fervor (Mark 3:17).[32] It is likely

---

29. This is a trick question. See J. R. Edwards, *The Gospel According to Mark*, PNTC (Grand Rapids, MI; Leicester, England: Eerdmans; Apollos, 2002), 363. Edwards rightly comments, "The question of the Pharisees and Herodians is, of course, intended to imperil Jesus in a compromise: support for taxation will discredit him in the eyes of the people, whereas his refusal to pay the tax will bring the Roman Imperium down on him."

30. Some dispute this and argue that he should be called "Simon the Canaanite." See for a brief discussion R. A. Guelich, *Mark 1-8:26*, WBC 34A (Dallas: Word, 1998), 163.

31. See Ben Witherington III, *The Gospel of Mark: A Socio-Rhetorical Commentary* (Grand Rapids, MI: Eerdmans, 2001), 152. Witherington writes, "The term 'Iscariot' might mean a person from Kerioth, a town possibly in Idumea, possibly in Judea (cf. Josh. 15:25 near Hebron, Jer. 48:24 in Moab, but in either case he is not a Galilean), but it is also possible that this label indicates he was one of the *Sicarii* or dagger men, the extreme faction and hit men among the revolutionary party."

32. See Guelich, *Mark 1-8:26*, 162, for a discussion concerning the difficulties of derivation and interpretation. There is a diverse range of views on what it implies. Combined with James and John's arrogant self-confidence (Mark 10:37-39) and their desire to call fire down on a Samaritan town that rejected Jesus (Luke 9:54), they too may have had nationalistic, militaristic, zealous desires for revolt against Rome.

these men were initially excited about the nationalistic and military possibilities they saw in Jesus.

THE ESSENES (QUMRAN COMMUNITY)

The Jewish historian Josephus refers to the Essene community as numbering about 3,000 to 4,000 people in Judea and throughout the nation (Josephus, *J.W.* 2.119–135). However, when the Qumran scrolls were found in caves beside the Dead Sea in 1947 from what appears to be an Essene community, much was revealed about this sect. The Essenes were characterized by an ascetic lifestyle, strict adherence to the ritual laws, belief that the temple and priesthood were completely defiled, and the hope of a coming messiah. They may have believed in two messiahs—one priestly and one Davidic. They believed they were living in the last days, in Sabbath observance and circumcision, community life, and a compulsory common purse.[33] Not many were married. They were led by a rebel priest. They opposed Roman rule, but not actively at this stage. They were apocalyptic in outlook, viewing themselves as the faithful "sons of light" who would join the battle against the "sons of darkness." They can be likened to members of a Christian cult who separate themselves from the church and society, perceiving it to be completely corrupted. Scholars ponder whether John the Baptist, Jesus, or his disciples had links to the Qumran community. No connections have been proven, but this remains an area of fascination and possibility.

THE COMMON PEOPLE: "THE PEOPLE OF THE LAND"

The "common people," or Israel's "people of the land," made up around 90 percent of the population. They were, overall, unaffiliated with any major sect but retained the essential faith of Judaism. In many ways, they were the key recipients of Jesus' message, that is, the people who made up the crowds he encountered and ministered among. There were common religious factors that held all groups and common people together, including:

---

33. This is different from New Testament giving in Acts and in Paul, which is "without compulsion" (2 Cor 9:7).

1. **The Shema:** "Hear, O Israel: the LORD our God, the LORD is one" (Deut 6:4). This guarded against pluralism and enforced monotheism. This was recited daily.

2. **Covenant and election:** This was the belief that Israel was God's chosen people, giving them a privileged position in the world. This gave Israel's people a strong sense of nationalism and hope.

3. **Anti-gentile sentiment:** While the populace was prepared to tolerate the gentiles for economic gain, many despised the Romans and longed for their defeat and destruction. The prophetic hope, apocalyptic literature, and the "golden" Maccabean period gave the Jews hope. As God's favored people, they believed in and longed for their oppressors' ultimate subjugation and destruction.

4. **The law (torah) and ritual practice:** The ordinary people lived in a general sense by the law. The core boundary markers[34] of Israel included circumcision, Sabbath observance, food laws, ritual purity, exclusive table fellowship (see, for example, Dan 1; 1 Macc 1:62–63), and calendric observance. Circumcision was expected for every male child on the eighth day in accordance with the law of Moses (see Gen 17). Jesus' circumcision is a great example (Luke 2:23–24). Sabbath keeping was mandatory, including a refusal to work (Gen 2:1–3; Exod 20:9–11). The clashes with Jesus over Sabbath healings exemplify this. Sacrifice was also expected at key times, adhering to the requirements of the torah. There were strict food laws, including hand washing (Mark 7) and a refusal to eat with gentiles (which becomes important in the feeding miracles and later evangelization). The primacy of the temple

---

34. "Boundary Markers" are those rituals that defined Israel over against the gentiles, those things that mark the boundary between them. See Paul R. Trebilco and Craig A. Evans, "Diaspora Judaism," in *DNTB* 292–93, who note four ritual features serving to mark off Jews of the diaspora from their gentile neighbors: (1) monotheism; (2) dietary laws; (3) circumcision; and (4) Sabbath.

was standard except among the Essenes.³⁵ The rhythms of the Jewish calendar were important. Israel's society revolved around feasts and festivals, which occurred on key dates on which they remembered God's acts and the harvest. Common people participated in these feasts and festivals and sought to travel to Jerusalem when they could. The common people were in the main, and were committed to synagogue worship each Sabbath.

5. **Messianic hope:** While it is disputed that all Israel was expecting a Davidic messiah redeemer and that the expectations were varied, there is ample evidence in the Gospels that many among the ordinary people dreamed of the day the messiah would come on God's behalf to put things right. This redeemer was expected to be a warrior-king figure who, with God on his side, would redeem Israel from the oppression of the Romans and gentiles. He would establish a theocratic state centered on Jerusalem, the temple, and the law. The world would convert to Judaism or be defeated (e.g., Pss. Sol. 17).³⁶

THE SAMARITANS

The Samaritans were hated by the Jews, who considered them half-Jews because they were descended from those who had been taken into exile in 722 BC by Assyria and had intermarried and mixed with other nations. The Samaritans had their own temple on Mount Gerizim. During the reign of Antiochus Epiphanies (168 BC) the Samaritans complied with his decrees and stopped observing the Sabbath and circumcising, and dedicated their temple to Zeus, causing the Jews to hate them even more. In 128 BC, their temple was destroyed by the Maccabean family as it was considered blasphemy. Like the Sadducees, they rejected all but the torah in the Scriptures. The Samaritans did worship the same God, however, and they observed the Sabbath and circumcision, the law of Moses, and the Pentateuch—and

---

35. There were exceptions, e.g., the Essenes saw themselves as the temple; there were temples in other places.

36. Mark J. Keown, *Jesus in a World of Colliding Empires* (Wipf & Stock, 2018).

they looked for a messiah deliverer. They were deeply despised by the Jews. They recur throughout the New Testament and often at the most surprising times as heroes in opposition to Jews (see Matt 10:5; Luke 9:52; 10:25-37; 17:16; John 4:7-42; 8:48; Acts 8:4-25).

THE DIASPORA

Another important feature of Israel at the time of Jesus was the number of Jews living in communities outside the nation itself. It is estimated that more than five million Jews lived outside of Israel, and only one to two million within. This came about not only through natural migration but also through enforced emigration after the exile and the continuous oppression of Israel. The diaspora, meaning "dispersion," was intense under Alexander the Great (332 BC). Significant Jewish populations developed in Alexandria,[37] Rome,[38] and Sardis. As Paul took the gospel to the Greco-Roman world, there were synagogues in every city he visited except Philippi, Lystra, and Derbe. The primary significance of the diaspora is that it enabled the spread of the gospel quickly through Jewish pilgrim converts (Acts 2) and through the ministry of Paul in synagogues. Here Paul found Jews, gentile converts (proselytes), and God-worshipers (not fully converted gentile seekers).

POPULAR PROPHETIC AND MESSIANIC MOVEMENTS

Prophetic movements popped up at various times and in various ways. When they came to the Romans' attention, they were usually immediately crushed as they were a threat to Roman rule (see Luke 13:1-2; Acts 5:37; 21:38).[39] The most well-known movements of this type are those of John the Baptist and Jesus. Both were considered as possible messiahs (John 1:19-28), and both preached and promoted repentance. However, neither advocated violence. John preached a message of repentance and good works. Jesus preached a "revolution" of repentance and love.

---

37. Philo numbered Jews in Egypt in the first century AD at one million. See Philo, *Flacc.* 43.
38. There were 20,000 to 50,000 Jews in Rome at the turn of the eras (see J. A. Overman and W. S. Green, "Judaism," in *ABD*, 3:1048).
39. Horsley, R. A. "Early Christian Movements: Jesus Movements and the Renewal of Israel," *HTS* 62.4 (2006), 1201-25.

OTHER FEATURES OF LIFE IN ISRAEL

PEASANT AND URBAN LIFE

In general, there was a distinction between rural and urban life in Israel. In the West, most people lived in cities, while most people of the ancient world were rural and agrarian. However, there were many significant cities and towns that were centers of political, economic, and religious life. As with the world today, rural people tended to be more conservative and biased against new ideas, such as those of Hellenism and Rome. Urban life tended to be more cosmopolitan, and these people were open to new ideas that could infiltrate. Interestingly, Jesus' ministry was focused almost exclusively in rural areas, while Paul focused on cities.

THE LIFE OF THE PEASANT

Most people in Israel lived in villages and small towns. They worked the land and had strong kinship bonds, valuing loyalty highly. They tended to have mixed views of the urban world. They distrusted city people, since cities were the centers of power, wealth, and privilege. On the other hand, they interacted economically with people who lived in the city.

Life was lived at a subsistence level. People were at the mercy of the weather and other natural disasters such as earthquakes,[40] droughts, and famines,[41] as well as the whims of those in power. Life revolved around the harvest, which needed to supply all that was needed for food, trade, and seed

---

40. The Jordan Rift Valley is a fault line. See Amos 1:1, which refers to an earthquake, which is likely an earthquake in Hazor (765-760 BC); see Billy K. Smith and Franklin S. Page, *Amos, Obadiah, Jonah*, NAC 19B (Nashville: Broadman & Holman Publishers, 1995), 38 (see also Exod 19:18; Num 16:31; 1 Sam 14:15; 1 Kings 19:11; Zech 14:5). See also the earthquake at Jesus' crucifixion and resurrection (Matt 27:54; 28:2). There was a shocking earthquake at the time of the battle of Actium in September 31 BC in Judea that destroyed many herds, and a huge number of people were crushed, while the army was spared (10,000 in Josephus, *Ant.* 15.120-121; revised to 30,000 in *J.W.* 1.370). The main centers for earthquakes are northern Galilee, Samaria near Shechem, and the western Judean mountains near Lydda (see "Earthquake," in *BEB* 1.647).

41. Famines were common due to drought, which was frequent in Israel and caused great suffering (Jer 14:1-6; Lam 4:9). Famines led to increased prices for food (2 Kgs 6:24-25). Drought and famine were greatly feared, and sometimes led to cannibalism (Deut 28:56-57; 2 Kgs 6:28-29; Jer 19:9; Lam 2:20; 4:10; Ezek 5:10). A great famine caused Israel to enter Egypt (Gen 41:27, cf. Gen 12:10; 26:1; Ruth 1:1). Other famines are also mentioned (2 Sam 21:1; 24:13; 1 Kgs 8:37; 18:2; 2 Kgs 4:38; 6:25; 7:4; 8:1; 25:3; Neh 5:3). Twice Paul took up collections for the Judean Christians experiencing famine (Acts 11:28; Rom 15:24-26; 1 Cor 16:2; 2 Cor 8-9).

for the following year while leaving enough to sell to pay taxes. Ceremonies such as weddings, births, funerals, and festivals were important. With no health or social services, personal health was of huge importance to survival. Jesus' ministry of healing, preaching, feeding, deliverance, and salvation was, for the most part, in such settings.

URBAN AND ELITE LIFE

There is little reference to Hellenistic Roman cities, such as Tiberias (established in AD 20) and Sepphoris, in the Gospels. This is somewhat surprising, especially regarding Tiberias, which is very close to Magdala and Capernaum, which lie on the western side of the Sea of Galilee. Sepphoris, too, is close to Nazareth. On the other hand, although there were Jews living in the cities, the cities were Greco-Roman in orientation. The primary setting for Jesus' ministry was small towns like Capernaum.

Hellenistic-Roman cities like Sepphoris and Tiberias provided markets where peasants sold their harvests to feed the people of the city and for export. These cities included harvest-based industries (mills, presses, granaries) and small businesses (e.g., bakeries, potteries) and served as the base for interregional commerce. They were self-governed.

The key city in the Gospels is Jerusalem. Its importance was based almost solely on its being the site of the temple, which brought together the religious, political, economic, and social strands of life in Israel.[42] The Roman base in Israel was Caesarea Maritima, a key port on the west coast. When the gospel expanded beyond Israel, the movement became based on urban centers.

A CORPORATE MINDSET

The European western mindset is characterized by rampant individualism in which the center of a person's world is self. This individualism is reflected in western law, which favors the individual (individual human rights) and in private attitudes to life and property (privatism). Israel at the time of Christ was, on the contrary, highly corporate. The primary social unit was the household (*oikos*), but it extended well beyond the nuclear

---

42. Jerusalem was not a trade center—it was located off the trade routes and had no river or port.

family, including other relatives, slaves, and sometimes clients. Social engagement and cohesion were based on hospitality and table fellowship, especially meals. The modernist mantra "I think, therefore I am" can be replaced by the African view of the person, which believes, "I am because we are, and since we are, therefore I am."[43] Or perhaps, "We eat together. Therefore, we are." Hence, the culture of the New Testament is more akin to indigenous cultures, like those in Polynesia, Asia, the Americas, and Arab communities rather than contemporary western European culture. It is critical when reading Scripture to remember that the individual, while not obscured, was always seen in the context of close-knit communities rather than western individualism.

THE FAMILY: "FICTIVE KINSHIP"

As in most pre-industrial societies, human identity at the time of Christ was formed in the context of family, genealogy, and community—that is, kin-groups. The family was the basic unit of the empire. It included the husband, wife, children, other relatives, clients, and slaves in the home. The authority rested with the senior male, the *paterfamilias*, who was at the same time father, husband, and master. Thus, in Paul's household codes, while children, wives, and slaves are addressed, the father, husband, and master is the same person, and the rhetorical force falls on the head male (Eph 5:21–6:9; Col 3:18–4:1). In Greco-Roman culture, the father's authority was widespread, including the right to divorce the wife, to retain or reject children,[44] to punish a child severely even to death, to take a child's property, and even to sell a child into slavery. Children and slaves were the most vulnerable. Women maintained their place through child bearing, child rearing, and engaging with other women. This background shows how radical Jesus' teachings were in relation to family. His kind treatment of children, his redefinition of family as those who do God's will, and his calling God "Abba"—an expression of intimacy—opposed normal practices.

---

43. Mbiti, John. *African Religions and Philosophies* (New York: Doubleday and Company, 1970), 141.

44. In Greco-Roman culture, it was common for a child to be aborted or exposed (left to die) if unwanted. Jewish culture found this abhorrent. See Michael J. Gorman, *Abortion in the Early Church: Christian, Jewish & Pagan Attitudes in the Greco-Roman World* (Eugene, OR: Wipf & Stock, 1982).

In the New Testament, the family is the primary model of the church. God is the Father, Jesus Christ the Son, believers the brothers and sisters, and the community meal of the word and communion is at the center of its "family life." Jesus is also considered the "bride of Christ." The church and other voluntary societies create what is called "fictive kinship" whereby the family circle is redefined in terms of allegiance to God and Christ and spreads to others who are not biologically family, even at the expense of those in one's natural family. The church also began in family groupings in homes and spread from home to home. These homes were, in a sense, opened and extended to the world.

RECIPROCITY

Reciprocity speaks of the common cultural practice of repayment or recompense whereby when one gives something to another, that person reciprocates. In many cultures, this is obligatory. There are two types of reciprocity in the New Testament world. First, there is "balanced reciprocity," which dominated the world at the time. This refers to the general expectation that when one person gave something, reciprocation was expected from the recipient. Thus, giving always came with strings attached. How this played out depended on the social relationships of the various parties. However, even in Greco-Roman friendship, there was a normal expectation of reciprocity. This is critical for understanding patronage. Second, there is what some call "generalized reciprocity," which refers to giving within close kinship ties. This tends to be one-sided and altruistic without the expectation of response.[45] If a person gave, he did so in expectation of return, and vice versa. Christian giving stands in contrast to this, with a person giving without expectation of reciprocation and without the giver having control over the recipient (as in Corinth with Paul). However, the principle of reciprocity is retained, but it is God who gives in return for his people's giving to others. He honors and rewards the giver.

PATRONAGE

Patronage was also a dominant feature of ancient interpersonal relationships. This involved a patron who resourced a client while the client

---

45. Oakman, D. E. "Economics of Palestine," in *DNTB* 306.

responded with loyalty and honor, which were useful to the patron. In fact, the whole social structure of the Roman Empire was based on a system of patronage whereby the emperor was seen as the ultimate patron to humanity, and the power structures of towns and communities were based on patronage. Because patronage carried with it the expectation of reciprocation, the wealthy would give to clients with the expectation of some return and often with public honor. Patronage could be public, whereby a wealthy member of the elite donates or funds a public amenity and gains honor and public acclaim. It was important for climbing the social ladder. This sort of thing is not uncommon in contemporary politics. Christian giving subverts this as the follower of Jesus gives unconditionally to God's work without public acclaim or a need to exert influence.

STATUS IN AN HONOR-AND-SHAME SOCIETY

In the ancient world, status was not based on class in a Marxist sense, but on power and privilege, which involved a complex interplay of religious purity, family heritage, land ownership, vocation, gender, ethnicity, education, wealth, and age. Essentially it related to ascribed honor based on others' estimation of a person's being and ability. Shame was the great enemy of honor. Personal reputation was critical, and great efforts were made among the more Romanized to seek personal glory through bragging, patronage, and selfish ambition. There was also the critical expectation of bringing honor to one's family and to the State. However, even one's family could be sacrificed to enhance one's own status, as seen in politics—those seeking glory often had a family member killed for personal gain. The Christian community was open to people of all levels of status and honor and ascribing to all equal honor, despite worldly status or one's role in the community. Understanding that the New Testament world was based on honor and shame—largely due to its highly stratified system, its corporate lifestyle, and the need to protect one's name—is critical. Honor-and-shame-based societies differ from individualistic societies based on personal sin and guilt. Rather, one's understanding of sin emphasizes not only guilt but communal shame.

PATRIARCHY

Women were essentially homemakers and expected to provide support to their husbands. In Jewish society, women did not own property but were at the mercy of their fathers and, when married, their husbands. Although there may have been the odd exception, women could not divorce husbands. Women had few legal rights, with their testimony in court worthless. Women were unable to be religious leaders such as priestesses, disciples, or rabbis. The goal of the unmarried young woman was to find a husband, through whom her identity was formed. Producing an heir was critical, and barrenness was shameful. In wider Greco-Roman societies, women sometimes had more freedom such as being able to own property (e.g., Lydia and Nympha, Acts 16:11–15; Col 4:15) and divorce a husband. However, as with Jewish society, women were generally confined to their sphere. A public conversation between a man and woman would arouse suspicions. Upon arriving at the New Testament, these ideas were being challenged and patriarchy radically subverted.

QUESTIONS TO CONSIDER

- What distinctive features of Jewish culture stand out to you?
- What key similarities and differences between Israel's first-century culture and your own culture do you need to consider as you engage in New Testament study?

THE GRECO-ROMAN CONTEXT OF THE NEW TESTAMENT

CHAPTER 3

This chapter discusses some of the historical, political, and social factors of the Greco-Roman[1] world important for New Testament study. This is particularly significant in understanding the spread of the gospel into the gentile world; Paul's missions; the world of the first readers of the Gospels of Mark, Luke, and John; and the letters of the New Testament, which were mostly written from and/or into the Greco-Roman environment.

HELLENISM

Hellenistic (Greek) culture remained strongly influential throughout the whole of the Roman world. Many of these factors also relate to the Jewish background of the New Testament because Judaism had been influenced strongly by Hellenism for more than 300 years and by Rome for 100 years—a significant time for the interpenetration of cultural ideas. The Romans loved the Greek culture. As their influence spread and they superseded Macedonian rule, they tended to retain the Greek influence that was well established. So, Koine Greek remained the lingua franca throughout the Roman world; life was more Greek than Roman.

---

1. "Greco-Roman" is the American spelling, "Graeco-Roman" the UK spelling. I have opted for the American for simplicity's sake, as both are commonly used today.

THE CITY

While Jesus' mission was primarily to the rural world of Galilee, Paul's mission led to a remarkable social shift in the early Christian church. The Christian faith shifted from being a predominately Jewish and rural movement to a mainly gentile and urban movement.[2]

The Greek world consisted of hundreds of *poleis* ("city-states"). Each *polis* was fiercely independent, with its own distinctive internal political and religious structure. The *polis* developed by the late sixth century BC and typically included an acropolis,[3] rock walls, a public square (*agora*), multiple temples and shrines, a theatre, fountains, springs and baths, and a gymnasium—all within the city walls.

The cities of the empire were located on important roads and ports. They were important centers of consumption and distribution. Their streets and marketplaces were bustling centers for traders and peddlers. Most had a main street with colonnades and a covered walkway from the city gate to the *agora*, where large buildings such as temples and palaces could be found. One of the key buildings was the "council house" or *bouleuterion* where the council (*boulē*) met. Another was the *prytaneion*, the magistrate meeting house, in which was found the sacred hearth of the city gods who oversaw the city.[4]

The *agora*, which was flanked with shops, functioned as a marketplace, a center for justice and public discourse (*bema*) concerning business and philosophy, and a venue for meetings. The *gymnasia* included physical training venues but also schools for the rich. While physical labor dominated rural life, it was not popular in the city. In fact, hands stained or marked by hard labor were dishonorable—something Paul would have had to deal with. Important values included virtue, character, self-sufficiency, and, if possible, a life of leisure. This was enabled by the huge number of slaves who carried the bulk of the work. Civic leadership, public service, and benefaction were greatly valued among the elite, especially among

---

2. For detail, see D. J. Tidball, "The Social Setting of Mission Churches," in *DPL* 883–91.

3. The acropolis (*akros*, "highest" and *polis*, "city") was a fort and lookout on top of a nearby mountain which housed soldiers and oversaw the area for the protection of the town or city. For example, there is one on the mountain overlooking Philippi, a large one on the Acrocorinth overlooking Corinth, and the famous acropolis in Athens which was surmounted by the Parthenon. See "Acropolis," in *TBD* 10.

4. See D. F. Watson, "Cities, Greco-Roman," *DNTB*, 213.

those wealthy with "old money" based on real capital, not work. Many in the city were not wealthy. They were workers, including leather workers (e.g., Paul), grocers, bakers, and slaves. Their children, especially sons, took over the family business.

Paul focused his mission on these cities, establishing the church in these centers and leaving the new communities of faith with the task of continuing the mission and extending it into the rural regions (e.g., Acts 13:49; 19:10; 1 Thess 1:8, see also Rom 15:19). The cities Paul visited lay on the east-west trade routes.

Antioch in Syria was the early base for his operations (Acts 13:1-3; 14:26-27; Gal 2:11). Antioch had a population of about 250,000 and was prosperous. It was located on the main road from Rome to the Persian border. It was the capital of the imperial province of Syria and an intellectual focal point. It had a long-standing and large Jewish population.

The other cities Paul visited were also on trade routes and were relatively prosperous. Laodicea, Hierapolis, and Colossae were centers of wool trade. Philippi was a small but highly important city and was granted the status of a Roman colony due to its support of Octavian in establishing his reign. It was highly favored and distinct in that it was more Latin in character and was an agricultural rather than a commercial center. While Ephesus does not have a harbor today, at the time of the New Testament it was well-known for its harbor and the amazing temple of Artemis. Corinth and Thessalonica were provincial capitals and important trading centers. The cities of Galatia, Antioch in Pisidia, Iconium, and Lystra were, like Philippi, Roman colonies.

While Latin was the Roman political language, the lingua franca of the educated populace in the cities was Koine Greek. Many other languages and dialects from the local populations were also spoken through the empire, especially in the hinterlands. The cities tended to be physically orientated toward Rome. They were conveniently located on a road or a sea. They varied in size; in Paul's missions, Antioch was the largest and Philippi the smallest. Ephesus was a government center for Asia Minor.

As much of their space was afforded to public facilities, their residential areas were densely populated with most people in apartment blocks, or *insulae*. There was, thus, little privacy. Apart from the wealthy who lived in big villas, due to heat and the close confines of the *insulae*, people only slept and stored possessions in their homes and lived, for the most part, outside. Because of this, people's lives were exposed and easily observable. This has important missional implications. People tended to gather in ethnic groups and were easily identifiable. For Paul's mission, the Jewish quarter with the synagogue at the center was most important. The Jews of the diaspora were well integrated but lived in their own areas and were politically quiescent and religiously focused. Jews were well distributed throughout the status system.

The many temples were important centers for city life, and Paul would have encountered a wide variety of religious and philosophical viewpoints in each center.

In terms of mission, cities were more strategic locations than villages because of the ease of communication through a common language and ongoing business and political activity. Rural contexts and villages tended to be conservative and closed. They were subsistence based and as such had few opportunities for upward social mobility. On the other hand, cities were open and changeable with people who were independently-minded and thus receptive to the new message of the gospel. Further, when the gospel was seeded in a city, the scope for its spread was far greater.

SOCIAL INSTITUTIONS

Three key social institutions are especially important for understanding Paul's mission in the wider Greco-Roman world.

THE SYNAGOGUE

There were synagogues throughout the Roman world due to the Jewish population throughout the diaspora. These synagogues provided Paul, as a Jew and highly honored Pharisee, with an immediate platform for his message and in many ways served as a model for the new churches. Synagogues were the centers of Jewish political organization and, as such, were recognized in the government structure of the cities. Synagogues were called *aedes sacrae*, or "sacred buildings" in Roman law. Those synagogues without a permanent fixture for the torah ark could be meeting houses for secular matters such as matters of justice, where slaves were released, where the poor were fed, and where community life was managed. Many functioned as schools for the youth. The *archisynagogos* was a Jewish political ruler within the local synagogue. We see these people regularly in Acts (Acts 13:15; 18:8, 17, cf. Jairus in Mark 5:22; Luke 13:14). Gentiles were also attached to the synagogue, some full converts like the proselyte Nicolaus in Acts 6:5, and others worshipers of God with a real interest in Judaism. Some of these mentioned in Acts include Cornelius (Acts 10:1–2), Lydia (Acts 16:14), and Titius Justus (Acts 18:7). Nero's second wife, Poppaea, was also a God-worshiper (Josephus, *Ant.* 20.195). Synagogues then gave Paul and others like Apollos (Acts 18:26) a ready audience and opportunity for the gospel to spread through Jew and gentile alike. However, this was usually short-lived, with the church moving to homes as a result of Jewish persecution. Christianity then became a separate movement.

THE HOUSEHOLD[5]

At the time of Paul's ministry, the household (*oikos*) differed greatly from the private picket-fenced residences of the western world today. Poor households crowded into apartments called *insulae*. Sometimes these *insulae* included shops at the front and living quarters at the rear. For the artisans, there would have been room for worship and living quarters for dependents and visitors. Such homes had room to accommodate itinerant preachers like Paul and provided opportunities for him to make his living as a tentmaker (e.g., Phlm 22). Like itinerant Cynic philosophers of the day, Paul used manual labor to model his philosophy to his disciples; however, he did not beg as was common with Cynic itinerant teachers.

The households were large inclusive communities consisting of the family, slaves, friends, tenants, partners, and clients who would have been involved in a common or agricultural enterprise. When the church developed, these homes provided an ideal context for church meetings. Households were hierarchical and patriarchal, under the authority of the father (*paterfamilias*). Wealthy homeowners, including some women, often acted as patrons of the early church communities (Rom 16:3–5, 14, 15, 23; 1 Cor 1:11; 16:19; Col 4:15; Phlm 2; Acts 16:11–14). Households were not based on the rampant individualism of contemporary western society; the leader of the household would make decisions on behalf of the remainder of the household. Hence, when the household leader became a believer

---

5. For detail, see Tidball, "The Social Setting," 883–91.

(e.g., Lydia or the Roman jailor), whole households were usually converted (Acts 16:15, 31-34, cf. Acts 18:8; 1 Cor 1:16). This meant that the mission was not always met with an equal commitment among the converted with some coming to Christ because of family allegiance and not a personal decision. However, there is also evidence in the New Testament of homes where not all were Christian (1 Cor 7:13-16; 1 Pet 3:1-2). It is also possible that the focus on house churches led to divisions based on an affiliation to particular preferred leaders (cf. 1 Cor 1:10-17). However, overall, in close-knit communities in which life was public, the household was a ready-made "basic cell" for the spread of the faith through existing relationships.

The houses in which the church met were owned by the wealthy who acted as patrons of the church, providing a base. The area around the *impluvium* (bath) is the atrium where they probably held their meetings, ate meals, and performed baptisms.

VOLUNTARY ASSOCIATIONS

There were many voluntary associations or *collegia* in Roman society, including private clubs based on a common trade or objective. Their corporate life revolved around festivity and meals. The associations often provided people with religious and emotional satisfaction, which was lacking in the more austere public or official cults. Rome tolerated these groups with suspicion. These groups included:

- Professional corporations or guilds, e.g., fisherman, fruit growers, ship owners

- Funerary societies (*collegia tenuirum*)

- Religious or cult societies (*collegia sodalicia*)

Rome viewed Judaism as a large international *collegia*. As Christianity emerged, it was viewed as an extension of Judaism. As Christianity became distinct from Judaism, the church remained a voluntary association in that it had private meetings, voluntary membership, an initiation ritual, meal fellowship, and a degree of exclusivity. The Christian church differed from these voluntary associations in that it crossed the social strata, was inclusive of women and slaves, called for a high degree of commitment, and was international. The category of voluntary association was important because it enabled the Pauline churches to be accommodated in the Roman world.

GREEK RELIGION

Numerous cults were devoted to the worship of the Olympian gods, the reigning emperor, mystery religions, and Oriental deities.[6] These were paramount for a city's economy as pilgrims brought in their money. Temples were among the most prominent buildings in the cities. Festivals shaped the annual calendar and the public holidays. The Imperial cult was a vehicle for reinforcing political allegiance and cohesion.[7] However, the more popular religions gave meaning and order to life. A common feature of religion at the time was syncretism—a blend of different religious ideas.

The religious and cultural institutions accessible to all Greeks included the Panhellenic games held every two to four years (e.g., the Olympic games, 776 BC onwards), the oracle of Apollo at Delphi, the healing cult of Asclepius at Epidauros, and the Eleusinian mysteries at Eleusis. In the late sixth century BC, the civic cult of the twelve gods was instituted in many Greek cities. Greek religion was not centered on a set of coherent doctrines but on the observance of traditional rituals such as processions, prayers, libations (drink offerings usually made up of a mixture of water and wine), sacrifices, and feasting.

THE GODS

Jews believe in one transcendent God (monotheism), who embodies the masculine and feminine, created all things other than himself, and is utterly good and just. Christians retained this, however, considering the son of God to be three in One, with all three persons of the Godhead good,

---

6. See further for details on this section in D. E. Aune's article, "Religions, Greco-Roman," in *DPL* 786-95.

7. From the time of Alexander the Great, there was an increasing tendency to deify kings (i.e., see them as gods). This was logical in a pantheistic environment based on religious heroes who were both human and gods. Julius Caesar and Augustus were deified and consecrated as part of the official Roman pantheon by acts of the Roman senate. The importance of the Imperial cult was greater away from Rome (especially in Asia) where the emperor was unable to be present while based in Rome. In the traditional form of the Imperial cult, the emperor was worshiped as a god only after his death and apotheosis. However, two emperors, Caligula (Philo, *Legat.* 353) and Domitian (Suetonius, *Dom.* 13.2), took the name Deus ("god") upon themselves in their lifetimes.

just, involved in creation, and not engaged in sexual relationships. Greeks had an utterly different view of the gods who are many (polytheism), male and female, and were capricious (capable of good and evil). These gods, through sexual relationships, could produce more gods.

The Greek gods were not transcendent (distant) and were relatively passive but, like the Hindu gods in India today, were immanent (present) and active. They did not create the cosmos but came into being *after* the cosmos, which is eternal. The god of the sun (*Helios*), the goddess of the moon (*Selene*), and the gods of the stars were "eternals," while Zeus (king of the gods, Hera's husband), *Hera* (Zeus' sister and consort), and *Poseidon* (god of the sea) were "immortals." Both gods and humanity were subject to fate (*moira, Tyche*). Ambrosia and nectar sustained the gods, and "ichor" flowed through their veins. They were neither omnipotent nor omniscient. Humans were mortal; the gods were immortal. In archaic or classical Greek religion, immortality was not possible for humans.

In Hesiod's *Theogony* (eighth/seventh century BC), the gods are genealogically linked. In Homer's *Iliad* and *Odyssey* (c. seventh century BC), the gods are depicted as a pantheon of Olympian gods. The cult of the twelve gods first appeared in the sixth century (c. 520 BC). They ruled after the overthrow of the Titans. These twelve were not identical with the later twelve Olympians. They include *Zeus* (*Dia*), who overthrew his father, *Cronus* (*a* Titan, the god of time), and after drawing lots with his brothers *Poseidon* and *Hades*, became the supreme ruler of the gods. *Zeus* is lord of the sky, the rain god, and his weapon is a thunderbolt. His wife and sister is *Hera*, whom he married after deceit and rape. While her relationship with Zeus is stormy, she is the protector of marriage and married women. He features in Acts 14:12 (see below). It is likely that *Zeus* is the "most high god" mentioned by the slave girl in Acts 16:17.

After the overthrow of *Cronus*, *Poseidon* was allotted the sea and was important for mariners. His weapon is a trident. He is second to *Zeus* in power. He is quarrelsome and greedy. After *Cronus'* defeat, *Hades* was allotted the underworld to rule over the dead. His desire is to see people die, and he is unpitying and capricious. While he is king of the dead, the god

Thanatos is death itself. *Hades* features in Jewish Greek literature[8] and in the New Testament not as a god, but as a place—hell—which Jesus triumphs over and which is ultimately destroyed in the lake of fire (Matt 11:23; Luke 10:15; 16:23; Acts 2:27, 31; Rev 1:18; 6:8; 20:13, 14).

Another sister of *Zeus* is the virgin goddess *Hestia,* who is a goddess of domestic beauty and the hearth, when a newborn child is received into the family. Each Greek city had a perpetually burning public hearth sacred to *Hestia.*

Zeus and *Hera's* son is *Ares,* the god of war. *Zeus'* favored daughter is *Athena,* another virgin goddess, who sprang from *Zeus'* forehead fully armed and has no mother. She protects the state and home. She enabled people to tame horses by inventing the bridle. She also invented a range of other things like musical instruments (e.g., the flute), farming utensils (e.g., the plow), and vehicles (the ship and the chariot). She is the goddess of wisdom. Her favorite city is Athens, as the city's name indicates. *Athena* features prominently in ancient architecture in Greece and Turkey, as does *Artemis.*

Apollo is *Zeus* and *Leto's* son, the daughter of Titans *Coeus* and *Phoebe,* and the twin brother to *Artemis.* He is the god of music and poetry, medicine and healing, light (he moves the sun), and the truth—he cannot lie (cf. Jesus, John 14:6). As the god of prophecy, he spoke through the Oracle of Delphi. The slave girl with the spirit of divination would have been understood to have spoken on behalf of *Apollo* (Acts 16:16). *Apollos* bears his name, a name culturally appropriate for his dynamic speaking (Acts 18:24–19:1; 1 Cor 1:12; 3:4–6, 22; 4:6; 16:12).

Artemis is another virgin goddess—the goddess of chastity and overseas childbirth. She is a huntswoman who protects the young and is associated with the moon and fertility. Her cult was especially important in Ephesus, and followers clashed with early Christians in that city (Acts 19:24–35). The goddess of love, desire, and beauty is *Aphrodite. Epaphroditus* was

---

8. *Hadēs* is found in the LXX 108 times, often translating the Hebrew *Sheol,* the place of the dead (e.g., Gen 37:35; Num 16:30; Deut 32:22; 1 Sam 2:6; Ps 6:6; Prov 1:12; Eccl 9:10; Song 8:6; Job 7:9; Hos 13:12; Amos 9:2; Jon 2:3; Hab 2:5; Isa 5:14; Jer 41:5; Ezek 31:16–17; Dan 3:88; Wis 1:14; Sir 9:12; Tob 3:10; Bar 2:17; 2 Macc 6:23; 3 Macc 4:8; Pss. Sol. 15.10). Common in other Jewish literature (e.g., *Sib. Or.* 1.81; *Gk. Apoc. Ezra* 4.32; *T. Reu.* 4.6; *T. Levi* 4.1; Josephus, *Ant.* 6.332; *J.W.* 2.156; Philo, *Post.* 31; *Mos.* 1.195; *Legat.* 235).

named with her in mind (Phil 2:25). In old Corinth, before its destruction (146 BC), a great temple to *Aphrodite* with many prostitutes sat on the Acrocorinth overlooking the city and contributed to the city's reputation as a den of sexual immorality. Aphrodite's husband is *Hephaestus*, Zeus and Hera's son. He is ugly and lame and the god of fire and metalwork who builds arms for the gods in a volcanic forge.

Hermes is another son of *Zeus*, this time born to *Maia*, daughter of *Atlas* and one of the Pleiades. He is speedy (the god of travel), wears winged sandals and a hat, and carries a wand. He is *Zeus'* messenger and the god of thieves and commerce. He is also the god of invention, inventing musical instruments (e.g., the lyre) and the music scale, and creating sports like boxing and gymnastics. One early Christian carried his name (Rom 16:14). He is also the god of eloquence. Barnabas and Paul are mistakenly associated with *Zeus* (father) and *Hermes* (messenger) in Acts 14:12.

While Jesus is the Son of God the Father in the New Testament, he is nothing like the literal genealogical relationships of the Greek gods in myth. There is no "mother goddess." God is both father and mother, and there is no sexuality in the Godhead. God creates by a word, not through sexuality and conflict. While God acts in judgment, he is nothing like the capricious gods of Greece. The one God of the biblical narrative is God of all.

Overall, the Greeks recognized three kinds of deity: (1) Olympian gods, (2) chthonic (earth) gods, and (3) heroes. Some were of Indo-European origin—for example, Zeus = Jupiter. Most of the chthonic gods appear to have been deities indigenous to the Greek world and associated with the earth, crops, and the underworld. The heroes were mortals who, due to their amazing exploits, were deified upon death and received cultic honors at their tomb. Some were seen as the product of a god or goddess and human sexual relationships. So, for example, *Hercules* was supposedly the son of *Zeus* and a mortal woman, *Alcmene*. In general, the Greeks were receptive to new deities and cults and often identified their own deities with foreign ones. This is evident in the cross-identification with Roman gods and Egyptian cults. This is also seen in the spread of Judaism and Christianity within the Greek world. The Greek gods were linked by a genealogy derived from sexual relations between gods and goddesses.

Thus, we can see that the Greco-Roman religious worldview was polytheistic with affinities to contemporary Hinduism. The concept of monotheism was alien to them. The Christian faith system, like Judaism, called for an exclusivity that stood in stark contrast to the syncretism, tolerance, and acceptance of new gods in Greek religion.

RITUALS

All religion has its rituals. Greco-Roman religions were based around certain rituals designed to keep the capricious and unpredictable gods happy. These were slavishly kept as the Greco-Roman world was superstitious and governed by fear that the wrath of the gods would be aroused. There was, thus, a range of practices maintained to ensure the *pax deorum*, "the peace of the gods."

Prayer

This involved various formulae to ensure the gods were not offended so as to bring judgment. Prayers were uttered with public sacrifices, public ceremonies, and before battle. Some Christian prayer would have taken on similar Greco-Roman prayer forms.

Sacrifice

The primary mode of sacrifice was the slaughter of approved domestic animals. Part of the animal was burned on the altar and part was consumed by those making the sacrifice. Animals were associated with divinities. For example, cows were associated with *Athena* and pigs with *Demeter/Hades*. Different gods required different sacrifices. An example was the great civil event Hyacinthia at Sparta. A procession of sacrifice victims and citizens was followed by the slaughter, the burning of part of the sacrifice, and the division of what remained for the populace.[9] Hence, Christ's death as a sacrifice was easily understood in the Greek context.

Festivals

Even more than in the Jewish world with its feast-and-festival calendar, festivals, called *heortai*, were regular and important. For example, in the *polis* of Athens, 120 days were devoted to religious festivals for such gods as *Athena, Dionysus, Apollo and Artemis, Aphrodite, and Hermes*. Most were rural

---

9. Aune, D. E. "Religion, Greco-Roman," in *DNTB* 920.

in origin, and every month was named after a seasonal festival. An example is the *Panathenaia*, which included games in Athens, involving all people in the city including slaves and foreigners.[10] Another is *Thesmophoria*, the most common festival, restricted to women only. It honored *Demeter* (goddess of the harvest) and her daughter *Persephone* (queen of the underworld) and especially with the sacrifice of pigs.[11] The *Thargelia* was an annual feast (May 6-7), where two ugly men (*Pharmakoi*) were chosen to die and sacrificed to the gods by stoning and burning, followed by a celebration. Paul alludes to this ritual when he describes the apostles as the "scum" of the world—they are like these sacrificial victims (1 Cor 4:13).[12] The development of the Christian calendar based on festivals grew out of this as well as the Jewish tradition of annual feasts. Some Christian festivals may have grown out of Roman as well (e.g., Christmas).[13]

Temples

The Greek temples originated in the early eighth century BC in conjunction with the rise of the *polis* (city). These buildings were rectangular with a central room (*cella*) including a half-size statue of the patron(ess) cult deity. Unlike a church, they were not meeting places for the congregation. Rather, offerings and dedications were stored inside. Sacrifice and worship occurred outside the temple. Temples were important centers of city life, and they feature across the New Testament such as a temple of Zeus in Lystra (Acts 14:13) and of Artemis in Ephesus (Acts 19:27, 35). Idolatry was also a major problem for early Christian gentile converts (e.g., 1 Thess

---

10. Guettel Cole, Susan. "Festivals, Greco-Roman," in *ABD* 2:793.
11. Aune, "Religion," 920; Cole, "Festivals," 793. See Cole, "Festivals," 793-94, who notes that in Athens there were festivals of the city, regions (demes), family, and social groups. Athens had more than thirty-five *heortai* and public sacrifices (*thysia*) each year. Some were agricultural, some for ritual purity. They included processions and contests (athletics, music, poetry, drama, ship races). The great Greek athletic and artistic games were often linked. Romans called their festivals "holidays" (*feriae*). An example is March 1, with sacrifices made to Mars, god of war (*Salii*). New festivals were added, including the emperor's birthday (cf. Queen's Birthday).
12. See Gustav Stählin, "περίψημα," in *TDNT* 6:84-93.
13. See "Christmas," in *EBD*, 210, which notes that it coincides with "the Roman feast *Natalis Solis Invicti* ('birth of the unconquered sun'), the birthday of Emperor Aurelius." See also "Christmas," in *ODCC*, 338, which notes the first association with 25 Dec is AD 336 (Roman Philocalian Calendar). Others argue it is worked out from the supposed date of the Annunciation.

1:9–10). Eating food sacrificed at temples and attendance of temple feasts is a major issue in 1 Corinthians. Paul endorses eating food sacrificed to idols unless someone objects, but warns against attending temple celebrations and meals (1 Cor 8–10; cf. 2 Cor 6:16). The body and the church as a temple would call to mind both Jewish and Greco-Roman ideas (1 Cor 3:16; 6:19; Eph 2:21). In the consummated world, there will be no temple—for all of creation will be God's temple (Rev 21:22), the original intention of creation.

Divination

Divination—the interpretation of signs or messages from the gods—was important in Greek religion. Methods of divination included *cleromancy* (casting lots), *ornithomancy* (observing bird flight), *hieromancy* (observing animal sacrifice and organs), *cledonomancy* (random omens or sounds), and *oneiromancy* (dream interpretation). The diviner was the *mantis*, which means "diviner," "soothsayer," "seer," and "prophet" (e.g., Simon Magus in Acts 8:9). The "oracle" was both the verbal response of a god and the place where the god was consulted. The most famous such oracle is the Panhellenic Oracle of Apollo at Delphi. On the seventh day of the month, inquirers could pose questions to the priestess (*Pythia*) who was a spokesperson for *Apollo* seated on *Apollo's* tripod-throne. The priestess would give *Apollo's* response. The oracle could relate to any area of life. It is possible that the oracle of Delphi gives background to the problems among the women of Corinth (1 Cor 14).[14]

Domestic Cults

The hearth was a fire that burned year-round and was used for cooking. It was ritually put out and restarted each year to symbolize new birth and life. Prayers were said each day and libations poured on the ground or on the hearth. The male head of the household (*paterfamilias*) acted as a priest, and offerings were made to dead ancestors who were divine upon death. This was also done at the tombs of ancestors.

---

14. See B. Witherington III, *Conflict and Community in Corinth: A Socio-Rhetorical Commentary on 1 and 2 Corinthians* (Grand Rapids: Eerdmans, 1995), 287.

ROMAN RELIGION

Those who were not Roman citizens did not adopt Roman religion in any significant way. Rather, they retained their traditional or Greek religious viewpoints. This was not a problem in a syncretistic and polytheistic context where mixing and mingling religious viewpoints was part and parcel of religious life. There were, however, some core features of Roman religion.

PAX DEORUM: "PEACE WITH THE GODS"

This involved maintenance of peaceful relationships with the gods. It was considered key to temporal prosperity (cf. prosperity teaching)[15] and success. A disaster such as an earthquake was considered a result of failure to maintain right relationships with the gods. Divination helped find the problem. Four measures were designed to maintain this peace:

- Sacrifice and prayer
- Exact fulfillment of vows and oaths
- The ritual of *lustratio* to preserve from hostile influences
- Strict attention to all outward signs of the will of the gods

In the imperial period, a fifth element was of great importance: support and protection of the emperor by the gods.

ROMAN GODS

The Romans had three types of gods. First, there were the *autonomous divinities*. Roman gods were often arranged in triads—for example, Jupiter

---

15. On the prosperity gospel (also called prosperity teaching or doctrine, or "the health and wealth gospel"), see D. W. Jones and R. S. Woodbridge, *Health, Wealth & Happiness: Has the Prosperity Gospel Overshadowed the Gospel of Christ?* (Grand Rapids: Kregel Publications, 2011). "The prosperity gospel is the assertion that God wants all of us to be wealthy. It expounds that Christians are entitled to greater riches, dwelling in abundance of wealth and health and enjoying everything the world has to offer. It also claims that as God's children, we have been called to enjoy all these privileges. All that is expected of us is to believe in those biblical promises and apply some biblical principles established by God to unleash them" (J. M. Prosper, *The Prosperity Gospel, Truth or Lie? Reviewing the "Wealth Gospel"* (Bloomington, In.: WestBow Press, 2012). This gospel is flawed. As K. O. Gangel, *Acts* (HNTC 5; Nashville, TN: Broadman & Holman, 1998), 45, rightly says, "The Bible never denotes money or celebrity status as a sign of God's blessing (2 Cor. 6:3-10). Trouble or struggle in our lives does not evidence the lack of God's blessing upon us or our families."

(light, sky, weather, state, welfare, laws), *Mars* (war), and *Quirinus* (early state god). Alternatively, *Jupiter*, *Juno* (Jupiter's companion, the goddess of light, birth, women, marriage), and *Minerva* (Jupiter's companion, the goddess of wisdom) were grouped. They were individually honored and of a fixed character. They could be called "mother" or "father" but, unlike the Greek gods, had no marital relationships or offspring. Hence, there is no genealogy corresponding to the Greek gods. The most important god, *Jupiter*, had two partners, *Juno* and *Minerva*, who were not wives but consorts. Archaic Roman religion linked *Jupiter* with *Mars* and *Quirinus*. It seems they were grouped as twelve as with the Greek gods and paralleled them:

Roman Name	Greek Name
Juno	Hera
Vesta	Hestia
Minerva	Athena
Ceres	Demeter
Diana	Artemis
Venus	Aphrodite
Mars	Ares
Mercury	Hermes
Jupiter	Zeus
Neptune	Poseidon
Vulcan	Hephaestus
Ennius	Apollo

FIGURE 6: ROMAN AND GREEK GODS

The second category of deities were the *secret beings*; these were jealous for their anonymity, and helped or hindered Roman people. They could not be named or influenced. Third, there are the *indigitimenta*, which are teams of minor deities with a minor function of hindering or assisting human activity.

PRIESTS

Different terms were used for priests including *pontifex* (a college of priests) and *flamen* (a priest of sacrifice and the later emperor's priest). Priesthoods were part-time positions to prevent a priestly class from forming. Two exceptions were *rex sacrorum*, the "king of sacrifices," and *Flamen Dialis*, the "priest of *Jupiter*." Four colleges of priests developed in the late period of the republic. Only the emperor could belong to all four simultaneously.

Public divination to discern the things that interrupted peace with the gods was central to religious life.

PRACTICES

Prayer

The invocation of god or gods by name was universal. Worshipers always prayed with their heads covered, which may relate to interpreting the difficult chapter of 1 Corinthians 11. Great care was taken to address the right god for appropriate circumstances. Worshipers used a kind of "to whom it may concern" formula. *Janus* was the first deity invoked in prayers, then *Jupiter*, *Mars*, and *Quirinus*. Vesta was last.

Sacrifice

As with the whole ancient world, public and private sacrifices were important. Male animals were sacrificed to male deities and female animals to female gods. It was a good sign when the animal went willingly to slaughter.

Temples

Temples were rectangular and built on a raised platform. They included:

- The inner room, the *cella*, with a statue of the deity and an altar of incense
- The room behind the *cella* with treasure
- The anteroom in front of the *cella*
- A roofed colonnade

A stone altar was placed in front of the temple for sacrifice. The priests ate the small sacrifices. The larger sacrifices fed bigger groups with the excess sold at the meat market (1 Cor 8). As with the Greek temples, these were not places to gather inside for worship but to come for sacred rituals performed by the priests.

THE IMPERIAL CULT

The Roman Imperial cult involved the "offering of divine honors to a living or dead emperor."[16] The concept originated in Egypt, Persia, and the Hellenistic ruler cults of Greece, and developed in the republic under Julius Caesar and Augustus. Julius Caesar and Augustus were deified after death and added to the Roman official pantheon. The Imperial cult tended to be of greater significance outside of Rome, especially in Roman Asia (e.g., Ephesus), giving a sense of presence for the absent emperor in these regions. The cult was also strong in Romanized cities like Philippi and Corinth. This gives important background to reading the letters to these cities where Jesus as Lord stands in contrast to Caesar as lord. Traditionally, the emperor was worshiped as a god after his death and *apotheosis*—his transformation into a deity.

Different emperors responded differently to the notion. During his life, the second Emperor Tiberius (AD 14-37) refused all such deification including refusing to let some Spaniards build a temple in his name. He declared, "I am a mortal, and divine honors belong only to Augustus, the real savior of mankind" (Tacitus, *Ann.* 4.37-38). Tiberius issued an edict refusing the swearing of allegiance and status (Suetonius, *Tib.* 26.1). However, the title *divus* (divine) was found on a denarius of Tiberius, and he was called "son of god" in some papyri.

The brutal *Caligula* (also Caius) (AD 37-41), by contrast, was convinced of his own divinity. He decided he was the incarnation of *Jupiter* (*Zeus*) and demanded that he be worshiped. Temples were erected in his honor in Miletus and Rome (Dio Cassius, 59.11.12; 28.1-2). He also declared his deceased sister, Drusilla, a deity (Dio Cassius, 59.11.3). Caligula deeply offended Jews when, in AD 39, statues were erected of him in Alexandrian synagogues, and he ordered that one be erected in the Jerusalem temple (Josephus, *J.W.* 2.184-203); he abandoned the latter idea. After his assassination, he was not deified.

While *Claudius* (AD 41-54) did not like to be considered divine, he did permit some statues to be erected, and some temples were built in his honor in Britain. He was also called "lord," "savior of the world," and "son

---

16. See Donald L. Jones, "Roman Imperial Cult," in *ABD* 5:806.

of god." When these ideas appear in the New Testament, this Roman background cannot be neglected.

Nero (AD 54–68) is especially important for understanding Christianity from the mid-50s to the 60s AD. Nero provides a backdrop to the events of Philippians, the Pastorals, Mark's Gospel, 1 Peter, and the deaths of Peter and Paul.[17] He deified Claudius, despite the ridicule of Seneca. Nero was depicted as a "god" on coins from AD 65. He saw himself as an incarnate *Apollo*, "the lyre player." He wore the radiant crown of a deified emperor. In AD 55, his statue was erected in the temple of *Mars Ultor* (Tacitus, *Ann.* 13.8.1)—the first such direct association since Caesar. While he rejected a proposed temple to "the divine Nero" in AD 65 on the basis that only dead emperors were divine, he did have a one-hundred-foot bronze statue of himself as the sun with a star-shaped crown erected. Imperial announcements such as, "Our Apollo … by thyself we swear" and, "O Divine Voice! Blessed are they that hear you" were also divine in intent (Dio Cassius, 62.20.5 and 63.20.5). He was also called "lord of the whole world" in a Boeotian inscription in AD 67. However, he was not deified upon his death but declared an "enemy of the state" by the senate. It is possible that this elevated self-perspective lies behind Revelation and the "man of lawlessness" in 2 Thessalonians 2:1–10.

Vespasian (AD 69–79) generally refused divine honors but joked on his deathbed, "I suppose I am becoming a god" (Suetonius, *Vesp.* 23.4) and was regularly labeled "lord" and "Savior."

Titus (AD 79–81), Vespasian's son, consecrated Vespasian and had a temple erected in his name. He himself was called "savior of the world" and was consecrated by *Domitian*, his brother.

Domitian (AD 81–96), who is of importance when reading Revelation, insisted that he be acknowledged as a *deus praesens* ("divine presence"). He is pictured on coins as sitting on a throne as "father of the gods" and had a huge marble statue of himself erected in Ephesus, where he became the focal point of the Imperial cult in Asia Minor. He demanded that he be addressed as "our lord and god" (Suetonius, *Dom.* 13) and punished those who refused. Notably, Thomas says these very words to Jesus in John 20:28.

---

17. His persecutions may also provide a backdrop to Hebrews and Revelation, although most date Revelation later in the persecutions of Domitian in the 90s AD.

By this time, emperor deification, offerings, incense, prayers, and vows were obligatory and were the basis for the punishment of Christians who refused to worship mere human beings.

Trajan (AD 98–117), who followed Domitian, generally rejected divine honors. However, his reign provides insight into the challenges faced by early Christians from an interchange between Pliny the Younger and Trajan concerning Christians in Bithynia and Pontus (Pliny the Younger, *Ep. Tra.* 10.96–97).

Pliny:

> This is the course that I have adopted in the case of those brought before me as Christians. I ask them if they are Christians. If they admit it I repeat the question a second and a third time, threatening capital punishment; if they persist I sentence them to death ... All who denied that they were or had been Christians I considered should be discharged, *because they called upon the gods at my dictation and did reverence,* with incense and wine, *to your image* which I had ordered to be brought forward for this purpose.

Trajan then offered this reply (*Ep. Tra.* 10.97):

> You have taken *the right line,* my dear Pliny, in examining the cases of those denounced to you as Christians, for no hard and fast rule can be laid down, of universal application. They are not to be sought out; if they are informed against, and the charge is proved, they are to be punished, with this reservation—that if anyone denies that he is a Christian, and actually proves it, *that is by worshiping our gods, he shall be pardoned as a result of his recantation,* however suspect he may have been with respect to the past [italics mine].

Although this interchange postdates Paul's letters, the underlying attitude toward Christians surely was prevalent from the earliest Christian reticence concerning Greco-Roman gods and the Imperial cult.[18] As such, the Christian gospel was a direct challenge to the supremacy and divinity of the emperor. New Testament documents declaring Jesus is "Lord," "King," "Son of God," and "Savior" call to mind the direct political and social

---

18. See Jones' essay, "Roman Imperial Cult," 806–809.

confrontation of the Christian gospel with the Roman Empire. They also demonstrate how dangerous it was to preach Christ in the Roman world and give a backdrop to the rise of pagan persecution.

THE "MYSTERY" RELIGIONS

The greatest religious inheritance from the Hellenistic period (336–31 BC) were the so-called "mystery religions." The "mystery religions" are a variety of ancient public and private cults that shared certain features. "Mystery" comes from the Latin *mystes*, which means "initiation." Hence, these religions had secret initiation rituals.

Many mystery cults trace their ancestry back to the oldest of the mystery cults, the Eleusinian Mysteries, from Eleusis in Attica, adopted in Athens and which flourished until AD 395. These initiations had three features:

- *Dromena*, "things acted out," the enactment of the cultic myth

- *Legomena*, "things spoken," the oral presentation of the cultic myth

- *Deiknymena*, "things shown," the ritual presentation of symbolic objects to the initiate

The initiates who experienced the ritual were sure of *sōteria* (salvation) in the sense of *present health and prosperity and a future blissful afterlife*.

The Eleusinian Mysteries revolved around a central myth whereby *Hades*—the god of the underworld—took his wife *Persephone*—the daughter of the goddess of the harvest *Demeter*—to the underworld as his wife. *Demeter* searched for her, and the sun god *Helios* revealed to her the truth. *Demeter* took revenge, causing a severe drought. Zeus sent Hermes to make a deal with *Hades*, and *Persephone* was returned to her mother on condition that she spend one-third of every year in the underworld with *Hades*. *Demeter* is called "earth mother" in the story, and *Persephone* is "grain." This myth is an explanation of the seasons. The vegetation deities were metaphors of life and death, and the initiate was guaranteed a blissful afterlife in the spirit world through identification with *Persephone*. Initiation was voluntary and in two stages—initiation into the lesser and then the greater mysteries. It began with the offering of a pig in Athens in honor of *Demeter* and a torchlight parade to Eleusis to the Teleserion, the "hall of initiation." When the initiates entered the inner room, the initiation was complete. It is probable there was an enactment and oral presentation of the myth and a display of grain and other symbols.

Another mystery cult was the cult of *Mithras*, the Persian sun god and god of light. This cult arose in the first century BC, flourishing until Christianity became dominant in the fourth century. Popular in Italy and the Danube, *Mithras* followers included soldiers, bureaucrats, merchants, and slaves, while women were excluded. Astral salvation was a central belief, the ascent of the deceased follower through the seven planetary spheres after death. There were seven grades of initiation, each with the protection of a planetary god.[19] Devotees worshiped in artificial caverns called *mithraea* below sea level. Artistic evidence suggests their ritual centered on the killing of a bull. The contemporary date of Christmas, December 25, is based on the birthdate of *Mithras* as the actual birth date of Christ is unclear.

PAUL AND GRECO-ROMAN RELIGION

Paul was a man of his era from Tarsus and was aware of this plethora of religions (cf. 1 Cor 8:5). An earlier group of New Testament scholars tried to place Paul in the context of the mystery religions. The so-called "history of religions school" (*Religionsgeschichte*, e.g., Bousset; Reizenstein), saw Christian interest in the Eucharist and baptism as intimately connected to the concept of a dying and rising god (Rom 6). Some argued that Paul was contending against such ideas in Romans 6 and 1 Corinthians 15 (Bultmann). However, Wedderburn has argued that:[20]

- The mystery cults were widespread in the time of Paul.

- They had no standard theology centered on the promise of immortality through participation in the death and resurrection of the deity.

---

19. These included: (1) Corax, "raven" (Mercury); (2) Nymphus, "bride" (Venus); (3) Miles, "soldier" (Mars); (4) Leo, "lion" (Jupiter); (5) Perses, "Persian" (Moon); (6) Heliodromus, "courier of the sun" (Sun); and (7) Pater, "father" (Saturn).

20. See Aune, "Religion," 793, referring to A. J. M. Wedderburn, *Baptism and Resurrection: Studies in Pauline Theology Against Its Graeco-Roman Background*, WUNT I.44 (Tübingen: J. C. B. Mohr, 1987).

- The offer of immortality to the initiate is not verified in evidence.
- The connection between baptism and the Spirit is not found in any mystery.

Paul may have been influenced by such cults, but it is more likely that he was simply using the general religious language of the time.

In the Imperial cult, which was particularly influential in Asia and Tarsus, the names commonly given to the emperor included *kyrios* (lord) and *sōter* (savior). "Son of god" was used of Augustus, Julius Caesar's son. The terms applied to Jesus may have been inspired by the Imperial cult. The concept of the gospel (*euangelion*) is no doubt influenced by the Old Testament, particularly Isaiah 40-66, where Isaiah refers to the good news of God's deliverance of his people from exile and the salvation of the world—the new heaven and the new earth. However, "good news" is also of importance in the Imperial cult, especially concerning the announcement of good news concerning the emperor, such as a military victory or birth of a son.

A good example is the Priene calendar inscription 105.40 (9 BC):

> It seemed good to the Greeks of Asia, in the opinion of the high priest Apollonius of Menophilus Azanitus: "Since Providence, which has ordered all things and is deeply interested in our life, has set in most perfect order by giving us Augustus [*ton Sebaston*], whom she filled with virtue that he might benefit humankind, sending him as a *savior*, both for us and for our descendants, that he might end war and arrange all things, and since he, Caesar, by his appearance (excelled even our anticipations), surpassing all previous benefactors, and not even leaving to posterity any hope of surpassing what he has done, and since the birthday of *the god Augustus* was the beginning of the *good news* (*euangelion*) for the world that came by reason of him,"[21] which Asia resolved in Smyrna.

---

21. Evans, C. A. *Mark 8:27-16:20*, WBC 34B (Dallas: Word, Incorporated, 2001), lxxxiii (adapted).

In this inscription, good news is associated with the peace Augustus established. Against this backdrop comes Christ, who establishes God's true *shalom*—not through war, but non-violent self-sacrifice to save humanity and the world.

Paul considered pagan sacrifice a sacrifice to demons (1 Cor 10:20), a view common in Judaism (Deut 32:17; Ps 95:5 LXX; 105:37; Bar 4:7). Paul also expressed no difficulty with eating meat from temple worship unless it caused others unbelief (1 Cor 10:28).

Acts regularly references the cults of Greco-Roman culture related to Paul's mission:

- In Acts 14:11–13, after Paul and Barnabas heal a disabled man, the people believe the gods have come in human form. Barnabas is identified as *Zeus* and Paul, the chief speaker, as *Hermes* (*Zeus'* spokesman). Since Homer, it was believed that the gods could take on human form.

- In Acts 16:16–18, Paul exorcizes a "spirit of divination" from a young slave girl, causing a loss of income for her owners and thus a threat to *Pax deorum*. This is a classic example of the sociological clash between Christianity and the status quo.

- In Acts 17:23, Paul picked up the Athenian concept of the unknown god as a basis for his message. Although no altar with the exact inscription has been found, it is consistent with altars to unknown gods found in Athens and Olympia.[22]

- In Ephesus, the new Christians rejected sorcery and burnt their magical books (Acts 19:18–19). Paul used these clashes with paganism as opportunities for proclaiming the existence and claims of the one true God and to reflect pagan hostility in response to his proclamation of the gospel. After this, in Acts 19:23–41, Paul's success threatened the livelihood of silver-workers from the temple. The temple of *Artemis* was one of the seven wonders of the ancient world, and the city was

---

22. See the discussion in B. Witherington III, *The Acts of the Apostles: A Socio-Rhetorical Commentary* (Grand Rapids: Eerdmans, 1998), 522–23.

entitled "temple-keeper." The acclamation "Great is Artemis of the Ephesians" was a popular title of the goddess.

Paul's ministry and the growth of Christianity were set in the context of a multitude of pagan cults. Paul's mission involved direct encounters with these cults and so threatened the economic and political stability of society. While it is difficult to make the associations accurately because of fluid use of language, it is certain Paul's selection of language and theological themes was governed by the religions of the day and his recipients. Paul considered these religions rooted in the demonic and, as such, enslaving to others.[23]

Paul's world was pluralistic—that is, it embraced various religious viewpoints. As such it was tolerant, granting many religions legal status. However, it is also apparent that where Christianity, Judaism, and other religions clashed—particularly with the economic, political, social, and religious powers of the Greco-Roman world—hostility resulted. This was intensified in mission as the gospel was proclaimed and converts were made, threatening the status quo. The exclusivity of Christianity based on salvation by faith was manifested in mission. It was at this point Paul experienced resistance.

In this regard, there are many similarities to today's society where tolerance and pluralism are becoming increasingly rampant in the western world. However, this "tolerance" masks a degree of hostility to Christian religion that is revealed when anyone seeks to be evangelistic and convert people from other belief systems. The tolerance is then revealed as a mask. It is tolerance of anything that does not demand a change of exclusive allegiance, particularly to Christian faith. As such, Paul is a critical biblical model for westerners who seek to do mission in the postmodern context.

PHILOSOPHY

It is important to understand first-century Greco-Roman philosophy to place Paul in his context.[24] Doing so will illuminate Paul's theology, letters, and mission praxis. There were *four main philosophies* held by intellectuals

---

23. Aune, D. E., "Greco-Roman Religions," in *DPL* 786–96.
24. See further on this section: T. Paige, "Philosophy," in *DPL* 713–18.

in the first century: the Middle Platonists, the Stoics, the Peripatetics,[25] and the Epicureans. Another important group was the *Cynics*. This group begged for a living and offered popular, moral advice. As Greeks believed in the immortal soul planted by the gods in the mind, philosophy was the path to enlightenment. As such, philosophy was highly valued and considered a normal part of education for public life or even for the military.

Its influence was widespread among the upper educated classes. While not many were professional philosophers, digests of school philosophy were commonplace. Paul's hometown of Tarsus had a philosophy school that Paul probably did not attend, but would have ensured circulation of philosophical ideas in the city. In addition, Paul would have encountered philosophy in Jerusalem, where Hellenistic ideas had infiltrated to the degree that any training under Gamaliel would have interfaced with Greek philosophy.

GREEK

Greek philosophical thought included the following:

- A *supreme deity* existed above and behind all supernatural forces. "Theology" was assumed and studied alongside physics, logic, and math.

- The *pantheon of gods* was considered children or servants of the higher power, and the concept of the supreme deity was seldom challenged.

- Philosophy remained *detached from popular religion* and was critical of myth, anthropomorphism (interpreting God through human categories), and the trivia of gods' struggles, passions, and activities.

- Middle Platonists and Peripatetics saw God as an utterly transcendent, immaterial, divine force, with a *pure mind and rationality*. Lesser gods carried out God's will so that the supreme

---

25. The Peripatetics were a minority group at a time when Platonism dominated. Peripatetics followed Aristotle (384-322 BC), Plato's disciple. He rejected Plato's immaterial soul, arguing that the soul and the body were inseparable, except for thought.

deity could avoid contact with physical matter. God dwelt beyond the moon in the stellar sphere. Stoics saw God as immanent and active in the world.

- Greek philosophical thought adhered to the concept of *dualism*, especially in Middle Platonism, which connected the world above with physical matter. Matter was despised and inferior, while the world above was ideal and perfect. Thus, death was seen as a blessed release.

- All four schools held the highest and most divine attribute of God to be mind (*nous*) or reason (*logos*). Human ability to reason was considered divine—the seed of God, the immortal soul. Each school had its own distinctive perspectives.

EPICUREANS

Epicurean philosophical thought included the following:[26]

- The gods were "blessed and immortal beings."

- The gods lived as though religion was irrelevant.

- Everything was explainable by natural forces (cf. naturalism) and composed of "atoms."

- Random collisions of atoms caused all events, and chance predominated.

- Man had free will and life was not left to fate.

- The goal of Epicurean philosophy was to free the mind of fear and trouble to reach a state of mental peace.

- *Pleasure* was the primary good. While Epicurus himself reviled excess as incompatible with true pleasure, his followers were lambasted as effeminate or extravagant.

---

26. Some Epicureans include Epicurus, the founder (341-270 BC), Polystratus (c. 290-250 BC), Basilides (c. 250-175 BC), Diogenes of Tarsus (c. 150 BC), Zeno of Sidon (c. 150-75 BC), Philodemus (c. 110-40 BC), and Horace, who created carpe diem ("seize the day") (65-8 BC).

Epicureans are directly mentioned in Acts 17:18 as dialogue partners with Paul who ridicule him as a *spermalogos*—someone who, like a bird picking up seeds, picks up crumbs of thought and peddles them.[27]

MIDDLE PLATONISTS

Middle Platonic philosophical thought included the following:[28]

- Plato believed that *the rational element of the human soul was immortal*. God bestowed this rationality on the universe. The rest of the human person was entrusted to lesser gods who were creations of the demiurge.[29] These included "irrational passions" and appetites (dualism between the body and the soul).

- By the first century, the demiurge was a lesser god and the supreme deity was remote from the material world. This led to a belief in *material things as inferior substances* and the *body as a hindrance* to progress toward God.

- The universe was peopled by a host of intermediary beings that acted as servants of the supreme God. These intermediaries were involved in oracles and attended sacrifices.

- Ascent to deity and freedom from the cycle of reincarnation was achieved via the pursuit of philosophy.

- Reason was also placed in other "bodies" such as stars and demigods.

Some have argued that Hebrews reflects a kind of Platonism seen in Philo and Alexandrian exegesis. For example, the law as a "shadow" and the heavenly tabernacle could reflect Platonic dualism. However, relatively

---

27. See F. F. Bruce, *The Acts of the Apostles*, NICNT, Third edition (Grand Rapids: Eerdmans, 1990), 331.
28. The period of Middle Platonism runs from Antiochus of Ascalon (c. 130-68 BC) to Plotinus who is the founder of Neoplatonism (AD 204-270). Other prominent Middle Platonists include the Jew Philo of Alexandria who interpreted Hebrew Scriptures with Platonism (30 BC-AD 45) and Plutarch (AD 45-125).
29. The demiurge is a divine mythical figure from Platonic and Neopythagorean thought who is responsible for fashioning and maintaining the universe.

recent discussions prefer to see these as reflective of Jewish typology and eschatology.³⁰

STOICS

Stoic philosophical thought included the following:³¹

- Stoics believed in pantheism (many gods, cf. Hinduism).

- They rejected "immaterial substance," that is, all is material, including God.

- God was fire, reason (*logos*) or spirit (*pneuma*), which was material, unlike the Holy Spirit.

- God existed in everything and shaped fate and reality through divine reason.

- There was a deep reverence for this God who shaped nature by wisdom.

- By the first century, ethics were central to Stoic thought, especially the question: "How can the wise man live in accordance with nature?" That is, how can the wise man live rationally while accepting his fate with God?

- Virtue was the only absolute good recognized. All else, including health, wealth, strength, beauty, and life from death, were *adiaphora* (indifferent).

- A Stoic was highly individualistic and self-centered in pursuit of "virtue."

---

30. G. R. Osborne, "Hermeneutics," in *DLNTD* 482-83.

31. Prominent Stoics include its founder, Zeno of Citium (c. 334-262 BC); Athenodorus of Soli (c. 275 BC); Cleanthes (331-232 BC); Chrysippus (c. 280-206 BC); Zeno of Tarsus, fourth leader of the Stoic school (c. 200 BC); Antipater of Tarsus, sixth leader (c. 200-129 BC); Archedemus of Tarsus (c. 140 BC); Cato the Younger (95-46 BC); Seneca (c. 4 BC-AD 65); Dio Chrysostom (c. AD 40-115); and Roman Emperor Marcus Aurelius (AD 121-180). There is a strong association of Tarsus with Stoicism; Seneca was Nero's advisor when Paul arrived in Rome. There are also links between Stoicism and Paul's hometown, Tarsus, suggesting Paul was familiar with Stoicism.

- Stoics believed in the cyclic re-creation of the cosmos. It was destroyed by fire, re-created, and started again.

The term "regeneration" (*palingenesia*), which means "creation again," is used for the restoration of the cosmos (Matt 19:28). Paul quotes a fellow Cilician, Aratus, in Acts 17:28: "we are his offspring." Other famous Stoics came from Tarsus, including Athenodorus, a friend of Emperor Augustus Caesar. Stoics also developed the literary form *diatribe* that Paul adopted (e.g., Rom 2).

CYNICS

Philosophical thought common to Cynics included the following:[32]

- Cynicism was more a way of life than a philosophy and was often combined with other philosophies.
- A key feature was to live "according to nature," meaning independence from external supports, that is, with the barest of essentials. Cynic Diogenes of Sinope, for example, lived in a barrel with only a cloak and a cup, eventually giving up the cup (cf. the monastic movement).
- Most Cynics begged for a living, although some worked.
- Cynics rejected social norms, were "shameless," and saw themselves as moral reformers.
- They often spoke publicly with caustic, abusive, and arrogant speech to expose the people's sin.
- Cynics were concerned with ethics and right living and not with abstract thought.

Some have tried to argue that Jesus is basically a Cynic preacher. However, this claim is tenuous as Jesus stands in the Jewish prophetic tradition rather

---

32. The key figures are Diogenes of Sinope, who lived in a tub on the street of Athens (c. 412-323 BC), and Crates of Thebes (c. 365-285 BC). Cynicism experienced a reemergence in the first century AD. Cynics were reviled for their disgusting behavior.

than Greek philosophy.³³ Malherbe has also noted points of connection between Paul and a mild Cynic philosopher in 1 Thessalonians (e.g., Dio Chrysostom).³⁴ However, if there is a connection, Paul re-orientates the material he has in common with the Cynics to a Christian worldview. Contrary to Cynicism, Paul does not support the notion of begging as a means of support, preferring self-support and, at times, the support of the churches.³⁵

CONCLUSION

Paul was a man familiar with the religion and philosophical ideas of his world. Paige aptly wrote, "As a man of his era, he was aware of intellectual currents."³⁶ However, where Paul drew upon Cynic ideas, he did so with Christian content and framework.

TRAVEL IN THE ROMAN WORLD

One of the great developments in the Roman era was the establishment of a comprehensive network of travel and communication. The construction of roadways connecting the far reaches of the empire and the systemization of sea travel were a key factor in the spread of the message.

Eckhart Schnabel has estimated that Paul traveled 25,000 km (15,500 mi) in his missionary travels by land and sea, including approximately 14,000 km (8,700 mi) by land.³⁷ Hence, Paul was probably the most widely traveled person in the New Testament and benefited hugely from Rome's travel developments. Three factors were vital to Paul's mobility—and the spread of the Christian message through other Christians.

---

33. For sustained critique, see N. T. Wright's *Jesus and the Victory of God*, 66-74.
34. Malherbe, A. J. *Paul and the Popular Philosophers* (Minneapolis: Fortress, 1989).
35. See further Paige, "Philosophy," 717.
36. Paige, "Philosophy," 717.
37. Eckhart J. Schnabel, *Early Christian Mission: Paul and the Early Church* (Vol 2; Downers Grove, IL; Leicester, Eng.: IVP, Apollos, 2004), 1288. R. Hock, *The Social Context of Paul's Ministry: Tentmaking and Apostleship* (Philadelphia: Fortress Press, 1980), 27, estimates Paul traveled a total of 10,000 mi or 16,000 km. L. J. Kreitzer, "Travel in the Roman World," in *DPL* 945-46, arrives at 6,200 miles or 10,300 km. Schnabel's thoroughness lends weight to the accuracy of his estimate.

ROADS AND HIGHWAYS

The Roman world was crisscrossed by a network of 80,000 km (50,000 mi) of main military highways and 300,000 km (186,400 mi) of secondary roads. Many were public building projects and bear the name of the benefactor who paid for them, for example, *Via Appia* (Rome-Capua), built by Appius Claudius in 312 BC. The highways were initially used for military movement and later for trade. Many survive today and are integrated into Europe's contemporary road system.

Paul used many major trade routes, including the *Via Egnatia* (146 BC), which ran from Dyrrachium (modern Durrës, Albania) on the Adriatic Sea, across ancient Macedonia, through Thessalonica and Philippi, and through ancient Thrace to Byzantium (Istanbul, Turkey). Paul's second missionary journey took him along this road from Neapolis (modern Kavala), through Philippi and Thessalonica, and on to Berea before heading south to Athens. He also claims to have visited as far west as Illyricum (Rom 15:19), which would have occurred during this second journey or later (Acts 20:1–3). Paul also traveled along a part of the *Via Appia* en route to Rome as a prisoner (Acts 28:14–16).

Travel was usually by foot with about 30 km (20 mi) covered in a day. Animal transport (e.g., camel, donkey, horse) ensured that about 8–10 km (5–6 mi) per hour could be covered. Horses were usually only used by the military, hunters, and dispatch riders. Paul traveled by horse from Jerusalem to Caesarea under guard (Acts 23:23–24). Otherwise, it is likely that Jesus, his disciples, and Paul made their overland journeys by foot. On occasion, Paul did this alone (Acts 20:13).[38] Land travel was more difficult in the north during the winter months between November and early March due to the cold. October, April, and May were also problematic due to wet weather.

SEA ROUTES

Emperor Augustus (27 BC–AD 14) boasted, "I made the sea peaceful and freed it from pirates" (*Res gest. divi Aug.* 25). In the New Testament period, the long-term problem of piracy had been stabilized through the establishment of permanent Roman fleets at key points in the Great Sea (Mediterranean).

---

38. Paul traveled by foot from Troas to Assos, a trip of around 50 km (30 mi).

This was critical, as the sea was important for trade between Egypt, Rome, Tyre, Caesarea, Ostia, and Pisidia Antioch.

The ships included warships (biremes and triremes) fitted with oars and manned by rowers. Most commercial ships were sailing vessels dependent on wind and weather. Winter travel was particularly dangerous. Hence, travel between May 27 and September 14 (northern summer), March 10 and May 26 (northern spring), and September 14 through November 11 (northern autumn) was considered risky—and November 11 to March 10 (winter) dangerous. Sea travel occurred mainly during the day with regular stops at night on routes that hugged the coastline.

Paul made use of sea travel in all four of his major recorded journeys. The events of the boat-trip in Acts 27:1–28:16 to Rome are typical of the hazards of winter sea-travel. The three shipwrecks referred to in 2 Corinthians 11:25 were before the shipwreck in Acts 27, and illustrate how dangerous sea travel could be.[39]

POSTAL SERVICES

Because travel within the empire was relatively easy, a regular postal system could be established. Paul did not use this postal system directly, although it is possible that some of his Roman letters were taken by friends in the imperial system (Phil 4:22). Timothy, Tychicus, Epaphroditus, and Phoebe operated as couriers for his letters (1 Thess 3:2; Col 4:7; Phil 2:25; Rom 16:1).

SOCIAL STRATIFICATION

Today, in western contexts, class is primarily based on economic position, although there is great prestige from aristocratic and royal links. In Paul's day, class (rank and status) was based more on birth and legal status. Greco-Roman society was highly hierarchical and classist with limited possibility of movement between classes. Early Roman society was split between the "orders" of Patricians. Patricians were the highly privileged aristocrats. Membership of this class was based on heredity alone. Plebeians were Roman citizens who were not Patricians. Marriage across these orders was originally forbidden. Between 500–287 BC, continuous

---

39. See B. M. Rapske, "Travel and Trade," in *DNTB* 1245–50.

conflict existed between the two. The aristocracy of birth was then broken down and replaced with an aristocracy based on holding political office and wealth (especially land-based wealth). However, this did not remove the hierarchy of rank in the culture or improve the lot of the poorer groups in Roman society. Greco-Roman society remained highly stratified with a great gulf between rich and poor. While it was possible to move upward with the acquisition of wealth, it was not easy to do so. A person's clothes marked their rank.

UPPER CLASSES

Senatorial Class (senatores)

These were men involved in the Roman Senate and their families. Hence, this was a class based on political power. The dominant group was the nobles (*nobiles*), families who included at least one consul[40]—the highest level of the political pecking order, the *cursus honorum*. Nobility was achieved through the family, often requiring three generations of senatorial involvement to establish noble status. Senators had to prove they had property worth one million *sesterces*.[41] This is because public office brought no salary and senators were forbidden from non-agricultural business, trade, or public contracts. Senators wore a toga with a broad purple stripe (*laticlavio*).

Equestrian Class

These were men who were wealthy, that is, they possessed stable wealth of 400,000 sesterces. The families of such men were included by extension. Sometimes an equestrian could move into the senatorial class. However,

---

40. Each year, two consuls (the more senior consul prior, consul posterior) were elected for a one-year term and together, month on and month off, they governed Rome, Italy, and the Roman provinces. In the empire, their position was more symbolic. The proconsuls worked on behalf of the consul (e.g., Sergius Paulus, proconsul of Cyprus, Acts 13:7-12; Gallio, proconsul of Achaia, Acts 18:12). Gallio went on to be a consul under Nero in AD 55. Quirinus of Luke 2:2 was likely Publius Sulpicius Quirinus, consul of Syria, in AD 12. Sometimes the emperor was consul prior. See also "Consul," *TBD*, 311. "Consul," in *ISBE*, 1:766; Klaus Haacker, "Gallio," in *ABD*, 2:901.

41. A Roman coin worth one-quarter of a denarius, which was a working man's wages for a day. A million sesterces added up to 250,000 denarii. Assuming a minimum US wage of $7.25/hour for an eight-hour day, this would be $14.5 million USD.

this was rare because equestrians were often involved in business dealings and business was forbidden for senators. In addition, the senatorial ranks were dominated by families who had maintained their position for years. It was possible but infrequent for a freeborn Roman citizen to move into the equestrian class through the acquisition of wealth. Equestrians wore tunics with narrow purple stripes (*augusti clavi*).

While families dominated the above orders, membership was defined by male activity and birth. Women belonged to their father's social class followed by their husband's. They wore no special dress to show their status. Great privilege and prestige were associated with being a part of these orders, including greater economic, political, and educational opportunities, and legal rights and benefits. Unlike contemporary western society, there was no middle class, but rather, an immense gulf between the classes.

LOWER CLASSES

Commons

All freeborn Roman citizens, except slaves, were considered commoners. The men wore togas. This was a position of great status with privileges including: protection from extreme forms of punishment like crucifixion and torture; the right to vote; attendance at games and theaters; exemption from many taxes including the standard Roman tribute and land tax, legal protection over property purchased, inheritance, legal contracts, adoption, and marriage; and the right of imperial appeal. Citizenship carried responsibility including military service and other taxes.[42] All Roman citizens were free to marry a Roman citizen and have legitimate children who were thus Roman citizens (*conubium*).

Freeborn residents of Italy, or *Latini*, were granted full citizenship until 89 BC. Former slaves freed by Roman citizens were a special group called "Junian Latins." All freeborn men and women outside of Italy who lived in Roman territories, *peregrini*, were granted full Roman citizenship until AD 212.

---

42. See James S. Jeffers, *The Greco-Roman World of the New Testament Era: Exploring the Background of Early Christianity* (Downers Grove: IVP, 1000), 198–99.

Freed People (liberti or libertini)

These were men and women who had been slaves but bought their freedom or had been liberated (manumission). They had some restrictions and were bound in some ways to their former masters, who were now their patrons. They became citizens if they were formally manumitted and their masters were Roman citizens. They were not eligible for public office. Hence, it was not possible to leave this class for a generation. Their children were granted full citizenship and could become equestrians if they were rich enough. There was a social stigma, however, in being a freedman's son. Freedmen tended to be of low social status and were poor, although, if they were successful in trade, they might become wealthy. They wore no special dress but tended to be identifiable by their names.

Slaves

People were born into slavery or sold into slavery through war or piracy. They were the property of their owners by law. They might be allowed to save (*peculium*) to buy their freedom. Alternatively, their masters might manumit (free) them. Roman slavery was not racially based, and there was no special dress. However, sometimes runaway slaves (e.g., Onesimus) might be made to wear metal collars with an inscription: "I have run away. Capture me. When you have returned me to my master, Zoninus, you will receive a reward." The notion of "Caesar's household" in Philippians 4:22 may include slaves from all over the empire who were part of a network that supported the emperor.

Women

In the lower classes, women were automatically members of their parents' social class, except with freedmen since only one generation could be thus named. If parents were Roman citizens and legally married, their children were Roman citizens. Latins, foreigners, slaves, and children retained the social status of their mother, even if their father was a freeborn Roman citizen.

Conclusion

During Roman Empire domination most of these classes continued. From the time of Augustus, the imperial household gained greater status, including women, who were often entitled *Augusta* and *mater castrorum* ("mother of the military camps") and even gained high levels of influence without a formal office. Freedmen associated with the emperor tended to gain prestige and wealth while *remaining in their social class*. Imperial slaves also gained a certain social prestige; hence, there were anomalies within the social orders of the day. During the empire, the Senate tended to lose political power, and membership depended on the favor of the emperor. However, rank was still pivotal to the empire and became more marked and formalized.

Membership of the churches of the New Testament crossed the social spectrum with few from the senatorial and equestrian classes and the lowest, peasantry. There were some wealthy people who owned homes in which the churches met. These include Priscilla and Aquila (Rom 16:3), Phoebe (Rom 16:1), Nympha (Col 4:15), Philemon (Phlm 1), and Lydia (Acts 16:14). Erastus is mentioned in Romans 16:23 as the "city *oikonomos*," meaning he was a significant Roman employee within the Corinthian government. An inscription has been found in Corinth: "Erastus, in return for his *aedileship*, laid this pavement at his own expense." The *aedile* was the commissioner of public works and a high-ranking public official belonging to the Roman ruling class in a city.[43] However, most of the church was probably from the lower stratum of society (see 1 Cor 1:26). The radical ethic of egalitarianism allowed poorer Christians to gain a higher status within the church than in the wider society.

PATRONAGE

Patronage was important in the Roman world. Greco-Roman society existed under the patronage and benefaction of the emperor and the gods. The whole empire was seen as being under the patronage of Rome and the emperor. Alongside military force, patronage was a critical way to maintain the allegiance of the people. To resist Rome was thus an act of rejection of the patronage of Rome.

---

43. On Erastus as an aedile, see D. W. J. Gill, "Erastus the Aedile," *TynBul* 40 (1989): 293–310.

In religious terms, festivals were held under the patronage of the gods and emperor.[44] This also provides a potential background to Paul's approach to eating food at temple meals (1 Cor 10:14–22)—the participant in the meal was placing themselves effectively under the patronage of the deity who was being worshiped, thus violating the monotheistic nature of the Christian faith.[45] Christianity challenged this system by its implicit suggestion that Yahweh was the only true patron and Jesus as Lord assumed the role ascribed to the gods and emperor. As such it was destabilizing.

At a local level, patronage was basic to the functioning of society—for example, the noble Greek-Roman aristocrat being generous to the city, contributing to civic developments (e.g., libraries) and the arts (cf. Erastus above). It was not uncommon for the nobleman to be a patron to writers, orators, and philosophers, patronage being one of the basic means of support. Other means included charging fees and, less commonly, self-support (often looked down upon) or begging (Cynics). The patronage system was based on friendship, and the whole Greco-Roman society functioned on a network of obligation.

At the core of the controversy in Corinth was Paul's refusal to place himself under the patronage of members of the Corinthian church. Rather, he chose to be self-supporting, which was not only considered demeaning among elite Romans, but violated the principles of patronage. His reticence may have been because of the constraints such a relationship might bring—the benefactor potentially being a limiting factor of the philosopher's freedom to teach the truth. Along with this violation of the principle of the gospel-worker being worthy of his hire,[46] this meant Paul was not considered an authentic apostle by some in Corinth.[47] In addition, the refusal of gifts in Greco-Roman culture was considered insulting and shaming because of the principle of general reciprocity.[48] One of the means of expressing power for the wealthy was patronage, and the basis

---

44. The meals in Luke-Acts and in Revelation (cf. "in the presence of God") may have this background.
45. I. Howard Marshall, "Lord's Supper," *DPL* 573.
46. See Paul's defense of this principle in 1 Corinthians 9:1–15.
47. See Paul's defense of his apostleship in 1 Corinthians 9.
48. J. M. Everts writes, "The giving and receiving of benefactions was an extremely important component of the social structure." See J. M. Everts, "Financial Support," in *DPL*, 295.

of benefaction was the principle of friendship. Hence, to refuse patronage was an act of enmity. This illuminates why Paul was at odds with sections of the Corinthian church. His refusal was seen by some as a rejection of friendship and/or refusing them the option of being involved in the ministry of the gospel. In addition, by choosing to work for his own support, he was demeaning both himself and the Corinthians. This may have been exacerbated by his acceptance of Philippian patronage, likely because the Philippians understood the basic "no strings attached" principle of Christian giving (Phil 4:10-20; 2 Cor 11:7-9).

This notion of patronage also underpinned the development of the church, as churches were primarily based in houses under the patronage of the wealthy ("the church that meets at their house"; Rom 16:5; cf. Col 4:15; Phlm 1). Hence, the problems in Corinth (1 Cor 1:10-11), Rome (Rom 14-15), and Philippi (Phil 4:2-3) may relate to conflicts across house churches under the patronage of wealthy members of the congregation. In some contexts, Paul was happy to be reliant on patronage, accepting the hospitality and friendship of Aquila and Priscilla (Rom 16:3, cf. Acts 18), Gaius (Rom 16:23), Philemon (Phlm 1, 22), and the Philippians (Phil 4:14-19). This may be due to these Christians not using patronage as a means of power, that is, not being concerned to influence Paul and violate his freedom and/or allowing him the freedom to earn his own living if he so chose.

Patronage was not confined to men; there is record of Roman women acting as patrons, of women being "the mother of the synagogue" in Jewish circles, including leadership, and of women being leaders in the Christian church such as Nympha, Phoebe (Rom 16:1-2), and supporters of Jesus (Luke 8:1-3).[49] Phoebe is described as a *prostatis* used of a female patron (e.g., Lucian, *Bis acc.* 9). Patronage was also central to family life. The *paterfamilias* was the patron (*patronus*) of the family, and the family was dependent on his patronage. This is probably one background aspect of Paul's use of familial language; God is the patron of the church, which functions as God's family.

Another feature of patronage was that it was often public. It was a feature of rank and had to be seen to be meaningful. Hence, privilege earned one the right to wear certain clothing that demonstrated one's

---

49. L. Michael White, "Christianity (Early Social Life and Organization)" in *ABD*, 1:932-33.

status. Privilege brought great honor, cherished in Greco-Roman culture. The whole society was based on "friendship" (*amicitia*) or mutual support among upper-class men of relative—though competitive—equality. Patronage worked based on publicly acknowledged inequality between patron (*patronus*) and client (*cliens*). Clients acted as a kind of clan to the patron, supporting him in political and military ventures and in legal contexts. The patron defended his clients in these same contexts. Loyalty was expected of the clients (*fides*) and was a prized virtue. Patronage passed through generations, the heir of the patron continuing the relationship with the client family.

There were two main types of patronage, *public* and *personal*.

PUBLIC PATRONAGE

Public patronage involved a wealthy patron becoming the protector and benefactor of a group (e.g., a craftsman's guild, a religious association, or a city). It involved giving money for infrastructure, public buildings, and entertainment; it could involve protection and advocacy. Such patronage was expected to lead to public acknowledgment from client groups with statues and inscriptions (e.g., Erastus). It thus brought great honor to the giver. It was expected that the recipients would support the patron politically and protect his or her honor.

PERSONAL PATRONAGE

Personal patronage involved a patron giving assistance to an individual in the lower classes through such things as money, gifts, hospitality, legal assistance, advice, or protection. Such a relationship could span generations. This often occurred with freedmen. Such patronage was expected to lead to public displays of deference, such as the morning greeting or salutation. In the morning, clients flocked to the house of their wealthy patron wearing togas and clustering in the atrium, vestibule, and the streets, waiting to be summoned individually to greet the patron at his *tabilum*. They then accompanied the patron to the forum for a court meeting, or something similar. As in the case of public patronage, the client was expected to support the patron politically.

Hence, public display and personal honor and prestige were essential to the system. This system led to a rich legacy of Roman literature; wealthy patrons supported authors in their writing and expected commemoration in their literature. For example, Maecenas, an equestrian, was a patron to Horace and Vergil. It is possible this is the situation in the New Testament with Theophilus perhaps being Luke's patron (Luke 1:3, 4; Acts 1:1). Patronage, in a sense, was the oil that kept the wheels of the Roman society turning.

While this was a male-dominated concept as with all aspects of Roman society, women participated in the patronage system as well to achieve great honor. This client system held the Roman Empire together, giving it stability based on the loyalty of clients who kept patrons and their families in power over the centuries. It almost functioned as a means of social welfare. It extended to protection, help in poverty, loans, dowry, and funerary costs.[50]

The principles of Christian giving cut against the patron-client system with Christians giving to others freely without expectation of personal reciprocity and without public visibility. However, the principle of reciprocity carried over into the idea that God would repay the giver (e.g., Matt 6:1–4; Luke 6:29–30, 35, 38; 2 Cor 8–9; Phil 4:10–20).

ADDITIONAL FEATURES OF GRECO-ROMAN SOCIETY

HONOR AND SHAME

As with many corporate cultures, Greco-Roman societies revolved around the notion of honor and shame rather than individual guilt. One's individual, family, tribe, and state's standing before others was critical. Reputation was all important. One sought to gain honor through fulfilling one's civic duty. Moving up the highly stratified society was managed, in part, through increasing one's honor. The patronage system was a means of sustaining honor. The flip-side of patronage was that the client was bound to enhance the honor of the patron. The court system was used in the pursuit of honor, with wealthy aristocrats seeking to shame others in court to enhance their own honor. This is the likely background to 1 Corinthians

---

50. It is interesting that the Italian word *padrino*, linked to the Mafia (Godfather) is derived from *patronus*. There are great similarities between the Mafia and the client system of Greco-Roman society.

6:1–8. Honor was gained through athletic or military prowess, brilliant rhetoric, wealth, political and legal maneuvering, and through demeaning or removing opponents (enemies). Friendship was important in enhancing one's honor. The converse of honor was shame. To fail to do one's duty brought shame on the person involved. This was in many cases a fate worse than death. In such situations, being shamed often led to suicide—seen as honorable.

SEXUAL IMMORALITY

One of the radical distinctions between Judaism and the Greco-Roman world was their attitude toward sexual immorality. Whereas Judaism at the time of Christ repudiated homosexuality, adultery, incest, and prostitution, and affirmed monogamous heterosexual marriage, at least as an ideal (e.g., Mark 10:1–12; 1 Cor 7), the Roman world was liberal in terms of its sexual ethic. Marriage was ideally "a life-long partnership, and a sharing of civil and religious rights" (*Modestinus Digesta* 23.2.1). However, it could be terminated by either party with a simple oral or written notification. Adultery was defined as a married woman engaging in sexual intercourse with a married man and was a serious crime punished with banishment or death.[51]

Prostitution, homosexuality, pederasty, and other forms of sexual immorality were common and often related to temple worship and the Greco-Roman symposia. Old Corinth was particularly infamous for its loose sexual mores so that a prostitute was colloquially termed "a Corinthian girl" and to engage in illicit sexual activity was "to Corinthianize."

Christianity refused to compromise in terms of sexual license. It emphatically sided with the Jewish ethic as the gospel spread, repudiating prostitution and homosexuality, and affirmed a monogamous heterosexual sexual ethic based on love.

LIFE AFTER DEATH

Another feature of the Greco-Roman world was that, unlike the Jewish belief in a bodily resurrection and a new heaven and earth, there was a complete lack of acceptance of the notion of bodily resurrection in the

---

51. See G. F. Hawthorne, "Marriage and Divorce, Adultery and Incest," in *DPL* 594.

hereafter. A good example is Aeschylus, who says, "But when the dust has drawn up the blood of a man, once he is dead, *there is no return to life (anastasis)*. For this, my father has made no magic spells."[52]

The afterlife was believed to be a disembodied existence. Achilles pondered in Homer's, *Iliad*, "Ah then, it is true that something of us does survive even in the Halls of Hades, but with no intellect at all, only the ghost and semblance of a man" (Homer, *Il.* 23.99–107). It was seen as a blessed release from the cage of the inferior body. As Cicero indicated: "Yes they are," he replied, "and freed from their chains, from that prison-house—the body; for what you call life is in fact death" (Cicero, *Rep.* 6.13).

Critically, across the whole New Testament corpus, when Christ was preached in the Greco-Roman world, there was a complete refusal to modify the gospel toward this disembodied spiritual resurrection (see esp. 1 Cor 15).

QUESTIONS TO CONSIDER

- What distinctive features of the Greco-Roman culture stand out to you?

- How does Greco-Roman culture differ from Jewish culture?

- What key similarities and differences between the Greco-Roman culture and your own culture should you consider as you engage in New Testament study?

---

52. *Aeschylus, Aeschylus, with an English Translation* by Herbert Weir Smyth, Ph. D. in Two Volumes. 2. Eumenides (ed. Herbert Weir Smyth; Medford, MA: Harvard University Press, 1926), 647–49.

UNDERSTANDING CRITICAL METHODOLOGIES

CHAPTER 4

The wonderful thing about studying the New Testament is that anyone can do it. The first step is to simply read it and observe the story while taking notes, memorizing texts, and noting interesting features like links and repetition. Deeper study might involve investing in a good study Bible, which will provide additional information. Another useful idea is to use simple aids like lexicons, which assist in identifying recurring words and themes. Simple Bible dictionaries give great background to the people, places, and themes in the Bible. There are many great commentaries that introduce each book of the Bible and then draw out the meaning (exegete) the text. Great Bible software applications are available, and websites abound that help explain the text. Books that teach the principles of hermeneutics—the study of the principles and methods of interpreting the text—are great resources, too. These resources help a reader negotiate issues of the various genres of Scripture and sound principles of interpretation.

The next level involves daring to read some of the more technical writings from the history of Christian scholarship. This might be through a Bible college, university, or seminary. There Bible students discover there is a whole world of technical language that can be surprising. Since the days of Christ, people have put the Bible under the microscope. It is not only Bible-believing Christians who have done this, but people of nominal faith, as well as unbelievers. That is not necessarily wrong—God's Word is gifted to humanity for the world. Still, it can be overwhelming to try and come to terms with biblical study and the range of critical approaches.

Keep this in mind when studying critical methodologies. The concept will be briefly introduced in preparation for technical terms that will surface throughout the chapter.

KEY TERMS

There are some basic terms to intuitively understand when studying the principles and methods of interpreting biblical text:

Exegesis: The term "exegesis" comes from the Greek *exēgeomai*, which can mean simply "to tell," but also can mean, "to set forth in detail, to expound."[1] It is used in John 1:18 of Jesus, who "exegetes" or "expounds, makes known" God. In biblical studies, it means to draw out the meaning of the text, usually in verse-by-verse or phrase-by-phrase exposition of the text. In a sense, it is a critical expository sermon. Good exegesis is faithful to the original intent of the writer but takes note of how the reader would understand it. Exegesis interprets the text in its context, both in the text and in the historical and social setting. The purpose is to draw out the intent of the passage. The converse is sometimes called "eisegesis," whereby people read into the text their own perspective.

Hermeneutics: This comes from the Greek word *hermēneia* and the associated verb meaning "translate" or "interpret."[2] The term is found in 1 Corinthians 12:10 and 14:26 speaking of the spiritual gift of interpretation. Applied to biblical studies, hermeneutics speaks of the principles of interpreting Scripture. Hermeneutics goes further than exegesis, not only seeking to draw out the meaning of the text, but interpreting it using a wide range of interpretative methods appropriate to the genre and context, and includes the application of the text to everyday life. Put simply, it speaks of how to interpret Scripture for daily living.

TEXTUAL CRITICISM

Textual criticism is focused on finding the original form of the biblical text (original "autographs") from the many textual witnesses that exist. This is important because Christians believe the Scriptures are sacred, and a vital way through which God speaks to humanity, and should thus want

---

1. BDAG 349.
2. BDAG 393.

to know the original text as best they can. No actual manuscript penned by the biblical writers exists. In fact, the oldest is P^{52}, a papyrus fragment from c. AD 125 with a few verses of John.[3] Across many witnesses, there are variant readings as the text has been passed down through the ages. Most are caused by mistakes in copying. A good example is Mark 1:1, where some manuscripts include the words "Son of God" and others do not. The text critic's task is to closely examine and weigh the readings to assess the best possible reading. In Mark 1:1, while "Son of God" is missing from many witnesses, the importance of the theme in his Gospel suggests to some that it is original.

In the process of textual criticism, two types of documents are examined to assess the original reading. First, there are some 5400 Greek manuscripts, which can be whole books (continuous-text mss, 3000 exist) or passages (lectionary mss, 2403 exist). These can be papyrus or parchments mss.[4] They are labeled with a $\mathfrak{P}$. Thus, $\mathfrak{P}^{52}$ is Papyrus 52. The second source of material is citations in the writings of the early church fathers, the "patristic" (*pater* = father) writings. The citations provide clues as to what text they worked with, and give a reasonably solid historical setting.

In many ways, textual criticism is the most important of the critical methods developed in scholarship, as it helps identify what ancient biblical writers originally wrote.

HISTORICAL CRITICISM

Historical criticism (the historical-critical method, or higher criticism) developed in the seventeenth century as western civilization became increasingly interested in science and sought freedom from the dominance of Christianity. It speaks of an approach to reading Scripture that sought to determine not only what is in the text, but the world behind it—what was really going on for writers and readers in their given historical setting. The interpreter sought to reconstruct the original context and the

---

3. Roger L. Omanson and Bruce Manning Metzger, *A Textual Guide to the Greek New Testament: An Adaptation of Bruce M. Metzger's Textual Commentary for the Needs of Translators* (Stuttgart: Deutsche Bibelgesellschaft, 2006), xi. Much of this section is drawn from pp. xi-xvi.

4. Papyrus mss are made from pressed strips of papyrus plant (116 exist today). Parchments are made from animal skins and found from around the fourth century AD (around 3000 exist). Many are uncials, written in Greek capital letters.

text's meaning in it. The focus was not so much on the final form of the biblical writings, but its origin and original meaning. Historical criticism looks at both "the history *in* the New Testament text and the history *of* the New Testament text."[5]

Many of the modern methods discussed below came from such an approach, especially source, form, and redaction criticisms. Contemporary biblical scholarship continues to utilize historical-critical methodology but without the claims of neutrality, and many come to the text with a much more trusting perspective. Historical criticism is "invaluable in saying what a text *can* or *cannot* mean, rather than what it *did* mean."[6] It provides a useful control against rampant reader-driven readings of the text that clearly violate its original intent. However, it can also limit the Spirit's power to speak from the text into the present.

HISTORY OF RELIGIONS (*RELIGIONSGESCHICHTE SCHULE*)

One historical-critical method that developed in the late nineteenth century is the so-called "history of religions school," a movement that sought to source the ideas found in Christianity in the world of comparative religions. For example, the death and resurrection of Jesus were supposedly derived from myths of the dying and rising god (e.g., *Osiris, Dionysus*). The emphasis became not on what happened, but how Christians "borrowed concepts, language, and practices from other religious movements."[7] Similarly, the so-called Greek *Theios Anēr* (divine man), who was a miracle worker, was the *real* basis for Jesus the miracle worker (Reitzenstein). Hellenism and the wider ancient Near East became the source for Christian ideas, which needed to be stripped away to find the real Jesus. Scholars who took this approach tended to diminish the historicity of the New Testament, arguing that many of its ideas were borrowed and non-authentic. They tended to play down the clear differences between the myths observed and the New Testament. New Testament readers subsequently tended to disengage with the Greco-Roman context, and Judaism became the primary background

---

5. Bruce Corley, et al., *Biblical Hermeneutics: A Comprehensive Introduction to Interpreting Scripture*, 2nd ed. (Nashville, TN: Broadman & Holman, 2002), 150.

6. Patzia and Petrotta, *PDBS* 58.

7. Patzia and Petrotta, *PDBS* 59.

for interpretation. In the last few decades, there has been a great rise in interest in interpreting the New Testament against a Greco-Roman background, but without the skepticism that drove these early scholars.

SOURCE CRITICISM

Source criticism is another branch of historical criticism, specifically seeking to find the original sources for the New Testament documents. Where did Matthew derive his material from? Mark? Luke? John? Where did the stories of Jesus come from? And, as there are similarities and differences between the four Gospels, where did the material come from to form those documents? A simple answer is that Mark was Peter's friend and gathered his material from him. Matthew was an apostle and used Mark and his personal recollections. John, too, was an apostle and deviates from Matthew and Mark including unique material drawn from memory. Finally, Luke gathered his material from reading Mark, Q, and other documents, some of which may be lost. Where both Luke's Gospel and Acts are concerned, he may also have interviewed eyewitnesses. However, over the history of biblical criticism, scholarship has come up with a range of answers to the questions posed. The most prominent ideas are that Mark is the first of the Gospels, another document called Q exists (common material in Matthew and Luke), and Matthew and Luke gained their material from other sources. Another question remains: From where did John draw his material? Some interesting ideas have been proposed.

FORM CRITICISM

Form criticism grew out of historical-critical approaches and seeks to find the oral tradition in the written text and to categorize it according to fixed forms (*Formgeschichte*, "history of forms") such as parables, miracles, legends, and pronouncement stories. Form-criticism followers sought to find the original setting, the *Sitz im Leben* (life setting), in which the saying originated. Major New Testament scholars with this approach include Martin Dibelius, Rudolf Bultmann, and Vincent Taylor. Rather than accepting that the sayings and actions of Jesus reported in the Gospels came from Jesus himself, they found the origin in the life of the early church. Much of the material in the Gospels was a construct. They built on the work of the history-of-religions school, arguing that the stories grew from a mix of real events and sayings of Jesus and a mythological worldview. They dug into these stories, seeking the original action and sayings of Jesus. They developed sophisticated criteria for weighing the historical veracity of each saying and action of Jesus.[8] With a tendency toward a repudiation of the supernatural as a remnant of an ancient worldview, they removed these aspects of the New Testament. Their Jesus became a greatly reduced Jesus. The work of the Jesus Seminar today carries on this tradition, its members voting on which parts of the Gospels are authentic and which are not, weighing them with a color-code system.

REDACTION CRITICISM

Redaction criticism grew out of form criticism, while initially retaining much of its skepticism. Whereas form criticism finds the origin of the material in the Gospels in the early church, redaction criticism finds it in the work of the redactor (editor)—the evangelist who compiled the Gospel. Early redaction critics still saw much of the Gospels as historical fiction, but now the source was the evangelist rather than the early church. Source criticism is vital for redaction criticism, as the redaction critic seeks to discern how the New Testament writer has handled their sources to discover their theology and tendencies. They are interested in how they selected their material (what they left in or left out), edited the material sourced from another document (e.g., Mark, Q), ordered the material, structured it, and shaped it. This gives insight into their theological perspective.

Importantly, it was the development of redaction criticism that saw the rise of evangelical biblical studies in the mid- to late twentieth century. Scholars like F. F. Bruce, I. Howard Marshall, Leon Morris, and others

---

8. See C. L. Blomberg, "Form Criticism," in *DJG*, 248–49, for a list of criteria and assessment: (1) Criterion of dissimilarity—where Jesus says or does something different to Judaism and the early church, it is likely authentic; (2) Criterion of multiple attestation—if something is found in multiple sources (Mark, Q, M, L, John) it is likely authentic, e.g., feeding of the five thousand; (3) Criterion of environment or language—if the action or saying is Semitic in style or background, rather than Hellenistic, it is more likely genuine; (4) Criterion of coherence—if the text aligns with another authenticated by the first three, it is more likely authentic. These criteria sound okay but, in fact, say nothing of historicity. Jesus was capable of originality. Something found in one Gospel may still be historical. Further, the criteria are not applied in all cases. So, form critics did not accept Jesus that fed five thousand miraculously, despite it being in all four Gospels. Further, miracles are found in all five sources, and yet are rejected by many.

could utilize its approach positively to explore how the Gospel writers shaped their material. Rather than seeing the material as an imaginative construct of the Gospel writer, using the tools of redaction criticism, they could explore the theology of each Gospel writer and help interpret the message they were trying to impart. It is fair to say that the rise of redaction criticism has seen the rise of a new era of biblical scholarship that continues today through the many faithful evangelicals producing sound biblical scholarship around the world.

RHETORICAL CRITICISM

Although rhetorical criticism is used in Gospel studies, its greatest contribution to New Testament studies is in the interpretation of the letters of the New Testament. Rhetorical critics argue that the letters of the New Testament should not be simply read as letters but as speeches. This is not baseless, as the letters were originally delivered by an emissary who likely read them out to the recipients. Rhetorical criticism looks at the principles of Greco-Roman rhetoric developed in rhetorical handbooks by Aristotle and others. Roman elite citizens were raised to be skilled in persuasion through public speaking. They were trained in rhetoric. Rhetorical criticism assesses the letters of the New Testament against their patterns. This includes classifying the letter against one of the three main forms of rhetoric found in Greek rhetoric. These are:

1. Forensic—to defend or accuse the readers of past action, to move them to right action

2. Deliberative—to exhort or dissuade them to future action

3. Epideictic—to affirm communal values by praise or blame[9]

For example, scholars have argued that Galatians is forensic (Betz), Philippians is deliberative (Witherington), and 1 Thessalonians is epideictic (Jewett). Other scholars have come up with different analyses, and still others reject this approach, seeing the letters as letters and not speeches. In most cases, while some scholars are convinced that the letter writers of the New Testament are utilizing the tools of rhetoric, others tend to

---

9. See G. W. Hansen, "Rhetorical Criticism," in *DPL* 822.

argue that the writers may be using some of the ideas of rhetoric, but not in a formal way.

Rhetorical critics also break down letters into constitutive parts, each of which has a particular purpose within the overall rhetorical approach. There are usually six parts: (1) introduction *(exordium)*; (2) narration *(narratio)*; (3) proposition *(propositio)*; (4) confirmation *(probatio)*; (5) refutation *(refutatio)*; and (6) conclusion *(peroratio)*.[10] Each part leads to the overall goal, dependent on which of the three approaches is being used.

Rhetorical critics also examine the letters for the use of well-established rhetorical devices used in the letter to achieve the overall goal. A good example is a *chiasm*, a device found in both the Old and New Testaments based on the Greek letter chi (X) which has an A-B-C-B"-A" structure. For example, consider Philippians 3:8-10:

> A   that I may gain Christ and be found in him,
>   B   not having a righteousness of my own
>   C   that comes from the law,
>   C"   but that which comes through faith in Christ,
>   B"   the righteousness from God that depends on faith
> A"   that I may know him and the power of his resurrection, and may share his sufferings, becoming like him in his death,

There is a wide range of such rhetorical devices (see further in Vol. 2). In particular, rhetorical criticism is a useful approach to reading the letters of the New Testament.

NARRATIVE CRITICISM

From the late twentieth century to the present, there has been a movement to dig behind the historical setting of the texts (the focus of historical criticism) to the text itself. There has also been a trend to read the New Testament documents as literature (literary criticism), leaving aside the unanswerable historical questions to interpret the texts of the New Testament in their own right. Among the range of approaches toward literary criticism, narrative criticism is arguably the most influential, especially in Gospel studies. With this approach, interpreters read the New

---

10. Patzia and Petrotta, *PDBS* 101.

Testament as stories, concentrating on the features of the narrative. The focus is not historical reliability or even the theology of the passage, but placement, plot, and characterization. This approach is appealing to many today because it frees people from having to engage with several centuries of historical criticism. For example, when interpreting Luke's Gospel, rather than seeking to determine whether Luke has used Mark, Q, Matthew, or another source, and how he has done so, the narrative critic focuses on what Luke is doing in the text and from there draws out its meaning.

However, the best narrative critics do not completely neglect redaction and source-critical insights. They still deal with the narrative with an eye to how the story has been shaped regarding the original source, especially if Mark is in view. Further, they recognize that legitimate readings of the text privilege the historical and social setting; otherwise, one can read into the text whatever one likes from a contemporary point of view. The focus remains how the writer is narrating the story.

THE QUEST FOR THE HISTORICAL JESUS

"The quest for the historical Jesus" is the name used to describe the search to find the historical Jesus behind the words of the New Testament. Just who was he? Most analysis suggests that, broadly speaking, there are three phases to the quest.

REIMARUS TO SCHWEITZER

The quest coincided with the rise of modernist rationalism and critique of Christianity. A range of writers interpreted Jesus in diverse ways other than the traditional view of the Christ of faith. H. S. Reimarus saw Jesus as a failed revolutionary, his body stolen, and his divinity a conception of his disciples. Other writers like David Friedrich Strauss rejected Jesus' miracles and saw them as fiction. Ernest Renan argued the Gospels are a work of romantic fantasy. Source criticism emerged in this period with writers like Heinrich Julius Holtzmann, who argued for Markan priority and Jesus as merely an ethical teacher of timeless truth. Weiss argued Jesus preached the end of the world, but it never materialized. Albert Schweitzer wrapped up this first phase, arguing that Jesus sought to keep his messiahship secret, was betrayed by Judas, and died believing God would intervene—but he didn't. Schweitzer rejected the views of the other writers, arguing that the

Jesus they constructed never existed. Jesus is meaningful, not in a historical sense, but because of the spiritual good he brings. In 1906, he effectively brought this initial quest to an end, declaring it a failure.

ALBERT SCHWEITZER TO ERNST KÄSEMANN

The launch of the second phase is attributed to Ernst Käsemann. Before his contribution, Karl Barth both critiqued the liberal "historical Jesus" who is far from the Gospel portrayals, seeing the earthly life of Jesus as irrelevant, and focused on a crucified Jesus who judges human religiosity. The other great figure was Rudolf Bultmann, a dominant man who rejected much of the Gospels as pre-scientific myth and claimed what matters is faith in the one who died on a cross. He argued Christianity was constructed from Hellenistic myth. In this period, source and form criticism dominated, their proponents believing they could reconstruct Jesus through them.

The second phase was inaugurated on October 20, 1953, when German Ernst Käsemann argued that if one removes Jesus from history, a docetic Christ is created (purely divine) and the cross loses relevance. His words hit home, and a second quest was underway. Scholars developed criteria for assessing the historicity of Jesus' sayings and deeds (see Form Criticism above). Bornkamm rejected Jesus' miracles, believed that Jesus did not regard himself as the Messiah, argued his ministry was fulfilled in the present, and accepted only a few events as historical (e.g., the calling of the Twelve).

Jeremias argued that understanding Jesus required consideration of the historical setting. He developed a list of words Jesus likely said (*ipsissima verba*) and spoke of an inaugurated eschatology. Some have argued Jesus was not a prophet or Messiah but a Cynic philosopher, a teacher of pithy wisdom sayings (Mack). The views held in these first two phases live on in popular critique of Christianity (e.g., Dawkins) and among some scholars.

THE "THIRD QUEST"

The debate continues today with a range of views. What stands out is the scholarly consensus that Jesus should be understood in terms of Second Temple Judaism rather than Hellenism and myth. How did Jesus fit into the world of first-century Judaism? B. F. Meyer (1979) believes that Jesus' table-fellowship with sinners is key, a picture of Jesus' hope for a new community. A. E. Harvey (1982) accepts the Gospels' portrayal of Christ's arrest, trial, and death. Jesus was Messiah, but not in a divine sense; rather, he was unique. Marcus Borg (1984) interprets Jesus as a nationalist traitor because he called for mercy and love rather than revolution, which would end in disaster. Mark 13 and parallel passages in the Gospels point to the fall of Jerusalem. E. P. Sanders (1985) sees the clearing of the temple as the key event in Jesus' ministry. Because of his attack on the temple, he was handed over to the Romans. He was not a revolutionary but died anyway.

CONCLUSION

The quest will go on. Accepting the Gospel accounts as faithful to the memory of those who were with Jesus still leaves students of the Bible with uncertainty of who the real Jesus is behind the four portrayals in the Gospels. What was he really like? What really mattered to him? What does he want of humanity?[11]

QUESTIONS TO CONSIDER

- Which methodologies seem the most useful to you?
- Which methodologies do you find difficult to understand?
- Which methodologies do not make sense to you?
- How would you answer the question: "Who is the historical Jesus?"

---

11. See for more detail, N. T. Wright, "The Quest for the Historical Jesus," in *ABD* 3:796-802.

THE SYNOPTIC GOSPELS

CHAPTER 5

The first four books of the New Testament are termed "the four Gospels." The term "gospel" is derived from the *euangelion*, which means "good news." The four books were grouped together in the early to mid-second century as they circulated as a unit.

A cursory examination of the four books shows that the first three books have much common material, whereas John is significantly different with some similarity, but a great deal of unique material. While it is argued by some that John personally knew of one or more of the Synoptics, John is written without literary dependency on any of the other three Gospels. The similarity in the first three Gospels has led to them being described as the Synoptic Gospels. The term "Synoptic" is derived from two Greek terms: *syn* (with), and *opsis* (seeing), and producing the idea, "seeing together." The Gospels can be viewed together and compared, hence their designation.

The common material in the Synoptic Gospels has led to much debate over their relationship.

NO RELATIONSHIP

Some have argued that while there is similar material, there is no relationship between the Gospels. However, this can be ruled out by comparing the similarities.

For example, compare the passages below. While in the Greek there are times when a word or word order is slightly adapted, there is a great commonality in language, especially in the first two verses, where there are twenty-eight common Greek words out of the thirty-seven in Mark, the thirty-eight in Matthew, and the thirty-nine in Luke.[1]

Matt 19:13-15	Mark 10:13-16	Luke 18:15-17
[13] Then children were brought to him that he might lay his hands on them and pray. The disciples rebuked the people, [14] but Jesus said, "Let the little children come to me and do not hinder them, for to such belongs the kingdom of heaven." [15] And he laid his hands on them and went away.	[13] And they were bringing children to him that he might touch them, and the disciples rebuked them. [14] But when Jesus saw it, he was indignant and said to them, "Let the children come to me; do not hinder them, for to such belongs the kingdom of God. [15] Truly, I say to you, whoever does not receive the kingdom of God like a child shall not enter it." [16] And he took them in his arms and blessed them, laying his hands on them.	[15] Now they were bringing even infants to him that he might touch them. And when the disciples saw it, they rebuked them. [16] But Jesus called them to him, saying, "Let the children come to me, and do not hinder them, for to such belongs the kingdom of God. [17] Truly, I say to you, whoever does not receive the kingdom of God like a child shall not enter it."

FIGURE 7: GOSPEL SYNOPSIS

It is evident from this and many other parallel passages that there is some relationship between these passages, suggesting some form of interdependence. However, there is also evidence of freedom to retell the story. In addition, there are similarities in order. For example, compare:

- Mark 8:27-10:52 with Matthew 16:13-20:34 and Luke 9:18-51; 18:15-43.

- Mark 3:31-6:6a with Matthew 12:46-13:58 and Luke 8:19-56.[2]

Furthermore, there are similarities in the parenthetical material placed by the redactors. For example:

---

1. The examples here are taken from ESV.
2. Robert H. Stein, "The Synoptic Problem," in *DJG* 784. For a more detailed and updated analysis, see A. D. Baum, "Synoptic Problem," in *DJG2* 911-19.

- "Let the reader understand" in Matthew 24:15 and Mark 13:14
- "He then said to the paralytic" in Matthew 9:6; Mark 2:5; Luke 5:24
- "For he was saying ..." Mark 5:8; Luke 8:29[3]

There are also similarities in biblical quotations (e.g., Mark 1:2 par. Matt 3:3 and Luke 3:4; Mark 7:7 par. Matt 15:9). Because there were multiple versions including the LXX and Hebrew texts, the exact correlation of these verses requires explanation.[4] Hence, this idea of total independence can be quickly ruled out.

AN ORAL UR-GOSPEL

One old idea is that the Gospels are dependent on a body of oral tradition. This idea says there is a *urevangelium* (*ur* means "early, original, primitive," plus *evangelium*, which means "gospel") behind the three Synoptics. This Ur Gospel idea originated with J. G. Herder, who originally promoted the idea that there existed a reasonably fixed *oral* summary of the life of Jesus and that this accounted for the similarities between the Gospels.[5] This view is diagrammatically represented below.

This perspective was elaborated by J. Geiseler (1818),[6] was popular in the nineteenth century, and retains support today from John M. Rist and Bo Reicke.[7] As in the case of the previous theory, this does not account for the similarities in detail concerning wording, sentence structure, and order found in the three Gospels.

---

3. Stein, "The Synoptic Problem," 784.
4. Stein, "The Synoptic Problem," 784.
5. J. G. Herder, "Vom Erlöser der Menschen," in *Herder Werke: Theologische Schriften* 9/1 (Frangurt: Deuscher Klassker, 1994), 671–87. He later shifted his perspective to a written Ur Gospel.
6. C. L. Gieseler, *Historisch-kritischer Versuch über die Entstehung und die frühesten Schicksale der schriftlichen Evangelien* (Leipzig: Engelmann, 1818).
7. See John M. Rist, *On the Independence of Matthew and Mark*. SNTSMS 32 (Cambridge: Cambridge University Press, 1978); B. Reicke, *The Roots of the Synoptic Gospels* (Philadelphia: Fortress, 1986).

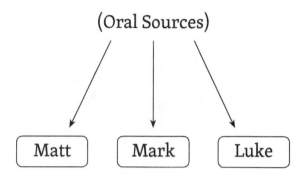

FIGURE 8: ORAL UR-GOSPEL

AN ARAMAIC PROTO-GOSPEL

Rather than a body of oral tradition, the Proto-Gospel theory argues that there was an original written but lost Aramaic or Hebrew Gospel from which the canonical Gospels were made:

This theory sees the differences between the Gospels coming from the different handling of the common original Aramaic or Hebrew Gospel. This was first proposed by German scholar G. E. Lessing in 1771 and was developed by others including J. Eichhorn, who argued for several lost gospels as the original sources for the Synoptic Gospels.[8] This did not find favor apart from C. C. Torrey in 1933.[9] Another similar view is that of F. Schleiermacher, who argues that several fragments of gospel tradition existed in the early church and formed the basis for the Gospels.[10] However, this does not account for the high degree of similarity in wording and order, which requires literary dependence.

---

8. G. E. Lessing, "Neue Hypothese über die Evangelisten als blos menschliche Geschichtschreiber betrachtet," in *Theologiekritische Schriften I und II* (Gotthold Ephraim Lessing, Werke 7; ed. H. G. Göpfert; München: Hanser, 1976), 614–36; G. Eichhorn, *Einleitung in das Neue Testament* (Vol. 1; Leipzig: Weidmann, 1804).

9. C. C. Torrey, *The Four Gospels* (New York: Harper, 1933).

10. F. D. E. Schleiermacher, *Ueber die Schriften des Lukas, ein kritischer Versuch: Erster Theil* (Berlin: Reimer, 1817).

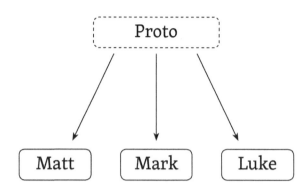

FIGURE 9: ARAMAIC PROTO-GOSPEL

THE AUGUSTINIAN OR GRIESBACH HYPOTHESIS

Traditionally, until the nineteenth century, it was commonly believed that Matthew was the first of the Gospels. Twentieth-century proponents included B. C. Butler and D. J. Chapman.[11]

Luke was then written using Matthew as a primary source, along with a variety of other material designated M. Mark was subsequently written using both Matthew and Luke. This is called Augustinian (after Augustine)[12] or the Griesbach hypothesis, so named after Johann Jakob Griesbach (1745-1812), who revived this idea.[13] Few scholars accept this understanding today, although William Farmer has supported it in the twentieth century.[14]

---

11. See B. C. Butler, *The Originality of St. Matthew: A Critique of the Two-Document Hypothesis* (Cambridge: Cambridge University Press, 1951); D. J. Chapman, *Matthew, Mark and Luke: A Study in the Order and Interrelation of the Synoptic Gospels* (London: Longmans, Green, 1937).

12. Augustine of Hippo (350–430 AD) is an early church leader and theologian whose theology is vastly influential in western thought. He is not to be confused with Augustine of Canterbury. See further J. Newton, "Augustine of Hippo" in *Who's Who in Christian History*, ed. J. D. Douglas and Philip W. Comfort (Wheaton, IL: Tyndale House, 1992), 47–52.

13. J. J. Griesbach, "Commentatio qua Marci Evangelium totum e Matthaei et Lucae commentariis decerptum esse monstratur." Pages 358–452 in *J. J. Griesbachii Opuscala Academica Vol 2*. Edited by J. P. Gabler, J. C. G. Goepferdt. Jena: Frommanni, 1825.

14. W. Farmer, *The Synoptic Problem: A Critical Analysis* (New York: Macmillan, 1964) & *New Synoptic Studies: The Cambridge Gospel Conference and Beyond* (Macon: Mercer University, 1983); H. Stoldt, *History and Criticism of the Marcan Hypothesis* (Macon: Mercer University, 1980); A. Bellinzoni Jr, *The Two-Source Hypothesis: A Critical Appraisal* (Macon: Mercer University, 1985).

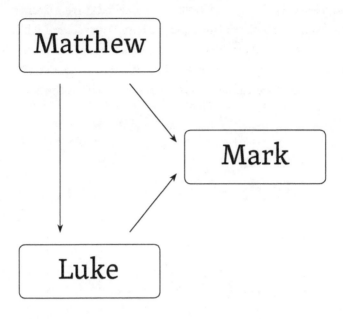

FIGURE 10: AUGUSTINIAN OR GRIESBACH HYPOTHESIS

MARKAN PRIORITY, Q, AND THE TWO- OR FOUR-SOURCE HYPOTHESIS

In the nineteenth century, led by scholars such as B. H. Streeter,[15] scholarship shifted from Matthean priority to Markan priority. Most scholars of all persuasions hold to this view— namely that Mark was written first. Matthew and Luke then both used Mark's Gospel in the writing of their biographies of Jesus. In support, Luke refers to many writings about Jesus (Luke 1:1). It is generally agreed that Mark was written at the earliest in the late 50s AD, but most likely in the mid-60s or early 70s AD.

While scholarship generally accepts that Mark was first and provides source material for Matthew and Luke, there is disagreement over the relationship between the Gospels. The majority view is that alongside Mark's Gospel is another source, which is made up of some combination of written and oral memory. The clue to this is the common material in Matthew

---

15. Burnett Hillman Streeter, *The Four Gospels: A Study of Origins Treating of the Manuscript Tradition, Sources, Authorship, Date* (London: MacMillan & Co., 1930).

and Luke's Gospels. This common material is called Q, from German *Quelle*, meaning "source." Some scholars consider it a written source, while others a blend of written and oral material. Copious amounts of research have gone into reconstructing Q; however, in truth, it does not exist.

The blend of Mark and Q leads to the designation the Two-Source Hypothesis:

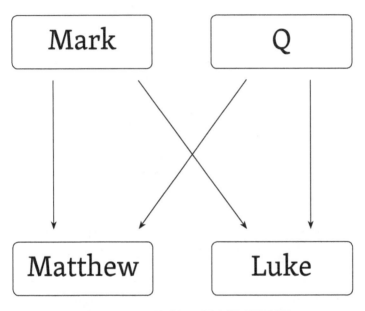

FIGURE 11: TWO-SOURCE HYPOTHESIS

The Two-Source Hypothesis has also been amended to the Four-Source Hypothesis, which recognizes there is material in Matthew and Luke unique to their Gospels. As such, it is held by many that Matthew had his own source (M) and similarly Luke (L). When Matthew and Luke wrote their Gospels, they drew on Mark, Q, and their own sources. One version of the Four-Source Hypothesis can be diagrammed like this:[16]

---

16. "JEDP Hypothesis, Q Theory, and the Critical Text ... Oh My!" *Redeeming God.* https://redeeminggod.com/jedp-hypothesis-q-theory-and-the-critical-text-oh-my/

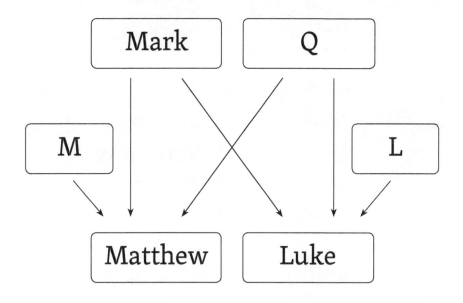

FIGURE 12: FOUR-SOURCE HYPOTHESIS

FARRER OR FARRER-GOULDER HYPOTHESIS

As no such document has been found, there is strong resistance to the Q hypothesis among many scholars. Yet, other ideas have been proposed. The Farrer or Farrer-Goulder Hypothesis derives from Austin Farrer, who argued that Mark was written first.[17] Matthew then wrote his Gospel using Mark and his own gathered material. Then Luke wrote his Gospel using both Mark and Matthew. He has been followed by Michael Goulder and Mark Goodacre.[18] This can be diagrammatically represented as:

---

17. A. M. Farrer, "On Dispensing with Q," in *Studies in the Gospels: Essays in Memory of R. H. Lightfoot*, ed. D. E. Nineham (Oxford: Blackwell, 1955), 55–88.

18. Michael D. Goulder, *Midrash and Lection in Matthew* (London: SPCK, 1974); Mark S. Goodacre, *Goulder and the Gospels: An Examination of a New Paradigm*, JSNTSup 133 (Sheffield: Sheffield Academic Press, 1996); idem, *The Case Against Q: Studies in Markan Priority and the Synoptic Problem* (Harrisburg, PA: Trinity Press International, 2002).

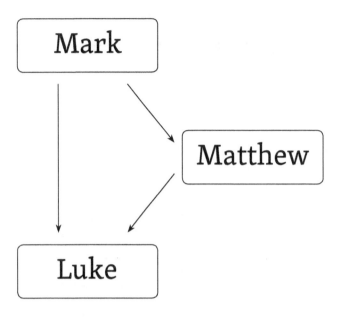

FIGURE 13: FARRER HYPOTHESIS

WILKE HYPOTHESIS

Some, like Christian Gottlob Wilke, writing in the early 1800s,[19] reversed the order of the Farrer hypothesis, contending Mark wrote first, Luke used Mark, and Matthew relied on both Mark and Luke.

---

19. C. G. Wilke, *Der Urevangelist oder exegetisch kritische Untersuchung über das Verwandtschafts-verhältniss der drei ersten Evangelien* (Dresden: Fleischer, 1838).

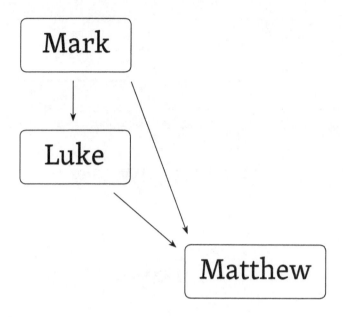

FIGURE 14: WILKE HYPOTHESIS

ADDITIONAL POSSIBILITIES

A range of other proposals has also been made. Some, like R. Morgenthaler,[20] believe Mark was influenced by a collection of sayings.

Matthew drew on both Mark and this source. Luke used both Mark and the sayings along with Matthew. Similarly, Martin Hengel argues that Matthew used Mark, Luke, and a sayings source.[21] This is the so-called three-source hypothesis:

---

20. R. Morgenthaler, *Statistische Synopse* (Zürich: Gotthelf-Verlag, 1971).
21. M. Hengel, *The Four Gospels and the One Gospel of Jesus Christ: An Investigation of the Collection and Origin of the Canonical Gospels* (Harrisburg, PA: Trinity Press International, 2000).

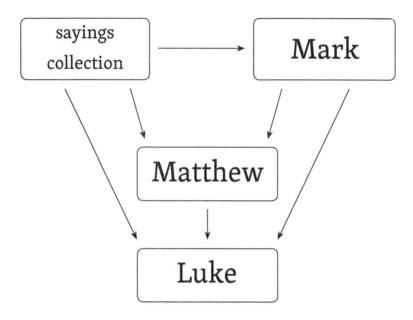

FIGURE 15: THREE-SOURCE HYPOTHESIS

In the Q + Papias Hypothesis, MacDonald argues that Q should be called the *Logoi* (sayings) of Jesus,[22] something Papias refers to.[23] Mark drew on the Logoi (Q), Matthew used both Mark and the Logoi, and Papias also wrote a gospel drawing on the Logoi, Mark, and Matthew. Luke is the final Gospel in the Synoptic process, and he also drew on Papias. Few scholars agree with this idea as Papias is a second-century writer and Luke was likely completed much earlier than Papias.

---

22. Dennis R. MacDonald, *Two Shipwrecked Gospels: The "Logoi of Jesus" and Papias' "Exposition of Logia about the Lord"* (Atlanta: Society of Biblical Literature, 2012), 96–97.

23. See Eusebius, *Hist. eccl.* 3.39.14–17: "Then, Matthew, in the Hebrew dialect (*dialektō*), organized the sayings (*logoi*) of Jesus."

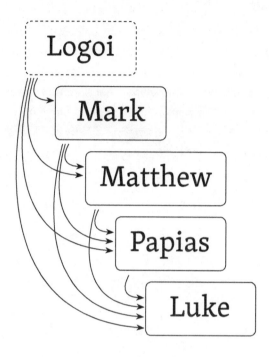

FIGURE 16: Q + PAPIAS HYPOTHESIS

The Jerusalem School of Synoptic Research focuses on the Hebrew language and argues that a Greek Anthology (A) existed, which is a translation of a Hebrew original. This was supposedly used for each Synoptic Gospel. The School argues that Luke is the first Gospel, drawing on a Reconstruction (R) of the life of Jesus and the anthology. Mark wrote second, drawing on Luke and A. Matthew is the final Synoptic, drawing on Mark and A, but not Luke. Again, this view is now commonly accepted.

CONCLUSION

How should Bible students handle such varying possibilities?

First, while there is a wide range of ideas, the overwhelming majority of scholars accept that Mark's Gospel was first. There are sound reasons for why this is the dominant view:

1. **Mark's brevity:** Mark (11,025 words) is shorter than Matthew (18,293) and Luke (19,376). Remembering that 97 percent of

Mark's words have a parallel in Matthew and 88 percent in Luke (410 verses, i.e., 40 percent of Luke, is dependent on Mark), it is more likely that Matthew and Luke took over Mark than Mark condensed Matthew and Luke. For instance, it seems unlikely that Mark would have omitted critical features including the Sermon on the Mount, the birth narratives, and the appearances of the risen Christ. Why Mark was written if Luke and Matthew already existed is difficult to comprehend.

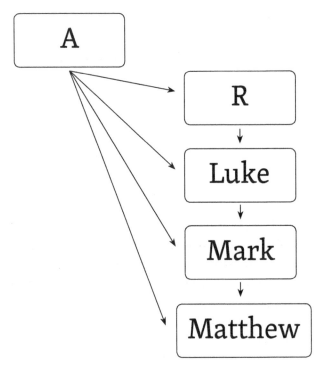

FIGURE 17: GREEK ANTHOLOGY HYPOTHESIS

2. **Verbal agreements and order among the gospels:** A deeper look at verbal parallels indicates Matthew and Mark frequently agree in their wording as do Mark and Luke. However, Matthew and Luke rarely agree. The same applies to the order of material in the three Gospels. This suggests Mark is the central work around which Matthew and Luke are based. If so,

Mark probably came first, and Matthew and Luke built on Mark's work. This is more likely than the other main options.

3. **Mark's less sophisticated literary style:** There are more grammatical irregularities and awkward Greek constructions in Mark. Because it is more likely later authors would smooth out irregularities for their gentile readers, rather than roughen them, it is probable Mark came first. Mark also includes a number of Aramaisms, which he translates for his readers. These are not found in later writings, suggesting that they were removed.

4. **Mark's more primitive theology:** Most scholars agree that there are more difficult theological statements in Mark than in Matthew and Luke. For example, Mark 6:5 states that Jesus "*could* not" do miracles in his home town, whereas Matthew 13:58 notes that Jesus "*did* not" do miracles due to their lack of faith. It is most likely later writers smoothed out such theological issues, rather than introduced them.

Second, since much of the material common to Matthew and Luke is so similar, it's possible to posit a common written source, Q. Yet, at other points, such as the Beatitudes and Woes of Matthew 5 and Luke 6, it is not clear whether the material chosen comes from a written or oral source, and while similar, there are differences. This could indicate points where Luke and Matthew drew on sources independently.

The notion of a sayings source for the Gospels may be traced to Papias (c. AD 150), who referred to a set of sayings—a gospel (*logia*)—that Matthew compiled and composed in the Hebrew dialect. Some believe this refers to the Gospel itself; others to Q.[24] In the nineteenth century, Schleiermacher, followed by others, proposed that Q is a written source of the sayings of Jesus made up of 250 or so verses common to Matthew and Luke. Others argue that Q is not a written source, but a common oral source known in the early church. It is a highly contentious area of New Testament research.

---

24. See G. N. Stanton and N. Perrin, "Q," in *DJG* (2) 713: "Most scholars now conclude that Papias was referring to canonical Matthew and not Q."

There are four main arguments for the existence of Q:

1. **Verbal agreement between Matthew and Luke:** This could be explained by Luke using Matthew or vice versa. About 250 verses—nearly 25 percent—of Luke is from this material. However, this is unlikely; in the Markan material, Matthew and Luke rarely agree with one another in terms of order and wording.

2. **Agreement in order:** Some argue that there is a similar order in the "Q" material in Matthew and Luke. However, this is disputed and not conclusive.

3. **Doublets in Matthew and Luke:** There are a few examples of the doubling-up of sayings such as "nothing is hidden (concealed) that will not be disclosed, and nothing concealed (hidden) that will not be known" (Luke 8:17; 12:2). Luke 8:17 is paralleled in Mark 4:22 and Matthew 10:26. This suggests that one came from Mark and the other from Q. This doubling-up could point to the existence of Q.

4. **Different placement of Q material:** The Q material is placed in different contexts by Matthew and Luke. Matthew clumps things together (e.g., Matt 5–7) and Luke tends to spread them throughout his Gospel. This suggests a common source, arranged differently.

Finally, there are clear points where Luke and Matthew have drawn on their own memory or source material. In Luke, about 455 verses are unique (just over 40 percent).

Other viewpoints cannot be ruled out, especially the Farrer-Goulder and Wilke perspectives. If Luke-Acts is completed not long after Paul's Roman imprisonment (Acts 28:30–31), then the latter is not at all unlikely. However, the Four-Source Hypothesis remains the most likely explanation of the relationship between the three Synoptics. Decisive is Luke 1:1, where Luke refers to "many" undertaking to write concerning the events of Jesus' life. This would suggest Luke had access to more than just Mark's Gospel and may include Matthew, Q, and other now lost written sources.

However, even if the Q hypothesis is accepted, this does not suggest that Q can be defined with certainty or that scholars should make excessive claims concerning it. For example, it is claimed Q is the earliest "Gospel." Some have produced editions of Q with commentary. Such ideas are tenuous, unhelpful, and misleading. Further, Q may be a much smaller document or set of written and oral material than is sometimes claimed. If Q can be narrowed to those parts of Matthew and Luke that are close in wording, then it is greatly reduced. On the other hand, sections like the Sermon on the Mount (Matthew 5-7) and the Sermon on the Plain (Luke 6:19-49) may come from independent oral sources. The differences in Gospel and ethical material may be due to Jesus saying the same or similar things across the nation of Israel. Memories of this would differ. Overall, Q should be understood as a blend of written and oral material.

The following chart shows a relationship between the Gospels that accepts Peter is behind Mark's Gospel, and that the writer of Matthew is the apostle:

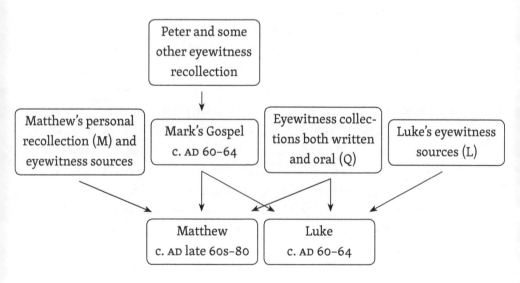

FIGURE 18: EYEWITNESS HYPOTHESIS

This preserves the Four-Source Hypothesis and Markan priority with Peter as Mark's primary source. It is also important to realize that Mark is connected to the Jerusalem community. If he is the fleeing young man of Mark 14:51, this means he had personal knowledge of the death and resurrection of Christ, and was an eyewitness to at least the crucifixion and resurrection and perhaps some earlier events. He also had access to the apostles and may have seen more of Jesus than at the end of his ministry. He was also from Jerusalem and was a part of the first Jerusalem Church with access to a wide range of sources including Barnabas and Peter (cf. Acts 12:12, 25). His home may have been the site of the Last Supper and the events at Pentecost. This construct also preserves the idea of eyewitness sources as the key, the apostle Matthew respecting Peter's account in Mark, and bringing his own material to his Gospel. Similarly, Luke gathered eyewitness recollections to supplement Mark and Q. It argues for an early date for Mark and Luke. Clearly, Luke must post-date Mark, but this gap may be quite short as both Luke and Mark were together in Rome in the early 60s AD (Col 4:10, 14; Phlm 24). Luke may have copied Mark or an earlier version early, and wrote his own soon after, with additional material gathered from others.

When readers engage with the material in Matthew and Luke also found in Mark's Gospel, one of the skills involved is consideration of how these later writers used Mark's source material. What did they amend? How did they change it? How did they restructure his order? This comparative work gives clues to Matthew and Luke's intent in writing their later Gospels. When dealing with material common to Luke and Matthew, this can be discussed with less concern for the alternative reading unless the reader is convinced that Luke used Matthew or vice versa. If so, then one can consider how Luke used Matthew or Matthew used Luke to gain an understanding of their purposes. In passages like the Sermon on the Plain (Luke 6:19–49) or the Sermon on the Mount (Matt 5–7), to interpret the material closely, readers need to decide whether Luke is dependent on Matthew or the converse, or that the material is independent. Where common material exists, although some make confident assertions, it is anyone's guess as to whether Matthew or Luke is closer to the original.

With so many questions concerning historical origins and relationships, some would argue it is better to interpret the Synoptic Gospels in their own right and merely posit possibilities concerning interpretations based on possible relationships.

In this approach to Synoptic research, Mark is interpreted regarding Mark's own material and where he has cited the Old Testament—a narrative criticism. Each reader of the Synoptics, however, must make up their own mind on such things.

QUESTIONS TO CONSIDER

- Which theories on the Synoptic problem make the most sense to you? Why?

- What do you think of the Q hypothesis?

MARK'S GOSPEL

CHAPTER 6

Mark's Gospel is a fast-moving presentation of the life of Jesus. Mark does not focus on Jesus' childhood, and instead launches his story with John the Baptist—the prophets are back. Jesus emerges to be baptized by John, anointed as the Servant King. The agenda is declared in Mark 1:14-15; "the kingdom of God" is breaking in. Israel and the world are summoned to repent and believe. Jesus then launches into ministry, gathering an assortment of young men to be his disciples. They join him, likely in the hope that Jesus will lead them to liberate their nation from Roman rule. Through the first half of Mark, Jesus enacts the kingdom, inviting his disciples and people to recognize his kingship. At Caesarea Philippi, Peter confesses Jesus' messiahship, the turning point of the gospel. From this moment, Jesus teaches them what kind of Messiah he is and what it means to be a subject of the kingdom. The disciples struggle to grasp that he is a humble servant who must die to bring redemption. They grapple with what the life of a person in this kingdom should look like—a life of cross-bearing love. The gospel climaxes with the horror of Jesus' betrayal, trial, and death. It ends with his disciples nowhere to be seen and the women at the tomb bewildered and fearful. What has happened? Who is this man? It is clear Mark knows, and his readers are challenged to come to their own conclusion.

THE AUTHORSHIP OF MARK'S GOSPEL

Traditionally, John Mark of Jerusalem is the writer of Mark's Gospel reflected in the title of second Gospel "According to Mark." However, many scholars question this assumption on authorship. While arguments about authorship can surprise people who have not considered the history of biblical interpretation, the doubt over authorship is not that surprising when one realizes Mark did not himself sign the document. The ascriptions are not part of the original text, and Mark was a common name at the time. These ascriptions were added sometime in the second century. Mark's story of Jesus is foundational to Luke and Matthew's account, and seeking to know by whom and when Mark was written is important.

EVIDENCE FOR MARKAN AUTHORSHIP

The Testimony of Papias

The earliest reference to the authorship of Mark is found in a quote by a certain Papias recorded by the fourth-century church historian, Eusebius. Papias was a bishop of Hierapolis in Asia Minor (Turkey) and, according to Irenaeus, was connected with the disciples, being "a hearer of John and a companion of Polycarp" (c. AD 60–130). Papias is quoted as saying of Mark:

> And the Elder said this also:
>
> "Mark, having become *the interpreter of Peter*, wrote down *accurately* whatever he remembered of the things said and done by the Lord, but *not however in order*." For neither did he hear the Lord, nor did he follow him, but afterwards, as I said, Peter, who adapted his teachings to the needs of his hearers, but not as though he were drawing up a connected account of the Lord's oracles. So then Mark made *no mistake in thus recording some things just as he remembered them*. For he took forethought for one thing, not to omit any of the things that he had heard nor to state them falsely.[1]

Hence, Papias recorded that Mark had been Peter's "interpreter" and had written down "accurately all that he remembered" although "not in order," which likely means, not chronologically. As Peter's interpreter (*hērmēneutes*), Mark probably interpreted and composed Peter's words into the

---

1. Eusebius, *Hist. eccl.* 3.39.15.

form of a written Gospel. The "elder" (*presbyter*) is commonly believed to be John, probably John the apostle himself.[2] Later Christian writers agreed that Mark was the writer of the Gospel.[3]

If this is correct, then sometime around the end of Peter's life, before he was traditionally crucified upside down during Nero's reign (c. AD 64),[4] Mark wrote down the essence of the gospel Peter shared, in Greek. If so, then Mark was not inscribed by an eyewitness to Jesus' entire life—although he may have been involved in some of the final events of Jesus' life—but as one who obtained most of his information directly *from an eyewitness*, namely Peter.[5]

Additional Arguments

Other arguments supporting Markan authorship include:

1. **Early church agreement to Markan authorship:** The early church was unanimous in agreement that the second Gospel is from the pen of Mark and the mind of Peter. Today, some dispute Papias' testimony because of his reference to early Hebrew Matthean texts that, it is argued, fail to take account of the material that is in Matthew's Gospel. However, this could point to proto-gospels and collections of sayings in Aramaic or Hebrew before they were formed into a Gospel. Significantly, there is *not one dissenting voice* in the early church suggesting another author.[6]

---

2. See the excellent discussion in Craig S. Keener, *The Gospel of John: A Commentary*. Vol. 1 (Grand Rapids, MI: Baker Academic, 2012), 95-98, who concludes on the identity of John the Elder, "When all this is taken into account, it is far more likely that John the elder was none other than John the apostle."

3. See Irenaeus, *Haer*. 3.1.2. (AD 180); Tertullian, *Marc*. 4.5 (c. 200); Clement of Alexandria, *Hypotyposes* (c. 200), according to Eusebius (*Hist. eccl.* 6.14.5-7); Origen, *Comm. Matt.* (early third century), according to Eusebius (*Hist. eccl.* 6.15.5) and probably the Muratorian Canon (c. 170-200). Justin Martyr the mid-first century apologist also mentions the "reminiscences of Peter" in conjunction with a quotation from Mark's Gospel (*Dial*. 106).

4. If this tradition is correct, cf. R. F. Stoops, Jr., "Passion of Peter and Paul," in *ABD* 5:264.

5. This is supported by the work of Richard Bauckham, who argues persuasively that Peter is the primary eyewitness relied on by the author of Mark (Bauckham, *Jesus and the Eyewitnesses*, 155-81).

6. Guelich, *Mark 1-8:26*, xxviii notes of the idea that author Mark is someone other than John Mark that, "We really do not have any basis for this distinction in the church tradition."

2. **The ascription "according to Mark":**[7] Martin Hengel argues that this title may have been added early when the Gospel was distributed beyond its founding community.[8] At the least, it indicates that by around AD 125, a significant portion of the early church believed that the second gospel came from a certain Mark. While the evidence has some degree of doubt and supposition, the alternative is not a strongly supported historical construct.

3. **1 Peter 5:13:** Peter's letter indicates Mark and Peter were together in Rome and that their relationship was close. Peter writes: "She who is at Babylon, who is likewise chosen, sends you greetings, and *so does Mark, my son.*" The attribution "son" suggests an intimate father-son relationship between Peter and Mark, not unlike that of Paul and Timothy. Additionally, if Philemon 24 and Colossians 4:10 are written from Rome, as is likely the case,[9] corroborating evidence indicates Mark was also in Rome at the time and in close contact with both Peter and Paul.

4. **The priority given to Mark by the Gospel writers:** Assuming Markan priority, it is significant that the other Synoptic writers, Matthew and Luke, based their Gospels on Mark's account. This is especially important if Matthew was an apostle who defers to Mark when telling of Jesus' life. That both use large portions of Mark indicates they attributed special authority to Mark. A credible reason for this may be that Matthew and Luke were aware that Peter was behind Mark's writing and valued it highly as a source.

5. **Peter's prominence in Mark:** Peter figures significantly in Mark, and some of the references are best explained as coming from Peter (e.g., Mark 11:21; 14:72, where Peter "remembered"

---

7. Greek: *KATA MARKON*.
8. M. Hengel, *Studies in the Gospel of Mark* (Philadelphia: Fortress, 1985), 74–81.
9. Some scholars argue that the imprisonments are Ephesus or Caesarea. Some dispute Paul wrote Colossians and see this as invaluable. See later on Pauline authorship.

events). Peter is named first and last of the apostles (Mark 1:16; 16:7), indicating he is probably Mark's primary source.[10] Furthermore, some believe the pattern of Mark's Gospel follows reasonably closely the arrangements of Peter's preaching in Acts (the *Kerygma*).[11]

6. **Latinisms, Semitisms, and Greek style:** Another factor cited in favor of Mark is his use of "Latinisms" in the text, suggesting he wrote in a Roman context. These are Greek words taken over from Latin, such as "centurion" (Lat. *centurio*, 15:39, 44, 45), "legion" (Lat. *Legio*, 5:9, 15), and "denarius" (Lat. *denarius*, 6:37; 12:15; 14:5).[12] In addition, his Greek style is "simple and unsophisticated."[13] Mark also has many translated Semitisms (Hebrew and Aramaic), which would align with a first-century Greek-speaking Jew from Jerusalem.[14] He regularly references Aramaic and Hebrew and gives the Greek translation. Martin Hengel wrote: "I do not know any other work in Greek which has so many Aramaic or Hebrew words and formulae in so narrow a space as does the second Gospel."[15]

7. **Naked man:** Some have suggested that there is a cryptic self-reference to the author himself in the reference to the young lad who fled naked during Jesus' arrest: "A young man, wearing nothing but a linen garment, was following Jesus. When they seized him, he fled naked, leaving his garment behind" (Mark 14:51–52). If so, then he was perhaps an eyewitness; at least to the end of Jesus' life. However, the idea that

---

10. Bauckham, *Jesus and the Eyewitnesses*, 165–72.

11. See C. H. Dodd, "The Framework of the Gospel Narrative," *ExpTim* 43 (1932): 396–400.

12. Others include *census* ("poll tax," 12:14), *modius* ("peck measure," 4:21), *praetorium* ("governor's official residence," 15:16), *quadrans* (a Roman coin, 12:42), *sextarius* (quart measure, "pitcher," 7:4), *speculator* ("executioner," 6:27), and *flagellum* ("to flog," 15:15).

13. Larry W. Hurtado, *Mark*, UBCS (Grand Rapids, MI: Baker Books, 2011), 11.

14. Andrew M. Bowden, "New Testament Semitisms," *LBD*. See also David Alan Black, "New Testament Semitisms," *The Bible Translator* 39.2 (April 1988), 215–23.

15. M. Hengel, "Literary, Theological and Historical problems in the Gospel of Mark," in *The Gospel and the Gospels*, ed. Peter Stuhlmacher (Grand Rapids: Eerdmans, 1991), 46.

this is John Mark is strongly disputed, not the least because Papias states Mark is *not* an eyewitness (see earlier quote).[16]

If Papias is accurate in his recollection, as is most likely, the Gospel was written by a certain Mark in Rome somewhere near the end of Peter's life. This is still the view of many contemporary scholars.[17] However, it must be acknowledged that while the evidence is not conclusive, it remains the best solution rather than a certain solution. Who wrote Mark does not matter much for interpretation. Clearly, the early church accepted the Gospel as genuine and worthy of inclusion in the New Testament, and regardless of authorship, it is to be reckoned with and interpreted as Scripture.

JOHN MARK IN THE NEW TESTAMENT

If Mark is the author, what is known about him? There are eight references to a "Mark" in the New Testament within Acts, Colossians, Philemon, and 1 Peter. Almost certainly these refer to the same person, making this figure by far the most likely author (Acts 12:12, 25; 15:37, 39; Col 4:10; 2 Tim 4:11; Phlm 24; 1 Pet 5:13). From these references, much can be discerned about him. He was also called "John" (Acts 13:5), hence the regular pseudonym, "John Mark." His cousin was Barnabas (Col 4:10).[18] His mother was a certain Mary, possibly a sister or sister-in-law of one of Barnabas' parents, whose home in Jerusalem was a place of prayer for the Jerusalem church (Acts 12:12) and possibly the scene of the Last Supper. When Barnabas and Saul brought a collection for the poor to Jerusalem during the reign of Claudius (Acts 11:27-30), they may have stayed with Mary and John Mark. They were possibly there during James' beheading and Peter's imprisonment. When they left to return to Antioch, they took John Mark with them as part of the team (Acts 12:25).

Mark became a missionary in the early church, traveling with Paul and Barnabas on their first missionary journey. Thus, Mark is gospel

---

16. James A. Brooks, *Mark*, NAC 23 (Nashville: Broadman & Holman Publishers, 1991), 238 rightly states, "The view that the reference is an autobiographical one pointing to John Mark may be the most probable, but it is still nothing more than a possibility."

17. So, for example, D. E. Garland, *Mark*, NIVAC (Grand Rapids, MI: Zondervan, 1996), 26-28.

18. LSJ 137 notes that the term means "first cousin," or more generally, "cousin."

summary by a missionary, and as such it is a "missional tract." However, Paul and Barnabas had a severe dispute concerning him. Mark, for reasons unknown, but which Paul clearly found inadequate, abruptly left the first missionary journey in Pamphylia (Acts 13:13; 15:38) and returned to Jerusalem. When the time came for Paul's second missionary journey, Barnabas wanted to take Mark with them again. However, Paul did not agree because of Mark's earlier desertion. Barnabas stood up for his cousin, they had "a sharp disagreement" (Acts 15:39) and split up. Barnabas and Mark went to Cyprus to engage in further mission, while Paul went with Silas to visit the churches he and Barnabas had planted on the first missionary journey. In Colossians 4:10 and Philemon 24 (c. AD 60-61) Mark turned up again with Paul in Rome as a coworker and possibly also a prisoner. Paul also described Mark as "very useful to me for ministry" in 2 Timothy 4:11. This suggests Paul and Mark reconciled and once again worked together, and that Mark was a prisoner for his bravery for the gospel. In 1 Peter 5:13 Peter also mentions Mark, again in a Roman context, in glowing terms as his "son." It is probable, then, that Mark wrote his Gospel while in Rome during this time. Peter's tender reference to Mark as his "son" makes it possible that, after his falling out with Paul and work with Barnabas, Peter took Mark under his wing. Whatever the exact situation, he was well positioned to write an account of Jesus' life.

THE ALTERNATIVE: AN UNKNOWN WRITER
LIVING OUTSIDE ISRAEL

Problems with Markan authorship

Markan authorship is disputed for a number of reasons:

1. **The questionable reliability of Papias:** Papias' reliability is questioned based on his words, "Matthew collected the oracles in the Hebrew language, and each interpreted them as best he could." Some argue there is no other evidence that the Gospel of Matthew was ever written in Hebrew, Aramaic, or any other language than Greek. Hence, if Papias is wrong on this count, is he to be trusted when he says Mark wrote the Gospel? Some believe, however, that Papias was referring to

a source for Matthew (Q) as having been written in Hebrew.

2. **Mark's Gospel is anonymous:** Some argue the second Gospel was originally anonymous, suggesting that Peter is unlikely to be behind it, as one would expect such an important figure to be named. If Mark did not write it, then it is wide open as to who did. However, none of the Gospel authors put their names on their writings; this may be explained by their desire to give God the glory, rather than themselves.[19]

3. **Questions about identifying the author with John Mark:** The identification of the author "Mark" with the John Mark of the New Testament has fallen out of favor with some scholars. Some question Mark's involvement at all, rejecting the early church belief. "Mark" was also "one of the most popular names in the Hellenistic age,"[20] leading some to believe that, even if it was a Mark, it could have been anyone.

The Challenges of Other Arguments

Some of the other evidence is also questioned. The "Latinisms" argument (1.2.2 above) is weakened in that such "loan words" were quite common over the whole Roman Empire at the time. The mention of the naked runner in the arrest account does not necessarily mean this is the author.[21]

Alternative Authors

These and other factors combine to lead some scholars to look for alternative authors. Many believe that before Mark's Gospel was written down, there was a period in which the material existed in an oral form in Greek

---

19. Garland, *Mark*, 26.
20. Paul J. Achtemeier, "Gospel of Mark," in *ABD* 4:542.
21. See Joel Marcus, *Mark 8–16: A New Translation with Introduction and Commentary*, AYB 27A (New Haven; London: Yale University Press, 2009), 1124–25, who notes these options: (1) Symbolism based on Amos 2:16 and the ideals of discipleship; (2) John, son of Zebedee; 3) James, Jesus' brother; (4) A resident of the Last Supper home; 5) John Mark; (6) Symbolic, linked to the young man at the tomb (Mark 16:5), so perhaps symbolizing baptism (clothes off, clothes on); (7) Christ himself (cf. 15:46); and (8) Symbolic, the Markan community.

and circulated among Christian communities. Hence, they believe that bits and pieces of Mark existed, perhaps even in collections, before the writer of Mark put them all together.

Such scholars agree that the writer is unknown but have come to a sort of consensus based on clues from the text itself. They argue that this unknown writer comes *from outside Israel* writing to *an audience also outside Israel* for several reasons. First, the fluency of his Greek and the writer's supposedly loose knowledge of geography suggest such a provenance.[22] Second, the author translated all Aramaic words and phrases in Mark into Greek (*talitha koum* in 5:41; *ephphatha* in 7:34; *Eloi, Eloi, lema sabachthani* in 15:34). This suggests that *his readers were outside Israel*; the author is assisting them through these translations. Furthermore, the Jewish customs to which Mark refers are carefully explained (e.g., Mark 7:2–4). Different suggestions for where the Gospel was written include Rome (traditional); Alexandria (based on comments by Clement of Alexandria); or Antioch, where the mission to the gentiles gained momentum (Acts 11:20–21).

CONCLUSION

Considering the early church's unanimous attestation, Papias' testimony, and the absence of any other known Mark, there is no strong reason to reject the idea that John Mark—missionary and co-worker of Barnabas, Paul, and Peter—was the author of the second Gospel. There are also sound reasons to accept that, in many ways, this is Peter's Gospel written down by Mark, probably from Rome. It is most likely the first written extant Gospel and, as such, is critical to understanding the historical Jesus and forming Christology.

THE DATE OF MARK'S GOSPEL

Clearly, the date of Jesus' resurrection (AD 30/33) is the earliest possible date for the Gospel of Mark. The latest possible date is the mid-second century when Mark begins to be quoted in references outside the New Testament. Overall, scholars have defended three dates for the Gospel.

---

22. For example, in Mark 7:31 he states that Sidon is south of Tyre and that the Sea of Galilee is in the midst of the Decapolis.

THREE POSSIBLE DATES

There are three main ideas concerning the date Mark was written. The first two are not popular, and tenuous; the third is most likely.

The 40s AD

An early date is held by a small number of scholars. C. C. Torrey suggests the "abomination that causes desolation" (Mark 13:14) is a reference to the attempt in AD 40 by Caligula to set his image up in the Jerusalem temple.[23] He also assumes an early Aramaic version of Mark existed. J. W. Wenham postulates that Peter left Jerusalem after being released from prison and went to Rome in AD 42 to establish the church and Mark's Gospel was written then.[24] Neither of these views is commonly accepted.

The 50s AD

A small number of scholars suggest Mark was written in the 50s AD. There is some evidence Peter may have been in Rome in the later 50s AD; he was in Corinth before AD 55 (1 Cor 1:12; 9:5). If 1 Peter is authentic, he was in Rome in about AD 63. Intriguingly, Eusebius, writing in the fourth century, states that Peter was in Rome during the reign of Claudius (AD 41–54):

> Close after him in the same reign of Claudius the Providence of the universe in its great goodness and love towards men guided to Rome, as against a gigantic pest in life, the great and mighty Peter, who for his virtues was the leader of all the other apostles. Like a noble captain of God, clad in divine armor, he brought the costly merchandise of the spiritual light from the east to the dwellers in the west, preaching the gospel of the light itself and the word which saves souls, the proclamation of the kingdom of God. (Eusebius, *Hist. eccl.* 2.14.6, LCL)

However, the absence of reference to Peter's presence in Rome at the time Paul wrote to the Romans (c. 56–57) argues that he may not have been there. He may have been in Rome before or after this time, but Paul may

---

23. Torrey, *The Four Gospels*, 261–62.
24. J. W. Wenham, "Did Peter go to Rome in AD 42?" *TynB* 23 (1972): 97–102.

not have been aware of his presence, or Paul may simply have chosen not to mention Peter.

Stronger support for a 50s AD date comes from the end of Acts. Acts ends abruptly with Paul in a Roman prison, about AD 62. If Luke ended his account at this juncture to send it to Theophilus, and if Mark was used as the basis for his first volume, the Gospel of Luke—as most scholars accept— then Mark may have been written sometime before AD 60. However, this is not conclusive, as Luke was possibly in Rome and may have had access to Mark's Gospel just after it was written, reducing the need for a considerable time gap between the Gospels. A late 50s date is possible, but is not the favored option.

The 60s–Early 70s AD

Those who accept that John Mark wrote the Gospel in connection with the death of Peter usually date it around the mid-60s to early 70s AD before or just after Peter's martyrdom in Rome, which probably occurred during the persecution of Nero (c. AD 64–65), immediately after this, or in the period around the destruction of Jerusalem (AD 70). This is the majority position for two main reasons. First, early tradition favors Mark being written around the date of Peter's death (i.e., the mid-60s AD). Second, the internal evidence favors a context of persecution in Rome. This is especially seen in the disciples "taking up their cross" to follow Jesus. Hence, this view argues that it was probably written during or after Nero's persecution of AD 65.

Another factor leading some in this direction is the fall of Jerusalem in AD 70. Some find explicit references to the fall in Matthew (Matt 22:7) and Luke (Luke 19:43), suggesting they wrote after this event. On the other hand, Mark 13 does have reference to the fall of Jerusalem but with a strong future orientation and with indistinct details (e.g., Mark 13:2, cf. 14:58; 15:29). If so, this supports a date before AD 70 and accords with the traditional dating of about AD 64–65.

The 70s–80s AD

A small minority of scholars believe Matthew was the first Gospel written, followed by Luke and Mark (the Griesbach hypothesis), and date it after Matthew and Luke and so in the 70s to the 80s AD.

CONCLUSION

The argument concerning the fall of Jerusalem does suggest that Mark was written before AD 70. Apart from these arguments, it is a close call between the late 50s and early 60s AD dates. It is likely the Gospel was written in the late 50s or early 60s AD since Acts was finished about AD 62 when Paul was in prison.[25] The argument that there is evidence of concern for persecution and for Nero is problematic, as persecution was a part of the world of the time and the comments are general. The "taking up of one's cross" perspective is a metaphor that relates to Jesus' death itself more than the Roman situation. If this is correct, a date in the late 50s or early 60s AD, just before Luke-Acts was written (the early 60s before Peter's, Paul's, and James's deaths), seems right.

THE PROVENANCE OF MARK'S GOSPEL

Rome is the most likely place where Mark was written. This is supported by early church tradition. For example, the so-called anti-Marcionite Prologue to Mark,[26] Irenaeus (*Haer.* 3.1.2), and Clement of Alexandria (150–c. AD 215, Eusebius, *Hist. eccl.* 6.14.6-7), all written in the second half of the second century, suggest Mark was written "in the regions of Italy." Other aspects that support Rome include: the use of Latinisms; the mention of Simon of Cyrene's sons Alexander and Rufus, who may have been known to Mark in Rome (Rom 16:13); the apparently gentile audience as evidenced by the Semitisms; the allusions to suffering; 1 Peter 5:13, which puts Mark and Peter together in Rome; Colossians 4:10 and Philemon 24, which also place Mark in Rome; and the historical connection of Mark's Gospel to Rome.

---

25. It seems most unusual to a number of scholars that Luke would write in the 70s or 80s AD and miss out the deaths of James (AD 62), Paul and Peter (c. AD 64–66), Paul's letters, and the fall of Jerusalem (AD 70). See for example Colin J. Hemer, *The Book of Acts in the Setting of Hellenistic History* (Tübingen: Mohr-Siebeck, 1989), 365–410, who suggests a date before AD 65 but possibly after Paul's release, seeing Luke as exercising discretion about Paul's whereabouts because of his enemies.

26. On the anti-Marcionite prologues, see Lee Martin McDonald, "Anti-Marcionite (Gospel) Prologues," in *ABD* 1:262–63. These are short prefixes added to the Gospels of Mark, Luke, and John contending against Marcion's views, he a first-century heretical Christian teacher. While some consider them fourth century, De Bruyne and others agree that they date from AD 160–180. John's Prologue is particularly debated, some seeing it as a faulty reading of Tertullian, *Marc.* 4.5.3.

However, while these reasons are convincing, some do not find them totally conclusive and argue for other options. Egypt has some support in Chrysostom (*Hom. Matt.* 1.3 [c. AD 400]) and possibly in a supposed letter of Clement that says Mark, after writing his Gospel in Rome with Peter, came to Alexandria, where he composed a "deeper" Gnostic-orientated gospel. Some suggest Antioch, noting Peter's connection with Antioch (see Gal 2:11), or somewhere in the east due to John (the elder) coming from the east. Both Galilee and Syria have also been suggested as options due to the prominence of Galilee in the narrative. Rome remains the most likely option.

THE SETTING FOR MARK'S GOSPEL

If Mark was written in Rome in the mid-60s AD, it was written during a time of tremendous turmoil. According to Tacitus, to put an end to the rumor that he had burned down Rome, Nero sought to blame Christians for the fire. Many who upheld the "mischievous superstition" based around *Christus* and which had infiltrated Rome were arrested, convicted "for hatred of the human race," and sentenced to death. "An immense multitude" suffered greatly: "they were wrapped in the skins of wild beasts and dismembered by dogs, others were nailed to crosses; others when daylight failed, were set afire to serve as lamps by night" in Nero's garden in a circus exhibition. According to Tacitus, this led to public pity as they were being killed to "satisfy the cruelty of a single man!" (Tacitus, *Ann.* 15.44). Some believe that one of the reasons for Mark's Gospel may have been to encourage the Christians in the face of such horrendous suffering.[27] Even if it was written just before this, persecution was still a factor. It was a time leading to the terrible period of state-enforced persecution in which Peter and Paul lost their lives. It makes sense that, at this time when the lives of the great founding leaders of the church were under threat, the church sought to conserve and stabilize the traditions about Jesus.

If this Roman setting is correct, Mark should be interpreted in light of this empire and the emperor. Against the backdrop of the maniacal despotic tyrant Nero, the story is told of a new type of king, a messiah who rather than inflicting death on the innocent, despite his doing no wrong, is

---

27. See further Garland, *Mark*, 28–31.

killed at the hands of the Jewish people colluding with the Roman authorities. Mark inverts the expectations of what an ancient triumphant king would be expected to look like in that historical setting. Jesus is not a military or political Alexander or Julius Caesar-type figure who seeks glory, fame, and honor through military force and political intrigue. He is not the Davidic military messiah figure of Israel's expectations. Rather, he is the humble Servant who comes in love, sacrifice, and death, rising to rule the nations and call his subjects to walk in his footsteps bearing crosses. Rather than impose death by crucifixion, he dies in this way to show humanity a new way—*the* Way. He is killed by the kings of this world but is himself King of the world. He experiences horrendous suffering, yet dies to end suffering. Unlike Augustus, who established the *Pax Romana* through military force, he comes to establish the *Pax Dei* (the peace of God), not through violent overthrow, but through being seemingly defeated and yet triumphing over death as *Christus Victor*. He is a miracle worker who heals and feeds people, the ultimate benefactor who serves his people and the world without discrimination—not a despot who rules through fear and favor.

THE AUDIENCE OF MARK'S GOSPEL

At the time of Mark, there were 40,000–60,000 Jews in Rome. Inscriptions and records indicate considerable tension existed among Jews in Rome in the years leading up to Mark's Gospel. Suetonius records that during the reign of Claudius (AD 41–54) "he expelled the Jews from Rome because they were constantly causing disturbances at the instigation of *Chrestus*" (Suetonius, *Claud*. 25.4). Most take this to mean clashes over Christ (*Chrestus*). This expulsion occurred about AD 49 and is also mentioned in Acts 18:2. Around the same time, the Jerusalem Council letter would have reached Rome with the ruling that gentile converts to Christ did not need to Judaize—to become Jews through circumcision. Faith was the only requirement. The combined effects of the Jewish expulsion and release from Judaizing requirements likely led to the church being increasingly gentile and more distinct from Judaism. The letter to the Romans written AD 56–58 likely addresses tensions between Jews and Christians in the Roman church, after the Jews returned (see Rom 9–11; 14–15; the names in Rom 16). These tensions may also be seen in the anti-Paulinism in Philippians 1 and Hebrews as some Christians gravitated to Judaism.

By the 60s AD, there are clear indications that the Christian church was predominately gentile in Rome and becoming recognized by the Roman Imperium as something other than a Jewish religion. This is also seen in Philippians 1, as Paul faced potential death in Rome. Further, Nero's blaming of Christians for the fire indicates Christianity was recognized as a threat and no longer seen as a Jewish sect. Mark was written for this context. The emphasis on suffering and cross-bearing, the use of Aramaisms and their translation, the explanation of Jewish customs, the regular use of Latinisms, and the presentation of the Romans in a neutral light suggests that the primary audience was gentile. Edwards agrees, writing: "These data indicate that Mark wrote for Greek readers whose primary frame of reference was the Roman Empire, whose native tongue was evidently Latin, and for whom the land and Jewish ethos of Jesus were unfamiliar."[28] Recognizing the Roman gentile audience means that Mark's presentation of Jesus in his Gospel is to be read against the backdrop of the Roman view of the emperor, and especially the despotic Nero. Belief in Jesus as Lord was a threat to the emperor and the empire.

THE SOURCES FOR MARK'S GOSPEL

Another fascination of biblical scholarship is the question, "Where did Mark (or the author) glean his/her material from?" If Peter is behind the Gospel, as is most likely, then the writer's primary source is Peter. If so, then it is important to keep this Petrine perspective in mind when reading Mark. However, the Gospel remains Mark's; it is *his* presentation of Christ drawn from his recollection of Peter's *kerygma*.

Advocates of the Griesbach hypothesis argue that Matthew was Mark's source—that is, Mark summarized Matthew's material. This is unlikely. Others hold that Mark drew on a prior sayings source, Q, or an Aramaic proto-gospel. If the latter, it could be that Peter was the source for this also. Some also argue for a pre-Markan passion narrative (an account of the cross). Others maintain the whole Gospel existed in oral form and Mark brought oral traditions of Jesus together. If so, Peter may remain the main source of these oral traditions.

---

28. Edwards, *Mark*, 10.

It is possible that there were Aramaic gospels or writings from earlier that were translated into Greek when the apostles' lives were ending and for the growing gentile mission. This is particularly possible in a culture where there was a tradition of secular historians, such as Josephus, Tacitus, and many others, recording events. In fact, common sense would suggest it is unlikely nothing was written down for thirty years. However, there is no access to this material, so speculating on possibilities and dealing with Mark's text is necessary.

Trusting the connection to Peter, the issue of sources is resolved. Mark recorded a summary of the *kerygma* (message) of Peter either just before or after Peter's death.

TEXTUAL ISSUES OF MARK'S GOSPEL

Looking closely at an English Bible (other than the KJV or NKJV),[29] it is notable that there are points in Mark where verses are left out, and footnotes are included referring to these missing verses. These point to verses considered by contemporary scholars to be additions to the original text found in the better manuscripts of Mark (these happen throughout the New Testament).

For example, after Mark 7:15, the text jumps over 7:16, and includes a footnote reading something like, "Some manuscripts add verse 16: *If anyone has ears to hear, let him hear*" (ESV)—words found in Mark 4:23. This indicates Mark 7:16 is not found in the earlier and better Greek manuscripts of the text. Somehow, it was added in as the text was dictated or copied and handed down.

Other texts that are dropped out in this way include Mark 7:16; 9:44, 46; 11:26; and 15:28. The most important of textual question is the longer ending to Mark's Gospel, 16:9–20. This is significant because there are no resurrection appearances and no Great Commission in Mark except in the disputed endings. If the original Gospel ended at Mark 16:8, it radically changes how Mark is read. It raises the question: Why end a document in

---

29. This is because the KJV and NKJV are based on the Textus Receptus (*Erasmus*, Greek New Testament), which is viewed by most textual scholars as less reliable than earlier manuscripts due to additions and mistakes that have crept into the text over time. A small minority of textual critics prefer the Textus Receptus. See Stanley E. Porter, "Textual Criticism," in *DNTB* 1212.

this strange way? Mark 16:8 reads, "and they said nothing to anyone. For they were afraid." It also begs the question: How and why are the disputed endings included in some texts? There are in fact a variety of endings of Mark, one shorter, and several longer ones.

THE "ORIGINAL" ENDING (MARK 16:6–8)

The best-attested manuscripts end dramatically in verse 8 with the angel reporting the resurrection to the women at the tomb, instructing them to tell Peter and the disciples to go to Galilee, and the women's subsequent incomprehension and fear:

> "'Don't be alarmed,' he said. 'You are looking for Jesus the Nazarene, who was crucified. He has risen! He is not here. See the place where they laid him.'
>
> But go, tell his disciples and Peter, "He is going ahead of you into Galilee. There you will see him, just as he told you." Trembling and bewildered, the women went out and fled from the tomb. They said nothing to anyone, because they were afraid. (Mark 16:6–8 NIV)

THE SHORTER LONGER ENDING

Some ancient manuscripts have additional material, including the women going to Peter with the news of the resurrection and then Jesus sending them out to preach the gospel throughout the world. This is found in some older uncial[30] Greek manuscripts from the seventh to ninth centuries and some old Latin and other versions. The additional material is therefore likely late and certainly not original to Mark:

> And all that had been commanded them they told briefly to those around Peter. And afterward Jesus himself sent out through them,

---

30. An uncial is a formal style of handwriting with large rounded letters, each separated from the next, found in Latin and Greek codices. As a classification of New Testament manuscripts, "uncials" is not used to refer to all New Testament manuscripts written in uncial characters (about 650), but only to *continuous-text manuscripts* so written on parchment (about 270). It comes from the Latin *uncia*, "twelfth" (the word *inch* is derived from it), apparently a reference to the size of the letter compared to cursive script. Uncial manuscripts are designated in the critical apparatus by capital letters (e.g., ℵ, A, B, Ψ) or numbers preceded by 0 (e.g., 0170). See further DeMoss, *PDSNTG* 126.

from east to west, the sacred and imperishable proclamation of eternal salvation.

THE COMMON LONGER ENDING (MARK 16:9–20)

The traditional ending that is found in the KJV (AV) is from Textus Receptus,[31] the majority text,[32] and is found in many texts, the *Diatessaron*,[33] and early church writers Irenaeus and Jerome. There are several versions.[34] Most Bibles aside from the KJV and NKJV, which work from the ancient text Textus Receptus and accept it as original, do not include these words in the main text, but place them in italics or a note of some sort indicating that they are probably an interpolation:[35]

---

31. This refers to the texts used as the basis for Luther's original German Bible, Tyndale's translation, and the KJV. However, most textual critics believe that there are earlier, more accurate texts. See Porter, "Textual Criticism," 672.

32. The Majority Text does not actually exist but is created by comparing all known manuscripts and creating a text with the readings that are most common across all known texts. However, this does not mean it is the most accurate. After Christianity became dominant, there were many texts created. However, this occurred in the fourth century onward, and many mistakes had crept into it by this time. As such, most consider that the earlier texts are more reliable—by this time less mistakes had crept in.

33. Elijah Hixon, *Diatessaron, LBD*. The Diatessaron, from the Greek *dia tessarōn*, "through four," is a harmony of the four Gospels traced to Trajan in AD 172. Only a single mss fragment exists (0212). It begins with John 1:1–5 and then Luke 1:1–4. It excludes John 7:53–8:11, indicating it is spurious, but he includes elements of the long ending of Mark, indicating it existed at the time. He ends with John 21:25. This indicates that this material was present in a version of Mark when Tatian composed the *Diatessaron* in the late second century. Tatian ends the *Diatessaron* as he began it—with a passage from John (21:25). It does not include the genealogies. It is faithful to the Gospels, but Tatian's reputation as a heretic likely saw it lose status.

34. One Greek manuscript, Codex Washingtonianus, includes the following after verse 14: "And they excused themselves, saying, 'This age of lawlessness and unbelief is under Satan, who does not allow the truth and power of God to prevail over the unclean things of the spirits [or, does not allow what lies under the unclean spirits to understand the truth and power of God]. Therefore reveal your righteousness now'—thus they spoke to Christ. And Christ replied to them, 'The term of years of Satan's power has been fulfilled, but other terrible things draw near. And for those who have sinned I was handed over to death, that they may return to the truth and sin no more, in order that they may inherit the spiritual and incorruptible glory of righteousness that is in heaven'" (from Bruce Manning Metzger and United Bible Societies, *A Textual Commentary on the Greek New Testament, Second Edition: A Companion Volume to the United Bible Societies' Greek New Testament (4th Rev. Ed.)* (London; New York: United Bible Societies, 1994), 103.

35. An "interpolation" refers to a portion of the text that is not original to the biblical book, but during the process of copying, other material was inserted into the text whether intentionally or unintentionally. If something is "an interpolation" it is deemed to not be original to the text (see DeMoss, *PDSNTG* 74). Usually there are clues, such as the text being absent from some manuscripts and witnesses.

When Jesus rose early on the first day of the week, he appeared first to Mary Magdalene, out of whom he had driven seven demons. She went and told those who had been with him and who were mourning and weeping. When they heard that Jesus was alive and that she had seen him, they did not believe it.

Afterward Jesus appeared in a different form to two of them while they were walking in the country. These returned and reported it to the rest; but they did not believe them either. Later Jesus appeared to the Eleven as they were eating; he rebuked them for their lack of faith and their stubborn refusal to believe those who had seen him after he had risen.

He said to them, "Go into all the world and preach the good news to all creation. Whoever believes and is baptized will be saved, but whoever does not believe will be condemned. And these signs will accompany those who believe: In my name, they will drive out demons; they will speak in new tongues; they will pick up snakes with their hands; and when they drink deadly poison, it will not hurt them at all; they will place their hands on sick people, and they will get well."

After the Lord Jesus had spoken to them, he was taken up into heaven and he sat at the right hand of God. Then the disciples went out and preached everywhere, and the Lord worked with them and confirmed his word by the signs that accompanied it. (Mark 16:9-20 NIV)

WHICH IS THE CORRECT READING?

It is likely the *shorter longer ending* is not authentic; the evidence is scant, and it dates from the seventh century.

The arguments *against the longer ending* being original are also strong, which is a disappointment to those who find it helpful for their evangelistic theology.[36] There are sound reasons for this:

---

36. Some contemporary evangelists base their evangelistic understanding to a large degree on Mark 16:15-18 due to the explicit appeal to "Go into all the world and *preach the gospel* to the whole creation." However, this is a tenuous biblical basis for an evangelistic theology. Rather, such a theology should be based on undisputed New Testament texts.

1. **Manuscript evidence:** The longer ending is missing from the two most important uncial manuscripts, the uncials ℵ (Codex Sinaiticus) and B (Codex Vaticanus).

2. **Jerome and Eusebius:** Both third- to fourth-century writers record that the best manuscripts do not contain the longer ending.

3. **The variety of endings:** Two longer endings exist—one with sixteen lines of text with Jesus chastising his disciples. The first of these is the shorter ending (see L Ψ 099 0112 among others) and a longer ending combined with an interpolation. This suggests uncertainty.

4. **The non-Markan material in the longer ending:** The longer ending contains several expressions and words unusual in Mark and more in line with reflections from Luke's account and hints of John's Gospel.[37]

5. **The lack of flow:** The longer ending does not flow naturally from 16:8. Hence, it is likely to be an interpolation added by someone familiar with Luke's account in Luke-Acts to fill out the sense of incompleteness in the story.

Overall, it is probable that Mark ended his Gospel at 16:8. However, this reading is not without its challenges as it lacks any reference to appearances and ends in a real note of ambiguity and with the Greek *gar*, "for, because"—an unusual way to finish a document. In addition, it is strange that Mark records no Galilean appearances considering the promises of Jesus' appearance there in 16:7. Some, therefore, argue that the longer ending is, in fact, original.

---

37. For example: Mary, being delivered from seven demons (cf. Luke 8:2); the road to Emmaus account (Luke 24:13-32); the commissioning (Luke 24:46-49 [but note the flavor is entirely different here]); speaking in tongues (Acts 2:1-4); Paul surviving a snake bite (Acts 28:1-6, cf. Luke 10:19); laying on of hands (Acts 3:1-10 etc.); and the ascension (Luke 24:50-53; Acts 1:9-11). The reference to Mary Magdalene blends John with Luke's references to Mary Magdalene (Luke 8:2; John 20:11-18).

If the long ending is to be rejected, scholars discuss possibilities for the "real" ending of Mark. Some believe that Mark intended to write more but was stopped, perhaps due to imprisonment or death. A scenario around Nero's persecution fits here. Others believe that Mark may have written a longer ending that has been lost from the scroll. Other scholars believe, however, that Mark 16:8 represents the *real* end of Mark. The abruptness of such an ending fits Mark's style, and the confusion of the disciples and the unraveling identity of Christ is a theme that is found running through the Gospel (see 10.2).

In the absence of any other evidence, the correct ending is likely Mark 16:8. This may be unusual but is the best reading of the evidence. If this is the case, Mark intentionally finished his Gospel with the disciples completely disheartened at the death of Christ, and the women visiting the tomb utterly bewildered and terrified. Jesus' followers had thought he was the Messiah, but once they had recognized this, he had acted in a non-messianic manner. Jesus talked about death and suffering and being arrested and killed on a cross, all the while refusing to aid his own deliverance—all seemed lost. The angel's testimony is left hanging as the women wonder what this is all about.

Further, the discerning reader will realize that this was not the end of the story. As the Gospel of Mark exists, then the women, while initially petrified, must have gained courage and delivered to Peter and the others the news that Jesus is risen. Otherwise, Jesus' story would not have been recorded at all. Further, if Peter is behind the Gospel, as is likely, Peter's testimony substantiated the women's claim. This ending prompts the reader to consider Mark's *euangelion* is now penetrating the world.

Ending with *gar* is also not as strange as people think. The word *gar* never leads a sentence but is found after an initial verb, adverb, conjunction, or another word. But it is translated first, "for ..." Here in Mark, this short sentence is grammatically appropriate and correct, "because they were afraid." Further, other documents have been found that end with *gar*.[38]

Clearly, this ending has not satisfied all in the church. The additional endings indicate there was a perceived need to complete the story with

---

38. Evans, *Mark 8:27–16:20*, 538.

summaries of the appearances and mission. This is not surprising, but arguably it robs the story of the uniqueness of its open ending.

Does this mean that there is no value in Mark 16:9–20? Some would say so and disregard it. On the contrary, the details correlate nicely and give additional witness to the appearance accounts of Luke and John. The longer ending should be considered another important witness to these events, albeit that it was added after the initial completion of Mark sometime in the second century. It is still an important testimony to the belief in the early church that Jesus rose from the dead. It also shows the importance of mission for the early Christians, who committed to proclaiming the gospel to all creation.

THE CONTEXT OF MARK'S GOSPEL

Mark's Jesus ministers primarily in the region west of and proximate to the Sea of Galilee. The maps below are not exclusively confined to Mark's Gospel but indicate the context of Jesus' ministry.

THE MINISTRY OF JESUS IN GALILEE, SAMARIA, AND JUDEA

Jesus ministered throughout the nation, including some ministries to the north.[39]

---

39. It is likely that the healing of the demoniac occurred on the northeastern side of the Sea at Geresa. See also the next map.

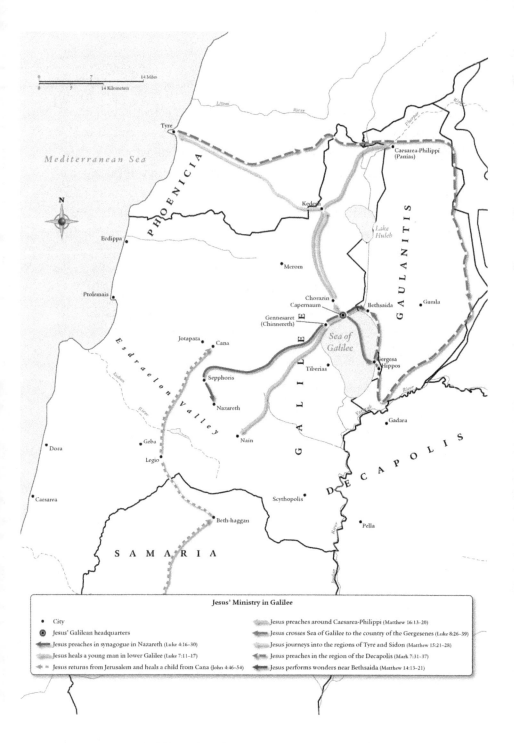

FIGURE 19: JESUS' MINISTRY IN GALILEE

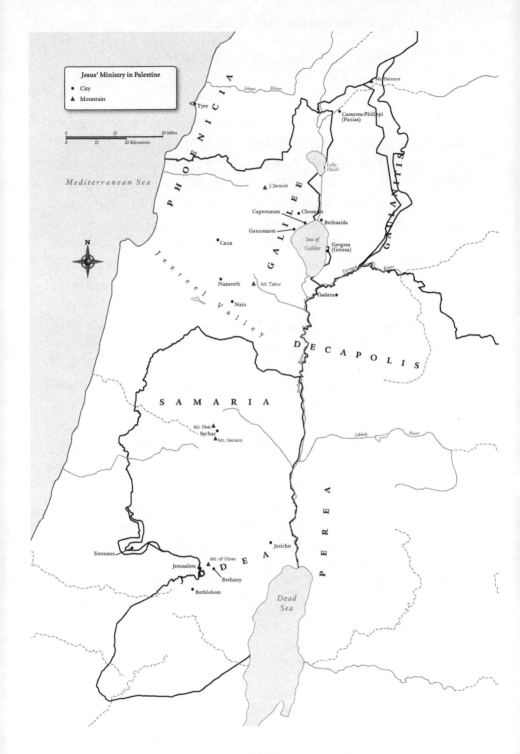

FIGURE 20: THE LAND OF THE GOSPELS

THE STRUCTURE OF MARK'S GOSPEL

THE QUESTION OF CHRONOLOGY

Papias stated that Mark did not record Peter's Gospel in order (*ou mentoi taxei*).[40] This perhaps suggests that Mark's layout of the life of Jesus is not to be taken as chronologically definitive. In the same passage, Papias tells readers that Peter had adapted his teaching to the needs (*chreia*) of his hearers. This leads some scholars to argue that Mark is written in a "*chreia* form,*"* which means it is not written in order but is a collection of the sayings of Jesus useful for Christian life.[41] Some would interpret this as a lack of historical interest. Certainly, from a modern historiographical point of view, there is some truth in this. However, the organization of the life of Jesus in terms other than straight chronology does not necessarily imply a disinterest in history or mean that the events are not historical. Rather, it shows that that the material has been arranged to suit Mark's purposes.

There are several points in the narrative that purportedly support the idea that Mark's writing is chronologically loose. It is argued that there are consecutive sea voyages crossing from "west to east" with no intervening return, either by boat or on foot (see 4:35 and 5:1 for the first voyage; 5:21 for the second). Mark has supposedly left out material about the return trips. This claim is based on the notion that "the other side" is a technical term— meaning the eastern side of the Sea of Galilee. However, Mark recorded that Jesus left to go to the other side (the east) in 4:35, he arrived there in 5:1, and he returned to his point of departure in 5:21. Further, Richard Bauckham argues that this is explainable from the perspective of a first-century Galilean fisherman (Peter) rather than modern cartography. The "other side" does not mean a west-east or east-west movement, but rather, "the other side" is from one point to the other as the fisherman experiences it.[42]

A second example of a so-called "loose chronology" is in 6:45 where Jesus directs his disciples to take their boat to Bethsaida while he dismisses

---

40. Eusebius, *Eccl. hist.* 3.39.15.

41. See for example, the discussion in Witherington, *The Gospel of Mark*, 9–16, who sees this form as influential in Mark's Gospel. DeMoss, *PDSNTG* 29, notes that the *chreia* form contained "a concise, pointed saying attributed to a well-known person and useful for daily living (χρεία)."

42. Richard Bauckham, "Mark's Galilean Geography and the Origins of Mark's Gospel." Paper presented at Laidlaw College, 2014.

the crowds. Then, in 6:53, after Jesus is in the boat, he and the disciples land at Gennesaret. Again, this can be satisfactorily explained as the telescoping of several journeys.[43]

A third example is the condensation of the events between Mark 4:35 (evening) and Mark 6:2 (Sabbath, beginning at sunset, i.e., 6:00 p.m.). This means the events took place within a couple of hours, or a twenty-four-hour period. Clearly, this is not the case. In fact, the whole of Mark is fast paced rather than a well-structured "life of Jesus" as one might expect in modern historiography.

THE ARRANGEMENT OF MARK'S GOSPEL

EXPLANATION

Mark opens his Gospel telling his readers it is a declaration of good news (*euangelion*)[44] of the gospel of "Jesus the Messiah, the Son of God" (Mark 1:1 NIV),[45] the theme of messiah will dominate his presentation. The account begins with John fulfilling the prophetic hope (Mal 3:1; Isa 40:3) by announcing the coming of the Messiah (Mark 1:2–13). John then baptizes Jesus, anointing him as the Servant King of Israel. Jesus faces temptation, and then sets off into ministry, gathering disciples and revealing his messiahship to the nation. The organizing principle of Mark's presentation is the kingdom of God (Mark 1:14–15). The gospel is the good news of the coming of the Messiah to bring God's kingdom. The response is repentance and faith.

---

43. See Guelich, *Mark 1–8:26*, 348. See also Bauckham, "Mark's Galilean Geography."

44. The use of *euangelion* is critical as it echoes both Isaiah's declaration of the good news of Israel's deliverance from Babylon (Isa 40:9; 41:27; 52:7; 60:6; 61:1, cf. Nah 1:15) and its use in Roman thought of the declaration of imperial news (e.g., the *Priene Inscription*). Mark, then, is an imperial herald or prophet declaring good news that Israel's messiah and Rome's emperor has come. On *euangelion*, see the succinct discussion in Edwards, *Mark*, 24.

45. The early manuscripts are split between two readings, some that add "Son of God" and others that do not. While some scholars prefer the shorter reading as this reading has better attestation in early manuscripts, there is ample evidence that "Son of God" was original to the text of Mark. The main reason for this is that "Son of God" is a recurring important theme through Mark's narrative and at important junctures like the baptism (Mark 1:11), on the lips of demons (Mark 3:11; 5:7), the transfiguration (Mark 9:7), in the parable of the tenants (Mark 12:6), in the discussion of Psalm 110:1 (Mark 12:37), at his trial from the high priest (Mark 14:61), and on the lips of the centurion (Mark 15:39). For a discussion, see Guelich, *Mark 1–8:26*, 6; Metzger, *Textual Commentary*, 56.

Focus	Beginnings	Revelation of Jesus as Messiah		Revelation of Jesus as Servant Messiah		
Ref	1:1–13	1:14–8:29		8:30–16:8		
Ref		1:14–8:26	8:27–39	8:30–10:46	11:1–15:27	16:1–8
Location	Wilderness	Galilee, Across Jordan, Tyre, Sidon	Caesarea Philippi	Judea	Jerusalem	Jerusalem
Theme	John the Baptist Baptism, Temptation	Messiah Revealed (Note: 2 Feedings, Sight Healing)	Messiah Recognized	Messiah Redefined as Servant King (Note: Sight Healing)	Servant Messiah Revealed Sacrifice Passion	Servant Vindicated Resurrection
Disciples	Gathered	Incomprehension	Understanding	Incomprehension	Confusion	Devastation Incomprehension
Narrative	Beginnings	Revelation	Climax Turning Point	Revelation	Despair	Climax (Open)
Time	ca. AD 29–33					

FIGURE 21: DIAGRAMMATIC SUMMARY

During his ministry, Jesus is careful to silence anyone, whether a person or a demon, who recognizes who he is (see 1:25, 44; 3:12). Some interpret this as suggesting Jesus was not Messiah and did not want to be known as such. However, he is more likely concealing his identity because people's false understandings of messiahship may lead them to gather around him for a revolution (John 6:15). Jesus takes care to minister in a way that is not an open declaration of his messiahship, speaking indirectly to the crowds in parables (Mark 4), performing miracles, but refusing to perform signs on demand. His miracles are extraordinary and include casting out demons, healing the sick, walking on water, forgiving sins, raising the dead, and feeding great crowds. Where people are concerned, his miracles are always acts of compassion and mercy for the good of the other. They are never performed to impress others or for his own self-aggrandizement. Through them, he invites observers to consider who he is. Through them, he calls people to him and to a new movement. This is not a movement of coercive force or power, but one that draws people to God with love, service, and healing. This Jesus stands in vivid contrast to the political and military approach of Caesar and the Herodian Philip. He also stands in marked distinction to the Jewish expectations of the Messiah as a military and political king.

Through the narrative leading up to Mark 8:29 there are different reactions to Jesus. The demons recognize him, but he silences them. The leaders antagonize him. He is popularly understood as a prophet (Mark 6:14-16; 8:27-28). Central is the struggle of the disciples to understand him. The final encounter of Mark 1:14-8:29 is the healing of the blind man (Mark 8:22-26). This healing symbolizes the disciples' journey from spiritual blindness to sightedness. He needs to be healed twice, perhaps reflecting the two feeding miracles. Later, another healing of a blind man will precede Jesus' entry into Jerusalem, where the full extent of his messiahship is revealed in his death on a cross.

In Mark 8:27-30, Jesus asks the disciples who they believe him to be. On behalf of the others, Peter answers, "the Messiah" (Mark 8:29). He is the Davidic Messiah King Israel longed for, here to redeem the nation. This is the climax of the first half of the Gospel and the turning point around which the narrative is arranged. Notice this occurs at Caesarea Philippi, named after two important political figures, Caesar (Rome) and Philip,

Herod the Great's son who was tetrarch of Galilee.[46] The city, named after the two dominant royal dynasties in Israel at the time (Julio-Claudian and Herodian), is a highly appropriate and perhaps ironic setting for the revelation of Jesus' messiahship. Gentile forms of leadership by political and military power set the backdrop for Jesus' redefinition of kingship of the world—not through violent force and intrigue, but through the lens of servanthood and sacrifice.

The confession that Jesus is Messiah in 8:29 is the pinnacle of the first half of Mark. This is the point Jesus has been working toward, when his followers—who will continue his mission—think they understand. Surely now he will head into Jerusalem and smite the Romans, gather the nation, and take over the world!

What follows is totally unexpected. He immediately tells them not to tell anyone about who he is (Mark 8:30). This is because Jesus would neither meet the expectations of the nation nor of his disciples—namely, to win the world through military and political conquest, which would violate human volition (cf. Caesar). Rather, he would win the world through humility, grace, sacrifice, service, and people yielding willingly by repenting and following him with faith. Jesus diverts attention from the title "Messiah" to the vague "Son of Man." When the story fully unfolds, he identifies himself with the "one like a son of man" in Daniel 7:13-14, who is given cosmic dominion (see also 1 En 37-71). For hearers, however, it would be ambiguous—is Jesus a prophet like Ezekiel (cf. Ezek 2:1), merely a human (cf. Ps 8:4), or is he Daniel or 1 Enoch's "son of man" figure? Jesus then plainly declares to his disciples he will suffer and die in Jerusalem and then rise from the dead (Mark 8:31-32).

Peter reacts by rebuking Jesus, probably because he feels it is nonsense to suggest that the agent of God's reign would be rejected, suffer, and be killed. Such a statement will not attract Israel's men to join the

---

46. Brian Algie, "Caesarea Philippi," *LBD*. Algie notes that around 20 BC, Augustus, just having taken office, gave the district of Panias (named after the god Pan) to Herod the Great. The town was Paneas or Panium where Herod built a temple dedicated to Augustus. He gave the city to Philip his son in 2 BC. He built it up into the region's capital and his place of residence, the city of Caesarea Philippi honoring himself and Caesar Tiberius. Later, it would be renamed Neronias to honor Nero (Josephus, *Ant.* 20.214). It was a mainly Greek city supporting the Roman armies in the Jewish War (Josephus, *J.W.* 3.443-444; 7.23-24). Today, the town is known as Banias.

coming conflict with Rome and the gentiles. Jesus, in turn, rebukes Satan, who, through Peter, is seeking to thwart his mission. Jesus then declares that anyone who wants to follow him must take up their cross and give their own life for the gospel to be saved. This statement was likely heard by the first disciples as a call to war beginning in Jerusalem with the Romans. Time will prove that is a call to *walk in the path the Messiah is about to show them*, the path to greatness through non-violent service and sacrifice. The experience of suffering, death, and vindication is the path of discipleship.

Jesus continues his ministry. He transfigures before Peter, James, and John, revealing his real glory, and God summons the disciples to "listen to him." Jesus is now God's chosen absolute Messenger to the world (cf. John 1:1; Heb 1:1-3). Jesus continues to teach what it means that he is the Messiah. He is God's Servant come to deliver and heal. Being his disciple means following him and serving the needs of others in their brokenness and pain. The path to greatness is not wealth (10:17-31) and power, but servanthood (9:33-35). It means valuing children (10:13-16), emulating their dependence (9:36), and not leading them to sin (9:42). It includes faithfulness in marriage, unlike the decadence of the age (10:1-12). True discipleship means repudiating the false patterns of leadership in the gentile world and ambition for power, and serving as Jesus serves the world (10:35-45). The final passage before Jerusalem is the healing of blind Bartimaeus—who recognizes Jesus' messiahship ("Son of David") and follows Jesus along the way. In Mark 9-10, Jesus twice more repeats predictions of his forthcoming suffering, death, and resurrection (Mark 9:31-32; 10:33-34). The disciples do not understand what Jesus is saying and doing, and neither do the political powers. Jesus is defining what sort of Messiah he is—he is not a triumphal, political, and military Davidic Messiah. Rather, he came as a servant Messiah. He renounces the use of political and military force and intrigue so common among the gentiles.

Jesus then enters Jerusalem, fulfilling the prophecy of Zechariah about riding a donkey and not a war horse (Mark 11:1-11, cf. Zech 9:9). This act fuses three concepts in the Old Testament together: the notion of the Son of Man (Dan 7:13-14), the Messiah (Isa 9:1-7; 11:1-9; Jer 23:1-8; Ezek 36), and the Servant (cf. Isa 42:1-6; 49:1-6; 50:4-10; 52:13-53:13; 61:1-2). The latter notion of servanthood, death, and vindication redefines the first two notions, which suggest military and political power.

Then, rather than gathering to him the people and leaders of the nation to take on the gentiles, beginning at the Roman base in the Praetorium and Fortress Antonia, he debates and challenges his own people, attacking the central symbol of God's presence, the temple, and continually arguing with the leaders in the temple courts (11-12). He shows little interest in doing the expected work of the Messiah. His interactions with the leadership are provocative, his parables challenging their desire to kill him (esp. 12:1-12). He predicts the fall of Jerusalem and a triumphal coming of a Son of Man on the clouds of heaven at the end of the age when the message of the kingdom has gone out to all nations (Mark 13:10). Thus, this first coming is one of a king coming in humility, going to his death without resistance, and then rising to spiritual, cosmic rule. Then there is an interim period of mission and world struggle, including the destruction of Jerusalem (Mark 13:1-25). He predicts that the work he has begun will be continued by his people and the message of the gospel will spread to the entire world (Mark 13:10). Then there will be a glorious climax, a second coming of the King-Messiah, his glorious return in power and victory (Mark 13:25-27).

A woman anoints Jesus King in the home of a leper in Bethany, declaring him Messiah (Mark 14:1-9). Again, he predicts that this gospel will be proclaimed throughout the world and it will include an account of this incident (this is fulfilled in the Gospels as Jesus predicted). He then celebrates the Passover, the great celebration of the salvation of Israel from Egypt (Exodus). From now on it will be a remembrance of another great redemptive event—the Lamb of God sacrificed for the liberation of the world from sin. He again predicts his death, this time stating that his body and blood are now symbols of a new covenant: the covenant yearned for since Jeremiah (Mark 14:23-25; Jer 31:31-33). Just as God delivered Israel from bondage to Egypt, he will deliver the world in a new second exodus from the forces of darkness and oppression. This meal will be celebrated across the Christian world from this time on (Communion, the Lord's Supper) to symbolize this deliverance, just as the Passover feast commemorates deliverance from Egypt.

Judas approaches the leaders of Israel seeking to see Jesus destroyed, perhaps he a Sicarii disappointed by Jesus' failure to behave like a true Messiah (Mark 14:10-11). At the meal, Jesus predicts that one will betray him (Mark 14:20-21) and that the disciples will deny and desert him (Mark

14:27, 29-31). The disciples have no idea what Jesus means, and are hurt and dismayed. Jesus experiences his deepest struggle and darkness in the garden as he faces his impending death; he pleads with his God for deliverance from the suffering he will endure. Yet, he completely submits to God's will, knowing that his death will bring the salvation of the world (Mark 14:32-42).

Jesus is then betrayed, rejected by his own people, and killed unjustly for political ends at the hands of the Romans (Pilate). Crucifixion was reserved for slaves, and thus Jesus the Son of God was killed in the most humiliating fashion imaginable at the time. The false messiah and royal claimant is thus destroyed. The Jewish faith and the Jews' reliance on the Mosaic covenant, Yahwism, nomism, and the temple system, are safe; the leaders have saved Judaism from being divided. Rome has vanquished this false messiah, and the political threat has been averted. Caesar, god and patron, and the gods of the Roman pantheon remain in control of the world. The hopes of the people and the disciples are shattered. They subsequently scatter—disillusioned, confused, and defeated.

Mark's Gospel ends with a surprising twist. The women go to the tomb and find it empty and a young man declares the good news that Jesus is risen and has gone ahead of them to Galilee, as predicted (Mark 14:28; 16:7). They are afraid and bewildered. The men know none of this, and their hopes remain shattered. The women have some hope but do not know what to do about it. At that time, the penny had not fully dropped. The existence of Mark's Gospel indicates the women did pass on the news to the disciples. This news sets a movement ablaze that, by the time of Mark's writing, had influenced Rome itself—the heart of the empire. The Messiah Man is now a messianic martyrdom movement. This happened under Caesar's nose— little wonder he unleashed persecution upon them.

Mark's Gospel is utterly subversive, challenging the politics of Israel and Rome. The whole narrative is based on the identity of Jesus as Messiah, particularly the Servant Messiah. Jesus fulfills the hopes of Israel through the ministry predicted by Isaiah in the Servant Songs, which prophesied a servant figure anointed by the Spirit who would be the light to the nations, bring God's justice, suffer, die, and be vindicated. The scene is set for a new world power and leader to take control, not through might, military force, and power, but through grace, love, servanthood, forgiveness, restoration, deliverance, faith, salvation, and hope.

THEOLOGICAL THEMES OF MARK'S GOSPEL

JESUS

The Gospel is anonymous, indicating Jesus is the intended focus for readers—not the writer Mark, nor the apostle Peter.[47] The Gospel is all about Jesus. He is the Messiah, the Son of God, come to establish God's reign (Mark 1:1). Mark wants his readers to respond with repentance and faith (Mark 1:14-15). For Romans, Jesus is the true Caesar, God's Son, who will save and bring God's deliverance. Without an infancy narrative (the story of Jesus' birth) and only a short resurrection account, the thrust is Jesus' ministry—his dramatic entrance into Judaism and humanity, his miracles, his preaching in parables, the struggle of the disciples to grasp who he is, his controversial encounters with Jewish leadership, and his striking entry to Jerusalem to fulfill the Old Testament hope. What was not expected was that he would fulfill the prophecy of the suffering servant of Isaiah, rather than the triumphant messianic deliverer in this first visit to planet earth (esp. Isa 53). The Gospel ends with the astonishing news of Jesus' resurrection and hope for all. Although rejected by his own people and killed by the Roman emperor's procurator Pilate, Jesus is the risen King over all kings.

JESUS' IDENTITY

Mark's presentation of Jesus clearly revolves around the issue of who Jesus is. It focuses on different groups and their responses to Jesus.

Clearly, Mark knows who Jesus is as he tells the story from the perspective of the resurrection. Jesus is the Son of God, the divine representative of God who addressed God as Abba, Father (Mark 14:36) and who walked in intimate relationship with him. Caesar was often known by this term, but Jesus is *the* true Son of God, king over all the nations. He is the Son of Man who fulfills the hopes of Daniel and many successive prophecies in

---

47. This humility is also seen in Origen's perspective of his death, where it is said he refused to be crucified right way up as this was reserved for Jesus, so was crucified upside down.

Judaism of one who would come like a Son of Man and bring God's kingdom (Dan 7:13-14; 1 En 37-71). He is the Lord, supreme over the Sabbath, God's agent to establish the kingdom. He is the presence of Yahweh who is truly Lord on earth; he is the Lord over all the world and so above all earthly claimants (including Caesar). He is the teacher, the one who teaches with authority and brings God's word to his people (Mark 1:22; 4:38; 5:35; 9:17, 38; 10:17, 20; 12:14, 19, 32; 13:1; 14:14). As such, he is the wisdom of God (cf. Prov 8:22-31; 1 Cor 1:30). He is the one who forgives sin, strongly suggestive of his divinity (Mark 2:9-10). He provides, heals, raises the dead, and performs amazing miracles over nature such as walking on water and calming a storm. For Mark, he is the risen Lord, the Messiah, the divine Son of God, fulfilling the hopes of the Old Testament and the world. As this Gospel declares, written in the heart of the Roman world, he *is* the ruler of Rome. He *is* the defeater of Satan, here to set the world free from his false tyranny. He overcomes Satan in the desert, drives him out in healing and deliverance, thwarts him on the cross, overcomes death, and opens salvation to the world. His mission will see this extend to all nations as the gospel goes global. He is the one in whom the Old Testament hope of the Law (Moses) and the Prophets (Elijah) come together, as symbolized by the transfiguration (Mark 9:1-13). In fulfillment of Isaiah, Jesus is the suffering servant who came as Messiah and died for the world.

The story includes different responses to Jesus. Some fully comprehend who Jesus is, like John the Baptist, who, from the start, prophetically recognizes Jesus (Mark 1:7-8).[48] Similarly, the demons reluctantly recognize him, shrieking when they see him, unable to withstand his authority and power (Mark 1:23-24; 3:11; 9:20). However, they continue to resist his sovereignty.

Some struggle to understand who he is, like the disciples, who follow him without hesitation (Mark 1:16-20; 2:13-17). However, while they follow him, fascinated and amazed by his character, miracles, and teaching, they struggle to comprehend who he really is. The Greek word *existēmi* recurs in 2:12, 5:42, and 6:51 and suggests "greatly astonished."[49] This incomprehension is seen at different points in the narrative, especially before Peter's confession.

---

48. Mark does not include the Q material (Matt and Luke) concerning John sending disciples to question Jesus as to his identity. These passages suggest that even John questioned who Jesus was, perhaps confused by his non-militaristic approach (cf. Matt 11:2-6; Luke 7:18-23).

49. See also 3:21 where it means "out of your mind."

For example, in the boat the disciples are fearful, crying out for help, and when Jesus saves them, they are terrified and incredulous (Mark 4:35-41). Again, when Jesus walks on water, the disciples are amazed, not understanding the force of the feeding miracle (Mark 6:48-52). They should have recognized that Jesus is the Messiah because of his feeding the people in the wilderness as God did for Israel (cf. Exod 16). The second feeding serves to repeat this and ends with Jesus asking, "Do you still not understand?" (Mark 8:21) and is followed by the healing of the blind man at Bethsaida (Mark 8:22-26). The healing serves to symbolize the spiritual healing of the disciples, who finally get it and recognize who Jesus is in 8:29.

The different responses to Jesus are outlined in the account of John the Baptist's death. A few, like Herod, consider Jesus to be John the Baptist raised from the dead (Mark 6:14; 8:28). Others consider that he is Elijah restored to earth after his translation to heaven in fulfillment of Malachi's prophecy (Mark 6:15; 8:28, cf. 2 Kgs 2; Mal 4:5-6). Some consider him merely a prophet in line with the Old Testament prophets (Mark 6:15). These perspectives prepare the ground for Peter's confession of Jesus being the Messiah in 8:29. The repetition in two contexts of these perspectives (Mark 6:14-15; 8:27-29) is significant. The disciples are like other Jews (cf. Herod) who do not recognize Jesus.

The disciples ultimately recognize Jesus as the Messiah (Mark 8:29); this is a critical moment in Mark's Gospel. However, the disciples are immediately plunged into confusion as their false expectations of the Messiah are exposed by Jesus' first prediction of his death and their own suffering (Mark 8:31-37). They do not fully grasp who Jesus is until after the resurrection.

The story of Peter dominates Mark. In the gospel Peter is the first and last mentioned disciple (Mark 1:16; 16:7); is among the first respondents to his call (Mark 1:16-20; 3:16); is part of the inner circle with John and James (Mark 5:37; 13:3; 14:33); recognizes Jesus as Messiah (Mark 8:29); experiences Jesus' rebuke for being Satan's emissary and challenging Jesus' passion prediction (Mark 8:32-33); responds to the coming together of the Law and Prophets at the Mount of Transfiguration by responding with an offer to "make three tents" (Mark 9:5); is the mouthpiece for the disciples (Mark 8:29; 10:28; 11:21); boldly declares that he will never deny Jesus but then does so and is humiliated (Mark 14:29, 31, 54, 66-72); stays with Jesus in the garden, but then falls asleep after being told to pray (Mark 14:37); and is nowhere to be seen after Jesus is taken for crucifixion. His story encapsulates the problem for the disciples—they don't quite get it.

From 1:16 to 8:29 the disciples continue to grow in their realization until Peter confesses Jesus' messiahship. However, they still do not completely understand in fullness who he is, even though three times Jesus explicitly states that he will suffer, die, and rise. Their worldview with its presuppositions is clouding their ability to grasp Jesus' divinity. They believe the messiah will establish God's reign through a spiritual and military power. This incomprehension is left unresolved at the end of the Gospel, but the resolution is anticipated in Galilee, where Jesus will appear to Peter and the others (Mark 16:7-8).

Some reject Jesus completely. The demons recognize Jesus but continue to work to destroy God's people and the world. Judas initially accepts the call to follow Jesus but then rejects and betrays him.[50] Those in Jesus' hometown also fail to understand who he is, unable to believe that this son of Joseph could be a miracle-performing prophetic healer, let alone a messiah. As a result, Mark records that Jesus can do no miracles except heal a few people there (Mark 6:1-6).

Throughout Mark, there is growing opposition to Jesus from Jewish leaders, beginning as early as 2:6 when Jesus forgives the paralytic, is seen in ongoing debates (Mark 2:16; 7:1-23; 9:14; 11:27; 12:14, 19, 28), accuses demonic forces at work in his ministry (Mark 3:22), and confronts the Jewish leaders' desire to kill him (Mark 8:31; 10:33; 11:18; 14:1, 43, 53; 15:1, 31). In many ways, this clash is the crux of the story—the whole of the Gospel building to the crescendo of his death and then the confusion of the empty tomb and the angel's report of his resurrection.

The crowds (*oklos*),[51] or the "the many" (*hoi polloi*),[52] are the people who come in masses. They too do not fully grasp who Jesus is. He clearly amazes them through his authoritative teaching (Mark 1:22, 27), healings,

---

50. Mark does not include the accounts of Judas' remorse. For Mark, unlike Matthew and Luke, his story ends at the arrest and what happens to Judas is left open (cf. Matt 27:3-5; Acts 1:15-19).

51. See Mark 2:4, 13; 3:9, 20, 32; 4:1, 36; 5:21, 24, 27, 30, 31; 6:34, 45; 7:14, 17, 33; 8:1, 2, 6, 34; 9:14, 15, 17, 25; 10:1, 46; 11:18, 32; 12:12, 37, 41, cf. 14:43; 15:8, 11, 15.

52. See Mark 1:34; 2:2; 3:7, 8; 4:1; 5:21, 24; 6:31, 34; 8:1; 9:14; 11:8; 12:37.

and exorcisms (Mark 1:32-33; 5:20, 42). Some of his other miracles have a similar effect, especially the feeding and walking-on-the-water episodes. Ultimately, he cannot enter towns because of these crowds, and he remains in the wilderness (Mark 1:45). There are various understandings of who he is—most seeing him as a great prophet (Mark 6:15; 8:28). By the time of his arrival in Jerusalem (Mark 11:1-11), messianic expectations are at fever pitch as he comes in on a donkey fulfilling Old Testament prophecy (Zech 9:9) while the crowds sing messianic psalms (Ps 118:25-26). Expectations are heightened by the clearing of the temple (Mark 11:12-19)—a public act challenging the authority of the religious leadership and inciting thoughts of rebellion. However, their expectations are not met, and they turn on him, rejecting his release at his trial (preferring Barabbas), and abusing him at his crucifixion. The Gospel ends with this note of rejection from the people of Israel echoing in the air.

Another feature of Mark is the so-called "messianic secret" where Mark repeatedly notes Jesus commanding demons and people not to disclose who he is (e.g., Mark 1:34, 44; 3:12; 5:43; 8:30). There appear to be two reasons for this. First, knowledge of his identity would excite messianic expectations, which could see people rise in revolt (John 6:15). Second, it would thwart his mission. This is seen where Jesus' warning is disregarded, and he must adapt his mission as a result (Mark 1:45).

JESUS' MINISTRY

Most of Mark revolves around *Jesus' ministry*. The key elements of his ministry are calling disciples and appointing and sending apostles (Mark 1:16-20; 2:13-14; 3:16-19), teaching and preaching (Mark 1:21-28, 38-39; 4:1-34), healing and deliverance (ten healings/deliverances/resurrections and three summaries), praying (Mark 1:35-37), feeding the poor (two accounts), miracles over nature (two accounts), and encounters with individuals (e.g., the Syrophoenician woman; the rich ruler) and groups (e.g., children). He is the friend of sinners, lepers, children, and others who are marginalized, defying the expectations of a Jewish rabbi who would not come into contact with such unclean people. In fact, these are the very people he came for—to restore their relationship with God and the community of God's people from which they had wrongly been shut out (Mark 2:17). He ministers to these people through servanthood and love, from alongside and not above, without using political and military revolution as is usual in this world.

Interestingly, apart from the rich ruler account (Mark 10:17-31) and the generous widow (Mark 12:41-44), there is little development of the matter of the poor which is so prominent in Luke's Gospel and, to a lesser extent, Matthew. However, the concern over materialism, a renunciation of greed, and the kingdom call for radical generosity are anticipated in Jesus' feedings (esp. Mark 6:37, "you give them something to eat").

Jesus' ministry is continually one of confrontation with the Jewish perspective and especially the Pharisees and scribes (without the developed view of Matthew 5–7), the pouring of new wine into old wineskins (Mark 2:19-22). In particular, Jesus calls into question their view of the Sabbath (Mark 2:23–3:6) and kosher food (Mark 7:1-23). The clearing of the temple and the cursing of the fig tree are also symbolic challenges to the Jewish leadership (Mark 11:12-25). The clearing of the temple hints at the Johannine idea of Jesus as the temple (John 2:18-22). The cursing of the fig tree points to the barrenness of Israel as the old covenant period ends and the kingdom is inaugurated through Jesus.

One of Mark's strengths is the way Jesus' ministry clashes with the powers of darkness. This is seen in a small mention of his defeat of Satan at his temptation (Mark 1:12-13), his deliverance ministry, the Beelzebub controversy where he declares that the kingdom has come to plunder Satan's realm (Mark 3:22-30), and Jesus' rebuke of Satan through Peter (Mark 8:33). The subtext of Mark is that Jesus has come to deliver the world from Satan's grip, setting all people free. Jesus' time in Jerusalem (Mark 11–12) tells of his confrontation with many of the Jewish rulers as they seek to trap him to justify killing him.

Jesus' proclamation in Mark to the crowds is done through parables (Mark 4:1-20). Jesus relates this to the Isaianic expectation that the word of God will result in the hardening of hearts rather than leading to repentance (Mark 4:11-12, cf. Isa 6:9-10), indicating that this approach was related to the purposes of God for the people of Israel at that time.

There is far less "teaching material" in Mark than in Matthew and Luke, who mostly prefer to cluster Jesus' teaching into "sermons" (cf. Matt 5–7; Luke 6). However, there are sayings scattered through the narrative embedded in encounters. These encourage bringing one's witness forward

(Mark 4:21-23), God's blessing (Mark 4:24-25), humility (Mark 9:33-35), welcoming children (Mark 9:36-37), the ideal of childlikeness (Mark 10:13-16), the renunciation of sin (Mark 9:47-50), divorce (Mark 10:1-12), wealth (Mark 10:17-31), present and future blessing (Mark 10:29-31), and servant leadership (Mark 10:35-45). During his theological engagement with the leading Jewish thinkers in the temple on arrival in Jerusalem, Jesus also taught about paying taxes (Mark 12:13-17), the absence of marriage at the resurrection (Mark 12:18-27), the greatest commandments—loving God and one's neighbor (Mark 12:28-34), the Lordship of the Messiah (cf. Ps 110:1), radical generosity (Mark 12:41-44), and his own return and need for steadfastness (Mark 13).

Hence, apart from a radical discipleship commitment and a call for taking up the cross and following Jesus (cruciformity), Mark is not as strongly interested in ethics or Christian living as Matthew or Luke.

FULFILMENT OF HOPE

Mark's Gospel begins with a blended quote (Mark 1:2-3 [Mal 3:1; Isa 40:3]) stating from the beginning that this gospel of Jesus Christ, the Son of God, is a fulfillment of long-held hopes in Israel's story—promise and fulfillment. The role of John the Baptist as the forerunner of Jesus and his ministry fulfills the commonly held Jewish expectation that one like Elijah (cf. 9:11; Mal 4:5) would come before the messiah to prepare the way for him. John's ministry bridges the gap from the Old Testament to New Testament. It was commonly believed prophecy ceased at Malachi (1 Macc 9:27, cf. 4:46; 14:41), and the emergence of John the Baptist announced a new era had dawned. John was a prophet not unlike Elijah (cf. 1 Kgs 17:1-7), living in the wilderness, surviving on honey, dressed as a wild man. He baptized people, calling them to repentance and fidelity to the covenant, and prepared them to meet their messiah. The huge response ("the whole Judean countryside and all the people of Jerusalem went out to him") indicates people recognized times were stirring. John's role is to point the reader away from himself to the main character, who would not merely baptize with water, but would "baptize ... with the Holy Spirit and fire"—Jesus (Matthew 3:11). His baptism of Jesus is a coronation as Servant-King. The dramatic sign of heaven torn open is seen, indicating that the eschaton has arrived—heaven is breaking into earth, and the chaos caused by the fall in

Genesis is being reversed. The coming of the dove harkens back to creation where the Spirit hovered like a dove; God is coming to restore creation.

JOHN THE BAPTIST

John the Baptist is an important forerunner to Jesus. He prepares the way and bridges the eons. He is the fulfillment of the old and points to the new. He is the last of the prophets of Israel[53] and the first witness to the Messiah, the first proclaimer of the good news that God has moved in Jesus. John's death is thoroughly related (Mark 6:14–29), in part due to the Herod's false understanding that Jesus is John the Baptist raised from the dead (Mark 6:14). John is the Elijah who was to come as a forerunner to the Messiah (Mark 9:13). His death is symbolic of the culmination of the era of Judaism, and the inauguration of the new era in which people from all nations come to God through his Messiah. His death means that the work of the prophets is now complete; the long-hoped-for Messiah is here. Thus, he is the greatest of all who have lived, but he is least in the kingdom of God (Matt 11:11). His influence remains strong; Acts speaks of believers like Apollos and twelve in Ephesus who know only John's baptism (Acts 18:25; 19:3).

THE ACTION ORIENTATION OF MARK'S GOSPEL

One of the features of Mark is its "action orientation." Mark is not concerned about exact chronology; what matters are the phenomenal actions of Jesus and demonstrating the dos and don'ts of discipleship with those Jesus encounters. Mark's account shifts scenes rapidly with few temporal markers. Interspersed throughout the accounts is the term "immediately" (*euthys*) (forty-two times).[54] Its regular use gives the impression of Jesus moving around constantly, performing miracles, dealing with opposition, and teaching his followers. Mark gives little sense of the length of Jesus' ministry with vague links. He employs "and it happened" (*kai egeneto*) nine times.[55] Often, no time indicators are given, only general statements of

---

53. The church will also have prophets who will prophesy in continuity with the gospel of Christ (e.g., Acts 21:10; 1 Cor 12:28–29; 14:29–32; Eph 2:20; 4:11; Rev 10:7). However, John is the last of the pre-Christ prophets looking forward to the Christ.

54. Especially in the account of Jesus' ministry (Mark 1, twelve times; Mark 2, two times; Mark 3, once; Mark 4, four times; Mark 5, four times; Mark 6, five times; Mark 7, once; Mark 8, once; Mark 9, three times).

55. Mark 1:9; 2:23; 4:4, 39; 9:7 (twice), 26.

movement-launching encounters or much longer sections. He spends forty days in the wilderness; this could be any time in a year (Mark 1:13). Jesus enters Galilee and preaches (Mark 1:14). He is then beside the sea (Mark 1:16; 2:13; 3:7-12), a leper comes to him (Mark 1:40), "after some days" he returns to Capernaum (Mark 2:1), he goes up a mountain (Mark 3:13), returns home (Mark 3:20; 6:1), is encountered by scribes coming from Jerusalem (Mark 3:22), and his family visits him (Mark 3:21, 31). He begins to teach (Mark 4:1), and launches a whole chapter of parables (Mark 4). He comes to the other side of the sea (Mark 5:1), crosses again to the other side (Mark 5:21), calls and sends the Twelve (Mark 6:7), and that same day walks on water (Mark 6:45-52). Jesus visits Tyre and Sidon (Mark 7:24), and returns to the Decapolis in Galilee (Mark 7:31). At times, Pharisees come to him (Mark 7:1; 8:11), and the disciples forget bread (Mark 8:14). They come to Bethsaida (Mark 8:22), to Caesarea Philippi (Mark 8:27), go up a mountain six days later (Mark 9:2), and then come down the mountain to the disciples (Mark 9:9, 14). They arrive at Capernaum, launching a whole list of encounters (Mark 9:33). Then, Jesus sets out on his journey (Mark 10:1), goes up to Jerusalem (Mark 10:32), and comes to Jericho (10:46).

The climactic final events are launched with Jesus and his team drawing near (Mark 11:1) and entering Jerusalem (Mark 11:1, 11). They then move back and forth from Bethany daily (Mark 11:12, 15, 19, 20, 27), with chapters 12 and 13 in one sequence. The passion begins with Jesus in Bethany (Mark 14:3), going to Jerusalem for the last events (Mark 14:13, 17), going to the Mount of Olives (Mark 14:26) and to Gethsemane (Mark 14:32), followed by his arrest and the events of Jesus' final evening and day of life.

Events can happen without any temporal markers, such as the encounter over fasting (Mark 2:18). Mark 1:21-34 occurs on one Sabbath, and seemingly Mark 1:35-39 on the next day, spring-boarding an undetailed period of preaching in Galilean synagogues. In Mark 6:6, Jesus teaches in the villages, without detail. Similarly, the mission of the Twelve is of unspecified length (Mark 6:7-13, 30) leading to Herod's feast, John's death, and the 5000 (Mark 6:14-44). Other events happen on Sabbaths, without any other time indicators (2:23-28; 3:1-6; 6:1). After Caesarea Philippi, he passes through Galilee—no time indication (Mark 9:30).

There are other dramatic features such as "heaven being torn open." Some of the elements found in Matthew and Luke are presented in shortened form, including the temptation, which is condensed to two verses (Mark 1:12-13, cf. Matt 4:1-11; Luke 4:1-13); and his ethical teaching, which, unlike Matthew's Sermon on the Mount (Matt 5–7) and Luke's Sermon on the Plain (Luke 6:19-49), is only one verse (Mark 2:13). The call of the disciples is punchy and immediate, especially compared with Luke and John (see Luke 5; John 1, cf. Mark 1:16-20). Mark's Jesus is on a mission, always looking to move to the next place to continue to preach the word and heal the sick (Mark 1:38-40). He won't be tied down and allow the people to harness him to their messianic expectations.

THE KINGDOM OF GOD

As in the other Synoptics, the rubric that defines Jesus' coming and who Jesus is in relation to God and humanity is the kingdom of God. The kingdom is the coming of the Messiah King (Jesus) to restore God's intention for Israel, all humanity, and God's world. The kingdom is the antidote to the fall, ultimately putting right every dimension of human existence and creation itself. It is the restoration of right relationship between God and his people—that is, salvation. It is the bringing of wholeness (*shalom*) to the world, beginning in Israel and spreading throughout the world.

The kingdom is the primary subject of Jesus' ministry throughout Mark. The kingdom has arrived in Jesus; therefore, people must respond and turn from sin (repent) and believe the good news (Mark 1:14-15). Jesus then is the inaugurator of this new kingdom. Herod and Caesar may rule as did kings of the past, but they are now trumped by Jesus. The Davidic Messiah, the Son of God has arrived. Satan's false realm is now being plundered. The kingdom is here because the King is here. The parables of Mark are orientated around this kingdom. They explain in pithy comparisons that the kingdom comes in a secret, hidden, unstoppable invasion rather than in glorious apocalyptic power (Mark 4:26-34). The miracles are signs of the kingdom, demonstrating the restorative nature of God's kingdom and anticipating the culmination of complete wholeness of the kingdom.

The passion narrative is dripping with bitter irony in terms of the kingdom of God with Jesus condemned for admitting before the high priest that he is the Messiah, the Son of God "the blessed one," and then stating that he will be the Son of Man seated at God's right hand coming in glory (Mark 14:61-62; Dan 7:13-14). This direct declaration of his kingship causes the leaders' violent response. Pilate's question, too, revolves around kingship. He asks Jesus if he is the "King of the Jews," that is, does he claim to be the Messiah (Mark 15:2)? Jesus again answers affirmatively. He *is* the Messiah, but not as they expected. The overall irony is that, in killing him, they are in fact bringing in the kingdom of God. The release of Barabbas ("son of God") is also ironic, as he *is* a military threat (Mark 15:7), yet he is released for Jesus, who is no direct threat. Pilate asks, "What shall I do, then, with the one you call the King of the Jews?" (Mark 15:12). Their answer is to "crucify him" (Mark 15:13)—a slave's death for the King. The soldiers' mockery involves parodying Jesus as king, *crowning* him with thorns, dressing him in royal purple, and mocking him, saying, "Hail, King of the Jews," while falling on their knees before him (Mark 15:17-20). The inscription on the cross drives this home: "The King of the Jews" (Mark 15:26). The leaders' ridicule involves them challenging Jesus: "Let the Christ, the King of Israel, come down now from the cross, that we may see and believe" (Mark 15:31-32).

They cannot comprehend that the kingdom is come, that Jesus is King. Like Israel who longed for a king like the surrounding nations in 1 Samuel 8, they had longed for the wrong kind of king. They cannot conceive that the one hanging on a tree is not being cursed, but is their ruler, taking humanity's curse (Deut 21:23; Gal 3:13). They are blinded by their false kingdom hopes. The Roman soldier who calls out "surely, this man is the Son of God" was probably stating Jesus' kingship as this is the phrase used of Caesar (Mark 15:39). He perhaps senses in Jesus what real kingship is: selflessness, sacrifice, suffering, and service to save one's people. Thus, written from Rome is Mark's story of the breaking in of the kingdom and King in an utter reversal of power and expectation. Jesus is rejected by Jew and gentile alike, crowned with thorns, crucified among thieves, and mocked—and yet, in this drama, when the King of the world was killed, the movement that would change all people was born.

DISCIPLESHIP

The notion of a disciple (*mathētēs*) suggests a student or, better, an apprentice. Moses and Joshua modeled such a relationship (Exod 24:13).[56] Such disciples were common in rabbinic Judaism, and John had disciples (Mark

---

56. "Then Moses set out with Joshua *his aide*, and Moses went up on the mountain of God."

2:18); however, the initiative lay with the apprentice to seek the teacher and ask to follow. In the Gospels, Jesus takes the initiative (Mark 1:16-20; 2:13; 10:21), although there are examples of some seeking to follow Jesus (Matt 8:19; Luke 9:57).

Disciples are urged to "come after (*deute*) me" (Mark 1:17), or to "follow (*akaloutheō*) me" (Mark 2:14; 8:34; 10:21, 28). Bartimeus "followed" Jesus along the way, indicating he joined the disciples in grateful response to his healing.

The disciples are key figures in Mark, a means for Mark to teach readers the ideals of discipleship. There is the dramatic calling of the four fishermen at the lake (Mark 1:16-20); through Christ, God is summoning people to his service. These four men respond, demonstrating the ideals of discipleship; they leave everything including community, kin, and livelihood to follow Jesus ("without delay"). Similarly, the tax collector, Levi (Matthew), responds dramatically, leaving his job and life of sin behind to follow Jesus (Mark 2:13-16). These disciples exemplify the right response to the call of Jesus and the kingdom—the giving up of everything to serve its King. The call recalls the calls of the prophets in the Old Testament and is not unlike the response of Isaiah (Isa 6:1-14) and Jeremiah (Jer 1:4-10, see also Moses, Exod 3). The healed demoniac also points to the ideal of obedience (Mark 5:1-20). Conversely, the rich ruler leaves despondent when challenged to sell his worth and follow Jesus (Mark 10:17-22). He and Judas, who ultimately betrayed his master, stand out as negative examples.

Jesus redefines family in Mark. When he is visited by his family, his response is culturally shocking. He challenges the priority of family and community by redefining kinship in a fictive sense to those who "do God's will"—any person who yields to Jesus. Throughout the narrative, Jesus challenges one's first allegiance and declares repeatedly that authentic discipleship places the people of God above commitment to blood relationships (Mark 3:31-34, cf. 1:16-20; 2:13-17; 10:19, 29-31).

Another dimension of discipleship in Mark is suffering. There is no blessing or prosperity doctrine in Mark. Jesus anticipates suffering for those who follow him (Mark 8:34-36). To be called to service is to be called to suffer. The motif of "take up your cross" is an invitation to walk in Jesus' footsteps of service, sacrifice, and suffering. This is the pattern of the cross (cruciformity) that undergirds Paul's theology and the whole

New Testament (esp. Phil 2:1-11). We must resist any notion that suggests Christian life will be pain-free if we have enough faith. This is spurious and leads to disillusioned people who give up on the faith when it gets hard.

Faith is also important on the part of the disciple. The expected response to the good news of the kingdom is "repent and believe" (Mark 1:15). Jesus' response is often conditional on the faith of those who approach him, whether those bringing the sick (Mark 2:5), or the sick themselves who are made whole (sōzō = saved) because of their faith (Mark 5:34; 10:52). The disciples are rebuked for their lack of faith (Mark 4:40), and the general populace is encouraged to have faith in Jesus as a healer (Mark 5:36). On the other hand, lack of faith leads Jesus not to heal in his hometown, suggesting that to receive God's healing in Mark the inquirers must have faith (Mark 6:6). With faith, one can achieve the impossible (Mark 9:23), which leads to one of the great prayers in Scripture from an enquirer: "I do believe; help me to overcome my unbelief!" (Mark 9:24 NIV). Children can believe and must be encouraged positively in the faith (Mark 9:42). Jesus encourages all to have faith and have a radical confidence in Christ to answer prayer (Mark 11:22-24). On the other hand, they are not to believe accounts of false messiahs (Mark 13:21). False faith is seen from those at the foot of the cross who demand that Jesus come down that they may believe (Mark 15:32).

The question at the end of Mark's account is—will they believe the word of the women and believe that he is risen? Faith features strongly in the long-ending accounts of belief and lack of belief in the resurrection appearances of Jesus (Mark 16:11-17). The existence of the Gospel of Mark, written some thirty years later based on Peter's experience of Jesus, indicates that they continued to walk by faith.

It is clear that faith in Jesus—that he is God's salvation, the Messiah, the King come to restore—is important to Mark's narrative. It is faith that he *can* intervene and restore. In the garden, Jesus shows that, while faith is critical, it is conditioned by God's will (Mark 14:36). Jesus believed God could deliver him from the cross, but he placed the outcome in the hands of God and his purposes: "yet not my will, but yours be done" (Luke 22:42 NIV). Ask in faith, and trust for the outcome.

While Mark does not say as much as Luke about women, there are positive perspectives. Jesus heals Peter's mother-in-law and accepts her service to him (Mark 1:30-31). The bleeding woman is commended and healed for demonstrating great faith in reaching out to touch Jesus' robe for healing. Jesus also heals the twelve-year-old girl in the same narrative (Mark 5:21-43) and extols and heals the gentile women (Mark 7:24-30). Another woman singled out for commendation is the widow who gives all she has to the temple treasury, perhaps having been oppressed by Jewish leaders, illustrating the all-or-nothing discipleship Jesus called for (Mark 12:41-44). The woman who anointed Jesus with oil is highly commended—Jesus stating that her story must be told throughout the world (Mark 14:9). The servant girl who hears Peter's denial of Jesus is faithful to her master, openly challenging Peter (Mark 14:69). In the passion narrative, it is the women who are the best examples of discipleship, remaining with Jesus through his suffering (although from afar), going to the tomb, and being the first to witness its emptiness (Mark 15:40-16:8). The end of Mark's Gospel can be read negatively with the women fleeing in fear, but Mark's narrative implicitly shows that they were faithful to the angel's command and eventually told the others—and the message began to spread through the world. This is especially important when remembering that the first witnesses were women, which is extremely surprising considering that in the first century a woman's testimony was legally worthless.

ONGOING MISSION

Mark records the missions of John the Baptist and Jesus and then moves to that of the disciples. John's mission is that of the prophet who foretells and announces the coming of the Servant King. Jesus' mission is mainly limited to Israel, but there are hints of a wider scope of his ministry in Tyre, Sidon, and the Decapolis including the healing of the Syrophoenician woman and the feeding of the four thousand, including many gentiles (Mark 7:24-8:9). In this meal, Jesus breaks food protocols by eating with non-Jews and with unwashed hands. In his teaching, he also speaks of the gospel being proclaimed to the world (Mark 13:10).

Mark records Jesus' commissioning his apostles to go with his authority to preach, heal, and deliver people from the power of evil (Mark 3:14). They are to continue the work of Christ to save and restore. Just as he was sent, they are sent. Unlike in Luke, there is no strong doctrine of the Spirit empowering the disciples (cf. Acts 1:8), but the Spirit's empowering presence for mission is not completely absent (Mark 1:8; 13:11). The mission of the disciples is not developed as fully as in Matthew (Matt 10) and Luke (Luke 9:1-6; 10:1-24), who add other dynamics (e.g., the Great Commission, the mission of the seventy-two, or seventy[57]).

The initial expectation in Mark is to go into mission with total dependence on God's provision (Mark 6:7-11). There is a small summary of the initial missionary encounter (Mark 6:12-13). As noted, ministry encounters north in Tyre and Sidon and Jesus' ministry in the Decapolis including feeding a crowd of four thousand, including gentiles (Mark 7:31-8:9), anticipate the statement that the gospel will be preached to all nations (further below). Jesus' expectation of witness is seen at different points such as the parable of the lamp, which speaks of his followers bringing what is hidden into the open (Mark 4:21-23); and at 8:38, where he warns his disciples not to be ashamed of Jesus or his words amid a fallen world. The impact of the mission is seen in the mustard-seed parable, where the seed becomes a tree filling the whole earth and into which the birds (nations) come (Mark 4:30-32).

If the longer ending is non-authentic, the commission to go to all the world is not directly stated in Mark as it is in Matthew, Luke, and even John (John 20:21). However, it is implied at several points. First, Jesus states in his eschatological Sermon on the Mount of Olives that "the gospel must first be preached *to all nations*" (NIV) before the end will come (Mark 13:10). This is not a command, but simply a statement of what will happen. This is occurring in Rome and all over the world (cf. Rom 1:8; Col 1:6). Second, he states that the story of the woman anointing his head will be told: "wherever the gospel is proclaimed *in the whole world*" (Mark 14:9). Finally, at the culmination, angels will gather the elect of God from "the four winds, from the ends of the earth to the ends of heaven," meaning the entire world (Mark 13:27). These examples indicate that Mark is working with an understanding that the gospel will be preached to every nation. Who is to do this is not clearly stated—it will happen through his followers. Mark's Gospel, written in Rome for the gentile world, is an expression of this.

---

57. As the ancient texts are evenly divided from seventy to seventy-two, scholars debate the merits of each. See Metzger, *Textual Commentary*, 126.

The absence of an explicit commission in Mark leaves an incomplete picture of the ongoing mission he envisages. It certainly includes the proclamation of the gospel, which in Mark is the narrative of the gospel itself centered on the kingdom and Jesus as crucified and risen King. It at least includes the continuity of the ministry of Christ, including suffering, preaching, healing, teaching, feeding the poor, and restoration. It seems all followers will take up the challenge, as there is no doctrine of various mission offices or spiritual gifts; it is Paul who develops this.

JESUS' DEATH

In 1892, Martin Kähler described Mark's Gospel as "a passion narrative with an extended introduction."[58] While this diminishes the value of the pre-passion material, he is right to highlight the sense of movement to a climax, which is Jesus' death. Even the resurrection is not fully explained. The movement is seen throughout with threats to Jesus flowing through the narrative. The story begins well (Mark 1:22, 28, 45), but things quickly begin to unravel after he takes on the divine prerogative of forgiving a paralytic with the teachers of the law questioning his authority (Mark 2:5-7). Pharisees and teachers of the law question his eating with sinners and defying purity laws (Mark 2:16). He is challenged when he takes food from grain fields and heals on the Sabbath (Mark 2:23; 3:6). The latter situation is highly ironic; Jesus heals on the basis that one should bring life on the Sabbath whereas the Pharisees, who should be pro-life, then seek his death! The Pharisees also balk at his deliverance ministry, believing him to be demonized (Mark 3:22). They are disturbed by his refusal to follow Jewish ritual purity concerning eating (Mark 7:1-15), and they clash with him over his understanding of divorce (Mark 10:1-12). Throughout, they are concerned with Jewish legal minutiae, ritual issues, and boundary markers, rather than the heart of the law, which is about justice and concern for others. In Jerusalem, tensions rise and the desire to kill Jesus is restated after the clearing of the temple. Jesus is full of zeal, striking at the heart of Jewish religious passion (Mark 11:18). After this, there is

---

58. M. Kähler, *The So-Called Historical Jesus and the Historic Biblical Christ* (Philadelphia: Fortress, 1964 [orig. 1892]), 80, n. 11. He described all the Gospels in this way. However, he was skeptical about the Gospels, seeing them as a construct of the early church.

continuous testing and public debate (Mark 11:27-12:34). Central to this is the parable of the tenants, which parabolically tells the story of the Jewish leaders' rejection of the prophets (and so God) and rightly predicts that the Jewish leaders will kill him (Jesus). Ironically, they do not hear but seek even more to arrest him in secret, fearing a riot if they do it publicly (Mark 12:12).

Throughout Mark, Jesus is clearly aware of his impending death—he was sent to minister and die at the hands of his own people. Three times he explicitly states that he will be tortured and killed at the instigation of the Jewish leadership. He will then rise from the dead (Mark 8:31-32; 9:31; 10:33-34, see also 9:9). Trapped in their worldview of an all-conquering messiah, the disciples cannot understand. There are other times Jesus reveals his knowledge of his forthcoming death, including the killing of the son in the parable of the tenants, a clear foretelling of his own death at the hands of the Jewish leadership (Mark 12:6-8). Especially significant is the Last Supper, where Jesus speaks of his body broken and his blood as the blood of a covenant poured out for many (Mark 14:24). In 14:27, Jesus quotes Zechariah 13:7 of the shepherd being struck, another allusion to his death. The thrust of the prayer in the garden is that God will release Jesus from his fate; Jesus is clearly in great pain knowing what is about to happen (Mark 14:36). Even the prayers of the one who claims that with faith everything is possible (Mark 11:24-25) are not answered with a "yes." He must die to save the world. In these passages referring to suffering and death, Jesus is picking up the notion of the suffering servant of Isaiah 53 and applying it to himself (cf. Ps 22). Jesus is that Servant, sent not to be served but to serve and give his life as a ransom (Mark 10:45).

The Jerusalem ministry period involves public debate in the temple courts (Mark 11:27-12:39), no doubt greatly provoked by Jesus' prophetic action in clearing the temple and declaring it to be a den of thieves rather than a house of prayer (cf. Jer 7:11; Isa 56:7[59]), and the subsequent parable of the talents. Throughout these theological debates and challenges, Jesus is presented as superior in his understanding of God's purposes, and defeats

---

59. Interestingly, at the entry to the temple area in modern-day Jerusalem, Isaiah 56:7 is prominent at the bottom of a sign one sees on entry. However, unsurprisingly, there is no reference to Jeremiah 7:11.

the religious leaders, thrilling the crowds and stilling the leaders' challenges. Roman readers well versed on the great philosophers of Greece would be impressed. Jesus recalls the wisdom of David's son, Solomon. Some of Jesus' proclamation is highly inflammatory, especially the parable of the tenants, which is directed at the Jewish leaders' rejection of the Son of God (Mark 12:1-12; see esp. v. 12). All these challenges further inflame them and lead inevitably to the passion.

The passion itself fills two chapters, a substantial portion of the narrative. It is a tragic story of treachery (Mark 14:1), great grief and love (Mark 14:1-9), betrayal by a friend with great deceit (Mark 14:10-11, 18-20, 43-45), farewells and final meals (Mark 14:12-26), denial by one of his first followers (Mark 14:27-31, 66-72), personal struggle and pain in the garden (Mark 14:32-42), violence (Mark 14:43, 47, 65; 15:16-20), Jesus' obstinate refusal to take up arms despite his immense power seen through the Gospel (Mark 14:48-50), tragic humor (Mark 14:51-52), legal injustice (Mark 14:53-59), political intrigue (Mark 14:60-64; 15:1-15), uninvited involvement (Mark 15:21), and brutal punishment, crucifixion, and painful death (Mark 15:22-37). The involvement of the Jewish Sanhedrin and Roman leadership (Pilate) is carefully balanced, but with the Jews as prime instigators. There is the bitter irony of the two forces coming together in their refusal to release Jesus—who had shown no indication of political, military, or revolutionary threat—preferring to release Barabbas, who was a genuine threat as an insurrectionist involved in an uprising (Mark 15:1-15).

The whole narrative is charged with Old Testament imagery. It takes place at the Passover, with Jesus as the Passover Lamb after he and his disciples have eaten the traditional Passover meal, so inaugurating a new covenant based on his sacrifice (Mark 14:12-26). It is highly symbolic, prophetic, and parabolic, the bread and wine representing Jesus' broken body (Mark 14:22-25). The tearing of the temple curtain at Jesus' death is a symbolic sovereign action pointing to a new era dawning in which all humanity can approach God through Jesus (Mark 15:38). Throughout the narrative, Mark indicates that the era of Israel has culminated in Christ and the future of God's relationship with humanity now lies with Jesus, who has inaugurated the new Israel in continuity and discontinuity with the old—effectively, Israel by faith continues "in Christ" and his people (cf. Rom 4; Gal 3). Participation in God's people is based on repentance and faith in Christ and resultant entry into the kingdom, transcending ethnicity and the need to become a Jew. The path is open to Jews but also to gentiles by the same means—faith and repentance (Mark 1:15). This latter notion is supported by the timely mention of the Roman soldier who confesses Jesus' divine sonship at his death (Mark 15:39).

The narrative places the blame squarely at the feet of the Jews with Pilate and the Romans acting out of political expediency against their better wishes (Mark 15:1-15).

THE RESURRECTION OF JESUS

Some argue based on the short ending of Mark that there is no resurrection in Mark. However, this is not so. More accurately, there are no resurrection appearances, but there are an empty tomb and the testimony of a young man (likely understood as an angel) that Jesus is risen. However, there is still much in Mark that supports that he believed in the resurrection.

First, Jesus' three predictions of his death all explicitly state that he will be raised (Mark 8:31; 9:31; 10:34). In addition, in 14:27-28, through the lens of Zechariah 13:7, Jesus predicts that he (the shepherd) will be struck, the disciples (sheep) scattered, and that this shepherd will rise and go ahead of them to Galilee, a specific allusion to the resurrection narrative in Mark 16.

Second, Jesus' statement that "some who are standing here will not taste death before they see the kingdom of God come with power" points, not to an imminent return, as some argue, but to the transfiguration (which follows in 9:1-13) and ultimately, the resurrection.

Third, the empty tomb in Mark clearly points to previous predictions of the resurrection (Mark 16:1-4). The declaration by the angel announces this resurrection (Mark 16:6-8). What is lacking in Mark is any specific appearances of Jesus. This may be due to the ending being cut short or lost. Or this is intentional. The longer ending was probably added early from a later source to resolve the dilemma of the strange ending. While there are no explicit appearances, they are supposed.

THE FALL OF JERUSALEM AND THE RETURN OF JESUS

Some see an imminent parousia in Mark in which Jesus is expected to return almost immediately. Hence, Mark has little development of the intervening period between the crucifixion and Christ's return when compared to Matthew and, especially, Luke (esp. in Acts). However, as has been noted, Mark 9:1 probably points to the transfiguration and resurrection, not the return of Christ. Furthermore, in Mark 13:10 (cf. Mark 13:27; 14:9) Jesus states that the gospel must first be preached to all nations. Considering that the first Christians were aware of a much greater world than the Roman Empire and that the gospel had only begun to penetrate that world, it is likely Mark's apparent expectation of an imminent parousia speaks more of urgency than an actual reality.[60] More likely, like other New Testament writers, Mark conceived of an unspecified but substantial period between resurrection and return.

Chapter 13, known as the Olivet Discourse, or the "Little Apocalypse," is given in response to the disciples' query about the temple (Mark 13:1). It is disputed whether it refers only to the events surrounding the fall of Jerusalem in AD 70 (e.g., N. T. Wright) or also points to the return of Christ (e.g., Edwards; see "The Consummation of the Kingdom"). Since Luke and especially Matthew interpreted this chapter with both the fall of Jerusalem and the future second coming in mind (Matt 24; Luke 21), it is probable that there is a double edge to the prophetic oracles referring to both the fall of Jerusalem (see esp. Mark 13:2-4, 30) and the return of Christ at the culmination of the age when the gospel has been preached to every nation (Mark 13:10, 13, 24-27). It is unclear whether the signs relate to one or other or are general apocalyptic references (Mark 13:5-8, 12-23), so great care must be taken not to form too tight a scheme concerning end-time events. More importantly, Mark's readers are encouraged to continue to serve (Mark 13:34) and watch the signs and be prepared (Mark 13:28-30, 35-37), not knowing when these events will occur (Mark 13:32-34).

QUESTIONS TO CONSIDER

- Which date for Mark's Gospel makes the most sense for you?
- Why might this be important or unimportant?

---

60. See Mark J. Keown, "An Imminent Parousia and Christian Mission: Did the New Testament Writers Expect Jesus' Imminent Return?" in *Christian Origins and the Establishment of the Early Jesus Movement*. Edited by Stanley E. Porter and Andrew W. Pitts. TENTS; ECHC 4; Leiden: Brill, accepted for volume, forthcoming.

- If Mark wrote his Gospel from Rome, Roman influences would be on the text in the 50s–early 70s AD which might affect its meaning?

- Because Mark wrote from the heart of the Roman Empire and in the Roman emperor's city, what might those influences have on understanding Christ for readers of his Gospel?

- Which ending of the Gospel seems the most likely to be original to you, and why?

- If the shorter ending is original, why does it end this way?

- If you agree that the shorter ending is original, what is the value of the longer ending? Should it be taken seriously? Why? Why not?

- How chronological do you think Mark's Gospel is?

- Why did Mark write his Gospel in this active manner?

MATTHEW'S GOSPEL

CHAPTER 7

If Mark is a gospel for Roman Christians, Matthew's Gospel is rightly understood as an expansion of Mark's Gospel with a specific message for the Jews: Jesus is the fulfillment of Jewish prophetic hope found in the Old Testament—he is Israel's Messiah! Matthew is much more extensive than Mark's Gospel, incorporating around 90 percent of Mark, and adding substantial extra material. While Mark's Jesus contends with the Jewish leadership, this theme is radically intensified with both John the Baptist and Jesus clashing with the leaders—at times, quite vehemently. The theme of Israel's rejection of Jesus is prominent, and her leaders are to blame (as in John). While there is a prominent apologetic focused on Jews and Jesus' ministry is confined to the "lost sheep of Israel," Matthew has a strong emphasis on mission to the gentiles—this Messiah is for the world and his followers will make disciples in all nations. This mission will culminate with Christ's faithful people receiving the kingdom prepared for them since the creation of the world. For those who do not, there are vivid warnings of God's wrath. This challenges Jews who reject Jesus and Christians who fail to hold firm to the end. While Mark clearly sees Jesus as Messiah, God's Son, and Lord, Matthew also has a heightened Christology: this Jesus is "God with us," and is to be worshiped as Lord.

THE AUTHORSHIP OF MATTHEW'S GOSPEL

The traditional view is that Matthew, the tax collector from the Twelve, otherwise known as Levi (Matt 9:9; 10:3, cf. Mark 2:14; 3:18; Luke 5:27, 29; 6:15), was the author of Matthew.

THE PRESCRIPT

The prescript "according to Matthew"[1] states that a certain Matthew is behind the Gospel. This indicates that by the beginning of the second century, the church believed that a certain believer named Matthew wrote it. There is only one Matthew in the New Testament, the apostle (Matt 9:9; 10:3; Mark 3:18; Luke 6:15; Acts 1:13). Traditionally, this is the Levi of Mark 2:14 whom Matthew and Luke identify as Matthew (Mark 2:14; Matt 9:9; Luke 5:29). So, it is believed that he is the writer.[2]

PAPIAS

1. **Papias wrote of Matthew:** "Matthew arranged the sayings *in the Hebrew language* (*Hebraidi dialektō*), and each interpreted them as best he could" (Eusebius, *Hist. eccl.* 3.39.14-16, emphasis added). This suggests Papias felt Matthew wrote material about Jesus down in Hebrew or Aramaic.

2. **Aramaic collection of sayings:** Some (e.g., Martin) believe this does not refer to an original gospel, but an original collection of Aramaic sayings and parables of Jesus. This would then be the mystical Q, which was translated and portions added to Markan traditions to create Matthew (c. AD 60-70). This is certainly possible, although this would suppose that Q was originally in Hebrew or Aramaic.

3. **Hebrew rhetorical style:** Some scholars argue that Papias, in saying the *Hēbraida dialektō* is not referring to the Hebrew language, but to a Hebrew rhetorical style. It is not a translated Gospel but shows that Papias is referring to Matthew's "orderly" or "Hebrew style," which is different from Mark's non-chronological "*chreia* form." Papias' comment that

---

1. Greek: KATA MATTHAION.
2. Hengel, *The Four Gospels*, 14, 16, 55, 71, 80-81, notes that the tradition of the four Gospels is older than Irenaeus (early AD second century-202), that there are no other divergent titles, and that the name Matthew is not mentioned elsewhere in early Christianity than in the few verses in the Gospels, making it unlikely that a Gospel would later be ascribed to him. He asks, "How could people have arrived at this name for an anonymous Gospel in the second century, and how then would it have gained general recognition?"

Matthew "interpreted" (*hērmēneusen*) Jesus' sayings refers to his style. Matthew is styled in an orderly Jewish way, whereas Mark is a *chreia*, unordered Gospel.[3]

4. **An original Hebrew or Aramaic Gospel:** Some argue Matthew recorded a gospel either in Hebrew or Aramaic, dependent on what is meant by *Hēbraida dialektō*.[4] They contend that this original Aramaic or Hebrew Gospel by Matthew was later translated into Greek by an unknown Christian or by Matthew himself. This is widely supported by early church writers. The most interesting of these is Irenaeus, who states that Matthew was a Gospel composed in a Semitic language, while Peter and Paul were founding the church in Rome (*Haer.* 3.1.1). This would date Matthew's Gospel before their deaths (before AD 68). Eusebius also relates this (*Hist. eccl.* 5.8.2). Origen,[5] Cyril of Jerusalem,[6] Epiphanius,[7] and Jerome[8] all understood Papias this way.

The strength of this tradition is impressive, and it is likely the second or third of the above options is to be preferred. Either way, Matthew wrote an Aramaic Gospel, or he made a collection of Jesus' sayings in Aramaic. If so, this is Q. It is certain that Matthew, as a tax collector, would have spoken Greek, the language of the day. He may have translated his sayings and/or his Gospel into Greek, or this was done later by others and his name attributed to the writing.

---

3. See S. McKnight, "Matthew," in *DJG* 527-28.

4. The Greek *hebrais* can refer to Hebrew, or as is more likely at the time, Aramaic (see BDAG, 270; "Ἑβραΐς," in *EDNT* 1:370; Walter Gutbrod, "ἑβραΐς," in *TDNT* 3:388-89). This is confirmed in that the exact phrase found in Papias (*Hebraidi dialecktō*) is used in Acts 21:40; 22:2 where Paul addresses the crowd at the Jerusalem temple, and in Acts 26:14 where Jesus addresses Paul on the Damascus Road. These are both likely Aramaic, as this is the daily language of Israel at the time.

5. Origen writes, "Concerning the four Gospels which alone are uncontroverted in the Church of God under heaven, I have learned by tradition that the Gospel according to Matthew, who was at one time a publican [tax collector] and afterwards an Apostle of Jesus Christ, was written first; and that he composed it in the Hebrew tongue and published it for the converts from Judaism" (Origen, *Comm. Matt.* 1, also cited in Eusebius, *Hist. eccl.* 6.25.4).

6. See Cyril, *Cat.* 14.

7. See Epiphanius, *Haer.* 30.3.

8. See Jerome, *Vir. ill.* 3; *Prol. in Comm. Matt.*; *Praef in quat. ev.*

ADDITIONAL ARGUMENTS

1. **Matthew in the text:** Matthew is mentioned at several points in the Gospel (Matt 9:9; 10:3), and this could point toward Matthean authorship.

2. **The shift from Levi to Matthew:** This shift of names the name of the called tax collector could mean the same person (Matt 9:9-13, cf. Mark 2:13-14).

3. **The tag "Matthew the tax collector":** (Matt 10:3): This is missing from the other Gospels.

4. **References to financial transactions:** Some note the references to financial transactions in Matthew, which may indicate the author had an interest in financial issues, as one might expect of a tax collector (Matt 17:24-27; 18:23-25; 20:1-16; 26:15; 27:3-10; 28:11-15).

ARGUMENTS AGAINST MATTHEAN AUTHORSHIP

Others do not find these arguments persuasive and prefer that Matthew the apostle is not the author.

1. **Papias is not reliable.** Some note that our only reference to Papias is a quote by a fourth-century historian, Eusebius, and as such it is unreliable. In response, it is important to note that the claims of Papias concerning Mark and Matthew were held widely across the early church, so they are not isolated but corroborated.

2. **The Gospel appears to have originally been in Greek and not Aramaic or Hebrew.** Some scholars argue that there is little evidence of translated Hebrew and Aramaic in Matthew. Therefore, the book was not penned by Matthew because it was composed in Greek (e.g., Beare, Kümmel). It has Greek word-plays (e.g., Matt 6:16) and refers to the LXX (Matt 1:23; 11:10). However, other scholars like Guthrie counter that

Matthew was a tax collector and so would have been linguistically versatile and would have known both Greek and Latin.

3. **Matthew as an apostle would not borrow from a non-apostolic writing (Mark).** Some question why an apostle and eyewitness writing his own Gospel would use Mark's version of events. He did so in the account of his own call (cf. Matt 9:9-13 with Mark 2:13-17). However, this can be countered if Peter was behind Mark—that is, Mark's Gospel carries apostolic authority from Peter, who was highly honored. Matthew lends his story to that of Peter.

4. **The Gospel appears to be written by a gentile writer.** Some note that aspects of the Gospel seem more likely to have come from a gentile writer than a Jewish writer, such as the Gospel's concern for universal gentile mission (e.g., Matt 28:19) and the torture of Matthew 18:34, which is more Roman than Jewish. However, neither is definitive; the former is common to all Gospels and the New Testament as a whole, while the latter may simply indicate Jesus referred to Roman practices in his parable.

5. **It is too late to be written by Matthew.** It is argued by some that, assuming Matthew uses Mark (60s-early 70s AD), Matthew's Gospel must date from ten years after Mark (c. AD 75-80 [e.g., Davies]).[9] This arguably rules out Matthean authorship. However, this theory is beset with problems. First, a good argument can be made for an earlier Mark. Second, the ten-year gap is pure speculation; Matthew may have been aware of Mark much earlier. Third, there is no evidence that Matthew died before AD 70, and he could have lived until the mid-80s AD.

---

9. The logic here is that Mark needed time to circulate and become authoritative.

CONCLUSION

It seems reasonable to accept Matthean authorship of the Gospel, particularly based on widespread agreement in the early church. Matthew's name is attached to it, and there is only one Matthew in the New Testament. Just who is this other Matthew, and how did his name get on a document venerated in the early church?

However, this perspective is not without its problems. The date is difficult to discern. If we trust Irenaeus and Papias, Matthew may have been written in the 60s AD and originally in Aramaic. It may precede Mark. On the other hand, if the majority view is accepted that Matthew used Mark, it was written *after* Mark, which means no earlier than the mid- to late 60s AD. It may date as late as the mid-80s AD. Whether Matthew was originally Hebrew or Aramaic, or some portions were Hebrew or Aramaic (e.g., Q and M material), is unclear—but plausible, especially with such a widespread acceptance of this in the early church. Perhaps Matthew's Hebrew/Aramaic material was by Matthew or a member of the Matthean circle with Mark's to form a Gospel in his name, based on his use of Matthew's sayings of Jesus, perhaps originally written in Hebrew or Aramaic.

WHO WAS MATTHEW?

Assuming that the apostle Matthew is the writer of Matthew, what is known about him? Of the Gospel writers, the least is known about Matthew. Here is what is known:

A TAX COLLECTOR

All three Synoptic writers mention Matthew as one of the twelve apostles (Matt 10:3; Mark 3:18; Luke 6:15), with Matthew adding the descriptor, "the tax collector." In each of the Synoptics, the call of a tax collector is recorded; in Mark and Luke, a certain Levi (Mark 2:13-17; Luke 5:27-32); and in Matthew, a certain Matthew (Matt 9:9-13). Mark adds he is the son of Alphaeus (Mark 2:14). He may be the brother of James, son of Alphaeus (Mark 3:18; Matt 10:3; Luke 6:14; Acts 1:13).

The comparison of the stories suggests that this is the same person, or at least the writer of Matthew believed that Levi was Matthew—either a correction of Mark or his other name.

While some modern scholars refute it is the same person, this is one of those instances where one wonders how a contemporary scholar, two thousand years removed, with nothing other than deductive powers and suspicion, can know better. As the adjustment to Mark is in the Gospel attributed to Matthew, it reinforces the likelihood that this is the same person with Matthew seemingly clarifying Mark's account to ensure readers know it is one and the same. He perhaps preferred to be known by this name rather than Levi.

Like others in the New Testament (Saul/Paul, Simon/Peter), he appears to have two names, either from his naming, by his own choice, or through Jesus (as with Peter). Perhaps Matthew preferred Matthew over Levi because it invoked Levitical and legal associations. He may indeed be from the tribe, but not functioning as a Levite, making a living from taxes. Perhaps this was intentional—having walked away from a life in the cloth, perhaps disillusioned with Israel's religious setup (like the Essenes). When he found Christ, or better, was found by him, he also found hope, and known as Matthew, left everything to follow Jesus (Luke 5:28). Certainly, he left his source of living, preferring Jesus over Caesar. He kept his home, using it to welcome others from his social contexts to meet Jesus.

Matthew is one of only five apostles whose call encounter is recorded in the Synoptics. This speaks of his importance in the early church community. Formerly employed by Rome and Caesar, he was now a citizen, ambassador, and emissary for the kingdom of God and its Messiah. He is an example of a disciple instantly yielding to Jesus' call to follow, leaving everything and abiding, and using what he had in service of the kingdom.

Prior to his call, Matthew may have been one of those who came to John to be baptized and who sought guidance on what to do—to be told by John not to collect any more than they were authorized to take (Luke 3:12–13; 7:29–30; Matt 21:32).[10] In his former life as a tax collector (or even a Levite-turned-tax-collector), Matthew would have had an interesting existence. He was previously an employee of Rome and Herod Antipas and perhaps a Roman citizen—maybe the only one among the Twelve. Hagner notes, "As a tax collector, Matthew probably lived in or near Capernaum and collected

---

10. Luke intimates that it is those who had been baptized by John who were open to Christ. Matthew also mentions tax-collector interest in Jesus.

tolls for Herod Antipas on the commercial traffic using the major road between Damascus and cities of Palestine."[11] He was wealthy, seen in his home ownership and capacity to host Jesus, the other disciples, and many other tax collectors and sinners to a "great feast" (as Luke describes it) in his home (Matt 9:10-11; Mark 2:15-16; Luke 5:29-30). This suggests a spacious home. As was common, he may have made his money through dishonest tax takings, drawing a bit on the side as he gathered levies. Like Zacchaeus (Luke 19:1-10), he was no doubt repudiated by many Jews; tax collectors were despised by many as being sellouts to Rome.[12] Initially, relationships within the disciples may have been strained—Simon the Zealot, Judas the Sicarii, and the Sons of Thunder James and John were previously bitter opponents of Romans and Roman workers.

As a tax collector, he would have had an eye for detail, a great memory, mathematical and writing skills, all ideal for someone who would write a Gospel. Papias posits Matthew collected Jesus' sayings in their original language, and this makes sense of a man used to recording financial records.

AN EVANGELIST

Matthew emerges instantly as one of those people who instantly sought to convert his or her friends. He is effective, immediately inviting a crowd of fellow tax collectors to a lavish meal to hear Jesus—classic invitational evangelism. The interest among tax collectors toward Jesus through the Synoptics could be due in no small part to Matthew's presence and witness to them (see the meal narratives referenced above, see also Matt 11:19; 21:31-32; Luke 7:29, 34; 15:1). Perhaps Jesus had Matthew in mind as he told the parable of the Pharisee and the tax collector (Luke 18:10-13). It may be through Matthew, too, that Zacchaeus knew of Jesus. The Gospel of Matthew is a brilliant work, structured around five great discourses, and clearly designed to teach new disciples the story and life of Jesus. Matthew is a great example of how God takes a person with a set of skills,

---

11. Donald A. Hagner, "Matthew," in *ISBE* 3:280.

12. This implicitly negative attitude is seen in Jesus' teaching where tax collectors are paired with sinners in Jewish critique of Jesus (Matt 9:11; 11:19; Mark 2:15-16). Although Jesus did not despise tax collectors, Jesus' teaching alludes to the widespread negative perception: he speaks of the fact that "even the tax collectors" show love to their families (Matt 5:46); he pairs them with gentiles, repudiated and shut out by Jews (Matt 18:17); he pairs them with prostitutes (Matt 21:31, 32).

brings them to faith, and then uses them with all that they have for his glory. Matthew exemplifies the right response. With other New Testament authors, his writings have changed the world.

OTHER SOURCES

Matthew is mentioned only once elsewhere in the New Testament, as a member of the Jerusalem community praying and awaiting Pentecost (Acts 1:13). Presumably, he was involved in the life of the early church with the others. Otherwise, little else is certain. Aside from the widespread belief he wrote the Gospel and the references from Papias, Eusebius records:

> For Matthew, who had at first preached to the Hebrews, when he was about to go to other peoples, committed his Gospel to writing in his native tongue, and thus compensated those whom he was obliged to leave for the loss of his presence.[13]

Later writers suggest that the "others" includes "Ethiopia, Persia, Parthia, Macedonia, and Syria."[14] Clement of Alexandria (AD 150-c. 215) commends Matthew for being a vegetarian who ate seeds, nuts, and vegetables without flesh (*Paed.* 2.1). It is unclear how he died; most traditions suggest he died as a martyr, although there are conflicting accounts.[15]

THE DATE OF MATTHEW'S GOSPEL

If Matthew used Mark, a date subsequent to Mark's production (mid-60s AD) is the earliest date for the Gospel. Quotations of Matthew are found in the writings of Ignatius, the Bishop of Antioch (c. AD 110).[16] This means that Matthew was completed at the latest by the turn of the first century.

---

13. Eusebius, *Hist. eccl.* 3.24.6.
14. Hagner, "Matthew," 280.
15. Hagner, "Matthew," 280 and others suggest Clement of Alexandria, *Strom.* 4.9 cites Heracleon, a second-century Valentinian Gnostic, that Matthew died of natural causes. However, this is not what the text says; rather, it says he departed after making a good confession. The manner of his death remains unclear.
16. There are three citations: (1) Ign. *Eph.* 14:2, a citation of Matt 12:33, "the tree is known by its fruit"; (2) Ign. *Smyrn.* 6:1, a citation of Matt 19:12, "The one who accepts this, let him accept it"; (3) Ign. *Poly.* 2:2, a citation of Matt 10:16, "Be as shrewd as snakes ... innocent as doves."

So, Matthew must have been written between AD 65–110. There are two main perspectives on the date.

A LATER DATE (AD 80–100)

Most New Testament scholars date Matthew during the period AD 80–100. This is based on the following arguments:

- **Matthew borrowed from Mark.** Assuming Markan priority and that Mark was probably written in Rome around AD 65, and factoring in sufficient time for Matthew to gain access to Mark, Matthew must be later, that is, the early 70s to the 80s AD.

- **Indications in the text of a later date.** Some references appear to show knowledge after the event of the destruction of Jerusalem (esp. Matt 22:7) and so point to a later date. Similarly, of the Gospel writers, Matthew alone references the church, which could indicate a more developed ecclesiology[17] and a later date (Matt 16:18; 18:17). Twice, the phrase "to this very day" is repeated, first of the name "Field of Blood" Judas purchased (Matt 27:8), and then in the story of Christ's stolen body that circulated among the soldiers (28:15). This could indicate a substantial period from the event to Matthew's Gospel. Matthew's higher Christology (e.g., the "Son of God" language; compare Mark 8:29 with Matt 16:16) and the Trinitarian formula of Matthew 28:19 could also indicate a later date where Christology is more developed.

- **The negative view of Jews in the Gospel.** Some believe there is anti-Semitism in Matthew's Gospel. It is argued that this suggests a post-85 AD date after the Council of Jamnia at Yavneh (c. AD 85), which expelled Christians from the synagogue.[18]

---

17. Ecclesiology, from the Greek *ekklēsia*, "church," is an aspect of theology that focuses on the church. Grenz et.al., *PDTT* 42 note that "Ecclesiology seeks to set forth the nature and function of the church. It also investigates issues such as the mission, ministry and structure of the church, as well as its role in the plan of God."

18. D. A. Hagner, *Matthew 1–13*, WBC 33A (Dallas: Word, 2002), lxxiii. A curse against the *minim* or "heretics" to the liturgy of the synagogue was put in place, the so-called *Birkat*

AN EARLIER DATE (60S–70S AD)

However, other scholars counter these arguments, proposing an earlier date, perhaps even before AD 70. Here are some of their arguments:

- **The dating of Mark and the time lag is speculative.** As noted above, Mark may have been written earlier, and Matthew may have learned of Mark far more quickly than the ten-year time lag theory presupposes.[19] If Mark was written in the late 50s or early 60s AD, then Matthew could easily be pre-AD 70. Even if Mark was written in the mid-60s AD, Matthew might have gained access to it earlier and incorporated it within a year of Mark's production. The Neronian persecution could have seen Mark and other early Christian documents removed from Rome perhaps to Antioch. Alternatively, Matthew may have visited Rome. There is a myriad of possible ways Matthew got a copy of Mark's scroll very soon after its production.

- **The so-called indications from the text are overplayed.** The supposed post-AD 70 reference in Matthew 22:7 could still be pre-70 AD. It remains a general statement and is found in a parable. It also resonates with Isaiah 5:24–25, and it could be that Jesus or Matthew draws it from there (Gundry). There are only two references to the church; this hardly constitutes proof of a late date, since the church had been in existence since Pentecost. The phrase "to this very day" is, at best, ambiguous; any date from the mid-50s AD on would be over twenty years since the events. The supposedly "higher Christology" and Trinitarian formula are also found in Paul's writings in the early 60s AD, rendering this argument void.[20] This is especially so if, as is likely, the Gospel of Matthew comes from the

---

ha-Minim in the twelfth of the Eighteen Benedictions, the *Shemoneh Esreh*.

19. Similarly, see Hagner, *Matthew 1–13*, lxxiii, who rightly notes only one to two years are needed.

20. On Christology, see Phil 2:5–11; Col 1:15–20; 2:9, both written in the early 60s. Some argue Philippians and Colossians were written from Ephesus between AD 53–55 and this would indicate the high Christology is earlier. Both passages may be hymnic material from the very early church. The Trinitarian formula is used by Paul in 2 Cor 13:14.

area of Syrian Antioch, where Paul and Matthew may have been in contact.

- **Continuity with the view of the Jews in Mark.** Matthew continues the theme of Mark in which the Jewish leadership is not pictured positively. Tensions between Christians and Jews are apparent from the earliest days, including the Sanhedrin's attempts to hinder the spread of the message, the martyrdom of Stephen, and Saul's persecution of Christians (see Acts 4–5, 7–8). The evidence that the Council of Jamnia at Yavneh was a key turning point is not strong.[21]

Additionally:

1. If Matthew the apostle is the author, then an early date is more likely, although knowledge of the death of Matthew is uncertain.[22]

2. The early church fathers unanimously ascribed an early date to Matthew. In fact, they argued that Matthew was the first of the Gospels. If taken seriously, the Griesbach hypothesis of Matthean priority should be considered and an early date ascribed to Matthew's Gospel. Matthew would then become the apostle on which the Synoptic Gospels are founded, rather than Peter.

3. Some sayings can be argued to indicate that the temple was standing when Matthew wrote (Matt 5:23-24; 12:5-7; 23:16).

As such, it is reasonable to take an earlier date. However, this earlier date is not firm; with the uncertainty over the traditional date of Matthew's death,[23] the Gospel can be dated anytime from the mid-60s to the 80s AD.

---

21. See Hagner, *Matthew 1-13*, lxxiii.

22. See William Stuart McBirnie, *The Search for the Twelve Apostles*, Rev. Ed. (Carol Stream: Tyndale House, 1973), Chapter 10, "Matthew," who notes that there are a variety of traditions: (1) A natural death (Clement of Alexandria, *Strom.* 4.9); (2) Condemned to death by the Sanhedrin (Talmud); (3) Death after the *Anthropophagi* tried to put him to death (Acts of Andrew and Matthew).

23. Tradition has it Matthew preached for fifteen years in Israel, then in Ethiopia, Macedonia, Syria, Persia, Parthia, and Medea. His death is uncertain with claims he died

Aside from historical and apologetic reasons, the date is not particularly important. What matters is Matthew's message.

THE PROVENANCE OF MATTHEW'S GOSPEL

Little evidence exists revealing where Matthew's Gospel was written. A popular suggestion is somewhere in Israel. This is based on five main ideas. First, there is the inclusion of untranslated Aramaic, indicating readers understood these words.[24] Second, Papias' perspective that Matthew was originally an Aramaic or Hebrew Gospel supports Israel as the point of origin. A third argument is the assumption that readers understand Jewish customs. Fourth, the Old Testament texts cited come from both the Hebrew Masoretic Text[25] (e.g., Matt 13:14-15; Isa 6:9-10) and the Greek LXX (most citations, e.g., Matt 3:3; Isa 40:2). Finally, there are examples of Semitic literary forms (e.g., Matt 5:2, "he opened his mouth").

However, these arguments could equally be explained by diaspora Judaism, in which there was a wide dispersal of Jewish people throughout the empire. As a result, some suggest Caesarea Maritima or the Phoenician cities of Tyre or Sidon as possible points of origin. Others propose it is from the Transjordan area of Pella. This idea is based on the phrase "across the Jordan" (Matt 4:15; 19:1). These ideas seem tenuous.

Most commonly, scholars prefer Syrian Antioch as the point of origin, because Matthew was likely written after the destruction of Jerusalem (AD 70). It is argued that Antioch in Syria would be a good context for the following reasons:

---

naturally in Ethiopia or Macedonia or was martyred by stabbing in Ethiopia. His martyrdom is remembered by Catholics on September 21, and in the Orthodox Church on November 10.

24. These words are: (1) *raka* = "fool" (Matt 5:22); (2) *mamōnas* = "mammon, money" (Matt 6:24); and (3) *korbanas* = "temple treasury" (Matt 27:6).

25. The Masoretic Text is the Hebrew text used for the Jewish Bible in Judaism and used as the basis for the Old Tesetament in the Protestant Bible and some Catholic Bibles, while the Eastern Orthodox Church prefers the LXX. The Masoretic Text was copied, edited, and distributed by Jewish scribes known as the Masoretes (seventh-tenth century AD). The term is based on the Hebrew *mesorah* referring to the transmission of a tradition. The oldest extant mss are from the ninth century AD.

1. **A large Jewish population** (Josephus, *J.W.* 7:43),[26] against which Christians would have to defend their perspective. This is seen in Antioch's importance in the initial spread of the gospel to Greeks and the Judaizing debate (e.g., Acts 11:19-26; 13:1-3; 15:1-2, 22-23, 30; Gal 2:11).

2. **Antioch as a center for outreach** (Acts 11:19-22). The city was the base for Paul's three great missions (Acts 13:1; 14:26; 15:35; 18:22). Matthew has a strong mission emphasis, which may reflect the missional tradition of the city.

3. **Citations in Ignatius, the Bishop of Antioch** early in the second century. Ignatius was the first to demonstrate knowledge of the Gospel of Matthew (for the citations see above).

4. **Links between Matthew and the Didache**, a book of Christian teaching written in the late first century or early second century, which is purportedly related to Syria.[27] Some have even tried to argue Matthew is dependent on the Didache; however, it is far more likely the dependence works the other way. In particular, the writer of the Didache shows a great awareness of the Sermon on the Mount and the Olivet Discourse.

---

26. Josephus writes, "The Jewish race, densely interspersed among the native populations of every portion of the world, is particularly numerous in Syria, where intermingling is due to the proximity of the two countries. But it was at Antioch that they specially congregated, partly owing to the greatness of that city, but mainly because the successors of King Antiochus had enabled them to live there in security" (Thackeray, LCL).

27. Some of the parallels include the "two ways" (Did 1.1, cf. Matt 7); the Great Commandments (Did 1.2, cf. Matt 22:37, 39); love for enemies (Did 1.3, cf. Matt 5:44-47); go the extra mile (Did 1.8, cf. Matt 5:48); not asking for the return of things borrowed (Did 1.4, cf. Matt 5:41); the humble inheriting the earth (Did 3.7, cf. Matt 5:5); the Matthean Lord's Prayer (Did 8.2, cf. Matt 6:9-13); giving holy things to dogs (Did 9.5, cf. Matt 7:6); the sin against the Spirit (Did 11.7, cf. Matt 12:31); lamps burning awaiting Christ's return (Did 16.1, cf. Matt 25:1-13); an increase in hatred and persecution (Did 16.4, cf. Matt 24:10-12); false Christs (Did 16.4, cf. Matt 13:22); many falling away and those enduring being saved (Did 16.5, cf. Matt 24:10, 13); signs on earth (Did 16.6, cf. Matt 24:30); trumpet sound (Did 16.6, cf. Matt 24:31); Christ coming with his saints (Did 16.7-8, cf. Matt 24:30). These are drawn from the footnoting in "The Didache" from M. W. Holmes, *The Apostolic Fathers: Greek Texts and English Translations*, updated ed. (Grand Rapids, MI: Baker Books, 1999).

The knowledge of Matthew in the Didache and by Ignatius lends good support to Antioch being the most likely point of origin for the Gospel. Jerusalem is unlikely, as it was destroyed in AD 70. However, Antioch remains only a "good guess." Blomberg notes:

> At least a plurality of commentators, however, would tentatively place Matthew's community in Syria and most probably in Antioch, home to a large Jewish community and a sizable Jewish-Christian congregation from at least the time of Acts 11:19–30 (no later than AD 46) and lasting well into the second century.[28]

THE STRUCTURE OF MATTHEW'S GOSPEL

There are three main views on the structure of Matthew's Gospel: Geographic, Christological, and Five-Discourse Didactic.

GEOGRAPHIC STRUCTURE

The oldest and perhaps simplest way of understanding Matthew is based around Jesus' ministry in Galilee, to the north in Tyre and Sidon, and then Jerusalem (e.g., Allen):

Matthew 1:1–4:11	Prologue and Jesus' preparation for ministry
Matthew 4:12–15:20	Jesus' ministry in Galilee
Matthew 15:21–18:35	Ministry to the north of Galilee
Matthew 19:1–20:34	En route to Jerusalem
Matthew 21:1–25:46	Confrontation in Jerusalem
Matthew 26:1–28:20	Passion and resurrection

However, many scholars believe this is not the best way to understand Matthew's structure. It developed from the nineteenth-century quest to write a life of Jesus and tries to read Matthew as if it were Luke, which includes the "travel narrative" in which Jesus resolutely travels to Jerusalem (Luke 9:51–19:27).

---

28. Blomberg, *Matthew*, 37.

CHRISTOLOGICAL STRUCTURE

Another proposal adopted more recently and gaining favor (e.g., Kingsbury) sees the key to understanding Matthew as the formula *apo tote* ("from that time on") found in Matthew 4:17 and 16:21:

Matthew 1:1–4:16	Introduction to Jesus' Ministry
Matthew 4:17–16:20	The Development of Jesus' Ministry
Matthew 16:21–28:20	The Climax of Jesus' ministry[29]

This is a good structure. However, it ignores clear markers such as the three chapters of the Sermon on the Mount (Matt 5–7), the missional discourse of Matthew 10, the chapter on parables (Matt 13), and the discourse on the church (Matt 18).

FIVE-DISCOURSE DIDACTIC STRUCTURE

The most common view of Matthew's structure originated with B. W. Bacon (1918, 1930). He held that Matthew is based around five discourses. He went further and proposed that these mirror the five books of Moses, so Matthew presents Jesus as a new Moses.[30] While few scholars accept that Matthew is mirroring the Pentateuch, the view that Jesus is a new Moses and that there are five discourse blocks remains influential among contemporary scholars. The key to this is the recurring phrase, "And it happened, when Jesus had finished saying these things, that …" (Matt 7:28; 11:1; 13:53; 19:1; 26:1). These statements function as markers of the shift in the narrative. *The collection of parables in Matthew 13 is the turning point of the Gospel* after which Jesus heads to Jerusalem, whichever structure is adopted.[31] There are various titles given for the five sections. Bacon structured it this way:[32]

---

29. Craig L. Blomberg, *Matthew*, NAC 22 (Nashville: Broadman & Holman Publishers, 1992), 49.

30. B. W. Bacon, "The 'Five Books' of Matthew against the Jews," *Exp* 15 (1918): 56–66.

31. See Blomberg, *Matthew*, 128.

32. Taken from R. T. France, *Matthew*, TNTC (Grand Rapids, MI; Leicester: Eerdmans; IVP, 1985), 61 (France does not follow this structure).

Matthew 1:1-2:23	Preamble
Matthew 3:1-7:29	Book One: Discipleship
	Narrative, Matthew 3-4
	Discourse, Matthew 5-7
Matthew 8:1-10:42	Book Two: Apostleship
	Narrative, Matthew 8-9
	Discourse, Matthew 10
Matthew 11:1-13:58	Book Three: The Hiding of Revelation
	Narrative, Matthew 11-12
	Discourse, Matthew 13
Matthew 14:1-18:35	Book Four: Church Administration
	Narrative, Matthew 14-17
	Discourse, Matthew 18
Matthew 19:1-25:46	Book Five: The Judgment
	Narrative, Matthew 19-22
	Discourse, Matthew 23-25
Matthew 26-28	Epilogue

The structure identifies large portions of discourse including the Sermon on the Mount in Matthew 5-7, the mission discourse in Matthew 10, and the parables of Matthew 13. However, while there is discourse material in Matthew 18, it is not clear that this is a discrete church administration discourse. The discourse of Matthew 23-25 is broken into two: the woes upon the scribes and Pharisees, and the Olivet Discourse. It is difficult to read this as one unit. Further, the titles are also forced as they do not quite summarize the material and a wider range of topics is addressed in each section. The structure also relegates the infancy narrative to a mere prologue and the passion and resurrection to an epilogue. This is flawed, as they should be seen as critical elements of Matthew's account. Indeed, the death and resurrection of Jesus and the commissioning are more a climax than an epilogue. This structure is rarely followed by today's commentators.

ALTERNATIVE STRUCTURES

Other scholars resist such structures and arrange their structure around clear blocks without overt concern for markers, which may or may not indicate a structure. For example, Nolland arranges Matthew in twenty-two sections.[33] While accepting the Christological approach above, Blomberg blends this with the "narrative/discourse" pattern.[34]

CONCLUSION

The correct structure depends on whether Matthew can be arranged around the recurring formula *apo tete* (Matt 4:17; 16:21) or the narratives and discourses. The former view ignores the fact that *apo tete* in Matthew 16:21 builds on Mark 8:31, and so it might not be part of such a structure. As such, it might be better to adopt the five-discourse structure along with Carson and Moo.

Nolland's approach of reading Matthew with clearly-delineated clusters of material is appealing. In this twelve-fold structure, *theme* dominates. There is no real attempt to force disparate parts into a thematic whole (e.g., the three sustained periods of mission). Further, no parts are relegated to merely prologue or epilogue. Each part can be broken down further. As Blomberg has noted, there is a movement from discourse to narrative.

---

33. See John Nolland, *The Gospel of Matthew: A Commentary on the Greek Text*, NIGTC (Grand Rapids, MI; Carlisle: Eerdmans; Paternoster, 2005), 44-62: 1) The Stock from Which Jesus Comes—and Its History (1:1-17); 2) Infancy (1:18-2:23); 3) John Proclaiming in the Wilderness (3:1-12); 4) Preparation (3:13-4:12); 5) Establishing His Ministry (4:13-25); 6) Sermon on the Mount (5:1-8:1); 7) Jesus on the Move in Ministry (8:[1]2-9:34); 8) Workers for the Harvest (9:35-11:1); 9) Seeing Clearly and Relating Rightly to God's Present Agenda (11:[1]2-30); 10) Conflict with the Pharisees (12:1-50); 11) Parables of the Kingdom (13:1-53); 12) Jesus Interpreted, but Also Rejected (13:53[54]-16:20); 13) Anticipating a Future through Suffering and Beyond (16:21-17:20); 14) Status and Behaviour in the "Royal Family" (17:22-18:35); 15) Family and Possessions in View of the Kingdom (19:1-20:16); 16) Redefining Greatness, Jesus Goes to Jerusalem to Die: Jericho, Bethphage, Entry into Jerusalem (20:17-21:11); 17) Provocative Ministry in Jerusalem (21:12-46); 18) Jesus Silences the Leaders Who Are His Opponents (22:1-46); 19) Jesus Criticises the Scribes and Pharisees (23:1-39); 20) The Shape of the Future: The Destruction of the Temple and the Coming of the Son of Man; with Appended Parables of Judgment and Reward (24:1-25:46); 21) The Passion Account (26:1-27:66); 22) Resurrection and Commissioning (28:1-20).

34. Blomberg, *Matthew*, 22.

1. The Birth of Jesus (Matt 1:1-2:23)

2. John the Baptist's Ministry, Jesus' Ministry Inauguration and Beginnings (Matt 3:1-4:25)

3. Sermon on the Mount (Matt 5:1-7:29)

4. Jesus Ministers 1 (Matt 8:1-9:38)

5. Jesus Commissions and Sends the Twelve into Mission (Matt 10:1-42)

6. Jesus Ministers 2 (Matt 11:1-12:50)

7. Parables of the Kingdom (Matt 13:1-52)

8. Jesus Ministers 3 (Matt 14:1-20:34)

9. Jesus Challenges Judaism in Jerusalem (Matt 21:1-23:39)

10. The Olivet Eschatological Discourse (Matt 24:1-25:46)

11. The Passion of Jesus (Matt 26:1-27:66)

12. The Resurrection and Commission (Matt 28:1-20)

THE PURPOSE OF MATTHEW'S GOSPEL

The content of Matthew reveals a series of purposes in his writings. He writes to convince his readers that:

1. **Jesus is the promised messiah:** Jesus is Israel's long-hoped-for Messiah. He is the Son of David, the Son of God, the Son of Man, and Immanuel; the one to whom the Old Testament points.

2. **The Jews have rejected Jesus:** In Matthew, while the crowds flock, the Jewish leaders fail to recognize Jesus during his ministry and oppose him. Jesus responds with great force, but they refuse his challenge. For Matthew, they are in extreme danger if they continue in this stance. This will involve the destruction of the nation and eschatological condemnation.

3. **The promised kingdom has come:** The promised eschatological kingdom has already dawned, inaugurated by the life, death, resurrection, and exaltation of Jesus. It will be gloriously consummated at the return of Christ.

4. **The mission of the kingdom is to go to all nations:** This messianic reign is continuing in the world as believers, both Jews and gentiles, submit to Jesus' authority, overcome temptation, endure persecution, wholeheartedly embrace Jesus' teaching, and thus demonstrate that they are the true people of God. They give authentic witness to the world with the gospel of the kingdom.

5. **The kingdom awaits its ultimate consummation:** This messianic reign is not only the fulfillment of the Old Testament hopes but the foretaste of the consummated kingdom that will dawn when Jesus the Messiah personally returns. At this time, Jesus will consign humanity that has rejected him to eternal destruction while his people will inherit the kingdom.

Jesus and the kingdom are presented in this way to encourage worship of Jesus, committed discipleship, and evangelism, and for Christians to know how to live in light of this new kingdom.

SIMILARITIES AND DIFFERENCES TO MARK

Matthew drew heavily on Mark's Gospel to put together his own story of Jesus. By assuming so much of Mark, Matthew undoubtedly accepts Mark's Jesus, so there are many similarities with Mark. However, he also develops Mark's narrative with much additional material indicating his emphases.

SIMILARITIES AND DIFFERENCES IN CONTENT

Matthew includes some obvious differences to Mark. Scholars have identified two bodies of material in Matthew that are not in Mark. One group of material is common to Luke (Q) and the other distinct (M).

1. Most of Mark is in Matthew: As noted above, 606/661 verses from Mark are in Matthew in some form (92 percent). Those sections excluded include "the exorcism at Capernaum" (Mark 1:21-28), the healing of the blind man in Bethsaida (Mark 8:22-26), and the widow's offering (Mark 12:41-44). It is difficult to explain why these would not be included by Matthew.

2. A great amount of additional material added in and amplified: There is a great deal of additional material, including teaching, parables, and details. On the whole, Matthew includes and expands the Markan account.[35] He adds the genealogy, stressing Jesus' Abrahamic and Davidic descent (Matt 1:1-17), the birth narrative (Matt 1:18-2:23), and the Sermon on the Mount (Matt 5-7). He adds significant detail to the sending of the Twelve into mission (Matt 10), some healings such as the centurion's servant (Matt 8:5-13), and a whole block dealing with church conflict and forgiveness (Matt 18:10-35). He adds in a number of parables including the parable of the unforgiving servant (Matt 18:23-35), the parable of the workers in the vineyard (Matt 20:1-16), the parable of the two sons in the vineyard (Matt 21:28-32), the parable of the wedding banquet (Matt 22:1-14), the parable of the faithful or unfaithful servant (Matt 24:45-51), the parable of the ten virgins (Matt 25:1-13), the parable of the talents (Matt 25:14-30), and the parabolic sheep-and-goats discourse (Matt 25:31-46). He also adds the apologetically significant detail of the Roman guard at the tomb (Matt 27:62-66).

A significant part of the additional material is found in the eschatological discourse (Matt 24:42-25:46). Matthew reworks the material in Mark 13 (the Olivet Discourse) to ensure readers recognize that it refers not only to the fall of Jerusalem but to the second coming. He thus has a heightened futuristic eschatology focused on the return of Christ.

Matthew also includes *fulfillment motifs*, particularly, the formula "this was to fulfill what was spoken through the prophet ..." (Matt 1:22; 2:15; 3:15;

---

35. Matthean priority proponents argue that Mark summarizes Matthew.

5:17; 8:17; 12:17; 13:35; 21:4). These motifs emphasize prophetic fulfillment in the coming of Christ. Matthew is seeking to confirm to his readers that Jesus is the long-awaited Christ.

While most of the early material is included, the order of the early part of Mark (Mark 1-8:26) is substantially reworked. However, there is substantial agreement with Mark (Mark 6:14-13:37) in the flow and detail from Matthew 14:1 to 24:44. The passion narrative agrees with Mark with some differences—the most significant difference being the guarding of the tomb. The resurrection narrative in Matthew builds on Mark's abrupt ending, giving the details of Jesus appearing to the women and in Galilee. A significant difference is the addition of the so-called Great Commission—to make disciples of all nations.

DEEPER DIFFERENCES

A Distinct Jewishness

When compared with Mark, there is a strong Jewishness to the Gospel of Matthew. This includes:

1. **Old Testament quotes and fulfillment sayings:** These are usually from the Hebrew Old Testament and not the Greek Old Testament, but not exclusively. For example, Matthew 1:21-22 says: "She will give birth to a son, and you are to give him the name Jesus, because he will save his people from their sins" (NIV). All this took place to fulfill what the Lord had said through the prophet: "The virgin will conceive and give birth to a son, and they will call him Immanuel" (NIV).[36]

---

36. Immanuel means "God with us" (cf. Isa 7:14, LXX). Others include the genealogy (Matt 1:1-17); Matt 2:6, cf. Mic 5:2; Matt 2:15, cf. Hos 11:1; Matt 2:18, cf. Jer 31:15; Matt 2:23 (disputed, possibly Isa 11:1; 52-53, or Nazirite in Num 6:2-21, Judg 13:5); Matt 3:3, cf. Isa 40:3; Matt 4:4, cf. Deut 8:3; Matt 4:7, cf. Deut 6:16; Matt 4:10, cf. Deut 6:13; Matt 4:15-16, cf. Isa 9:1-2; Matt 8:17, cf. Isa 53:4; Matt 10:35, cf. Mic 7:6; Matt 11:3, cf. 3:1; Matt 12:7, cf. Hos 6:6; Matt 12:18-21, cf. Isa 42:1-4; Matt 13:13-15, cf. Isa 6:9-10; Matt 13:35, cf. Ps 78:2; Matt 15:8-9, cf. Isa 29:13; Matt 19:4-5, cf. Gen 1:27; 2:24; Matt 21:5, 9, cf. Zech 9:9; Ps 118:26; Matt 21:13, cf. Isa 56:7; Jer 7:11; Matt 21:16, cf. Ps 8:2; Matt 21:42, cf. Ps 118:22-23; Matt 22:32, cf. Ex 3:6; Matt 22:37-39, cf. Deut 6:5; Lev 19:18; Matt 22:24, cf. Deut 25:5; Matt 22:32, cf. Exod 3:6; Matt 22:37, cf. Deut 6:5; Matt 22:39, cf. Lev 19:18; Matt 22:44, cf. Ps 110:1; Matt 24:29, cf. Isa 13:10; 34:4; Matt 26:31, cf. Zech 13:7; Matt 27:46, cf. Ps 22:1.

2. **A positive view of the law and Jesus as the fulfillment of it:** Matthew has a positive view of the law in terms of its fulfillment and not its abolition. The best example is the summary of Matthew 5:17-20. However, Jesus defines what is important to the law, moving attention from purity rituals and Sabbath observance to justice, righteousness, and mercy.

3. **More references to Old Testament stories and accounts in the narrative:** Matthew recalls Jesus' use of Old Testament accounts to a greater degree than Mark or Luke. For example, his genealogy covers the sweep of Israel's history from Abraham, to David, the exile, and to Jesus (Matt 1:18). He also refers to Abraham, Isaac, and Jacob (Matt 3:9; 8:11; 22:32), Sodom and Gomorrah (Matt 10:15; 11:21-24), creation (Matt 19:4-5), Jonah (Matt 12:40-41), and Noah (Matt 24:37-38). David is mentioned seventeen times.

Ethics—Especially the Sermon on the Mount

A strong development in Matthew and Luke from Mark is their gathering of a collection of Jesus' teaching in the Sermon on the Mount. The sermon teaches the radical ethics of the kingdom for a disciple of Christ. It is also addressed to the crowds, so it is an invitation to humanity to participate in the kingdom and its lifestyle.

While there is a range of interpretative approaches to the Sermon, the ethics expressed should be understood as ethical principles of the kingdom Jesus is inaugurating. While they set the bar high and all people fall short, Matthew's Jesus is urging followers of Jesus to seek to live them in every context of life. He desires that the ideals of the sermons should shape communities. While the ethic is for all the world, if it will yield to its Creator King, it will be rejected by many, including most of the Jewish leadership at the time of Christ. Jesus in Matthew urges God's people to hold on to these ethics, whatever those in wider society choose to do. Matthew's vision is that by living them, kingdom people will be salt and light in a flavorless and dark world. Through living the Sermon's values, believers bring God's reign to the world and others are drawn to Christ. As they are faithful to it, the powers of the world are subverted, transformed from the inside out.

The Church

Mark does not mention the church at all. Neither does Luke or John, although Luke does refer to the church in Acts frequently.[37] Matthew is the only Gospel in which the church is mentioned. This leads some to see the passages or references to church as interpolations, the church as an idea placed on the lips of Jesus. However, there is no need to take these references in this way, as it is used around 100 times in the LXX, and the parallel Hebrew notion of *qāhāl* is common in the Hebrew Scriptures, often describing Israel. It is reasonable that Jesus appropriated for his followers. Matthew mentions the church twice (emphasis mine; cf. Matt 18:20):

1. **Matthew 16:18:** "Upon this rock I will build *my church*; and the gates of hell shall not prevail against it" (KJV). The rock here is perhaps Peter; alternatively, it refers to the messianic confession and/or Jesus as Messiah, who is the foundation of the church.[38] Jesus predicts that even if persecution comes, Satan will never dissolve God's people.

2. **Matthew 18:17:** "If he refuses to listen to them [witnesses accusing a brother of sin], tell it to *the church*. And if he refuses to listen even to the church, let him be to you as a Gentile and a tax collector." Here, a process is given for church discipline, where one member wrongs another. The whole of Matthew 18 is about church life and particularly the need for discipline and forgiveness in the church. These references are the only

---

37. *Ekklēsia* is mentioned twenty-three times in Acts, nineteen times of the Christian church or churches (Acts 5:11; 8:1, 3; 9:31; 11:22, 26; 12:1, 5; 13:1; 14:23, 27; 15:3, 4, 22, 41; 16:5; 18:22; 19:41; 20:17, 28). Once it is used of Israel as God's congregation (Acts 7:38) and three times of the Ephesus City Assembly (Acts 19:32, 39, 41).

38. Most scholars argue that the most natural reading of the passage is that Peter is the rock based on the same Aramaic word being behind these two texts (*kepha*) and that there is little difference between the two words in question (see the discussion in Hagner, *Matthew 14-28*, 470-71). However, this view is questionable when the Greek is considered. "Peter" is the *masculine* Greek word *Petros* meaning "rock." "Rock" is the *feminine* word *petra*, which is also preceded by the feminine "this" (*tautē*), which grammatically can't refer to Peter, as the genders do not align (they would have to for Peter to be in mind—this is Greek 101). So, the rock may be the confession just made, or better, the one whom they confessed—Jesus! (Some also consider it may refer to Matt 7:24-27.) Christ is the foundation of the church and upon him, the Messiah and Son of God, the church is built (see C. C. Caragounis, *Peter and the Rock* [Berlin: de Gruyter, 1990].)

references to *ekklēsia* in the Gospels and are important in that they place the notion of the church in the mouth of Jesus before it is fully inaugurated at Pentecost.

Discipleship

Mark has a real interest in discipleship. Matthew and Luke take that further. Matthew adds to the Markan references to Jesus' call for wholehearted discipleship, for example: "Seek first the kingdom of God and his righteousness" (Matt 6:33). In Matthew 8:18–22, he recalls two encounters that speak of potential homelessness and the call to place allegiance to the kingdom above family and culture, even when a loved one dies. The Sermon on the Mount also challenges disciples to take up its radical ethic of living righteously. Followers of Jesus must have a righteousness that surpasses the scribes and Pharisees (Matt 5:20). They are to be perfect, as God the Father is perfect (Matt 5:48). "It is a call for unalloyed commitment to the will of God as expounded by Jesus ... The call is to go all the way with the will of God, now seen with fresh clarity."[39] For Matthew's Jesus, discipleship is all or nothing—disciples are to give everything they have in service to God and his kingdom, or walk away and face destruction.

Mission

Mark's Gospel has a strong implicit sense of ongoing mission in the sending of the Twelve (Mark 6:7–13) and references indicating that the gospel will go to all nations (esp. Mark 13:10). These are included in Matthew as well (10:1–42; 13:31–32; 24:14; 26:6–13). However, the sense of mission in Mark is weak in comparison to Matthew and Luke, especially when considering the longer ending of Mark may not be the original.

In Matthew's case, Jesus' focus is "the lost sheep of Israel" (Matt 10:6; 15:24). This could suggest that Jesus was concerned only with Jewish mission. However, there are many indications that while Jesus limited his mission, his vision was for the whole world to hear his message and become disciples. His focus was the Jewish people, God's chosen, but his followers would take his message to the world. This is seen in a variety of ways:

---

39. Nolland, *Matthew*, 271.

1. **Hints of a concern for universal mission:** These include the Magi who come from the east to worship the King (Matt 2:1-12), the Canaanite woman's daughter healed in Tyre and Sidon (Matt 15:21-28), the Roman centurion's exemplary faith (Matt 8:5-13), and as with Mark, the centurion soldier at the cross (Matt 27:54).

2. **The statement that believers are the salt and light of the world:** This emphasizes the imperative that the disciples live the values expressed in the Sermon on the Mount in wider society so that people can be saved and society and the world transformed (Matt 5:13-16).

3. **Commission to love enemies:** In context, this would include the love of their gentile rulers, the Romans, Jewish opponents, and others. God is given as the primary model, blessing good and evil alike. So should followers of Jesus (Matt 5:43-47).

4. **A long development of the initial mission:** Matthew 10 builds on Mark's call narrative (Mark 6) adding detail and emphasizing witness before Jewish and gentile authorities (Mark 10 [esp. v. 18]).

5. **Bearing fruit:** People outside of Israel would bear fruit for the kingdom (Matt 21:43).

6. **The gospel preached to all nations:** Matthew restates Mark 13:10 that the gospel of the kingdom will be preached in the whole world before the consummation (Matt 24:14). From all nations, angels will gather God's elect (Matt 24:31). The story of the woman who anointed Jesus will be spread to the world (Matt 26:13).

7. **Universal judgment:** The whole world, including all nations, will be judged by Jesus (Matt 25:31-46).

8. **Initial limitation and ultimate extension of mission:** While there is an initial limitation of mission to the Jews (Matt

10:5-6, 23 15:24), there is an extension of the mission to the whole world post-ascension (Matt 28:18-20).

The Great Commission

The climax of Matthew's Gospel is the resurrected Jesus, now with complete authority over all creation, commissioning a crowd of disciples to go[40] and make disciples of all nations, baptizing them, and teaching them, assured of his presence with them.

The statements limiting Jesus' mission concern to the Jews should not be read absolutely (i.e., him only coming to Israel) but as representing his intention to establish the gospel in Israel before it is extended into the world after his death and resurrection. Hence, when Jesus gave the command to preach the gospel to all nations, the initial work had already been done in Israel, although mission to Israel's people will go on. It is the responsibility of the disciples and the remainder of the church to take the gospel to all nations (Matt 24:14). That this was the ultimate purpose of God is seen in hints throughout. Matthew's hope is that his readers will continue the work of making disciples of all nations.

The Kingdom of Heaven

While Matthew at times uses "kingdom of God" (see 6:33; 12:28; 19:24; 21:31, 43), he uniquely replaces it with "the kingdom of heaven" (twenty-four times).[41] Most scholars believe these are interchangeable terms. Matthew may have avoided "God" here because of the Jewish preference for avoiding using the name of God (i.e., Yahweh). Seven times he introduces parables with "The kingdom of heaven is like" (Matt 13:31, 33, 44, 45, 47, 52; 20:1), the parables similitudes, comparing the kingdom to things and situations, aiding understanding.

---

40. The central command is to "make disciples." "Go" is a participle, and some argue it should be translated "as you go." Often Matthew "uses 'go' as an introductory circumstantial participle that is rightly translated as coordinate to the main verb—here 'Go and make' (cf. 2:8; 9:13; 11:4; 17:27; 28:7)" (see Blomberg, *Matthew*, 431). Hence, the right translation is "Go," but this can be overstated.

41. Also "the kingdom" (Matt 4:23; 8:12; 9:35; 13:19, 38; 24:14; 25:34), "your kingdom" (Matt 6:10; 20:21), "his kingdom" (Matt 13:41; 16:28), and "the kingdom of their Father" (Matt 13:43; 26:29).

The use of "heaven" also emphasizes eschatology. That is, the realm of heaven has broken into the present in the person and ministry of Jesus Christ, another Matthean emphasis. With his stronger futuristic eschatology, Matthew also gives greater emphasis to the consummation of the kingdom. Matthew's vision is of this creation renewed (Matt 19:28). At the judgment, God's people do not "go to heaven," but receive the kingdom prepared for them from the foundation of the world (Matt 25:34). This kingdom is the renewed creation. This fits with Paul's view of the liberation of creation from decay (Rom 8:19-23) and the new heavens and earth of Revelation 21-22.

A Higher Christology

Mark has a high view of Jesus, speaking of him as the Messiah or Christ (see esp. Mark 1:1; 8:29; 9:41; 14:61), Daniel's Son of Man (fourteen times, e.g., Mark 2:10), the Son of God (Mark 1:1, 11; 3:11; 9:7; 12:6, 36–37; 14:61; 15:39), Lord in a sovereign sense (six times, e.g., Mark 1:3; 2:28; 5:19; 12:36–37); and the servant (Mark 10:43-45).

However, Matthew emphasizes a higher Christology than Mark and a number of themes concerning the person and identity of Jesus. His intention is to convince his readers of Jesus' messianic identity, and that he is more than a human: he is God the Son.

Some of the main christological dimensions of Matthew include:

Jesus as Teacher and "New Moses." Jesus is presented as a teacher and as a new Moses bringing a fresh revelation that directs people of the kingdom concerning the way they should live. This is not an abolition of the law, but its fulfillment (Matt 4:23; 9:35). The Sermon on the Mount is a sustained piece of teaching on a mountain reminiscent of Moses, who received the torah on Mount Sinai. He reinterprets Moses in this sermon, interacting with the law and bringing a "new law." He teaches with authority, unlike the lawyers (Matt 7:29, cf. 22:33) and is even addressed as "teacher" by a Jewish teacher who promises to follow him (Matt 8:19). Jesus is now the authoritative spokesperson of God's will for life. He defeats the Jewish leaders continually in the temple debate narrative (Matt 21:23–22:46). He states in his woes to the Pharisees: "nor are you to be called 'teacher,' for you have one teacher, the Messiah" (Matt 23:10 NET). He meets Moses and Elijah—two great prophets of Israel who encountered God on Mount Sinai—on the Mount of Transfiguration, and the disciples are told to "listen to *him.*" For Matthew and the other New Testament writers, Jesus is not just a new Moses; he is *the* Moses, the Prophet in the Mosaic tradition who brings the complete revelation of God's being and will (cf. Deut 18:15).

Additional connections between Jesus as Moses:

1. Miracles around his infancy (Matt 1–2), cf. Moses' birth (Exod 2).

2. Jesus' birth causes turmoil among political leaders (Herod, Magi [Matt 2:1–11], cf. Pharaoh [Exod 5–12]).

3. Jesus survives a massacre of children (the slaughter at Bethlehem [Matt 2:16–18], cf. the birth of Moses [Exod 1:15–22] and the killing of the firstborn at Passover [Exod 11–12]).

4. Jesus retraces the exodus journey to Egypt and out (Matt 2:13–15, cf. Exodus [Gen 46–47; Exod 12–14; Hos 11:1]).

5. Jesus remains in the wilderness for forty days and forty nights (temptation [Matt 4:1–11], cf. Moses on Mount Sinai [Exod 24:18; 34:28]).

6. Jesus reveals the "new law" (Matt 5–7), cf. the Mosaic law (Exod 20–23).

Son of David, King, Messiah. Matthew continues and heightens Mark's identification of Jesus as the Davidic Messiah or Christ. He refers to Jesus being Christ or Messiah eleven times (e.g., Matt 11:2: "When John heard in prison what the *Messiah* was doing, he sent a message by his disciples," emphasis added; HCSB). Jesus is also called "Son of David" nine times, unparalleled in any other Gospel (four times in Luke; three in Mark; none in John). This fits the "Jewish orientation" of Matthew and his desire to demonstrate from his Jewish heritage that Jesus is Messiah.

God the Son. Matthew presents Jesus with a higher Christology than Mark, especially in terms of Jesus' divine sonship. He uses the term "Son of God" more than Mark. The term was associated with the Messiah (Ps 2:7), and in Mark, this is its sense. Luke has a slightly higher Christology but emphasizes Jesus as Lord. However, in Matthew the Son of God notion moves toward a recognition that Jesus is not just a human Messiah, King, and Son of God, but *he is God the Son.* John takes this further and speaks of a completely divinized Son. Matthew's interest is seen at various points (emphasis added):

1. Matthew 1:18-22: As in Luke and not mentioned in Mark, Jesus is conceived *by the Spirit* (Matt 1:18); she will give birth to *a son* who will be called Immanuel, or *"God with us"* (Matt 1:23). In other words, he is God's presence with humanity. He is the divine Son of God.

2. Matthew 2:15: "Out of Egypt I called *my son.*"

3. Matthew 26:63-64: "The high priest said to him, 'I charge you under oath by the living God: Tell us if you are the Messiah, *the Son of God.*' 'You have said so,' Jesus replied. 'But I say to all of you: From now on you will see the Son of Man sitting at the right hand of the Mighty One and coming on the clouds of heaven'" (NIV).

4. Matthew 4:3, 6: The devil assumes Jesus is the Son of God.

5. Matthew 14:33: The disciples confess him as the Son of God when he walks on water.

6. Matthew 16:16: Peter's confession in Matthew includes the term "Son of God" (Mark's does not).

Hence, what is mentioned in Mark's Gospel is made more explicit in Matthew; Jesus is God the Son. John will draw it out fully.

Wisdom Incarnate. In some texts in Matthew's Gospel, Jesus' wisdom is emphasized. This resounds with the notion of God's wisdom personified in the intertestamental book of "wisdom literature," Ecclesiasticus, which is attributed to Jesus, son of Sirach. Some see Jesus as God's wisdom incarnate (cf. Prov 8-9). Some examples of this wisdom attribution include:

1. Matthew 12:42: "The Queen of the South will rise at the judgment with this generation and condemn it; for she came from the ends of the earth to listen to Solomon's wisdom, and now one *greater than Solomon* is here" (NIV).

2. Matthew 13:54: "'Where did this man get *this wisdom* and these miraculous powers?' they asked" (NIV).

3. Matthew 11:19: He and John the Baptist vindicate God's wisdom.

4. Matthew 11:25–30: Jesus calls the lowly to himself and promises them rest, a motif-like wisdom.

Divine Lord. Matthew does not use "Lord," or *kyrios*, as much of Jesus as Mark and Luke do. Sometimes, it is God who is *kyrios* rather than Jesus (e.g., Matt 1:20; 4:7; 11:25; 21:9; 22:37). Often, he employs it as a form of address by people coming to inquire of Jesus, especially for healing or deliverance of some sort (fourteen times). For example, Matthew 20:30 says, "Two blind men were sitting by the roadside, and when they heard that Jesus was going by, they shouted, '*Lord*, Son of David, have mercy on us!'" (NIV). In these instances, it speaks of Jesus' recognized status and authority, rather than his cosmic lordship. However, it is used of Jesus in a cosmic sense as well on several occasions. One example is Matthew 7:21: "Not everyone who says to me, 'Lord, Lord,' will enter the kingdom of heaven, but the one who does the will of my Father who is in heaven" (see also Matt 9:38; 24:42; 25:37, 44). "Lord" can also carry the sense of Messiah on occasions, especially from Peter's lips (Matt 16:22; 17:4; 18:21, cf. 20:30; 21:3).

Jesus as the Object of Worship. On several occasions, Jesus is the object of worship. In the infancy narrative, the Magi come to worship him (Matt 2:2, 8, 11). After the calming of the storm, the disciples worship him as the Son of God (Matt 14:33). Some of the disciples worship him on the mountain as he gives them the Great Commission (Matt 28:17). In a zealously monotheistic environment where worship of anything or anyone other than Yahweh was *verboten*, this speaks of followers recognizing his divine status. This is stunning from first-century Jews.

Conflict with Jewish Authorities

Throughout Mark's Gospel, Jesus clashes with the Jewish scribes and Pharisees, and they ultimately conspire to kill him. Luke has a similar thrust. However, John and especially Matthew speak of even deeper antagonism between Jesus and the Jewish leadership. This perhaps reflects the situation in the 70s and 80s AD where Judaism and Christianity are parting ways. If Matthew wrote after the fall of Jerusalem, as is likely, he may also be theologically explaining the destruction of the nation—it is because the Jewish leadership rejected Jesus and his Son the Jews were exiled. In John, Jesus' opponents are simply called "the Jews."

In Matthew, John the Baptist's language toward the Jewish leadership is stronger. He even calls them "a brood of vipers" in danger of God's coming wrath (Matt 3:7). Through the Gospel, with great vitriol, Jesus challenges the scribes, Pharisees, and the Sadducees. This is especially strong in the "Woes" of Matthew 23 and in 27:25 where the crowd cries out, "His blood be on us and on our children." The Olivet Discourse of Matthew 24 predicts the demolition of Jerusalem and the temple (Matt 24:2). While Mark and Luke mention the Sadducees once in the final-week marriage debate (Mark 12:18; Luke 20:27), Matthew mentions them in seven passages, all negative (Matt 3:7; 16:1, 6, 11, 12; 22:23–34). He refers to Jewish houses of worship as "their" synagogues, as if distancing himself from the Jewish leadership (Matt 4:23; 10:17; 12:9; 13:54). However, while Matthew strongly condemns Jewish leadership, this is not anti-Semitism. He does not target *all* Jews, but those who reject Jesus. Further, all of Jesus' disciples were Jews including the author, Matthew. His critique is that of an insider, a Jew speaking to other Jews. He is a Semite critiquing other Semites. Through Matthew, Jesus is positive toward a range of Jews, including prophets, kings, Old Testament figures, and John the Baptist; and in his ministry, he prioritized Jesus' mission to Israel (Matt 15:24). While Matthew's Jesus challenges the torah, he endorses it, quotes it, and affirms it (esp. Matt 5:17–20). Some see in this conflict with Jewish authorities Matthew reflecting the clash between Judaism and Christianity after the fall of Jerusalem and culminating in the expulsion of Christians from the synagogue. This seems likely.

Eschatological Judgment and Hope

Mark's eschatological outlook is debated, with some seeing his focus in Mark 13 being on the fall of Jerusalem and that he was also looking forward to an imminent parousia. Others argue that Mark 13 is double-focused, with both the fall of Jerusalem and a distant parousia in view. Whatever is correct concerning Mark, indisputably Luke and particularly Matthew take the future dimension of Mark's account (Mark 4:29; 10:30, 37–40; 12:18–27; 13:1–36; 14:62) and give it a sharper and more detailed eschatological edge.

In Matthew, this comes through warnings of eschatological judgment because of wrong action. Sometimes the metaphor of fire is used powerfully to speak of unspeakable misery for those who experience eschatological rejection by God. This is seen in John the Baptist's ministry (Matt 3:9–12) and in the threat of judgment for those who do not live the ethic of the Sermon on the Mount (e.g., Matt 5:22). Matthew also has a strong emphasis on judgment in Jesus' parables, often referring to "weeping and gnashing of teeth," a vivid description of eschatological torment (e.g., Matt 8:12; 13:42; 22:13; 24:51).[42] There are also strong notes of eschatological reward for the faithful who live out the kingdom ethic (Matt 6:4, 6, 18; 7:14; 12:35–37; 20:1–16; 25:19–23, 34–40). Often, his eschatological discourse is couched in the language of dualistic contrast, that is, two paths, one to life and one to destruction (Matt 7:13–14), or the sheep and the goats (Matt 25:31–46). Matthew highlights two ways of living, and the ultimate outcome is either eternal life or eternal destruction. Readers are to make their choice through their response to Jesus. There is also warning to Christians of severe judgment for a fake faith, one not based on a genuine relationship with Jesus (esp. Matt 7:21–23).

The return of Christ also features more prominently in Matthew than in Mark. It is more obviously the context for the Olivet Discourse (Matt 24). The question that launches the Olivet Discourse in Matthew explicitly refers to both the temple's devastation and Jesus' future coming, whereas in Mark it refers only to the destruction of the temple (cf. Matt 24:3; Mark 13:4). Matthew adds to Mark's material a series of parables that all speak of

---

42. See on this strong note of eschatological judgment 5:20, 22, 29–30; 7:13, 21–23; 8:10–12; 10:15; 11:21–24; 12:31–32, 35–37; 13:29–30, 40–43, 49; 18:7–9, 30–35; 19:24; 21:31–32; 22:11–14; 23:13; 24:51; 25:10, 41–46.

being fully prepared for the coming of Jesus. The parable of the ten virgins speaks of always being awake and ready (Matt 25:1-13). The parable of the talents refers to believers investing what God has given them in the interim (Matt 25:14-30). The sheep and goats' judgment scene speaks of the final judgment concerning the way the people of the nations have responded to the gospel and God's people (Matt 25:31-46).

QUESTIONS TO CONSIDER

- What aspects of Matthew's portrayal of Jesus stand out to you?
- What is the special value of Matthew's Gospel for you?

LUKE'S GOSPEL

CHAPTER 8

Luke's Gospel is the third of the Synoptic Gospels. It is generally agreed that Luke is the first part of a two-part work with Acts. The general agreement that Luke and Acts had a common author is primarily because of the similar prologues, both of which are addressed to Theophilus (Luke 1:3; Acts 1:1). In Acts, the writer refers to "my former book" (*prōton logon*, or "first message/book/word"). Other reasons include the similarity in style, vocabulary, and theology. One could say that the books could be renamed with Acts as Luke 2, or Luke as "The Acts of Jesus." Some scholars (e.g., Witherington) believe that Luke-Acts was one work but, because of the size of the document, it was cut into two to fit onto two scrolls.[1] Alternatively, Luke was written first, and sometime later, Acts was penned. Either way, the two are closely related, and Lukan scholars work with both documents. What follows functions as both an introduction to Luke and to Acts. Material from both documents is considered when introducing Luke.

Luke-Acts was written by an educated Greek man and should be considered among the great historical Greek writings. It tracks the story of Jesus and his movement, first in Luke from Jesus' humble birth to his resurrection

---

1. Witherington III, *The Acts of the Apostles*, 4–8, who notes that Acts is about "the maximum one could include on one normal papyrus roll writing in medium-sized Greek script, following the normal procedure of leaving no gaps between words and sentences." Scrolls were about forty feet (approx. twelve meters). A thirty-foot scroll would have about 100 columns of thirty to forty lines per column and twenty characters a line. Luke's Gospel (19,404 words) would fit on a thirty-five-foot scroll, and Acts (18,374 words) on a thirty-two-foot scroll with normal handwriting and spacing. Thematically there is also clear continuity.

and exaltation, then in Acts from his resurrection appearances to Paul in prison in Rome, where the gospel is well established. Luke's account of God's work of salvation stands in continuity with the Deuteronomic writings of the Old Testament. What makes the two-part work so useful is that it not only gives an excellent account of Jesus, but tells the story of how his followers initially lived after his ascension. As such, believers are instructed concerning how they are to live.

THE AUTHORSHIP OF LUKE

ARGUMENTS IN FAVOR OF LUKE

As in the case of Mark and Matthew, as well as John, there is no explicit internal evidence that Luke, a doctor and traveling companion of Paul (see below), is the author of the Third Gospel or Acts. However, unlike these other two Gospels, scholars are generally in agreement that Luke is the author. Here are some of the reasons:

The external ascription

The ascription reads "according to Luke." This suggests that in the early second century it was believed that someone called "Luke" wrote this Gospel (see the discussion on authorship and the ascriptions in Mark and Matthew).

The unanimous agreement of early church writers

There is convincing evidence that the early church believed that Luke is the writer. These include Marcion, Justin (c. 160, *Dial.* 103.9 = "a memoir of Jesus"), the so-called anti-Marcionite Prologue (c. 160-180), the Muratorian Canon (c. AD 170-180), Irenaeus (c. AD 175-195; *Haer.* 3.1.1; 13.1-3; 15.30-35); Tertullian (c. 160-220, *Marc.* 4.2.2; 4.5.3), and Eusebius (early fourth century; *Hist. eccl.* 3.4.2). The oldest manuscript of Luke, the Bodmer Papyrus XIV, cited in 𝔓75 (AD 175-225), ascribes the work to Luke. There are also allusions in 1 Clement (*1 Clem.* 13:2; 48:4) from the early 90s AD and in

---

2. Frank E. Dicken, "Luke," *LBD*. Dicken notes that the Bodmer Papyrus (𝔓75) XIV/XV includes a fragmented copy of the Gospels (c. AD 175-225). It includes Luke with the words "gospel according to Luke."

2 Clement 13:4 (c. AD 150). No other name has ever been attached to the work. The unanimous agreement is strong support for Lukan authorship.

The four "we passages" in Acts

There are four points in Acts where Luke writes in the first-person plural ("we/us") after writing in the third person plural ("them/they") (see Acts 16:10-17; 20:5-16; 21:1-18; 27:1-28:16). While there are other arguments,[3] the best interpretation of this is that the writer of Acts was with Paul and his team at these points. From these passages it is clear Luke was a participant in some of Paul's missions. He joined Paul on his second Antiochian mission in Troas, remained in Macedonia when Paul traveled on to Achaia, rejoined him on his third Antiochian mission, and traveled with Paul to Jerusalem and to Paul's Roman imprisonment. These passages indicate Paul was in both Jerusalem and Rome, perfectly positioned to gather material to write his two works. From Paul's prison letters—especially Philemon and Colossians 4—it is possible to identify other writers. These people include the likes of Titus, Demas, Crescans, Jesus Justus, Epaphras, Epaphroditus, Timothy, Mark, and Luke. There is no reason to ascribe the authorship to any of the others, so Luke is the most likely.

Acts 20:13 in the Western text

While Luke is not mentioned in the preferred texts of Luke, the so-called Western text of Acts 20:13 reads: "But I Luke, and those who were with me, went on board." While this is an interpolation, it confirms that the scribe considered Luke the writer and was with Paul. F. F. Bruce dates the Western text at AD 120, arguing that this gives early evidence for Lukan authorship of Acts—and so also the Gospel of Luke.[4]

---

3. For example, that Luke is using a source, diary, or journal (see the discussion in Witherington, *Acts*, 53). However, such ideas are unlikely. The language and theology are consistent with the rest of Acts. It was important in ancient history that the person writing was a part of the events narrated. By these "we passages" Luke indicates that he was involved, and so adds to arguments for historical integrity. He rightly says (p. 52), "On the face of things, the 'we' passages which show up in the second half of Acts suggest that our author was a sometime companion of Paul." See also pp. 480-86.

4. F. F. Bruce, *The Acts of the Apostles: The Greek Text with Introduction and Commentary* (London: Tyndale, 1962), 4. Dated AD 120, along with the prescript (if we accept Hengel), this is the earliest clear evidence of Lukan authorship. Other scholars date it in the mid-second century (Bruce M. Metzger and Bart D. Ehrman, *The Text of the New Testament: Its Transmission,*

OBJECTIONS TO LUKAN AUTHORSHIP

While most agree Luke is the author, not all are completely convinced that Luke was a traveling companion of Paul. Here are some reasons:

The "we passages" can be read in other ways

Some believe that the "we passages" do not indicate the author was with Paul but indicate snippets of a Pauline diary or journal or from some other source written in the first person and inserted into the Acts account. Alternatively, Luke has not edited his sources. However, the most straightforward explanation is that "we" should be read to include the author.

Discrepancies between Paul in his letters and Acts

Some also find too many discrepancies between the Paul of Acts and the Paul of the Epistles, which suggests to them that the writer of Acts was not a traveling companion of Paul. For example, Luke does not stress Paul's doctrine of justification by faith and inclusion in Christ, which is so important in his letters. Further, Paul's maintenance of the law at times in Acts supposedly stands at variance with his law-free attitude in the letters.

However, justification by faith is found in only two of Paul's letters, both addressing issues of Judaizing and legal observance (Romans and Galatians). Further, Luke does cite Paul referring to both inclusion in Christ and justification in Acts 13:38–39: "and from everything which you have not been able in the law of Moses to be justified (*dikaioō*) from, in this man (*en touto*), everyone who believes has been justified (*dikaioō*)." This speaks both of inclusion in Christ (*en touto*) and justification. The content in Paul's letters is not what Paul preached as he initially preached the gospel. Rather, they are occasional letters to converts.

Where observance of the law is concerned, Luke's Paul is consistent with the Paul of the Epistles. In 1 Corinthians 9:19–22, Paul emphatically states that he has no need to observe the law, but chooses to follow Jewish cultural protocols when among Jews, and gentile social protocols when among gentiles. He does this for missional purposes: to win as many as

---

Corruption, and Restoration, 4th ed. [New York: Oxford University Press, 2005], Kindle Edition, the Western text) or the third century (Kurt Aland and Barbara Aland, *The Text of the New Testament: An Introduction to the Critical Editions and to the Theory and Practice of Modern Textual Criticism* [trans. Erroll F. Rhodes; 2nd ed.; Leiden: Brill, 1989], 54–56).

possible to Christ. Acts is consistent with this approach. In general, Paul exists comfortably among gentiles, living and meeting in their homes (e.g., Acts 16:15; 18:7), and enjoying fellowship with them. At the Jerusalem Council, Paul vehemently rejects the Judaizers who demand Mosaic legal observance and especially circumcision (Acts 15:1-12). Paul does have Timothy circumcised in Acts 16:3, while he does not circumcise Titus in Galatians 2:3. However, this is easily explainable, as Timothy is a Jew on his mother's side (Acts 16:3), and circumcising him would enable him to move freely between Jews and Greeks. Titus, however, is a gentile, and Paul will not force him to Judaize. Both decisions are missional, consistent with Paul's perspectives on freedom from the law and cultural accommodation. He does cut his hair on a vow in Acts 16:3, but there is nothing said of the law here; this may be a vow based on some other reason (Acts 18:18).[5] If it is due to Jewish law, he then left Cenchreae and traveled to Ephesus to engage in Jewish mission in the synagogue (Acts 18:19). In Jerusalem, his decision to join others in a vow of purity was in preparation to enter the temple, consistent with 1 Corinthians 9:19-22.

As such, these so-called discrepancies are barely significant, with the Paul of Acts preaching the same gospel. The congruency between Acts and the letters of Paul far outweighs any discrepancies.

Conclusion

There is good evidence, external and otherwise, that Luke is the author of the Third Gospel. He is also the author of Acts and one of the most important writers in the New Testament.

INTRODUCING LUKE

If Luke is the author, who was he? The name *Loukas* (Luke) is found three times in the New Testament (Col 4:14; Phlm 24; 2 Tim 4:11). These likely refer to the same person and author. There are also references to two people by

---

5. Most scholars take this as a Nazarite vow (Num 6:1-21)—Paul wanting to indicate his preparedness to submit to the law to heal relationships with Jews (e.g., Dunn). Alternatively, it may be due to an act of thanksgiving for protection. However, Bruce, *Acts* (Greek Text), 398 argues it may be a private vow thanking God for his protection in Corinth and is not related to Jewish law, but is a customary Greek protocol. See the discussion in Eckhart J. Schnabel, *Acts*, ZECNT (Grand Rapids: Zondervan, 2012), 767-68.

the name of Lucius (*Loukios*), one in Antioch who was from Cyrene (Acts 13:1), and another who is either a relative of Paul or, more likely, a companion who is with Paul in Corinth and who greets the Romans (Rom 16:21).[6] It is unlikely that the figure in Acts 13:1 is Luke, as he is the author and gives no indication of this. Most likely he is designated Lucian of Antioch to distinguish him from other Lucians, including the author.[7] Some scholars including Origen (c. AD 184–254) believe that the figure in Romans 16:20 is the same person. However, modern scholarship is cautious.[8]

The three mentions of *Loukas* help identify who he was:

Paul's beloved companion

Luke is described as "beloved" in Colossians 4:14. While Paul often uses *agapētos* (beloved) of congregations, he also uses it of fellow gospel-workers who are especially dear to him, including Timothy (1 Cor 4:17; 2 Tim 1:2), Tychicus (Eph 6:21; Col 4:7), Epaphras (Col 1:7), Onesimus (Col 4:9; Phlm 10–16), and Philemon (Phlm 1).[9] Paul and Luke then are friends, and Luke is important to Paul.

A doctor

Colossians 4:14 also reveals Luke was a physician (*iatros*).[10] Dunn notes that this "indicates a man of some learning and training (though at this time medicine was only just becoming a subject of systematic instruction)."[11] Some suggest Luke was a Jewish physician. However, this is unlikely; he was probably a gentile, trained in the Greco-Roman art of healing. Either

---

6. The Greek translated "my fellow Jews" in the NIV (*syngenēs*) can be literal as the NIV (and more translations) assume, or figurative (companion). If it is literal, it could indicate that Luke was a Jew and even possibly a relative of Paul. It is also unclear whether Paul wants the Roman reader to recognize that all three named are *syngenēs* or the last two named, Jason and Sosipater, although the former is the best reading of the Greek, which joins the names with *kai*, "and."

7. Witherington, *Acts*, 392. I. Howard Marshall, *Acts*, TNTC (Grand Rapids, MI; Leicester: Eerdmans; IVP, 1984), 253 n. 1 notes that a later reading from Africa identified him as Luke the evangelist and as a brother of Titus. However, Marshall sees the link as "improbable."

8. E.g., Douglas J. Moo, *The Epistle to the Romans*, NICNT (Grand Rapids, MI: Eerdmans, 1996), 934.

9. See also Rom 16:5, 8, 9, 12.

10. On physicians see R. K. Harrison, "Physician," in *ISBE* 3:865.

11. J. D. G. Dunn, *The Epistles to the Colossians and to Philemon: A Commentary on the Greek Text*, NICNT (Grand Rapids, MI; Carlisle: Eerdmans; Paternoster, 1996), 283.

way, he would have been an educated man. He would also have been wealthy. As Paul was committed to self-provision as a missionary (a tent maker), he may have continued to work as he traveled with Paul, providing for his own means. He may also have provided medical care for Paul and his team. Certainly, Paul's many travails would have seen him need a doctor on a regular basis. He may be the first medical missionary, although this is speculation. Luke may have been significant in the recovery of Epaphroditus (Phil 2:25-30).

Paul's coworker

Paul describes Luke as one of his coworkers (*synergos*) in Philemon 24. This is another term Paul used for his fellow gospel workers such as Prisca and Aquila (Rom 16:3), Timothy (Rom 16:21), Titus (2 Cor 8:23), or Philemon (Phlm 1).[12] He is thus not merely a passenger, but a gospel worker—a missionary and preacher in his own right. Luke-Acts should be recognized as a vital aspect of his ministry.

A loyal man

In 2 Timothy 4:11, as Paul faces his final challenge, trial, and death at the hands of Caesar Nero, he says of him, "Luke alone is with me." With Colossians and Philemon likely written in the early days of Paul's imprisonment in Rome around AD 60-61, Luke remained faithful to the end of Paul's days (c. AD 65-66). He is a truly loyal man. Lea and Griffin suggest of this verse, "Luke's presence with Paul showed his personal devotion and may also indicate that Luke had given a physician's care to Paul for his physical needs."[13] Perhaps with Timothy, Luke was Paul's most important coworker.

From the "we passages" (Acts 16:10-17; 20:5-16; 21:1-18; 27:1-28:16), in which Luke was with Paul, more can be gleaned:

Luke traveled extensively with Paul

Luke initially appears in Acts in Troas, perhaps indicating this was his home. There are no details on why he joined Paul here. He was likely a God-worshiper in the local synagogue. He may have already been a follower of

---

12. See also Rom 16:9; Phil 2:25; Phil 4:3; 1 Thess 3:2; Phlm 24.
13. Lea and Griffin, *1, 2 Timothy, Titus*, 253.

Jesus, although this is unlikely. Perhaps he was converted by Paul, if Paul preached there, although Luke says only that he passed through. It may have been later that he evangelized the city (2 Cor 2:12). It remains a mystery how and why he and Paul joined up.

Whatever the circumstances, Luke, Paul, Silas, and others in the party traveled across the Aegean Sea to Macedonia to Neapolis and Philippi (Acts 16:10–17). Present through Paul's ministry in Philippi, Thessalonica, and Berea, Luke remained behind when Paul moved on to Athens (Acts 17:1 shifts from "we" to "they"). It is likely Luke played a key role in the initial phase of the churches of Macedonia. However, he could equally have traveled in this time. For example, he may have traveled further west to Rome, even delivering the letter from the Jerusalem Council to Rome (Acts 15:22–35).[14] On that journey, he may have ministered to the west as far as Illyricum. Otherwise, Luke likely gave pastoral leadership to the budding Macedonian churches.

Luke rejoined Paul and his team when they returned through Macedonia after ministry in Thessalonica, Athens, and Corinth (Acts 20:5). They traveled to Troas, and it appears Luke remained with Paul and his team as they traveled on through Assos, Mitylene, Samos, Miletus (where Paul gave his final speech to the Ephesian elders), Cos, Rhodes, Patara, Tyre, Ptolemais, Caesarea Maritima (staying with Philip), and on to Jerusalem. Luke shifts back to the third person at Acts 21:19, and it is likely that he was no longer with Paul, although Paul was imprisoned from that time on. In Jerusalem, Luke was present with the local Christian community, and it is likely that during this time Luke gathered a substantial portion of his Gospel material. The "we passages" resume in Acts 27:1, Luke with Aristarchus (Acts 27:2), traveling with Paul in the epic sea journey to Rome (Acts 27:1–28:16). He and Aristarchus were not part of the party of prisoners but may have bought their own tickets as passengers, or Luke may have traveled as a doctor.[15] As evidenced by Colossians 4:14 and Philemon 24, Luke was with

---

14. The Jerusalem Council Letter was sent with Silas and Paul on his second visit to the churches of Galatia and on to the Macedonian and Achaian missions. It is possible Paul and/or Silas wanted to take this to Rome. However, Claudius had expelled the Jews from Rome in AD 49 and it would need to be delivered by a gentile. This may explain why Luke is not with Paul and reconnects with him. He may also have led a mission to western Greece on behalf of Paul (Illyricum, Rom 15:19).

15. Bruce, *Acts* (Greek Text), 511.

Paul in Rome. This accords with the evidence from the explicit references to Luke in the Pauline Epistles (Col 4:14; Phlm 24; 2 Tim 4:11). This would put him in contact with Peter, Mark and his Gospel (Col 4:10; Phlm 24; 1 Pet 5:13), and potentially the writer of Hebrews—and hence, he was in a great position to compile Acts.

Early church writers confirm that Luke was a traveling companion (e.g., Justin, *Dial.* 103.19 [c. AD 150-55]; the Muratorian Canon [c. 170-200]; and Eusebius, *Hist. eccl.* 3.4.2 [early fourth century]).

In addition, evidence suggests:

Luke was not a Jew, but a gentile Christian convert

If Romans 16:20 refers to this same Luke, then he *may* be a Jew. However, although some argue that Luke was a Hellenistic-Jewish Christian (e.g., Ellis)[16] or a Jew (Fitzmyer),[17] this can be almost certainly ruled out. Most scholars rightly contend that Luke was a gentile Christian. This is based on Colossians 4:11, where Paul states that Mark and Jesus (Justus) are his only coworkers of the circumcision. Paul then goes on to mention Luke, clearly implying he is a gentile.

He was a second-generation Christian

Luke makes it clear in the Prologue of his Gospel that he was not an eyewitness to the events surrounding Christ. Rather, he drew on the work of eyewitnesses and ministers of the gospel in putting together his Gospel (Luke 1:1-4).[18] He is a second-generation Christian, likely converted by Paul in Troas.

Luke was a good Greek writer

Luke's Greek is respectable and versatile. The prologue to the Gospel is written in classical Greek (Luke 1:1-4). Marshall says of the prologue, "The preface is written in excellent Greek with a most carefully wrought

---

16. Earle E. Ellis, *The Gospel of Luke*, 2nd ed., NCBC (Grand Rapids, MI; London: Eerdmans; Morgan & Scott, 1974), 52-53.

17. Joseph A. Fitzmyer, *The Gospel According to Luke (i-ix)*, AB 28 (Garden City, NY: Doubleday, 1981), 42-47.

18. Darrell L. Bock, *Luke: 9:51-24:53*, BEC (Vol 2; Grand Rapids, MI: Baker Academic, 1996), 6.

sentence structure."[19] He then shifts to a Hebraic style reminiscent of the LXX in the remainder of chapters 1 and 2, suggesting he is intentionally writing a continuation to the Deuteronomic history. Again, Marshall comments on these chapters: "It must be admitted that the style of the whole section is Lucan, and that he often adopts a Septuagintal style … There is a greater degree of Hebraic style in Luke 1-2 than elsewhere in his writings."[20] Beginning in Luke 3, the author works with Mark, tidying up his more rustic Greek and adding his own renderings of Q and other material he gleaned in his research. This fits with what is known of Luke as an educated doctor, likely raised in the traditions of Greek and Roman rhetoric.

Luke was perhaps a client of Theophilus

Luke wrote to a certain individual, Theophilus (Luke 1:3). His description of Theophilus as "most excellent" (*kratiste*) indicates he is an elite and likely a Roman official. The term *kratiste* is used by Josephus of his patron Epaphroditus (Josephus, *Ag. Ap.* 1.1), likely the same kind of arrangement. However, later in Acts, Luke uses it of the governors Felix and Festus, so it may simply refer to his status.[21]

Luke was possibly from Antioch

It has already been suggested that Luke was from Troas, where he links up with Paul for the first time. However, there is some evidence from the so-called anti-Marcionite Prologue of the later second century that he may have been from Syrian Antioch (c. AD 160–180). The Prologue also indicates he was eighty-four years old, confirms he was a doctor and was never married, that he wrote in Achaia, and died in Boeotia (Greece). The fourth-century historian Eusebius also wrote that Luke was "of Antiochian parentage," likely because of the Prologue (Eusebius, *Hist. eccl.* 3.4.6).

THE PROVENANCE OF LUKE'S GOSPEL

Where did Luke write from? The references to Luke's origins in Antioch make it possible that it originated from Antioch. The evidence of the

---

19. I. Howard Marshall, *The Gospel of Luke: A Commentary on the Greek Text*, NIGTC (Exeter: Paternoster, 1978), 39.
20. I. Howard Marshall, *Luke*, 46.
21. See Witherington, *Acts*, 13.

anti-Marcionite Prologue suggests he wrote from the "regions of Achaea" (southern Greece, where Corinth is found). Another possibility is that he wrote from Rome, as Luke is with Paul in Rome during the writing of Colossians, Philemon, and 2 Timothy. This fits with the end of Acts. However, if he wrote later, he may have left Rome after Peter and Paul died and written elsewhere.

THE DATE OF LUKE'S GOSPEL

The date of Luke is usually linked with the end of Acts, which ends with Paul in Roman prison at the beginning of the 60s AD. So, the earliest date for Luke and Acts is AD 62, allowing time for Paul to spend two years in Roman prison (AD 60–61). The latest possible date for Luke is AD 170, as it is cited by Irenaeus (*Haer.* 3.13.3; 3.15.1). Scholars usually settle on one or two dates: 1) The early to mid-60s AD; or 2) Between AD 75 and 90 with the 80s AD most popular.

AN EARLY DATE: THE MID-60S AD

A minority of scholars argue that Luke and Acts were written within a few years of the end of Acts, before the death of James (AD 62) and the Neronian persecution in AD 64–65.[22] The assumption is that the ending of Acts indicates the time proximate to the completion of the two-part work. Arguments used for the earlier date include:

The abrupt end of Acts

Acts ends abruptly when Paul is in Roman prison (Acts 28:31), about AD 62. It is argued that this indicates Luke has brought his account up to the time of writing (his present).

The absence of reference to key events from the 60s–70s AD

This argument builds on the previous one. If Luke wrote much later than AD 62, there are significant events he does not refer to. First, there is the stoning to death of James—the brother of Jesus—in AD 62, which is referred to by Josephus (Josephus, *Ant.* 20.200). James is a prominent person in the

---

22. E.g., Darrell L. Bock, *Luke: 1:1–9:50*, BECNT (Vol 1; Grand Rapids, MI: Baker Academic, 1994), 16–18.

second half of Acts (Acts 15:13-21; 21:18). Furthermore, Luke has been careful to record the deaths of Stephen (Acts 7:54-60) and James, the brother of John (Acts 12:1-2). It seems strange that Luke would write years later but exclude some reference to the death of such an important figure, James. Second, the Neronian persecution occurred around AD 64, and yet is not referenced in Acts. As with James's death, Luke is careful to chronicle important events such as the deaths of significant Christians. During the persecution, multitudes were killed by being thrown to the dogs wearing animal skins. Others were crucified, and others set alight in Nero's circus (Tacitus, *Ann.* 15.44). If he wrote later, why would he not mention this? Paul and Peter were put to death sometime after the Neronian persecution and before Nero's death in AD 68. It doesn't make sense that Luke would not mention these, particularly with Paul and Peter dominating large portions of Acts and Peter's prominence in Luke. Finally, there is the fall of Jerusalem in AD 70, which Jesus predicted in Luke 21:20.[23] It seems strange that such important events around Jerusalem and key figures critical to Luke's narratives are not included if Luke-Acts is to be dated later. Many would argue that this is decisive for dating Luke-Acts in the mid-60s AD.

The friendly picture of Rome

Luke-Acts is generally kind to Rome, blaming Jesus' death squarely on the Jews and emphasizing Jewish persecution through Acts. Examples of this friendly portrayal include the Roman centurion (Luke 7:1-10) and Pilate's extreme reluctance to crucify Jesus (Luke 23:13-25) and his readiness to release Jesus' body (23:52). In Acts, there is no reference to gentile negativity toward Christianity until Paul's missions. Even in Paul's mission, persecution is generally Jewish aside from Philippi, where Paul is flogged illegally, imprisoned, and asked to leave the town (Acts 16:19-40); Thessalonica—but those involved were rabble-rousers stirred up by the Jews (Acts 17:5-9); and Ephesus—but this was stirred up by local metalworkers who were losing money, and authorities were not interested (Acts 19:21-41).

---

23. Some also argue that the absence of mention of Paul's letters is a factor. However, his earlier letters written before the end of Acts are also not mentioned, so the argument is moot—Galatians, the Thessalonian and Corinthian correspondences, Romans, Ephesians, Colossians, and Philemon were all likely written before the end of Acts. Some would also add Philippians, although I would date it just after the conclusion of Acts.

In Corinth, Gallio refused to act against Paul (Acts 18:11-17). The Roman authorities also treated Paul kindly through his arrest and imprisonment in Acts 21-28, culminating with him in his own lodgings openly preaching and teaching the kingdom. For good reason, some scholars argue that this friendly picture of Rome fits better if the Neronian persecution had not yet occurred.

Theophilus

If Theophilus is an individual, as is likely, some speculate that he may be a significant Roman associated with Paul's trial. This could reflect a key purpose of Luke's writings: an apologetic defense of Christianity as it came under pressure from the Imperium. Evidence suggests that after Paul's "friendly" incarceration (Acts 28:30-31), his situation worsened. This is seen in Philippians 1, where Paul faces trial and the genuine possibility of death (Phil 1:19-26). Some from among the Praetorium and others connected to Paul's situation became aware of his being in Roman prison for Christ (Phil 1:12-14). One of these may be Theophilus. Luke may end his narrative here because this is the historical setting. Challenging this is the question of why Luke would write such a sustained narrative, including a life of Jesus, which also emphasized Peter. Luke states that Theophilus has been taught about Christ (Luke 1:3-4). Luke writes his Gospel to reinforce what he has learned through a comprehensive account of Christ's life from the beginning, explaining its origins, its spread, and how it arrived in Rome. Peter is the second dominant missionary of the first years of the faith, was also associated with Rome in the 60s AD (1 Peter), and he too would face trial and be killed by Nero. He is featured because of his prominence—because Theophilus knows of him, is involved in Rome, and perhaps too is facing impending trial. Anyone learning of Christianity at the time would hear of his remarkable transformation from a passionate young Jewish fisherman to the initial leader of the Christian movement.

A LATER DATE IN THE 70S–90S AD

A majority of Lukan scholars argue that the evidence for an earlier date is not conclusive. They believe that while Luke's narrative ends with Paul in Rome, it is written substantially later for these reasons:[24]

The details concerning the fall of Jerusalem in Luke

These details are explicit and may therefore indicate Luke's knowledge of Jerusalem's fall as a past event (see Luke 19:43-44;[25] 21:20-21, 24).[26] Others suggest, however, that the details are general and that it is inconsistent to consider some of the prophecies in Luke 21 to be after the event and others before the event.[27] Further, the details are simply the sorts of things that happen in a war and need not suggest post-event knowledge.

The date of Mark

A key argument is Markan priority. It is supposed that Luke's use of Mark suggests a post-60s AD date on the assumption that Mark was completed in the early to mid-60s AD, and that time was required for Luke to gain access to Mark and for it to have gained sufficient authority for Luke to use it. This supposedly pushes Luke's date into the mid-70s AD or beyond. However, this is not certain. First, some believe Mark was completed in the late 40s or mid-50s AD. Even if Mark is dated in the mid-60s AD, as is likely, if it was written from Rome as is supposed, the "we passages" in Acts 27 and three of Paul's letters place Luke in Rome at that time. Colossians 4

---

24. For example, Fitzmyer, *The Gospel According to Luke (i-ix)*, 53-57. Some even date it in the second century; however, its tone is different to the documents of *1 Clement* (AD 95) and the letters of Ignatius (AD 117).

25. "For the days will come upon you, when your enemies will set up a barricade around you and surround you and hem you in on every side and tear you down to the ground, you and your children within you. And they will not leave one stone upon another in you, because you did not know the time of your visitation."

26. "When you see Jerusalem being surrounded by armies, then you will know that its desolation is near. Then let those who are in Judea flee to the mountains, let those in the city get out, and let those in the country not enter the city ... They will fall by the sword and will be taken away as prisoners to all the nations. Jerusalem will be trampled on by the gentiles until the times of the gentiles are fulfilled" (NIV).

27. Bock, *Luke: 9:51-24:53*, 1675-78 argues that Luke, writing in the 60s, "sees the handwriting on the wall for Jerusalem, based on covenant unfaithfulness, just as Jesus did. As such, Luke makes his focus the approach of the fall, using Jesus' teaching as a base."

and Philemon 24 confirm that Luke and Mark were there simultaneously. As such, Luke would have been aware of Mark's Gospel and would know of its Petrine origin and authority. Consequently, no time lag is required for Luke to use Mark's Gospel; he may well have had a copy within days of its completion.

Common use of Q material with Matthew

Assuming the four-source hypothesis, some consider the common use of Q by Matthew and Luke indicative of a date similar to Matthew. This theory has many challenges. Even if true, a good case can be made for Matthew being produced earlier. Further, a common use of Q says nothing about its date. It merely says that both Matthew and Luke had access to it; this could have been decades apart. Then there is the question of whether Q exists. Alternatively, Luke may have used Matthew, or Matthew may have used Luke. This is, at best, one possibility among many.

The "many" writings of Luke 1:1

Perhaps the strongest argument for a later date is Luke 1:1, where Luke refers to "many" who had written about Jesus before him. This could include Mark, Q, and/or Matthew, and any other lost documents. If so, this may suggest a later date. However, Luke was written at least thirty years from the time of Christ's ministry, so there was time for "many" writings—some of which may be incorporated into the Gospels, or are now lost.

The rhetorical structure of Acts

While Luke ends his account with Paul in Rome in the early 60s AD, it doesn't necessarily follow that this indicates the likely date. Some argue that Luke finishes his account in Acts, not because he has brought the account up to date, but because his rhetorical purpose—implied in Acts 1:8—is complete. This purpose is that the witness empowered by the Spirit has been given in Jerusalem, Judea, and Samaria, and now has gone to Rome and so can go from the heart of the empire to the "end of the earth." Hence, its abrupt ending is rhetorical and not temporal. However, it is disputable that the "end of the earth" fits Rome. Rather, as Schnabel has argued, it would be more appropriate to speak of Spain to the west, Britain and Scandinavia to the north, Sierra Leone and Ethiopia to the south, and Seres (China) to the east.[28] As such, this argument lacks credence.

The picture of Paul

It is argued Paul is presented as a hero-figure, something that needed time to emerge. However, in 2 Peter 3:15–16, Peter states: "And count the patience of our Lord as salvation, just as our beloved brother Paul also wrote to you according to the wisdom given him, as he does in all his letters when he speaks in them of these matters. There are some things in them that are hard to understand, which the ignorant and unstable twist to their own destruction, *as they do the other Scriptures*" (ESV). While this indicates some anti-Paulinism, Peter speaks positively of Paul's letters, likening them to the Scriptures (LXX). If Petrine authorship is accepted, this must have been written some time before his death between AD 65 and 68. Further, Paul is clearly well known throughout the church by the 60s AD, as evidenced by his wide travel in Acts and letters. In addition, there is no need for anyone other than Luke to see Paul as a hero-figure for him to write positively of Paul. As his traveling companion, he had plenty of time to see Paul in a positive light. Scripture indicates the feeling was mutual (Col 4:14; Phlm 25).

The Catholic perspective of Acts

Another argument sees Acts as a conciliatory document resolving tensions in the early church concerning Paul and Peter. Based primarily on the clash between Paul and Peter at Antioch (Gal 2:11–14), many critical scholars hold that early Christianity was characterized by factions with different theologies based on these two great figures. Peter represented a Jewish perspective and Paul a law-free Hellenistic viewpoint. The Pastoral Epistles and Luke's writing represent an attempt to reconcile these two conflicting points of view. In Acts then, both Peter and Paul are represented as heroes. They come to an agreement in the Jerusalem Council (Acts 15). As such, Luke-Acts is late, intent on resolving issues in early Christianity.

This construct is flawed from start to finish. While Paul and Peter did clash in Syrian Antioch, this likely occurred in the late 40s AD. After this

---

28. See Eckhart J. Schnabel, *Early Christian Mission: Jesus and the* Twelve (Downers Grove, IL; Leicester, Eng.: IVP; Apollos, 2004), 444–99.

time, there is absolutely no evidence of ongoing issues. In 2 Peter 3, Peter speaks warmly of Paul's letters. Further, Luke's Paul is hardly perfect, clashing with Barnabas (Acts 15:36–40). This reading of early Christianity is an imposition of later denominational clashes in the European church with little support. This view has nothing to commend it.

CONCLUSION

While not conclusive, evidence is weighted toward an earlier date. In particular, Luke and Mark, both being in Rome in the early 60s AD, the ending of Acts, and exclusion of key moments in the 60s AD argue persuasively for it. The only argument of substance against an earlier date is the multiplicity of documents mentioned by Luke in his prologue. Either way, Luke is written in the period AD 62–95, and, aside from being a useful argument apologetically, it matters little when in that period it was written.

THE RECIPIENTS OF LUKE'S GOSPEL

Luke clearly states that his Gospel was written to a certain, "most excellent Theophilus" (Luke 1:3; Acts 1:1). On the surface, this refers to an individual. However, there are two main ways of reading these verses. Even if Theophilus is an individual, he likely represents a broader group as well.

TO ALL "MOST EXCELLENT LOVERS OF GOD"

The term "Theophilus" means "lover/friend (*philos*) of God (*theos*)." As such, it could be symbolic of all believers who are friends or lovers of God. Luke then is not writing to an individual, but to all people who are lovers or friends of God in Christ. If so *kratistos*, "most excellent," would be a designation of all believers as a statement of their elite status in Christ. Alternatively, it refers to God-fearers.[29] Taking it as a pseudonym makes good sense in a book that is strongly concerned for the poor and marginalized. However, the likelihood is lessened when in Acts 1:1 Luke reminds Theophilus of his earlier book, clearly referring to the Third Gospel. If the Gospel had been sent to a general set of recipients, it is unlikely that Luke would have been confident that they had read it. If an individual is in mind, this makes better sense. Further, as will be argued below, *kratistos* is used

---

29. John Nolland, *Luke 1:1–9:20*, WBC 35A (Dallas: Word, Incorporated, 2002), xxxiii.

of individuals later in Acts. Few contemporary scholars take Theophilus in a general sense.

THEOPHILUS, A PERSON

The most obvious way to understand it is that Luke was writing to a real person named Theophilus. The Greek name is found in Greek writings (e.g., Plutarch, *Alex.* 32.5; Plato, *Crat.* 394e; Josephus, *Ag. Ap.* 1.217; *Let. Aris.* 49). If so, he may have been Luke's patron, which meant he probably paid the costs of the publication of the work. "Most excellent" (*kratistos*) then indicates that Theophilus was a Greek man of Roman rank, as the adjective is used by Luke in Acts of high-ranking Roman officials (of Felix [Acts 24:3]; of Festus [Acts 26:25]). Scholars today find the weight of evidence supports his being a significant individual. Some scholars see a link to Paul's situation in Rome. It is unclear what his role is. He may be directly involved in Paul's situation, already a Christian, he may be facing doubts, he may be a God-worshiper exploring the faith, or he may be an interested seeker.

THEOPHILUS, A WIDER GROUP—ELITE ROMANS

If Theophilus was a person, this does not necessarily imply it was written *only* for one person. It is probable that he represents the group for which it was written. This wider group would include people of higher rank and status in the Greco-Roman world with an interest in the Christian movement. The content of Luke points in this direction. It has far greater concern for status and wealth issues than Mark's Gospel.

Some indicators that suggest gentile Christians are in view include:

1. **Theophilus:** Theophilus is a Greek name, and he is of some status, indicating Luke is directing his Gospel to Greeks and Romans.

2. **Gentile concern:** Luke has a great concern for gentiles and universal salvation through the Gospel and strongly in Acts (Luke 2:32; 7:1–10; Acts 1:8; 28:28–31).

3. **Style:** The preface is written in the Greco-Roman classical style (Luke 1:1–4). Luke uses the Greek Old Testament (the LXX) consistently throughout Luke-Acts.

4. **The absence of Aramaic:** The lack of Aramaic compared to Mark—for example, "Rabbi" (Mark 9:5) and "Abba" (Mark 14:36).

5. **Perspective on Romans:** The Romans are generally viewed positively through both books.

This means Luke should be read with the Greco-Roman world in mind (as opposed to Matthew, who has Jewish issues in mind). Thus, understanding issues such as the empire, wealth-status, honor-shame, meal protocols, patronage, polytheism, and patriarchy helps with interpretation.

THE COMPOSITION OF LUKE'S GOSPEL

As discussed, it is probable that Luke used Mark to put together his Gospel. One analysis argues that 88.4 percent of material from Mark is paralleled in Luke (cf. 97.2% of Mark's material in Matthew).[30] Another analysis suggests that 380 out of 661 of the verses in Mark appear in Luke.[31] However, Luke uses Mark differently than Matthew. Whereas Matthew uses Mark without too much adaptation, Luke is far more creative. Luke also used other material that is common to Matthew (Q) and unique material he gathered himself (L). He accessed his own material through meeting eyewitnesses when traveling with Paul (Acts 1:2) or on his own, especially in Jerusalem (Acts 22) and in Rome (Acts 28).

TRACKING THE KEY POINTS OF DIFFERENCE
IN LUKE'S ARRANGEMENT

Major Structural Differences

An analysis of Luke reveals some similarities and differences with the other Gospels:

1. **The infancy narrative is unique (Luke 1-2):** This is unique material that differs in detail if not in substance from Matthew.

---

30. See Stein, "Synoptic Problem," 787.
31. Bruce, "Gospels," 428.

2. **The ministry preparation phase (Luke 3-4):** The pre-ministry preparation—including John the Baptist, baptism, and temptation—uses the same content as Mark and Matthew except for Luke's unique genealogy (Luke 3:23-38, cf. Matt 1:1-17) and the Nazareth synagogue encounter, which varies considerably from Mark and Matthew (Luke 4:14-30, cf. Mark 6:1-6; Matt 13:53-58).

3. **Jesus' ministry in Galilee (Luke 3:1-9:50 and esp. 4:14-9:50):** This material follows Mark's Galilean ministry outline with some additional material in Luke 6 and 7, including the Sermon on the Plain, which has many similarities to Matthew's Sermon on the Mount (Luke 6:17-49, cf. Matt 5-7). He also adds a series of encounters.[32]

4. **The majority of the travel narrative (Luke 9:51-18:37):** This section forms a large portion of Luke's travel narrative (Luke 9:51-19:28) as Jesus resolutely turns toward Jerusalem and moves toward the city and his death. In this section, Luke is most creative, including teachings from Jesus' itinerant ministry, which is mainly non-Markan, so drawn from Q and L material.[33]

5. **The conclusion to the travel narrative, passion, and resurrection (Luke 18:15-24:53):** The final sections of Luke follow Mark's outline with more insertions of distinctly Lukan or Q texts than in 3:1-9:50.[34]

---

32. Luke 7 includes unique material inserted into the Markan material: The Resurrection of the Widow's Son (Luke 7:11-17); The Anointing by the Woman (Luke 7:36-50); and Q Material: The Healing of the Roman Centurion's Servant (Luke 7:1-10, cf. Matt 8:5-13); John the Baptist (Luke 7:18-35, cf. Matt 11:2-19).

33. Most of the section is L and Q. The only Markan material in these nine chapters is: The Beelzebub Controversy (Luke 11:14-26, cf. Mark 3:23-27); Be Ready for Service (Luke 12:35-48, cf. Mark 13:33-37); Parables of the Mustard Seed/Yeast (Luke 13:18-21, cf. Mark 4:30-32); and The Salt Parable (Luke 14:34-35, cf. Mark 9:49-50).

34. The unique material includes The Zacchaeus Encounter (Luke 19:1-10); The Sword Encounter (Luke 22:35-38); Jesus before Herod (Luke 23:8-12); Jesus' Journey to the Cross and the Thieves Narrative (Luke 23:26-43); Unique Resurrection Material Including the Emmaus Road (Luke 24:13-32); Appearance to Simon (Luke 24:34); The Ascension (Luke 24:50-53).

Summary of Detail

Luke's arrangement reveals much common material from Mark and especially Matthew (Q). He includes a unique genealogy that is difficult to reconcile with Matthew 1 (later).[35]

Interspersed throughout Luke, and especially in the travel narrative (Luke 7 and 9:51-18:27), is a large amount of unique L material, including parables, encounters, teachings, and healings such as: Jesus' rejection at Nazareth (Luke 4:14-30), the resurrection of the widow's son (Luke 7:11-17), the Samaritan rejection of Jesus (Luke 9:51-56), the parable of the good Samaritan (Luke 10:25-37), Mary and Martha (Luke 10:38-42), the rich fool (Luke 12:13-21), the parable of the barren fig tree (Luke 13:6-9), the healing of a woman in the synagogue on the Sabbath (Luke 13:10-17), further teaching on the cost of discipleship (Luke 14:24-30), the parable of the lost coin (Luke 15:8-10), the parable of the prodigal son (Luke 15:11-32), the rich man and Lazarus (Luke 16:19-31), the healing of the ten lepers (Luke 17:11-19), the parable of the persistent widow (Luke 18:1-8), the parable of the Pharisee and the tax collector (Luke 18:9-14), and the encounter with Zacchaeus (Luke 19:1-10).

Luke also leaves out a whole block of miracles from Mark 6:45-8:26 including Jesus walking on water (Mark 6:45-51; cf. Matt 14:22-32; John 6:16-21); the ritual purity clash (Mark 7:1-23; cf. Matt 15:1-20); the healing of the gentile woman (Mark 7:24-30, cf. Matt 15:21-28); the healing of the deaf and mute man (Mark 7:31-37); the feeding of the four thousand and dialogue (Mark 8:1-21; cf. Matt 15:32-16:12); and the healing of the blind man (Mark 8:22-26). This is labeled "Luke's Great Omission."[36] It is unclear why he omitted Jesus' walking on water and healings. However, he might have avoided the miracle of the feeding the four thousand (cf. "the 5000" in Luke 9:10-17), the blind healing (Luke 18:35-43), and the deaf healing (Luke 11:14) to avoid repetition—something he seems to do. The issue of

---

35. There are different ways of reconciling this: 1) Matthew gives Joseph's natural lineage; Luke gives Joseph's legal lineage (Julius Africanus, AD 170-245); 2) Matthew gives Joseph's legal lineage; Luke gives Joseph's natural lineage (several modern scholars); 3) Matthew gives Joseph's natural lineage; Luke gives Mary's natural lineage (Annius of Viterbo, AD 1490); 4) Matthew gives Mary's natural lineage; Luke gives Joseph's natural lineage (Tertullian, second century AD). See D. S. Huffman, "Genealogy," in *DJG* 258. The truth is that it is unclear.

36. R. T. France, *The Gospel of Mark: A Commentary on the Greek Text*, NIGTC (Grand Rapids, MI: Eerdmans; Carlisle: Paternoster Press, 2002), 269.

ritual versus inner purity is dealt with in a way that does not involve the Jewish law in Luke 6:43-45 (cf. Acts 10). He may have left out the healing of the Syrophoenician woman because of the cryptic and controversial use of the word "dogs." This may have been potentially offensive to his intended gentile readers.

Some of the material from the Sermon on the Mount (Matt 5–7) and the sending of the Twelve (Matt 10) is dispersed throughout Luke at different points. The material is also expressed slightly differently (e.g., compare the Lord's Prayer [Luke 11:1-4; Matt 6:9-13]).

Unlike Mark and Matthew, which record only the sending of the Twelve (Mark 6:6-13; Matt 10:5-15), Luke includes two sending narratives, one for the Twelve (Luke 9:1-6) and one for the seventy-two in Luke 10:1-24. Luke's perspective on mission encompasses a much broader group than the Twelve.

The account of the entry into Jerusalem is much the same, but Luke omits the cursing of the fig tree. The debates in the temple are almost directly in line with Mark and Matthew. The signs of the end of time cohere with Mark 13 and Matthew 24 in outline, but differ in detail. The passion account is similar in content, except in Luke Jesus is taken before Herod (Luke 23:8-12). The crucifixion is similar except one of the thieves does not mock Jesus but asks him to save him. The burial is the same except there is no guard as in Matthew. Luke's resurrection account is the most complete and includes some of the shorter longer ending of Mark, which may suggest that the longer ending of Mark drew on Luke. Luke alone includes an ascension narrative. The material in Luke 24 is reworked in Acts 1:1-11, giving an interesting insight into the way Luke uses his sources—in this case, his own material.

Additional Notes on Composition

There are two other aspects of the composition of Luke that should be mentioned at this point. These include:

1. Luke alters Mark, and probably Q, and improves their style and language. For example, he abbreviates the parable of the sower from 151 words (Mark) to ninety words.

2. Luke often removes references to Jesus' feelings. For example, compare Luke 18:22 with Mark 7:21.[37] His focus seems more on what Jesus did and said.

All in all, Luke takes Mark's account, tidies it, edits it, rearranges its order slightly, places before it a unique infancy narrative, and inserts into it much Q material and unique L material, especially in Luke 7 and in the travel narrative.

THE STRUCTURE OF LUKE'S GOSPEL

THE GEOGRAPHICAL STRUCTURE OF LUKE-ACTS

It is important to remember that Luke is effectively part one of a two-part work, Luke-Acts. As such, Luke must not be examined in isolation but considered within the context of both books as a structural unity.

In Acts, it is quite easy to discern a geographical structure based on Acts 1:8: "But you will receive power when the Holy Spirit comes on you, and you will be my witnesses in Jerusalem and in all Judea and Samaria, and to the end of the earth."

Acts then tracks the empowering work of the Spirit in the first believers who generate the geographical spread of the gospel. It radiates out from Jerusalem to the ends of the earth. This is seen in three reasonably clear, but overlapping mission phases:

1. Jerusalem (Acts 1–7)
2. All Judea and Samaria (Acts 8–12)
3. To the ends of the earth (Acts 13–28)

Craig Blomberg suggests that the reverse can be discerned in Luke:

1. The birth of Jesus in the context of Galilee *of the gentiles*, world history, and *Roman rule* (Luke 1:5; 2:1; 3:1). Jesus then ministers in Galilee *of the gentiles* (Luke 3:1–9:50).

2. Jesus in Samaria and Judea (Luke 9:52; 17:11; 18:35; 19:1, 11, 28).

---

37. However, there are exceptions, e.g., Luke 7:13.

3. Jesus in Jerusalem (Luke 24; Acts 1).

4. While the comparison between the first sections might be strained, there is definitely a move from Galilee through Samaria toward Jerusalem and an outward movement from Jerusalem to Samaria and then to the world in Acts.

ADDITIONAL KEY STRUCTURAL CLUES

There are several other key things to note to understand the structure of Luke.

The infancy narrative

After the prologue in 1:1-4, Luke 1-2 focuses on Jesus' origins with a definite parallel to the infancy of John the Baptist. Whereas Matthew focuses on Joseph, Mary is the key focus; she may be Luke's source for his material. There are distinct parallels with the beginnings of David with Elizabeth and John the Baptist's story paralleling Samuel. These include Elizabeth's barrenness (cf. Hannah). The Greek is like the LXX and Luke is intentionally continuing the Old Testament narrative—the long-awaited hopes are coming to pass. The stories of John and Jesus are parallel—but Jesus is greater. It places the Jesus story in world history. Many of the key themes of Luke are anticipated.

Jesus' baptism, the role of the Spirit, genealogy, and Jesus' temptation

In Luke 3-4, Luke tells the story of Jesus' baptism, his genealogy, and his temptation. Luke's version of the baptism highlights that Jesus was at prayer, introducing this important theme. Luke 3:16; 4:1, 14, and 18 all mention the role of the Spirit in Jesus' life. For Luke, the Spirit is the empowering force for mission—for Jesus, and for the disciples (Acts). Unlike Matthew's genealogy, which starts with Abraham and focuses on Israel, Luke's genealogy starts with Adam, bringing the whole world into the story, nicely balancing "the ends of the earth" (Acts 1:8). Luke's description of Jesus' temptation reveals that the real battle in Luke-Acts is not contending with "flesh and blood," but with the forces of evil (cf. Eph 6:12). The story that follows tells of how Jesus defeats Satan. The temptation order is different to that in Matthew. It ends in Jerusalem, which is the geographical hinge of Luke-Acts.[38]

The Nazareth synagogue encounter

In Luke 4:14-30, Jesus returns from defeating Satan in the wilderness and declares the basis of his ministry, that he will deliver the world from the power of Satan. He will do it in a totally unexpected way, not with the sword and political might, but through the power of the Spirit in love, mercy, suffering, and sacrifice. He declares he is God's anointed (Messiah) come in fulfillment to the prophets (Isa 61:1-2) bringing Jubilee to set the world free spiritually and materially (Luke 4:18-20). This mission statement launches Jesus' public ministry, and the narrative of Luke tells how it is played out. Later, in 19:10, Jesus gives another mission statement at the end of his public ministry. The two statements (Luke 4:18-20 and 19:10) function as bookends for his ministry (inclusio).[39] This reflects Luke's holistic approach to salvation as spiritual and material, especially releasing the poor from oppression.

The Sermon on the Plain

In Luke 6:20-49, Jesus teaches the disciples, giving them the ethical basis for the ministry of the kingdom. Luke's narrative gives illustrations of the ethics of the Sermon on the Plain as it does with those in the Nazareth manifesto (Luke 4:18-20).[40]

The turning point

In Luke 9:51, Jesus turns his face toward Jerusalem. This is seen by scholars as the turning point in Luke launching the travel narrative. The section until the entry into Jerusalem in Luke 19 shows Jesus determinedly "on the way" to the cross to die to release the world from oppression.

---

38. Luke places the temptation for the whole world before the Jerusalem temptation. In other words, Jesus will begin the deliverance of the whole world in Jerusalem (see Luke 4:5-13). Luke ends in Jerusalem; Acts flows out of Jerusalem.

39. An "inclusio" is a technical term for such a bookend, i.e., parallel statements at the beginning and end of a passage, which creates a kind of frame. Sometimes called bracketing. See DeMoss, *PDSNTG* 71.

40. See Christopher J. H. Wright, "Sabbatical Year," in *ABD*, 5: 861.

The travel narrative

From the turning point in Luke 9:51 Luke highlights the travel narrative (Luke 9:51-19:27) where Jesus is en route to his death. He is the Servant King showing "the way" of the Christian life. In Acts, faith is called "the Way" (e.g., Acts 9:2; 18:25; 19:23).

The lost parables

In Luke 15, Luke groups together three parables based on the notion "lost." The lost sheep and coin speak of Jesus seeking the lost people of the world. These parables are gender balanced—one for the men (shepherd), one for women (coin). This is another reflection of Luke's concern for the marginalized and his gender inclusiveness. The familiar story of the prodigal speaks of the love of the Father for lost humanity and the resistance of the older son.

The Son of Man came to seek and save the lost

Another critical mission statement that, with Luke 4:18-20, frames Jesus' public ministry is the summary of the Kingly Son of Man's mission to find the lost and bring salvation to them. This is found in Luke 19:10.

The death and resurrection of Jesus

Luke 4:22-24 is the highlight of the story, with Jesus dying and rising from the dead, the servant of God crucified, raised, and exalted to save God's world.

The mission commission, Spirit promise, and ascension

Luke 24:44-53 links Luke to Acts. Acts sees the Spirit come as promised, the Lukan Commission being fulfilled, and Jesus reigning as ascended King. The ascension is in a way the climax. Jesus' work is completed. He is commissioning his people, rising to sit at God's right hand, exalted as Lord. From there on his Father's behalf, he rules, by his Spirit sent to clothe and empower his people for life and mission. His exalted status fulfills Ps 110:1 and features in Acts (e.g., Acts 2:25, 33-34; 5:31; 7:55, 56) as does the name "Lord" for Jesus (105 times with most referring to Jesus).

THE TEXT OF LUKE

There were two main forms of Luke-Acts in the early church. The first is the so-called "Accepted Text," expressed in Sinaiticus (א), Vaticanus (B), upon which most versions of the New Testament are based. The second is the so-called "Western text." The Western text is found in old Latin manuscripts and Codex Bezae (D 05) including the Gospels and Acts, and secondarily, Codex Claromontanus (D 06), including Paul's letters. The text is characterized by "addition, omission, substitution, and 'improvement' of one kind or another."[41] In the Western text, the text of Acts is 10 percent longer than the Byzantine text, which is longer than the Accepted Text (and forms the basis of the KJV). The Accepted Text is preferred in most situations by most contemporary New Testament scholars. The Western text has some differences from the text favored by contemporary scholars for the New Testament.

Some of the different readings in the Western text are interesting. For example, it says the stone over Jesus' tomb was one "which twenty men could scarcely roll" (cf. Luke 23:53). It adds clauses to the Lord's Prayer so that it reads more like Matthew's version rather than the shorter version in the Accepted Text and most Bibles (Luke 11:2-4). It omits some sentences, including Jesus' words to Martha: "You are worried and upset about many things, but few things are needed—or indeed only one" (Luke 10:41-42 NIV). It adds that Paul ministered in the lecture hall in Tyrannus in Ephesus from 11:00 a.m.-4:00 p.m., or during the siesta (Acts 19:10). As noted above, it adds that Luke joined Paul and others on board a ship (Acts 20:13).

Most scholars believe the accepted text is to be trusted. However, every reading must be assessed according to its merit. In some cases, scholars refer to or adopt the Western text, believing that it may be authentic (e.g., Acts 19:10).

KEY EMPHASES IN LUKE'S ACCOUNT

Luke has the same essential emphases as do Mark and Matthew, including the centrality of the kingdom of God; Jesus as an amazing miracle worker,

---

41. Metzger and Ehrman, *The Text of the New Testament*, Kindle Edition, The Western Group of Texts.

preacher, ethical teacher, the Messiah who ministered and was crucified to save the world (the passion); and Jesus the resurrected Lord. Luke adds the ascension of Christ (Luke 24:51; Acts 1:9); this is important for his theology in Acts of Jesus as reigning Lord.

However, there are some distinctive features of Luke's approach that emphasize different dimensions of Jesus and the impact of his coming.

AN IMPLICITLY TRINITARIAN EMPHASIS: GOD'S
PLAN, JESUS MESSIAH, SPIRIT POWER

Although it is incorrect to say a particular New Testament writer is Trinitarian in the sense of the formulas developed at later church councils, as with Paul, undergirding Luke's account is an implicit Trinitarian construct. Luke emphasizes God's plan, providence, and purpose working itself out in human history. In Luke's Gospel, this is worked out particularly in and through Jesus—his Son, the Messiah and Lord. Conceived of the Spirit, as a human, he is empowered by the Spirit sent from on high to conduct his phenomenal ministry. In Acts, these same themes will continue with the emphasis shifting from Jesus' personal presence to the Spirit empowering God's people for life and mission.

God the Father and His Plan

The whole of Luke is based on God's plan of salvation. The story of Jesus' birth (infancy narrative) is written intentionally in line with the Greek Old Testament (LXX). This approach puts the God of Israel at the center of the story from the beginning. Although the focus is Jesus, God is the dominant figure in Luke with human events, including the work of Jesus, the fulfillment of God's providential plan.[42] This is seen in the fulfillment of angelic predictions (Luke 1:11-21, 26-38, 56-66; 2:1-7). Jesus' life is the fulfillment of God's promises to the people of Israel in the Old Testament, particularly the Greek LXX.[43] One example is John the Baptist, who comes as the expected forerunner to the Messiah (Luke 3:4-6; cf. Isa 40:3-5; 7:27;

---

42. Darrell L. Bock, "Gospel of Luke," in *DJG* 502.
43. Bock, "Luke," 502. He notes Luke's use of the suffering Son of Man texts, which are unique to him (e.g., Luke 9:22, 44; 17:25 [L]; 18:31-33 [L]; 22:22 [L]; 24:7 [L]).

Mal 3:1-2). Similarly, the resurrection and Jesus' whole life and ministry are foretold in the Scriptures (Luke 20:37-38; 24:25-27, 32, 44-45).

Throughout Luke, despite apperances that might suggest otherwise, God remains in control. For example, Luke 1:32 predicts that "the Lord God will give to him the throne of his father David." Mary's song celebrates the providence of God in history and particularly in Israel (Luke 1:46-55). John and Jesus proclaim the "word of God" (Luke 3:2; 5:1; 8:11, 21). Jesus is sent from God (Luke 10:16) and his ministry reveals the tremendous power and the authority of God in forgiveness (Luke 5:21; 7:48; 23:34), his correct interpretation of the law (Luke 6:1-3; 13:10-17), his power expressed in miracles, and his exclusive role in revealing the Father (Luke 10:22). On the Mount of Transfiguration, God summons humanity to listen to his chosen one (Luke 9:35). Jesus is intentionally and willingly subservient to God the Father, for example, "my Father's house" (Luke 2:41-49) and "Son of God" (Luke 4:3, 9; 22:70).

The repeated use in Luke-Acts of the Greek *dei*, meaning "it is necessary" (forty of 101 uses in the New Testament), often carries the sense of a "divine imperative" and points to the fulfillment of God's plan (e.g., Luke 4:43; 13:16). While Caesar and the Herodians appear in control, God rules his world and is working out his plan, and nothing can stop him (even if it is most unexpected).

The concept of God in control and his plan continues in Acts (see Acts 2:23; 4:27-28; 13:32-39; 24:14; 26:22-23).[44] In Luke, "today" (*sēmeron*) is the time of fulfillment. Yet there is more to come; the fulfillment is not complete.

Jesus the Messiah and Lord, and His Salvation

If God is the prime character *behind* the Gospel of Luke working mysteriously in history, Jesus is the primary character in the *foreground* of part one of Luke's work, the Gospel. In Acts, Father and Son govern in the same way through the Spirit. As such, Christology is central to Luke's purpose.

He uses a range of royal notions from Israel's heritage, stressing Jesus' kingship. These indicate that Jesus is the Messiah of Israel and Lord of the world; he is Lord over all, including Caesar (cf. Ps 110:1). He is Yahweh's

---

44. Bock, "Luke," 502.

son who is divine and who has come to take back his world from all spiritual and political powers.

For example, Luke takes over the notion of *Son of Man* from Mark (Luke 9:22), Q (Luke 6:22), and L (Luke 19:10), using it twenty-seven times. While the title is ambiguous, it is drawn from "one like a son of man" who has cosmic authority in Daniel 7:13-14 (see also 1 En 37-71). The Gospel is about Jesus as God's agent bringing his salvation. All key points of his life illustrate his identity as *Messiah*, the anointed King that Israel and the world have yearned for. He is born of a virgin by the Spirit amid an amazing array of spiritual events that involve colliding world powers (especially Rome [Luke 2:1; 3:1]), angels (e.g., Luke 2:9, 13-14), and Israel's faith.[45] He is *the Son of God* (Luke 1:32, 35; 3:22; 4:3, 9, 41; 8:28; 9:35; 22:69). He is a *prophet* in a similar sense to Moses (cf. Ps 2; Isa 42, see also Luke 11:29-32 where Jesus compares himself to Jonah), but his prophetic identity is fused with his messianic role and should probably be seen as subordinate to and a component of his messianic role.

Jesus' ministry begins with an intense but triumphant test and clash with Satan in the wilderness (Luke 4:1-13). This is the first battle, but the war continues through his whole ministry as he plunders Satan's realm through proclamation, love, touch, and mercy (Luke 11:14-27). Christians continue this work by the Spirit as they engage in mission (Luke 10:17). Using Isaiah 61:1-2 in the Nazareth synagogue, he declares himself to be God's anointed King who will usher in a new age of God's work among the needy. Sadly, this proclamation alienates the people of his hometown who reject him and seek to kill him (Luke 4:16-30). This anticipates his later rejection by Israel's leaders and his death. He is a teacher (Luke 4:31-32), exorcist (Luke 4:33-37; 7:21; 9:37-42), healer (Luke 4:38-40; 13:10-17; 17:11-17), raises the dead (Luke 7:11-17, 8:40-56), feeds the poor (Luke 9:10-17), performs miracles that defy nature and science (Luke 7:22-25), preaches the kingdom of God (Luke 4:43), and teaches in pithy memorable stories (e.g., Luke 8:1-15; 10:25-37; 12:13-21; 13:18-20; 15; 16:1-12, 19-31). These activities remain at the center of his ministry until his death. In so doing, he is performing the work of the ultimate Patron—this one born in utter humility

---

45. See the references to Zechariah's priesthood, his presence in the temple, Simeon, Anna, circumcision, dedication, and prophecy and fulfillment.

among shepherds, who would be killed at the hands of Jew and Roman alike, the Shepherd King of the world over Israel, Rome, and all the nations.

Jesus established a community around a mission team. He called others to join him (Luke 5:11, 27-32) and sent them as apostles, or "sent ones" (Luke 6:12-16). He called seventy-two and sent them to heal and preach in order to continue the restorative and salvific work of the kingdom. Counterculturally, he encouraged women to be his disciples (Luke 10:38-42). He called people to radical holistic discipleship (Luke 5:27; 6:17-49; 9:21-27; 9:57-62; 14:15-35; 19:11-27).

Luke's Jesus defied the expectations of Israel and the status structures of the Greco-Roman world, hanging out with sinners (Luke 5:30) and the marginalized (see below). He clashed with Israel's religious leaders over his involvement with sinners (e.g., Luke 7:36-50), his claims, and the excitement his ministry caused.

In contrast to the greed of the leaders of Israel and the Greco-Roman greed for status and rank, he taught a radical ethic of material generosity, renunciation of wealth, and humble generosity (Luke 6:20-26; 12:13-34; 18:18-30; 20:45-21:4). He taught a practical merciful love for all, including enemies, refusing to use military might and power (Luke 6:27-36; 10:25-37; 14:12-14; 15:19-31). He taught self-judgment and acceptance of others (Luke 6:37-42), humility (Luke 9:46-48; 18:9-14), prayer (Luke 11:1-13; 18:1-8), fear of God (Luke 12:4-6), servanthood (Luke 12:35-48), faithful monogamous heterosexual marriage (Luke 16:18), salvation (Luke 10:25-33; 13:22-30; 18:18-30), forgiveness (Luke 17:2-3), and faith (Luke 17:5-6). He encouraged lives focused not on Jewish law but on his own teaching, claiming an authority that was unacceptable to the Jewish religious authorities (Luke 6:43-49). He taught of a God who loved humanity with an inestimable concern (Luke 12:7).

He defied the expectations of those around him that he would restore the nation of Israel (Luke 24:21; Acts 1:6) and rather accepted the path of suffering and the cross, knowing he had to die to save the world (Luke 9:21-26; 18:31-33). He was frustrated at his rejection, especially by the people of Jerusalem (e.g., Luke 13:31-35).

He called his followers to mission. He spoke of the culmination of the kingdom at the time of his return (Luke 17:20-37), predicting a range of signs with application both to the fall of Jerusalem and to his future return (Luke 21).

The culmination of his ministry came as he determined to go to Jerusalem (Luke 9:51) to face debate with the leaders of Israel and death. Nothing would stop his resolve to go and face the religious and political powers of Judaism and Rome. One of his own, Judas, betrayed him to the Jewish authorities (Luke 22:1-5) and he went to the cross. He rose from the dead, appeared on a number of occasions, and commissioned the disciples to testify to the entire world (Luke 24:1-49). Finally, Luke records Jesus' ascension (Luke 24:50-53).

The Spirit's Power

The final piece of the implicit Trinitarian structure of Luke is the role of the Spirit. Luke places more emphasis on the work of the Spirit (*pneuma*) than the other two Synoptic writers. Of the Gospel writers, only John has a similar emphasis. However, in Luke's writings, the emphasis on the Spirit is strongest in Acts. Yet, the Spirit is also mentioned more in the Gospel than in Mark and Matthew.[46] Luke especially stresses the Spirit's role in mission, first in Jesus (esp. Luke 4:14) and then in the life of the believers in Acts (Acts 1:8). The Spirit is God's empowering presence in the life and ministry of Christ in Luke.

His pneumatology[47] is introduced in the infancy narrative, where Jesus' coming sparks amazing spiritual activity—God is breaking in.[48] For example, the Spirit is on John the Baptist even from birth (Luke 1:15), after Elizabeth's miraculous conception and John's jumping in the womb of Spirit-filled Elizabeth as she met the also-pregnant Mary (Luke 1:21, 44). Jesus is also conceived by the Spirit, a truly miraculous conception

---

46. There are several examples of the word *pneuma* being used of the human spirit, i.e., the inner being (e.g., Luke 1:17, 47, 80), and a few other references to *pneuma* are to evil spirits (e.g., Luke 4:33, 36). The spirit and power of Elijah are also understandable in terms of the Holy Spirit, who empowered his ministry (Luke 1:17).

47. Pneumatology, from the Greek *pneuma*, "spirit," is an aspect of theology that focuses on the Spirit. Grenz et al., *PDTT*, 92, states, "Pneumatology explores the person and work of the Spirit, especially the Spirit's involvement in human salvation."

48. An interesting feature of Luke's pneumatology is the intensified activity of the Spirit at key points of inbreaking—Jesus' birth, his ministry launch (Luke 4), Pentecost (Acts 2), Samaria (Acts 8), Paul (Acts 9), Cornelius and gentile conversion (Acts 10), and Ephesus (Asia Minor).

(Luke 1:35). John's parents are filled with the Spirit (Luke 1:41, 67), Zechariah prophesying under the Spirit's power concerning the ministry of his son (Luke 1:67-78). The Spirit also directs and impels Simeon to the temple to prophesy over Jesus (Luke 2:25-27). These moments in the infancy narrative anticipate the Spirit anointing Jesus at his baptism and coming upon *all* believers in Acts.

Jesus' work is a ministry of the Spirit in different ways. Jesus is described by John the Baptist as the one who would baptize with the Spirit and fire (Luke 3:16), anticipating Pentecost and the five initial comings of the Spirit on the infant church, groups, and individuals in Acts (Acts 2:1-4; 8:17; 9:17; 10:44-48; 19:6).[49] At his baptism, Jesus is filled with the Spirit, who descends upon him from heaven (Luke 3:22), empowering him for ministry. The first work of the Spirit is somewhat surprising. The Spirit leads the freshly anointed Servant King into the desert, where he fasts for forty days and is challenged by Satan, triumphing over Satan's temptations (Luke 4:1). This indicates that the overall purpose of God is for Jesus to defeat Satan through the power of the Spirit (cf. Acts 10:38). Under the direction of the Spirit, Jesus returns to Galilee, empowered (Luke 4:14), and he begins to teach and minister in the synagogues (Luke 4:15-16). Although Luke only mentions the direct role of the Spirit sparingly from this point on in Jesus' ministry, this verse indicates that everything Jesus does from this point on is empowered by the Spirit. This includes Jesus' application of Isaiah 61:1-2 to his ministry, when he says, "The Spirit of the Lord is upon me" (Luke 4:18), that is, the anointing of the Spirit is bringing forth his ministry as Servant King of preaching to the poor, setting the prisoners free, healing the blind, and proclaiming the freedom of Jubilee.

Luke records Jesus is "full of joy through the Holy Spirit" (Luke 10:21) at the return of the seventy-two from their mission and their account of their ministry. He teaches that the Spirit will give the disciples all they will need (Luke 12:12), that God will give the Spirit to those who ask him (Luke 11:13), and that the disciples will be "clothed with power from on high" (Luke 24:49).

---

49. There are also other instances such as Acts 4:31 where the Spirit comes afresh on people, filling them again and empowering them for further service (cf. Acts 4:8; 13:52).

This emphasis on the Spirit flows over into Acts, growing out of the Pentecost event; the Spirit is the power source for the apostolic community (see later Acts).

JESUS IN HISTORY

Luke writes a *bios* (biography) of Jesus as a historian in the Greco-Roman tradition (compare the prologue of Josephus' historical work, *Against Apion* 1.1–5 with Luke 1:1–4). He writes a particular type of history, which blends Greco-Roman historical style with Old Testament historical narrative style. The prologue (Luke 1:1–4) reflects this blend where, like other contemporary historians, he recalls previous attempts from "the first eyewitnesses and servants of the word" (NIV) to write an account of Christ. He speaks of his own "careful investigation" of "everything from the beginning" and of writing an "orderly account" to give certainty to his readers. Hence, his purpose is historical and theological. Luke wants his readers to place Jesus in the sweep of history, including that of Israel—but more importantly for Luke, of the world, beginning with the Greco-Roman world.

SALVATION HISTORY

Luke is described by many (esp. Conzelmann) as the theologian of *Heilsgeschichte* (salvation history), in that he links the story of Jesus and salvation with events in world history, and not just Israel's story. Luke's core theme for many scholars is salvation. This salvation includes all people who will yield to Jesus, especially the lost and marginalized, and includes the transformation of the present material state of people, the ultimate gift of eternal life, and the restoration of the cosmos.

This emphasis on salvation is seen before Jesus begins his ministry, from the mouths of Zechariah, Simeon, Mary, angels, and Isaiah (see Luke 1:46–47, 67–71, 77; 2:10, 25–30; 3:6). It is found in Jesus' teaching (Luke 8:12; 9:24; 13:23; 18:26) and in his encounter with Zacchaeus (Luke 19:8–10). This salvation is universal and not limited to Israel. So, for example, Luke includes, "and *all people* will see God's salvation" (Luke 3:6 NIV) in his recollection of Isaiah 40:3–5. His genealogy ends at Adam, not Abraham, indicating that salvation is for all (Luke 3:38, cf. Matt 1:2). He has a great interest in Samaritans (Luke 9:51–55; 10:30–37; 17:16, cf. Acts 8) and others outside of Israel (Luke 4:25–27). The story of Acts is a narration of the spread of this salvation through Samaria to "the end of the earth" (Acts 1:8). Another point of interest is the way in which Jesus' public ministry in Luke is flanked by two mission statements: Luke 4:18-20 and Luke 19:10 (the "Son of Man came to seek and save the lost"). Luke wants his readers to recognize that Jesus is the only means of salvation for all people and wants them to turn to him and be saved.

MISSION

The concepts of salvation and the Spirit are connected intimately to mission and conversion. Luke's account in both Luke and Acts is the story of God's mission to save humanity through his Son and Spirit. In the Gospel, Jesus is the primary figure, empowered by the Spirit to save humanity. Acts continues this account with Jesus reigning on high as Lord, and ministering through his Spirit. The Spirit becomes the central figure empowering key individuals to lead the mission to fulfill the task that Jesus made possible and began. In the Gospels, only Matthew rivals Luke in his mission emphasis, but in a different way,[50] and without the story of what happens next: Acts. In Luke, the elevation of mission is seen in a range of ways including:

1. The importance of salvation—in particular, Jesus' mission statements, which pepper the Gospel, especially Luke 4:18-19; 5:30-32; 19:10, and the summary in Acts 10:38.[51]

2. Throughout Luke, Jesus states his purpose in missiological terms. At Nazareth (Luke 4:18-19) he defines his ministry in terms of Isaiah 61:1-2: "The Spirit of the LORD GOD is upon me, because the LORD has anointed me to bring good news to the poor; he has sent me to bind up the brokenhearted, to proclaim liberty to the captives, and the opening of the prison to those who are bound, to proclaim the year of the LORD's favor." Only Luke records this event. This highlights a number of aspects of Jesus' mission:

---

50. Through the Great Commission, which climaxes the gospel and points the Jewish readers to the wider meaning of Jesus' mission: to make disciples of all nations. This has been anticipated at various points (Matt 5:13, 16; 9:36-10; 24:14).

51. Bock, "Luke," 502.

a. The fulfillment of the Old Testament hope of God's deliverance (cf. Isa 1:1-2, cf. Luke 4:21, "Today this scripture is fulfilled in your hearing" NIV).
b. The role of the Spirit in empowering ("is on me" ... "anointed me") this mission.
c. The Christocentric nature of the mission ("anointed *me*").
d. The nature of the mission as a message preached (note the three-fold use of verbs of proclamation: *euangelizomai* and *kērrusō* (twice). However, what follows is not merely verbal, but everything Jesus is, does, and says is proclamation. Little wonder John called Jesus the Word of God (*logos*) in John 1:1.
e. The wider nature of the mission includes salvation ("freedom for the prisoners"), healing ("recovery of sight"), and social, material, physical, and spiritual deliverance (release the oppressed). Each clause can be interpreted either as present deliverance from suffering, or future eschatological deliverance. People don't need to choose, for both are in Luke's mind. Jesus is changing the present. He will return, and everything will be transformed; all will know *shalom*.
f. The mission includes the marginalized and oppressed of society.
g. The eschatological dimension of mission, the "year of the LORD's favor" brings fulfillment of the Old Testament hope, especially the "year of Jubilee."

In this regard, the unique account of Zacchaeus' transformation climaxes with Jesus' summary statement of intent: "the Son of Man came to seek and save the lost" (Luke 19:10).

THE MARGINALIZED AND OPPRESSED

As noted above, Jesus' ministry of release involved spiritual salvation through faith and salvation in holistic terms, that is, spiritual salvation from sin and its consequences, and salvation from material and physical oppression and from marginalization from society. Jesus came to release the marginalized and oppressed and bring their Jubilee (Lev 25:8-55).

He came to restore people to relationship with God, to restore their human relationships, and to restore society itself. The vision is of a new world with God and all humanity united in love. Luke promotes an eschatological reversal and radical egalitarianism, which clashes with the Greco-Roman world of status and rank. Specific groups feature in the narrative, illustrating the egalitarian nature of the kingdom:

Samaritans and gentiles

Only Luke records the parable of the good Samaritan (Luke 10:25-37) and the story of the ten healed lepers with one grateful recipient being a Samaritan (Luke 17:11-19). Jesus refuses John and James's request to smite the Samaritan town, despite its people utterly rejecting and shaming him (Luke 9:51-55). Their time will come, but destruction won't be now. First, there will be the offer of salvation through the ministry of Philip (Acts 8:5-25). Jesus also foreshadows gentile mission in the healing of the servant of the commended Roman centurion (Luke 7:1-10) and the details of the parable of the banquet, which includes people from all contexts (Luke 14:23). In Luke-Acts, Samaritan and gentile mission are dominant themes, especially in Acts 9, 10-11, and the mission of Paul.

Women

Rabbinical teaching forbade the teaching of women, yet Luke's Jesus teaches women and encourages them to learn at his feet (Luke 10:38-42). Luke mentions women leaving their lives, traveling with Jesus, and supporting him (Luke 8:2-3, cf. Mark 15:41). There are also other women featured, including the widow of Nain (Luke 7:11-15), the disabled woman in the synagogue (Luke 13:11), and the "sinner" who anointed Jesus' feet (Luke 7:36-50). The women in the birth narrative—Elizabeth, Mary, and Anna—are affirmed as positive role models (Luke 1-2). The paired parables of the mustard seed and the leaven (Luke 13:18-21) and lost sheep and the lost coin (Luke 15:3-10) neatly balance the traditional roles of men and women. Incredibly, though some of these women are "sinners" in the eyes of the people, Jesus accepts them, forgives them, heals them, and delivers them (Luke 7:36-50; 8:2; 13:10-17). Ultimately, it will be women who first deliver the good news of the resurrection (Luke 24:10). Priscilla will be an important teaching disciple in Acts (Acts 18:26), and Lydia will be the first convert, hostess, and likely the first leader[52] of the Philippian church (Acts 16:11-15).

Children

Luke continues Mark's emphasis on children, but builds on it. This is seen in his references to "the only son" or "the only daughter" in some stories (Luke 7:12; 8:42; 9:38). Jesus also puts "a little child" by his side to rebuke his disciples (Luke 9:47) and encourages that children be "welcomed" (Luke 18:15-17). He also uses children in his stories and teaching, stressing their importance (Luke 10:21; 17:2; 18:16).

The poor

Luke's interest in the poor is seen throughout and is one of the dominant features of the Gospel; indeed, it is fair to call Luke the evangelist for the poor. As such, Luke profoundly challenges the rich and those in nations that have a disproportionate amount of the world's resources. This emphasis is seen in Jesus' own childhood when Joseph and Mary opt for the "poor" sacrifice at the temple (Luke 2:24, cf. Lev 12:8), indicating Jesus' family was not wealthy. Jesus' ministry is from the bottom up; he works among the powerless. Luke's Jesus preaches "good news to the poor" (Luke 4:18, cf. Luke 7:22), indicating that the era of God's *shalom* for the poor has come. He states, "Blessed are you who are poor ... are hungry" (Luke 6:20-21). Now that he has come, through his ministry and that of his followers, the poor across God's world will be transformed, and eschatologically, all poverty will end. Conversely, Jesus strongly warns against riches in Luke's Gospel. The rich, while apparently blessed (at least in popular theology), are also oppressed and must be set free from their bondage to greed and mammon through their salvation reflected in their radical generosity to the poor and needy (e.g., Zacchaeus, Luke 19:1-10; Barnabas, Acts 4:36-37).

---

52. Although this is to some extent supposition, it may be inferred Lydia led the church, at least initially. She is the only convert from the group by the river, and likely as a "worshiper of God" (a gentile attracted to Judaism, but not fully converted), the only one with a knowledge of the Scriptures. It is likely she gave leadership to the church, although this cannot be proven. Later Euodia and Syntyche are key leaders in Philippi of enough importance to feature in the letter (Phil 4:2-3).

Luke includes woes to the rich and well fed (Luke 6:24), and has unique parables (L) warning the wealthy, including the rich fool (Luke 12:16-21), the rich man, and Lazarus (Luke 16:19-31). He includes accounts of good and bad examples in the handling of money, including Zacchaeus (Luke 19:1-10), the poor widow (Luke 21:1-4), and the rich ruler (Luke 18:18-27). In Luke, Jesus balances examples of good role models where wealth is concerned (e.g., Zacchaeus, the widow, the disciples), and the not-so-good (e.g., the rich ruler). In the coming of the kingdom, there is thus an economic eschatological reversal. Great reward is promised to those faithful to Jesus in the consummation of the kingdom—to those who heed the call of the kingdom to be generous to the poor in the present.

The disreputable

Luke includes accounts of those who were not so respectable in society, including the shepherds who are the first recipients of the message (Luke 2:8-10), the tax collectors and "sinners" whom Jesus ate with (Luke 5:30; 7:34), the sinful woman who anointed Jesus' feet (Luke 7:37-50), the parable of the Pharisee and the tax collector (Luke 18:9-14), and the conversion of Zacchaeus (Luke 19:1-10). There are also mentions in Jesus' parables of the unrighteous, including the Pharisee and the tax collector (Luke 18:11, cf. Matt 5:45; Luke 16:10-11).

Luke wants his readers to turn from the love of wealth, rank, and status, to live always with an eye to the needs of others and respond with lavish generosity. They are not to do so according to the rules of Greco-Roman patronage—for public acclaim and expecting reciprocity. God will reciprocate and more. Yet, this reward from God is not to be their motivation—out of gratitude to God and his Son they are to emulate Jesus, moved with compassion, and let God respond as he wills. He wants believers to be radically inclusive of others, leaving aside any notions of status and rank. The marginalized are to be an equally important part of the community. These are the lost people of Luke 15 and 19:10 and Jesus is seeking them out. So, also, must God's people in their given locations.

PRAYER

Mark clearly sees prayer as important,[53] and Matthew even more so.[54] However, it is Luke who emphasizes prayer more than the other Synoptic writers including references to Jesus' praying in Mark, such as the Gethsemane prayer (Luke 22:39-46, cf. Mark 14:32-42). Like Matthew, who has the longer version, Luke includes a shorter version of the Lord's Prayer but includes other teaching on prayer at different points.

First, there are examples of prayer warriors among the New Testament saints who anticipate the coming of Christ, such as Zechariah, Elizabeth, Simeon, and Anna. Second, seven times Luke adds a Markan account that Jesus was praying at the time of an event including his baptism (Luke 3:21, cf. Mark 1:9-11), the healing of the leper (Luke 5:12-16, cf. Mark 1:40-44), praying all night at the selection of the Twelve (Luke 6:12, cf. Mark 3:16-19), the confession of Jesus' disciples (Luke 9:18-20, cf. Mark 8:27-29), the transfiguration (Luke 9:28-29, cf. Mark 9:2-8), the teaching of the Lord's Prayer (Luke 11:1-4, cf. Matt 6:9-13), and over Peter's denial (Luke 22:32, cf. Mark 14:26-31). He has Jesus praying nine times overall. Significant in these references is Luke 5:16: "But he [Jesus] would withdraw to desolate places and pray"—such prayer was his customary practice.

Third, there is other material on prayer throughout the Gospel. This includes direct teaching on prayer in response to requests (Luke 11:1-13), and several parables about prayer urging perseverance and humble penitence (Luke 11:6-13; 18:1-8, 10-13). Considering the many references to prayer in Acts, it is clear Luke wants to emphasize the importance of prayer for effective Christian living and mission. In Acts, the community is always prayerful, and praying is directly linked to the power of the Spirit seen in their mission (cf. Acts 1:14; 2:1-4; 4:29-5:16;[55] 10:3-23).

---

53. Mark includes: Jesus praying (Mark 6:46), the power of prayer over demons and difficult situations, with faith (Mark 9:29; 11:24-25), the temple as a gentile house of prayer (Mark 11:17), Jesus repudiating hypocritical prayer (Mark 12:40), and the importance of praying in a crisis (Mark 13:18; 14:32, 38).

54. Matthew includes: praying for enemies (Matt 5:44); repudiates hypocritical long-winded prayers, preferring private short prayers (Matt 6:5-7); records the Lord's Prayer (Matt 6:9); urges prayer for mission workers (Matt 9:38); records Jesus' praying (Matt 14:23) including for children (Matt 19:13); the temple as a house of prayer (Matt 21:13); the power of prayer with faith (Matt 21:22); praying in a crisis (Matt 24:20; 26:36, 41).

55. The amazing events of this section flow from the courageous prayer of the disciples, including the radical generosity of the believers, the spread of the gospel, and miracles. The

RADICAL DISCIPLESHIP

Compared to Mark, Matthew has a heightened sense of discipleship with the inclusion of the "follow me" accounts (Matt 8:18–22). Luke also emphasizes discipleship, presenting a challenging view of kingdom life for the disciple. Luke includes the same two "call encounters," adding a third (Luke 9:57–62). One of the themes of the parable of the banquet is not placing one's property and interests over the invitation to the eschatological feast (Luke 14:18–20)—nothing is as important as accepting the invitation. The parable is followed by a discourse appealing for wholehearted commitment in Luke 14:25-33. Here Jesus makes some strong statements including:

1. "If anyone comes to me and does not hate father and mother, wife and children, brothers and sisters—yes, even their own life—such a person *cannot* be my disciple" (v. 26 NIV, emphasis added), clearly hyperbole to make the point that being Jesus' disciple is first priority.

2. "So then, none of you can be My disciple who does not give up all his own possessions" (v. 33 NASB).

3. Like Matthew, Luke has two references to the notion of taking up the cross, emphasizing the importance of suffering and possibly dying for Christ for those who accept his call to follow (Luke 9:23; 14:26, cf. Matt 10:38; 16:24).

Considering Luke's emphasis on the marginalized and his call for radical generosity, his Gospel reflects a sense of a strong call to discipleship in his understanding of Jesus.

ISRAEL'S REJECTION OF JESUS

Throughout his narrative, Luke makes evident the rejection of Jesus by Israel. Some level the accusation of anti-Semitism at Luke for this. However, this cannot be sustained, as throughout Luke and Acts, the key figures of the faith are mostly Jews. Luke's criticism is not of Jews per se, but of Judaism as it existed at the time and those Jews who rejected Christ and persecuted him and his movement. Like all the Gospel writers, he targets

---

deaths of Ananias and Sapphira are also "miraculous," though in a different sense.

most of the Jewish leadership. Particularly in Acts, there are shades of Romans 9-11 where Paul proposes that the rejection of the gospel by the Jews led to the spread of the gospel around the world.

Examples of Jesus' challenging the Jewish leaders pepper Luke's Gospel. The declaration of Luke 4:16-20 leads to Jesus' rejection at Nazareth, especially because Jesus refers positively to gentiles, while criticizing Israel's rejection of the prophets (Luke 4:20-30). The Markan Sabbath controversy is retained (Luke 6:1-11, cf. Mark 2:23-3:6). Luke records three meal encounters in which Jesus powerfully challenges the exclusivism and hypocrisy of the Jewish authorities (Luke 7:36-50; 14:1-24), including his powerful invective against the Pharisees and lawyers (Luke 11:37-54, cf. Matt 23). These can seem particularly harsh as Jesus is a guest of the Jewish leader and yet challenges them powerfully. Parables such as the prodigal point to Israel's rejection of the gospel; Israel as the older son fails to welcome the lost son (Luke 15:11-32). Similarly, the rich man and Lazarus highlights the rich man's failure to understand Scripture, which leads to an inability to understand a resurrected messenger (Luke 16:19-31). The destruction of Jerusalem is more directly accounted for than in Mark (Luke 21:24), and in the passion, the prime movers are Jews; the Romans are merely involved out of political expediency. In Acts, this rejection continues as the church spreads (Acts 4-5; 7:1-8:4).

HOSPITALITY AND TABLE FELLOWSHIP ENCOUNTERS

One of the features of Luke is his emphasis on table fellowship in the stories Jesus told. In the ANE, meals were critical points of welcome into a home, symbolizing oneness. These emphasize community and the welcome of God and Jesus to all, including the marginalized. Luke features Jesus eating with sinners and tax collectors, who were viewed negatively. In Jewish Pharisaic protocol, it was strictly forbidden for a holy man to participate in table fellowship with sinners.[56] In Luke 5:29, Jesus is eating with tax collectors and "sinners." This leads the Pharisees and the teachers of the law to strongly condemn him (Luke 5:30). In Luke 7:33-35, Jesus

---

56. Nolland, *Luke 1:1–9:20*, 246, goes further: "Pharisaism had strong separatist tendencies, and because of the prominence in Pharisaic piety of food and ritual cleanliness rules, Pharisees *would only accept hospitality from one another*" (emphasis mine).

is scornful of their inconsistency in criticizing John the Baptist for fasting and refusing alcohol and censuring Jesus for enjoying food and wine. For Jesus, this demonstrated their hypocrisy. He appeals to his and John's fruit as evidence of their godliness: "Yet wisdom is justified by all her children" (v. 35).

Jesus' repudiation of the Pharisaic refusal to enjoy fellowship with sinners is brought home when he allows a sinful woman (probably a prostitute [not Mary Magdalene]) to anoint him with perfume and tears. In response, the Pharisees condemn him (Luke 7:36–50), yet Jesus dares to forgive her.

Equally scandalous is Jesus' behavior at a Pharisee's home in Luke 14 where Jesus challenges the host's concern for status and urges him to invite the marginalized and gentiles. The parable of the great banquet speaks of God's open invitation to humanity to his meal, an invitation that is sadly rejected by many with concern for possessions and life. Through Jesus and his emissaries, all people from every nation, no matter how broken, are invited. The parable of the rich man and Lazarus also revolves around the failure of the rich man to accept the beggar Lazarus into table fellowship (Luke 16:19–31).

Table fellowship is a symbol of God welcoming everyone to the feast of salvation. It symbolizes celebration, Jubilee, and unity. It speaks of the acceptance of the marginalized into the eschatological community. It anticipates the eschatological banquet (cf. Isa 25:6–8). God's table is to be open to all. The Pharisaic rejection of the marginalized and any notion of status in table seating is anathema to the principles of the kingdom.

WORSHIP

Another standout theme in Luke-Acts is worship. Worship is a full response to God including love for God (vertical dimension) and for others (horizontal dimension). Luke strongly emphasizes the communal dimensions of worship. For example, Jesus calls his followers to serve each other (cf. Luke 12:35–48) and all people, even enemies and the utterly marginalized.

Luke emphasizes worship in the vertical sense—worship and adoration of God. This theme begins in the infancy narrative with the righteous Jews faithful to the worship of Israel. This includes the priest Zechariah who faithfully fulfills his call as a priest of the line of Abijah (Luke 1:5, 8–10, 23) and his wife Elizabeth, also a descendant of the priestly line of Aaron

(Luke 1:5). They are both upright in the sight of God (Luke 1:6). It is in the context of gathered worship that the angel appears to Zechariah (Luke 1:10). There are references to glorious praise in the songs of Mary (Luke 1:46-56 [*Magnificat*]), Zechariah (Luke 1:67-79 [*Benedictus*]) and Simeon (Luke 2:29-32 [*Nunc Dimittis*]). Each gives glory to God for his work in history and for bringing Jesus to save his people. These likely formed important songs that were sung in the early church. There is praise at John the Baptist's birth (Luke 1:58, 64, 66), at Jesus' birth from angels and shepherds (Luke 2:14, 20), and from Simeon and Anna (Luke 2:25-27, 38).

The theme of worship runs through Jesus' ministry. Jesus appeals for worship that embraces mercy to others in need (see esp. Luke 6:17-36; 10:30-37; 11:41). Honoring God in song and prayer is good, but on its own, not enough; it must be accompanied by mercy and justice. Jesus himself participated in Jewish worship (Luke 4:14, 16, 31, 44; 13:10). He is passionate about prayer (Luke 6:12; 9:18), teaching more about prayer in Luke than in the other Gospels. Luke records that Jesus cleared the temple because the commerce being carried out within its courts was a violation of the invitation to the gentiles to pray and worship—the temple was to be a house of prayer (Luke 19:45; cf. Isa 56:7). Jesus is Peter's object of worship (Luke 5:8), and the woman's anointing of Jesus is a radical act of emotional, expensive worship that Jesus accepts (Luke 7:36-38, 44-48).

Jesus' ministry regularly leads to the praise of the Father, rather than of Jesus himself. So, after forgiving and healing the paralytic, the healed man returns home praising God (Luke 5:25; cf. 7:16; 9:43; 18:43).

The entry to Jerusalem is a time of praise as the disciples herald Jesus as King and throw their cloaks on the road as they joyfully praise God in loud voices, singing from Psalm 118:26 (Luke 19:28-39). Jesus' response to the criticism of this praise is that even the rocks will cry out in praise if the disciples do not (Luke 19:40)—creation declares praise to God and his Son. The parable of the minas demonstrates true worship; the believer directs all work for the kingdom (Luke 19:11-27). The disciples are to set aside competitiveness and a desire for greatness and adopt a servant-leadership pose rather than the elitism and power games of the world of politics (Luke 22:24-30). Luke pictures worship extending to the whole world. While many in Israel will be rejected because their worship is false ("away from me, you evildoers"), people from the wider world will come to the feast (Luke 13:22–30, cf. 14:12–24). The passion-resurrection narrative includes the worship of the Roman centurion (Luke 23:47), anticipating mission to Rome. The Gospel ends in worship filled with joy (Luke 24:52) as, "they stayed continually at the temple, praising God" (Luke 24:53 NIV). The emphasis on worship flows into Acts. Luke mentions joy more than any other New Testament book (Luke 1:14, 44, 47; 2:20; 7:16; 10:21; 13:13, see also Luke 6:21; 15:6–7, 9–10, 23, 32; 19:6).[57] Worship is the correct response to God in both a vertical and horizontal sense; both are indispensable, and they are inextricably linked.

QUESTIONS TO CONSIDER

- What aspects of Luke's portrayal of Jesus stand out to you?

- Do you think Luke-Acts is one work? If so, how does that affect the way you interpret Luke's Gospel?

- What date do you prefer for Luke-Acts?

- What do you consider to be the main value of Luke's Gospel?

---

57. The noun *chara*, or "joy," is used eight times; the verb *chairō*, "rejoice," twelve times; and *synchairō*, once. A synonymous verb, *agalliasis*, is used twice; and *skirtaō*, "leap for joy," once.

JOHN'S GOSPEL

CHAPTER 9

John's Gospel is characterized by its rich theology and his Christology. Whereas the three Synoptics are very similar, John blazes his own trail telling the story of Jesus. He unambiguously speaks of Jesus' divinity. Jesus is not secretive about his messianic statement. Whereas in the Synoptics Jesus is mostly in Galilee, in John, while he does spend time in Galilee, Jesus is in and out of Jerusalem. Rather than pithy parables, John's Jesus engages in dialogue with the Jewish leaders who oppose Jesus as a group, "the Jews." Some of Jesus' most memorable sayings are in John, notably the "I am" sayings. While the Synoptics emphasize Peter, James, and John, John gives an account of other disciples, like Philip, Andrew, and Thomas. Like Paul, for John, Christian life is about faith and love, with the language of repentance. Like the Synoptics, Jesus is a miracle-worker, but aside from two exceptions (John 6:1–20), John tells of different miracles. These he calls "signs," not a response by faith, but which generate nascent faith. Through John, the picture of Jesus and what God wants from his people is greatly enriched.

THE AUTHORSHIP OF JOHN

The authorship of John is one of the more contentious issues in biblical scholarship, with a range of views. There are four general ideas as to who wrote John. The first is the traditional view that John the apostle, the son of Zebedee, is the writer—or it is his writings that have been compiled. Many are not convinced, arguing for another John of the early church, John the Elder—the most common alternative. Others suggest writers including Lazarus, John Mark (supposedly the writer of Mark's Gospel), or an unidentified writer.

THE CASE FOR JOHN THE APOSTLE AS AUTHOR OF THE GOSPEL OF JOHN

The Superscription

As with the other Gospels, the superscription "according to John," added sometime in the early to mid-second century (c. AD 125), indicates that the infant church believed that someone by the name of John wrote it. There are a number of "Johns" in the New Testament. John the Baptist is dead by this point (Mark 6:14–29; and parr., cf. John 3:24), so he is not an option. Peter's father was named John in John 21 (John 21:15, 16, 17), but there is no indication that this is the writer of John's Gospel. Mark, otherwise known as John (Acts 12:12, 25; 13:5, 13; 15:37), is a third John. It could be argued that John Mark wrote the Gospel; however, the Greek is profoundly different to Mark's Gospel, and it is unlikely he wrote both. If he wrote John, he didn't write Mark. The best argument in support of John Mark is that he is from Jerusalem and he fits better being an acquaintance of the high priest (John 18:15). It may have been his home in which the Last Supper was held; if so, it makes sense that he is seated close to Jesus at the Lord's Supper, since he was part of the host family (John 13:23; 21:20). Third, it is possible that John Mark is the young man who flees the garden. He may have left the Supper and followed Judas. However, while this is a tempting possibility, it has no real support as John Mark is not associated with the Johannine school, and the early church was monumentally confused over the Johns of history.

Without question, the most well-known John in early Christianity is John the brother of James, the son of Zebedee, and an apostle of Jesus—one of Jesus' Synoptic inner circle. All circumstantial evidence points to John the apostle.

External Evidence

Most writers in the early church felt John the apostle wrote the Gospel. For example, Theophilus of Antioch (c. AD 170–185) ascribes the work to John (Theophilus, *Autol.* 2.22). The strongest argument from external sources is the testimony of Irenaeus, who became bishop of Leon in AD 177 and died in 202. Irenaeus writes refuting Gnosticism, including the claim that the false teachers claim to be "improvers of the *apostles*." Irenaeus states that he and his generation of believers ("we") have learned of the plan of salvation from no one else other than those who passed on the gospel (i.e., the apostles). These apostles were preachers who, by God's will, penned and handed on the Scriptures "to be the ground and pillar of our faith." These apostles[1] were imbued with the Spirit and his gifts and perfect knowledge, and preached. Irenaeus says they "all equally and individually possess the Gospel of God." He then lists Matthew, whom he specifies as a disciple and interpreter of Peter, and Luke "the companion of Paul." He then says of John, "Afterwards, John, the disciple of the Lord, who also had leaned upon his breast, did himself publish a Gospel during his residence at Ephesus in Asia" (*Adv. Haer.* 3.1.1).[2] The use of "disciple" could count against his apostleship, as in the case of Mark. However, where Mark and Luke are concerned, Irenaeus states their link to the apostles Peter and Paul. In the case of John, there is no mention of another apostle, making it likely that he has in view the apostle.

The case for John the apostle in Irenaeus does not end here. Eusebius records a letter from Irenaeus to a Roman presbyter, Florinus, to warn against the Gnosticism of the Valentinians (Eusebius, *Hist. eccl.* 5.20.5-6). He speaks of his intimate relationship with Polycarp including reference to John:

> While I was still a boy I knew you in lower Asia in Polycarp's house when you were a man of rank in the royal hall and endeavouring to stand well with him. I remember the events of those days more clearly than those which happened recently ... so that I can speak even of the place in which the blessed Polycarp sat and disputed, how he came and went out, the character of his life, the appearance of his body, the discourses which he made to the people, *how he reported his intercourse* **with John** *and with the others who had seen*

---

1. While the Latin does not have "the apostles" as the subject of the verb, the use of the noun in the previous verse suggests that they are the subject.

2. Cited from Irenaeus of Lyons, "Irenæus against Heresies," in Alexander Roberts, James Donaldson, and A. Cleveland Coxe, ed(s). of *The Apostolic Fathers with Justin Martyr and Irenaeus*, Vol. 1, The Ante-Nicene Fathers (Buffalo, NY: Christian Literature Company, 1885), 414.

the Lord, how he remembered their words, and what were the things concerning the Lord which he had heard from them, and about their miracle, and about their teaching, and how Polycarp had received them from the eyewitnesses of the word of life, and reported all things in agreement with the Scriptures. (Kirsopp Lake, LCL)

This indicates Irenaeus knew Polycarp, who knew John. This is certainly feasible as Polycarp ministered in Smyrna (modern Izmir). He died at age 86 in AD 156, meaning he was born in AD 70 and was a "boy" in the 80s AD when the Johannine literature was likely written. Smyrna is just over a 70 km (40 mi) walk from Ephesus, where John was reputed to live out his days. Both Ephesus and Smyrna are mentioned in another Johannine writing, Revelation, as the two of the seven churches of Asia Minor. Eusebius also claims that "those who had seen the Lord" entrusted the oversight of the Smyrna church to Polycarp (Eusebius, *Hist. eccl.* 3.36.1).

The so-called anti-Marcionite Prologue to John (c. AD 160–180) also states that John wrote the Gospel, perhaps through dictation to Papias, one of John's disciples. Clement of Alexandria (AD 150–c. 215) also confirms that John wrote the Gospel: "But that John, last of all, conscious that the outward facts had been set forth in the Gospels, was urged on by his disciples, and divinely moved by the Spirit, composed a spiritual Gospel" (Eusebius, *Hist. eccl.* 6.14.7). The Muratorian Canon (c. AD 170–200) also records that John wrote the Gospel after it was revealed that he should do so in a dream or prophecy to Andrew. The *Diatessaron* of Tatian (c. AD 175) uses John's Gospel as the framework for his harmony of the four Gospels, indicating that the apostolic origin of John was assumed at that time.

Consequently, external sources affirm that by the end of the second century, aside from Gaius who was possibly of the *Alogoi*,[3] there was total agreement that the apostle John was responsible for the Gospel. Eusebius,

---

3. Gaius, in his response to Montanism, challenged the apostolic authority of John's Gospel and attributed Revelation to Cerinthus. Irenaeus responded. Many believe Irenaeus was responding to the *Alogoi* or *Alogi* and that Gaius was a part of this group. The *Alogoi* were supposedly a small second-century splinter group from Rome reacting against Montanism. Their name *Alogoi* means, "those who refuse the *logos*." It originates with Epiphanius (AD 374-376). Many contemporary scholars do not believe this group existed; see R. Culpepper, *John, the Son of Zebedee: The Life of a Legend* (Minneapolis: Fortress, 2002), 122 (see also in the discussion of the authorship of Revelation).

the historian, argues that the Gospel is unquestionably the work of the apostle John.

Internal Evidence

In John 21:20, the writer narrates that Peter turned and saw "the disciple whom Jesus loved." This is clearly not Peter. He is identified as the one who leaned back against Jesus at the Last Supper and asked about Judas' betrayal. Peter then asks Jesus about this disciple. This leads to the writer of the Gospel explaining that this led to the rumor that the beloved disciple will never die. John 21:24 reads: "This is *the disciple* who testifies to these things and who wrote them down" (emphasis added). This means two things: 1) A disciple wrote down the Gospel and testifies to its truth; 2) and "we" indicates the author used the plural for self-authentication or indicates some degree of editing or a signing of an authorization from a group, probably in Ephesus. Who is this disciple? Who may have edited it and what was their role? It is not Peter, Judas, or James the son of Zebedee. So what can be gleaned about authorship from John?

The Beloved Disciple

One clear possibility is Lazarus, who is described as "the one you love" (John 11:3, 5 NIV), which could mean he is the author (Witherington). However, it is not likely that a Gospel by someone of his standing would have been accepted in the Johannine community.[4] He was not an apostle or in the right places at the right time to be the "beloved disciple." He is not mentioned anywhere else in the New Testament. Neither is it likely that the author is Mary or Martha, both of whom are described as being loved by Christ (John 11:5).

---

4. See Gerald L. Borchert, *John 1-11*, NAC 25A (Nashville: Broadman & Holman Publishers, 1996), 86. He writes off John Mark for the same reason. One who sees John Mark as the writer is P. Parker, "John and John Mark," *JBL* 79 (1960): 97-110. See also J. E. Bruns, "The Confusion between John and John Mark in Antiquity," *Scripture* 17 (1965): 23-26. On Lazarus see B. G. Griffin, "The Disciple Whom Jesus Loved," *ExpTim* 32 (1920-21): 379-81; F. Filson, "Who Was the Beloved Disciple?" *JBL* 48 (1949): 83-88. Other suggestions for the authorship of the Fourth Gospel have included such persons as Benjamin (the elder of 1, 2 John, who is conceived of as other than John), Matthias, even Paul, and the rich young ruler. See Culpepper's comments in *John the Son of Zebedee*, 79-84.

So, who is this person? Throughout John, there are five references to "the disciple whom Jesus loved" (John 13:23 NIV; 19:26; 20:2; 21:7, 20). In addition, he is likely the one referred to as "another disciple" in John 18:15, one known to the high priest. He is also likely the disciple from John 19:32-35 whose testimony concerning Jesus' pierced side is true. The beloved disciple is also with the women at the cross, which could be any of the disciples of Jesus (John 19:26). He also went to the tomb with Peter (John 20:2, 8). None of these references reveal the identity of the writer of the Gospel of John, other than affirming the apostle John was the best known John in the New Testament. Because he was known by the high priest could suggest he is from Judea; however, this is unclear as John may have encountered him in a range of ways—fishing, or while in Jerusalem with Jesus.

Aside from the evidence from early church sources, there are four strands of evidence that point to John the apostle.

First, John 13:23 says that at Jesus' final meal, the Last Supper, the disciple Jesus loved "was reclining at table at Jesus' side" (NIV). Hence, this person sat at the table during the Lord's Supper directly beside Jesus (John 13:23). The other three Gospels clearly state that those who sat at the table with Jesus were the Twelve (Mark 14:17-18; Matt 26:20; Luke 22:14). This means that unless John disagrees with this, the writer is one of the Twelve. While there is no way to be certain, those named are all from the Twelve, and so, this is likely. The Markan reference is especially important, as many scholars, including some who argue against the apostle John as the author, accept that John was familiar with Mark's Gospel. In John's Last Supper narrative, four disciples are named: Judas (John 13:2), Peter (John 13:6), Thomas (John 14:5), and Philip (John 14:9). Clearly, the unnamed "loved disciple" is not one of these.

Also, the New American Standard Version of John 13:23 states that the disciple whom he loved "was reclining on Jesus' bosom," meaning his head was alongside Jesus' chest. As they ate with their right hand, they reclined on their left side, feet away from the table. Hence, the loved disciple was to the right of Jesus with his head alongside Jesus' chest. The position at the right hand of Jesus was the position of greatest status. This makes it unlikely that the person was from outside the Twelve, and most likely, it was one of the three apostles from Jesus' inner circle—Peter, James, or John. The most likely person is John the apostle. Although Jesus repudiated seeking status and sitting in the privileged positions at meals (Mark 12:39; Luke 14:8-11), there is ample evidence that the disciples were concerned about status. The two most concerned were James and John, who in one memorable moment asked Jesus to grant them the honor of sitting at his right and left hands—the positions of highest honor (Mark 10:35-45; Matt 20:20-28). Intriguingly, Luke's version of the clash over places of honor is not before the entry to Jericho and Jerusalem, but at the Last Supper (Luke 22:24-30). This is undoubtedly the same story, and one of Luke's stated intentions was to write an ordered account, whereas Papias suggested Mark did not (see earlier on Luke and Mark).[5] There are also hints that John was familiar with Luke, especially the catch of fish in John 21, which seems to intentionally recall the call of Peter in Luke 5. Whether this is the case, it is probable that Luke retains the correct setting for the clash over status. With their clear interest in the places of highest status, it is likely that the right and left places beside Jesus were taken by James and John. Further, John records Peter observing Jesus address Judas and signaling the loved disciple to ask Jesus who it is. This suggests Peter is proximate to the loved disciple. If Peter, James, and John were part of Jesus' inner circle, this makes sense. If some or all of this is correct, the position of the loved disciple here would suggest one or other of these disciples is a possibility. As he is not James, and he is not Peter, the most likely candidate is John.

The second helpful piece of evidence is from John 21:2. As the discussion over the loved disciple and Peter later in John 21 is set in this context, the loved disciple is one of the Seven who met Jesus by the sea. He is not Peter, nor James, the other son of Zebedee. This leaves Thomas, Nathanael, the apostle John, or one of the two unnamed disciples. Candidates include Andrew, Bartholomew, Matthew, Philip, James son of Alphaeus, Thaddeus, Simon the Zealot, or Nathanael. While one or even a few others could be possible, Andrew, Philip, and Nathanael are ruled out. It is John who is in

---

5. As James and John are not specifically mentioned, it can be argued that this is a different situation; however, Jesus' response concerning gentile patterns of leadership would suggest it is the same situation. While the source may differ, John Nolland, *Luke 18:35-24:53*, WBC 35C; Dallas: Word, 1998), 1062 rightly states, "There can be little doubt that Luke 22:24-27 is a version of the same tradition as Mark 10:41-45 (note especially the degree of structural parallelism)." What is less certain is the source. However, whatever the source (if not Mark), Luke is familiar with Mark and will no doubt be acquainted with James and John's role in this. See also Bock, *Luke: 9:51-24:53*, 1736.

the right place at the right time and remains as good a possibility as any of the others.

The third strand of evidence is not explicit. As the writer of the Gospel claims to have borne witness to the material given in the Gospel, he must have been there at the start. As such, some scholars recognize that the author may be introduced in John 1:35-42. Two disciples are introduced to Jesus by John the Baptist; one is Andrew, and the other is unnamed. The Synoptics list Peter, Andrew, John, and James at the first calls of the disciples (Mark 1:16-20; Matt 4:18-22; Luke 5:1-11). Peter and James can be ruled out, and Andrew is the second of the two disciples. Nathanael and Philip are also ruled out in what follows (John 1:43-51).

A fourth possible piece of evidence is the speculative idea that the introduction of John in John 1:6 may not necessarily refer to John the Baptist, which is assumed by most scholars because of John 1:15. Could this have double intent? Further, in John 1, Peter's father is again John (John 1:42). Such ideas are at best tenuous, but intriguing.

Finally, aside from being two of Jesus' three disciples in his "inner circle," Peter and John are paired frequently in the early days of Acts (Acts 1:13; 3:1-4, 11; 4:13, 19; 8:14). Here, Peter and the loved disciple are paired (John 13:23-24; 20:2, 4-6, 20).

Significantly, James and John are not mentioned in the Gospel, which is most intriguing. This person is also mentioned alongside Peter regularly and is noted favorably. As such, along with the external evidence, there is no real reason to dispute the likelihood that the apostle John is the author. If so, why is he anonymous? Revelation reveals John was imprisoned at that time on Patmos. It could be that the Gospel is anonymous to protect him, either because he wrote it while in Patmos or before or after when under threat from Domitian. Alternatively, it is anonymous out of humility—John wants the focus to be Jesus.

The Editing of John

The additional statement "*we* know that his testimony is true," along with 19:35[6] and the issues noted below, lead some to argue that John the

---

6. "The man who saw it has given testimony, and his testimony is true. He knows that he tells the truth, and he testifies so that you also may believe" (NIV).

apostle is *not* the actual author of the fourth Gospel. Others believe that the Gospel is John's, but that it has been authenticated or edited by others in the Johannine churches or communities.[7] The Johannine community appears to have certified the claims of the Gospel. Others write off the "we" as a kind of royal "we," meaning John himself (e.g., John 21:24).[8] Some, like R. Culpepper, R. Brown, and L. Martyn see a kind of Johannine school or community behind the Gospel and have created complicated historical stages of development for it.

If John was edited, this raises the difficult question of how much is due to the editor and how much is due to John. It is an incredibly complex discussion and scholars are deeply divided over it. Suffice to say, many interpreters believe that the editing is minor, being limited to the comments at the end of the Gospel in John 21:23-25, and other additions and comments added to give clarity or guidance to readers. Link texts like John 2:12; 2:23-25; 3:22-24; 4:43-45 may also be examples of edits. However, many of these may be the work of John himself. Other scholars are prepared to see wider editorial work; however, it is a highly subjective exercise. Whatever is correct, if John is edited, the work remains John's with another writer gathering his data.

PROBLEMS LEADING TO MANY DENYING
JOHN THE APOSTLE AS AUTHOR

Many scholars, including some conservatives, deny that the apostle John is the John who is behind the production of the Gospel. There are good reasons for this.

Questions Over the External Evidence

First, for some, the testimony of the early church concerning John is "ambiguous, inadequate, wrong, legendary, or polemical."[9] For example, Irenaeus is seen as unreliable as his testimony is from the late second

---

7. Borchert, *John 1-11*, 83, 89 writes: "[w]hereas it is John 'who stands behind the gospel tradition,' the gospel itself suggests that there was more than one mind and one hand at work in bringing the work to its final form."

8. E.g., D. A. Carson, *The Gospel According to John*, PNTC (Leicester, England; Grand Rapids, MI: Inter-Varsity Press; Eerdmans, 1991), 683-84.

9. M. M. Thompson, "John, Gospel of," in *DJG* 369.

century and is secondhand—despite the link to Polycarp and to John himself. Some argue the evidence may refer to another John, such as John the Elder. Others argue that the evidence of Clement of Alexandria is legendary. Important here again is Papias, Bishop of Hierapolis (c. AD 130). As recorded in Eusebius he wrote:

> And if anyone chanced to come who had actually been a follower of the elders, I would enquire as to the discourses of the elders, what Andrew or what Peter said, or what Philip, or what Thomas or James, or what *John* or Matthew or any other of the Lord's disciples; and things which Aristion and *John the elder*, disciples of the Lord, say.

This is perhaps a reference to a second John outside of the apostles who was recognized as an elder (Eusebius, *Hist. eccl.* 3:39.4-5). Some argue that this is the John behind the Gospel. However, others contend that Papias really meant, "Aristion and the aforementioned elder."[10] It should be conceded that this may suggest the existence of another elder, sufficiently well-known to be mentioned by Papias. It cannot be ruled out that he is the writer of John's Gospel. However, no one else in early church history made this connection. Further, can the wide testimony concerning John the apostle be so simply ruled out, especially the link between Irenaeus, Polycarp, and John.

Questions Over the Identity of the "Beloved Disciple"

Many scholars question the identity and role of the "beloved disciple." Some scholars believe it could be one of the unnamed disciples or another follower who was not one of the Twelve. Others in the Gospel are said to be loved by Jesus, including Lazarus (John 11:3, 36), Martha, and Mary (John 11:5). Some, clutching at straws, have even suggested the rich ruler whom Jesus looked at and loved (Mark 10:21). These arguments are circumstantial.

Other Arguments

The statement in John 21:24 concerning the truth of the witness given is argued by some as referring to the passage or chapter rather than the

---

10. See the discussion in Carson, *The Gospel According to John*, 69-70.

whole Gospel. As such, this disciple is only responsible for this small part of the Gospel.

Other strands of evidence against John's authorship include the observation that the Gospel focuses on Judea, whereas John was a Galilean, making it less likely he is the author. Some question how a first-century Galilean fisherman could be known to the high priest. It is also noted that Peter and John are called "unschooled, ordinary men" by Luke (Acts 4:13), so John could not have written such a well-constructed, well-written, theologically astute work. John (with James) is called a "son of thunder," which is incongruous with the tone of the book. John was also vengeful toward Samaritans (Luke 9:54), yet writes about them kindly (John 4). However, these arguments are strongly refuted by some.[11]

These and other arguments lead many to reject John the son of Zebedee as the author and to postulate other candidates, including another John, John the Elder, Lazarus, the unnamed disciple (John 1:35-40), or an unknown Jewish follower of Jesus.

Conclusion to Authorship

Because of a combination of the almost unanimous external evidence and especially the link between John and Irenaeus, along with the most likely identification of the "beloved disciple" as both the author and John the disciple and brother of James, it is most likely that the apostle John is behind the Gospel. It is possible that John's work was gathered by others and that there was a process of editing (John 21:24-25). However, this position should be held tentatively. Except in affirming that the Gospel was penned by an eyewitness, it is not important for interpretation.

THE PROVENANCE OF JOHN'S GOSPEL

There is a range of suggestions for the origin of John's Gospel. Aside from the traditional view that it was written in Ephesus by the apostle John, there are three main ideas for John's origin in recent scholarship: Alexandria, Antioch, and Israel.[12] Some, like Sanders, argue for Alexandria in Egypt because of similarities in thought with Philo of Alexandria (e.g.,

---

11. See Carson, *John*, 68-81.
12. See Borchert, *John 1-11*, 93-94 for details.

logos). Other possible links to this include the Gnostics, who frequently used John, Clement of Alexandria, and the discovery of the Egerton Papyrus 2 in Egypt.[13] However, this idea has fallen out of favor.

Some scholars, like Burney and Kümmel, prefer Antioch because of allusions to John in the Odes of Solomon, and in the letters of Ignatius the Bishop of Antioch (died c. AD 115).

Finally, there is the traditional view that the Gospel was written in Ephesus, which is based on the patristic evidence, especially that of Irenaeus, who states John wrote it from Ephesus ("while he was a resident at Ephesus in Asia" [Irenaeus, *Haer.* 3.1.1, see also Eusebius, *Hist. eccl.* 5.20.5-6]). Concluding the apostle John is the author, Ephesus would seem to be the best suggestion.

THE DATE OF JOHN'S GOSPEL

In the past, some have sought to date John in the second century. However, this has been effectively ruled out by manuscript discoveries. For example, fragments from John 18 dating as early as AD 130 have been discovered—John 1-14 and some of the remaining chapters in the Bodmer Papyri (P^{66}), and John 1-11 and parts of 12-15 (P^{75}) from the end of the second century. Hence, most now date John somewhere between AD 55 and 95.

John 21:19 suggests it was written after Peter's death (c. 64-66), while John 21:23 could indicate it was written around the time of John's death. If the tradition that John died an old man in Ephesus is correct, this would point to a date late in the century. However, some argue it was written not long after Peter's martyrdom, also noting an absence of reference to the destruction of Jerusalem and the temple and John's references to the temple. For example, he mentions the destruction of the temple in John 2:19 metaphorically, but does not clarify this in terms of AD 70. He also uses the present tense concerning the temple (e.g., "Now there *is* in Jerusalem near the Sheep Gate a pool," [John 5:2 NIV]). However, John uses the present

---

13. Papyrus Egerton 2 is a codex fragment now in the British Museum from around AD 200 or perhaps even the first century of an unknown gospel of Johannine flavor found in Egypt and published in 1934. It includes: (1) a controversy like John 5:39-47; 10:31-39; (2) the healing of a leper (cf. Matt 8:1-4, Mark 1:40-45, Luke 5:12-16; 17:11-14); (3) a controversy about paying taxes (cf. Matt 22:15-22, Mark 12:13-17, Luke 20:20-26); and (4) an incomplete miracle-account about Jesus filling the Jordan and seeds growing and bearing fruit miraculously.

tense of the past in other places and, if it was edited in the late first century, then only some parts of it need be earlier. Further, John is narrating a story that happened before the temple's destruction, so the present is neither here nor there.

Most scholars opt for a date between AD 85-95 because:

1. of the *tradition* that it was written during the reign of Domitian (AD 81-96); however, this is disputed;

2. the idea of Christians being "put out of the synagogue" (John 9:22; 12:42; 16:2) may point to a time after the Council of Jamnia at Yavneh (AD 85) when Christians were banned from the synagogue (again this is disputed);

3. some details point to this later date. For example, there is no mention of Sadducees, whose influence declined after AD 70; and

4. of the argument that high Christology fits a later date (esp. 1:1-18; 5:18; 8:58; 10:30; 20:28).

It seems appropriate to side with the tradition that John wrote the Gospel from Ephesus as an old man. The links to Revelation suggest a time in Domitian's reign (AD 81-96).

THE RECIPIENTS OF JOHN'S GOSPEL

As with every aspect of Johannine study, the original recipients are disputed. Some think the Gospel was written for the so-called Johannine community. However, the existence of the so-called Johannine community is uncertain. Because there is no reason to dispute the traditional view that the Gospel was written in Ephesus, then the Christian community in and around Ephesus is in view. The best clue in this regard is the seven churches of Revelation, which indicates John's sphere of influence extended through Asia Minor. The map below shows the region.

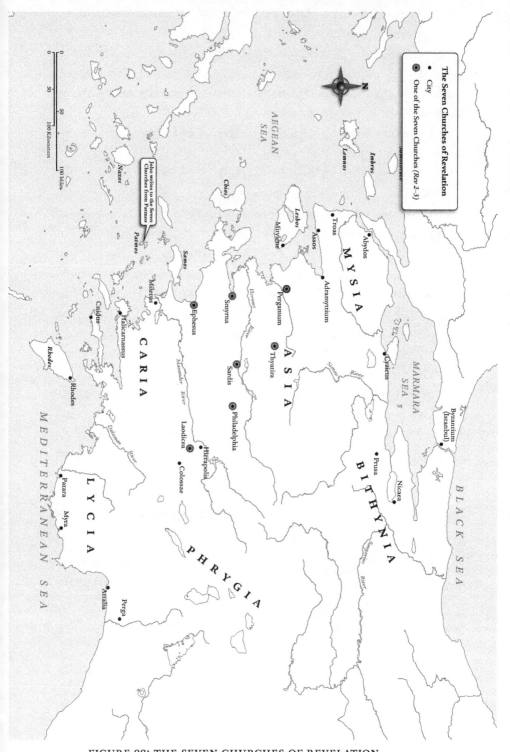

FIGURE 22: THE SEVEN CHURCHES OF REVELATION

John's Gospel, like Revelation, was likely written for the churches of Asia over whom John had authority. It is also possible that, at this late stage of his life, with the spread of Christianity into the gentile world, John and those who edited the Gospel were aware of the wider implications of his book and wrote also with a general gentile audience in mind.

THE TEXT OF JOHN

There are many points of discussion concerning the text of John. For example, John 5:3 is omitted from the best manuscripts.[14] The main point of interest is the account of the woman caught in adultery in John 7:53–8:11. This passage is missing from the oldest Greek manuscripts (e.g., P66 and P75), while in other manuscripts it is located elsewhere or missing entirely. It is also full of words not found elsewhere in John—fourteen out of eighty-two words, or 17 percent.[15] There is also an absence of standard Johannine ideas. Hence, it is almost certainly an interpolation.

However, this does not mean that the account is unhistorical or of no value.[16] It aligns with Jesus' whole approach to women (especially in Luke) and speaks profoundly of his grace. Hence, although not Johannine, it is perhaps authentic or at least of some value. Borchert notes that it is found after Luke 21:38 in some Greek manuscripts and that it looks more like a Synoptic pericope[17] than part of John. He also notes the mention of scribes (John 8:3) and the Mount of Olives (John 8:1), and that Jesus is addressed directly as teacher (*didaskale*) (John 8:4), suggesting that it may be placed in Jesus' ministry in his closing days (cf. Luke 20–21). A reference in Papias

---

14. Some have part or all of: "waited for the moving of the water. From time to time an angel of the Lord would come and stir up the waters. The first person into the pool after each such disturbance would be cured of whatever disease they had."

15. These include "olive" (*elaia*) (John 8:1), "daybreak" (*orthros*) (John 8:2), "adultery" (*moicheia*) (John 8:3), scribes (*grammateus*) (not mentioned by Köstenberger); "the very act" (*autophōros*) (John 8:4), "commit adultery" (*moicheuō*) (John 8:4), "bend down" (*kuptō*) (John 8:6), "accuse" (*katagraphō*) (John 8:6), "remain" (*epimenō*) (John 8:7), "straighten up" (*anakuptō*) (John 8:7, 10), "guiltless" (*anamartētos*) (John 8:7), "bend down" (*katakuptō*) (John 8:8), "elder" (*presbyteros*) (John 8:9), "leave behind" (*kataleipō*) (John 8:9), "condemn" (*katakrinō*) (John 8:10–11). See Andreas J. Köstenberger, *John*, BECNT (Grand Rapids, MI: Baker Academic, 2004), 245.

16. For example, Köstenberger, *John*, 248, says that it should be omitted from preaching in churches.

17. "Pericope" comes from the Greek *perikoptō* ("cut off, cut out") and is the technical term for a literary unit or section of the text. See Patzia and Petrotta, *PDBS* 92.

to a story of a woman charged with many sins in the presence of Jesus may suggest this account originated from the lost "Gospel to the Hebrews."[18]

THE SO-CALLED JOHANNINE COMMUNITY AND SOURCES FOR JOHN

One idea that has complicated Johannine study is the question of John's sources, an additional complex area of research. In the zenith of source and form criticism, when scholarship focused on the historical origin of every part of the Bible, the texts of John were sifted through with this question in mind.

The reasons for this interest include John's strange transitions. For example, "come now, let us leave" in John 14:31 (NIV). However, they do not leave until John 17:26. Another example is the seeming conclusion in John 20:30-31,[19] followed by John 21. There is also a repetition of material, such as material in John 14 and 16 (see also John 6:51-58). There are geographical shifts from Galilee to Jerusalem, leading some to think John 6 should be placed before John 5. There are also shifts in eschatology from the future (John 5:28-29) to present (John 5:24-25).

There is a range of theories concerning John's sources, some tenuous. Some earlier scholars tried to find an "original John" within the extant canonical version—a *Grundschrift*, or original composition. Rudolf Bultmann developed a highly speculative three-source theory:

1. **A revelation-discourse source:** written in Aramaic, translated into Greek that is poetic and like the Jewish Odes of Solomon, and supposedly like Mandean[20] Gnosticism theologically. It included an earlier form of the prologue in John 1 written by a disciple of John the Baptist.

2. **A signs source:** including the miracle-type stories from John 2-11 and the call narrative in John 1. Supposedly, it is unreliable and full of imported ideas from Hellenistic myth. This

---

18. Borchert, *John 1-11*, 370.
19. "Jesus performed many other signs in the presence of his disciples, which are not recorded in this book. But these are written that you may believe that Jesus is the Messiah, the Son of God, and that by believing you may have life in his name" (NIV).
20. A region in southern Iraq and south-eastern Iran.

source treated Jesus as a *Theios Anēr* (divine man)[21] to prove his divinity.

3. **A passion source:** including the resurrection accounts. Supposedly, this source was made up in early-church Easter preaching, and was in Greek with Semitisms (remnants of the original Aramaic/Hebrew).

Bultmann argued an editor arranged this material to suit his purposes and inserted mentions of "the beloved disciple," who is not a true figure, but an ideal model of a disciple. He also added material referring to the Lord's Supper and baptism (sacramental material), for example, "bread of life" and "born of water." After this, Bultmann could rearrange the material and demythologize it to produce an original Johannine Gospel for the modern reader. His theory is highly convoluted and impossible to verify. Most consider it incorrect. Borchert notes even Bultmann's own followers rejected his source theory.[22]

The dimension others (esp. Fortna) have picked up from Bultmann is the idea of a "Signs Source," based on the miracles in the Gospel. Fortna gave a detailed analysis of the signs featured in John's Gospel, seeking to isolate the source John used for this material.[23] His analysis is highly subjective and unconvincing.

Both Martyn and Brown have studied the development and history of the so-called Johannine community from source reconstructions of John's Gospel. They look at the stages of the text's development and construct a picture of the Johannine community from this perceived development.

---

21. On "Divine Man" (*theos anēr*) see B. L. Blackburn, "Divine Man/*Theios Anēr*," in *DJG* 189-91. It is the theory of a supposed Hellenistic legendary or historical human hero figure who demonstrated "moral virtue, wisdom and/or miraculous power so that they were held to be divine." It arose from the History of Religions School. The myth of Jesus supposedly developed in the church and he is presented as one of these; much of the Gospels is then myth and not to be taken historically (e.g., his miracles). See Blackburn for critique.

22. Borchert, *John 1-11*, 44.

23. These include signs themselves (John 2:1-11; 4:46-54; 6:1-25; 9:1-8; 11:1-45; 21:1-14), John's testimony and the call of the disciples (John 1:19-51), and the sign dimensions of Jesus' death and resurrection (John 2:14-19; 5:2-9; 11:47-53; 12:1-8, 12-15; 13:1-20; and most of chaps. 18-20).

In 1966 Brown[24] developed a five-stage approach:

1. The gathering of oral material independent of the Synoptics.

2. The development of this material by a preacher or teacher, including the devices of misunderstanding and irony (which are found throughout John).

3. A first Greek edition of John by the evangelist, including signs and stories from Galilee and Judea.

4. A subsequent editing by the evangelist to deal with issues, including problems from the disciples of John the Baptist and the excommunication from the synagogue of Jewish Christians.

5. Another editing by another person (a redactor), a friend of the evangelist, who added other material such as John 3:31–36; 6:51–58; 11–12; 12:44–50; 15–17; 21.

While this construct may be argued to be brilliant, it is utterly speculative and based at best on sniffs of possibility fused together to create a historical fiction. In the end, the remaining construct is far less convincing than the traditional idea that John wrote the Gospel as a coherent whole allowing for a degree of editing.

Brown revised his ideas in 1979, modifying them to a four-stage process:

1. He began with two groups who combined: first, Jewish Christians with a low Christology who saw Jesus as a Davidic Messiah, and second, an anti-temple group who saw Jesus as a prophet like Moses. They have a strong leader and spokesman, and develop a high Christology, seeing Jesus as God. This leads to their expulsion from the synagogue.

2. Gentiles are then welcomed into the group, which is interpreted as a sign from God. However, the community is persecuted and

---

24. Raymond E. Brown, *The Gospel According to John: John i–XII* (AB; Garden City, NY: Doubleday, 1966), lxxxiv–ix.

leaves Israel. The Gospel is written with a universal scope, and this upsets Jewish Christians, who break away.

3. The Johannine Epistles are written, condemning those who broke away.

4. The Johannine community ends, with those who broke away joining Gnostic groups, which denied the incarnation (cf. 1 John 4:2-3). Those remaining join the "Great Church" and cease to exist independently.

Clearly, this is ingenious historical speculation.

J. Martyn in 1968/1979[25] developed his own three-stage theory of the development of the Gospel and the Johannine community:

1. A period from the establishment of the community to the mid-80s AD in which they tried to convince Jews that Jesus is the Messiah. The disputes lead to a split from the synagogue.

2. The split with Judaism intensified, and the curse of Jewish heretics in the late 80s AD is introduced (*Birkat ha-Minim*) (e.g., John 5:18-24; 9:1-41).

3. Christians are forcibly ejected from synagogues, resulting in a time of identity formation for the Christian group. The Paraclete notion is developed as a basis for Christian relationships.

Again, this is a fanciful construction. If John is dated in the mid-80s AD, relationships between Jews and Jewish Christians may be a factor in interpreting the Gospel. However, this theory gives no recognition to gentile mission. The linear development remains speculative in the extreme.

While these ideas are fascinating, they reveal the dangers of reading too much speculative historical detail from New Testament texts. There is no clear agreement about the "Johannine community." Some believe it was John's church or his addressees, or even a larger gathering of believers with a particular theological perspective. One thing these discussions

---

25. J. Martyn, *History and Theology in the Fourth Gospel*, rev. ed. (Nashville: Abingdon, 1979).

do highlight is the probability the Gospel was written at a time of tension between Jews and Christians, and this may be important to interpretation. However, this tension existed from the time of Christ, and it is not necessary to resort to speculative constructs to explain them. In terms of sources, if John is the writer of the Gospel—or behind its writing in its final form—*then John himself must remain the key source* for his own work.[26] If there are other sources, it is impossible to find them with confidence. The text should be handled in its final canonical form rather than interpreted against a speculative construct.

THE RELATIONSHIP TO THE SYNOPTICS

In many ways, John's presentation of Jesus correlates with the Synoptics. John's Jesus is a preacher, teacher, healer, and evangelist. Some of the Synoptic stories are found in John with different details. These include some aspects of John the Baptist (John 1:6, 15, 19-42; 3:23-27; 4:1), clearing the temple—although at a different point in Jesus' ministry (John 2:12-25), feeding the five thousand (John 6:1-14), walking on water (John 6:16-24), Jesus' anointing (John 12:1-11), the entry into Jerusalem (John 12:12-19), predictions of betrayal and denial (John 13:18-38), the outline of his death (John 18:1-19:42), and resurrection appearances (John 20:1-21:23).

UNIQUE MATERIAL

At the same time, there is much unique material in John. This includes:

1. The prologue focused on the *logos*, Jesus' pre-existence and role in creation, and incarnation (John 1:1-18).

2. The details of John the Baptist and accounts of the calls of the disciples (John 1:19-51).

3. The highlighting of the involvement of figures not prominent in the Synoptics including: i. Andrew (John 1:35-40, 44; 6:8; 12:22); ii. Philip (John 1:43-45; 6:5; 12:21-22; 14:8-9); iii. Nathanael (John 1:45-49; 21:2); iv. Thomas (John 11:16; 14:5; 20:24-28; 21:2); and v. Lazarus (John 11-12).

---

26. See further the discussions in Borchert, *John 1-11*, 43-50.

4. Three unique personal encounters including Nicodemus (John 3:1-21), the Samaritan woman (John 4:1-42), and Greeks seeking to see Jesus (John 12:20-26).

5. Five unique miracles including: i. his turning water into wine in Cana (John 2:1-11); ii. the healing of the official's son, again in Cana (John 4:43-54); iii. the official's son's healing at the pool (John 5:1-15); iv. the healing of the blind man (John 9:1-41); and v. the raising of Lazarus (John 11:1-44).

6. Long discourses including: i. eternal life (John 5:16-47); ii. bread of life (John 6:25-71); iii. at the Feast of Tabernacles (John 7:1-51); iv. the light of the world (John 8:12-58) and the Good Shepherd (John 10:1-42); v. love, the paraclete, and the true vine (John 14-17).

7. The details of the Last Supper including: i. washing the disciples' feet (John 13:1-17); ii. the way to the Father (John 14:1-14); iii. the promise of the Spirit (John 14:15-31); iv. the true vine (John 15:1-8); v. the love of the Father, hatred of the world (John 15:9-16:4); vi. the work of the Spirit (John 16:5-16); vii. joy and hope (John 16:17-33); and viii. Jesus' prayer (John 17:1-26).

8. The miraculous catch of fish and Peter's restoration (John 21:1-23).

LESS OBVIOUS UNIQUE MATERIAL AND EMPHASES

In addition to these obvious content differences, there are other subtle distinctions. One distinction is John's heightened "from above" Christology. John begins declaring Jesus' divinity, but then his narrative expounds Jesus' divinity and humanity. Unlike the Synoptics, he ascribes divinity to Jesus. For example:

John 1:1	"the Word was God"
John 1:18	"no one has seen God except God the one and only"

John 5:18	"making himself equal with God"
John 8:58	"before Abraham was, I am"
John 10:30	"I and the Father are one"
John 20:28	"my Lord and my God"

He also employs a series of "I am" sayings.

There are other differences. John leaves out or uses sparingly many expressions common to the Synoptic Gospels. These include: "the kingdom of God/heaven," which he uses twice (John 3:3, 5; cf. 18:36). He makes no mention of "Sadducees," "scribes," "forgive/forgiveness," "repent/repentance," "demons," or "tax collectors."

In addition, he includes other expressions with great frequency such as "life," "light," "darkness," "truth," "the world," "the Jews," "know," "Counsellor," and "Son" as a title for Jesus. The notion of "Father" is also more developed.

John's style is different from the Synoptics. It has a deceptive simplicity. It is possible there was an Aramaic original from which it was translated. Certainly, the Aramaisms, including *messias* ("messiah" [1:41; 4:25]) and other phrases, suggest the writer is from a Jewish background. The Gospel also has a poetic feel with literary features indicating that the material may have been intended to be read out loud.

The flow of the Gospel is dramatic; it has a sense of progress and building tension. There is stronger characterization than in the Synoptics and an obvious interplay of narrative (story account) and discourse (speech) — the discourses flow out of the narrative and develop the story theologically. Often this is connected to a sign like the feeding of the five thousand, leading into the discourse about the bread of life (John 6). The healing of the blind man and spiritual blindness of the Pharisees illuminate the light of the world discourse (John 8–9). John is also rich in symbolism, including metaphor in which Jesus is likened to another reality such as light (John 8:12; 9:5), water (John 4:10-11; 7:38), or bread (John 6:35, 48) to amplify the meaning of his presence. There are also dualistic contrasts such as light and darkness (John 1:5; 3:19), life and death (John 5:34; 8:51), or above and below (John 8:23) symbolizing acceptance or rejection of the revelation of

God. There is also great symbolism in Jesus' actions, which develop into dialogues exploring their full meaning.

Through the story, there is irony and misunderstanding as Jesus says something and his opponents misunderstand. An example is Nicodemus, who misunderstands being "born from above" as "born again," and ponders the ridiculous idea of returning to his mother's womb (John 3:3-8). Similarly, the Samaritan woman takes Jesus literally and wants to drink the water of life (John 4:10-15). In John 6, John's Jesus declares himself the "bread of life," and his opponents are offended at the thought of eating him (John 6:26-58).

The characters of the Gospel inevitably fall into two categories: believers or opponents. The opponents harden in their opposition through the narrative. Some who started as believers fall away (e.g., John 6:60-65). Those who are believers demonstrate varying levels of maturity, and their faith develops. Nicodemus is intrigued about Jesus, but cannot understand him (John 3:1-9); he then defends Jesus (John 7:50-51) and then appears to be a believer (John 19:39). The Samaritan woman moves from incomprehension, to belief, to mission (John 4). Similarly, the blind man comes to faith through the narrative of John 9; he is healed both physically and spiritually. The royal official demonstrates profound faith (John 4:46-54). Martha demonstrates growth in faith (John 11), while Thomas models coming to faith from a place of doubt (John 20:24-29).

RECONCILING DIFFERENCES

Though there are clear links between the Synoptics, the acute differences between John and the Synoptics lead to the inevitable question: What is their relationship? There are two main solutions proposed: (1) Either John knew of one or more of the Synoptics and wrote to supplement them and interpret Jesus differently. (2) He wrote completely independently.

John Wrote to Supplement and Interpret the Synoptic Gospels

Until the twentieth century, the dominant view was that John was aware of one or more of the Synoptics and wrote to add to the well-known pictures of Jesus in his writings. Many conservative scholars still hold this view. This was a view held as early as Clement of Alexandria (AD 150-215). He recognized John had a different agenda, writing: "John, last of all, realizing that the physical facts had been made clear by the Gospels, urged by his friends and divinely moved from the Spirit, composed a spiritual gospel" (Eusebius, *Hist. eccl.* 6.14).

In this hypothesis, it is argued that John knew at least some of the Synoptics and wrote his Gospel to add additional detail and/or a different perspective on Jesus' ministry. If Clement is taken seriously, John wrote from a different "spiritual" angle, bringing more theological and spiritual interpretation to the text. Some who take this position suggest that John is more about doctrine and theology and less about historical exactitude. Some note that much of the Gospel is based in Judea rather than Galilee, which nicely supplements the Synoptics that focus on Galilee. Another idea is that John is a commentary on or an elucidation of the Synoptics.

John Wrote Independently of the Synoptic Gospels

The idea that John knew the Synoptics has been challenged since the beginning of the twentieth century. Two scholars, P. Gardner-Smith and C. H. Dodd,[27] have argued that John wrote his Gospel without knowledge of, or reference to, the Synoptics. Rather, he had access to a different stored tradition. Any similarities are due to common material in the different traditions circulating in the early church. Others believe that John *did* know the Synoptics but did not use them as sources for his Gospel as Matthew and Luke used Mark and Q.

Conclusion

There are hints that John knew something of the Synoptic Gospels, including the feeding of the five thousand, the walking on water, and the structure of Jesus' life (his ministry, the clearing of the temple, the Lord's Supper, his betrayal, his arrest, his trial, his death, and his resurrection). These might suggest an awareness of Mark's Gospel. The miraculous catch of fish and Mary and Martha may reflect knowledge of Peter's call from Luke 5 and the Martha-and-Mary encounter in Luke 10:38-42.

---

27. P. Gardner-Smith, *St John and the Synoptic Gospels* (Cambridge: Cambridge University Press, 1938); C. H. Dodd, *Historical Tradition in the Fourth Gospel* (Cambridge: Cambridge University Press, 1963).

However, if he knew one or other of the Synoptics, John clearly put his own spin on the material. If this is John the apostle or a Judean disciple John, he likely drew on his own recollections. If it is another author, he must have gained material from eyewitnesses or written sources, which are now uncertain other than the disciples featured in the Gospel. The emphasis on other characters may indicate that they were eyewitnesses for the writer.

Two options remain. First, John knew the Synoptics but wrote independently. Second, John *did not* know the Synoptics. Any conclusion must be partially related to the dating of the Gospels. The earlier John is dated, the more likely it is to be independent of written sources. If John is dated later than the Synoptics, dependent on the time gap, the more likely he was aware of the other Gospels.

If, as has been argued, John was produced in the 80s AD and even the 90s AD while Mark and Luke wrote in the 60s AD, then it is likely he knew of their writings and wrote to supplement and build on Mark and Luke's accounts. If Mark and Luke were produced in Rome, as suggested, their gospels would have been dispersed through the Neronian persecution. Further, Mark and Luke are linked to Paul and Ephesus, and the Asia Minor area was initially evangelized by Paul (Acts 19). While there are great distances between the centers of early Christianity, there was also great movement, and preachers and documents no doubt moved across vast differences. With this in mind, assuming the schema of dates in this work, it is likely that in two decades, copies came to Asia and were read by John. As such, it is more likely John knew of at least Mark and Luke and wrote to give an additional supplementary account of Jesus for early Christians well versed in these two Gospels.

Still, so much is shrouded in mystery it is impossible to make a safe decision on this question. Two alternatives remain.

THE HISTORICITY OF JOHN

Can John be taken seriously as history? On the one hand, it is important to acknowledge that the Gospels are not pure history (not that such a thing exists)—they are *theological* history. They recount historical events with theological intent: to convince Jews that Jesus is the Messiah (Matthew); to tell the story of Jesus to Roman gentiles (Mark); and to give a historical account of Jesus and salvation for all humankind to educated gentiles

(Luke-Acts). Extremists recognize the theological dimension and reduce the historicity of the Gospels almost to a redundancy. That is not necessary. All history is slanted with a purpose. If, as is likely, John wrote to supplement the Synoptic material, then his purpose is more theological than historical (or as Clement says, "spiritual"). This does not mean that John is ahistorical; rather, it means that the Gospel's emphasis is more theology than history, whereas the Synoptics are more intentionally historical and less theological.

Whether this is the case, there are sound reasons to accept that John's Gospel is "historical" in the sense that the material can be trusted as an authentic record of events in the life of Jesus. John's Jesus is still patterned in the same way: Jesus is in Israel, he calls disciples, he engages with Jewish leaders and Samaritans, he preaches and teaches, he feeds the poor, he enters Jerusalem, he celebrates the Last Supper, he is betrayed by Judas and denied by Jesus, he is arrested and tried, he is crucified, and he rises. Through the narrative, it is clearly the same Jesus. While there are significant differences of detail, the Gospels are clearly about the same man in space and time.

The major sticking point is the clearing of the temple. In John, this event launches Jesus' ministry, while in the Synoptics, it precedes Jesus' entry into Jerusalem. In the Synoptic portrayal of Jesus' death, the clearing of the temple along with the parable of the tenants is critical in his subsequent arrest. It seems pivotal. In his trial, it is Jesus' threat to the temple that is used as an accusation. This detail is found in John's account (John 2). If this happened three years earlier in Jesus' ministry, then it seems strained that it would play such a significant role. This seems key to recognizing that the clearing occurred at the end of Jesus' life rather than earlier. If the readers already know Mark and/or Luke when reading John, then they would recognize this move as theological rather than historical.

Whether John wrote independently or in some sense his Gospel was a supplement to the Synoptics, Jesus' three-year ministry would have involved a great deal more than the Synoptics as John reveals (see John 21:25). In addition, much of John is based in Judea, which seems to strengthen the theory that John intentionally records information not included in the Synoptics. The discourses arise out of a dispute with Jews in Jerusalem or with disciples, and could well be historical reminiscences not contained in the Synoptics. The details concerning the events and the feasts involved seem realistic.

Furthermore, even with different details, Jesus' *modus operandi* as preacher and miracle worker is similar in John to that in the Synoptics. Although Jesus mainly speaks in parables in the Synoptics and not so in John, parabolic material is not completely absent in John. In his discourses, Jesus draws on a wide range of images to convey truth such as: wine, birth, water, bread, light and darkness, sight, shepherding, and vines (e.g., John 10:1-18; 15:1-17). Jesus' teaching is parabolic, if not full of parables. If, as most agree, Jesus lived according to the practice of a faithful Jew of the day and attended the key feasts, engagement with Jews on these occasions makes good sense.

The Synoptic portrayal was not necessarily strictly chronological, so confusion over chronology when comparing them with John may be explained by different authorial intent and theology. The theology of John does not contradict the theology in the Synoptics, but develops it in different directions, such as with deity, the Spirit, and servanthood.

The Synoptics offer a better historical feel than John. John, knowing his readers knew the basic outline of Jesus from the Synoptics, arranged his material with more freedom to give theological meaning. However, other scholars prefer the Johannine historical shape to Jesus' ministry.

The Gospel of John seems to reflect the depiction of Jesus in both the Synoptic Gospels and in Paul. Paul's understanding of the faith has a strong emphasis on faith and love. Whereas the Synoptic Jesus calls people to divest themselves of their lives and follow him, John's Jesus summons people to believe in him. Whereas the Synoptics focus in the ethical sermons on a range of responses, John and Paul tend to wrap up the Christian ethic in the overriding attribute of love. John seems to reflect a point in Christian thought development, whereby Paul and the Synoptic Jesus are coming together.

John, then, is different because he is not seeking to present a *bios* of Jesus focusing on events; rather, he is focusing on the theological meaning of Jesus. This does not mean the events did not happen, but John has shaped the telling of the stories to his missional purpose.

THE PURPOSE OF JOHN

Whereas in the Synoptics the purpose of the writer must be deduced, John is explicit concerning his objective in writing his Gospel. He writes in John 20:31: "But these are written so that you may believe that Jesus is the Messiah, the Son of God, and that by believing you may have life in his name" (NIV). Clearly, the reason John wrote was to help people believe in Jesus as Messiah and Son of God. His purpose is that through this faith they may receive eternal life through Christ.

While this is clear, there has been a lively debate over whether John's purpose is evangelistic (helping people come to faith) or pastoral (encouraging believers to continue to believe). This debate is fueled by the alternative possibilities concerning the text of "believe" and the presence of a sigma or not in the verb "believe" (*pisteuō*) in John 20:31. "Believe" can either read the aorist subjunctive *pisteusēte*, which arguably speaks of an evangelistic purpose, people "coming to faith in a moment."[28] Alternatively, it can be the present subjunctive *pisteuēte*, indicating "continuing to believe," so pointing more to a pastoral message, encouraging believers in the faith.[29] John probably had both ideas in mind.[30] John, writing in the 80s AD, knows that his Gospel will have a variety of readers, some believers and some not. He is hoping unbelievers who read his Gospel will be convinced that Jesus is the Christ and God the Son, and place their trust in him. He hopes that believers will continue to have faith and so experience life in Jesus' name, especially in the face of Jewish persecution and false teaching. There is probably an apologetic intention as well: John is reinforcing in his account notions that counteract Jewish rejection of Jesus as Messiah and false teaching such as proto-gnostic ideas, a diminishing of Christ's supremacy, docetism, and/or Arianism.[31] Note the word "life" is present

---

28. Carson, *John*, 661 takes it evangelistically.
29. Beasley-Murray, *John*, 387 additionally notes that John breaks these supposed "rules of grammar" in the Gospel.
30. See, for example, Gerald L. Borchert, *John 12–21*, NAC 25B (Nashville: Broadman & Holman, 2002), 319; Köstenberger, *John*, 582; Ramsay J. Michaels, *The Gospel of John*, NICNT (Grand Rapids, MI; Cambridge, UK: Eerdmans, 2010), 1022.
31. Derek Brown, "Docetism," *LBD*. Docetism is an early church heresy that argues Jesus did not have a physical body, but appeared to be human and die on a cross. It thus downplays his humanity. Conversely, Arianism is an early church heresy propagated by Arius that argues Jesus was created and ontologically subordinate to God the Father, and so not divine.

subjunctive in this verse, indicating this life starts at the point of faith, now. John wants his readers to *be* saved and *stay* saved.

John's purpose includes an evangelistic intent (that readers come to faith), a pastoral purpose (to encourage believers in their faith), and an apologetic objective (to defend Jesus and Christianity against false teaching and/or Jewish refusal to accept Christ as Messiah). John clearly portrays Jesus as both God and man. He defends Jesus against those who might regard him as merely an angel or a great person. And he defends him against those who might regard him as less than a real man—for example, the heresies of docetism and Gnosticism.

THE STRUCTURE OF JOHN

Beasley-Murray says of the structure of John: "The fundamental plan of the Gospel is plain, and it is acknowledged by most exegetes."[32] The Gospel is usually divided into two main sections framed by a prologue (John 1) and an epilogue (John 21).

1. **Prologue** (John 1:1–18).

    a. **Signs** (John 1–12):[33] In John 1–12, Jesus performs wondrous deeds, engages in discussion with opponents and crowds, and moves freely. In these chapters, Jesus' "hour has not yet come" (John 2:4; 7:30; 8:20). Within the book of signs, there are seven miracles or signs and other encounters that lead to faith, but there is also rising opposition that peaks in John 11 when authorities seek Jesus' life.

The church ruled that "Christ was co-equal and co-eternal with the Father." Contemporary Jehovah's Witnesses have a similar theological perspective to the early Arians.

32. Beasley-Murray, *John*, xc. For this standard structure, see also Köstenberger, *John*, 9–13; Gary M. Burge, *John*, NIVAC (Grand Rapids, MI: Zondervan Publishing House, 2000), 40–45.

33. There are various other analyses; see Carson, *John*, 103–108. Carson himself sees the shift not at the end of John 11, but the end of John 10, with John 11:1–12:50 as the turning point. Michaels, *John*, 36–37 argues for this structure: Preamble (John 1:1–5); The testimony of John and transition (John 1:6–3:36); Jesus' self-revelation to the world (John 4:1–12:43); Jesus' self-revelation to the disciples (John 13:1–16:33); Verification of Jesus' self-revelation in his arrest, crucifixion, and resurrection (John 18:1–21:25).

b. **The pivot of the letter** (John 12): Jesus is anointed for death and burial (for John, his glorification) and enters Jerusalem, and events move toward his death and resurrection. John 12:23 announces the advent of the crucial time of revelation (the cross and resurrection), and in John 13-20, the hour has come (John 13:1; 17:1).

c. **Glory** (John 13-20): In John 13-20 Jesus talks to his disciples alone, followed by the passion and resurrection accounts.

2. **Epilogue** (John 21).

KEY DIMENSIONS OF JOHN'S GOSPEL

John's presentation develops Synoptic notions such as the treatment of John the Baptist,[34] the calling of the disciples,[35] Jesus' engagement with non-Jews (John 12:20-22), and Jesus as the servant (John 12:38; cf. Isa 53:12), exemplified and demonstrated supremely when Jesus washes his disciples' feet (John 13:1-7). The Gospel, like the others, climaxes with Jesus crucified[36] and raised. While the three Synoptic passion predictions are absent (cf. Mark 8:31; 9:31; 10:33; 14:27; and parr.), throughout John there are numerous allusions to Jesus' ultimate suffering and death, indicating that John's Jesus was aware of his fate and the need for his death (John 12:23,

---

34. There is additional information concerning John the Baptist in John's Gospel, perhaps indicating his ongoing influence in the Ephesian Christian community (cf. Acts 19:1-5). His role as the forerunner and witness to Jesus as Messiah is highlighted (John 1:6-9, 19-20, 29-38; 3:30; 5:31-36; cf. Isa 40:3; Mal 3:1-2; 4:5). The first disciples in John's account also come from among John's disciples (John 1:29-35).

35. The accounts of the call of Andrew, Peter, Philip, and Nathanael are different in John's Gospel to those in the Synoptics (John 1:35-51). Throughout the narrative there are those who fall short of the ideal of discipleship, such as Nicodemus initially (John 3:1-15), but who ultimately appear to have become a disciple (John 7:50; 19:39; the deserters of John 6:60-66, and Judas). There are others who reflect authentic response such as the disciples (John 6:68-69), the Samaritan woman (John 4:1-42), the healed blind man (John 9:38), Martha (John 11:27), Mary (John 12:1-8), and Joseph of Arimathea (John 19:38-42).

36. The Johannine passion narrative has some differences including: the name of the servant Malchus (John 18:10); the names of the high priests (Annas and Caiaphas); details of Jesus' interrogation before the high priest and his appearance before Pilate (John 18:19-24, 28-38); emphasis on Pilate's view of Jesus' innocence (John 19:6); Jesus carrying his own cross (John 19:17); three languages of the *titulus* "King of the Jews" (John 19:20); the presence of John ("the beloved disciple," John 19:25-27); that his legs are not broken and his side is pierced and the blood separates (John 19:31-34); and the presence of Nicodemus at his burial (John 19:38-42).

27-28, 32-33). The raising of Lazarus is the key event, as Jewish authorities react to the rise of popular support for Jesus (John 12:9-11). John, like Luke and Matthew, ends his Gospel with resurrection appearances including to Mary Magdalene (John 20:1-18, cf. Matt 28:9), the Thomas encounter (John 20:24-28), and the seven disciples fishing in Galilee (John 21:1-14, cf. Mark 16:7; Matt 28:16-20).

THE "I AM" SAYINGS OF JESUS

One of the distinctive features of the Gospel is the so-called "I am" sayings in which Jesus states aspects of his identity through the formula *egō eimi* ("I am"). While there are other "I am" sayings, seven have a predicate[37] and are designated the "I am" sayings, which define Jesus metaphorically. Each has important theological significance.

- I am *the bread of life* [and variants] (John 6:35, 41, 48, 51).
- I am the *light of the world* (John 8:12; 9:5).
- I am *the gate* (John 10:7, 9).
- I am *the good shepherd* (John 10:11, 14).
- I am the *resurrection* and the *life* (John 11:25).
- I am the *way*, the *truth* and the *life* (John 14:6).
- I am the *true vine* (John 15:1, 5).

There are also other places where John uses the "I am" construction in the narrative. These include:

- "I am [the Christ], the one speaking to you" (John 4:26).
- "I am, do not be afraid" (John 6:20): to the fearful disciples in the boat as he walked toward them.

---

37. DeMoss, *PDSNTG* 100: a "predicate" is "The part of a clause consisting of a verb and often other components that complement the subject, expressing (predicating) something about it; the element or construction around which the sentence is organized." For example, in "I am the bread of life," "I" is the subject (Jesus), "am" is the verb, and "the bread of life" is the predicate, as it expresses something about the subject, Jesus.

- "I am the one who testifies for myself" (John 8:18).

- "For unless you believe that I am, you will die in your sins." I am! (John 8:24).

- "When you have lifted up the Son of Man, then you will know that I am" (John 8:28).

- "Before Abraham was born, I am" (John 8:58).

- "I am telling you this now, before it takes place, that when it does take place you may believe that I am" (John 13:19).

- "Jesus said to them, 'I am'" (John 18:5, 8).

The statements with predicates all define Jesus in terms of his role in salvation and as the giver of life in different ways. As the bread of life, he is the spiritual sustenance of the world, giving the food that yields eternal life. Whereas food sustains physically, he is the true Manna of God that feeds God's people daily. As the light of the world, Jesus enlightens humanity and lights the way to salvation in a dark, fallen world. He drives out the darkness (evil). As the resurrection and the life, Jesus is the solution to humanity's ultimate problem—death. He created life (John 1:2), and he not only gives physical life to all who believe and all flesh, but he gives eternal life, beginning in the present spiritually, and into the age to come both physical and spiritual. As the gate, Jesus is the entry point into salvation, eternal life, God's people, the temple, and the city of God (cf. Rev 21–22). He can be likened to the narrow gate (cf. Matt 7:13–14). As the Good Shepherd, Jesus is the shepherd and pastor of the world. He is a guide, protector, and provider, who cares for his sheep (his people). He is the fulfillment of the hope of a Davidic shepherd in Ezekiel 34. He is a true shepherd, unlike other false claimants. He is "good," and the embodiment of "the LORD is my Shepherd" (Ps 23:1). As the way, the truth, and the life, Jesus is the path to salvation, the only authentic claimant to spiritual reality, and the source of life—physical and eternal—the celestial city. He is "the truth" in a world of relativism and false claims. In John's world—unlike Judaism, which claims Mosaic law and the gentile world with its many philosophical ideas—it is Jesus who is the truth. He is the answer to Pilate's question: "What is truth?" (John 18:38). He is "the life," that is, the source of all life, present life, and eternal life. As the true vine, he is the source of life giving sustenance to believers. He is the true Israel into which people come (Isa 5). In him, the people of God continue.

There is debate over the absolute "I am" sayings and whether they indicate a claim to divinity or are simply identity statements. The latter can be argued to be the case in those instances in which Jesus is clarifying his identity (John 4:26; 6:20; 8:18, 8:24, 28; 13:19). However, in 8:58, Jesus is clear: he is stating that before Abraham was born, "I am," that is, "I exist"—this both suggests his existence before Abraham and his divine status, as seen by the response to kill him (John 8:58). In the garden, as Jesus says, "I am" to the arresting party, they fall to the ground (John 18:6). This speaks of Jesus' power and likely points to his changeless theophanic[38] divine authority. These two and the force of the predicated "I am" sayings suggests that John does not use the construct neutrally or merely as an identification device. Most likely, they point to Jesus' divinity in terms of Exodus 3:14 (LXX): "I am the one who is" (*egō eimi ho ōn*). It also calls to mind Isaiah 40-55 where "I am" is used as a title for God (Isa 43:10, 25; 45:18; 46:4; 51:12; 52:6). This is confirmed by the Jews' response; they recognized it as a radical claim to divinity and sought to kill him (John 5:18; 8:59; 10:33).[39]

The sayings are also connected to the discourses and teaching of John—the bread of life is followed by a lengthy discussion of Jesus' teaching (John 6). The light of the world is followed by the healing of the blind man (John 8-9). The gate and shepherd sayings are tied into a chapter stressing the assurance of Jesus' protection (John 10). The "resurrection and life" saying relates to the resurrection of Lazarus (John 11). "I am the way" is connected with Jesus stating he will go to prepare a place for the disciples (John 14). "I am the vine" is nestled in a discourse to the disciples concerning abiding in Christ (John 15).

---

38. Jeffrey E. Miller, "I Am Sayings in John's Gospel," *LBD*. Miller notes, "The consistent use of the present-tense 'I am'—rather than the past-tense 'I was'—suggests that the phrase has changelessness in view." Miller continues: "John may be presenting this event as a theophany, since the people react as though God's presence were manifested before them."

39. Jeffrey E. Miller, "I Am Sayings of John," *LBD*. Miller writes, "In passages where Jesus makes an 'I am' statement, the negative reaction of His opponents reinforces the view that the phrase amounts to a claim to deity."

THE SIGNS OF JOHN

Jesus performs some astonishing miracles in John. John calls these "signs" (*sēmeion*) rather than "miracles of power" as in the Synoptics (*dynameis*) (John 2:11, 18, 23; 3:2; 4:48, 54; 6:2, 14, 26, 30; 7:31; 9:16; 10:31-32; 11:47; 12:18, 37; 20:30). They are thus recorded as indicators of Jesus' identity.

This is confirmed in John's purpose statement for the Gospel in John 20:30-31: "Now Jesus did *many other signs* in the presence of the disciples, which are not written in this book; *but these are written* so that you may believe that Jesus is the Christ, the Son of God and that by believing you may have life in his name."

The miracles or signs selected by John are designed to convince his readers that Jesus is indeed the Messiah and Son of God. For Jews, signs were extremely important. Despite his many miracles, Jesus was regularly asked to perform them on demand (Matt 12:38-39; 16:1), which Jesus repudiated (Matt 16:4; Mark 8:11-12; Luke 11:16, 29-30). Paul notes this desire in 1 Corinthians 1:22, stating the "Jews demand signs." This fits with John's desire to present an apologetic for Jesus to Christians combatting Jewish perspectives. He is seeking to demonstrate the signs of Jesus he records, among the many others he performed, are sufficient to prove Jesus is Messiah and God's Son so that people will believe and receive eternal life.

Another distinctive in John is that whereas faith generates miracles as in the Synoptics (e.g., Matt 9:29; 15:28; Mark 2:5; 5:34; 10:52; Luke 7:50; 17:19), in John, they *generate* faith. However, the faith they generate is not yet saving faith, but a shallow faith that attracts people to Jesus that sometimes grows to a saving faith (see John 2:11; 3:2; 4:48), but sometimes does not (John 2:23-25; 6:14-65). John also calls the miracles "works," indicating that the miracles are the work of God, the work of restoration (John 5:20; 7:3, 21; 8:41; 10:25, 32-33, 37-38; 14:11-12; 15:24). These should authenticate Jesus but are insufficient for his Jewish opponents. John deems them sufficient.

It is often said that there are seven signs in John:[40]

1. The turning of water into wine (John 2:1-12)

2. The healing of the nobleman's son (John 4:46-54)

---

40. E.g., Carson, *John*, 274.

3. The healing of the man at the pool of Bethesda (John 5:1-47)

4. The feeding of the five thousand (John 6:1-4)

5. Jesus' walking on water (John 6:16-21)

6. The healing of the blind man (John 9:1-41)

7. The raising of Lazarus (John 11:1-57)

The eighth and greatest sign is the resurrection of Christ himself. As signs, these function to demonstrate who Jesus is. There are other signs mentioned in general terms throughout the narrative, usually in reference to debates over Jesus' identity. John also intimates that these are selected for his argument that Jesus is Messiah and Son of God.

In the first sign, the turning of water into wine at Cana (John 2:1-12), Jesus reveals his glory suggesting his identity as Messiah and God the Son. This leads the disciples to respond with faith (John 2:11). Aside from Judas, who for John is a demonized devil, betrayer, and son of perdition (John 6:70-71; 12:4; 13:2), this grows into authentic faith and the disciples' refusal to desert Jesus (John 6:67-69). John specifically notes that this is Jesus' first sign. The amazing transformation of water into fermented grape juice demonstrates Jesus is the Creator and has supremacy over the created order (see John 1:2-3). It is also a miracle of provision and deliverance; Jesus provides his host with wine and what is socially necessary to ensure that the host is not shamed.[41]

There is a distinction between the type of sign that Jesus would perform and that which the Jews demanded. Jesus refused to perform signs on demand or without the motivation of genuine concern for the recipient. When they demanded a sign of his authority (after he cleared the temple), he states ambiguously that the resurrection is the only sign he would show them (John 2:18-22). This is consistent with Matthew and Luke's "sign of Jonah" (Matt 16:4; Luke 11:29). For John, the signs Jesus did perform are sufficient.

---

41. Carson, *John*, 169 notes: "To run out of supplies would be a dreadful embarrassment in a 'shame' culture; there is some evidence it could also lay the groom open to a lawsuit from aggrieved relatives of the bride."

Jesus performed many other signs in that initial Passover visit to Jerusalem, and many believed (*pistis*) in him as a result (John 2:23). However, their *pistis* appears inadequate as Jesus refuses to "*entrust*" (*pistis*) himself to them (John 2:24). This indicates that signs in and of themselves do not guarantee a person will respond in faith. The signs may excite interest and even a level of faith. But they must be read at a deeper level, the recipient perceiving the full identity of Jesus—he is no mere prophet, he is Messiah and Son of God—and believe in him. Belief is more than cognitive acceptance; it involves yielding oneself completely to Jesus in trust and commitment. Nicodemus is one of these Jews attracted to Jesus because of his signs but who does not understand Jesus or who he is. Unlike the disciples in 2:11, he is spiritually blind (John 3:1-7). As the story unfolds, it seems he became a full believer (John 7:50; 19:39).

The second Johannine "sign" Jesus performed is the healing of the official's son, again in Cana in Galilee, although the son is at Capernaum (John 4:43-54)—the completion of the so-called Cana cycle. Some think he may have been a Roman soldier as the healing is similar to that of the centurion's servant in the Synoptics (Matt 8:5-13; Luke 7:1-10); however, this is unlikely in that there are great differences between the two stories.[42] The Greek word to describe the official means "royal official, " and so he may have been an official of Herod Antipas, the tetrarch of Galilee.[43] Again, Jesus bemoans the constant appeal for signs and yet he responds to the official's genuine need (John 4:48-50). The climax of the story is the official and his family believing—he is a model of the right response to the miracles of Jesus for Jewish and other readers (4:53).

The third sign is the healing of the man by the pool of Bethesda (John 5:1-14). The man has been severely disabled for thirty-eight years and is unable to step into the pool, which is renowned for healing. Jesus heals

---

42. While there are similarities such as an official, a child, and a distant healing, there are significant differences: (1) In John, unlike Matthew and Luke, Jesus has just returned from Judea; (2) John's miracle is in Cana and the sick child is in Capernaum, while Matthew and Luke's official and child are in Capernaum; (3) John's recipient is a royal official and Matthew and Luke's a centurion; (4) the interaction between the official in John and the centurion is significantly different, with John focusing on signs, and Matthew and Luke on authority.

43. This leads to interesting ponderings over the connection to Herod's hearing about the fame of Jesus (from this official?) (Matt 14:1; Mark 6:14, 16; Luke 9:7) or the connection to Chuza, whose wife traveled with Jesus (Luke 8:3).

him and him alone rather than the whole crowd at the pool. This shows Jesus' freedom to heal at his whim—he did not heal everyone he encountered—and reveals his compassion for a man disabled for many years.[44] This becomes a great issue of controversy as it occurs on the Sabbath. This and the previous healing demonstrate Jesus' power to restore and heal a genuine enquirer in need. He heals the rich and poor. These are "great works" that should lead people to believe (John 5:20, cf. 7:21). They give testimony to his identity as the Son of God working on behalf of his Father (John 5:36).

In John 6, Jesus performs two more signs back-to-back, both of which are found in the Synoptics. The first (fourth overall) is the feeding of the five thousand (John 6:1-13), found in all four Gospels. The story is essentially the same in John as in the Synoptics, but with extra detail—especially concerning the supply of food and Andrew and Philip's involvement. The crowd's response is to describe Jesus as "the prophet," the fulfillment of the common Jewish hope of a prophet like Moses (Deut 18:15). This leads Jesus to withdraw because he is concerned that they will try to make him king by force (John 6:14-15). Jesus is not here to lead a rebellion. This coincides with John's emphasis on the impact of signs on observers of Jesus' miracles. Their response is inadequate, however; it is not full-fledged, saving faith. These verses are critical to understanding Jesus, and his silencing of messianic hopes expressed about him (e.g., the messianic silencing in Mark). Although he is Messiah, he refuses to be one who lines up with Jewish expectation of military might. He will express his messiahship through mercy and sacrificial death by crucifixion. For John (and the other Gospels), Jesus is Messiah, *but not that sort of Messiah*. This feeding miracle is picked up later in John 6 in the discourse built around the saying, "I am the bread of life." Jesus is compared to Moses, who provided manna, which nourished physically (Exod 16). However, Jesus doesn't merely provide bread; he is God's true Manna who nourishes spiritually, giving eternal life. This is not understood by his hearers who are offended at the thought of cannibalism. This discourse leads to the dramatic rejection of Jesus in John 6:61-70 by all but the disciples. Thus, there is a contrast between those who read the

---

44. Köstenberger, *John*, 179, notes that this man had been in this place for longer than many lived at the time with the average life expectancy around forty.

signs and understand them (the disciples) and those who do not (those who walk away). John wants his readers to emulate the disciples, not those who walked away.

This miracle is followed by the fifth of John's signs, Jesus' walking on water (John 6:16–24). This demonstrates Jesus the Creator's supremacy over the created order as he achieves the "ludicrous" (cf. John 1:3–4). It also recalls God's control over the waters at the flood, the exodus, and the crossing of the Jordan. John's telling of this story highlights Jesus' supremacy as he responds to the disciples' fear with the "*I am*" before "do not be afraid." While these words are found in Matthew and Mark's versions, and possibly only speak there of his identity ("it is me"; see Mark 6:50; Matt 14:27), considering the other "I am" sayings in John, this likely speaks of Jesus as God the Son. John ensures his readers know Jesus crossed the lake miraculously; he records that the crowds followed Jesus when they realized he had left and had not stepped into a boat. This miracle adds to the effect of Jesus being the Messiah and Son of God. Again, John summons his readers to recognize who Jesus is: the Creator, the *logos*—God.

In John 6:30–31, after the feeding and the water miracles, there is yet another request for a sign. This time the request is for one that supersedes the giving of manna in the wilderness (Exod 16:31–35). The request demonstrates the failure of many to perceive the "signs." Jesus rejects their request and explains that he is the bread of life, which must be eaten to have eternal life (John 6:35–40).

In John 7:25–31, signs lie at the heart of debates among Jews in Jerusalem concerning Jesus' identity. The signs cause astonishment (John 7:21) and many "believed in him" because of them (John 7:31). This faith is not saving faith, for later all will reject him as he is arrested and goes to the cross.

John 9 revolves around the sixth sign, the healing of a blind man. The restoration of sight to the blind man powerfully illustrates Jesus' statement, "I am the light of the world" (John 8:12, cf. 9:5). The healing challenges the idea that personal or prior generational sin is the cause of disease. The reason for this man's blindness is not due to his sin, or those of his parents or ancestors, but that God will be glorified through his healing (John 9:3). Jesus heals him using saliva and mud, and by washing in a pool.

The healing leads to further controversy as the Pharisees reject Jesus because he has performed his signs on the Sabbath (John 9:16). The people are divided in their opinion of Jesus (John 9:17). There is a heated debate between Jewish leadership and the healed man. Eventually, the leaders reject the man's testimony on the basis that he is a sinner. There is a progression in the development of faith in the blind man, who states Jesus is a prophet (John 9:17), then that he is "from God" (John 9:31-32) and then, after an encounter with Jesus, that he is the Son of Man (John 9:35-38). The climax is John 9:38 where the healed man states, *"Lord*, I believe," and he *worshiped* him. He is thus a paradigm of right response to Jesus—he recognizes who Jesus is, and worships him. Later, Martha will do the same but before the raising of Lazarus (John 11:25). There is a play on the notion of blindness here; the man is now spiritually sighted, whereas the Jewish leaders, who should perceive who Jesus is, are spiritually blind (John 9:40-41). This speaks powerfully into John's context where Jewish leaders cannot accept Jesus. This is a sign of the healing power of Christ, not only to heal the *physically* blind, but also to open the eyes of the *spiritually* blind so that they will be saved. Through the signs, there is an increase in tension over Jesus. The miracles ("works") testify to Jesus' authority, but they are rejected by the Jewish leaders (John 10:25). They do not satisfy them—they want specific signs of authentication as Moses presented to Israel's leaders before the exodus (Exod 4:18-31). There is irony in Jesus' dialogue in John 10 as he challenges the leaders about his works and their desire to kill him (John 10:32-38). Clearly, for John, the miracles should lead people to acknowledge Jesus' Lordship. For his enemies, they increase their resolve to kill him.

The most dynamic sign, aside from the supreme sign of the resurrection which this anticipates, is the seventh in John 11—the raising of Lazarus (John 11:1-45). The sign is made more impressive in that Lazarus has been dead for four days. Again, the power of Jesus as Creator is evidenced: he is the resurrection and life full of creative power to raise the dead. This leads to contrasting responses—while more believe in Jesus, there is further opposition from the leaders. They are concerned that many more people will turn to Jesus if he continues to perform miracles.

In John 14, Jesus appeals to his followers to believe in him because of his miracles (John 14:11); if they believe, they will do even more of the same (John 14:12). He pronounces judgment on those who reject him because they have seen the signs and yet do not believe in him (John 15:24). John's Gospel is a quasi-legal presentation of the signs of Jesus as evidence to believe in him. John's readers must make a choice.

The ultimate sign in John, and especially so for the first disciples including John, is the resurrection. Mary Magdalene at first believes that opponents have removed Jesus from the tomb to an unknown location (John 20:2). Peter and another disciple (possibly John) are perplexed (John 20:4-10). Then, as she meets Jesus, Mary's grief turns to joy, worship, and proclamation (John 20:11-18). The disciples' fear turns to joy (John 20:19-20). Thomas' doubt transforms to worship (John 20:24-28). This sign and others are recorded that readers will believe (John 20:30-31).

Throughout John's Gospel, the signs and works of Jesus are pointers that lead to discussions (dialogues) about Jesus' identity and claims. John is inviting his readers not to be like the "Jews" (Jewish leaders) who rationalize Jesus' signs and works (e.g., claiming they are from the devil, e.g., John 7:20; 8:48-52; 10:20-21), reject them because he performs them on the Sabbath (e.g., John 5:1-18; 9:1-41), or deny them for any other reason. John calls readers to identify with him and other believers, and follow and worship Jesus as Messiah and Son of God.

THE FEASTS OF JOHN

Much of the narrative of John occurs at Jewish annual festivals.[45]

1. **Passover 1:** In John 2, Jesus travels to Jerusalem to the Passover, clears the temple, and performs many signs. There is no indication of a shift in context for Nicodemus' visit and the subsequent discourse until John 3:22, suggesting these are situated by John in Jerusalem.

2. **Unspecified Feast:** John 5 takes place at an unspecified feast that may be Passover and Unleavened Bread,[46] although

---

45. The wedding feast in John 2 could be added.
46. See Irenaeus, *Haer* 2.22.3. Carson, *John*, 240 acknowledges this possibility. Some argue for the Feast of Trumpets (Yom Teruah, later called *Roch ha-Shanah*; see Lev 23:23-25) or Purim (Esther, see J. Bowman, "The Identity and Date of the Unnamed Feast of John 5:1," in *Near Eastern Studies in Honor of William Foxwell Albright*, ed. H. Goedicke [Baltimore: Johns Hopkins Press, 1971], 43-56). F. Braun argued strongly for Pentecost. F. Braun, *L'Evangile selon Saint Jean* (Paris: du Cerf, 1946), 351.

John specifies Passovers elsewhere. If not Passover, this could be Pentecost/Weeks, or Tabernacles; many scholars opt for the latter.[47] However, others argue the use of the article could indicate Passover. There is no way to know.[48] What matters is not the feast, but that Jesus is back in Jerusalem. En route he healed the royal official's son and in Jerusalem, the man by the pool. He does so on the Sabbath of the feast, and this creates controversy and a desire to kill Jesus.

3. **Passover 2:** In John 6:4, John mentions the Passover being at hand, but does not record Jesus going. Some argue that John 5 and 6 should be inverted, but that is not supported in any ancient version. Hence, there is uncertainty as to whether Jesus went, although, as a faithful Jew, he likely did. Here, Passover invokes the memory of the exodus, and the feeding of the five thousand and "bread of life" discourse recall the wilderness wanderings. Jesus is the "new Moses" who does not only give bread as did Moses, but whose body is the bread of life. To believe in Jesus is to "gnaw" on him.[49]

4. **Tabernacles:** John 7:1–10:21 seems to be set in Jerusalem with most of John 7 and 8 at the Feast of Booths/Tabernacles. Again, this invokes the exodus and wilderness. Jesus does not respond to his unbelieving brothers insisting he go and market himself there, but makes his own way there later (John 7:8-10). There he teaches, challenging Jewish interpretation of the law of the Sabbath, which is for healing. Jesus' invitation to come to him and drink on the last great day of the feast (a special Sabbath) is set in the context of the daily delivery of a golden pitcher of water from the Siloam Pool to the temple and the drink offering made on the seventh day.[50] Jesus is the

---

47. Köstenberger, *John*, 177. He even dates it, suggesting October 21-28, AD 31.

48. Similarly, Carson, *John*, 241, who writes, "The truth of the matter is that we do not know what feast John has in mind."

49. The Greek *trōgō* used four times in John 6:54-58 has the sense of "chew," and is used of animals (BDAG 1019).

50. Beasley-Murray, *John*, 113.

living water. "Streams of living water" can refer to Jesus as the source of the water, or the water flowing from believers.[51] Either way, Jesus is the source of the water. Later, at the feast, Jesus declares himself the light of the world. This likely happened the same evening at the festival of lights, when golden lamps were lit filling the temple area with light while people danced in celebration.[52] The feast was associated with hopes of Israel's redemption and the nations gathering to worship God in Jerusalem (e.g., Zech 14:16–17). Jesus is declaring himself the fulfillment of those hopes. Again, the healing of the blind man in John 9 occurs on a Sabbath, Jesus again challenging the Jewish leaders' interpretation.

5. **Dedication:** In John 10:22, Jesus is still in Jerusalem during the Feast of Dedication (or the Feast of Lights). This is the feast that celebrates the Maccabean liberation of the temple from Antiochus Epiphanes, who had set up a pagan altar within it (167 BC). While walking in the temple, Jesus is challenged concerning his messianic status, appealing to his works as evidence, speaking of his gift of eternal life to his sheep, and his oneness with the Father.

6. **Passover 2 or 3:** Jesus' final festival is his final Passover coinciding with his death.

THE IDENTITY OF JESUS

The "I am" sayings and signs serve to help readers recognize that Jesus is the Messiah and Son of God. Running through the Gospel is the question: "Who is this man?" John highlights many dimensions of Jesus' identity in answering this question—ideas from the context, the "I am" sayings, and the testimony of others. Some of these include:

---

51. Carson, *John*, 323.
52. Beasley-Murray, *John*, 126–27.

The Logos

Picking up an idea from the Old Testament of Jesus as wisdom, torah, and dā·bār (word), and a concept from Greek philosophy (esp. Stoicism), John first presents Jesus as the incarnate pre-existent divine Word who has come from heaven (John 3:13) to reveal the nature and person of God to humanity. Jesus is not just the final preacher of God's word to humanity; *he* is the Message. His whole being is God's proclamation, his revelation, to the world.

Creator

As divine *logos*, Jesus is the one through whom the world was formed. He is the Creator, who has become a part of his creation ("flesh," John 1:14), come to redeem his creation. This idea is found in Paul and Hebrews (Col 1:16; Heb 1:2).

God

Throughout John, there are implicit and explicit indications of Jesus' divinity:

1. Jesus is the *logos* who was with God and *was* God (John 1:1). Some point out that because the Greek lacks the definite article "the" John is not saying Jesus is God, but that he has God-like qualities. If so, John would have used *theios* (divine) rather than *Theos* (God). The absence of the article is not important and emphasizes the point, "was God."[53]

2. Jesus is "the unique and beloved one, [himself] God"[54] (John 1:18).

3. Jesus is also accused of "making himself equal to God" (John 5:18) and "making himself God" (John 10:33).

---

53. For detail, see Carson, *John*, 117, 137. Note also that *Theos* is used in John eighty-three times and all refer to God except in John 1:1, 1:18; so why would these two not also be saying that Jesus in some sense is God? Further, in John 1:18 both references to God lack the article. The first relates to God the Father, the second to Jesus—"God (*Theon*, accusative of *Theos* without the article) no-one has ever seen, the one and only God (*Theos*, no article), who is at the bosom of the Father (with article) him, he has made him known."

54. Carson, *John*, 139.

4. Jesus declares, "Before Abraham was born, *I am*" (John 8:58). This takes up the name of Yahweh, *egō eimi* (cf. Exod 3:14; Isa 41:4; 43:13). The response of the Jews is to take up stones to kill him, clearly indicating that they understand these words as blasphemous, that is, Jesus was claiming divinity.[55]

5. In John, Jesus is *worshiped* by some, including the healed blind man when he realizes who Jesus is and experiences spiritual healing (John 9:38). After the resurrection, Thomas confesses of the resurrected Jesus, "my Lord and God" (*ho kyrios moy kai ho Theos moy*), a direct confession of Jesus' divinity. Interestingly, this phrase was applied to the Roman Emperor Domitian (John 20:28).[56]

6. The Jew's *desire to kill Jesus* in John is also directly linked to his claims to be God. At the Feast of Dedication, some seek to stone him for claiming oneness with God, and so divinity (John 10:33, cf. 10:30).

The Lamb of God

Jesus is the servant (Isa 53), and the one who fulfills the whole sacrifice system of Israel. He takes away not only the sins of Israel but the sins of the whole world. He is the Lamb of God (John 1:29).

God the Son

This notion is first implied when John refers to Jesus as the one and only unique Son of the Father (John 1:14). John here uses *monogenēs* of Jesus alone, a word once translated "only begotten," and now generally understood as "unique" or "one and only" (John 1:18; 3:16, 18).[57] His divine sonship is then found on the lips of John the Baptist (John 1:34)[58] and Nathanael (John 1:49).

---

55. Carson, *John*, 358.

56. The Roman historian Suetonius reports that Domitian claimed the title "*Dominus et Deus noster*" ("Our Lord and God," *Dom.* 13), cf. Borchert, *John 12–21*, 316.

57. Köstenberger, *John*, 43.

58. The NIV (cf. NET, TNIV) records "God's chosen One"; however, the reading "Son of God" is favored (B rating) by Metzger, *Textual Commentary*, 172 and other translations (e.g.,

John preserves the Greek *huios* (son) for Jesus alone. He uses *teknon*, or "children," for believers who are children of God through him (e.g., John 1:12). The concept of sonship suggests the closest identification. As the Son, Jesus acts in dependence on and in obedience to God. He does and says nothing of his "own accord" (John 3:34; 7:28; 8:26, 42; 10:32, 37; 12:49). He and the Father share reciprocal knowledge (John 10:15). They work in unity in revelation and salvation (John 8:16; 10:25-30; 14:10-11; 17:10). The actions and words of Jesus, then, are truly the actions and words of God. For John, Jesus being the Son of God means he is God, just as being the son of a human father means being human. For John, Jesus is God the Son.

The Son of Man

This is Jesus' self-designation, especially in the Synoptics (sixty-nine times), but also in John although to a lesser extent (thirteen times, e.g., John 1:51; 3:13-14).[59] An elusive term connoting in the Old Testament a human (Ps 8:4-5) and a prophet (e.g., Ezek 2:1-6), it has its origins in the cosmic ruler of Daniel 7:13 and is developed in 1 Enoch 37-71. As a distinctly Jewish concept, it is not nearly as frequent in John's Gospel as in the Synoptics, perhaps indicating that John is writing for the gentile who would not understand its full implications.[60] However, when Jesus heals the blind man, he asks if the healed man believes in "the Son of Man." The man is uncertain of who he is but is prepared to believe in him if Jesus can define who he is. This could suggest the man is familiar with the Jewish expectation, but clearly, he has yet to recognize that Jesus is that person. When Jesus states that he *is* that person, the healed man declares his belief and worships him (John 9:35-38). This suggests that among the Jewish expectations of the time, there was some popular expectation of a "Son of Man" figure. The use of the Son of Man figure could indicate awareness of one or other of the Synoptics.

ESV, NAB, NIV 1984, NKJV).

59. See also John 6:27, 53, 62; 8:28; 9:35; 12:23, 34; 13:31.

60. "Son of Man" drops out of Christian use through the remainder of the New Testament, found only on the lips of Stephen (Acts 7:56), in a citation from Psalm 8:4-6 in Hebrews 2:5-8, and Revelation (Rev 1:13; 14:14). "Christ," also Jewish, is retained, perhaps due to its lack of ambiguity.

The Temple

In John 1:14, Jesus, the *logos*, becomes flesh and tabernacles amidst humanity. After the clearing of the temple in John 2, Jesus refers to himself becoming "the temple" ("this temple"), which will be destroyed and rebuilt (John 2:19). The locus of God's presence on earth will no longer be the Jewish temple or any of the multitude of temples in the Greco-Roman world, but the resurrected Jesus. This leads to great confusion as to whether Jesus intended to destroy the temple (John 2:19-22) and becomes one of the arguments used by Jews to convict (Mark 14:58) and mock him (Mark 15:29). Jesus is often in Jerusalem at festival celebrations at the temple. As noted earlier, these too may point to Jesus as the fulfillment of Israel's feast traditions; to dine on Jesus is to believe in him and receive eternal life.

Jesus is Life (Eternal)

In John's prologue, it is written that in Jesus is "life" (John 1:4). The theme of *eternal life* runs throughout John and is the most significant concept defining salvation (see below). The notion of "kingdom of God," which is used in the Synoptics, is rare in John's Gospel (John 3:3, 5, cf. John 18:36), but the concepts of "life" and "eternal life" are spoken of in a similar way. Jesus is the author of life (John 1:3-4). Through him comes life (John 5:16-30). He raises the dead (John 5:21). He judges all and assigns them eternal life or eternal destruction (John 5:21-22, 24-30). He provides life in all its fullness, speaking of the joy of God's presence with believers as they travel through life, and of eternal life to come (John 10:10). Jesus' resurrection of Lazarus and his statement, "I am the resurrection and the life" (John 11:25) also point to his power over life in terms of both literal and spiritual resurrection. Knowing Jesus *is* eternal life (John 17:3).

The Bread of Life

"I am the bread of life" (John 6:35) is Jesus' response to the request for a sign that supersedes the sign of manna from heaven (John 6:30-31). He refuses to do the sign but declares that he is the bread that must be eaten (John 6:33-40) to receive eternal life (John 6:44, 53-58). Unlike manna, which has a temporary effect, he gives eternal satisfaction. This is a metaphor for believing in him for salvation, which is the work of God (John 6:29). Connecting John's thought to the temptation narratives of Matthew and

Luke—"people do not live by bread alone, but every word that comes from the mouth of God"—Jesus is the totality of this Word, and is the ultimate sustenance for humanity (Matt 4:4; Luke 4). Jesus is the feast upon which people eat.

The Light of the World

Jesus is the light of the world, who lights the way to eternal life for those who follow (John 8:12; 9:5, 19; 12:35, 46). Followers are to believe in the light and become children of light (John 12:36). John focuses large portions of his narrative around a dualism of light and darkness, an important aspect of his theology. In John's theology, Jesus is the light of God's goodness coming to shine into the darkness of the world (John 1:4–5). The darkness cannot quench Jesus' light (John 1:5). Thus, remembering the first creative act of God, "Let there be light" (Gen 1:4), Jesus is both the Creator of the world's light and "the light" come to restore its goodness. Now, he has entered his creation as "light" to conquer the darkness that cannot overcome him (John 1:4). He is true light (John 1:9). In contrast, John is merely a witness to the light, as are all who share Christ with others, including the author. As the moon reflects the sun's light, so they merely reflect the Son's glorious light (John 1:7–8, cf. John 5:35). Considering John's dualistic cosmology, seemingly innocuous references to night and day could have theological meaning such as Nicodemus coming to Jesus "by night"—that is, in the darkness of his unbelief and ignorance (John 3:2). Similarly, Judas went out after the Last Supper, "and it was night" (John 13:30). Simon Peter and the fisherman caught nothing "that night," but then, "just as day was dawning, Jesus stood on the shore"; the contrast is with the darkness of the light of the world seemingly quenched, and the light of the world breaking afresh (John 21:3–4). Sadly, most of fallen humanity prefers darkness in its evil (John 3:19–20). Without God's light in their hearts, they stumble in the dark (John 11:10, cf. John 12:35). Yet, there are those who revel in the light (John 3:21). The healing of the blind man in John 9 illustrates Jesus as the light of the world, his story of physical and spiritual healing contrasted with the blindness of the Pharisees.

The Messiah, the Christ

Unlike the Synoptics, in which Jesus' messiahship is veiled (esp. Mark), John's Gospel does not have a secret-Messiah motif. From the beginning, Jesus is the Messiah. John starts with Jesus' identity and then demonstrates it.[61] Using the transliterated Aramaic *messias*, Andrew recognizes that Jesus is the Messiah and introduces Peter to him (John 1:41). John the Baptist denies he himself is the Messiah (*messias*); rather, he is the one who points to *the* Messiah, Jesus (John 3:28). Jesus' encounter with the Samaritan woman also raises the issue of his messiahship. There is a progression in the woman's understanding of who Jesus is until, based on his prophetic insight, she accepts and proclaims him as Messiah. This includes an explicit statement from Jesus that he is indeed the Messiah (John 4:25-26). In John 7:25-31 at the Feast of the Tabernacles, the crowd is divided over whether Jesus is the Messiah. This is an example of the Gospel's theme of acceptance or rejection of Jesus' messiahship. Some accept him as the Christ because of his miracles (John 7:31, 41). Others reject him because they know he is from Galilee and know nothing of his birth in Bethlehem (John 7:42).[62] At this, they want to seize him, but no one lays a hand on him because his time has not yet come. In John 10:24, Jesus is directly challenged as to whether he is the Christ. He affirms he is based on his miracles (John 10:25-26). Some believe, but most reject him and seek to kill him. The raising of Lazarus also sees one of the great confessions of the New Testament. Jesus states that he is "the resurrection and the life" and asks Martha whether she believes in him. She responds, "I believe that you are the *christos* [Greek for 'messiah'], the Son of God, who was to come into the world" (John 11:27). The fundamental purpose of John's Gospel is that readers believe Jesus is the Messiah, the Son of God (John 20:31).

The Savior (John 3:15-19, 35-36; 4:41-42)

Significant in these verses is the outcome of Jesus' encounter with the Samaritans of which it is said "many ... believed in him" and declare that

---

61. John's reasoning is deductive (i.e., he begins by stating Jesus' identity and then displays the evidence for it). The Synoptics are inductive. They tell the story and let the reader work out who Jesus is.

62. This is a good example of John assuming his readers know the other Gospels. They would have laughed at the irony.

he is the "Savior of the world" (John 4:41-42). The title "savior," *sōter*, was used in Judaism of God (Deut 32:15 LXX) and in the Greek world of the gods like Apollo (Aeschylus, *Ag.* 512) and especially of Zeus (e.g., Pindar, *Ol.* 5.17). It was also applied to rulers like Ptolemy I (Callimachus, *Hymn. Del.* 166). This encounter with Samaritans also demonstrates Jesus' breaking of boundaries and anticipates later Samaritan mission (Acts 1:8; 8). Hence, for John, Jesus is Savior of the world.

The Holy One of God (John 6:69)

Peter confesses that Jesus is the "Holy One of God," a parallel saying to the confessions of the Synoptics (Mark 8:29). This name is also used of Jesus by demons in Mark 1:24 and Luke 4:34. The name "holy one" was also used of God, identifying Jesus closely with Yahweh (e.g., 2 Kgs 19:22; 1 En 1.2; Philo, *Somn.* 1.254).

The Prophet (John 1:21, 25)

John the Baptist is asked if he is "the prophet" (John 1:21, 25). Jesus is similarly considered "the prophet" by some (John 6:14; 7:40, cf. Mark 6:15; 8:28). The prophet was an eschatological figure expected to come in the end times to fulfill Deuteronomy 18:15: "The LORD your God will raise up for you a prophet like me." Such a person was expected by the Samaritans (John 4:19) and at Qumran (4QTest 5-8). This title acknowledges Jesus' divine commissioning and authority. It links him to Moses. So, in a sense, the Muslim understanding of Jesus as a prophet is not wrong by identifying him prophetically; their error is their failure to recognize that Jesus is the Prophet, not Muhammad.

The Good Shepherd (John 10:1–18, esp. 11, 14)

Jesus describes himself in one of the "I am" sayings as "the Good Shepherd." In contrast to Satan (John 10:10), Jesus knows his sheep, and the sheep know him, i.e., they recognize him. He lays down his life for his sheep, pointing to his death on the cross. This invokes the Old Testament concept of God as a shepherd (e.g., Ps 23:1) and the Synoptic idea of Jesus as the shepherd who seeks the lost sheep (Matt 18:12-14; Luke 15:1-7). Jesus is the long-awaited Davidic Shepherd King who will come and restore the people of God when their leaders have failed (cf. Ezek 34; Zech 10-11). He is both the

Lamb of God who saves and the shepherd who saves. He gathers people to himself, provides for them, and protects them from enemies (false shepherds)—especially Satan, the false shepherd who seeks their destruction.

The Source of Living Water

Water is an important motif in John. Water is used in baptism by John (John 1:26, 31) and Jesus (John 3:22). John's baptism is contrasted with Jesus, on whom the Spirit descends and remains, baptizing with the Holy Spirit. The contrast evokes ideas of the Spirit as water from God drenching, immersing, and saturating believers, washing their hearts completely (John 1:33). Water is invoked as a metaphor for the Spirit when John's Jesus tells Nicodemus that a person must be born of water and Spirit to enter the kingdom, likely an emphatic construct indicating the Spirit.[63] In John 4, in contrast to the water from Jacob's well, Jesus is the giver of living water (John 4:10-15). In John 7:38 Jesus gives the Spirit so that rivers of living water flow from believers' hearts. Symbolically, water is used to wash the disciples' feet. Peter's refusal is rebutted by Jesus, and Jesus tells the disciples they are completely clean—referring to the cleansing work of the Spirit (John 13:8-10).

In John 2, water is turned into wine, perhaps symbolic of the new wine Jesus is instituting (recall the wineskins, Mark 2:22). Again, in John 5:7, the stirring of the waters supposedly brings healing. However, it is Jesus who heals the man. Jesus also walks on the sea in John 6:19, showing his command of the elements, as when he turned water into wine. Blood and water also come from Jesus' side, invoking memories of the water of life and Jesus as the bread of life who must be eaten (John 19:34, see also 4:14; 6:41-58)—from his death flow the elements of eternal life that is gained through "drinking and eating" Jesus, i.e., believing in him. It is beside the sea that Jesus reveals himself to the disciples (John 21:1-7).

---

63. Burge, *John*, 115-16 notes four: (1) Literal birth, but this is not an idea found in the context; (2) male semen, which is possible but obscure; (3) baptism, whether John the Baptist's or Jesus', but this creates the problem that one must be baptized to enter the kingdom, whereas, for John (and Paul) faith is all that is required; (4) "water and Spirit" as one concept recalling the use of pouring out and/or water in the Old Testament as a motif for renewal by the Spirit (e.g., Isa 32:15-20; 44:3; Ezek 36:25-27; Joel 2:28). The latter is rightly favored by many scholars.

Other Images

Jesus is the gate or the door—the path to salvation (John 10:7-9). He is also the way (John 14:6). He is not merely the entry point to life, but life itself. As the gate and the way, John links the Matthean notion of the narrow gate and path (Matt 7:13-14). He is also the embodiment of the Christian faith as "the way" (e.g., Acts 9:2; 19:9). He is also the truth, the embodiment of God as the faithful and true one (John 14:6). He is the vine, Israel embodied (Isa 5). Life is sustained through incorporation into Christ. This resounds with Paul's olive tree motif in Romans 11.

Conclusion

John powerfully portrays Jesus as the Messiah and God the Son working to bring God's salvation and mediating between God and humanity. So close is the identification of Jesus with God that to encounter Jesus is to encounter God, to see Jesus is to see the Father, and to know and receive Jesus is to know and receive the Father (John 14:9-10). This was new revelation for Jews, who did not believe that one could look upon God and live, let alone touch him (see 1 John 1:1-3).

JESUS CLASHES WITH "THE JEWS"

John's Gospel highlights the clashes between Jesus and his Jewish opponents, often labeled "the Jews" (used sixty-three times in John). Many believe these events did not happen as written, but that the Johannine writer wrote them in the light of later clashes between Jewish Christians and Jews when Christians were expelled from the synagogue (see John 9:22; 12:42; 16:2).[64] While hotly disputed,[65] it is argued that, toward the end of the first century around the time of the Council of Jamnia at Yavneh, the Twelfth Benediction was rewritten to include a curse on the Nazarenes and heretics (*minim*). This is the so-called *Birkat Ha-minim* attributed to Rabbi Samuel the Minor. It is said that these benedictions were recited three times a day and the curse was employed as a test of exclusion from the

---

64. C. K. Barrett, *The Gospel According to St. John*. 2d edition (Philadelphia: Westminster, 1978), 361; Martyn, *History and Theology*, 37-62.

65. R. Kimelman, "Birkat Ha-Minim and the Lack of Evidence for an Anti-Christian Jewish Prayer," in *Jewish and Christian Self-Definition*, Vol. 2, *Aspects of Judaism in Greco-Roman Period*, ed. E. Sanders et al. (Philadelphia: Fortress, 1981), 226-44; 391-403.

synagogue.⁶⁶ However, this anachronistic interpretation is not necessary as there is evidence of a development of condemnations.⁶⁷ It is likely that Jews were strongly antagonistic to those who confessed Jesus as Messiah from the early days, as the Synoptics and Acts reveal (cf. John 9:22). The references in John are then probably authentic but perhaps crafted to make sense to those in John's world when a full ban was in place.⁶⁸

John has a strong interest in clashes between Jesus and "the Jews," a term he uses often of Jesus' opponents (e.g., John 2:18; 5:10, 15-16, 18).⁶⁹ The term refers to leaders and those who oppose Jesus. All Jews are not involved, however,⁷⁰ which removes the stigma of anti-Semitism. For example, in John 10:19 the Jews are divided over Jesus, indicating that some of the Jewish people viewed him favorably. In Matthew 11, many Jews comfort Mary and Martha (cf. John 11:19, 31, 33, 36) while many of these Jews seek to kill him (John 11:46), and still others put their faith in him (John 11:45). Not all Jews were Jesus' opponents. John 12:11 says, "*many* of the Jews were going over to Jesus and believing in him" (NIV, emphasis added). The first disciples were Jews, as was John. As such, John's negativity about "the Jews" is about those Jews who oppose and are antagonistic to Jesus; essentially, they are those opponents of Jesus who are called "Pharisees," "scribes," "members of the Sanhedrin," and "Sadducees" in the Synoptics, i.e., the NIV's "Jewish leaders" (e.g., John 1:19; 5:10, 15, 16; 7:1).

Jesus' clashes with "the Jews" run throughout the Gospel, increasing as antagonism to Jesus grows. They clash over the temple clearing (John

---

66. The text reads, "For the apostates let there be no hope, and the dominion of arrogance do Thou speedily root out in our days, and let the Nazarenes and the heretics perish as in a moment, let them be blotted out of the book of the living, and let them not be written with the righteous. Blessed art Thou, O Lord, who humblest the arrogant." Gamaliel II demanded that this be recited three times a day in Jewish worship and it continued for centuries (see R. M. Novak, *Christianity and the Roman Empire: Background Texts* [Harrisburg, PA: Trinity Press International, 2001], 34). Epiphanius confirms that Christians were cursed three times a day in synagogues (Epiphanius, *Pan.* 29.9.2). Some question this (e.g., N. T. Wright, *The New Testament and the People of God* [Minneapolis: Fortress, 1992], 164-65).

67. See Brown, *John*, 1.374, who argues for a three-stage development: *nezifah* (a minor ban), *niddūy* (a thirty-day banishment), and *hērem*, a permanent exclusion from the synagogue.

68. Borchert, *John 1-11*, 319.

69. See also John 6:41, 52; 7:1, 11, 13, 15, 35; 8:22, 48, 52, 57; 9:18, 22; 10:24, 31, 33; 11:45, 54; 18:14, 38; 19:7, 12; 20:19.

70. The term is also used neutrally of "the Jews" concerning the people, their customs and institutions (see John 1:19; 2:6, 13; 3:1, 22; 4:9, 22; 5:1; 6:4; 7:2; 11:55; 19:40, 42).

2:13-22), the nature of spiritual birth (John 3:1-12), Jesus' claim that he is the "bread of life" (John 6:35-70), their failure to recognize Jesus despite the Scriptures (John 5:39), his miracles (John 7:30-49), his claim to be the light of the world (John 8:12) and to supersede Abraham (John 8:31-59), his opponents' claims that Jesus is possessed and a Samaritan (John 8:44, 48), his healing on the Sabbath (John 5:9-10; 7:22-23; 9:14-16), his claim to messiahship (John 10:23-33), and his popularity after raising Lazarus (John 11:54-12:9). This opposition culminates with his death as the Jewish leadership succeeds in seeing Jesus killed (John 18:14, 28, 36; 19:7, 12, 31).

JESUS, THE INTERCESSOR

John does not record Jesus' Gethsemane prayer, nor does he refer to Jesus' frequent prayer ministry (cf. Luke 5:16). However, John 17 records the great prayer of Jesus after his teaching of the Spirit in the context of the Last Supper (just before Gethsemane). It can be broken up into three sections:

1. Jesus prays *for himself* that he and the Father will be glorified by people gaining eternal life through him (John 17:1).

2. Jesus prays *for his disciples* that the Father will protect them (John 17:11-12, 15) and sanctify them by the word of truth (John 17:17) as they go out into mission (John 17:18).

3. Jesus prays for *future believers* who will believe the disciples' message that they would be one together with the Father and Son (John 17:21-22).

THE ROLE OF THE SPIRIT

While the Spirit is mentioned throughout the New Testament, three writers place great emphasis on the Spirit: Paul, Luke, and John.

Paul stresses the role of the Spirit in personal conversion (2 Cor 1:21-22; Eph 1:13-14), the Spirit in believers and the church as "the temple of the Spirit" (1 Cor 3:16; 6:19), and the Spirit in ongoing Christian life through spiritual gifts and ethics, or Spirit-fruit (see esp. Rom 8:1-27; 12:4-8; 1 Cor 12-14; Gal 4-5; Eph 4:11).

In Luke's Gospel, the Spirit is key to Jesus' powerful ministry (esp. Luke 4:1, 14, 18-19). Throughout Acts, Luke stresses the role of the Spirit in mission (e.g., Acts 2:1-41; 9:15-17), guidance (e.g., Acts 8:29; 16:6-7), and signs and wonders (Acts 4:31; 5:12).

John also stresses the role of the Spirit in Jesus' ministry. Jesus received the Spirit like a dove resting on him (John 1:32-33), poured out by God without measure (John 3:34).[71] Whereas John and Jesus' disciples baptize in water, Jesus baptizes believers in the Spirit (John 1:33).

Jesus' interaction with Nicodemus highlights the importance of the Spirit in giving spiritual understanding and enabling a person to perceive and enter the kingdom by being born from above by the Spirit (John 3:1-8). The sovereign freedom of the Spirit is also emphasized (John 3:8).

While at the Feast of Tabernacles, Jesus announces that he is the source of living water, the Spirit. He invites people to come to him and drink to receive eternal life (John 7:37). The concept of drinking, as in the case of eating in John 6, refers to faith, i.e., believing in Jesus as the Messiah. For those who believe, he promises the Holy Spirit, which had not yet been given (John 7:39). This Spirit will overflow from the believers, spreading life ("streams of living water," 7:38).

One of the most interesting and innovative ideas John develops is the Spirit as the *paraklētos* in John's extended Last Supper discourse in John 14-16. The *paraklētos* has a wide semantic range including "helper, comforter, counselor, encourager, mediator, intercessor."[72] God's Paraclete will indwell believers and be God's personal presence with them (John 14:17-20). The Spirit will teach and remind them of Jesus' life and teaching (John 14:26) and give them peace (John 14:27). The Paraclete will remind believers of Jesus' teaching and revelation (John 15:26), bring conviction of sin (John 16:8-11), and guide them into truth (John 16:13)—Jesus. Thus, the Spirit is the key, not only for Christian living but also to salvation, as the conviction of the Spirit leads to conversion. The Paraclete will glorify Jesus (John 16:14). The Paraclete then, is the presence of God indwelling the believer, empowering them, giving comfort and guidance, and encouraging and caring for them in their Christian life of struggle and challenge. John

---

71. While this is sometimes read as general, this refers to the imbuing of Jesus with the Spirit, and as such, he speaks the words of God. See Köstenberger, *John*, 139, who writes, "Jesus, on the other hand, was the one on whom the Spirit had come to rest in all his fullness, as the Baptist had previously testified (cf. 1:32-33)."

72. BDAG 766.

16:15 speaks of the intimate perichoretic[73] connection between Father-Son-Spirit—all that the Father has belongs to Jesus, and the Spirit will take what is his (and the Father's) and declare it to John's readers and, by implication, to all of God's children. John reveals the connection between the Father who gives to Christ all that he has, and through the Spirit, conveys this to believers. As with Paul and Luke, John's rich pneumatology brings to the fore the importance of the Spirit for Christian living.

AN EXTENDED LAST-SUPPER DIALOGUE

In Mark's account of the Last Supper, Mark accounts for the setting up on the meal (Mark 14:12-16), the sinister note of Judas' betrayal (Mark 14:17-21), and a short account of Jesus taking bread and wine and announcing the covenant in his blood (Mark 14:22-25). A song is sung, and then they leave for the Mount of Olives. Jesus predicts his demise and Peter's denial, and Jesus prays at Gethsemane (Mark 14:26-42). With some differing details, Matthew follows the same sequence. Luke varies Mark more, but keeps the same basic material, changing details and in some places the order, and adding in the controversy over greatness (Luke 22:24-30, cf. Mark 10:35-45). The three narratives are reasonably consistent.

Where the final meal is concerned, John's account is markedly different. He keeps an account of Judas' betrayal and Peter's denial. Otherwise, he diverts in his own direction, leaving out the preparation for the meal, the sharing of the bread and wine, mention of the covenant, the prediction of Jesus' death, and the song. He adds in the account of Jesus washing the disciples' feet—an act of servitude and example to the disciples (John 13:1-20). He includes an account of where Jesus is going (i.e., to his Father's house with many rooms).[74] He encourages his disciples that they, too, will

---

73. On perichoresis see "Circumincession," in Grenz et al., *PDTT*, 26. Also called circumincession, perichoresis affirms "that the divine essence is shared by each of the three persons of the Trinity in a manner that avoids blurring the distinctions among them. By extension, this idea suggests that any essential characteristic that belongs to one of the three is shared by the others. Circumincession also affirms that the action of one of the persons of the Trinity is also fully the action of the other two persons." The idea is important in discussions of the social Trinity, God moving in unity as he acts in his Threeness. It connotes the idea of perfect unity, into which believers are drawn in Christ, and so is the basis for Christian ideals of *koinōnia*, community.

74. Some scholars repudiate the idea of "going to heaven" stating that there is no reference to going to heaven in the New Testament. However, while they have a good overall point

go there if they place their trust in him (John 14:1-8). There is teaching on the oneness (unity) of Father and Son and the power of prayer (John 14:9-14). There is a developed concept of the coming and role of the Spirit (John 14:15-31; 16:5-15). It is unclear whether John 15-17 should be read as part of the Last Supper dialogue, or whether Jesus and the disciples leave the room and walk to the Kidron Valley (see John 14:31 NIV, "Come now, let us leave"). If this is so, then the events of John 15-17 may have happened en route to the garden. Some suggest so, and that Jesus and the disciples may have passed vineyards as they walked to Gethsemane. Another possibility is that the golden vine that hung over the temple's main entrance may have been the site.[75] However, considering John 18:1, where Jesus and his disciples cross Kidron Valley to the garden,[76] it is likely that John 15-17 continues the Last Supper discourse.[77]

Whatever the venue, Jesus continues to teach and uses the vine analogy to emphasize the importance of remaining close to God and to explain the love of God, who "prunes" believers, acting to bring their lives into accord with his will (John 15:1-8). The vine imagery calls to mind Israel as God's vine, especially in Isaiah 5. God is renewing Israel as the international people of God gathered around Jesus, his Messiah and Son. There is a strong emphasis on the importance of love and obedience (see esp. 15:1-8). There is also a warning of opposition from the world and coming grief, along with the promise of God's comfort and presence (John 15:18-25; 16:17-33).

---

that ultimately heaven and earth will be one entity (cf. Rev 21-22), there are references such as these to believers dying and going to the Father's house with many rooms (i.e., heaven).

75. Köstenberger, *John*, 446 notes this possibility. On the vine at the temple, Köstenberger notes Josephus, *J.W.* 5.210; *Ant.* 15.395; *m. Mid.* 3.8; Tacitus, *Hist.* 5.5.

76. Brenda Heyink, "Kidron, Brook of," *LBD*. Heyink notes that the Kidron (Heb: *qidron*) was "[a] dark, turbid brook located beside Jerusalem. Part of a wadi, the brook is frequently low or dry. Separates Jerusalem and the Mount of Olives. May act as a boundary, designating the edge of an area that belongs to the Lord." It exists today, between Jerusalem and Gethsemane. Hence, harmonizing with the Synoptics, Jesus and his disciples left the site of the Last Supper and traveled there at this point.

77. Borchert, *John 12-21*, 136, notes several proposals, including: putting John 14 after John 13-17 (Bultmann); however, there is no textual evidence for this; suggesting that John 13-14 are the Last Supper and John 15-17 are from another context (Brown); that the words were spoken on the way (traditional solution); that they were slow to exit and so Jesus continued to teach (Morris); a pause in the discussion (Hoskyns and Davey); and some avoid the issue. Beasley-Murray, *John*, 223, notes that while John 14:29 states they are to leave, John 18:1 suggests that it was at this point that they did leave. Thus, Morris is probably correct.

Finally, John includes Jesus' prayer in John 17. None of this contradicts the other accounts, but rather fills out the events of the night.

THE IMPORTANCE AND EXCLUSIVITY OF
FAITH IN CHRIST FOR SALVATION

Unlike the Synoptics, John is explicit about the importance of "faith in Christ" as the means of salvation (e.g., John 3:15-18).

The role of faith in the Synoptics is different to that in John. While "believe" as a right response that saves is not absent from the Synoptics (Matt 18:6; Mark 1:15; 2:5; 9:42), faith usually generates healing and answered prayer (Matt 8:10, 13; 9:2, 22, 28-29; 15:28; 21:21-22; Mark 5:36; 9:23-24; 11:22-24; 16:16-17; Luke 7:50). Conversely, Jesus does not perform many miracles in his home town because of the lack of faith of those who knew him as merely a carpenter's son (Matt 13:58; Mark 6:1-6, cf. Matt 14:31; 16:8; 17:20; Mark 4:40). The characteristic concepts for responding to Jesus and God in the Synoptics are "repent" and "follow," although faith is important in the programmatic[78] Mark 1:15.

In John, however, the characteristic term for responding correctly to Jesus is "faith" (*pistis*) or "to believe" (*pisteuō*) (e.g., John 1:12; 2:22-23; 3:12-18; 4:39-42; 5:24; 6:69; 7:5; 8:24; 9:35-38; 10:25-26; 11:15; 12:42-46; 13:19; 14:10-12, 29; 16:27-31; 17:8; 20:25-31).[79] So, in John, the work of God is "to believe in the one he has sent" (John 6:29 NIV). In addition, as noted earlier on John's signs, rather than generating miracles as in the Synoptics, faith is generated *by* miracles in John (John 1:50; 2:11, 23; 4:53; 10:38, 42). However, this is not uniform. The miracles work parabolically as signs on those who observe them: some believe, and others ("the Jews") do not (John 12:37). Usually, the faith is embryonic and must grow to full salvation faith (see earlier).

Salvation is a more dominant theme in John than in the Synoptics. While the notion is not completely absent, there are fewer references in the Synoptics to salvation or "being saved" (Matt 10:22; 19:25; 24:13; Mark

---

78. In biblical scholarship, "programmatic" is often used of an important passage that sets the agenda (program) for the book in which it stands. It implies an importance to the passage in terms of the content and structure of what follows. Examples include Luke 4:18-19, which sets the agenda for both Jesus' ministry and Luke's Gospel. Similarly, Acts 1:8 is seen as setting the program for Acts.

79. See also John 1:7, 50; 3:36; 4:39-42; 5:38-47; 6:69; 7:31, 38-39; 8:30, 31, 45-46; 10:37-38; 11:15; 12:42-46; 14:29; 16:9; 17:20-21; 19:35; 20:8.

8:35; 16:16; Luke 8:12; 13:23; 19:9-10).[80] Salvation is more often reckoned as "entry into the kingdom of God/heaven" in the Synoptics (Matt 5:20; 7:13, 21; 18:3; 19:23-24; 21:31; 23:13 [or "enter life," cf. Matt 18:8-9; 19:17]). In John, "salvation" and "being saved" are vital concepts (John 3:17; 5:34; 10:9; 12:47). The realm of eternal life, also so important in John, is the realm of salvation. The purpose of Jesus' incarnation is to save rather than condemn, i.e., to give eternal life to those who believe. John's Gospel is written to that end (John 20:31).

THE PRIORITY OF LOVE

Only Paul can rival John as the apostle of love (e.g., Rom 5:8; 13:8-10; 1 Cor 13; Gal 5:14-25), especially if one accepts that the same John wrote the Johannine letters where love is also prominent (esp. 1 John 3-4). Love is mentioned in the Synoptics—both love of God and love for one another (see Mark 12:29-31; Luke 10:25-31). Yet John goes further and speaks of God's love for humanity as the driving force for the revelation of Jesus and salvation.

Humanity is called to love God and, most prominently for John, the overriding ethical response of believers in Jesus is love—his catch-all ethical phrase. This is seen particularly in John 3:16 where love for the world is the motivating force that caused God to send his Son, Jesus. The primacy of love is seen in imperatives to the disciples to love others as evidence of their faith and God's presence among them (esp. John 13:34-35). This love is derived from the love the Father has for the Son (John 3:35; 5:20; 10:17; 15:9; 17:23-24, 26). The Father's love is reciprocated by Christ (John 14:31) and seen in his complete adherence to his Father's commands (John 5:19-20). The enemies of Jesus in the Gospel are those who do not have this love within them (John 5:42; 8:42). Jesus' attitude is one of love for his disciples (John 11:5, 36; 13:1, 23; 15:9; 17:23). The disciples are to emulate the love Christ demonstrated to them (John 13:1-2, 15, 34-35 ["just as I have loved you, you also are to love one another"]; 15:9, 11-12, 17).

Such love leads to obedience if the love is genuine, for the one who loves is keen to obey—it is love working out through obedience (John 14:15, 21, 23-24; 15:9-10). John sees an integral link between espoused love and action, i.e., love without characteristic action is not true love (cf. 1 John 3:16-17).

---

80. Also of physical salvation (Matt 8:25; 14:30; 27:40, 49; Mark 3:4).

If the believer has a love for God, then this is demonstrated in obedience to Christ. Then, the believer is guaranteed the love of the Father and of Christ (John 14:21, 23-24; 17:23). True love involves self-renunciation and the giving of one's life for others, something supremely demonstrated in the self-sacrifice of Jesus for the salvation of the world (John 15:13, cf. 3:16). The threefold questioning of Peter, "Do you love me?" illustrates that true love for Christ will lead to service and suffering and forms the basis of all ministry (cf. John 21:16-19). This love for God and each other is contrasted with love *for* the world and being loved *by* the world (John 12:25; 15:19).

Hence, John illustrates a kind of "network" of love:

1. **God is love (1 John 4:8).** Although this is not in the text of the Gospel, John's Epistles are clear this is his starting point.

2. **God loves the Son and the world.** He sends his Son as an expression of his love.

3. **The Son loves the Father.** This is seen in Jesus' obedience to the Father, to the point of death.

4. **The Son accordingly loves humanity and dies for it.**

CONCLUSION

The Gospel of John is an indispensable and powerful presentation of Christ. It complements and supplements the Synoptic Gospels through its unique understanding of Christ. Its deep spirituality and enriched Christology draw the reader further into understanding the identity of Jesus and challenge readers of the gospel to reflect deeply on his person.

QUESTIONS TO CONSIDER

- What do you like about John's Gospel?
- How do you account for the differences between John and the Synoptic Gospels?
- What stands out as the dominant features of John's Gospel?

THE ACTS OF THE APOSTLES

CHAPTER 10

It can be argued that Luke-Acts should be introduced together, as they are likely one work arguably separated due to scroll length (see Introduction to Luke's Gospel). However, while they are indeed one narrative, Acts is also a discreet unit. Whereas Luke centers on Jesus and his life, Acts's focus is the extension of the gospel from Jerusalem to Rome. This chapter will build on the material in Chapter 8, which introduces Luke's Gospel, and will present Acts and some of its important themes.

The importance of the Acts of the Apostles cannot be overestimated. It traces three decades of the church (c. AD 30/33–61/62), including the story of the first church in Jerusalem, the spread of the Christian faith north into Samaria, the first gentile conversions, and the church's spread along the northeastern rim of the Mediterranean Sea as far as Rome. It describes how those who had been with Jesus throughout his ministry on earth sought to fulfill his teaching and establish the church.

Many New Testament scholars agree that Luke's central theme in Acts is salvation or, as some put it, "salvation history" (German: *Heilsgeschichte*). Luke narrates the story of Jesus, self-consciously continuing the story of Israel in the LXX. Acts takes up the story beginning with Luke 24 retold—Jesus rising from the dead and appearing to his disciples, telling them they will receive the Holy Spirit and be his witnesses from Jerusalem to the world, and Jesus' ascension (Acts 1:1-11). He then narrates the story of the genesis of the church from the selection of Matthias to replace Judas, Pentecost, the church in Jerusalem, and the subsequent astonishing expansion of the church as the Word is preached.

Because Acts continues the story of Jesus in Luke, the story of the first church in Jerusalem is vital in providing an understanding of what Jesus had in mind when he called his disciples to establish his church. The church in Jerusalem, while not perfect, is paradigmatic for a proper conception of the church today. Luke's account of the church offers a sense of what was important for the first Christians. This does not necessarily mean that believers should read the book of Acts and then model church the same way as the first Christians. It is important to think carefully concerning how living for Jesus looks across the sociological and cultural divide. Acts should be read prudently, and the ideals and principles of the first church applied thoughtfully in their proper context.

The story of Acts is also especially important for understanding the nature of the mission Jesus left to his followers. Each canonical Gospel ends with some kind of commission to take the message of Jesus and the kingdom to the world (Matt 28:18–20; Mark 13:10 [cf. 16:15–20]; Luke 24:46–49; John 20:21). In Acts, Luke recounts the story of how the first disciples obeyed this commission and, more importantly, how God worked through human agency.

Acts is significant in telling of the first generation of Christians and how they established Christ's church, a tradition that continues in this age. First, the main critical issues concerning the book of Acts will be briefly introduced. Then the major themes will be examined from the point of view of ecclesiology and mission. Some of the critical issues concerning the book of Acts are also applicable to the Gospel of Luke, so at times we will refer back to the chapter on Luke.

THE TITLE

The title "the Acts of the Apostles"[1] is not original to the text but was probably added by later Christians in the second century as the works of the New Testament writers were gathered together for circulation.

---

1. Greek: *PRAXEIS APOSTOLŌN*. We can instantly see a difference to the four Gospels, which all begin with the Greek KATA, "according to …" The title comes from Codex Vaticanus (B) (c. AD 325–350) and Codex Bezae (D) (c. AD 400). This title was used by some early Christians including Athanasius, Origen, Tertullian, Cyprian, and Eusebius. The title is simply *PRAXEIS* (Acts) in manuscript A, Origen, Tertullian, and others. "The Acts of the Holy Apostles" is used by others (A2 E G H A K Chrysostom, etc.). See A. T. Robertson, *Word Pictures in the New Testament* (Nashville, TN: Broadman Press, 1933), Acts, Ch. 1.

Other suggestions for a title were made by later writers, including "The Memorandum of Luke" (Tertullian [c. AD 200]) and "The Acts of the Apostles" (Muratorian Canon [c. AD 170-200]). The term "Acts" (Greek: *praxeis*) indicates an ancient literary genre describing the lives and actions of important people.[2] Other names Acts might be given include Luke 2, or the Acts of the Holy Spirit.

THE AUTHORSHIP OF ACTS

THE SAME AUTHOR AS THE THIRD GOSPEL

It is generally agreed that the author of Acts is the same person who wrote the Third Gospel. This is because of the similarities between the prologues, including:

1. A reference to "the first book," which clearly refers to the Third Gospel, Luke ("In the first book, O Theophilus, I have dealt with all that Jesus began to do and teach, until the day when he was taken up" [Acts 1:1-2]).

2. The same addressee, "most excellent Theophilus" (Acts 1:1, cf. Luke 1:3).

3. Continuity from the end of the Third Gospel, especially the appeal to witness, the anticipation of the Holy Spirit coming to the disciples as they wait in Jerusalem, and the ascension and teaching on the kingdom (Luke 24:46-49; Acts 1:1-11).

Many consider Luke-Acts a two-part work broken up because it was too long to fit on one papyrus roll. Witherington believes that it may be in two parts because of its length. The maximum length of a papyrus roll was 40 feet (12m). Luke's Gospel (19,404 words) would fit on a 35-foot roll, and Acts (18,734) on a 32-foot roll.[3] On the other hand, the phrase "in my first book" (Acts 1:1) may suggest there was a gap between the two works. Either

---

2. Robert James Utley, *Luke the Historian: The Book of Acts*, Study Guide Commentary Series 3B (Marshall, TX: Bible Lessons International, 2003), 1.
3. Witherington, *Acts*, 6.

way, the first of the two works focuses on "the man" (Jesus Christ) and the second on "the movement" (the church and the mission).

LUKE AS AUTHOR

Unlike Paul's letters, neither Luke nor Acts is signed by the author, so some people doubt Lukan authorship. However, there are sound reasons to believe Luke is the author of Luke-Acts. Most of the arguments for Lukan authorship of Acts relate to the same set of data concerning the authorship of Luke's Gospel (see Ch. 8 on Luke), including the ascription, early church agreement, the "we passages" (Acts 16:10-17; 20:5-16; 21:1-18; 27:1-28:16), the specific mentions of Luke in Paul's letters (Col 4:14; Phlm 24; 2 Tim 4:11), and the Western text of Acts 20:13, which mentions Luke directly. Arguments against Lukan authorship are not strong. Luke is almost certainly the author.[4] He was probably from Antioch, a friend and companion of Paul, a well-educated physician, and a gentile convert. He wrote well as a first-century historian. He is highly important for understanding the New Testament.

THE DATE OF ACTS

The date of Acts relates to the date of Luke (see Ch. 8). There are two main views regarding the dating of Luke-Acts. First, there is the argument that Acts was written between the time of the events that mark its end and before the Neronian persecution, the martyrdoms of Peter and Paul, and the fall of Jerusalem (c. AD 62-64).[5] The second major view argues that it is later, well after Mark's Gospel was written (mid-60s to early 70s AD), and sees the culmination of Acts in Rome as a rhetorical device related to Acts 1:8—the gospel has come to the heart of the empire (Rome) and so will go to the ends of the earth. Therefore, some believe Acts to have been

---

4. See for example I. H. Marshall, *Acts*, 44-46; Bruce, *Acts*, NICNT, 6-8; Longenecker, *Acts*, 240, writes: "The tradition that Luke wrote the third Gospel and Acts goes back at least to the second century, that it was unanimously accepted within the church, and that it would be very strange were it not true."

5. Those who take it around AD 63 include Longenecker, *Acts*, 235-38, who suggests AD 62-64.

written in the 70s or even the 80s or 90s AD.⁶ Scholarship is split on this issue, which can clearly go either way.

THE RECIPIENTS OF ACTS

As noted above, Acts and Luke are written to a certain Theophilus who is most likely a Greek aristocrat and representative of well-to-do Greco-Roman society. As such, the two works have a strong Greco-Roman edge and speak into that world. This is important for interpretation.

THE HISTORICITY OF ACTS

The historical accuracy of Acts is the subject of great debate. In the nineteenth century, the German Tübingen school of biblical criticism argued that Acts was of dubious historical worth. They argue it was a largely fictitious attempt to soften the supposed conflict between Peter and Paul that was widely believed to dominate the whole New Testament and the early years of the church (esp. Gal 2:11-14).[7] Toward the end of the nineteenth century, Sir William Ramsey countered, arguing that Acts is an excellent piece of history and that Luke could be relied on as an accurate historian.[8] According to his analysis, Luke is extremely accurate in matters related to background such as geography and secular history and so should be trusted on other matters that cannot be verified with cross-referencing to secondary historical sources. In the twentieth century and into the twenty-first, many scholars such as F. F. Bruce, C. S. W. Williams, R. Longenecker, B. Witherington, D. Bock, and others have also argued that Acts can be trusted. In addition, others, such as A. N. Sherwin White and C. Hemer, have further demonstrated Luke's accuracy in the details of provincial

---

6. I. H. Marshall, *Acts*, 46-48, for example, suggests AD 70 with Luke bringing "his story up to a significant point, the completion of the process of bringing the gospel to Rome, as symbolized by Paul's unhindered preaching there for two years. This was a fitting climax to the story, and here Luke was happy to terminate his account." Bruce, *Acts*, NICNT, 10-13, suggests between AD 69-96 and probably midpoint (i.e., around AD 80).

7. This is not without some support such as Gal 2:11-15; 1 Cor 1:10. However, the latter reference does not indicate tensions between Peter and Paul; rather, it suggests problems with the Corinthians' perceptions of Peter and Paul. In reality, apart from the Antioch incident, there is little evidence of tension between the two men; if anything, they appear to be unified (cf. Acts 15:7; 2 Pet 3:15-16).

8. See W. M. Ramsay, *St. Paul the Traveller and the Roman Citizen* (London: Hodder & Stoughton, 1907).

government, geography, social and religious customs, navigational procedures, and more.[9] While some argue that accuracy in background issues does not mean accuracy in unverifiable matters, the inference of reliability seems fair. As I. H. Marshall points out, if it were not authentic, Luke would have been writing a historical novel based on authentic historic events. There is no evidence at all that Acts should be read as a novel.[10] Rather, as he says in his prologue to his "first book," Luke was extremely careful to rely on eyewitnesses and first-generation sources. He participated in the events of Acts, having excellent access to those involved. The use of eyewitnesses and his participation are both marks of excellent first-century historical research.

THEOLOGY (EARLY CHURCH AND/OR THE AUTHOR) AND NOT HISTORY

Historical skepticism concerning Acts has been seen in the work of form and redaction critics who have argued that the narrative is a construct of the early church and/or an editor, and has little historical validity. Writers such as M. Dibelius, H. Conzelmann, and E. Haenchen see Acts as baseless except for some oral tradition that is difficult to discern within the text. Another form of historical skepticism sees Luke's motivation as purely theological rather than historical. Hence, Luke (for redaction criticism) and/or the early church (for form criticism) had theological intentions in writing a narrative with minimal historical authenticity. Acts, then, is essentially interpreted like a movie that is purportedly based on true events but is really a creative construct with little relation to what actually happened.

Luke's writings do have theological emphases. After all, writings always come from a certain angle, and the biblical material is written from a theological perspective. However, this does not mean that Luke neglects history.

---

9. See A. N. Sherwin-White, *Roman Society and Roman Law in the New Testament* (London: Oxford, 1963); Hemer, *Book of Acts*. Some examples of Luke's accuracy include the death of Herod Agrippa I (Acts 12:19-23), the famine in the 40s AD (Acts 11:27-30), Claudius' edict (Acts 18:2), and the replacement of Felix with Festus. See also: Longenecker, *Acts*, 228-29, which has an excellent summary of the same main points of historical issue; M. Hengel, *Acts and the History of Earliest Christianity* (London: SCM, 1979), 67-68, who sees Luke as trustworthy as any ancient historian.

10. I. H. Marshall, *Acts*, 37.

All history is biased to some degree or another and is crafted according to the historian's viewpoint.[11] Acts is no different. It is theological history telling the story of the Christian church's early growth.

SOURCES FOR ACTS

Another factor causing people to doubt the historical accuracy of Acts is the problem of sources: Where did Luke acquire his information? Even if readers accept that Acts was written by a traveling companion of Paul's, this does not disclose where he derived his information from for the first sections. The lack of evidence of verifiable sources (which can be traced) suggests to some that Luke made it up. However, this completely ignores the fact that Luke would have known people who were there. He simply wrote what he learned from them in his own style and words.[12] Prior to Luke's joining Paul, Paul had visited Jerusalem on several occasions (see Acts 9:26-30; 11:30; 15:1-19; Gal 1:18-2:10), so he had knowledge of the Jerusalem church. Luke could have gained some insight from Paul's reminiscences. Luke records that he arrived in Jerusalem with Paul where he met the brothers, James, and all the elders (Acts 21:17-18). Luke also records that he traveled from Caesarea Maritima with Paul to Rome several years later (Acts 27:1). Colossians 4:14 and Philemon 24 also place Luke with Paul in Rome.[13] It seems reasonable to surmise that Luke took the opportunity to talk to apostles and other first-generation eyewitnesses while in Judea and Rome (cf. Luke 1:2).[14] These would include Barnabas, Mary, John Mark, and any others present. Hence, sections such as the infancy narrative of Luke could easily be drawn from discussions with these people. His analysis

---

11. See further Longenecker, *Acts*, 214-16.

12. There have been elaborate attempts to find Luke's sources beneath the text. Harnack, for example, notes: (1) A Jerusalem-Antiochian source (Acts 11:19-30; 12:25-15:35); (2) A Jerusalem-Caesarean source underlying sections of 1-12; (3) A "recension B" of the Jerusalem-Caesarea source underlying other parts of 1-12; (4) Another separate source 6:1-8:4; (5) Another at 9:1-28; (6) Legendary material in Acts 1. Harnack claimed Acts 4 and 5 were different sources of the same event. Some have found evidence of Semitisms underlying the Greek, pointing to sources beyond Luke (see further Longenecker, *Acts*, 221-23).

13. Some consider Colossians and Philemon were written from Ephesus; however, as will be argued concerning these letters, there is no reason to doubt the unanimous early church tradition that Paul wrote these letters and from Rome.

14. According to Bauckham in *Jesus and the Eyewitnesses*, 39-66, some of those are people named in the text such as Mary and Martha (Luke 10:38-39), Jairus (Luke 8:41), and Cleopas (Luke 24:18).

of the Pauline mission would come from Paul himself; he was in Rome at the same time as Mark, meaning he may have had access to Mark and his material from the first moment of writing Mark. This is all consistent with Luke's own testimony that he "carefully investigated everything" (Luke 1:3 NIV) and consulted eyewitnesses (*autoptēs* [Luke 1:2]). In fact, placing Luke in Jerusalem gives great confidence concerning the accuracy of the first part of Acts. Knowing Luke was Paul's travel companion in Rome means readers can have a high level of confidence in the historicity of the second half of Acts.

Luke's use of sources in his Gospel can also be tested where he used Mark, Q (or Matthew), and his own unique material gained from his own research (L). It is clear from Luke that he used his sources carefully and accurately while slanting the source material theologically toward his particular emphases. Unlike the Gospel, which in large part is a creative reworking of Mark's Gospel, Acts has a freer feel than Luke's Gospel as Luke crafts his account with fewer written sources. In Acts, he uses a wide range of source material gained from his own interviews and experiences.

SPEECHES

Another factor leading to historical skepticism is the speeches of Acts. Some believe that these speeches are constructs based on the structure and details of early church preaching (form critics) or constructs of Luke himself (redaction critics). They argue that the speeches differ from supposed fragments of sermons in the rest of the New Testament and are really Lukan or early church theology. In other words, Luke made up his own sermons and placed them on Peter, Stephen, and Paul's lips.

There are significant problems with this view. First, there is no evidence of a process by which the sermons of the early church were gathered, distributed, and venerated as Scripture. Postulating such a process requires quite a vivid imagination. Second, a plain reading of the sermons gives no indication at all that they are Lukan constructions. They differ greatly, although they are all recorded in Luke's writing style. Third, the use of the Old Testament and Jewish elements suggests that they had their origin in the preaching of Jewish Christians, rather than the gentile Luke's creativity (e.g., quotes from Old Testament passages concerning resurrection e.g., Acts 2:17–20; Joel 2:28–32). Fourth, the speeches are not uniform and have touches of originality. For example, Paul's speeches to the synagogue in Pisidia Antioch and to the Areopagus in Athens are markedly different in terms of culture and emphases, indicating Paul spoke to the specific context (cf. Acts 13:16-41; 17:22-31). One would expect more uniformity if these were constructs.[15] Finally, most of the speeches would have been in Aramaic, which Luke would have paraphrased, which is probably the main reason they are all in Lukan Greek.

Because the speeches show signs of originality, they are, without doubt, summaries of original speeches rather than complete sermons.[16] This is indicated by their brevity, each taking only a few minutes to read (one to seven minutes). In addition, the memories of the early church were focused on Jesus and not the first sermons; this may suggest they are general accounts. Furthermore, Luke was not concerned with word-for-word accuracy. This is seen by comparing the messages of the angel to Cornelius in Acts 10 where the details differ throughout the passage (cf. Acts 10:4-5, 22, 30-31; 11:13-14). Similarly, it is worth comparing Luke 24:44-53 to Acts 1:1-11 where Luke speaks of the same events with different details and substantial freedom.

Finally, there is the problem of how Luke could have known the details of some of what he records, for example, what Festus and Agrippa said to each other in private (Acts 25:13-22; 26:30-32) or the words of the Sanhedrin in closed session (Acts 4:15-17; 5:34-40). However, these can be explained as Luke's best summation based on what was said in public, and/or him encountering an eyewitness of these events (or some other source). This is entirely feasible considering that he was in Jerusalem and Caesarea and able to make connections with Christians and others present in these situations.[17]

While it is not necessary to view the speeches as fiction, they are general summaries of what the first Christians preached. There is no real reason to reject them as unhistorical.

---

15. I. H. Marshall, *Acts*, 41.

16. A point Luke himself makes in Acts 2:40: "with many other words …"

17. In relation to Acts 4-5, Nicodemus and Joseph of Arimathea were in the Sanhedrin and were likely a source. Luke also mentions other priests who came to Christ, perhaps from these groups (cf. Acts 6:7).

PAUL AND ACTS

Another historical issue is how to correlate the Paul in Acts with the Paul who wrote the Epistles. Some scholars see a great disjunction between the chronology and theology of Paul's letters and Acts. Some cannot correlate the journeys to Jerusalem mentioned in Acts with those in Paul's letters. They argue that the Epistles only mention three trips to Jerusalem (see Gal 1:18; 2:1; Rom 15:25), whereas Acts mentions five (Acts 9:26; 11:30; 15:4; 18:22; 21:17). Similarly, some find a tension between Paul's theology of grace and justification by faith and his sermons in Acts (esp. Rom 1–8; Gal 2–3).[18] However, these differences are exaggerated and have perfectly reasonable explanations. It is possible to harmonize the chronology of the visits to Jerusalem with a reasonable degree of certainty.[19] Theologically, it is important to remember that the sermons of Acts are summaries written in Luke's style and give insufficient grounds for fully assessing Paul's theology. Rather, Acts gives a wonderful background picture to the letters of Paul and does include a theology of grace, as does Luke (cf. Luke 18:13–18; Acts 13:38–39; 16:31). When it comes to assessing Paul's theology, one should always favor the first-hand accounts of his letters. However, Luke provides an excellent second point of reference from a traveling companion of Paul. When assessing Paul's theology, it is superficial to only consider his Epistles without any reference to Acts.

ANCIENT HISTORIOGRAPHICAL STANDARDS

Some argue Acts cannot be considered solid history because ancient historians were much looser with information than contemporary historians. That is, they wrote to give moral lessons or to edify, rather than to record what happened as a contemporary historian would.

This is not completely wrong. Many ancient "historians" blended fact with fiction rather freely. However, there is evidence that ancient

---

18. See Ellis, *The Gospel of Luke*, 45–47; F. F. Bruce, "Is the Paul of Acts the Real Paul?" *BJRL* 58 (1976): 282–305; I. H. Marshall, *Acts*, 42–43.

19. See L. C. A. Alexander, "Chronology of Paul," in *DPL* 115–23. If Luke's accuracy is accepted, then the three trips of the Epistles (Gal 1:18; 2:1; Rom 15:24) can be reconciled with the five trips of Acts (Acts 9:26; 11:27–30; 15; 18:22; 21:17). In this scheme, Gal 1:18 = Acts 9:26; Gal 2:1 = Acts 11:27–30 (the famine visit); and Rom 15:24 is a projected planned visit that was fulfilled in Acts 21:17 when Paul was sent to Rome for trial. This proves Paul did not mention all his visits to Jerusalem in his letters.

historians were not as loose as some think. There are ancient criticisms of historians of the time who neglect the facts. These critics appeal to historians that they should present what happened and what was said. Indeed, ancient authors speak of a concern for accuracy in historical reporting which is not unlike what is expected today.[20]

Longenecker discusses the approach of ancient historians in some detail. He notes that ancient historical writing was not mere chronicling but was "the conviction that the actions and words of distinctive people in their respective periods represent more adequately the situation than any comments by the historian."[21] Similarly, Bauckham has extensively defended the historicity of Luke and the other Gospels, arguing persuasively, in the case of Luke, that he used eyewitnesses and participated in the events.[22] Thus, through the "acts" recorded in Acts, the accounts give insight into the ethos of the period and the character of the person in mind. Some historians took a chronological approach (e.g., Tacitus), but most favored a thematic approach (e.g., Plutarch). Luke, who used

---

20. See Longenecker, *Acts*, 215. Two examples show this: Polybius, *Hist.* 2.56 (mid-second century BC), who writes, "Surely an historian's object should not be to amaze his readers by a series of thrilling anecdotes; nor should he aim at producing speeches which might have been delivered, nor study dramatic propriety in detail like a writer of tragedy: but *his function is above all to record with fidelity what was actually said or done, however commonplace it may be.*" He adds that the purpose of history is "to strike and delight *by words as true to nature as possible*" so that the effect is "permanent" and not temporary. He adds that in history "the thing of primary importance is truth, because the object is to benefit the learner" (see Polybius, *Histories* [Medford, MA: Macmillan, 1889], 151–52). See also Dionysius of Halicarnassus, *Thuc.* 1.22 (Charles Forster Smith, LCL, late-first century BC), who writes of speeches recorded in his work: "I have adhered as closely as possible to the general sense of what was actually said." He continues, "But as to the facts of the occurrences of the war, I have thought it my duty to give them, not as ascertained from any chance informant nor as seemed to me probable, but only after investigating with the greatest possible accuracy each detail, in the case both of the events in which I myself participated and of those regarding which I got my information from others. And the endeavour to ascertain these facts was a laborious task, because those who were eyewitnesses of the several events did not give the same reports about the same things, but reports varying according to their championship of one side or the other, or according to their recollection. And it may well be that the absence of the fabulous from my narrative will seem less pleasing to the ear; but whoever shall wish to have a clear view both of the events which have happened and of those which will some day, in all human probability, happen again in the same or a similar way—for these to adjudge my history profitable will be enough for me. And, indeed, it has been composed, not as a prize-essay to be heard for the moment, but as a possession for all time."

21. Longenecker, *Acts*, 212.
22. See Bauckham, *Jesus and the Eyewitnesses*.

eyewitness sources and participated in the events of that period, is an excellent first-century historian.

CONCLUSION

Readers can be confident that the story in Luke is historically sound. However, the account is selective and theological. Luke picks and chooses what is vital to his purposes; he tells the story along the lines of Acts 1:8. In addition, the account is slanted theologically and couched in Lukan terms and understanding, rather than the language of the original sources. As such, while accepting the material is selective and theological, this analysis will work from a general acceptance of the historicity of the account and take it as the basis for this discussion.[23]

EMPHASES IN ACTS

The Lukan emphases have already been discussed in Chapter 8. Some of these continue in Acts. In constructing his history of the first Christian church in Jerusalem and the expansion of Christianity, Luke has emphasized certain issues.

THE SOVEREIGNTY OF GOD

One of the strong themes of Acts is the sovereignty of God. It is God who is at work in the world and church. He guides history. He continues the story of his people in the newly forming people of God. This growth is through the work of the Spirit. Key events such as Pentecost, the persecution of Saul inspiring the scattering of the church and the evangelization of Greeks in Antioch, Cornelius' story where God moved dynamically in the lives of Peter and Cornelius and poured his Spirit out on gentiles, and the conversion of Saul and the incidents leading to Paul ending up in Rome are sovereign works of God—or God at work through apparently negative circumstances. Acts is the story of the unstoppable mission of God through his Spirit.

---

23. Further on historicity see I. H. Marshall, *Acts*, 36-44 and Longenecker, *Acts*, 212-16, 221-25, 229-31; both are positive concerning the historicity of Acts.

THE LORDSHIP OF CHRIST

In Luke, Jesus Christ is at the center of God's purposes, from his birth, to his ministry in Israel, and finally, his death, resurrection, commissioning of the disciples, and ascension to cosmic Lordship. In Acts, he is called the Lord Jesus (eighteen times), is seated at the right hand of God, and is Lord (e.g., Acts 2:33; 5:31). Acts 10:36 says, "he is Lord of all." By his Spirit, he continues his ministry of salvation.

THE POWER OF THE SPIRIT

The role of the Spirit is fundamental to Acts, mentioned fifty-seven times. Most often, he is the "Holy Spirit" (forty-one times), emphasizing the purity and consecrating power of the Spirit. On occasion, he is the "Spirit of Jesus" (Acts 16:7) or of the "Spirit of the Lord" (Acts 5:9; 8:39) emphasizing that Christ continues his work in the church through his Spirit. Much of the expansion of the church through Acts is based on works of the Spirit rather than human strategy or design.

THE CHURCH

In Luke's Gospel, the church (*ekklēsia*) is not explicitly mentioned. Contrastingly, in Acts, the term features twenty times. Churches are established in Jerusalem (Acts 5:11; 15:4) and experience persecution (Acts 8:1, 3; 12:1) from where Christians flowed into the gentile world with the gospel (Acts 11:22). Churches are also founded in Judea (e.g., Acts 18:22), Galilee, and Samaria (Acts 9:31). They are established in Syrian Antioch, and are multicultural and full of faith, charismatic life, and mission zeal (Acts 11:26; 13:1-2; 14:27; 15:4). Acts describes the rich life of the Jerusalem Church (esp. Acts 2:42-47, cf. 12:5). Churches are established through Syria, Cilicia (Acts 15:41), Galatia (Acts 14:23; 16:5), and Asia Minor (Acts 20:17, 28). Acts provides deep insight into the life of the early church, the way in which it dealt with issues, its expansion, its pneumatology,[24] and its missionary emphases.

---

24. Pneumatology is the study of the Spirit (i.e., a theology of the Spirit).

MISSION

1. **The Church:** Acts reveals the way the church intentionally and unintentionally expanded along the lines of Acts 1:8, in Jerusalem, Judea and Samaria, and to Rome.

2. **The Spirit:** God, through his Son and Lord, by his Spirit, governs this expansion. Even persecution becomes an "agent" for evangelization (Acts 8:4; 11:19).

3. **Key people:** The importance of key figures in the expansion of the church is highlighted, especially Peter and Paul. Other important figures include John, Stephen, Philip, James, Apollos, Priscilla, and Aquila.

4. **Inclusiveness:** Acts reveals the way in which Christianity crossed racial, gender, and social boundaries as it spread. Hence, it has a strong emphasis on the spread of the gospel to the Jews first and then to the gentiles (and Samaritans)—the development of the multicultural church with a commitment to interculturalism. As in the case of Luke's Gospel, women are freely mentioned. Particularly in the early part of Acts, concern for the poor and needy is important. However, these emphases are subsumed in the generality of the mission to the "ends of the earth" as the narrative develops. The emphasis throughout is on the inclusion of people of all races and cultures as the gospel breaks free from Jewish cultural distinctives and becomes a multicultural gospel based on inclusion by faith alone. The narrative ends with the church established from Jerusalem to Rome, from where the gospel will penetrate the world.

THE TEXT OF ACTS

The text of Acts has been preserved in two key forms:

1. **The accepted text:** This is represented by the fourth-century Uncial[25] Sinaiticus (א) and Vaticanus (B), which form the basis for most modern Greek texts and English translations.

2. **The Western text:** This is represented by the Codex Bezae (D). It is 10 percent longer than the accepted text. As mentioned in the Gospel of Luke in Chapter 8, it is probably dated about AD 120. Some of the additions are of interest, including:

    a. Acts 11:28: "… and there was much rejoicing. And as we were gathered together …" If authentic, it indicates the joyful state of the Antiochian church.

    b. Acts 19:9: Paul rented the hall of Tyrannus in Ephesus "from 11 a.m. to 4 p.m." This is possibly a genuine remembrance, giving the time frame for the use of the hall—the Asian Siesta.

    c. Acts 15:20 adds to the list of things prohibited: "and not to do to others what they would not like to be done to themselves." This adds to the Golden Rule (Matt 7:12), which is likely a later addition.

A small minority of scholars argue that the Western text should be preferred. Others argue that the Western text is a different line of textual transmission (recension) emanating from the original and should be taken as seriously as the accepted text. However, the best approach sees the Western text as a secondary modification of the accepted text. So, as the text was copied and spread out, various additions were made seeking to smooth out grammatical difficulties, resolve ambiguities, expand mentions of Christ, and add historical notes.

STRUCTURE AND PURPOSE OF ACTS

Luke 4:18–19 is programmatic for understanding Luke. Even more clearly, most scholars agree that the key point of reference for understanding the structure and purpose of Acts is Acts 1:8: "But you will receive power when the Holy Spirit has come upon you; and you will be my witnesses in

---

25. The word "uncial" is derived from *uncialis* (Lat), meaning "inch-high." It refers to Greek and Latin writing in capitals. The manuscripts have few spaces or punctuation. There are approximately 267 uncials. Three important ones are the fourth-century manuscripts Sinaiticus (א) and Vaticanus (B) and the fifth-century Codex Alexandrinus (A).

Jerusalem and in all Judea and Samaria, and to the end of the earth." This verse points out some of the purposes and key themes of Acts.

1. **The People of God:** The verse begins with "you," indicating the first Christians who receive the empowerment of the Spirit at Pentecost. The story of the expansion of the faith is intimately linked to people who work synergistically with God by the power of the Spirit. In his grace, God chooses to work with and through the likes of human beings.

2. **Spirit Power:** This restates Luke 24:49 where, prior to his ascension, Jesus states that he is sending the promise of God and that they are to stay in Jerusalem until they are "clothed with power from on high." They are told to stay in Jerusalem until they receive the Spirit, and the implication is that they then leave to preach repentance and forgiveness of sin to the nations. They do not quite obey this explicitly, remaining in Jerusalem until persecution by Saul, at which time they are thrust into the nations. In Acts 1:8 they are told they will receive power when the Spirit comes upon them. This primarily points to Pentecost when the first believers had a radical experience of the Spirit (Acts 2:1–4). It also anticipates the other moments when the Spirit fell on new converts (Acts 8:17; 9:17–18; 10:44; 19:6) and on the church again (Acts 4:31). It looks forward to the ongoing story of the Spirit empowering God's people into the future until Christ's return. All believers (Acts 2:38–39) will receive power when the Holy Spirit comes upon them.

3. **Witnesses:** The story of Acts is the account of God's mission centered on Christians being Christ's witnesses (*martyrs*) empowered by the Spirit. They testify to who he is and what he has done across the world (Acts 2:32; 3:15; 5:32; 10:39, 41; 13:31; 22:15; 22:20; 26:16). Some become "martyrs" in the full sense of the word, dying for Christ. In Acts, these include Stephen and James son of Zebedee (Acts 7:54–60; 12:1–2). Others in biblical times include Jesus' blood brother James (Josephus,

Ant. 20.200), many including Paul and Peter under Nero, and Antipas in Pergamum (Rev 2:13). Those who follow Christ experience persecution as they give witness to God, and many will even die. Yet nothing will stop them (esp. Acts 4:19-20, 29-31; 5:29; 8:4; 11:19).

This verse also gives a good indication of the structure of Luke-Acts:

1. **Jerusalem (Acts 1:1-8:3):** Luke ends in Jerusalem where Jesus dies and is raised, where the disciples gather and meet him, and where they are told to wait until the Spirit comes upon them (Luke 23-24). Acts 1:1-8 tells this story again. This first section of Acts focuses on Jerusalem and the establishment of the church in the heart of Judaism. While at times the story returns to Jerusalem (e.g., Acts 15), after Saul's persecution, the focus shifts away from Jerusalem as the gospel radiates out.

2. **All Judea and Samaria (Acts 8:4-12:25):** The central section of Acts focuses on the mission to Samaria through Philip the Evangelist, and to Judea, particularly through Peter. Other aspects of this section anticipate what will come in the third part of Acts—the conversion of Saul who becomes Paul, apostle to the gentiles (Acts 9:1-31); the conversion of the first gentile family (Acts 10:1—11:18); and the establishment of the church in Antioch with a gentile mission (Acts 11:19-30).

3. **To the end of the earth (Acts 13:1-28:31):** The threefold structure of Acts is not perfectly balanced, with the greater emphasis on Jerusalem and Paul's mission. Parts of Acts 9-12 lead into this section. Acts 13:1-28:31 focus on "the ends of the earth" and trace the spread of the gospel into the nations of the world. The key figure is Paul. It ends in the heart of the Roman Empire with Paul in prison preaching the gospel (Acts 28:30-31). While Rome is not the "end of the earth," it is the then "center of the earth," and from Rome, the gospel mission can go on through subsequent generations. Luke's initial readers will be inspired to be a part of this. Believers today

should similarly be excited to join the great mission to the "end of the earth."

Acts 1:8 functions to outline the program of Acts with its focus on the Spirit, witness, and the geographical spread of the gospel of Christ and the Christian movement.

THE FIRST CHURCH IN JERUSALEM

This section will focus on the first church in Jerusalem. This is because the account of the first church in Jerusalem is vital for understanding Christianity and its ideals. It imparts insight into how those who lived with Jesus for his whole ministry and who conversed with the risen Lord over those remarkable forty days of appearances (Acts 1:3) sought to live as the people of God. A cursory reading of the text shows that the initial unity and growth of the church are inspirational and dynamic. Where ecclesiology is concerned, readers can glean from the text features of this church that provide insight into God's vision for his church and mission. These dimensions are important and must be carefully and thoughtfully applied to church life today, remembering that this church was established in a much different world—even if people remain people. However, the principles are of vital importance in understanding what the church should be like. The factors that led to the dynamism of the first church will be summarized, while the focus of these notes is the first church in Jerusalem. Where appropriate, reference will also be made to other examples in Acts 9–28.

A GOD-HONORING CHURCH

Just as Luke's Gospel is implicitly Trinitarian[26] in emphasis, so is Luke's account of the early church. First is his emphasis on God (also sometimes "Lord").[27] As in the case of Luke, the story of God's salvation is behind the narrative of Acts. Aside from pronouns, God is mentioned directly 180 times in Acts. He is the Creator (Acts 4:24; 17:24), who cannot be contained

---

26. While the Trinity is not fully defined as in later church creeds, it is reflected implicitly in the freedom of movement between the three persons of the Trinity in Luke-Acts. While the relationship of the members of the Trinity is not defined, the notion of the unity and intimate relationship of the three-persons of the godhead is apparent if not explicit (perichoresis).

27. *Kyrios* or Lord is used sometimes of God, and sometimes of Jesus in Acts.

in buildings (Acts 17:24). He is the source for Jesus, the Spirit, his salvation, and the dynamics of the mission. And it is the kingdom of *God* that is established through Jesus (Acts 1:3; 8:12; 14:22; 19:8; 28:23). God is the object of the believers' praise and reverence (Acts 2:5, 11, 47; 3:8–9; 4:21, 24; 5:29–32; 7:55–56; 10:2–4, 22, 31; 12:5, 23; 16:14, 25; 17:4; 18:7, 13; 21:20; 24:14; 26:29; 27:35; 28:15, 28). It is God who pours out his Spirit in accordance with Old Testament expectation (Acts 2:22). God is the empowering agent who fulfills his promises. He sends angels as emissaries (Acts 8:26; 12:7, 11). In Acts, God works sovereignly through sending his Son Jesus to bring his salvation by allowing his Son to be crucified according to his will, raising him from the dead, and exalting him to God's right hand. This view of God features prominently throughout, and particularly in the sermons of Acts (Acts 2:22–39; 3:13–15, 18–26; 4:10; 10:34–46; 13:6–37; 17:23–31; 21:19; 22:14; 26:7–8).[28]

The apostles' proclamation is the "word of God," indicating that this message of salvation stands in continuity with the proclamation of the Old Testament prophets and with Jesus himself (Acts 4:31; 6:2, 7; 8:14; 11:1; 12:24; 13:5, 7, 46; 15:7–14; 17:13; 18:11, cf. 20:27). God answers prayer (Acts 4:24–31). Stephen's sermon in Acts 7 highlights the first Jerusalem Christians' understanding of the continuity between the God of the Old Testament, Jesus, and the church (cf. Acts 7 mentions God eighteen times alone). Jesus is God's Son (Acts 9:20), who brings the ministry of God into human history to Jews and gentiles alike (cf. Acts 11:17–19; 14:27; 15:4; 16:10; 28:28). This gospel is the "grace of God" (Acts 6:8; 11:23; 13:43; 14:26; 20:24) and to believe in Christ is to believe in God (Acts 16:33–34, cf. 20:21; 26:18, 20; 27:25). Those who believe follow the "way of God" (Acts 18:26). God (the Lord) adds new converts to the movement (Acts 2:47). The church is described as "the church of God" (Acts 20:28). God sends angels who guide the movement (Acts 5:19; 8:26; 10:3–7; 12:7–11; 27:23) as in the Old Testament (Acts 7:35, 38). Just as Acts begins with the resurrected Jesus teaching the disciples about the kingdom of God, it ends with Paul preaching God's salvation and kingdom in Rome (cf. Acts 1:3; 28:28–31). The early Christians look forward to the "day

---

28. God works through Jesus in wonders by his providence and then raises Jesus from the dead. God's name is used frequently in the sermons of Acts, where he is mentioned as the one who providentially brought his salvation through Jesus.

of the Lord" (Acts 2:20; Joel 2:20). God the Father is the central character of Luke-Acts.

A CHRIST-CENTERED CHURCH

Jesus, the Second Person of the Trinity implicit to Luke's work, features prominently in Acts as God's agent of salvation. It is clear from the start that the risen Christ was the foundation of the first church in Jerusalem. This is apparent from the introduction, where Luke reminds Theophilus of his first book, which was focused on Christ, and then stresses the resurrection appearances of Jesus (Acts 1:3). In both Luke and Acts, the last instruction of Christ is to wait to be empowered for the mission by the promised Spirit (Luke 24:49; Acts 1:4-5). The disciples obey him and are "clothed with power from high" as Jesus promised (Luke 24:49). Through the believers, the Spirit sovereignly extends the work of God and his Son. Obedience to Christ is seen from the beginning, as the disciples obey Jesus' command to remain in Jerusalem (Acts 1:5, 12). Their emphasis on prayer indicates their reliance on Jesus. The importance of Jesus as the building block of the new church is also reflected in their determination to replace Judas with someone who had been with Jesus throughout his ministry and who was a witness to the resurrection (Acts 1:21-23).

Jesus also forms the basis of the message they take to Jerusalem and beyond. He is the main subject of Peter and Paul's sermons, which speak of his earthly ministry of miracles, his suffering and death, his resurrection, his ascension and exaltation, the giving of the Holy Spirit, the need to respond by repentance, and baptism into "the name of Jesus Christ" (Acts 2:22-39; 3:12-26; 4:8-12; 10:34-43). Notably, receiving the Spirit is linked to the proclamation of Christ (e.g., Acts 10:44). In a summary statement, Luke records that they "continued to testify to the resurrection of the Lord Jesus," illustrating how central Christ and his resurrection were to their life and message (Acts 4:33 NIV). Similarly, Luke writes that Philip went to Samaria and "proclaimed the Messiah there" (Acts 8:5 NIV) and "preached the good news of the kingdom of God and the name of Jesus Christ" (Acts 8:12 NIV).

Miracles are performed "in the name of Jesus Christ," and Jesus is given the credit for empowering the healing of the disabled beggar at the gate Beautiful (Acts 3:6; 4:10). When Peter and John were released from prison by the Sanhedrin, their response was to pray to Jesus ("Sovereign Lord"

[Acts 4:24]) that they might do further miracles and that he might empower their proclamation (Acts 4:30). When Peter healed Aeneas, the bedridden paralytic, he stated, "Jesus Christ heals you" (Acts 9:34). In other words, Peter was a mere messenger and agent of Jesus the healer—so it is with believers today.

When commanded not to speak of Jesus, the apostles refused, considering it more important to obey God than the Sanhedrin, despite their political power. The magnitude of what they had seen and experienced in Christ meant that they could not hold back. Obedience to Christ ruled the Jerusalem church (Acts 4:17-20). To obey Christ's appeal to preach the gospel was to obey God (Acts 5:29). After being rebuked again by the Sanhedrin, "day after day, in the temple courts and from house to house, they never stopped teaching and proclaiming the good news [*euangelion*] that Jesus is the Messiah" (Acts 5:42 NIV).

The believers were baptized "in the name of the Lord Jesus" (Acts 8:16; 10:48), indicating that they had entered a new realm and way of living; to use Paul's phrase, they were "in Christ." On his conversion, in which he saw and heard Christ (Acts 9:1-6), Paul also centered his message on Jesus' preaching that he "is the Son of God" (Acts 9:20) and "proving that Jesus [was] the Christ" (Acts 9:22).

This emphasis on Christ extended as the church spread out in Acts 11-28. Christ brings messages to believers and is the object of worship (Acts 13:2) and prayer (Acts 11:8). He is the one who imparts the Spirit (Acts 11:16). This Spirit of Jesus guides the mission (Acts 16:7; 18:9; 22:8-21; 23:11). He is the "Lord" and supreme over all Greco-Roman and other "lords," including "Caesar" (e.g., Acts 11:17, 20, 21; 17:7 ["another king"]; 19:7; 20:21). He is the center and content of their message: "the good news about the Lord Jesus," and "the word of the Lord" (Acts 11:20; 13:12, 38, 44, 48-49; 15:35-36; 16:32; 17:3; 18:5, 25; 19:10, 20; 24:24; 28:23; 28:31). He is Messiah, the long-awaited Christ who suffered and rose again. Paul constantly sought to prove to the Jews that Jesus was the Messiah, often to little avail (Acts 17:3; 18:5, cf. Apollos, Acts 18:28). Conversion was based on believing in Jesus as Lord (Acts 11:21, 23-24). Miracles are attributed to Jesus (Acts 13:11; 14:3; 19:13). He is the Savior (Acts 13:23). The sermons of Paul center on Jesus (Acts 13:23-24, 27, 33, 38; 17:3). He is the fulfillment of prophecy (Acts 13:33, cf. Ps 2:7). He is the one who brings forgiveness. He is the one who commissioned believers to take the gospel to the gentiles (Acts 13:47; 20:24) and empowered them to do so (Acts 14:3). Followers place their faith in Jesus (Acts 14:23; 16:15; 18:8). His grace saves where faith is found (Acts 15:11, 40; 16:31; 20:21). It is for Jesus that believers work and serve (Acts 20:19), risking life and limb (Acts 15:26). He is sovereign over the mission, opening hearts to receive the message (Acts 16:14). The name of Jesus Christ brings power for miracles (Acts 16:18). He converts (Acts 22:8). His teaching is the blueprint for life, "the way of the Lord" (Acts 18:25). This teaching and example are the basis of the Christian ethic (Acts 20:35). It is into Jesus' name that new believers are baptized (Acts 19:5), by his name that they minister (Acts 19:14, 17), and for his name that they are prepared to die (Acts 21:13). His death and resurrection are central to their proclamation (Acts 17:31-32; 25:19; 26:23).

It is overwhelmingly clear that Christ formed the foundation of the first church. The implication that can be drawn from this is that Christ must form the foundation of *any* church (cf. 1 Cor 3:11). His power and name sustain, empower, and animate the church. He is the subject of the message. He is the locus of life and the focus of the believer's attention. Man's effort is merely continuing his work as he commands. Obedience to Christ is foundational for any church of Christ. There is no room here for a truncated Christ, a reduced Christ with certain parts taken out or sanitized. He is the Messiah Lord and Son of God revealed in Scripture. He is Jesus, who is continuous from his earthly existence—and this earthly existence recorded in the Gospels is the believer's foundation. He is the resurrected Lord, resurrected in the body, not merely in spirit. He is Christ the Lord. The mission the believer engages in, on behalf of his Father, is his mission—the *missio Christi*. All preaching and songs should center on him and the historical event of his full life and, particularly, his death and resurrection—the linchpin of history.

A SPIRIT-EMPOWERED CHURCH

The Third Person of the Trinity is the Spirit. In Acts, the Spirit runs through the narrative like a thread. One might say the Spirit "broods" over every sentence of the book. Luke's Gospel stresses, more than the other Synoptics, the Spirit-dimension of Jesus' ministry (Acts 10:38; Luke 3:16, 22; 4:1, 14, 18; 10:21). The Spirit's coming upon believers is anticipated in Luke from John's ministry on, and is fulfilled in Acts (cf. Luke 3:16; 11:13; 12:12; 24:49).

In Acts, the Spirit is everywhere, from the beginning to the end. If God is the underground well and Christ the fountain, the Spirit is the water who runs from the fountain, feeding the first disciples in the first church and empowering them for the task at hand.

Missional Empowerment

The disciples are told to wait for the Spirit until he comes (Acts 1:4, 8, 12; 2:1-4). There must be empowerment before mission! This empowerment is the Spirit's primary function in Acts, to "be my witnesses" (Acts 1:8). Sometimes, tongues play a part at the coming of the Spirit in Acts. Yet, contrary to some popular opinion, the gift of tongues is not the decisive sign of Spirit-reception—mission is. Indeed, the first coming of tongues is profoundly missional, as believers speak the languages of Pentecost pilgrims, and they are converted.

When the Spirit comes upon the disciples, he has a dramatic effect on them, and subsequently on the general populace, through Peter's proclamation, the healings, and the phenomenal *koinōnia* (fellowship) of the Jerusalem church. After Paul's conversion and Spirit-baptism, he almost immediately travels to the synagogues of Damascus to preach the message that Jesus is the Son of God and Messiah (Acts 9:20-22). This mission emphasis is seen when Peter faces the Sanhedrin and courageously refuses to yield to their command to stop preaching the message. Luke describes Peter as "filled with the Spirit" (Acts 4:8) and the Sanhedrin are amazed at Peter and John's courage (Acts 4:13). Boldness to proclaim is the work of the Spirit. This power is seen when the believers pray for God to move in signs and wonders and for empowerment for mission (Acts 4:24-31). The response is a shaken room, a fresh infilling of the Spirit, and renewed boldness to preach the gospel (Acts 4:31). Stephen was a man full of the Spirit who spoke by the Spirit—so much so that his opponents could not stand up spiritually to him (Acts 6:10). However, they then killed him.

Guidance

In addition, the Spirit is the guiding force for the mission in all of Acts. This is seen when Philip is led by an angel to intersect the journey of an Ethiopian eunuch. He is then directed by the Spirit to stand near the eunuch's chariot (Acts 8:29). This leads to a discussion over Isaiah 53 that climaxes in the African's conversion and baptism. After this, Philip is suddenly taken away by the Spirit of the Lord. Peter, too, is guided specifically by the voice of the Spirit (Acts 10:19), who tells him that he should not hesitate to go with the visitors from Cornelius. It is God who led Cornelius to reach out to Peter through an angel (Acts 10:3-4). This leads to the conversion of the first gentiles. This Spirit-led dynamic is seen later where Paul's first mission is released because "the Holy Spirit said, 'Set apart for me Barnabas and Saul for the work to which I have called them'" (Acts 13:2). It is also seen when Paul is forbidden by the Spirit to preach in Bithynia and Asia and is directed in a vision to go to Macedonia (Acts 16:6-9). It is this compulsion of the Spirit that encourages Paul to go to Jerusalem, despite prophetic warnings from the same Spirit warning of the consequences of doing so (Acts 20:23; 21:4). The only truly authentic evangelism is that which is Spirit-guided.

The Scriptures

The Scriptures find their origin in the Spirit. In Acts 1:16, Peter introduces the discussion over replacing Judas with these words: "the Scripture ... which *the Holy Spirit spoke beforehand* by the mouth of David" (Acts 1:16, emphasis added). When Philip connects with the Ethiopian eunuch, he finds the Ethiopian reading Isaiah 53:7-8, where the good news about Jesus was prophetically written centuries prior. These Scriptures also point to the importance of the Old Testament and the word of God to the first Christians. When considering the eunuch conversion in Acts 8, the Spirit was in action leading Philip and speaking from Scripture. It is a story saturated in the presence of the Spirit.

The Coming of the Spirit

The importance of the Spirit is seen in the Spirit's dramatic comings throughout Acts. There are seven explicit[29] examples or receptions[30] in

---

29. This discussion could be extended to other references to conversion in Acts where the Spirit (*pneuma*) is not mentioned explicitly. For example, the conversions of the Ethiopian (Acts 8), Lydia, and the jailor (Acts 16). In none of these does the convert speak in tongues; rather, they demonstrate a desire for baptism and mercy, and demonstrate hospitality.

30. There is another point where believers are filled with the Spirit, including individuals who have already received the Spirit, being filled at moments of witness including Peter before the Sanhedrin (Acts 4:8), and Paul before Elymas on Cyprus (Acts 13:9).

Acts. These seven moments of reception are at critical points: (1) The first Jewish believers empowered (Acts 2:1-4); (2) The Jerusalem Church reignited (Acts 4:31);[31] (3) The first Samaritan believers empowered (Acts 8:17); (4) Paul, the great missionary to the gentiles, empowered (Acts 9:17-18); (5) The first gentiles empowered (Acts 10:45; 11:15); (6) The disciples of Antioch filled with the Spirit (Acts 13:52); and (7) The believers in Ephesus empowered (Acts 19:6). However, they are the first Asian converts, so it is possible that this is also a pivotal point in mission.

The table and notes below summarize the different experiences. Note the variety of venues, modes, recipients, agents, manifestations, and timing in relation to faith and baptism. There is no clear pattern, and this should guard against overly schematic theologies of Spirit-reception.

Pentecost. The first and most powerful coming is the initial outpouring at Pentecost. This was anticipated by the disciples based on Jesus' promise (Acts 2:1-4). It came on Pentecost, a day of great spiritual significance to Israel that was associated with the first fruits of the harvest. This outpouring, then, is the first fruits of the Spirit's harvest on earth. It is noticeable that there are three visible and powerful manifestations at Pentecost. First, there is a *sound* like a violent wind filling the house. Second, there is the *sight* of what appeared to be tongues of fire. Third, there is the disciples speaking in known languages or tongues (*glossolalia/xenoglossy*).[32] These manifestations indicate that sometimes when the Spirit comes, strange things happen. Believers should be wise and discerning but not

---

31. This includes both the recipients of Pentecost and others converted since. This is not an initial experience for some, but perhaps so for some.

32. Glossalalia comes from the Greek *glōssolalia* from *glōssa* meaning "tongue, language" and *laleō*, "speak." Xenoglossy, of which this incident is an example, is from *xenoglōssia* compounding *xenos*, "foreigner," and *glōssa* meaning "speaking in a foreign known language spontaneously." Paul refers to the tongues of angels and humanity (1 Cor 13:1). It is highly unlikely that the tongues in 1 Cor 14 are known languages, as they are in Acts 2. It seems they are something different, perhaps mysterious Spirit-given languages, because: (1) the speaker does not speak to people but to God (v. 1); (2) no one understands the speaker (v. 2); (3) the speaker utters mysteries with his spirit/the Spirit (v. 2); (4) whereas one who prophesies speaks to people in a known language (v. 3); (5) the speaker does not edify the church (vv. 4, 5); (6) tongues are like indistinguishable or meaningless sounds (vv. 7-10); (7) the mind is unfruitful when one speaks in a tongue (v. 14); (8) others cannot concur with the prayer (if it was a language, someone would be able to translate it as they did in Acts 2) (v. 16); and (9) unbelievers think the speakers are mad. If they were speaking foreign languages, unbelievers would not think they had gone crazy, although they might not understand (v. 23).

Text	Venue	Mode	Recipient	Agent	Manifestations	Timing
Pentecost 2:1-41	Jerusalem, Temple Courts	Sovereign Outpouring	Jerusalem, Believers	God sovereignly	Tongues, mission	After faith, water baptism
Jerusalem Church 4:24-31	Jerusalem, Unspecified	Sovereign, In answer to prayer	Jerusalem, Believers (Again)	God, In response to prayer	Bold evangelism, Material generosity, Signs and wonders	After prayer, a subsequent experience, the Pentecost people and new converts
Samaritans 8:1-17	Samaria, Public Setting	The laying on of hands	Samaritan, Believers	God through Apostles Peter, John	Something unspecified but visible, opposition	After faith, water baptism
Paul 9:1-22	Home of Judas on Straight Street	The laying on of hands	Paul	God through Ananias, an ordinary 'disciple'	Healing, mission	After faith, before water baptism
Cornelius' Family 10:44-48	Home of Cornelius, a Gentile soldier	Sovereign Outpouring	Cornelius, a Gentile family	God sovereignly	Tongues, praise	During a sermon (after faith?) and before water baptism
Psidian Antioch 13:52	Unspecified	Unspecified	The disciples of Psidian Antioch	God? Unclear	Joy	Unspecified
Ephesus 19:1-20	Unspecified	The laying on of hands	Ephesian believers	God through Apostle Paul	Tongues, prophecy	After faith and water baptism

FIGURE 23: THE SEVEN OUTPOURINGS IN ACTS

be utterly surprised when people report strange spiritual phenomena and experiences.

Critically, immediately after the outpouring, *mission* flows from the experience—through Peter and into the narrative of Acts. The impact of the tongues-speaking spreads to the bemused crowd who hear Jews speaking their languages. While some think the believers are drunk, crowds gather, and Peter preaches boldly, promising the crowds the Spirit. There is a huge response with three thousand people baptized in one day. Peter links this event to Joel's prophecy of the Spirit being poured out in the last days, interpreting the coming as the awaited "Spirit of prophecy" (Joel 2:28-29). Throughout Acts, the dominant impact of the Spirit is missional.

Notably, the Spirit is impartial, falling on *each one* of the 120 or so, including men and women (Acts 1:14-15), so that *all* are filled. Those who receive the Spirit at Pentecost are Jews gathered from nearby nations. They receive the Spirit spontaneously without human agency, but after baptism and faith. It is likely that the Pentecost experience catalyzed the spread of the gospel as these pilgrims returned home full of the Spirit and believing Jesus is Messiah. It is also likely that the church spread from this point to Rome, Africa, and perhaps northern Asia Minor (cf. 1 Pet 1). Note that it is the sovereign work of God through the Spirit that causes this spread, which is a feature of Luke's Acts narrative.

Jerusalem Again. Luke records a "second Pentecost" in Jerusalem,[33] where the Spirit again falls upon the Jerusalem church and fills the believers, including those at the first outpouring, and new converts since. This occurs after the number of Christians swells to five thousand (Acts 4:4) and the Sanhedrin forbids the first believers from preaching the gospel (Acts 4:5-22). Rather than yield to this command that violates Jesus' commission (Luke 24:46-49; Acts 1:8), the believers in Jerusalem gather and respond through non-violent resistance. They pray for courage to preach and for

---

33. Some scholars repudiate seeing this as a second Pentecost, and in a sense, they are correct; Pentecost was a one-off event (e.g., John B. Polhill, *Acts*, NAC 26 [Nashville: Broadman & Holman Publishers, 1992)], 150). However, this is clearly a second experience of the Spirit for the church including the 120 from Pentecost, and demonstrates that the Spirit is free to fall at his leisure and does so, even on those who have previously received the Spirit. One should not be surprised to hear that Christians have more than one overwhelming experience of the Spirit.

God to act powerfully in healing, signs, and wonders (Acts 4:29–30). The results are dramatic. Believers are filled with the Spirit, the place they are in is shaken (another manifestation of the Spirit),[34] and they are emboldened to preach Christ in the face of opposition. There is no reference to speaking in tongues, and again, mission flows from the receipt of the Spirit. This boldness flows into the courage demonstrated in what follows with the apostles in Acts 5, Stephen in Acts 6–7, Peter in Acts 9, and the scattered Jerusalem Christians—including Philip and those who evangelized Antioch—in Acts 8–11. The subsequent narrative also indicates that radical generosity toward each other to alleviate need existed, and signs and wonders followed (Acts 4:32–37; 5:12–16). This shows the Spirit impels more than just evangelism, important though this is. Ananias and Sapphira's death is also a manifestation of the Spirit's power—though of judgment (Acts 5:1–11).

Samaria. The third dramatic outpouring of the Spirit is in Samaria during Philip's mission to the town. Philip was filled with the Spirit at Pentecost and/or the prayer event, and preaches and performs signs with dramatic effect, exorcising many demons. Great joy fills the city (Acts 8:7–8). There is also a power encounter with the local magi (cf. Acts 19:11–19). Peter and John become aware of what is happening, and travel from the mother church to Samaria to take note. While there, they lay hands on the new converts, who "[receive] the Holy Spirit" (Acts 8:17). This could suggest that the impartation of the Spirit must be apostolic. However, this is ruled out in Acts, as the Spirit comes in a range of ways—including God's sovereign action, and through Ananias, a disciple in Damascus (Acts 9:17–19). On this occasion, there are *no explicit manifestations,* but certainly, something happens because Simon is aware of some spiritual effect and seeks to purchase the power (Acts 8:18). Some claim that this must be tongues. However, tongues are only *one* possibility among the range of manifestations seen

---

34. The Greek is the aorist of *saleuō*, a strong term used in the New Testament of a reed shaken by wind (Matt 11:7; Luke 7:24), astral objects shaken (Matt 24:49; Mark 13:25; Luke 21:26), a measure of grain shaken together (Luke 6:38), a home shaken by a stormy flood (Luke 6:48), David unshaken because of God's support (Acts 2:25), a room shaken by an earthquake (Acts 16:25), a crowd stirred up for violence (Acts 17:13), shaken in one's mind (2 Thess 2:2), and God's voice shaking the earth (Heb 12:26–27). Here it could refer to the people being shaken up, or as is more likely (as the place is mentioned, not the people), the place itself (i.e., an earthquake-like experience).

through Acts such as joy, praise, prophesying, healing, visible experiences (wind, tongues of fire, and shaking), and missional engagement. Those who received the Spirit in Acts received him through the apostles, after faith and baptism (Acts 8:12).

Paul. The fourth outpouring of the Spirit comes after *Saul's conversion*. After he experiences the risen Lord, Luke describes Saul blind and fasting in Damascus. A local Jewish disciple named Ananias lays hands on him, and Paul receives the Spirit. The agent of this anointing is not an "ordained" leader or a recognized "apostle," but a "disciple"— an "ordinary" believer. Here there is one physical manifestation: Paul's eyesight is restored (Acts 9:17-19). There is no reference to tongues. Although Paul did speak in tongues (1 Cor 14:18), Bible interpreters must not automatically associate receiving the gift with this event; he may have received the gift on a subsequent occasion. Significantly, Saul's response, after a few days, is to preach the message in synagogues. Again, mission is the primary sign of the coming of the Spirit (Acts 9:20). Importantly, Paul received the Spirit after faith, but before baptism (Acts 9:18). This shows there is no absolute sequence of faith, baptism, and Spirit-reception.

Cornelius' Family. The fifth outpouring is what might be called the "gentile Pentecost," where the Spirit pours out upon Cornelius and his family— the first uncircumcised gentile family to experience the Spirit in this way. Peter enters the house of the uncircumcised gentile. In itself, this is a radical breaking of Jewish protocol, which precluded such fellowship with "unclean" gentiles. He then preaches the message to them. As he is speaking, the Spirit falls upon the hearers of the message. There are two manifestations: speaking in tongues, and praise of God (Acts 10:44-46; 11:15-17). This is the only example of an outpouring in Acts that is not immediately followed by the new believers embarking on mission. However, later in the narrative, the importance of this event for the mission is seen, as this event leads church leaders to endorse gentile mission (Acts 11:15) and reject the need for new gentile converts to be circumcised (Acts 15:8).

Pisidia Antioch. In Acts 13:52, after Paul's missionary team moves on from Pisidia Antioch, Luke notes that "the disciples were filled with joy and with the Holy Spirit." "The disciples" would appear to be distinguished from "Paul and Barnabas" in the previous verse and the one that follows, likely speaking of the local followers of Jesus. It is disputable that this constitutes an outpouring, as in previous instances. It is a summary statement. However, it does indicate that at some point the Antiochians received the Spirit. The only manifestation mentioned is joy.

Ephesus. The final explicit experience of the Spirit comes in Ephesus, the capital of Asia Minor, or modern western Turkey. Paul travels to Ephesus, where he finds some disciples who have neither been baptized into the name of Jesus, nor been filled with the Spirit. He baptizes them in water (Acts 19:5) and places his hands on them.[35] There are two manifestations on this occasion: speaking in tongues, and prophesying (Acts 19:6). Mission is also important, as these believers and others who join Paul in the lecture hall of Tyrannus share the gospel throughout Asia over two years (Acts 19:10). During this time, Epaphras plants the Colossian and Laodicean churches (Col 1:7). It is likely that the seven churches of Revelation, and arguably the churches of northern Asia Minor, are also planted (cf. Rev 2–3; 1 Pet 1:1). The Spirit is received after initial faith and baptism, through the laying on of Paul's hands.

Summary

In each outpouring, something evidentiary occurred with some common elements but also substantial variation. The claim that tongues is *the* sign of receiving the Spirit in Acts and/or in the New Testament does not stand up to scrutiny. First, outside of Acts, there is no evidence of believers speaking in tongues in the New Testament apart from Paul and some in the Corinthian church. There is no instance given of Jesus speaking in tongues.[36]

---

35. Luke doesn't give the exact timeline of events. This appears subsequent to the baptism, either as they came out of the water or later.

36. Jesus speaking in tongues is not mentioned in the writings of Matthew, John, Peter, James, Jude, or in Hebrews. It is mentioned in the longer ending of Mark, but this text is a later addition. This longer ending known in the mid- to late second century would imply that speaking in tongues continued in the church at least until the date of this ending.

Paul made it clear that, although he spoke in tongues himself (1 Cor 14:18) and wished that all spoke in tongues (1 Cor 14:5), not all do—just as not all are apostles, prophets, or teachers; not all speak in tongues (1 Cor 12:28).[37] For Paul, the sign of having received the Spirit is that believers will not dare to curse Christ but will confess from their heart that Jesus is Lord (1 Cor 12:3, cf. Rom 10:9).[38]

In Acts, tongues are specifically mentioned in three of the seven Spirit-moments: Pentecost, Cornelius' baptism, and Ephesus. On other occasions, it is unspecified (the prayer-experience, Samaria, Paul, and Pisidia Antioch).[39] Other manifestations include prophesying, praise, healing, and joy. Mission is the dominant effect of the Spirit-experiences, including Peter's sermon at Pentecost (Acts 2), the bold evangelism of Acts 4:31 and Acts 5, Paul's missions (Acts 9:19-22, 27-30; 13-28), and the evangelization of Asia Minor (Acts 19:10-20). The only exceptions are the Samaritans, Cornelius, and Pisidia Antioch. However, the receipt of tongues by Cornelius' family is a decisive factor in the opening up of gentile mission at the Jerusalem Council (Acts 15:7-8).

There is no necessary *immediate* connection in Acts between conversion and the receipt of the Spirit. On most occasions, the disciples believe before receiving (Pentecost, Samaria, Paul, and Ephesus). Nonetheless, in Cornelius' case, the coming of the Spirit and conversion seem to occur at the same time or immediately after. Perhaps more importantly, there

---

37. This is often missed by English readers but agreed by the vast numbers of scholars who work with Greek. The Greek involves a series of questions that begin with the Greek μή (mē) and so expects the answer "no." As Anthony C. Thiselton, *The First Epistle to the Corinthians: A Commentary on the Greek Text*, NIGCT (Grand Rapids, MI: Eerdmans, 2000), 1022 says, "It is important to render the rhetorical questions in in English idioms which take full account of the use of μή to express hesitant questions which demand negative answers." Some seek to avoid this by saying that the gift here is different to that of 1 Cor 14, but this is flawed as the same Greek word is used in 1 Cor 14, and 1 Cor 12-14 are written specifically in parallel (a chiasm).

38. The whole issue in 1 Cor 12:1-3 is the Corinthian obsession with spiritual gifts, especially tongues. Paul states that tongues or any other gift is not the prime mark of having received the Spirit; rather, the prime mark is that a person with the Spirit would never curse Christ (e.g., under interrogation), but would confess Jesus as Lord (and live out this confession). The other mark of the Spirit for Paul is love (1 Cor 12:31-13:13: "the most excellent way"). He also states in a different context (Rom 8:16) that there is an inward witness from the Spirit that confirms our reception of him.

39. It is possible that the visible sign in Samaria is tongues (cf. Acts 8:18); however, this is not certain. Equally, the converts may have experienced healing, praise, prophesying, or some other unspecified manifestation.

is no direct connection between water baptism and receipt of the Spirit.[40] Sometimes Spirit-reception precedes water baptism (Cornelius, Acts 10), sometimes it is experienced simultaneously (Ephesus, Acts 19), and sometimes it follows (Pentecost, Acts 4, Samaria). It is hard to systematize the receipt of the Spirit on the evidence of Luke's writing. What can be said is that on most occasions it occurred after or at the point of faith. As Dunn has argued, there is a nexus of conversion events, including initial faith, water baptism initiating the person into the people of God, and Spirit-reception. The Spirit in Luke is sovereign and acts according to God's will.

For the early Christians, the coming of the Spirit is the fulfillment of the hope of the Old Testament. This is explicit in Peter's first sermon, where the Spirit is explained in terms of the promise of Joel 2:28-32. Peter declares that day to be the "last day" when the Spirit will come on *all people*, whether young men, old men, or women, causing them to prophesy, have visions, and Spirit-inspired dreams. The Spirit is inclusive, falling not only on male Jewish leaders (e.g., Acts 2:1-4; 4:31), but also on women (Acts 2:1-4 [cf. 1:14]), on Samaritans (Acts 8:17), on the persecutor Paul (Acts 9:17), and on uncircumcised unbaptized gentiles (Acts 10:46-47; 13:52; 19:6, cf. Luke 3:16). Thus, the coming of the Spirit fulfilled Old Testament expectations of the messiah filled with the Spirit (cf. Isa 11:1-3; 42:1; 61:1-2; Luke 4:18-21; Acts 10:38) and a new era where the Spirit is written on the hearts of God's people from every nation (Isa 44:3; Ezek 11:19; 36:26-27; 39:29; Joel 2:28-29, cf. Zech 12:10). He is thus "the promised Holy Spirit" (cf. Acts 2:33; Luke 24:49; Eph 1:13), given as a gift (cf. Acts 2:39) to all who believe and obey the gospel (Acts 5:32). He is the "Spirit of prophecy" predicted by Joel, poured out on all people.

In Luke-Acts the source of the Spirit is not only the Father. Believers at Pentecost "received from the Father the promised Holy Spirit and has poured out what you now see and hear" (Acts 2:33 NIV). Yet, it is Jesus who is "sending the promise of my Father upon you" (Luke 24:49). It is Jesus who baptizes with "the Holy Spirit and fire" (Luke 3:16; Acts 11:16). This is of importance for students of church history and the study of the Filioque

---

40. Just as some Pentecostals will argue that tongues should be read into those instances where there is no mention, some older scholars argue that water baptism should be assumed in instances where it is not mentioned. Both arguments are flawed; this cannot be assumed.

controversy, which divided the church between East and West at the turn of the first millennium (see also John 16:7).[41]

Luke's account of the history of the first Christians indicates they clearly believed that all who subsequently came to believe in Jesus and were baptized would receive the Spirit (Acts 2:38-39; 5:32). In these texts, the Spirit is also connected to healing and miracles. Although the Spirit is not directly mentioned, the prayer, "stretch out your hand to heal" (Acts 4:30) indicates the work of the Spirit as the hand of Jesus. After the prayer, they were "filled with the Holy Spirit and spoke the word of God boldly" (Acts 4:31 NIV), and God moved powerfully in healing and the miraculous (Acts 5:12-16).

The receipt of the Spirit is also linked to the wonderful material *koinōnia* of the church. This connection is implicit. The disciples prayed for God to move in power in signs and wonders (Acts 5:12-16) and to enable bold proclamation (see Acts 4:31), but as well the Spirit brought dynamic *koinōnia* and radical sharing to the church (Acts 4:32-5:11).

Where there were outbreaks of spiritual power and renewal in Acts, there were often clashes with the authorities and persecution and spiritual clashes—the arrival of the Spirit excites opposition. For example, while initially Pentecost saw the Christians enjoying the favor of the community (Acts 2:47), Peter and John were subsequently hauled before the authorities after the healing of the disabled man (Acts 4:1-20) and the aftermath of Acts 4:31 in Acts 4:32-5:16 (see also Acts 5:17-40). Ultimately, the church was broken up after the Stephen's death (Acts 8:1-4). The coming of the Spirit in Samaria led to a spiritual clash with Simon the Magician (Acts 8:9-24). Paul's initial mission after his Spirit-reception led to persecution in Damascus and Jerusalem (Acts 9:20-30). The Ephesus spiritual awakening led to violent riots and resistance from worshipers of Artemis (Acts

---

41. "Filioque" is from the Latin, "and the Son." It is also called the "Double procession of the Holy Spirit." The Western church argued that the Spirit proceeds from God the Father and Jesus Christ. This was added to some later versions of the Nicene Creed after the words, "the Holy Spirit ... who proceeds from the Father," and became a part of many churches' worship. After AD 1000, it was adopted by Rome. Leading to this decision, there were intense debates in the latter part of the first millennium. The Eastern Orthodox Church argued that the Spirit proceeds from the Father alone and *not* Jesus. This controversy was key to the split between the Orthodox and Catholic Churches (1054). Luke 24:49 and Acts 2:38 would appear to support the Western church, although the theological arguments grow complex on both sides. See "Filioque," the *ODCC*, 614.

19:21–40). There were also constant outbreaks through Paul's missions. Such opponents of the early Christians are described as those who "resist the Holy Spirit" (Acts 7:51).

The mode of the Spirit's reception is described in different ways throughout the narrative. There is the notion of baptism in (*en*) the Spirit. There is a contrast between John the Baptist's baptism which is *in* (*en*) water and Jesus' baptism which is *in* (*en*) the Holy Spirit (Luke 3:16; Acts 1:5; 11:16). *En* can be translated "with" or "by," but the contrast with water baptism suggests being immersed in the Spirit as in water. The Greek for "baptize" (*baptizō*) means "to dip, immerse, wash." In non-Christian literature, it can also mean to "plunge, sink, drench, overwhelm" or, figuratively, "to soak" (as in Plato, *Symp*. 176b).[42] In other words, baptism in the Spirit means to be immersed in or thoroughly overwhelmed by the personal presence of God.

Although the term "baptism" is not used in Acts 8:17, it would seem that the experience of receiving the Spirit through the apostolic laying on of hands in this passage is the same experience. Luke uses different language to describe the experience, most employing the motif of water. Here he writes, "they received (*lambanō*) the Holy Spirit" (Acts 8:17; 10:47). He also states that the Spirit "had not yet fallen (*epipiptō*) on any of them" likening the receipt of the Spirit to being overwhelmed from above by the Spirit (rains upon, falls as in rain, a shower, or waterfall; see Acts 8:16; 10:44). In Acts 10:45, the Spirit is "poured out" (*ekchunnō*) upon the first gentile believers, as if God and Christ are standing above the believer and pouring the Spirit upon them from a cosmic Spirit-bucket or tap. Luke also employs the idea of "being filled" (*pimplemi*) with the Spirit, which moves the metaphor to an inward experience of water filling as in a hot water bottle. The human body, then, is likened to a water-receptacle. For example, Acts 2:4 says, "All of them were filled with the Spirit" (NIV). There are also examples of believers being "filled" afresh, often in the context of boldness in a mission situation (Acts 4:8, 31; 13:9). This suggests that the filling experience may occur multiple times, rather than a once-for-all situation (cf. Eph 5:18). Luke uses the language fluidly and interchangeably to seek to describe the indescribable and wonderful experience of receiving the Spirit.

---

42. BDAG 164–65.

Conclusion

John highlights the function of the Spirit in entry into the kingdom (John 3:3, 5-6), Jesus' ministry (John 3:23-24), worship (John 4:23-24), eternal life (John 6:63), mission (John 7:38),[43] support and comfort (John 14:16), bringing truth (John 14:17; 16:13), reminding the believer of Jesus' teaching (John 14:26), giving testimony to Christ (John 15:26), conviction (John 16:8-11), and bringing glory to Christ (John 16:14). Paul emphasizes the work of the Spirit in generating gifts for the good of the church (Rom 12:3-8; 1 Cor 12:1-31; Eph 4:11-16) and in sanctification (Rom 8:1-17; Gal 5:22-25).

Luke accentuates the coming of the Spirit, the experience of the baptism of the Spirit, and the importance of the Spirit for church unity, life, and especially mission. He has a rich theology of the Spirit placing the Spirit in the driving seat of church life and mission. Contemporary church life and mission should be no different. It should be led by the Spirit, empowered by the Spirit, and the verbal witness of the church should be placed alongside acts of grace, justice, and healing as God chooses to exercise his reign (i.e., signs and wonders).

While classical Pentecostalism has appealed to Luke for a theology of second blessing and tongues as evidence of the receipt of the Spirit, this is far from clear in Luke's writings. Luke presents a pneumatology of multiple blessing, where the Spirit comes on the same people more than once to do his work. Tongues are not always received when the Spirit comes. Other signs are found, and often not repeated, such as the sound of wind, tongues of fire, a room shaken, joy, prophecy, praise, and healing. Luke's theology is resistant to tight systematization. The Spirit comes at different points, whether at the moment of faith or before, during, or after baptism, in a range of contexts and ways (spontaneously, through the laying on of hands), and with a wide range of manifestations. Readers should be wary of seeking to schematize the work of the Spirit—like the wind (from the point of view of pre-scientific first-century people), the Spirit blows where he chooses (John 3:8). One thing is certain: God pours his Spirit out on all his people, immersing them in his being, and filling them. The experiences

---

43. Although this can refer to the Spirit flowing from Jesus to believers, the majority take it of the Spirit flowing from believers (see the discussion in Carson, *John*, 322-25). Either way, the metaphor "living water" flowing from the heart of Jesus or the believer speaks of mission: life flowing from the believer to others.

will vary, but all believers—leaders and followers, men and women, Jew and gentile, rich and poor, old and young—receive the Spirit. He is God's gift to those who trust him, enabling them to live by his leading and power.

A WELL-LED CHURCH

Another feature of the Jerusalem Church is its high-quality (if at times flawed) leaders. Peter is prominent through the first half of Acts. He has a strong role in preaching and the miraculous. He is clearly the initial leader of the church, standing as a spokesman at the appointment of Matthias (Acts 1:15-26; 3:12). Peter's importance is also seen in the Gospel narratives where he acts as spokesman and is singled out by Jesus (e.g., Matt 14:28-29; 15:15; 16:18; 18:21; Mark 3:16; 5:37; 8:29-33; 9:1, 5; 10:28; 11:21; 13:3; 14:29-37), in the priority of Mark's Gospel, in the putting together of Matthew and Luke, and in Paul's letters (Gal 1:18; 2:7-14). The decision, however, is not made by Peter alone, but rather by the group at his initiative (Acts 1:26).[44] This indicates that Peter and the first apostles did not exercise autocratic leadership, preferring a consultative model. Peter is the spokesman on other occasions (Acts 2:11-41; 3:1; 4:8). Likely due to the dangers to his life (Acts 12:1-19), he fades out of the limelight after Acts 12, although he does play a prominent and important role in the circumcision debate (Acts 15:7-11). He travels to Corinth at some point, may have continued into the north Galatian region (see 1 Cor 1:12; 9:5; 1 Pet 1:1), and is found in Rome (e.g., 1 Pet 5:13).

John is mentioned in relation to Peter on a few occasions, indicating he had a prominent role alongside him; however, Peter seems to do most of the talking (Acts 3:1-6; 4:8-12, 13; but see Acts 4:1, 19). There is surprisingly little mention of other apostles, except in general (e.g., Acts 5:29). The appointment of Matthias indicates they initially felt a need to maintain an inner circle of Twelve (Acts 1:13-26). However, there is no sign that this apostolic succession was to be continued. Indeed, if the two qualifications for apostleship had remained, the apostolic ministry would have died out as those who were with Jesus died. However, there is some evidence of the development of the wider concept of "apostle" in Acts 14:14, where Luke refers to both Barnabas and Paul as "apostles."

---

44. After the casting of lots.

Flexibility in leadership is seen when the church leaders appoint a group of seven Greek-speaking disciples, including Nicolaus the proselyte,[45] to distribute food to the Greek-speaking Jewish widows (Acts 6:4). Rather than stretching themselves to resolve this issue, the apostles establish another group to take on the role while they concentrate on prayer and preaching (Acts 6:4). Again, it is significant that, while the proposal came from the leaders, the "proposal pleased the whole group." This indicates their commitment to a degree of egalitarianism in decision-making under the guidance of wise leadership. The establishment of this ministry leads to further spreading of the word and sees the release of a new group of leaders. Prominent in this group is Stephen, whose ministry is powerful and effective and ultimately ends unjustly (Acts 6–7); Philip, who leads the mission to Samaria (Acts 8:4–40); and Barnabas (Acts 11–15).

This flexibility is seen in the ministry of Saul, a converted Pharisee who took the Greek name Paul. His acceptance as a leader was especially significant in the spread of the Gospel. Other key leaders in the spread of the gospel are Barnabas and Silas. While women are not listed as apostles, among the Seven, or as elders in Acts, Priscilla (also Prisca in Paul's letters) is active in mission, hosting others for worship and teaching alongside her husband, Aquila. She is most often named before Aquila (five out of seven times) and this possibly indicates she had some level of priority over him (Priscilla first: Acts 18:18–19, 26, cf. Rom 16:3; 2 Tim 4:19; Aquila first: Acts 18:2; 1 Cor 16:19).[46] In Acts 18:26, Luke uses the plural, ensuring that the reader knows that *both* Priscilla and Aquila were involved in the

---

45. The seven names are all Greek, suggesting that these are Greek-speaking men, perhaps from the diaspora. Aside from the proselyte Nicolaus, a full circumcised convert to Judaism, they are all likely Jewish Greeks. He is perhaps a founder of the Nicolaitans (Rev 2:6, 15) and a convert in Syrian Antioch (see Thomas W. Martin, "Nicolaus," in *ABD* 4:1107). Bruce, *Acts*, NICNT 121 notes that Prochorus is in later tradition the apostle John's attendant, bishop of Nicomedia, and martyred at Antioch (see also Jon Paulien, "Prochorus," in *ABD* 5:473). Tradition sees Timon as one of the seventy (Luke 10:1), later bishop of Arabia, and martyred in Basrah (Jon Paulien, "Timon," *ABD* 6:558). Parmenas is supposedly also one of the seventy and bishop of Soli in Cyprus, martyred at Philippi (John Paulien, "Parmenas," *ABD* 5:165). It is unlikely any were from the seventy as they are Greek speaking. Likely, they are early Christian converts.

46. See Witherington, *Acts*, 539, who observes, "This couple is always mentioned together in the New Testament, and in most of the instances Priscilla's name comes first (Acts 18:18, 26; Rom. 16:3; 2 Tim. 4:19). This is somewhat surprising and may well reflect her having higher social status than her husband, or greater prominence in the church, or both" (see below on 18:26).

instruction of Apollos.[47] Thus, Luke's gospel affirms a woman instructing a man.[48] Lydia, too, hosts Paul and his team at her house, indicating she is the patron of the church and a woman of means (Acts 16:14). As Luke's account suggests, there were no male Jews in the Philippian church (Acts 16:13);[49] Lydia, a church patron and a God-fearer with knowledge of the Scriptures and Judaism, was most likely the initial leader of the church. Some of the converts were women of high standing (Acts 17:4, 12, 34). Building on Luke's interest in women who traveled with Jesus (Luke 8:1-3), women were engaged in mission in Luke's account. For Luke, the decisive factor appears to be the empowering of the Spirit and godly wisdom, rather than the gender, age, or race of those involved.

A strong feature of all the leaders mentioned in Acts is that they modeled Christian living. They are found preaching, praying, and laying hands on others. They show amazing courage in the face of persecution, refusing to relent on the call of mission. Stephen and James even died for the cause (Acts 7; 12:1-2). They are not distant figures in offices directing troops into battle while they themselves are separate and safe. Although not military in a real sense, the first Christian leaders are more akin to Alexander the Great and others of history who led their armies into battle (spiritual). They are engaged and led by example. This is appropriate, for Christianity is more caught than taught. These leaders know this and lead the way. Paul calls for believers to imitate his life (e.g., 1 Cor 4:16; 11:1; Phil 3:17; 4:9). Paul's approach here reflects Jesus' teaching (Mark 1:17; 2:14; 8:34; 10:21; Matt 8:22; 10:38; Luke 9:59).

There are indications of the leadership struggling and at times failing. The selection of the leaders of Acts 6 indicates that leadership had failed to ensure that the distribution of welfare for the widows was equitable (Acts 6:1). This was due to overwork and possibly a degree of ethnocentrism as

---

47. Literally: "*they* (*proselabonto*) took him aside and *they* more accurately explained (*akribesteron ezethento*) the way [of God]."

48. See Witherington, *Acts*, 567, who rightly states, "That *both Priscilla and Aquila instructed Apollos is significant*, for Luke wishes to show the variety of roles women played in early Christianity."

49. A synagogue required ten males (see B. Chilton and E. M. Yamauchi, "Synagogues," *DNTB* 1145). There is no synagogue in Philippi, but a prayer-place by the river outside the town. Luke also carefully states there were only women by the river, confirming that there were no Jewish males in the town and likely indicating anti-Semitism in the town (see also 16:21).

they, even if inadvertently, favored the Hebrew-speaking Jews over those who spoke Greek; it is acknowledged and dealt with. Additionally, the first leaders do not appear to have fully grasped the full cosmic implications of the mission; they focus only on Jews and believe becoming a Christian requires becoming a Jew. In Luke 24:49, Jesus had instructed them to remain in Jerusalem *until* they were clothed with the Spirit. However, after Pentecost, they remain in the city. It could be that they should have immediately set out to share Christ with the nations after receiving the Spirit. However, one can argue this is a simplistic literal read of this verse and that Acts 1:8 gives a more nuanced understanding of God's purposes, which they did follow. It took some terrible persecution (Acts 8:1-4; 11:19-21) and dynamic work from God in Samaria, with regard to the Ethiopian, in Paul's conversion, and the Cornelius-event, for them to recognize the full implications of the gospel of grace (Acts 10-11; 13-15). This process is painful and involves some real contention (Acts 15:1-5). Paul and Barnabas clash sharply over John Mark, and their mission team divides (Acts 15:36-41). While this rift appears to have been restored later (Col 4:10; Phlm 24; 2 Tim 4:11), it indicates tension existed. However, Luke's account suggests the first phase of the church included wise leadership.

In conclusion, the issue of leadership is always crucial. The early church had great leaders who were not scared to make decisions and lead, yet they led in a non-autocratic manner, including all believers in their decision-making. One of the great stories of the New Testament is the journey of Peter from the spontaneous and stumbling fisherman to the great leader portrayed in Acts. Clearly, he is not perfect (see his development in the Synoptics and John 21, and his clash with Paul in Gal 2:11-14), but he is a great paradigm of the progress of a Christian leader. The role of other leaders cannot be overlooked, especially John and the other apostles: Barnabas, Philip, Stephen, Paul, John Mark, James, Timothy, Silas, Apollos, and Priscilla and Aquila. The leaders of the Jerusalem Church were people of genuine faith able to bring together flexibility, participative leadership, and leadership by example.

AN EVANGELISTIC CHURCH

Another powerful feature of the Jerusalem church is its commitment to evangelism. The term "evangelism" refers to the proclamation of the gospel: *euang* means "a set of words" (good news), or the verbal communication of the gospel message with the intention of convincing someone to believe that Jesus is Savior and Lord that they may accept God's gracious offer of salvation by faith. This can include personal one-on-one evangelism (Acts 5:42), family evangelism (e.g., "households" in Acts 11:14; 16:15, 31; 18:8, cf. 1 Cor 7:17), marketplace (*agora*) evangelism (Acts 14:8-18; 17:18), proclamation in a Christian gathering (e.g., Acts 14:1; 18:4), apologetic defensive proclamation (cf. Acts 4-5; Col 4:6; 1 Pet 3:15), verbal witness to Christ (Acts 1:8), and prison evangelism (Acts 16:25-26, cf. Phil 1:12-13). In the New Testament, it is always linked to a whole life given over to Christ, to ethical witness (living Jesus' way) and, supremely, to love. It is a collective rather than merely an individual notion—the church proclaims through its life, words, and through each person, as God leads and enables.

The emphasis on evangelism in the first churches of the Christian movement is prominent from the outset. In Acts 1:8, the Spirit empowers the believers for witness from Jerusalem to the nations. It is significant that the Spirit comes upon *all* the church, including the women, suggesting that the witness included all believers, not just apostles and evangelists (Acts 2:4). This is confirmed in Acts 8:1-4 where the church, aside from the apostles, is scattered but God's people continue to preach the gospel as they go. However, while their evangelism is inclusive, it also focuses on key leaders. This accords with the New Testament pattern of specially gifted and called evangelistic leaders leading the mission and equipping others for evangelism, the people of God sharing Christ in their social contexts as part of their Christian lives (cf. Eph 4:11-16).

Outside of the apostles, prominent among the disciples are two from the Seven of Acts 6: Stephen (Acts 6:5) and Philip (Acts 8:4-40). There are also wider groups involved in the extension of the gospel from Pisidia Antioch (Acts 13:49) and Ephesus into Asia Minor (Acts 19:10-20).[50]

---

50. M. J. Keown, "Congregational Evangelism in Paul: The Paul of Acts," *Colloquium* 42.2 (2010): 231-51.

There is evidence of systematic evangelism in Acts, especially believers going into synagogues and seeking to convince Jews to accept Jesus as Messiah and Lord (e.g., Acts 17:1-2; 18:26).[51] In particular, Paul's preaching begins with his "custom" of going to synagogues to preach and debate whether Jesus is the Christ (Acts 17:2-3; 18:4). Paul's sermon in Acts 13:16-41 is the only example of a "systematic" sermon taking place in the synagogue, and could reflect what Paul typically preached to the Jews on other occasions.

Aside from these situations, evangelism is more opportunistic than systematic in Acts. Peter's first sermon comes from a dynamic move of God that leads to the disciples speaking in known languages, which, in turn, leads to inquiry from the community. Peter embraces the opportunity and preaches a sermon based on the Spirit, and a huge number are saved (Acts 2:1-41). The second great evangelistic opportunity comes after the healing of the disabled man, which leads to great interest in what had happened. Again, Peter takes the opportunity to preach the message, this time referring to Jesus' miracle power (Acts 3:11-12). The third occasion for evangelism is linked to persecution rather than the Spirit or a miracle. Peter and John take the opportunity to witness before the Sanhedrin and refuse to yield to its appeal to desist (Acts 4:1-3). Another example of this opportunism is seen when the church, apart from the apostles, is scattered. Luke records that those "who had been scattered preached the word wherever they went" (Acts 8:4 NIV). He notes that some went as far as Antioch, which becomes a center for the next phase of the mission, northeast to Rome. And so, the gospel goes to the gentiles (Acts 11:19-21).

Paul's evangelism in Acts is also largely opportunistic. In Derbe, Paul's message is sparked by a healing, perhaps indicating one of the few times Paul speaks in public.[52] The message is catalyzed by the locals' subsequent desire to deify Paul and Barnabas as Hermes and Zeus.[53] Paul then preaches

---

51. E.g., Acts 9:30; 13:5, 14-43; 14:1; 17:10, 17; 18:4, 7-8, 19; 19:8; cf. 16:13. This also featured in Jesus' ministry (e.g., Matt 4:23; 9:35; Mark 3:1; Luke 4:15-30) and that of Apollos (Acts 18:26).

52. This is unclear. The context is not given. However, the impact of the healing indicates something perhaps in the public arena.

53. Paul as the main speaker is likened to Hermes, the god of oratory and inventor of speech. Barnabas is likened to Zeus, the head of the Greek pantheon. There is an ancient legend associated with the region in which Zeus and Hermes descend to earth in human guise, and this could be linked to the response of the people (see Polhill, *Acts*, 314). The myth

against idolatry around the familiar Greek themes of the God of nature and morality (Acts 14:15-18). In Athens, Paul is engaged in discussion with Epicurean and Stoic scholars in the Agora. There is interest, and Paul then accepts an invitation to speak at the philosophical guild of the Areopagus. He then picks up the Greek notion of the unknown god and he quotes Greek poets (Acts 17:17-31).[54] This sermon is paradigmatic for cross-cultural gospel communication.

This opportunist approach to evangelism in Acts is intimately linked to the work of the Spirit. This is evident at Pentecost, where the outpouring of the Spirit generates the interest of the people, and Peter preaches with great effect. Similarly, the healing of the disabled man at the Beautiful Gate leads to the preaching of the word. The link is also seen after the prayer in Acts 4 where many are healed, the disciples preach boldly, and more and more are added to their number (Acts 4:31; 5:18-21, 29-32, 42). In Philip's mission to Samaria, he proclaims and performs signs and wonders, including deliverance (Acts 8:4-7). The leading of the Spirit is also decisive in the ministries of Philip (Acts 8:29, 39-40), Peter (Acts 10:19), and Paul (Acts 16:6-9). Each of these opportunities is a result of the work of the Spirit. Evangelism, then, does not stand separate from the leading and power of the Spirit. As in the Gospels, in Jesus' ministry—which is often opportunistic and always Spirit-led—healing by the Spirit and preaching work together in harmony in effective evangelism.

Evangelism is also effective in the first part of Acts. This is seen in the astonishing growth of the community of believers:

---

from Ovid, *Metam.* 8.626 is noted in Witherington, *Acts*, 421, which speaks of "Jupiter [Zeus] *in the guise of a mortal*, and with his father came Atlas' grandson [Mercury or Hermes], he that bears the caduceus, his wings laid aside. To a thousand homes they came, seeking a place to rest; a thousand homes were barred against them." They found an old humble couple, Baucis and Philemon, who showed them great hospitality, and the gods kept replenishing their food miraculously. Because of their generosity the gods did not bring judgment on them and granted them their wish to be priests of Zeus' temple.

54. The *Areion pagon* (Areopagus) could refer to the location of the council, the council itself, or both—here Paul is clearly before the Council including Dionysius who is a member of the council (v. 34). At the time of Paul, the council met in the *Stoa Basileios*, just off the agora, rather than on Mars Hill, where it originally met. Witherington, *Acts*, 515 notes, "In a free city like Athens the appropriate place to prompt an official hearing of some new teaching or ideas was before the Areopagus. Among other things the council would have had the responsibility for maintaining religious customs and order in the city, and to act as a court dispensing verdicts and justice when necessary. That Paul was probably led here forcibly suggests that Luke is painting a picture of an adversarial situation."

1. The people were cut to the heart and sought salvation (Acts 2:37).

2. Three thousand were added in one day (Acts 2:41).

3. The number of people added up to five thousand (Acts 4:4).

4. More and more men and women believed in the Lord and were added to their number (Acts 5:14).

5. "The word of God spread. The number of disciples in Jerusalem increased rapidly, and a large number of priests became obedient to the faith" (Acts 6:7 NIV).

6. "There was great joy in that city" (Samaria; see Acts 8:8 NIV).

7. After the conversion and preaching of Paul in Jerusalem, "The church throughout Judea, Galilee and Samaria enjoyed a time of peace and was strengthened. Living in the fear of the Lord and encouraged by the Holy Spirit, it increased in numbers" (Acts 9:31 NIV).

8. After the gospel reached Antioch in Syria through the scattered disciples, "The Lord's hand was with them, and a great number of people believed and turned to the Lord" (Acts 11:21 NIV).

9. In the conclusion to Acts 12 Luke writes, "But the word of God increased and multiplied" (Acts 12:24), and the scene is set for Paul and Barnabas to launch the next phase.

10. After the mission in Pisidia Antioch, "The word of the Lord [spread] throughout the whole region" (Acts 13:49).

11. From the base of the lecture hall in Tyrannus, "all the residents of Asia heard the word of the Lord, both Jews and Greeks" and, "the word of the Lord continued to increase and prevail mightily" (Acts 19:1-20). The Colossian church (Col 1:6), the seven churches of Revelation, and the north Galatian churches (1 Pet 1:1) were likely planted at this time (Rev 2-3).

Evangelism does not always have this effect; the word was not always received with joy but was often rejected, especially by the governing authorities. It often led to outbreaks of persecution from Jewish leadership (Acts 4, 5, 7-8) and Herod (Acts 12). Paul constantly experienced rejection from Jews (e.g., Acts 13:44-45; 18:6, 12-17), from Greeks (e.g., Acts 16:16-40), or from both groups (e.g., Acts 13:50-52; 14:5-6, 19; 17:5-9, 13; 19:21-40). Paul is incarcerated for the final seven chapters of Acts. When the situation intensifies, Paul moves on. However, the Christians continue to engage in fervent proclamation.

The message of the first Christians is contained in the speeches of Acts, which, although summarized through the lens of Luke, give important insight into the evangelism of the early Christians.[55] There are a number of these summaries:

1. Peter at Pentecost in Jerusalem (Acts 2:14-41)

2. Peter in the Jerusalem temple (Acts 3:12-26)

3. Peter at Cornelius' home at Caesarea Maritima (Acts 10:34-42)

4. Stephen before the Sanhedrin in Jerusalem (Acts 7:2-53)

5. Paul in the synagogue in Pisidia Antioch (Acts 13:16-41)

6. Paul in the marketplace of Lystra (Acts 14:15-18)

7. Paul at the Areopagus in Athens (Acts 17:22-31)

8. Paul at the temple in Jerusalem (Acts 22:1-21)

9. Paul before Agrippa II in Caesarea Maritima (Acts 26:1-23)

---

55. This has been noted by scholars since C. H. Dodd, *The Apostolic Preaching and Its Developments* (London: Hodder and Stoughton, 1936 [1963 edition]). On pages 21-24 he noted a six-fold structure of the early Christian kerygma: 1) The age of fulfilment has dawned, promise is fulfilled (Acts 2:16; 3:18, 24); 2) This has taken place through the ministry, death, and resurrection of Jesus including: a) His Davidic descent (Acts 2:30-31); b) His ministry (Acts 2:22; 3:22); c) His death (Acts 2:23; 3:13-14); His resurrection (Acts 2:24-31; 3:15; 4:10); 3) By virtue of his resurrection, Jesus has been exalted to the right hand of God as messianic head of the new Israel (Acts 2:33-36; 3:13; 4:11; 5:31); 4) The Holy Spirit in the Church is the sign of Christ's present power and glory (Acts 2:33); 5) The messianic age will ultimately reach its climax in the return of Christ (Acts 3:21); 6) The *kerygma* always closes with an appeal for repentance, the offer of forgiveness and of the Holy Spirit (Acts 2:38; 3:15; 5:31; 13:24; 17:30).

Aside from the range of things mentioned opportunistically, the *main* emphases include:

1. **God:** God and his work in creation and history, whether from a Jewish (e.g., Acts 2:23; 3:13, 24-25; 7:2-50; 13:16-23) or a Greco-Roman perspective (Acts 14:15; 17:24).

2. **Old Testament fulfilment:** The fulfilment of Old Testament hope (not in the gentile sermons; e.g., Acts 2:17-21; Joel 2:28-32), or of Greek poets and philosophers (Acts 17:28).[56]

3. **Jesus:**

    a. *His identity:* The identity of Jesus as the Messiah, Lord, Savior, Righteous One, and Holy One, is stressed (e.g., Acts 2:31, 36; 3:14, 20; 5:31; 13:23; 22:14; 26:23).

    b. *His ministry:* Relevant aspects of his ministry and especially his miracles are mentioned (e.g., Acts 2:22; 10:38).

    c. *His crucifixion:* Jesus' death is mentioned in all the Jewish sermons, but not the Greek ones, except Peter to Cornelius (Acts 2:23; 3:15; 7:52; 10:39; 13:29).

    d. *His resurrection:* In most of the sermons, Jesus' resurrection is mentioned (e.g., Acts 2:32; 3:15; 10:40-41; 17:31).

    e. *His exaltation:* Jesus' exaltation to the right hand of God is commonly mentioned (Acts 2:33).

4. **The Spirit:** Some of Peter's sermons, especially Pentecost, refer to the gift of the Spirit (Acts 2:38; 7:51; 10:38, 47).

5. **Response:** The expected response including repentance (e.g., Acts 2:38; 3:19; 5:31; 13:38; 17:30), baptism (Acts 2:38, 41; 10:48), and renunciation of idolatry (to gentiles) (e.g., Acts 17:29-30).

---

56. Other citations include: Acts 2:25-28; 13:35/Ps 16:8-11; Acts 2:34/Ps 110:1; Acts 3:26/Gen. 22:18; 26:4; Acts 13:33/Ps 2:7; Acts 3:23; 7:37/Deut 18:15, 18; Acts 13:22/1 Sam 13:14/Isa 44:28; Acts 13:34/Isa 55:3. The two Greeks cited are Epimedes of Crete and Aratus from his poem "Phainomena."

The sermons are God- and Jesus-centered, but vary considerably. These evangelistic messages were Spirit-led and contextually relevant, while focusing on God and Jesus. Those in a Jewish setting emphasize Israel's salvation history and are Old Testament-based sermons, and interpret Christ from the perspective of Israel's story and the Old Testament (Acts 2, 3, 7, 13). The sermons to gentiles speak of God in creation and his impartiality, and with poetic, philosophical, and religious elements common to gentiles and Judaism (Acts 10, 14, 17). In the final two messages, the dominant theme is Paul's testimony as he defends himself and explains his Christian faith and mission to Jews (Acts 22, 26). It is especially interesting to compare the sermons of Peter and Paul to the Jews (Pentecost, the temple, Cornelius, and Pisidia Antioch) with Paul's gentile sermons (Lystra, Athens). They are markedly different, indicating Paul's contextualization of the message for his audience.

Evangelism in the Jerusalem church is non-negotiable. Even on the threat of death before the Sanhedrin on two separate occasions, the apostles refused to stop sharing the message. For example, in Acts 4:19-20 they respond to threats saying, "Judge for yourselves whether it is right in God's sight to obey you rather than God. For *we cannot help speaking* about what we have seen and heard." In Acts 4:30, the church responds to being forbidden to preach by praying for more boldness and for God's power to be unleashed. In Acts 5:19-20, after again being forbidden to preach, Luke writes: "In addition, after further imprisonment, an angel released them and *commanded them to continue preaching* the full message of this new life." They are further interrogated and say to the Sanhedrin: "*we must* obey God rather than people" (Acts 5:29 NET, emphasis added). This verse and Acts 4:20 indicate that, for them, obedience to God required that they share the message, despite persecution. In Acts 5:42, after a flogging, Luke records: "day after day, in the temple courts and from house to house, they *never stopped teaching and proclaiming* the good news that Jesus is the Messiah" (Acts 5:42 NIV, emphasis added). Stephen, too, exemplifies this commitment, prepared to die while sharing the faith (Acts 7:54-8:1). James is also killed for his faith (Acts 12:1). Throughout their missions, Paul, Barnabas, and Silas encounter terrible persecution but continue to proclaim the gospel.

The command to share Christ was an absolute for the first Christians despite the persecution and suffering that resulted. Luke's story is designed to encourage his readers to do the same who should be challenged to take up the mission.

Evangelism in Acts is also intimately *connected with experience*. The emphasis is on witness and testimony to "what we have seen and heard" (Acts 4:20). The apostles are witnesses to the resurrection. This is not just individual experience, but the collective experiences of God's people communicated to the world through their attitudes, deeds, and words. Paul's two defenses in Jerusalem and before Agrippa (Acts 22, 26) are full of his testimony of conversion. They communicate what the disciples had seen and heard.

Evangelism in Acts is a *priority* for the church leaders. The establishment of the Seven is not only to solve the problem of feeding the widows, but to ensure that the apostles are free to focus on prayer and preaching (Acts 6:2, 4). This indicates evangelism is such a priority that leadership structures had to be reordered to preserve it. The result was that the "word of God spread. The number of disciples in Jerusalem increased rapidly, and a large number of priests became obedient to the faith" (Acts 6:7 NIV). Neither are the Seven merely focused on the administration of food; two of them become great evangelists of the early church (Stephen and Philip, esp. Acts 21:8).[57]

Evangelism in Acts is governed by the sovereignty of God through his Spirit.[58] It is clear from Luke's narrative that the gospel almost has a life of its own, fueled by the Spirit. It is a force that cannot be stopped (Acts 6:7; 13:49; 19:10, 20). It will not be limited; it cannot be chained! (2 Tim 2:9, cf. Col 1:6; Phil 1:12–13). When the apostles face persecution they continue to preach wherever they go (e.g., Acts 8:4). God moves by his Spirit in healing and signs and wonders, causing the gospel to spread. Jesus appears to Paul and converts him from his antagonist into his agent to take the gospel to "the ends of the earth." He causes Peter to have visions that lead to the first gentile conversions. He directs Philip, Peter, and Paul into mission situations. In Acts, nothing will stop the growth of the church and evangelism.

---

57. Philip is the only person in the New Testament explicitly called an evangelist. Timothy is told to "do the work of an evangelist" (2 Tim 4:5).

58. An excellent book that examines this is J. I. Packer's *Evangelism and the Sovereignty of God* (Downers Grove, IL: IVP, 1961).

There is, however, one note of "failure" concerning evangelism. In the Great Commission, recorded in Luke 24:46-49 and Acts 1:8, Jesus stresses that the disciples must take the message to "all nations" and "every nation." Yet, the first Christians seemed to have no initial interest in going to the gentiles or even the Samaritans until God moves sovereignly to move them. First, Saul's persecution scatters the believers, and they take the gospel with them to the wider world (Acts 8:1-17; 11:19-23). Second, God moves dynamically in the lives of Peter and Cornelius with visions, angels, and Spirit-impulsion to share the gospel with an uncircumcised man (Acts 10:1-48). Third, the resurrected Christ reveals himself to Paul and commissions him for mission (Acts 9; 10-11; 13-28). It also takes non-apostles to take the message to the wider world. This could indicate that the first Jewish Christians did not initially grasp what Jesus meant and that God had to move sovereignly to cause them to realize the cosmic scope of mission. Similarly, the Judaizing dispute and Jerusalem Council (see Acts 15 and Galatians) indicate that they struggled to understand how the gospel could reach gentiles without them having to come under the Mosaic law to receive God's blessing. Peter required a three-fold vision (Acts 10) to realize that it was legitimate to go to gentiles with the Gospel. The Jewish Christians' surprise at the outpouring of the Spirit on the uncircumcised gentile converts reinforces their lack of understanding (Acts 11). Luke does not include the material from Mark 7 and Matthew 15 concerning eating kosher food. Rather, he focuses on Peter's vision in Acts 10, where Peter receives instruction from God to eat "unclean" food. It may be that Luke simply wanted to highlight the sovereignty of God in evangelism—that is, God intended to unfold his cosmic plan in this way. However, reading between the lines of Luke's account, it seems that the first Christians remained locked into a Jewish mindset concerning the salvation of the gentiles: they believed gentiles would be saved by being attracted to Judaism (centripetal mission) and becoming Jews through being circumcised and following Christ in the context of Judaism. They failed to grasp the truly gracious and cosmic nature of God's mission—that they were sent to go to the world with a gospel of grace without the requirement of circumcision and submission to Mosaic law (centrifugal mission).

In conclusion, the determination to continue in evangelism is undoubtedly one of the dominant features of the Jerusalem Church. It set examples for believers today that are difficult to emulate. Their leaders paved the way, and the people followed when the chance arose, taking the gospel as far as Antioch. Their determination to let nothing stop them from preaching the gospel is an attribute today's church needs above all else.

A PRAYERFUL CHURCH

Another key to the success of the Jerusalem church is its dynamic and committed prayer life. This is seen from its inception. This continues the emphasis on prayer in Luke's Gospel, in which Jesus is frequently portrayed as a man of prayer (esp. Luke 5:16), and at significant points in his ministry such as the appointment of the Twelve and the transfiguration (Luke 6:12; 28-29, cf. 3:21; 6:28; 9:18; 11:1-13; 18:1-8, 10-11).

Continuation with the Prayer Life of Judaism

A feature of the first Christians' prayer life is their continuation of their Jewish commitment to prayer. In Acts 3:1, for example, Peter and John are en route to pray at the temple at the ninth hour (3:00 p.m.). This fits the three Jewish times of prayer, which included:[59]

1. Early in the morning at the time of the morning sacrifice

2. At the ninth hour (3:00 p.m.) at the time of the evening sacrifice

3. At sunset (6:00 p.m.)

In addition, in Acts 10:9 Peter is praying at noon. This could indicate that the first Christians were not constrained in keeping to the traditional Jewish prayer times. Alternatively, it could indicate continuity with devoted Jews who prayed at noon based on Psalm 55:17: "Evening, morning and noon I cry out in distress, and he hears my voice" (NIV; cf. Dan 6:12). Several other aspects of Jewish prayer come through in Acts. First, there are gentiles, either converts to Judaism through circumcision (proselytes [if male]), or God-fearers, who prayed with the people of Israel (e.g., Cornelius, Acts 10:2). Luke records that the generous gifts and prayers of the God-fearer Cornelius bring pleasure to God (Acts 10:4, 30-31). Second, in Philippi, there

---

59. See Longenecker, *Acts*, 293.

is a gathering of women praying by the river at a "place of prayer" (*proseuchē*) on the Sabbath (Acts 16:13, 16). This indicates that there were not enough Jewish men to form a synagogue.[60]

A Church Bathed in Prayer

There are some general statements that show that the first believers, men and women, met regularly to pray. In Acts 1:14, Luke records, "They all joined together constantly in prayer, along with the women and Mary the mother of Jesus, and with his brothers" (NIV). In Acts 2:42, Luke writes that they "devoted themselves to ... prayer" (NIV), alongside devotion to the apostles' teaching, fellowship, and to communion. The Greek *proskatereō* in these two texts indicates that they "busied themselves, were busily engaged in, or were devoted to" prayer.[61] "All" (*pas*) and "the women and Mary the mother of Jesus, and ... his brothers" in Acts 1:14 is inclusive of the whole church. Prayer was thus corporate and not just private and individual.

As with Jesus—who is found praying at key times like his baptism, the appointment of the Twelve, and before his death—the church gathered in prayer at critical points. For example, Matthias' appointment to replace Judas is made through prayer (Acts 1:24-26): "Lord, you know everyone's heart. *Show us* which of these two you have chosen to take over this apostolic ministry, which Judas left to go where he belongs" (NIV, emphasis added).[62] Interestingly, the disciples used lots for the decision.[63] The casting of lots was a method of divination (*cleromancy*) used by the Greeks. This means of divining God's will was also common in Israel.[64] The use of lots by Christians

---

60. Some take "place of prayer" as a name for a synagogue. However, elsewhere in Acts Luke uses the term freely, and so he would have used the term if this was indeed one. Rather, it suggests that there is no synagogue in Philippi. See Bruce, *Acts*, NICNT 310, who notes that according to Rabbinic teaching, ten males were required to form a synagogue.

61. BDAG 881.

62. Some argue the church should have waited for God to appoint Paul to that position. Longenecker, *Acts*, 267 notes in response: (1) Paul was not with Jesus in his earthly life; (2) The necessity of twelve was symbolic and religious, i.e., to match the twelve tribes of Israel for Jewish mission, whereas Paul's focus was "the gentiles"; (3) Paul himself recognized his apostleship was focused differently to the Twelve (cf. to the gentiles), and he was illegitimately born (1 Cor 15:7-8).

63. Witherington, *Acts*, 126, notes that they likely used marked stones in a container or jar and shaken until they came out (cf. 1 Chr 26:13-14).

64. Lots were used to choose the scapegoat on the Day of Atonement (Lev 16:8-10; Philo, *Her.* 179), the allocation of the land to the tribes (Num 26:55-56; Josh 18:8-19:49), for priestly

is unique in the New Testament (cf. Mark 15:24 and parr.); it happened before the Pentecost anointing and is not seen after. So, it is probably not a model to be emulated (cf. Prov 16:33).[65] However, the decision was still bathed in prayer to ensure it was God's will. There is also a prayer at the "commissioning of the Seven" (Acts 6:1-7 esp. v. 4). Paul and Barnabas are set apart for their mission while the church is worshiping (*leitourgeō*)[66] and fasting (Acts 13:1-3). In this setting, the Spirit spoke to the church, calling it to set Paul and Barnabas apart for their mission (Acts 13:2). Subsequently, they again "fasted and prayed" and "placed their hands on them and sent them off" (Acts 13:3 NIV). The elders (*presbyteros*) in the Pauline churches were chosen by Paul and Barnabas and "with prayer and fasting" they were entrusted to the Lord (Acts 14:23).

The church is found in prayer at times of crisis, and Luke records that the church's prayers are effective. When the Sanhedrin tells the apostles to stop preaching, the church gathers and responds in prayer for courage to preach yet more (Acts 4:23-30, cf. Isa 37:16-20). The prayer is corporate. It is directed to God as "Sovereign Lord" (*despotēs*)[67] and interprets their current crisis through the Old Testament—specifically Psalm 2:1-2, a messianic psalm that anticipates global opposition to God's Messiah. Herod, Pilate, Romans, and Jews are all part of this opposition. Yet, these Christians recognize their opponents are merely acting out the will of God, despite appearances.[68] Then they appeal directly to God: "consider their threats and enable your servants to speak your word with great boldness. Stretch out your hand to heal and perform miraculous signs and wonders

---

duties (e.g., 1 Chr 25:8), to find the guilty (Josephus, *Ant.* 5.43), and to find a king (Josephus, *Ant.* 6.61). In the New Testament, the soldiers cast lots for Jesus' clothing in fulfilment of Ps 21:19. Nations cast lots for Jerusalem (Obad 11). Casting lots for God's people is rebuked by Joel (Joel 3:3). It is used by non-Jews (e.g., Esth 3:7). Jonah was discovered by sailors casting lots (Jon 1:7). It is used by Jewish soldiers killing one another rather than face defeat (Josephus, *J.W.* 3.388-391) (See also *Sib. Or.* 7.139; *T. Levi* 8:12; Josephus, *Ant.* 7.396; 1QS 5:3, 6:16).

65. See Polhill, *Acts*, 95.

66. *Leitourgeō* has the double meaning of service in a religious sense and of worship in the more contemporary sense.

67. Dennis Gaertner, *Acts*, CPNIVC (Joplin, MO: College Press, 1995), Acts 4:30 (no page, Logos edition): This term is found often in the LXX and calls attention to the supreme authority of God as ruler of the universe, cf. Exod 20:11; Neh 9:6; Ps 146:6; Isa 42:5. In the New Testament, see Luke 2:29 and Rev 6:10.

68. This is consistent with Old Testament examples of anti-Israel world leaders fulfilling the will of God (e.g., Nebuchadnezzar and Cyrus).

through the name of your holy servant Jesus" (Acts 4:29-30 NIV). This is a radical prayer. It is an appeal for increased boldness for evangelism and for increased manifestations of the Holy Spirit in miraculous signs.

The impact of the prayer is dramatic. First, its effect is immediate, the place is shaken, and the disciples have a fresh experience of being filled with the Spirit, which recalls Pentecost. Second, they experience increased boldness to speak the word in the public domain, the camp of the enemy. Finally, the long-term impact of their prayer is seen in subsequent events, including radical economic sharing within the community (Acts 4:32, 34-37); powerful and effective evangelism (Acts 4:33); signs and wonders, including healing by Peter's shadow (Acts 5:12-16); death (Acts 5:1-10); and growth (Acts 5:14). Ultimately this leads to further persecution and a renewed determination to continue to proclaim (Acts 5:17-42).[69]

This commitment to pray in a crisis is also seen in prison in Acts 12. James has been beheaded, and Peter imprisoned. The church's response is to gather to pray at the home of Mary, the mother of John Mark. The Greek says the church was there (Acts 12:12) praying earnestly (Acts 12:5 [*ektenos*]). The result is that Peter is released by an angel.

The leaders of the church also prioritize prayer alongside proclamation, as when the Seven were selected in Acts 6, which released the leaders into prayer and declaration. This is successful; after the Seven are appointed, the apostles can focus on these central tasks. Prayer and proclamation impact the growth of the church and penetrate the heart of Judaism: "so the word of God spread. The number of disciples in Jerusalem increased rapidly, and a large number of priests became obedient to the faith" (Acts 6:7 NIV).

Prayer and the Spirit's Power

Luke wants his readers to recognize an intimate connection between prayer and the enhanced experience and release of the power of the Spirit. Believers do not control the Spirit, but God honors the prayers of his people by moving in answer to their earnest requests.

---

69. During this time, Peter is released miraculously from prison by an angel. Although the text does not mention the church praying, it is probable they were at the time (Acts 5:18-19).

This link of Spirit-power and prayer is seen at Pentecost when the church gathered in prayer and experienced the Spirit (Acts 1:14; 2:1). Similarly, it is the persecuted church gathered in fervent prayer that experiences the shaking of the room, a fresh infilling of the Spirit, and the empowerment for further witness, signs and wonders, and radical generosity (Acts 4:23-5:16). It is seen in Samaria and at Saul's conversion as the Spirit comes through the laying on of hands (Acts 8:17; 9:11, 17). Miracles of the Spirit come through prayer—for example, Tabitha's healing (Acts 9:40). Peter's vision to go to Cornelius' home, a gentile, occurs during prayer (Acts 10:9; 11:5). There is a strong connection between powerful spiritual manifestations and prayer in the early church. As noted, Paul's mission is catalyzed by worship and fasting (Acts 13:1-3), while God is most definitely the initiator, the one who works the miracles and sends the Spirit. As evidenced in Acts, God answers sincere human prayer—prayer changes things (Jas 5:16).

The Link Between Prayer and Fasting

Prayer is intimately linked with fasting. In the Old Testament, fasting is often associated with mourning, confession, great emotion, and intercession for deliverance.[70] The importance of fasting is found in the Gospels in the example of the exemplary Jewish saint, Anna (Luke 2:36-37), and at Jesus' temptation (Matt 4:4). Christian fasting is assumed in the Sermon on the Mount (Matt 6:16-18). It is something future believers will do when Jesus is gone (Matt 9:14). However, hypocritical fasting is also critiqued in Luke 18:12 (cf. Matt 6:16-18). Fasting is mentioned three times. In Acts 27:9, reference is made to "the Fast," referring to the Day of Atonement. Twice it is paired with prayer, and the assumption is that it is a positive act that enhances the power of prayer (Acts 13:2-3; 14:23).

---

70. See Judg 20:26; 1 Sam 7:6 (with confession); 1 Sam 31:13 (seven days after death of Saul, cf. 2 Sam 1:12); 2 Sam 12:16 (David for the Lord's mercy for his son); 1 Kgs 21:9, 12 (national day of fasting); 21:27 (Ahab); Ezra 8:21, 23; Neh 1:4 (with prayer); 9:1 (repentance); Esth 4:3, 16; 9:31; Ps 35:13 (humility); 69:10; 109:24 ; Isa 58 (here Isaiah critiques empty fasting without concern for justice, compassion, and love, cf. Jer 14:12); Jer 36:6 (a day of fasting); Dan 9:3; Joel 1:14; 2:12; Jonah 3:5; Zech 7:3, 5 (fasting every fifth and seventh month for God's deliverance from Babylon); Zech 8:19 (they will fast on the fourth, fifth, seventh, and tenth months).

CONCLUSION

The importance of prayer flows through the second part of Acts as well (see later in Paul's mission strategy). The Jerusalem church is a praying church. Is it any coincidence it is also a church that impacts its community, has radical community life, is successful in evangelism, and sees the power of God released in its midst and mission?

The lessons for today's church are clear. An effective church must be founded on its commitment to prayer. From a Western point of view, believers need to relearn the importance of corporate prayer, gathering, and fasting, all of which are emphasized in Acts. Every dimension of church and individual life should be bathed in prayer to be effective as Christians. In Acts, prayer appears to have been daily—at least three times a day—as Christians continued the prayer life of Judaism. The prayer life of the first church was persistent, individual and corporate, expectant, and effective, something the modern church should seek to emulate.

A WORSHIPFUL CHURCH

Worship has two dimensions in the biblical material: (1) The traditional notion of the worship of God through ritual and prayer, either corporately or individually; and (2) The wider idea of service in all of life, including work. Authentic living in every sphere of life is in this latter sense worship. In this section, the focus will be on the first dimension: worship directed to God in the Jerusalem church. Prayer is a critical dimension of the Jerusalem community's worship life. However, prayer is not the only dimension of worship mentioned in Luke's narrative. This is seen in the Gospel of Luke, which ends with the believers worshiping Jesus (Luke 24:52, cf. e.g., 1:46-55, 67-79; 2:13-14, 20, 28-32; 4:7-8; 5:26; 7:16; 10:27; 13:13; 16:13; 17:15; 18:43; 19:37-38; 23:47). In Acts, there are a number of features of worship.

Gathering

It is common to speak of an "unchurched faith" today, but there is absolutely no concept of this in the New Testament or in Acts. Throughout Acts, the people of God gather together to worship God, experience community, and radiate out to engage in mission. Faith is not merely pietistic and individualistic; those who followed "the Way" gathered together. The gathering was inclusive, and both male and female were involved (Acts 1:14). As the church extended, Greek Jews were included (Acts 6:1) and gentiles (e.g., Acts 10–11; 13–21). Initially, they demonstrated their commitment by gathering regularly in the temple courts (Acts 2:46; see also 5:42). This shows they were not limited to one day to worship, whether the Sabbath or the first day of the week. They also met in homes for prayer (Acts 12:2–10), to break bread (eat together and celebrate the Lord's Supper, Acts 2:42, 46), and to teach and evangelize (Acts 5:42). In Acts, as early as the mid-50s AD, there is evidence of a shift from Saturday gathered worship (the Jewish Sabbath) to Sunday (first day of the week) worship (Acts 20:7, cf. 1 Cor 16:2; Rev 1:10 ["the Lord's Day"]).

Charismatic or Pneumatic Worship

Another feature of worship is the pivotal role of the Holy Spirit in Jerusalem and Antiochian churches' worship (e.g., Acts 2:1–4, 42–47; 4:29–31; 13:1–2). There was a profound sense of "experiencing" the Spirit in guidance, spiritual gifts (*charismata*), signs and wonders, and of being "filled with the Spirit." This is seen in the context of worship in Acts 2:43 in the description of church worship, whereby "many wonders and signs were being done through the apostles."

Baptism

Baptism is the pivotal initiation rite of the Jerusalem church. There are four types of baptism referred to in Luke's narrative:

John's baptism. As detailed in Luke 3, John's baptism is described as a baptism of repentance,[71] a preparation for the coming of the Messiah—and the marker-point for the beginning of Jesus' ministry. This features in Acts in recollections of John's ministry as the starting point of Jesus' work (Acts 1:22; 10:37; 13:24). His baptism anticipates Jesus' baptism of believers with the Spirit and fire (Luke 3:16),[72] which Peter recalls at Cornelius' baptism (Acts 11:16). Apollos and the Ephesian believers had been baptized by John (Acts 18:25; 19:3–4), but this baptism was inadequate so they were further

---

71. In Luke 3:3, it is "a baptism of repentance for the forgiveness of sin" (see also Acts 10:37; 11:16), a fulfilment of Isaiah 40:3–5 heralding God's salvation. His conception, gestation, and birth are also described in Luke 1–2.

72. In Luke 3:17, he also anticipates Jesus bringing judgment.

instructed and baptized, receiving the Spirit (Acts 19:5-6).[73] John's baptism is a key preparatory ritual anticipating water and Spirit baptism, which mark inclusion into the people of God.

Baptism of suffering. Luke 12:50 refers to Jesus' cross as a "baptism" of suffering, something Mark states James and John will experience (Mark 10:39). Christ's death is an immersion in suffering, so Christian suffering is a form of baptism—participation in the suffering of Christ. Believers can anticipate such a baptism as they follow Jesus.

Baptism in the Spirit. Baptism in the Spirit refers to the profound experience of being overwhelmed or filled with God's presence and power (Acts 1:5; 11:16).

Initiation water baptism. Water baptism is the most common form of baptism in Acts. Water was used for ritual cleansing through Judaism's religious practice, which stressed purity (e.g., Lev 13-17; Num 19; Ps 51:2, 7; Isa 4:4, cf. Mark 7:4; Heb 9:20). The healing of the leper Naaman is another example of washing, not unlike baptism (2 Kgs 5; Luke 4:27). While it is debated whether it began before or at the same time as the Christian movement, proselyte baptism used in conversion to Judaism has similarities to Christian baptism. Eventually, proselyte baptism was required seven days after circumcision. Later, Judaism expected three things to convert to Judaism: (1) Circumcision; (2) Baptism or ritual bath; and (3) Sacrifice. A woman needed to fulfill (2) and (3).

Water baptism is the key marker of initiation into the people of God in Acts. Whereas in Matthew 28:18-20 where the Trinitarian formula is used, in Acts, it is baptism "into the name of Jesus Christ."[74] In Acts 2:38-39, Peter tells the crowds who have heard the message, "Repent and *be baptized*,

---

73. It is likely that Apollos was baptized by Priscilla and Aquila in their instruction, although this is uncertain (Acts 18:26). See the discussion in Witherington, *Acts*, 567.

74. Reference to baptism into the name of Jesus leads to speculation as to whether there are two forms of baptism (the other being baptism in the name of the Father, the Son, and the Holy Spirit, Matt 28:19), or whether one should be preferred over the other. This is unnecessary. There is "one baptism" (Eph 4:5), and the exact formula used, while important, is not absolutely critical. Rather, baptism signifies inclusion in Christ and being welcomed into his family.

every one of you, in the name of Jesus Christ for the forgiveness of your sins. And you will receive the gift of the Holy Spirit. The promise is for you and your children and for all who are far off—for all whom the Lord our God will call" (NIV, emphasis added). Luke links water baptism to repentance, turning from sin and alternative faith objects to Jesus as Savior and Lord. In addition, baptism is linked to forgiveness and the receipt of the Spirit, which is promised to those who are water-baptized. Mass baptisms were not unusual in Acts. In Acts 2:41, for example, three thousand people were baptized in one day.

While there is immediacy between the receipt of the Spirit and water baptism on this occasion, subsequent events indicate that the immediate temporal link between water baptism and Spirit baptism cannot be established based on Acts. So, for example, in Acts 8 Philip preaches the message to the crowds, and many believe and are water-baptized (Acts 8:12-13). However, there is no immediate receipt of the Spirit in any evidential manner. It is not until Peter and John come up from Jerusalem and lay hands on the believers who have already been water-baptized that they receive the Spirit (Acts 8:17). Here, Luke seems to draw a clear distinction between being baptized into the name of Jesus Christ (initiation) and baptism in the Spirit. In other situations, the relationship of water baptism to Spirit reception is not consistent. For example, at the baptism of the Ethiopian eunuch, there is *no* evidence of Spirit reception (Acts 8:38, cf. 16:15, 33; 18:8). Paul's baptism *follows* faith and receiving the Spirit (Acts 9:18). Similarly, when Cornelius' family converts, baptism *follows* faith and receiving the Spirit (Acts 10:44-48). There may be an example of water and Spirit baptism occurring at the same time at Ephesus; however, Luke's words could mean that Spirit baptism followed water baptism (Acts 19:5).

In Acts, baptism followed *immediately* after expression of faith. This is seen in Peter's sermon (Acts 2:39-41), Philip's ministry in Samaria (Acts 8:14), the Ethiopian eunuch (Acts 8:36-38), Saul (Acts 9:18), Cornelius' family (Acts 10:47-48), Lydia's household (Acts 16:15), the jailor's household (Acts 16:33), Crispus' household (Acts 18:8), and the Ephesus believers (Acts 19:5).

It is not clear who performed the baptisms, and in most cases, it is unspecified. There is evidence it was not merely the evangelist or apostle; there may have been other believers present. These may have included: the apostles in Acts 2:38-41; Philip in Acts 8:14, 36; Ananias in 9:18; others commissioned by Peter in Acts 10:47-48; unspecified believers in Acts 16:15, 33; 18:8; and probably Paul in Acts 19:5, as he seems to be the only baptized Christian there. Interestingly, in 1 Corinthians Paul states that he did not baptize many of the Corinthians. This indicates others did. This may include members of his team, Timothy or Silas, or the first local converts (see 1 Cor 1:12-17). This calls into question that the baptizer must be ordained as in many contemporary denominations. Again, this developed over time to ensure that baptism was conducted adequately and by someone who is approved by the church.

The final issue is the question of children's baptism (paedobaptism). The cases of "household" (*oikos*) baptism, where whole households are baptized when the leader of the home comes to faith, certainly raise the possibility of children being baptized.[75] The ancient family was an extended family including slaves, clients, and wider family members. It was usually led by the oldest male, the *paterfamilias*, or the matriarch in the case of a widowed or divorced woman, like Lydia (Acts 16:14-15; see also Nympha, Col 4:15). This head usually defined the religion of the family. As such, where a head-male or female was converted and baptized, it is not unlikely that the whole family was automatically baptized, including slaves and children. This may be the case in the homes of Lydia, the Roman jailor, and Crispus (Acts 16:14-15, 29-33, cf. 18:8).

However, while this is possible, it is not explicit. In most occasions in Acts, baptism is linked to response—whether faith (Acts 8:12-13; 16:33; 18:8; 19:5),[76] receiving Peter's message (Acts 2:41), repentance (Acts 2:38), or other indicators (Acts 8:36; 9:18; 10:47-48; 16:15).[77] It is arguable, then, that where children were baptized (if they were), they had also become

---

75. For the case of infant baptism, see J. Jeremias' *Infant Baptism in the First Four Centuries* (London: SCM, 1960).

76. In the case of the Philippian jailor his question, "What must I do to be saved?" and Paul's response, telling him to "believe," suggest he responded positively. The faith of the remainder of his household is not mentioned. Faith is implied in Ephesus (Acts 19:1-10).

77. In Acts 8:36, faith is expressed in the Ethiopian's desire to be baptized. This shows that reference to baptism had been made in Philip's explanation of Isaiah 53 and the gospel. Similarly, in Paul's case in Acts 9:1-17, having seen Jesus, Paul believed, even if it is not explicitly stated. In the case of Cornelius, the water baptism is granted on the evidence of the Spirit coming, i.e., they must believe because they have received the Spirit (Acts 10:45-48). One of the most beautiful descriptions of conversion is portrayed through Lydia: "The Lord opened her heart to respond to Paul's message" (Acts 16:14 NIV).

believers.[78] However, it remains possible that there were children under the age of cognition in these families that were baptized. Thus, while the evidence leans away from infant baptism (before cognition), it is not a totally conclusive argument.[79] Certainly, it should not be divisive.

The Centrality of the Apostles' Teaching and Word

Acts 2:42 begins: "They devoted themselves to the *apostles' teaching* ..." This suggests that the first Christians prioritized the teaching of the apostles. It can be assumed this teaching was centered on Christ since one of the criteria for apostleship in the early part of Acts was having been with Jesus and having witnessed the resurrection (Acts 1:21-22). This meant the apostles could teach the ministry and life of Christ firsthand. Further, the apostolic records held in the Gospels certainly have their focus on the life, ministry, death, and resurrection of Jesus. Likely, it also included much of the parabolic and ethical teaching of Jesus found in the Gospels.

One of the key dimensions of this teaching was finding Christ in the writings of Israel—the Old Testament. Luke also mentions in the prologue to his Gospel other writers who have "undertaken to compile a narrative of the things that have been fulfilled (*plēeophoreō*) among us," which led to his desire to write his own orderly account for Theophilus (Luke 1:2-3). Fulfilment of the Old Testament Scriptures is a key theme of Luke. It is not surprising that Acts is replete with quotes from the Old Testament, which the church interpreted as pointers to Jesus the Messiah. Luke's account of the resurrection appearances of Christ also includes Jesus unpacking the Scriptures for the disciples and how the Scriptures anticipate the hope of a crucified and raised Messiah (Luke 24:26-27, 32, 44-47). Some of those Scriptures Jesus cited include:

---

78. See G. R. Beasley-Murray, *Baptism in the New Testament* (Exeter: Paternoster, 1972), esp. 312-20 for the arguments for believers' baptism.

79. One can also note that the common Christian ritual of "dedication" of an infant is not recorded in the New Testament, except in the case of Jesus (Luke 2:22-24). In the Old Testament, it is only the firstborn that was dedicated to God (e.g., Exod 22:29; 32:2, 13-16), and the Levites in their stead (Num 3:12). As such, "dedication" of all children in the church lacks strong biblical support. What is evident is the "touching" (blessing) of children by Jesus (Luke 18:15, see also Mark 10:16).

1. A replacement leader for Judas (Acts 1:20, cf. Ps 69:25; 109:8)

2. The Spirit poured out (Acts 2:17-21, cf. Joel 2:28-32)

3. Jesus' exaltation and resurrection (Acts 2:25-28, cf. Ps 16:8-11)

4. Jesus' exaltation over enemies and cosmic lordship (Acts 2:34-35, cf. Ps 110:1)

5. Jesus, the fulfillment of the hope of a prophet (Acts 3:22-23, cf. Deut 18:15, 18-19)

6. Blessings of Abraham to all nations through Jesus (Acts 3:25-26, cf. Gen 22:18; 26:4)

7. Jesus, the rejected capstone (Acts 4:11, cf. Ps 118:22)

8. Opposition to the Messiah (Acts 4:25-26, cf. Ps 2:1-2)

9. Jesus, the suffering servant (Acts 8:32-33, cf. Isa 53:7-8)[80]

This high view of Old Testament Scripture is seen in the references to the work of the Spirit through the human agency in its writing (e.g., Acts 1:16; 4:25).

The presentation of the history of Israel in Stephen's final speech also points to the disciples' knowledge and reinterpretation of the Old Testament in light of Jesus' coming (Acts 7:2-53 [full of references and allusions]). With a great deal of scriptural detail, Stephen's sermon in Acts 7 retraces the whole history of Israel including (1) the election of Abraham; (2) the patriarchs, Isaac and Jacob; (3) Joseph in Egypt; (4) suffering in Egypt; (5) Moses and the exodus with the hope of a prophet (Deut 18:15); and (6) the tabernacle and temple. Most of this is drawn from the Pentateuch, which is not surprising as the Sanhedrin was dominated by Sadducees, who only accepted the Pentateuch.

---

80. See also Paul's speeches in Acts, including Jesus' divine Sonship (Acts 13:33, cf. Ps 2:7); Jesus, the fulfillment of the blessings promised to David (Acts 13:34, cf. Isa 55:3); Jesus resurrected (Acts 13:35, cf. Ps 16:10); the rejection of the message (Acts 13:41, cf. Hab 1:5); the apostolic fulfillment of the servant's mission (Acts 13:47, cf. Isa 49:6); and the message going to the gentiles (Acts 15:16-17, cf. 9:11-12).

Similarly, in his sermon in Acts 13:17-22, Paul retells the whole story of Israel including: (1) the election of Abraham to conquest—the 450 years including election, Egypt, the exodus, wilderness wandering, and the conquest; (2) the judges to Samuel; and (3) the kingdom from Saul to the Davidic dynasty. Paul points out how the Messiah is descended from the line of David. He quotes Psalm 2:7 in Acts 13:32 concerning the Davidic King being a Son to God the Father, Psalm 16:10 of Jesus' resurrection (Acts 13:35), Habakkuk 1:5 as a warning not to reject the message (Acts 13:41), and Isaiah 49:6 of his ministry to the gentiles (Acts 13:47). Paul here sweeps the whole of the Old Testament narrative including the Pentateuch, historical Writings, and Prophets.

Overall, the intertextual links are drawn from the Pentateuch (Gen 22:18; 26:4; Deut 18:15, 18, 19), Stephen's narrative, Paul's Antiochian sermon, the Deuteronomic historian, the psalms (Ps 2:1-2, 7; 16:8-11; 69:25; 110:1; 109:8; 118:22), and the Prophets (Isa 49:6; 53:7-8; Joel 2:28-3:2; Hab 1:5). The two Isaianic references both come from Servant Songs of Isaiah—Jesus is the Servant of Isaiah's Servant Songs.

The Breaking of Bread (Hospitality and Communion)

Acts 2:42 speaks of the church being devoted to the "breaking of bread." Here it probably means not only table fellowship (so important to first-century culture), but also regular participation in the Lord's Supper, which probably initially formed part of an ordinary meal.[81] At some point in the gathering, bread was broken and wine drunk to symbolize the unity of the church around the death and resurrection of Christ.[82] The use of the same phrase in 2:46 may indicate merely eating meals together at each other's homes, or may refer to the same combination of meal and Lord's Supper. Either way, the fellowship of the community was constant, daily, and involved sharing food. It was no doubt wealthier Christians like John Mark's mother, Mary (Acts 12:12-13), who opened their homes for the rest of the church for these gatherings.

---

81. See the discussion in Witherington, *Acts*, 160.
82. See Bruce, *Acts*, NICNT, 73; Longenecker, *Acts*, 289-90.

Material Generosity and Care for the Needy

The amazing generosity and voluntary redistribution of resources within the church is also discussed, including the sale of land and the redistribution of wealth for the needy by the apostles and the Seven. Suffice to say, care for the needy by the voluntary redistribution of wealth was an essential component of the worship of the first church.

Praise

In Acts 2:47, Luke records that the Jerusalem church gathered to praise God. The same Greek term, *aiteō*, meaning "to give glory to God," is used in Luke 19:37 at Jesus' entry into Jerusalem and in Acts 3:8-9 of the healed disabled beggar, who walks, leaps, and *praises God* after his healing. The word has a strong sense of genuine joy and opens enthusiastic expression of adoration for God.

A GENEROUS CHURCH (ECONOMIC KOINŌNIA)

The community life of the Jerusalem church was remarkable. Men and women were involved on equal terms, and they were committed to daily gatherings, table fellowship, prayer, and worship. Aside from the issue of feeding the Greek-speaking Jewish widows, Paul's clash with Barnabas and Mark, and the later issue of circumcision, there is no evidence of disunity. However, one dimension of their communal life stands out above all else: their radical material generosity. Scholars sometimes call this "economic *koinōnia*" (fellowship, participation, sharing).

This radical corporate sharing of resources is recounted in Acts 2:44-45. The emphasis is on communal possession rather than private ownership. There is no sense of coercion here, but a free desire to share. This stands in continuity with the common purse that Jesus and the disciples kept during his ministry (see John 13:29) and the material support of women recorded by Luke (Luke 8:1-3). Their sharing lived out Jesus' command to "sell your possessions and give to the poor" (Luke 12:33 NIV). This indicates that the disciples took his commands about money seriously (e.g., Luke 12:33, cf. 14:33; 18:22).

The recipients of generosity were those in "need," and it seems that those within the community are particularly in mind. These certainly include widows (Acts 6:1-2) and would have included others who were poor (Acts 4:34-35). The importance of the practice of caring for the poor is reflected in the apostles' governance of the distribution (Acts 4:37; 6:2) and the subsequent institution of the Seven for the task (Acts 6:1-4).

In Acts 4:32-37, Luke gives more detail concerning generosity. He speaks of the unity of the church ("one in heart and soul") and corporate ownership ("no one said that any of the things that belonged to him was his own, but they had everything in common"). The result of this was the eschatological fulfillment of Deuteronomy 15:4: "There will be no poor among you." The radical generosity involved some selling land or houses and giving the proceeds to the apostles for distribution to the needy. Luke gives two examples, one positive and one negative. Barnabas, the "Son of Encouragement," sells a piece of land and gives the money to the church. It is unclear whether the land is from his native Cyprus or is family land in Jerusalem.[83] On the other hand Ananias and Sapphira sell property, but only give a portion *while claiming to give it all*; as a result, they are put to death by the power of the Spirit.

Qumran and Acts 4

Radical material sharing is also seen in Qumran in the community that lived in the Judean desert beside the Dead Sea. In the "Book of the Community Rule" (1QS), the sharing of possessions was compulsory. Members of the community were expected to bring their "possessions into the community of God." Their property and earnings were handed over to the bursar of the community and held for a year, and if the initiate was accepted after a year, his property was merged into the shared purse of the community. If a member of the community lied about his property, he was excluded from the community meal and gave up a quarter of his food as penance (1QS 1). Philo of Alexandria confirms that the Essenes shared houses, expenses, clothes, and food, and money earned was shared as an integral part of community life (Philo, *Prob.* 85-88.).

Unlike Qumran, the selling of possessions in the early Jerusalem church was voluntary.[84] Interestingly, there is no mention of compulsory tithing

---

83. Some note that he was a Levite who should not have owned land (Num 18:20; Deut 10:9). However, this principle was not always adhered to (see Jer 32:7-12).

84. I. H. Marshall, *Acts*, 84.

in Acts. Rather, the emphasis is on radical generosity without compulsion. This silence regarding tithing spans almost the whole New Testament and might suggest tithing was so entrenched it was not worthy of comment, or, as is more likely, that tithing is not part of the new covenant.[85] New Testament giving is less about a set percentage and more about radical giving without compulsion.[86]

Communism and Acts 4

These are examples, positive and negative, of living out the ideals of Jesus. However, some scholars see the story of the Jerusalem church as an example of "failed communism." The selling of land left the church vulnerable to the famine that struck and eventually led to Paul needing to lead an aid mission, raising funds from the newly formed churches (the Jerusalem Collection, Acts 11:26-30).[87]

However, this view is unnecessarily cynical. Rather, there is a sincere attempt to live out the ideas of Jesus for economic *koinōnia*. There is no evidence of any resulting poverty; rather, the church grew, and people were attracted to it. Later, the church faced privation due to a severe famine, not

---

85. Most aspects of Israel's institutions are transformed in the New Testament. For example, the priesthood becomes the priesthood of all believers (1 Pet 2:9); the temple becomes Jesus (John 2:18-20), the church (1 Cor 3:16; Eph 2:21), and the body (1 Cor 6:19); the sacrificial system is completed in Christ's final, absolute sacrifice (Heb 10:1-18); and the law is summed up in the law of love (Mark 12:29-31). The tithe seems consumed in a much more radical, material ethic where everything the believer has is put at the service of God.

86. There is also no reference to tithing in Paul, John, James, Mark, or Jude. Hebrews 7:1-10 does not endorse tithing, but uses the Abrahamic tithe to Melchizedek as an argument for Jesus' priesthood surpassing the Levitical priesthood. Matthew 23:23, Luke 10:42, and Luke 18:12 are texts in which Jesus critiques attitudes to tithing. One possible interpretation of the first two texts is that Jesus reinforces the tithe when he says, "without neglecting the others" (Hagner, *Matthew 14-28*, 670; Stein, *Luke*, 341; I. H. Marshall, *Luke*, 498). However, this is a disputed interpretation. Blomberg, *Matthew*, 346, for example, notes, "The last sentence of v. 23 does not imply that Jesus is becoming more conservative with respect to the law or that tithing is mandated of Christians, merely that as long as the Mosaic covenant remains in force (up to the time of Jesus' death and resurrection); all of it must be obeyed, but with discernment of its true priorities."

87. Scholars are divided as to whether the Acts 11 famine collection is the same as that referred to in the letters of Paul (1 Cor 16:1-3; 2 Cor 8-9; Rom 15:26-28, 31). Those who accept Luke's chronology is accurate argue there were two collections, and Acts 11 does not match the Pauline collection that happened in the mid-50s AD, whereas the famine under Claudius was in the mid-40s AD (matching Gal 2:1-10). Those who consider Luke was not accurate see it as one collection. The former is to be preferred (see Paul and his chronology, and Witherington, *Acts*, 372-75).

the pooling of resources (Acts 11:28). There is good evidence from writings of such a famine in AD 45-47 precipitated by a once-in-a-hundred-years flooding of the Nile in Egypt, the "breadbasket for the whole region" (e.g., Josephus, *Ant.* 20.51-53; Suetonius, *Claud.* 18).[88] The pooling of resources did not lead to inequality, but reduced it.

Wealthy members of the Jerusalem church had clearly taken to heart Jesus' frequent appeals for radical giving, renunciation of greed and wealth, and seeking first the kingdom. They took the responsibilities that go with great wealth seriously—to care for those in need. The protocols of Greco-Roman benefaction were turned on their head. True Christian giving is unconditional.

Ananias and Sapphira

In the context of the New Testament, and Acts to this point, the Ananias[89] and Sapphira[90] account in Acts 5 comes as a bit of a shock. Like Barnabas, they sell a piece of property, but unlike him, Ananias and Sapphira do not bring *all* the proceeds to the apostles while claiming to. From the Spirit or through knowledge of the transaction, Peter challenges Ananias for retaining some of the money. The core of Peter's critique is Ananias' lying. It is implied in verses 3 and 5 and made clear in verse 8 that the problem was not the retention of the money per se, but claiming to have given all the proceeds to the church when in fact he and Sapphira had kept some back for themselves. In his challenge, Peter exposes Ananias' lie is to the Spirit—to God (Acts 5:3, 5). Ananias drops dead,[91] causing the church to be greatly afraid. He is then buried. Three hours later, Sapphira comes in, unaware of her husband's encounter with Peter and his death. Like her husband, she lies about how much the land was sold for. Peter accuses her

---

88. Witherington, *Acts*, 372-73. He also notes that "the whole world" is an example of Lukan hyperbole, but speaks of a serious situation ("the whole Empire" is in view).

89. This Ananias is not to be confused with Ananias of Damascus, who comes to Paul after his experience of Jesus (Acts 9:10).

90. The two names are Hebrew: Ananias from חֲנַנְיָה (ḥănăn·yā(h)) and Sapphira from סַפִּיר (săp·pîr), or "sapphire." This suggests they are Hebrew-speaking Jews.

91. The suddenness of their deaths indicates they likely died of heart attacks, perhaps through shock. See Witherington, *Acts*, 216: "For all we know, Ananias may have died of a heart attack caused by shock, as sometimes happens to those who are suddenly found out, especially if they have at least somewhat sensitive consciences."

of testing the Spirit and prophesies that she, too, will die and be buried. She dies instantly and is buried with her husband. As one might expect, this causes great fear in the church.[92]

The story recalls Joshua 7 where Achan and his family die as a result of secretly taking plunder from Ai, despite God's prohibition against doing so.[93] As Bruce puts it, "In both narratives, an act of deceit interrupts the victorious progress of the people of God."[94] It also resonates with the Eden story in which Eve and Adam together eat of the fruit (Gen 3:6) and are banished from the garden. Certainly, the passage demonstrates the seriousness of sin to the Jerusalem Christian community and to Luke. The consequence of sin is death (Rom 6:23), and this incident demonstrates that vividly.

The Ananias and Sapphira account also shows the power of God to bring judgment on Christians who fail ethically. God's judgment on Israel is a dominant aspect of the Old Testament. Yet, God's present judgment is not absent from the New Testament, also seen in Acts in the death of Agrippa I (Acts 12:20-23) and the blinding of Elymas through Paul (Acts 13:8-11).[95] It is not surprising that "Luke's view is that the God of the Hebrew Scriptures is the same God Jesus and the disciples served, and so one should expect continuity of character and action."[96] God's present judgment is also seen in the death of Corinthian church members for abusing the Lord's Supper (1 Cor 11:29-30). For the sake of his glory and church, God at times acts in judgment. He is indeed a God of love, but love leads to bringing justice for those he loves. His action appears punitive. However, there is no mention

---

92. Scholars have reacted negatively to the story in a range of ways including intellectual and ethical incredulity. Some rationalizations include that it was not sudden, nor the result of Peter (Klausner), but an explanation of the first deaths in the Jerusalem community because of sin (Menoud). After his own restoration, Peter is commonly criticized for a lack of grace and a spirit of judgment (like Elijah and Gehazi, see 2 Kings 5:7; see also Bruce, *Acts*, NICNT, 103-104).

93. There are also significant differences including their whole family's murder, and death by stoning. Witherington, *Acts*, 214 notes also Leviticus 10:1-5 where Nadab and Abihu "died before the LORD."

94. Bruce, *Acts*, NICNT, 102. The language of "kept back" in verse 2 may be an echo of Joshua 7:1.

95. Some scholars class this as a punitive or rule (violation) miracle (see Witherington, *Acts*, 213).

96. Witherington, *Acts*, 214.

of punishment.[97] Rather, it is better to view this as protective justice, God protecting his church[98] from corruption, for "a little leaven leavens the whole lump" (1 Cor 5:6, see also Gal 5:9).[99]

A third lesson is the importance of Christians behaving ethically in the financial arena, for God is watching. These two were clearly wealthy, as they owned sufficient property to sell some for the church. They are like those who declare false tax returns, duplicitously claiming to give all when they only gave some of the proceeds, and they are caught out. Ananias and Sapphira did not sin in retaining some of the money; it was theirs to keep or give away (see Acts 4:4a). Their sin was lying about giving it all when they retained some. Christians must be above reproach in ensuring they do not steal and defraud the state or others. Not only might they face criminal charges, but the spiritual results could be catastrophic.

Likely, they were driven by a desire for seeking status in the church to rival the likes of Barnabas, esteemed as "son of encouragement" (Acts 4:36). This leads to a fourth lesson: selfish ambition is to be repudiated (Phil 2:3) and especially using falsehood and deception to gain it. This encounter shows that being a Christian and acting unethically can be a deadly business.

Fifth, this episode shows the power of God's Spirit in Peter. Peter perceives in the Spirit their lie and predicts their death. Some criticize him for his actions; however, Peter did not kill the couple; God did, by his power. This passage speaks of Peter the prophet. Interestingly, in his first letter, he tells his readers, "It is time for judgment to begin at the household of God; and if it begins with us, what will be the outcome for those who do not obey the gospel of God?" (1 Peter 4:17). Writing some thirty years after this event and perhaps recalling this event, Peter understood that God's judgment is reserved for believers and unbelievers alike. In the next passage, Peter's shadow has the power to heal (Acts 5:15), and in Ephesus, healings

---

97. As Witherington writes in *Acts*, 216, "Notice that it is not said that Peter either killed Ananias or uttered a curse that killed him. In other words, it is possible that we do not have punitive miracle here at all, unlike the cursing of the fig tree."

98. Acts 5:11 includes the first reference to *ekklēsia*, "church," in Acts. This is significant—the church was protected, realizing God will not trifle with sin.

99. Interestingly, in 1 Corinthians 5:6 the saying "a little leaven leavens the whole lump" is preceded by the line, "Your boasting is not good." As here, the problem is pride and status seeking.

are conducted through Paul's tent-making cloths (Acts 19:12). We should never underestimate God's power, both to heal and to bring judgment.

Sixth, there are lessons for married couples. This account warns how easy it is for spouses or family members to become perverted by those they love. Hard choices must sometimes be made to challenge a spouse or family member, resist them, or even report them to the authorities. Sapphira had gone along with the lie from the beginning (Acts 5:1-2), and refused to come clean, even when given space to repent (Acts 5:8). Their story is another tragic example of greed and pride claiming the lives of people who could have turned from their sin and lives would have been saved.

Seventh, lies—whether about finance, to protect oneself or others, or to enhance one's status—are lies to oneself but also to God. Lying tests the Spirit of God (cf. Luke 4:12; Acts 15:10) and presumes on his offer of grace. God is all-powerful, and while he protects and provides, he is also described as a consuming fire (Heb 12:29), jealous for his church and purposes. He judges and sees everything his people do. Ananias and Sapphira seemed to have forgotten this, and they paid the price. His forgiveness and grace should lead people to act in a manner opposite Ananias and Sapphira.

Eighth, while the narrative indicates Ananias and Sapphira are clearly personally responsible,[100] demonic influence is clear. This shows that some in the church can be subject to Satan (cf. 1 Cor 7:5; 1 Tim 5:15; 2 Tim 2:26, see also 2 Cor 2:11; 12:7). Scripture says Satan filled Ananias' heart (Acts 5:3), as he entered Judas (Luke 22:3). It is not clear that the couple were Christians, but they were members of the community. In Luke's writings, Satan is not often mentioned—only fifteen times, four of which are in Jesus' temptation (Luke 4:2-3, 5, 13). Jesus resists Satan, the report on the submission of demons in the mission of the seventy-two leads Jesus to declare that he saw him fall from heaven (Luke 10:18, 20), the disciples drive demons out of people (Acts 5:16; 8:7; 19:12), Jesus comes to set free those oppressed by his power (Acts 10:38, cf. Luke 4:36; 6:18; 7:21; 8:2), and Paul's ministry turns people from Satan's power to God (Acts 26:18). Yet, in Luke-Acts, Satan still has real power. This includes his ability to steal the word from people's hearts so that they are not saved when they hear

---

100. Ananias and Sapphira sold the property, kept back some proceeds, and brought some to the apostles (vv. 1-2). Sapphira directly lied to Peter's face (v. 8).

the gospel (Luke 8:12). He binds a woman with a crippling disability for eighteen years (Luke 13:16). He enters Judas and leads him to betray Jesus (Luke 22:3). He sifts Simon like wheat (Luke 22:31). He corrupts the magician Elymas (Acts 13:8-10).[101] Like Judas and Elymas, Satan has corrupted Ananias and his wife. As the wider New Testament testifies, believers must not give the devil a stronghold and seek to live lives of love and personal integrity (Eph 4:27). They must resist the devil (Jas 4:7) who, like a roaring lion, seeks to devour people (1 Pet 5:8).

Finally, Bruce rightly notes:[102]

> The incident shows, too, that even in the earliest days, the church was not a society of perfect people. Luke's picture of the primitive community is no doubt idealized, but it is not over-idealized. Lest his readers should overestimate the unity and sanctity of the first believers, he has recorded this incident, which not only illustrates his honest realism, but is also intended to serve as a warning to others.

Conclusion

It cannot be overemphasized that the gift of the Spirit should lead to the demonstration of the fruit of the Spirit. The fruit of the Spirit is best exhibited in love—not merely words or emotion, but love in action. Luke's Gospel and this early part of Acts powerfully state that true Christianity is shown in communities where people are deeply concerned about the needs of others, even to the extent of personal material sacrifice.[103] Three other New Testament writers who were members of this dynamic community state this same principle in different ways:

1. **Paul:** Paul writes, "Contribute to the needs of the saints, and seek to show hospitality" (Rom 12:13). This should extend to enemies: "If your enemy is hungry, feed him; if he is thirsty, give him something to drink" (Rom 12:20). Paul also says to

---

101. Jesus is also accused of casting out demons by his power (Luke 11:18); throughout the New Testament, Satan is a real adversary.
102. Bruce, *Acts*, NICNT, 104.
103. See Luke 4:18-19; 6:20-36; 9:13; 10:25-37; 12:13-34; 14:13-24; 16:1-31; 18:18-30; 19:1-10.

"Remember the poor" (Gal 2:10). Paul also shows this commitment in the Jerusalem Collection (1 Cor 16:1-4; 2 Cor 8-9; Rom 15:24-31) and in his concern for the widows (1 Tim 5).

2. **John:** John says, "By this we know love, that he laid down his life for us, and we ought to lay down our lives for the brothers. But if anyone has the world's goods and sees his brother in need, yet closes his heart against him, how does God's love abide in him? Little children, let us not love in word or talk but in deed and in truth" (1 John 3:16-18).

3. **James:** James encourages, "Religion that God our Father accepts as pure and faultless is this: to look after orphans and widows in their distress and to keep oneself from being polluted by the world" (James 1:27 NIV).

A radical commitment to material generosity toward one another is sadly missing from many contemporary churches. The sin of materialism has such a grip on the world and has tamed the church; the radical edge of voluntary sacrificial giving is missing in many instances. Believers tend to consider Luke's radical challenge as unrealistic, and soften its power (cf. Luke 6:20-36; 9:57-62; 14:26-34). The challenge as individuals and in Christian community is to rediscover what it means to have voluntary economic *koinōnia* in today's world. Believers must move beyond the compulsory "tithe," which can be oppression for the genuinely poor and a soft option for the genuinely wealthy, to something like the radical giving of this first church. If anyone is blessed, they are blessed to give, and should give because God has given first—without expectation of reward, and with a generous heart.

Emulating the Jerusalem church is a complex issue in a capitalist economy where profits are the driving force; where society is based on expensive technology; where many justice issues are global; where a complex global economy of investment, banking, and shares exists as well as a social welfare system; and where the best way to use resources for the poor may not be selling possessions and giving the money to the needy but rather investing money carefully and using what is gained for the good of those in need. The challenge is to start with Jesus' commands, and work through what that looks like in individual situations. What would modern churches look like if there was no need?

A PERSECUTED CHURCH

Persecution is not a positive attribute *of* the church. It is something inflicted *on* the church by an angry world. However, the way the early church courageously stood up to the challenge was one of its greatest strengths. Luke also sees persecution through the lens of the sovereignty of God with the perseverance of the first Christians playing a huge part in the development of the Jerusalem and worldwide church. He sees it as something that brings blessing for which believers should rejoice (Luke 6:22-23).

As in Luke's Gospel, where opposition to Jesus intensifies through the narrative, persecution of the first Christians increases through Acts. There is a slight hint of opposition in Acts 2:13 where some accuse the Spirit-filled tongues-speaking Christians of drunkenness. In its initial phase, the church is held in great favor with *everyone* "filled with awe" and the church "enjoying the favor of *all* the people," presumably including the Jewish leaders who turn against them as the story unfolds (Acts 2:43, 47 NIV).

The healing of the disabled beggar in Acts 3 sparks a great response from the throng, and Peter's sermon in the temple is decidedly provocative; he directly targets the Jews for their responsibility in the killing of Jesus (Acts 3:13-15, 17-18, 23, 26). This excites a strong reaction from the Sanhedrin that attacks the leaders of the movement, imprisons Peter and John, and, although its members are in some ways surprised and impressed by them (Acts 4:13-14), demands they desist from preaching the message. The apostles' response is not to hold back or withdraw, but rather a renewed determination to preach (Acts 4:19-30).

After this prayer, there is a period of growth. Their prayer is answered dramatically, many turn to Christ, signs and wonders are performed, and the church experiences radical fellowship. However, while many experience the wonderful miracles God is doing and the people hold the Christians in high esteem, "no one dared join them" (Acts 5:13 NIV). This could indicate that the Christian community was marginalized, and joining it held some fear (based on Ananias and Sapphira)[104] or perceived danger (perhaps due to Peter and John's arrest in Acts 4:2-3).[105] Peter and John are arrested and placed in prison again. Then, miraculously, they are released by an angel and told to continue to preach the message in the temple courts. This leads to confusion, further persecution, and threats. Yet, the apostles are unfazed and, rather than desist, they rejoice that they "had been counted worthy of suffering disgrace for the Name" (Acts 5:41 NIV) and they continue to preach in the temple and in homes (Acts 5:42). The first church clearly expected and embraced persecution, seeing it in continuity with the sufferings of Christ on their behalf (cf. Phil 3:10; Col 1:24; 1 Pet 4:12–16). At no time did these early believers respond with violent resistance or by withdrawing from evangelism. Rather, they prayed for their persecutors as Jesus urged (Luke 6:28) and, despite ongoing persecution, continued to proclaim the gospel.

The persecution of the church comes to a head with the martyrdom of Stephen and Saul's attack on the church. The Jewish leaders, having failed to stop the growth of the new movement by attacking its leadership, now attack the church itself—and the church scatters. This persecution is led by the zealous Pharisee Saul (Acts 7:54–8:3), who had been severely persecuting and ravaging the church, dragging men and women to prison (Acts 8:3), and even persecuting them to death (Acts 22:4; 26:10).[106] In a great irony, before his conversion, while he was an enemy of the gospel, God used Saul/Paul to spread the gospel by scattering the church. However, by God's sovereignty, while a horrific experience for all concerned, this scattering turned out to be positive for the mission. The believers, dispersed "throughout Judea and Samaria," were how the Spirit spread the

---

104. Bruce, *Acts*, NICNT 109.

105. Witherington, *Acts*, 225.

106. The persecution was certainly severe. It involved a "great persecution" (*diōgmos megas*; see Acts 8:1). *Diōgmos* is related to *diōkō*, which is a hunting term and speaks of being pursued. For example, in Plutarch, *Alex.* 33.3, the Barbarian ranks give way to Alexander and are pursued. It is a strong word (cf. Dionysius of Halicarnassus, *Ant. rom.* 3.25.3; see also Xenophon, *Cyr.* 1.4.21). The Greek in v. 3, *lumainō* (*elymaineto*), indicates "smashing" the church as in the demolition of a city or a lion destroying its prey. The term is rare, but powerful. It is used in Josephus of bodies being torn to pieces by Antiochus' forces (Josephus, *Ant.* 12.256) and the merciless destruction of cities (Josephus, *J.W.* 2.278). It is also used in the *Testament of Abraham* (A) of the demon Death who "ravages the world" (*T. Ab* (A). 17.5; 19.7). In the LXX, it is used of the destruction of those who forsake God, as of a lion on its prey (Sir 28:23; cf. Isa 65:25, see also Isa 65:8).

gospel into Samaria (Acts 8:5-25), Judea (Acts 8:26-40; 9:30-11:18), and into Antioch (Acts 11:19-21). Hence, persecution is a vital aspect of the fulfillment of Acts 1:8. Even persecution is interpreted positively by the early Christians; it another tool in the hands of God to spread his message into new and unlikely places (see Phil 1:12-14). To be persecuted was an honor, as participation in the sufferings of Christ and part of the cost of "taking up one's cross" (e.g., 1 Pet 4:12-16). After the scattering of the church in Acts 8, Luke records little of the influence of the church in Jerusalem. However, its impact in the world beyond Jerusalem and Judea is dramatic.

In Jerusalem, James is killed and Peter imprisoned (Acts 12:1-10). Yet, from Antioch, where the church had flourished due to the mission being set ablaze by Saul's persecution, a fresh mission is launched that culminates in Paul preaching in Rome within twenty-five years. There is a consistent pattern of persecution against Paul in his mission. He begins in the synagogue ("to the Jew first, and also to the Greek" [Rom 1:16]), but experiences rejection from his own people (Acts 13:44-45; 17:5-9, 13; 18:4-6; 19:8-9). Scorned and with a few converts, he goes to the gentiles (Acts 13:46-47; 18:6; 19:9), establishing a church with a few Jews and gentiles in a home. In this he experiences significant success (Acts 13:49; 18:7-8; 19:10, 20), but often faces further Jewish persecution (Acts 13:49-51; 14:19; 18:12-17), opposition in the Greco-Roman city where he is working (Acts 16:16-39; 19:23-41), or a blend of both (e.g., Acts 17:5-8). The Roman culture and state are threatened socially, economically, religiously, and politically by the new movement. Ultimately, it is persecution that leads Paul to Rome, when he appeals to Caesar as a Roman citizen following imprisonment in Caesarea (Acts 25:12). Yet, even this is the fulfillment of God's purposes: that Paul must testify in Rome (Acts 23:11).

Through it all, the glorious hand of God can be seen using the persecution of God's people for his mission. The pattern of the cross is the pattern for the church's mission as the people of God serve the Lord and face hostility from the forces of darkness and the ignorance of humanity. While many suffer greatly and even die for the cause, the gospel triumphs as it spreads, and the people of God are greatly rewarded in eternity.

Consequently, the impact of persecution in the growth of the early church should not be underplayed. The refusal of Christians to respond with violence is critical in demonstrating the love of God toward enemies.

Similarly, the refusal of Christians to withdraw from evangelism in the face of persecution affirms the reality of the faith they espoused. Over subsequent generations of the Christian church, these two dynamics would be critical in the growth of the church. As Tertullian said, *Sanguis martyrum est semen ecclesiae*, or "the blood of the martyrs is the seed of the church" (Tertullian, *Apol.* 50).

The *Epistle of Mathetes to Diognetus* (c. AD 130) describes the first Christians' commitment to Christ despite persecution:

> They love all people (orig. "men"), and are persecuted by all. They are unknown and condemned; they are put to death, and restored to life. They are poor, yet make many rich; they are in lack of all things, and yet abound in all; they are dishonoured, and yet in their very dishonour are glorified. They are evil spoken of, and yet are justified; they are reviled, and bless; they are insulted, and repay the insult with honour; they do good, yet are punished as evil-doers. When punished, they rejoice as if quickened into life; they are assailed by the Jews as foreigners, and are persecuted by the Greeks; yet those who hate them are unable to assign any reason for their hatred. (*Diogn.* 5)[107]

It is clear in the New Testament in such places as 1 Peter 3:1-2 that there is a time not to preach. In this text, Peter exhorts believing wives not to preach the word to their husbands who have heard the word and disobeyed it. Rather, followers of Jesus must work with what might be called a "soteriological imperative," living among unbelievers with the goal that they come to Christ and are saved (see 1 Cor 10:24-11:1). In New Testament terms, this involves the sharing of the gospel message graciously, respectfully, and holistically in attitude, word, and deed, and out of communities of love.

CONCLUSION

The factors discussed were critical for the expansion of the early church. God gave a detailed account of this church as a beacon of hope and possibility.

---

107. Adapted from Alexander Roberts, James Donaldson, and A. Cleveland Coxe, ed(s). "The Epistle of Mathetes to Diognetus," in ANF 1:26-27.

This is achieved by believers giving their lives in service to God and his church. It comes to pass when people stop being spiritual consumers, judging the church on whether "it meets my needs," and accept that it is an imperfect organization and resolve to serve within it. Such churches have existed and continue to do so, usually where the leaders and enough others in the church take such an attitude. The believer's charge is to be certain in the vision given in the first chapters of Acts, believe in the church no matter how big a mess it is in, be open to the Spirit, and be ready to contribute to see the church be what it was designed to be. The church is the broken and resurrected body of Christ, and it exists so a lost world may know the love and salvation of God!

THE EXPANSION OF THE GOSPEL TO SAMARIA AND JUDEA; THE JERUSALEM COUNCIL (ACTS 8–12)

Acts 8–12 reveals the way in which the gospel spread up to the time of Paul's gentile mission, which dominates the second half of Acts (Acts 13–28). This section aligns loosely with Acts 1:8, "in all Judea and Samaria."

Acts 8–12 is a critical section because it sees the promise to Abraham in Genesis 12:1-3 reach fulfillment. It also sees the hope of the prophets for the restoration of Israel and Judah begin to come to pass in the church, as the first Jewish disciples realize the gospel must go beyond Israel, a major development in salvation history.

The catalyst for the mission beyond Jerusalem and Judea in Luke's account was not so much a passion to complete the Great Commission, but rather, Saul's persecution.

THE EVANGELIZATION OF SAMARIA (ACTS 8:4–25)

Luke records that those who were scattered went on their way into Judea and Samaria preaching the gospel (Acts 8:4). These included Philip, one of the Seven, who went to Samaria with the gospel. Samaria is the name of both of a province and a city.[108] As a region, it is the area between Judea and Galilee, both of which were Jewish. After Herod the Great rebuilt Samaria and renamed it Sebaste, the name Samaria was used exclusively

---

108. Maynard-Reid, P. U. "Samaria," in *DLNTD* 1075-77; and H. G. M. Williamson, "Samaritans," in *DJG* 724-28.

of the province, which is how the term is used in the New Testament (Luke 17:11; John 4:4-5, 7; Acts 1:8; 8:1, 14; 9:31). However, it can refer to the city Sebaste, or Gitta (Acts 8:5, 8). The town of Sychar also features in Jesus' ministry, and some believe this to be where Philip experienced so much success in John, although this is conjecture (John 4:5). It is unclear what town Luke had in mind when Jesus is rejected in Luke 9:52. Other towns are alluded to in the New Testament (Matt 10:5), which Philip also evangelized (Acts 8:25).

The Samaritans were the natives of this region. However, just who these people are is shrouded in some mystery. Samaritans considered themselves to be direct descendants of Israel, believing that the nation's center should never have been moved from Gerizim to Shiloh in the period before Jerusalem was capital. The Jews believed they descended from the people who colonized the area under the Assyrians (2 Kgs 17:24-41). These colonizers adopted the Israelite faith alongside their own religion, the so-called Cutheans[109] (2 Kgs 17:41). However, many scholars now believe 2 Kings 17 is not relevant as it refers to the "people of Samaria" (2 Kgs 17:29 NIV) rather than Samaritans. Josephus documented that the priest Manasseh was expelled from Jerusalem and a sanctuary was built for him at Mount Gerizim in the fourth century BC, and that other priests from Jerusalem joined him. This accounts for the Jewish character of the Samaritans' religious practices.

The city of Samaria itself had been built by Omri in the ninth century BC (1 Kgs 16:24), and was the capital of the Northern Kingdom until it was destroyed by Sargon II, the Assyrian king, in 721 BC (2 Kgs 17). It was rebuilt by the Assyrians, but little is recorded in the biblical record until 4 Ezra where the people of Samaria opposed the rebuilding of the Jerusalem temple, suggesting that some Jews remained in the city. The city was destroyed again by Alexander in 332 BC and rebuilt as a Greek town. Thus, at the time of the New Testament, the area was recently populated — the earliest references being to Shechemites from Alexander's city (Sir 50:26; 2 Macc 5:22-23; 6:2; Josephus, *Ant.* 11.340-47; 12.10).

Some have been able to trace their heritage back to pre-exile days, but there may not have been many. Others descended from Israelites who

---

109. Another name for the Samaritans, found in the Talmud.

had returned from exile (2 Chr 30; 34:6; Jer 40:1–5). Others were probably Greeks, as the city was highly Hellenized. Some of these would have adopted the Samaritan religion in some form, but in a highly syncretistic manner. Others may have been priests forced out of Jerusalem due to the strictures of priestly leadership from the time of Ezra and Nehemiah. This may be why the Samaritans claimed a legitimate priesthood.

The strong resentment between Jew and Samaritan may also be due to political tensions between the different post-Alexander Greek kingdoms of the Ptolemies and the Seleucids, Jewish resentment of Hellenization, and the Samaritans' non-involvement in Jewish revolt (e.g., against Antiochus Epiphanes), among other things. In addition, in 128 BC, the Jewish reformer John Hyrcanus destroyed the temple at Mount Gerizim in Shechem, and then sometime between 111–107 BC, destroyed the city itself. It was rebuilt by Herod the Great in honor of Caesar Augustus and called Sebaste, but soon destroyed by the Romans in AD 66 during the Jewish revolt. Another aspect that would have caused tension was the Samaritans' exclusive acceptance of the Pentateuch as Scripture (like the Sadducees) and their preference for Mount Gerizim over the Jerusalem temple as the center of their faith. As seen in John 4:25–26, they also believed in the Messiah (Taheb), a "prophet like Moses." In AD 6–7, some Samaritans scattered bones in the Jerusalem temple during Passover (Josephus, *Ant.* 18.29–30); in AD 52, some killed a group of Galilean pilgrims (Josephus, *Ant.* 20.118).

Samaritans were not viewed as gentiles, but as schismatics, heretics, or half breeds; they were neither Jew nor gentile. The city (*polis*) in which Philip ministered is unlikely to have been Sebaste, as it was primarily Greek. It could have been Shechem (Acts 7:16). However, Shechem was destroyed in 128 BC.[110] Another possibility is Gitta, the traditional birthplace of Simon Magus.

Wherever Philip engaged in mission, his ministry included the proclamation of Jesus as the Christ. This suggests he was preaching to believers in Yahweh who had hopes of a messiah (cf. John 4:25). He sought to convince them that the crucified prophet Jesus of Nazareth is, in fact, the risen Messiah (Acts 8:6). His ministry also included signs, including deliverance

---

110. Witherington, *Acts*, 282.

and healing (Acts 8:7), the classic New Testament combination of preaching with signs and wonders.

The response in the city is positive, with joy, faith, and baptism (Acts 8:6-12). This evangelization of Samaria is important. Luke records that Jesus had been rejected by the Samaritans, and James and John had sought the city's destruction—something Jesus refused to do (Luke 9:51-56). This incident is the turning point of Luke's Gospel, and so there began the journey from Samaritan rejection of Jesus to Jesus' death, resurrection, ascension, and Pentecost, to the Samaritan conversion through the Spirit-empowered proclamation of Jesus the Christ by Philip. There is an interesting contrast between the patterns of world power through domination and the way Jesus seeks power—through forgiveness and willing submission to the gospel of a crucified and risen Lord, not the sword. Jesus did not bring the wrath of God on the renegade Samaritans who had deserted temple-based Yahwistic faith, but gave an opportunity for them to be saved through his death and resurrection. Jesus' attitude toward the Samaritans is anticipated in the good-Samaritan story and ten lepers' healing, where the focus is the Samaritans (see Luke 10:25-37; 17:11-19).

The evangelization of the Samaritans in the broader biblical redemptive story is also significant. This was God's undoing of the division of his people that happened when the north broke away under Jeroboam (1 Kgs 12), thus fulfilling the hope of the prophets of a reunified Israel (e.g., Jer 3:18; 23:6; 30:3; 31:1-37 [esp. vv. 27, 31]; Ezek 37:15-28; Hos 1:10-11; 2:2). In some places, these hopes are linked to the hope of a Messiah (Hos 1:10-11; 11:1-4, 10-12; Ezek 37:15-28).

One of the features of Philip's time in Samaria was the encounter with Simon, a sorcerer who was highly regarded in the city (Acts 8:9-11). Many from the city came to believe and were baptized, including Simon himself (Acts 8:12-13). However, when Peter and John visited, and the Holy Spirit came upon the new believers, Simon offered to pay money to receive the Spirit. Peter was not impressed and refused, urging Simon to repent, which he did (Acts 8:18-24).

This Simon is significant in later Christian tradition where he is labeled Simon Magus ("magician") and is supposedly the father of the second-century heretical movement, Gnosticism. Justin Martyr indicates Simon Magus was from the village of Gitta, and during the reign of

Claudius had a large following in Samaria and Rome. He was accompanied by a former prostitute, Helen; was demonized to imitate Christianity; was divinized by his followers; and persuaded people that he would never die (see Justin Martyr, *1 Apol.* 1.26).[111] In the late second-century drawing on Justin, Irenaeus views his conversion as fake and sees Simon as a source of heresy. Irenaeus says Simon claimed to be a god, the "absolute authority," and that Helen was an incarnation of the Gnostic goddess, Sophia. These two were gods to the Simonians in Irenaeus' time (Irenaeus, *Haer.* 1.23-27). According to Hippolytus (c. AD 230), Simon died claiming he would rise on the third day, but did not do so (Hippolytus, *Haer.* 6.2, 4-15). There were other such figures in the early church.[112]

Another feature of this evangelization of Samaria is the visit from Peter and John. When they came, they prayed for the new converts who received the Spirit (Acts 8:14-17). This suggests that the Jerusalem leaders were active in overseeing the expansion of the gospel, as in the Cornelius incident (Acts 10). It also indicates to some that the transmission of the Spirit had become institutionalized with the Jerusalem apostles' laying on of hands. However, this is unlikely, for at times in Acts the Spirit comes spontaneously (Acts 2:1-4; 10:44); is transmitted through a mere "disciple," Ananias (Acts 9:17); and through Paul (Acts 19:6). There is a variety of means by which the Spirit is transmitted in Luke's account (e.g., Luke 3:15-22). The outpouring of the Spirit on the Samaritans is also symbolic of the reunification of Jew and Samaritan, the restoration of Israel.

The great significance of this event in the Acts narrative is the expansion of the gospel along the lines of Acts 1:8, "to all Samaria," which is anticipated in Luke's Gospel (cf. Luke 9:52-56 [Jesus rejected in Samaria]; Luke 10:25-37 [the good Samaritan]; Luke 17:10-19 [the grateful Samaritan leper]).

THE GOSPEL GOES TO AFRICA (ACTS 8:26–40)

After Philip's evangelization of Samaria, he encounters an Ethiopian eunuch from the court of Candace, the Queen of Ethiopia. Ethiopia was the region south of Egypt. Ethiopians were romanticized in Greek literature

---

111. Supposedly, he had a statue erected in his name on the river Tiber with the inscription *Simoni Deo Santo* (To Simon, the Holy God).

112. See R. F. Stoops, "Simon (Person)," in *ABD* 6:29-31.

as the most handsome and tallest of all (e.g., Herodotus, *Hist.* 3.17–20; Homer, *Od.* 1:22–23). It is likely, then, that Luke's first readers would have reacted positively to the Ethiopian eunuch. Since eunuchs were unable to become full proselytes because they could not be circumcised (cf. Deut 23:1; Josephus, *Ant*, 4.290–91), it is likely he was a gentile. However, Luke's account clearly indicates that Cornelius was the first gentile convert, meaning Luke did not consider him a gentile in the strict sense. As the eunuch had been worshipping in Jerusalem and reading Isaiah 53, it is likely that he was a "God-fearer"[113] with a great interest in Judaism, if not able to be a full proselyte.[114]

The encounter is characterized by dynamic guidance by the Lord through an angel (Acts 8:26), the Spirit (Acts 8:29), and Scripture.[115] Luke records that the eunuch had "come to Jerusalem to worship" (Acts 8:27) and was reading Isaiah 53:7–8. Philip, led by the Spirit, used the text as a basis to share the gospel. A feature of the account is the Ethiopian requesting immediate baptism and Philip obliging (Acts 8:36–38). Another interesting element of the story is Philip's apparent translation by the Spirit from the point of baptism to the town of Azotus, where he continued to preach the message (Acts 8:39–40).[116]

The significance of this story lies in the spread of the gospel through this encounter *to Africa*. There is indeed no biblical account of the evangelization of North Africa, but plenty of indications that the Ethiopian and unknown believers took the gospel there (cf. Acts 2:10; 13:1; 18:24). However,

---

113. See F. S. Spencer, "Philip the Evangelist," in *DLNTD* 930.

114. See Beverly Roberts Gaventa, "Ethiopian Eunuch," in *ABD* 2:667, who notes that this anomaly leads to discussions of Luke's sources. Some think Luke's source here is Philip and this is an account of the first gentile conversion, but that Luke wished to preserve Peter's primacy in his account in Acts 10–11. Some see it as a legend about the conversion of a prominent individual. I would argue it came from Philip the Evangelist as he is named in the account (unlike the unnamed evangelizers of Acts 11:19–20) and Luke had ample opportunity to gather material when in Caesarea Maritima with Paul (see Acts 21:16; 27:1–2).

115. Based on Luke's theology of the Spirit involved in Scripture (e.g., Acts 1:16; 4:25).

116. The language of "snatching" here is *harpazō*, which is used of being snatched either for negative purposes—such as seizing by force or plunder (Matt 11:12; 12:29; 13:19; John 6:15; 10:12, 28–29; Acts 23:10; Rev 12:5). Alternatively, it is used positively such as God rapturing someone to heaven in a vision (2 Cor 12:2, 4), at the consummation (1 Thess 4:17), or of a believer snatching someone from the fire of judgment (Jude 23). Here it would seem that the sense is positive—the Spirit snatching Philip away from the situation, perhaps like Elijah or Jesus on the road to Emmaus. This can be read as a supernatural event. Or Philip was simply compelled by the Spirit to go to Azotus.

for Luke, while apostles and named others are important, the gospel is an unstoppable force propelled by the Spirit, who ensures the gospel arrives through people known or unknown. This is Luke's understanding of the mission of God—a pneumatological missiology.

THE CONVERSION OF THE APOSTLE TO THE GENTILES (ACTS 9:1–31)

Acts 9 shifts the emphasis from the Jerusalem church to the story of Saul's conversion. From this point on in Luke, Saul/Paul will play a critical role in Luke's presentation of the spread of the gospel. This is due to his importance to the mission for Luke, Luke's close relationship with Paul (see the "we passages"), and perhaps a desire to defend Paul's contribution either against other Christians or, more likely, to Theophilus and others in Rome. If Paul is in prison in Rome, it may be that Luke-Acts has an apologetic purpose in relation to Paul and his imprisonment.

Originally known as Saul,[117] he has been previously introduced to readers as a persecutor of Christians, including an approving bystander to Stephen's stoning and the architect of the persecution of the church in Acts 8:1-4. He reappears in the narrative this time seeking and receiving letters of commendation from the high priest, Caiaphas (Acts 22:5; 26:10). This indicates his status in Judaism. He is then en route to Damascus, a journey of around 218 km (135 mi) to arrest followers of "the Way" and return them to Jerusalem prison (Acts 9:1-2). As he is traveling, he has a spiritual encounter involving the manifestation of a great light. He hears Jesus' voice, and is blinded (Acts 9:3-4, 8). Jesus instructs him to go into Damascus and await instructions. His companions take him into Damascus, where he fasts (Acts 9:7-9).

The story is another example of God at work by his Spirit. While Saul is in the city, God instructs a disciple named Ananias to go to the house of Judas where Saul is staying and place his hands on Saul, heal him, and commission him to be God's instrument in taking his message to the gentiles

---

117. Σαῦλος (Saul) is a Grecized form of the Hebrew שָׁאוּל (Shaul). It is the name of the first king of Israel (1 Sam 9:2). It is also used of a king of the Edomites (Gen 36:37), a son of Simeon (Gen 46:10), and a son of Kohath (1 Chr 6:24).

(Acts 9:10-16).[118] Ananias is reluctant but, showing great courage and obedience, goes and prays for Saul. Saul is baptized in the Spirit and healed. He is then baptized (presumably by Ananias) and eats, regaining his strength (Acts 9:13, 17-19). Ananias is an important figure, as he is not an apostle, but a "disciple," yet baptizes Saul and instructs him. Ananias shows it is not necessary for a person to be a Jerusalem apostle to be used of God as a conduit for his Spirit. Ananias commissions Saul for his ministry to be God's chosen instrument to initiate the gentile mission. Ministry is not just for the apostles in Acts. Ananias is also a courageous man, obeying God despite his fear, as he acts despite perceiving that Saul was a danger to him and the movement.

At this point, Saul's life takes a dramatic turn as he acts in obedience to his call. Instead of going to the Christians of Damascus and arresting them, he enters the Jewish synagogues of Damascus no longer preaching that "the Way" is heretical, but that this crucified Jesus is the Son of God and Messiah, totally confounding the expectations of the Jews in Damascus (Acts 9:19-22). Not surprisingly, this leads to a death threat, the first of many against Paul (e.g., Acts 9:29; 20:3; 21:31; 23:12, 15, 30; 25:3; 26:21). Fortunately, Saul became aware of the plot, and "his disciples" lowered him in a basket through an opening in the Damascus wall (Acts 9:23-25).[119]

From Damascus, Luke records that Saul returned to Jerusalem as a follower of Jesus. In Jerusalem, he sought to join the disciples but, understandably, they are terrified, imagining that he has returned to continue his crusade against them (Acts 9:26). Barnabas' high character—the "son of encouragement" who comes to Saul, hears his story, and presents him to the apostles (Acts 9:27; cf. 4:36-37)—is revealed again. This begins a partnership that includes ministry in Antioch and Paul's Galatian ministry (Acts 13-14). However, this relationship is ruptured before Paul's

---

118. Further detail is given in Acts 22:12-16. Ananias is a devout Jewish man. He healed Saul, saying "Brother Saul, receive your sight." His words from Paul are recorded as: "The God of our fathers appointed you to know his will, to see the Righteous One and to hear a voice from his mouth; for you will be a witness for him to everyone of what you have seen and heard. And now why do you wait? Rise and be baptized and wash away your sins, calling on his name" (Acts 22:14-16). In Acts 26:14-18 Paul's testimony converges the words of Jesus and Ananias into one message on the lips of Jesus.

119. Paul also refers to this incident in 2 Corinthians 11:32-33, noting that the king and governor, Aretas, was seeking to stop him from escaping, but he escaped anyway—in a basket.

second great mission (Acts 15:36-41). After his acceptance by the Jerusalem Christians, Paul engages in evangelism with the Hellenistic Jews, those who had previously clashed with Stephen (Acts 9:28-29, cf. Acts 6:9). Old friends had become enemies. As with Stephen, they sought to kill him, the second plot against his life (Acts 9:29-30). The Jerusalem believers learned of the plot and sent Saul north from Jerusalem to Caesarea Maritima and home to Tarsus (Acts 9:30). These journeys may have been by ship. In this time, Paul may have met believers in Caesarea, perhaps including Cornelius and Philip the Evangelist, whom he would meet again (Acts 18:22; 21:8-15; 23:23-27:1). Saul's conversion brought the persecution period to an end, and the church in Judea, Galilee, and Samaria stabilized and experienced peace and growth (Acts 9:31).

Saul's conversion is one of the most important moments in the history of the church, alongside the call of Moses, Samuel, Isaiah, and the first disciples. It speaks of God's decisive intervention to set ablaze Paul's ministry to the gentiles, which established the gospel firmly from Jerusalem through to Macedonia and on to Spain. Again, the sovereignty of God in mission is evident.

THE GOSPEL SPREADS THROUGH JUDEA (ACTS 9:32—42)

Luke now turns his attention to the missionary journeys of Peter, the dominant apostolic figure in Luke and the first five chapters of Acts. Aside from his departure in Acts 12 and his contribution to the Jerusalem Council in Acts 15, this is Peter's last mission activity in Luke's story. From this point on, Paul will dominate. This does not mean that Peter's importance is diminished, as his mission appears to be more Jewish and it is likely he traveled widely from this point (e.g., 1 Cor 9:5). Luke picks up "the end of the earth" theme from Acts 1:8, which is not Peter's focus (Gal 2:7-8).

In this section, Peter's mission purpose appears to have been pastoral rather than for evangelism. He goes "here and there among them all" and visits "the saints who lived in Lydda" (Acts 9:32). This points to Peter's apostolic role, including not only evangelism (Acts 2-3), but the strengthening and following up of converts. He fulfills Jesus' appeal to him to "feed my sheep" (see John 21:15-18).

Earlier, Luke mentions Peter's healing ministry (Acts 3:1-10; 5:15), and this continues in Acts 9:32-42. Through God, Peter heals Aeneas, who had been bedridden for eight years with paralysis. Peter speaks directly to him: "Aeneas, Jesus Christ heals you; rise and make your bed!" (Acts 9:34). Healing was immediate. The centrality of healing to the ministry of the first Christians is once again evident. While Peter's trip was pastoral in intent, the impact of the healing was evangelistic. The healing triggered a huge turning to the Lord in Lydda and the region of Sharon, which extended north from Joppa (Tel Aviv) to Caesarea Maritima, south of Mount Carmel[120] (Acts 9:33-35).

While in Joppa, Peter had a second miraculous encounter with Tabitha (Dorcas), an important female disciple particularly known for her good works and acts of charity, especially toward widows (Acts 9:35, 39). She is another positive female Christian example in Luke's writings recalling the women who supported Jesus (cf. Luke 8:1-3) and anticipates the likes of Phoebe in Paul's writings (Rom 16:1-2). This also shows that the generous giving ministry in the Jerusalem Church (Acts 2, 4) is now spreading through Judea. When Tabitha becomes ill and dies, the believers send for Peter, who comes to her amidst the mourning widows who had received her ministry. Peter removes the mourners (cf. Jesus and Jairus' daughter, Mark 5:37). He directly addresses the deceased woman, telling her to "get up." She responds by opening her eyes and living again (Acts 9:41-42). The impact of this is evangelistic, with many coming to Christ. Thus, resurrection from the dead is another of the miracles in the early church. They call to mind the raising of the widow of Nain's son (Luke 7:11-17) and anticipate that of Eutychus (Acts 20:9-10). They were also signs of the kingdom, demonstrating that the time of salvation had come.

THE GOSPEL GOES TO THE GENTILES (ACTS 10:1–11:18)

Acts 10 tells the story of the spread of the gospel beyond Judaism to the gentiles. The expansion of the faith from a monocultural Jewish church to a truly multicultural one is not a result of strategy or intentional mission. However, it is linked to prayer, which seems to be the starting point for mission-engagement in Luke's writings. It is God who sparks the event,

---

120. Sharon is a fertile coastal region that extends north from Joppa to south of Mount Carmel and included Caesarea.

working dynamically in two contexts simultaneously to engineer Peter's encounter with the devout Cornelius.

Cornelius is a Roman centurion, and while he is not a circumcised proselyte, he is clearly a devout God-fearer. He calls to mind earlier Roman centurions who figure in Luke's account, including the Capernaum centurion whose servant Jesus healed, the centurion at the cross who both leads the crucifixion and yet recognizes Jesus' innocence, the centurion in Jerusalem who nearly flogs Paul, and Julius the centurion who escorts Paul and others to Rome (Luke 7:1-10; 23:47; Acts 22:26; 24:23; 27:1-43). Paul emphasizes such Romans perhaps to inspire Theophilus. Despite being Roman, Cornelius is an exemplary God-worshiper. Along with his family, he participates in Jewish prayer life and gives to the poor (Acts 10:1). During one of his thrice-daily Jewish prayer times, an angel speaks to Cornelius telling him that God has heard his prayers and that he must send for Peter, who is staying with Simon, the tanner in Joppa. Cornelius demonstrates his piety and obeys (Acts 10:2-7).

The following day Peter is praying on the roof at noon, indicating his dedication to prayer since noon was not one of the three official prayer times. Luke again emphasizes the importance of prayer. During prayer, Peter has a vision in which three times he is urged to eat unclean animals. Peter, in accordance with torah,[121] refuses and three times he is instructed to eat. Finally, the Lord says, "What God has made clean, do not call common" (Acts 10:9-16). This threefold experience can be linked to Peter's threefold denial of Christ (Luke 22:54-62) and his threefold restoration (John 21:15-19). Intriguingly, in Mark 7 and Matthew 15, the two evangelists record Jesus' teaching of the creation principle (cf. Gen 2:15; 9:3), that all food is good: "It is not what goes into the mouth that defiles a person, but what comes out of the mouth" (Matt 15:11). Luke does not record this account. This could suggest that a subtext of the Lukan narrative (as noted earlier) is the failure of the church to fully grasp the cosmic scope of Jesus' teaching and mission. Peter should not have needed the vision but, just as he and the other disciples failed to fully understand Christ's suffering and death,

---

121. See e.g., Lev 10:10; 20:25; Ezek 4:14; Dan 1:8-12; 2 Macc 5:27; 6:18-25; Tob 1:10-11; Jdt 10:5; 12:2.

they were slow to respond to the call to go to all nations with the gospel. It took the sovereign work of God to break through to them.

While Peter is considering what to make of the vision, Cornelius' men arrive and request that he come with them as the angel has instructed. Peter interprets the arrival as the purpose of the vision. The Spirit instructs him to go with them, and Peter invites them to stay the night—an astonishing act of hospitality from a Jew to a gentile (Acts 10:17-23).

The next day, Peter and other follower of Jesus from Joppa go north to Caesarea by horse, a trip of 63 km (40 mi), which would be traveled in a day. Here, when meeting Peter, Cornelius falls at his feet in worship. This calls to mind Luke 7:1-10 and the account of Jesus' preparedness to go to the home of the Roman soldier. Peter asks Cornelius why he, a gentile, had sent for him, a Jew, who by his own law is not to associate with gentiles (Acts 10:24-29). Cornelius then recounts the story of the angel (Acts 10:30-33).

Peter clearly accepts this story and recognizes that God is instructing Peter to move beyond the ethnocentrism of Israel's laws, and he begins to preach the message to Cornelius' household. Beginning with God's acceptance of all nations, he recounts the story of Jesus' ministry, death, resurrection, commission, and prophetic fulfillment (Acts 10:34-43).

Then comes a fifth critical moment of the coming of the Spirit in Acts (Acts 2:1-4; 4:31; 8:17; 9:17-18), and the first outpouring of the Spirit on gentiles. The Spirit falls spontaneously upon Cornelius' family in the middle of Peter's sermon (Acts 10:44). This demonstrates God's acceptance of the gentiles into the community of God on the same footing as Jews. This happens before any profession of faith or baptism, showing the freedom of the Spirit in Acts—something that should caution believers today from being too systematic in their pneumatology. The descent of the Spirit on uncircumcised, unbaptized gentiles, in the middle of a sermon, stresses God's acceptance and guards against any Jewish believers insisting that gentiles must be circumcised before incorporation into God's people. God is the God of the gentiles as well as the Jews (cf. Rom 3:29). The power of this event is seen in Peter and the other believers' astonishment (Acts 10:45) as they see Cornelius and his family speaking in tongues and praising God (Acts 10:46). The members of Cornelius' household are then baptized, and Peter stays with them for several days (Acts 10:47).

The significance of this event for Peter and salvation history should not be underestimated. In Acts 10, gentiles are received fully into God's people by the sovereign act of God and without prejudice. Previously, Jewish believers had thought gentiles would be saved and integrated into God's kingdom by becoming Jewish through being circumcised and adhering to the law and, in particular, its boundary markers (circumcision, Sabbath, ritual purity protocols, and food laws). Becoming a child of Abraham is now a matter of faith and not conforming to a culture, Jewish or otherwise (cf. Luke 3:8; 13:28; 16:22-30; 19:9). Abraham is now truly becoming a blessing to the nations (Gen 12:1-3). As such, today's churches must be culturally inclusive, without status and prejudice. Multiculturalism is an essential part of the gospel and mission.

The gravity of the encounter is seen when Peter returns to Jerusalem to face the criticism of Jewish believers for eating in the home of the uncircumcised (Acts 11:1-3). This confirms that, aside from the Pauline mission, to this point, new converts also had to become Jews. The Cornelius episode and the Antiochian mission sets ablaze the movement toward absolute inclusion of all peoples by faith, irrespective of cultural identity, something ratified at the Jerusalem Council in Acts 15.

Peter defends his actions by recounting the vision (Acts 11:4-11), the Spirit leading him to the gentiles and into their home (Acts 11:12-13), the coincidence that God had spoken to Cornelius through an angel (Acts 11:12-14), and the way the Spirit fell upon Cornelius' family as he spoke (Acts 11:15-16). Peter then interprets the outpouring as a fulfillment of John the Baptist's prophesy that Jesus would baptize with the Spirit (Luke 3:16). Peter then asks how he could stand in the way of God (Acts 11:17, cf. Acts 4:19-20; 5:29). This silences the criticisms, and the Jewish believers accept that "to the Gentiles also God has granted repentance that leads to life" (Acts 11:18). This event became decisive in the discussion over circumcision at the Jerusalem Council where the outpouring of the Spirit on an uncircumcised man and his family is critical in the decision not to enforce circumcision for new gentile believers (Acts 15:18).

THE GOSPEL SPREADS INTO SYRIAN ANTIOCH

At this point, the narrative shifts to a further account of the Christians scattered by the persecution of Saul. Acts 8:1 says the scattered went into

Samaria and Judea. Here it is clear they went much further into Syria, more evidence of the impulsion of the Spirit in spreading the gospel.

Some traveled to Phoenicia (north of Galilee, modern Lebanon),[122] Cyprus (an island in the Mediterranean off the coast of Phoenicia, Lebanon), and Syrian Antioch, preaching the word wherever they went (Acts 11:19). In Antioch, some from Cyprus and Cyrene (modern Libya, North Africa) shared the gospel, not only to Jews, proselytes, and God-fearers, as had the first Christians, but also to Greeks (i.e., general gentiles, the uncircumcised). A great number of gentiles believed (Acts 11:21).

The news reaches the church in Jerusalem and, as in the case of the Samaritan mission (Acts 8:14-17), they send an emissary to check out what is happening. Appropriately they send the Cyprian Levite Barnabas (the "son of encouragement"), who "was a good man, full of the Holy Spirit and faith" (Acts 11:21-22, 24 NIV). His response to the church in Antioch is positive, and he exhorts them in their faith and is a part of further evangelization (Acts 11:23-24). Barnabas then finds Saul in his hometown of Tarsus, and together they return to Antioch, where they continue to teach the converts.

It is in Syrian Antioch that the disciples are called "Christians" for the first time (see Acts 11:25-26, cf. Acts 11:26; 1 Pet 4:16). The word used here is *Christianos* (pl. *Christianoi*). The ending of the singular *-ianos* is equivalent to the Latin *-ianus* and describes ownership, or "people who belong to Christ," perhaps in the sense of slaves.[123] While not widely used, it was commonly used by non-Christian writers of believers (cf. Josephus, *Ant.* 18.64; Tacitus, *Ann.* 15.44; Pliny the Younger, *Ep. Tra.* 10.96-97; Lucian, *Alex.* 25, 38).[124] Christianity was beginning to be identified as separate from Judaism.

---

122. The region as understood by the Greeks and Romans included Canaan and the Syria-Lebanon-Israel coastal region. They experienced a time of great expansion forming Greater Phoenicia (Phoenicia proper) and Western Phoenicia (coast regions of North Africa, Southwestern Spain, Sicily, and some other Mediterranean islands). The center was Carthage. It had declined by New Testament times and Luke here means a hundred-mile-long (160 km) and fifteen-mile-wide (24 km) coastline: "the Mediterranean seacoast area of Syria, with Tyre and Sidon as its main cities" (D. L. Bock, *Acts I*, BECNT [Grand Rapids: Baker Academic, 2007], 412). See also Charles R. Krahmalkov, "Phoenicia," in *EDB* 1053-56.

123. Gaertner, *Acts*, Ac 1:1 (no page).

124. See also Lucian, *Alex.* 38; *Peregr.* 11, 12, 13, 16. In the Pseudepigrapha in interpolations (Gk. *Apoc. Ezra* 1.6; 2.7; 5.1; *Apoc. Dan.* 2.15; 8.6; 12.8; 13.7; 14.4, 6, 8, 9, 13). More regularly in the Apostolic Fathers (nineteen times, e.g., Ign. *Magn.* 4.1; *Mart. Pol.* 12.1; *Diogn.* 2.6, 10; 6.5; *Const. Ap.* 8.6.8).

This is further evidence that the gospel is now spreading spontaneously through the power of the Spirit to the gentiles (cf. Acts 1:8).

Again, the importance of social action in the early church is highlighted. Agabus, a prophet of Jerusalem, came to Antioch and predicted a famine throughout the world. This happened in the reign of Claudius (AD 41-54), during which there were several famines. One mentioned by Josephus in AD 44-48 hit Judea hard (Josephus, *Ant*. 3.320-21).[125] The response of the Antiochians was to raise money and send it to Judea through Barnabas and Saul (Acts 11:27-30). While some dispute this, seeing Paul's Galatians 2 visit to Jerusalem as Acts 15, this is most likely the visit of Paul to Jerusalem in Galatians 2.[126] This also indicates that accurate predictive prophecy was a part of the life of the early church (see also Peter in Acts 5:3 and Agabus in 21:10-11).[127] It also hints at the beginnings of itinerant prophetic ministry. This event is also significant because it introduces the financial partnership between churches across nations. The faith is now going truly global, and unity should transcend geography.

FURTHER NEWS FROM JERUSALEM

The account then returns to Jerusalem and relates another outpouring of persecution upon the Jerusalem church. This time it is initiated by King Herod Agrippa I. He imprisoned James, the son of Zebedee and brother of John, and had him killed by the sword (Acts 12:1-2).[128] Agrippa I (10 BC-AD 44) was the grandson of Herod the Great, the son of Aristobulus, who was killed by Herod the Great in 7 BC (see further Ch. 2). Herod Agrippa I was raised in Rome with his mother. He was appointed by Caligula to rule the

---

125. Bock, *Acts* I, 417-18, notes that during the reign of Claudius (AD 41-54) there were famines in the first (41), second (42), fourth (44), ninth (49), and eleventh (52) years of his reign. One inscription indicates a famine hit the whole world (CIG 2973.5-6). We have records of famine in Judea in AD 40-41 and 46-47.

126. Some believe that Galatians 2 refers to Acts 15, but this is unlikely. See the discussion in Ch. 24.

127. We can also mention Jesus' predictions of the fall of Jerusalem and destruction of the temple (e.g., Mark 13).

128. Polhill, *Acts*, 278, notes that if Herod killed James in a Roman way, which is most likely, he would have had him beheaded with the complicity of the Romans (Herod had no right to inflict capital punishment). If James was killed in a Jewish way, which forbade beheading as a desecration of the body, he would have had the edge of the sword thrust through his body. James may also have been a Roman citizen; hence he was not crucified.

north in AD 37 and the area under his authority was increased until by AD 41, under Claudius, he was the ruler of all of Judea, Samaria, Galilee, the Transjordan, and the Decapolis. Because of Roman political volatility, he needed strong support in Israel, so he did all he could to please the Jews, including supporting the Pharisees. This could explain his treatment of the Christians.[129]

The killing of James meets with widespread acclaim from the Jewish community, indicating a growing level of resentment from Jews to Christians. Consequently, Agrippa also imprisons Peter, no doubt with the intention of also killing him. The response of the *church* is fervent prayer, no doubt in the hope of saving him from the same fate as James (Acts 12:3-5). Luke again emphasizes the power of God in response to prayer (cf. Acts 4:26-5:16). While Peter is asleep, bound between two guards, an angel appears in bright light, releases him, and directs him to get up, get dressed, and follow him (Acts 12:6-9). Believing he was dreaming, Peter follows. He passes through the gates, which open automatically, and finally comes to himself in the street (Acts 12:10). Realizing what has happened, he goes to the home of Mary, the mother of John Mark, where the church has been praying (Acts 12:11-12). The servant Rhoda opens the door to him, thinking the visitor is Peter's angel.[130] Upon realizing it is indeed Peter, he is welcomed in, and he recounts his story (Acts 12:15-17). The guards are interrogated and put to death while Peter goes to Caesarea Maritima, up the coast.[131] There he would have encountered his friends Cornelius and Philip.

---

129. Polhill, *Acts*, 277.

130. N. T. Wright, *The Resurrection of the Son of God: Christian Origins and the Question of God* (London: SPCK, 2003, 690) argues this may indicate a Greek understanding of resurrection, thinking that this is an appearance of Peter's spirit. The presence of Rhoda as a female slave (*paidiskē*) indicates that John Mark's family was wealthy with a home and slaves.

131. That the soldiers were killed on this occasion strongly contrasts with the guard at Jesus' tomb who were not put to death, despite the disappearance of the body (i.e., his resurrection, cf. Matt 27:62-64). The killing of soldiers who escape is commonplace. See the *Cod. justin.* 9.4.4, which notes: "The custody and care of imprisoned persons devolves upon the jailer, who must not think that some abject and vile dependent will be responsible, if a prisoner should, in any way escape, for we desire that he himself shall suffer the same penalty to which the prisoner who escaped is shown to have been liable. When, however, the jailer is necessarily absent from his post, we order that his assistant shall be bound to exercise the same vigilance, and shall be punished with the same severity" ("Enactments of Justinian." *The Code*. Book IX, 4. "Concerning the custody of accused persons" in *The Roman Law Library*).

The first half of Acts finishes with the account of Herod's death when he accepts the crowd's praise of him as divinity and is struck dead by an angel and eaten by worms (Acts 12:20-23). Like Ananias and Sapphira, this is another example of Luke interpreting events as God's action in judgment (Acts 5:1-11; 13:9-11, cf. 1 Cor 11:30). This is followed by the continued growth of the gospel and the return of Saul, Barnabas, and John Mark to Jerusalem (Acts 12:24-25).

CONCLUSION TO ACTS 8–12

There are some key issues in these sections including:

1. The continuation of the redemptive story with the hope of the restoration of Israel and the bringing of gentiles to faith in God.

2. The continued work of the Spirit in spreading the message throughout the world.

3. The importance of signs and wonders and social action alongside evangelism.

4. The importance of pastoral ministry for the strengthening of believers alongside continued evangelistic mission.

5. The importance of cross-cultural mission and God's desire that all cultures and nations be saved.

6. The role of persecution in the spreading of the gospel in the church's initial phases.

7. The role of courageous and obedient key figures set apart by God for mission, e.g., Philip, Paul, Peter, Barnabas, and the unnamed disciples in Antioch.

TO THE END OF THE EARTH (ACTS 13–28)

Paul's missionary journeys will be discussed in some depth in the second volume of this series. Thus, this section will give a cursory overview of this section of Acts. This third part of Acts focuses on the final element of Acts 1:8, "to the end of the earth." The emphasis remains on the Spirit, this time working in Paul in particular. This perhaps indicates that Luke writes to Theophilus with apologetic intent, perhaps explaining the story of Paul to someone interested in him and his Roman imprisonment. This section can be broken down into six parts: (1) Paul's first Antiochian mission (Acts 13:1-14:28); (2) The Jerusalem Council (Acts 15:1-35); (3) Paul's second Antiochian mission (Acts 15:36-18:22); (4) Paul's third Antiochian mission (Acts 18:23-20:16); (5) Paul in Jerusalem and Caesarea Maritima (Acts 20:17-26:32); and (6) Paul's journey to Rome (Acts 27:1-28:31).

PAUL'S FIRST ANTIOCHIAN MISSION (ACTS 13:1–14:28)

In Acts 13:1-12, Paul and Barnabas are set apart for the mission to which they are called, indicating God's call upon them to take the gospel west. They take John Mark of Jerusalem with them. They travel west by boat to Cyprus, where they preach the gospel and Paul engages in a spiritual power clash with the Jewish magician, Elymas, who is blinded. The gospel penetrates the highest echelons of power, as the Roman proconsul Sergius Paulus becomes a believer.[132]

They sail from Cyprus to Perga in Pamphylia (modern Perge), and John Mark leaves the mission for Jerusalem, which will later lead to the fragmentation of Paul's team. In Pisidia Antioch, Paul preaches in the synagogue; Luke gives his readers a taste of a typical Pauline synagogue sermon replete with the fulfillment of the Old Testament. After a second Sabbath, some gentiles are converted, the word spreads, and Jews persecute the missionaries, so they move on. From here, Paul moves north to major city centers—Iconium, Lystra, and Derbe of Lycaonia—and then returns to the same cities, to Attalia, and on to Syrian Antioch. The major highlights of this period are continued resistance from Jews, a dramatic healing in Lystra after which Paul and Barnabas are labeled gods and they preach, Paul's stoning in Lystra, the appointing of elders in each church, and a joyful report of God's opening of "a door of faith to the gentiles."

THE JERUSALEM COUNCIL (ACTS 15:1–35)

The Jerusalem Council is a pivotal moment in the early church's history, the first great council to resolve important theological questions. The event is

---

132. On proconsuls, see Chapter 2.

catalyzed by Jewish Christ-followers who believe that a new gentile believer must come under Jewish law to be saved and incorporated into God's people. Most especially, they must be circumcised and yield to the other boundary markers. This clashes with Paul and Barnabas' gospel of grace and faith. The issue is resolved in a gathering of Christian leaders in Jerusalem. At the meeting, Paul and Barnabas present their case, while converted Pharisees clash with them arguing the converse. The key leaders of the Jerusalem church, Peter and James, side with Paul and Barnabas based on the spontaneous giving of the Spirit to the uncircumcised family of Cornelius and Amos 9:11-12. It is agreed that circumcision will no longer be a requirement of Christian conversion, with gentiles encouraged to desist from eating idolatrous food, sexual immorality, strangled animals, and blood—concessions to the Jews for the sake of unity and ongoing mission. A letter is sent to the churches to be carried by two prophetic leaders, Silas and Judas, who duly deliver the letter to Antioch with Paul, Barnabas, and John Mark. This decision marks the Christian faith's transition from the theological and ethnic limitations of Judaism—anyone can be a Christian, Jew or gentile. There is no racial preference in God's people. As Paul declares in Galatians 3:27-28: "For as many of you as were baptized into Christ have put on Christ. There is neither Jew nor Greek, there is neither slave nor free, there is no male and female, for you are all one in Christ Jesus."

PAUL'S SECOND ANTIOCHIAN MISSION (ACTS 15:36–18:22)

Paul and Barnabas decide to travel back through the cities they evangelized on their first Antiochian mission. Their purpose is pastoral: to strengthen them. This no doubt means taking the letter from the Council to back up what Paul had already said to these churches concerning the Judaizers in Galatians, his first letter (Acts 16:4).[133]

Before they set out, however, Paul and Barnabas cannot agree on taking John Mark after he had deserted them in Perga to return to Jerusalem (Acts 13:13). As such, they separate, another indication that the early mission involved some clashes. Barnabas and Mark travel to Cyprus, while Paul

---

133. This assumes Galatians 2:1-10 aligns with Acts 11:26-30 rather than Acts 15 and means Galatians was written to the churches evangelized on Paul's first Antiochian mission during the years between his first mission and the Jerusalem Council (AD 48), that is, AD 46-47.

takes Silas into Syria and Cilicia. Paul returns to Lycaonia to Derbe and Lystra and takes Timothy with him after having him circumcised because his mother was a Jew. They take the decision of the Jerusalem Council, to once and for all convince the Galatians not to yield to the Judaizers.

Paul then decides to head west to fresh fields. The Spirit leads him past Asia and Bithynia (Asia Minor) and on to Macedonia. At this time, Luke joins the team (a "we passage"). They first evangelize Philippi, a key Roman colony. The mission involves the conversions of Lydia and a Roman jailer, the deliverance of a fortune-telling demon from a slave girl, Paul and Silas' severe flogging, a miraculous escape from prison, and being asked to leave the city.

From there, they go to the Macedonian capital, Thessalonica. Paul engages in debate in the synagogue, and though he plants a church, he has to move on due to resistance from both Jews and gentiles: he is accused of challenging the rule of Caesar.

In nearby Berea, Paul is initially well-received by the Jews, only for the mission to be disrupted by Thessalonian Jews who force Paul to leave. Silas, Timothy, and Luke remain behind. It is possible during this time Luke traveled to Rome with the Jerusalem Council letter, something that may have had a big impact on Roman Christianity.

Paul travels to the great Greek capital, Athens, where he engages in debate with Greek philosophers at the Stoa and is invited to speak to the famous philosophical guild, the Areopagus. Luke records a summary of his sermon, which provides an interesting contrast with the synagogue sermon in Acts 13, focusing on theological ideas common to Jews and Greeks, and citing Greek sources. The impact is limited, with a few converts, and general resistance.

From Athens, Paul continues to Corinth, joining a Jewish missionary couple recently expelled from Rome by Claudius' expulsion edict (AD 49). Together they make tents and engage in evangelism. He is rejoined by Timothy and Silas. After making a few Jewish converts and then being rejected by the Jews, he establishes a base at the home of Titius Justus and enjoys substantial missionary success, staying there for eighteen months. He is then attacked and taken before the proconsul, Gallio, whose role and date of proconsulship is mentioned in inscriptions, confirming the accuracy of Luke's account (AD 51–52). Gallio sees no threat in Paul and releases him. Some days later, Paul travels to Ephesus, where he left Priscilla and Aquila, and on to Caesarea Maritima and to Syrian Antioch. Now, the gospel has extended west through Galatia across the Aegean through Macedonia and Achaia.

PAUL'S THIRD ANTIOCHIAN MISSION (ACTS 18:23—20:16)

Paul remains in Antioch for a while and then resolves to travel back through the churches planted, strengthening them. Although not mentioned by Luke, his letters indicate that Paul also purposed to gather funds for the Jerusalem church from these churches, the so-called Jerusalem Collection, referenced in 1 Corinthians 16, 2 Corinthians 8-9, and Romans 16. Luke then introduces Apollos, a firebrand preacher from Egypt, whom Priscilla and Aquila instructed, and who preached both in Ephesus and Corinth. First Corinthians indicates Apollos had a profound effect in Corinth, leading many to Christ, but inadvertently creating division among the Corinthians (1 Corinthians deals with this issue). After passing through Galatia, Paul establishes a base for three years in Ephesus. In Ephesus, Paul finds some Jewish followers of John the Baptist who were baptized in water and Spirit. Luke gives an account of the amazing Ephesus mission in which, from daily lectures in a lecture hall, the Asia Minor region was evangelized over two years. This included Colossae (Col 1:6) and the seven churches of Revelation (Rev 2-3). Other features include the demonic beating of Jewish exorcists and the burning of a significant number of magic scrolls. The success of the mission also leads to a riot among the silversmiths who were losing business, showing how Christianity could disrupt the social and economic harmony, leading to persecution. With his Jerusalem collection team, some of which are named in Acts 20:4, Paul then travels from Ephesus to Macedonia, on to Corinth in Achaia, back to Macedonia (where Luke rejoins Paul, as another "we passage" begins), and on to Troas. This may be cross-referenced with 2 Corinthians and the account of the Jerusalem collection, including the radical generosity of the Philippians and Paul's urging to the Corinthians to give lavishly. Titus is a significant player, although Luke does not mention him.

Paul then travels back to Jerusalem via Troas (where he raises Eutychus from the dead after he falls out of a window and dies during a midnight sermon), Assos, Mitylene, Samos, and Miletus (where Paul gives a long, passionate address to the Ephesian elders), Cos, Rhodes, Patara, Tyre, Ptolemais, and Caesarea Maritima (where he stays with Philip and is warned of impending suffering by Agabus of Acts 11 fame), and finally, to Jerusalem.

PAUL IN JERUSALEM AND CAESAREA MARITIMA (ACTS 20:17—26:32)

There is no mention of the Jerusalem collection, but Paul is welcomed into Jerusalem by James and the other believers. Paul takes up James' suggestion of taking a vow of purity and entering the temple. However, Paul is recognized and accused of bringing a gentile into the temple leading to a mob seeking his death. After fending off the accusation that he is a rebel and assassin (Sicarii), Paul convinces the Roman tribune to allow him to address the furious crowd. He gives his testimony, which goes well until he mentions his call to go to the gentiles; this provokes the crowd to seek his death. He is led away and avoids being flogged because of his Roman citizenship. He then appears before the Sanhedrin, and after provoking a dispute about resurrection between the Pharisees and Sadducees, the Pharisees support him, and he is taken to the barracks. God then appears to him, telling him he will testify about him in Rome.

Some Jews then plot to kill him, and this is discovered by his sister, who tells the Romans. Paul is then transported to Caesarea Maritima under armed guard. He is imprisoned in Caesarea Maritima for two years. He appears twice before governors—first Felix, and then Festus. During his second appearance, as was his right as a Roman citizen, he appeals to Caesar; this means he would travel to Rome to appear before Nero's judiciary. He also appears before Agrippa II, the son of Agrippa I who killed James, the brother of John (Acts 12:1). This section features two of Paul's sermons, both retelling his conversion story. It explains the circumstances of his going to Rome. It speaks of the sovereignty of God over his situation.

PAUL GOES TO ROME (ACTS 27:1—28:31)

Acts 27:1-28:16 is Luke's account of Paul's trip to Rome. It features another centurion, Julius, who seems to have a great relationship with Paul. Paul travels with others, including Aristarchus of Thessalonica and Luke (another "we passage"). The trip takes them from Caesarea to Sidon, past

Cyprus, Cilicia, and Pamphylia, to Myra in Lycia, past Cnidus and Crete, to Fair Havens near Lasea. Despite Paul's warnings of the dangers of the season, rather than waiting until winter was past, they travel on to reach Phoenix in Crete to winter there. A storm comes up that nearly kills them all. Luke records Paul encouraging all on board after God told him no one would die. The ship is beached on Malta, where Paul is bitten by a snake but survives unscathed, leading to his being deified. Paul prays for Publius, the leading man of the island, and he is healed, leading to others coming for healing. They then travel to Rome via Syracuse, Rhegium, the port of Puteoli, and to Rome. There he is met by Christians. Paul is kept under house arrest. He meets with the local Jewish leaders to whom he preached, and while some believe, others reject the message, leading Paul to castigate them through the words of Isaiah 6:9–10. Luke's narrative ends with Paul in Roman prison, welcoming visitors, and "proclaiming the kingdom of God and teaching about the Lord Jesus Christ with all boldness and without hindrance" (Acts 28:31). Through this final section of Acts, the sovereignty of God and the missional zeal of Paul are the focus. Paul engages in mission as he travels to face the emperor.

While it is disputed, it is likely that this marks the time of the writing of Luke-Acts. During this imprisonment, tradition holds that Paul wrote Ephesians, Colossians, and Philippians. He either died in this imprisonment or left on one final journey, which may have included Spain and a range of other places in Asia and Greece. Tradition holds that he was then taken again to Rome, where he wrote Titus and 1 and 2 Timothy, after which he was beheaded by Nero. Other events in the 60s AD of significance include the killing of James in AD 62, the fire of Rome and the persecution of Christians by Nero, and the Judean rebellion leading to Rome's demolition of the temple. Rome then becomes the center of Christianity for many centuries. With Paul in Rome, Roman Christianity is set on a sure footing, and from Rome, the gospel can continue to be preached to the end of the earth.

QUESTIONS TO CONSIDER

- What is the purpose of Acts?

- Do you think Acts can be trusted as a historical record of the early church?

- Of the features of the Jerusalem church, what is lacking most in the contemporary church?

- Why do you think the emphasis on social justice is strangely absent from Acts 13–28?

- What, for you, is the main value of Acts?

THE KINGDOM OF GOD

CHAPTER 11

The most important theme found in the Synoptic Gospels is the kingdom of God. Each of the three writers stresses the kingdom above all else; it is the idea upon which the Gospels are formed. Closely related is that Jesus is God's appointed and anointed King, establishing God's reign. His ministry of miracles, teaching, feeding, and restoring is the manifestation of the inbreaking of this reign. His rejection, suffering, death, and subsequent resurrection are the means by which the power of the kingdom is liberated, as it brings God's redemption and opens the way for the Spirit to fill believing humanity so that through believers Christ can extend his kingdom by the Spirit.

TERMINOLOGY

There are three main phrases used of the kingdom in the New Testament:[1] (1) "the kingdom of God" (*hē basileia tou theou*),[2] (2) "the kingdom of heaven" (*hē basileia tōn ouranōn*),[3] and (3) "the kingdom" (*hē basileia*).[4] The primary

---

1. Also, in Paul: "the kingdom of Christ and God" (Eph 5:5); "the kingdom of his beloved Son" (Col 1:13).
2. "Kingdom of God" is used sixty-seven times—Matthew five times; Mark fourteen times; Luke thirty-two times and Acts six times (thirty-eight times overall in Luke's writings); John twice; and Paul's letters eight times. Revelation has "the kingdom of our Lord" (Rev 11:15) and "the kingdom of our God" (Rev. 12:10), once each. It is not found in the other letters.
3. "Kingdom of heaven" is found only in Matthew, thirty-two times.
4. "The kingdom": Matthew eight times; Luke twice, Acts twice (four times overall in Luke's writings); Paul's letter's once; James once; Revelation once. Mark, most of Paul's letters, Hebrews, Jude, and John's writings—other than Revelation—do not use it.

meaning of the Hebrew măl·kût, măm·lā·kā(h), melû·kā(h), and the Aramaic măl·kû, and the Greek *basileia* is "sovereignty" or "royal rule." Most Jews avoided the term "God" (Yahweh) out of reverence, and replaced "God" with "heaven" (*shamayim*). This likely influenced Matthew's preference for "kingdom of heaven"; however, "kingdom of God" and "kingdom of heaven" are interchangeable.

OLD TESTAMENT ANTECEDENTS

The Gospels introduce the kingdom without explanation, suggesting that the kingdom of God was a well-known concept.[5] Yet, surprisingly, the actual phrase "kingdom of God" is absent from the Hebrew Old Testament.[6] Yet, on closer examination, the idea of God's kingdom saturates the Scriptures and Jewish thought.

First, a range of formulations invokes the notion of the kingdom of God. "The kingdom of the LORD" is used in 1 Chronicles 28:5 and 2 Chronicles 13:8, of Israel. However, in Psalm 103:19, "his kingdom" is used of God's reign in heaven. Similarly, in Daniel 6:26, "his kingdom" is used of God's indestructible and eternal reign. "His kingdom," with God in view, also features in the Pseudepigrapha (e.g., Odes Sol. 18.3). In the Assumption of Moses 10.1, "his kingdom will appear throughout his whole creation. Then the devil will have his end." "The kingdom" is used of God in 2 Bar. 73 and 3 Bar 11.2. Similarly, in 1 Chronicles 29:11: "Yours is the kingdom, O LORD, and you are exalted as head above all."

Second, the actual phrase "kingdom of God" is found once in the Greek Old Testament, in Wisdom 10:10, where Wisdom shows the one who runs from his brother's wrath, "the kingdom of God," and knowledge of holy things. Significantly, "the kingdom of our God" is used in the highly messianic Pss. Sol. 17.4, a psalm with military messianic expectations.[7] The Matthean phrase "kingdom of heaven" is found once in the Pseudepigrapha (3 Bar 11:2). In Isaiah 37:16, Hezekiah prays to God "enthroned above the cherubim, you are the God, you alone, of all the kingdoms of the earth."

---

5. Christopher D. Marshall, *Kingdom Come: The Kingdom of God in the Teaching of Jesus* (Auckland: Impetus, 1993), 22.

6. C. D. Marshall, *Kingdom Come*, 22 esp. n. 1.

7. See also its use in the highly Christianized Hist. Rech. 12.9c; see also Odes Sol. 23.12.

This invokes the idea of the ark of the covenant, where God inhabits and rules. The Qumran writings also regularly refer to God's kingdom.[8]

Third, the whole context of the Scriptures and their history is saturated with the notion of human kingdoms, reign, and kingship. This is seen in the Old Testament (e.g., Gen 10:10; Num 32:33; Deut 3:4; Josh 13:12; 1 Sam 10:18; 1 Kgs 4:24; Esther 1:2)[9] and in other Jewish literature where kingship is everywhere.[10] Israel's whole history was enmeshed in a world of kings and kingdoms from the time of Abraham (e.g., Gen 14:1–3), so much so that Israel cried out for a king "to judge us like all the nations" (1 Sam 8:5). These include the Egyptians (Pharaohs), Assyrians, Babylonians, Persians and Medes, Macedonians and Greeks (esp. Alexander), and the Romans (Caesar and the Roman Empire). In the ancient world, a king had *all* authority over his kingdom and subjects, so kingship could be a positive or a negative concept, depending on the relationship between the king and his kingdom. It is fair to say that kingship was the dominant political model in the world of the Bible.

Fourth, the concept of God as king is seen in a variety of other ways:

1. **God is presented as king:** For example, in Psalm 10:16 the psalmist declares, "The LORD is king forever and ever; the nations perish from his land" (cf. Job 41:34). Similarly, in Psalm 24:7 David sings: "Lift up your heads, you gates; be lifted up, you ancient doors, that the King of glory may come in" (NIV).[11]

2. **God is ascribed a royal throne:** For example, Psalm 45:6 says: "Your throne, O God, will last forever and ever; a scepter of justice will be the scepter of your kingdom" (NIV).[12]

---

8. For example, 1QSb 3.5; 4Q200 Frag. 6:5; 4Q400 Frag.1 ii.1–2. See also rabbinic writings, *m. Ber.* 2.2, 5; *y. Ber.* 4a; 7b.

9. In terms of kings: X the king of Y, e.g., Og the King of Bashan. In terms of kingdom: the kingdom of Y, e.g., the kingdom of Persia. There are 134 references to kings in Esther alone (ESV).

10. The Greek *basileus* (king) is found 3,172 times in the LXX, 647 times in the Pseudepigrapha, 2,235 times in Josephus, and 337 times in Philo.

11. See also Deut 9:26 [LXX]; 1 Sam 12:12; Pss 5:2; 29:10; 44:4; 47:2–9; 68:24; 74:12; 84:3; 95:3; 98:6; 145:1; 149:2; Isa 6:5; 8:21; 33:22; 41:21; 43:15; 44:6; Jer 8:19; 10:7, 10; Zeph 3:15; Zech 14:9, 16–17; Mal 1:14.

12. See also Ps 9:4; 47:8; Isa 6:1; 66:1; Ezek 1:26; Sir 1:8.

3. ***His reign is affirmed:*** Occasionally, texts affirm his reign. For example, Psalm 10:16: "The Lord is king forever and ever; the nations perish from his land" (cf. Ps 146:10; Isa 24:23; Wis 3:8).

Fifth, the concept has roots in the covenantal relationship between God and Israel. The covenant forged at Sinai is in the form of a Suzerain-Vassal treaty in which God, the king over all the earth, having delivered Israel from the oppression of the king of Egypt (Pharaoh), agrees to reign over the people of Israel if they agree to uphold the terms of the covenant (see Exod 20).[13] While God dwells in the heavens, the temple was God's palace on earth and his throne the ark of the covenant. Hence, God's kingship and reign are basic to Israel's cosmology.

Sixth, a closer look at Israel's history reveals certain points that are critical to understanding the notion of the kingdom of God in Jesus' ministry. God's kingship is indicated in the initial settlement of the land where Israel functioned without a king and was led by judges. Israel's desire for a king (1 Sam 8:4-5) was in effect a rejection of Yahweh's rule (1 Sam 8:6-8). Over time, the king came to be understood as God's representative and under God's rule. Because of this, the role of the prophets within the royal court to hold the king to account before the true King—God—may be realized afresh (e.g., Nathan, Gad, Elijah).

Finally, another significant point in the Old Testament understanding of kingship was the promise to David of an eternal kingdom in 2 Samuel 7:12-16. God promises to establish a kingdom through David's son, and he will build God's house. He will be to him as a father to a son. David's house and his kingdom will endure forever.

Because this promise was followed by the rejection of Solomon (1 Kgs 11:1-13) and the division of the kingdom (1 Kgs 12), hope began to grow for a future messianic king who would rule over David's kingdom in righteousness and prosperity. This built on earlier glimpses, particularly Genesis 3:15, "you will strike his heel" (NIV) and Genesis 49:10, "the scepter will not depart

---

13. Note also Exodus 19:6: "You will be for me a kingdom of priests and a holy nation" (NIV). See Suzerain-Vassal treaties, Michael L. Barré, "Treaties in the ANE," in *ABD* 6:653-56 esp. pages 654-55.

from Judah, nor the ruler's staff from between his feet, until he to whom it belongs shall come and the obedience of the nations shall be his" (NIV).

This hope grew as Israel fell further into idolatry and sin (Isa 9:7; 16:5; Jer 23:5-6; 33:15; Ezek 34:23-24; 37:24; Amos 9:11). This is strongest in Daniel—especially Daniel 7—and the hope of one like a son of man, who would have complete dominion. However, the conception of the kingdom of God by Daniel is transformed under the impact of the new situation. The divine sovereignty is set vis-à-vis human kingdoms.

These references can be summarized into two Old Testament strands.

GOD AS REIGNING KING

Whether people, the animal world, and all creation realize it, God presently reigns—not only over Israel, but over all humanity and the entire created order. This is the realized notion of the kingdom being here now. It is illustrated in texts that speak of God as present King over Israel and all humanity (e.g., Isa 33:22).[14]

GOD AS COMING KING

However, while God reigns as King now, much of his creation and sinful humanity is not yielded to his reign. Thus, there is the hope of God's future coming to restore complete submission to his kingship, either directly, through a Davidic messiah, or another figure (prophet, Son of Man, etc.). This is seen in texts that look to God coming to establish his kingdom in a yet unfulfilled way (e.g., Isa 40:9-11).[15]

There is a tension between these two ideas: God *is* King and reigns over all. Yet there is rebellion and resistance to this reign across humanity and creation. The mission of the kingdom is to see all of creation recognize God's kingship and bow willingly in volition, or ultimately face destruction as God purges his creation of corruption. The mission of the "coming King" is to see the "reigning King" reign fully as he should.

---

14. C. D. Marshall, *Kingdom Come*, 23-25.
15. C. D. Marshall, *Kingdom Come*, 25-29.

ESSENTIAL FEATURES

God's kingdom has three other essential features.

1. **The universality of God's reign:** God reigns over all the earth and all creation.[16]

2. **The righteousness of the kingdom:** God will make all things right, removing injustice and unrighteousness. This is reflected in the dream of a new covenant whereby humanity will be righteous, and injustice and oppression are utterly removed (Jer 31:31-33).

3. **The peace of the kingdom:** This is the hope for peace (*shalom*) in the Old Testament being fulfilled in the coming kingdom (Isa 11:6-9).[17]

THE KINGDOM OF GOD IN JUDAISM

The notion of the reign of God developed in Judaism in many ways.[18] First, it was believed that God is the judge. At the climax of this age, God will appear in judgment to punish the wicked (Israel's enemies) and reward the just (Israel). For example, Psalm 7:11 says God is a righteous judge (cf. Ps 50:6; Eccl 3:17). Second, many Jews expected God to exercise his reign through his chosen messianic king, God's "anointed," his "Christ," who will be a descendant of David and who will bring in a time of bliss for Israel (e.g., Ps 18:50; 45:7; Isa 61:1; Dan 9:25-26; Hab 3:13; Pss. Sol. 17.36; Josephus, *Ant.* 18.63). Third, God would act to save his people (Isa 25:9; 49:6; 52:10; Jer 3.23; Pss. Sol. 12.7). Finally, a critical aspect of this salvation was the belief that the oppression of Israel by the nations would come to an end (3 Macc 5:13; 6:13, 15; Pss. Sol. 17.22). While the term "kingdom of God" was not common, the *idea* was common, usually related to the kingdom of the

---

16. G. R. Beasley-Murray, *Jesus and the Kingdom of God* (Grand Rapids: Eerdmans, 1986), 20. See also C. D. Marshall, *Kingdom Come*, 26.

17. On *shalom* as "wholeness," rather than merely the absence of war, see C. D. Marshall, *Kingdom Come*, 27.

18. For a breakdown of the kingdom of God in the various streams of Judaism, see C. D. Marshall, *Kingdom Come*, 30-38.

messiah or descriptions of the messianic age. These concepts were blended together in different ways.

There were two general poles of thought concerning the way this kingdom would be exercised. Common was the view of a Davidic political kingdom, God's reign exercised in the world centered on Jerusalem, Zion, the temple, torah, and the elect people of God—the Jewish people. Often, this was to be followed by judgment and then a new reign involving a new world and *shalom*.

The other trend was a transcendent apocalyptic kingdom, which involves a heavenly everlasting kingdom encompassing the whole cosmos brought about by God's direct intervention. This would be established and ruled by a heavenly pre-existent figure called the Son of Man (see Daniel; 1 Enoch 37-71; 2 Ezra). The figure will take part in the judgment, and the kingdom that follows will be the eternal kingdom of God.

However, across Judaism, there were varying details. Some of these include:

1. **Tribulation:** A number of works speak of a time of tribulation and upheaval in heaven and earth preceding the messiah.[19] These are called the birth pangs of the messiah in rabbinic literature.[20]

2. **The Coming of Elijah:** Sometimes, the messiah's appearance is preceded by the coming of Elijah[21] or a prophet like Moses.[22] Alternatively, the prophet may be the messiah himself. Often, he is a fully human Davidic messiah[23] who conquers the wicked.[24]

---

19. See *Sib. Or.* 3:796-808; 2 *Bar.* 70:2-8; 4 *Ezra* 6:24; 9:1-12; 13:29-31; 1QM 12:9; 19:1-2; see also Matt 24:7-12 par.
20. See *b. Sanh.* 98b; Str-B I.950.
21. See Mal 3:1-2, 4:5; Sir 48:10-11; see also Matt 17:10 par; Justin, *Dial.* 8.
22. See Deut 18:15; 1QS 9:11; 4QTestim 5-8; John 1:21.
23. See Pss. Sol. 17:5, 23; *Sib. Or.* 3:49.
24. See *Sib. Or.* 3:652-56; Pss. Sol. 17:23-32.

3. **A Supernatural Being:** Sometimes the expected figure is a pre-existent, supernatural being who has power over all God's enemies and vindicates the righteous.[25]

4. **A Messianic Kingdom:** The coming of the figure, whether a messiah, Son of Man, or another epithet, involves establishing the messianic kingdom, which includes a wide range of notions including:

    a. The gathering of the scattered Israelites from the exile.[26]

    b. The restoration of Jerusalem.[27]

    c. The reign of God over his people.[28]

    d. The kingdom centered in Jerusalem, "the jewel of the world" (Sib. Or. 3:423).

Additional features of a messianic kingdom are mentioned in other writings. For example, Jubilees (mid-second century BC), features the first reference to a temporary messianic kingdom of 1,000 years brought about by human development in which evil is restrained (Jub. 1:29; 23:26-30; cf. Rev 20:1-6). In the Testament of Moses (first century AD), the kingdom is earthly and covers all creation, lacks a Messiah (T. Mos. 10:1), is brought about by repentance (T. Mos. 1:18; 9:6-7), and seeks glory for Israel and punishment for the gentiles (T. Mos. 10:7-10). In the *Second Apocalypse of Baruch* (pre-70 AD), there is a revelation of the Messiah bringing peace and prosperity (2 Bar. 27-30). The Messiah annihilates his enemy, the fourth empire (cf. Dan 7; see also 2 Bar. 36-40), and reigns until corruption is ended (2 Bar. 53-74). 1 *Enoch* and 4 *Ezra* are influenced by Daniel as they associate the kingdom with a "son of man." The Messiah is the judge and universal

---

25. See 1 En 46:1-6; 48:2-6; 62:5-7; 4 Ezra 12:32; see also Dan 7:13-14. In 1 En 90:16-38 he appears *after judgment*. In most others, he conquers and judges his enemies (Sib. Or. 3:652-6; Pss. Sol. 17:14-41; 1 En 46:4-6; 62:3-12; 69:27-9; 4 Ezra 13:32-8; cf. Matt 25:31-46). Some have a final attack by the ungodly on the Messiah to stop the messianic kingdom (Sib. Or. 3:663-68; 1 En 90:16; 1QM 15-19; 4 Ezra 13:33-34, cf. Ps 2:1-3). Sometimes the powers are destroyed by God (T. Mos. 10:2-7; 1 Enoch 90:18-19), or the Messiah (4 Ezra 12:32-33; 13:27-28, 37-39; 2 Bar. 39:7-40:2). Sometimes the messiah is presented as a warrior (Tg. Isa. 10:27; Gen 49:10), others in judicial terms (1 En 45:3; 46:4-6; 52:4-9; 55:4; 61:8-10, cf. Matt 25:31-46).

26. See Bar 4:36-37; 5:5-9; Philo, *Praem.* 28; 4 Ezra 13:39-47.

27. See Pss. Sol. 17:25, 33; 1 En 53:6; 90:28-29; 4 Ezra 7:26.

28. See *Sib. Or.* 3:704-6, 756-59; Pss. Sol. 17:1-4; 1QM 19:1.

ruler.[29] 4 *Ezra* sees the Messiah as transcendent and earthly and who dies after reigning for 400 years (or 1,000/30 years; see also 4 *Ezra* 7:28-29). At Qumran *malkuth* (sovereignty) occurs twelve times, but usually of Israel and only once of God's kingdom (1QM 12:7). The Essenes believed they were the true people of God fighting a battle against God's enemies.

THE KINGDOM IN THE DIFFERENT STRANDS OF JUDAISM

Clearly, different strands of Judaism had different views of the kingdom of God.[30] These views can be broken down further:

1. **Jewish apocalypticism:** In broad terms, apocalyptic literature conceived of a cosmological dualism that sees the world as a battleground between good and evil, God and Satan. This age is characterized by suffering and struggle, and ultimately God will intervene and overthrow evil and establish his reign. The book of Revelation falls into this category as a Christian apocalypse.

2. **Qumran/Essenes:** At Qumran, the separatist group saw themselves as participating in the eschatological era. They also looked to a future in which God would intervene and destroy the gentiles and give triumph to the people of light.

3. **Pharisaic Judaism:** The Pharisees focused on the law through which God was present in the world. They also looked to a future consummation of God's reign. This would be achieved by God alone, but may involve messianic agency.

4. **Targums:** These Aramaic paraphrases of Scripture understood the kingdom as God revealing himself dynamically and personally in the present and future. There is great interest in Mount Zion and the Davidic Messiah in the Targums.

---

29. See 1 *En* 46:4-6; 62:3-12; 63:4; 69:27-29); the messiah ushers in the messianic age (1 *En* 71:15-17, cf. 62:12-16).

30. See C. D. Marshall, *Kingdom Come*, 30-39.

5. **Zealots:** The Zealots believed that the kingdom could be ushered in through violence against the gentile invaders of Israel. This conflict, it was hoped, would ignite a messianic war.

6. **Sadducees:** The Sadducees were more cooperative with the occupying Romans and concerned to maintain the status quo. They believed the age of God's promise had begun with the Maccabees and was sustained under their own leadership. They rejected a future intervention of a Messiah, seeing the kingdom as a process, not a future event.

JESUS AND THE KINGDOM OF GOD

The human concept of kingship in Jesus' parables, such as the wedding banquet (Matt 22:1-14), is evident.[31] It is also seen in various other instances (Matt 4:8; 24:7; Mark 6:23; 13:8; Luke 4:5; 21:10). The notion of a supreme king was familiar to Jesus' listeners, as the Roman world had Caesar and Israel was subject to him. However, if one dynamic defined the ideal of kingship to Jews at the time, it was an idealization of the Davidic reign.

CONTINUITY AND DISCONTINUITY

Jesus' view is continuous with many threads of Judaism, and the Old Testament, but is distinct in a few ways:

1. **From Israel to the world:** The kingdom is a dynamic and not a geographic concept; it stretches across and within the whole world and is not geographically localized in Israel.[32] Rather, it is found in any locale where Christ is honored as King, and his Spirit fills the heart. It is exercised through God's people in every part of society where these people serve their King.

---

[31]. See also the sheep and goats (Matt 25:31-46); Luke 14:31; 19:12-27; the divided kingdom (Matt 12:28-29).

[32]. See also C. D. Marshall, *Kingdom Come*, 23, 43. A scholar associated with this is Dalman (1898), who argued for the dynamic character of the kingdom of God in Judaism and the New Testament, i.e., that the kingdom has no territorial or geographical reference but is dynamic in the sense that it is the kingly rule of God.

2. **Jesus Christ at the center:** It is a concept intimately linked to a person, Jesus the Christ, Son of God, Son of Man, and Lord.

3. **Entrance not through becoming Jewish but through faith in Jesus:** Entrance into the kingdom is through relationship with Jesus (repent, follow, believe, obey) rather than being based on the covenant, law, or Jewishness. Hence, new believers are under no obligation to yield to torah—especially its boundary markers, circumcision, Sabbath and feasts, food laws, and purity protocols.

4. **A present and future kingdom:** Whereas for Israel that viewed the kingdom as a purely future hope, the kingdom is here in the present in Christ and by God's Spirit, and will be consummated in the future at the return of Christ. In other words, it is imminent and not merely a future hope. The kingdom has come in the middle of history, not at the end of history as expected (further below).

5. **A subversive kingdom:** The kingdom appeared in a quiet, gentle manner, not through dramatic upheaval involving God's glorious intervention to subdue the world to his rule. It is extended unobtrusively, permeating the world quietly through humble service, proclamation, and works of justice.

DEFINITIONS OF THE KINGDOM

The kingdom of God can be defined as the "governing activity of God as ruler; the time and sphere in which God's kingly power [sic] will hold sway."[33] This definition suggests that the kingdom is primarily what God does, and secondarily, the sphere in which God's reign is experienced and accepted.

A. M. Hunter describes the kingdom as "a power breaking into this world from the beyond, through the direct action of the living God. It is God invading history for us men [and women] and for our salvation."[34]

---

33. C. D. Marshall, *Kingdom Come*, 44.
34. A. M. Hunter, *Christ and the Kingdom* (Edinburgh: Saint Andrew Press, 1980), 2.

C. H. Dodd, based on its Old Testament and Judaistic background, suggests that the kingdom of God "is the idea of God, and the term 'kingdom' indicates that specific aspect, attribute or activity of God, in which He is revealed as King or Sovereign Lord of His people, or of the universe he created."[35]

G. E. Ladd describes the kingdom as God's "kingship, His rule, His authority."[36]

While in one sense the kingdom of God in terms of God as reigning king can be defined "the reign of God over all creation," sadly, God's dominion has been resisted, and his world and people have been corrupted (or corrupted themselves). Thus, the world and its people need saving and transforming in accordance with God's original intent in creating humanity and placing them in the world to have dominion over it on his behalf. Thus, the kingdom spoken of by Christ carries the sense of God as coming King. In this sense, the kingdom is:

> "...the intervention of the world's ultimate Ruler and God into his creation, through his Son and King Jesus, to exercise his reign on his behalf and so resolving the problem of evil, by defeating it through his death, resurrection, ascension, and exaltation, and through people entering his kingdom by turning from corruption and believing the good news that God's salvation has come, and becoming agents in his restoration project as they live out the values of the kingdom, goodness and love, and ultimately the final and complete transformation of the cosmos when the King returns."

The Ruler is God exercising his rule through his Son, Jesus. The sphere is the whole world (not one nation, e.g., Israel). The historical means for this is the work of God's Son, especially his death and resurrection, in which he triumphed over evil and made possible the transformation of people and the world. The present means for this transformation is the sovereign work of the Spirit through all people who have received the Spirit having entered the kingdom by faith, and who work for the transformation of the

---

35. C. H. Dodd, *The Parables of the Kingdom* (Glasgow: Collins, 1961 [orig. 1935]), 29.

36. A. M. Hunter, *The Gospel of the Kingdom: Popular Expositions on the Kingdom of God* (Grand Rapids: Eerdmans, 1959), 21.

world with faith, love, and goodness. The time of completion is when the gospel of this kingdom has penetrated the whole world to God's satisfaction. This will be marked by the return of the King when his people will welcome him into his world. At this point, the transformation of the world will be completed and evil removed from God's creation. In the meantime, God reigns as King and his people live out their kingdom mandate to serve him with total commitment every minute of every day.

THE KINGDOM AS BOTH PRESENT AND FUTURE

Scholars have proposed different ways of understanding when and how the kingdom has or will come. The main Jewish idea was that the kingdom would be established by God through the Messiah *at the climax of human history*. Thus, it was a future hope. Some believe this is the position of the New Testament. However, others believe the kingdom came in Christ fully, or is inaugurated awaiting final consummation.

The kingdom as here, now, and purely personal and ethical

Ritschl (1822–89), a naturalist, rejected anything supernatural or apocalyptic ideas such as eternal life, evil spirits, angels, miracles, and the resurrection. He saw Jesus as an ethical teacher and understood the kingdom in purely ethical terms as a redeemed humanity that acted in accordance with love. His view gave birth to a tradition of Protestant liberalism, which sees the kingdom in primarily ethical, personal, and spiritual terms (i.e., a matter of the heart exercised in care for the poor and needy). Christianity is then based on "the fatherhood of God and the brotherhood of all people" (e.g., von Harnack, 1886). Another extension of this idea is the "social gospel," a view of the kingdom associated with liberalism in the early twentieth century. As there is no future eternal kingdom, its emphasis is purely on present social and political transformation based on love and human relationships. Such Christianity becomes purely social and political, limited to this world, and working for the end of oppression and poverty (e.g., C. Blumhardt, c. 1900; W. Rauschenbusch, 1912).

This led to a reaction that emphasizes the futuristic kingdom view. After this over-emphasis on the futuristic dimension of the kingdom, some scholars returned to over-emphasizing the present dimension of the kingdom of God, notably T. W. Manson (1931) and especially C. H. Dodd. Dodd, in *The Parables of the Kingdom* (1935), argued that the kingdom of God is already a present reality in Jesus' ministry. His healings and exorcisms are proof of this reality. To support this idea, Dodd downplayed Jesus' futuristic statements concerning the kingdom.

Contemporary theologies that resonate with this are some amillennial views, or post-millennialism. These views see the kingdom as present and expanding within this world spiritually, socially, and politically. Some modern examples of this tendency would be N. T. Wright and, to a lesser extent, Chris Marshall, who lacks any real discussion of the future coming of Christ. These scholars do not deny a future element, but primarily interpret the kingdom as present and downplay the future intrusion of God. They speak of a restored and a renewed heaven and earth rather than a new creation of heaven and earth (i.e., continuity, rather than discontinuity).

The kingdom as apocalyptic and future

J. Weiss (1892)[37] countered Ritschl, seeing the kingdom of God primarily as a future eschatological and apocalyptic concept that would see the sudden in-breaking of God to overthrow the forces of Satan and evil (called *Konsequente Eschatologie* = "consistent," "futuristic," or "thoroughgoing eschatology"). Albert Schweitzer, writing from 1901–1910, took Jesus' whole ministry apocalyptically, as did Weiss. Schweitzer believed Jesus expected the end to come through the work of the Twelve (Mark 6:7–13 and parr.), and when it didn't, Jesus gave his life to force God to set up his kingdom. This didn't happen, and Jesus is ultimately a failed Messiah.

Extremes of this point of view are found in classical dispensationalism and pre-millennial views that see the coming of the kingdom primarily occurring at the return of Christ. This view sees no real hope of restoring the world, but awaits an abrupt intrusion of God into human affairs to destroy this present order and replace it with a new order—a new heaven and earth.

The kingdom of God as inaugurated, present and future

Since Dodd, there have been some mediating positions between the futuristic and present interpretations of the kingdom of God. For example, W. G.

---

37. Weiss was Ritschl's son-in-law.

Kümmel, G. Beasley-Murray, R. Schnackenburg, N. Perrin, J. Jeremias, G. Florovsky, and A. M. Hunter speak of an "inaugurated eschatology." G. E. Ladd argues for both a fulfillment of the kingdom of God in history in Jesus' ministry and a full consummation to come. Thus, the kingdom came in Christ and is growing within this world. Yet, it awaits its climax at the return of Christ.

Toward a Synthesis

There are elements of truth in all the above views, although the final view is essentially correct. There is clearly a sense in which the kingdom has come in Christ. There is also a future hope of the full consummation of the kingdom. There is a strong ethical and social dimension to the kingdom. There is a spiritual and apocalyptic aspect to the kingdom, and a present earthly dynamic.

The kingdom has come in Christ. A close analysis gives evidence that Dodd is correct to say that the kingdom of God has come in the person and ministry of Christ and is continued through the work of the Spirit.[38] This is seen in Matthew 12:28, where Jesus says, "But if it is by the Spirit of God that I drive out demons, then the kingdom of God has come [aorist; *ephthasen*] upon you" (NIV).[39] Similarly, in Luke 17:21 (NIV), Jesus states that "the kingdom of God is in your midst" (or within [Greek: *en*], in the sense of "within your purview").[40]

This present dimension is also indicated in Jesus' statement: "From the days of John the Baptist until now [that is the point of Jesus' speaking], the kingdom of heaven has been subjected to violence, and violent people have

---

38. Similarly, C. D. Marshall, *Kingdom Come*, 46-48.

39. This is in the aorist tense implying that it has come in the past and this would be in the person of Christ. C. C. Caragounis, "Kingdom of God," in *DJG* 423 disputes that the aorist implies this. Rather he argues that it is an aorist that points to a future event. While this is possible, it is more likely that the aorist carries the usual past, punctiliar sense. See C. D. Marshall, *Kingdom Come*, 47. See also Hagner, *Matthew 1-13*, 343, who rightly notes: "The verb ἔφθασεν means, 'to come upon' and necessitates the conclusion that the kingdom of God has in some sense actually become present."

40. J. B. Green, *The Gospel of Luke*, NICNT (Grand Rapids: Eerdmans, 1997), 630 n. 54., and C. D. Marshall, *Kingdom Come*, 47, and Caragounis, "Kingdom of God," 423-24, dispute that this should be taken in this way. Rather it points to the kingdom being "within you" in the sense of a personal spiritual presence within the person. This is unlikely, as Jesus is addressing the Pharisees and, as Green points out, is totally without parallel in Luke-Acts.

been raiding it" (Matt 11:12 NIV). This states that the kingdom has been growing from the time of John's ministry, a point strongly reinforced by the mustard seed parable, which speaks of a seed planted and growing (Mark 4:30-32; and parr.). It also points to the pivotal role of John the Baptist in the coming of the kingdom in Christ. The human dynamic in the advancement of the kingdom, seen in the current age of the Spirit and the church, is seen in the second part of this statement: "and violent people have been raiding it." The transition from John the Baptist's ministry to Jesus' ministry points to a new order of things, the end of the pre-kingdom phase ("the law and the prophets"), and the beginning of the kingdom phase of history marked by the arrival of the King (Matt 11:11-14; Luke 16:16).

The eschaton (the end) then is active on earth in the person and ministry of Jesus. The heavens have been ripped open, and God has intervened dramatically, anointing his Son as Servant King with his Spirit, and releasing him to do the work of the King. The miracles of Jesus are "the kingdom of God in action." This does not imply that the kingdom of God is completed; rather, it is inaugurated in the life and ministry of Christ. Beasley-Murray considers the present dimension of the kingdom "unambiguously plain," and believers should not look for ways to reinterpret it.[41] Hence, an inaugurated eschatology is the best way of understanding the kingdom.

The kingdom is extended by Christ through the work of the Spirit in his people. Taking the entire New Testament into account, Christ remains present through the work of his Spirit (Rom 8:9). By his Spirit, God exercises his reign, often through the people of God who believe and are filled and led by the Spirit to live lives through which the kingdom is seen and extended. Thus, the body of Christ continues the earthly ministry of the person of Jesus. This idea is seen in John's theology of the Paraclete (John 14-16), in Luke's theology of the Spirit, in Jesus, through the early church in Acts (see Acts 1:8; 2), and in Paul's theology of spiritual gifts and fruit working in the body of Christ (e.g., Rom 12; 1 Cor 12-14; Eph 4). The appeals for mission, which climax each Gospel and launch Acts, strongly indicate the role of the Spirit in mission (Matt 28:18-20; Mark 16:15-20, cf. 13:10; Luke 24:46-49; John 20:22; Acts 1:8). The parables of growth, such as the

---

41. Beasley-Murray, *Jesus and the Kingdom of God*, 75-76.

mustard seed parable, the parable of the sower, and the parable of the seed, all point to this same thing.

The kingdom will be consummated at some future point at Christ's return. Jesus taught about a point in history where he (the King) will return to enact the ultimate overthrow of evil and the establishment of the kingdom in its fullness (see especially Matt 24-25, cf. Matt 26:29; Mark 14:25; Luke 22:16-18). Some argue that Jesus believed the kingdom of God would come in all its fullness during the disciples' lifetime. This seems to be indicated in Matthew 16:28 (and parr.): "Truly, I say to you, there are some standing here who will not taste death until they see the Son of Man coming in his kingdom" (see also Mark 9:1; Matt 16:28; Luke 9:27). However, while this is a possible interpretation, it most likely points to the transfiguration that follows and, more pointedly, the coming resurrection at which time the disciples will realize who Jesus is—the King! It could also point to Pentecost, when the power of Christ filled believers purified by the redemptive death and resurrection of Christ. This seems particularly likely since death and resurrection are strongly indicated in the context (see Matt 16:23-27; 17:1-13).

One possible dimension of the prayer, "Your kingdom come" (Matt 6:10; Luke 11:2), is that it is a prayer for the full coming of the kingdom. It probably also has realized dimensions, asking God for the extension of the kingdom in the present (i.e., for the kingdom to come and grow). The subjects of the King are to be constantly ready for his return, watching for the signs and seeking to be constantly vigilant (Matt 24-25).

In effect, the establishment of the kingdom is both an event and a process. As an event, it has a beginning point when the King comes. As a process, it begins with the ministry of Christ in the interim period, continues through the ministry of the Spirit in his people and world, and culminates with the return of Christ and the events that surround it. However, the full experience of the kingdom remains a future hope, when the Son will return and make all things right.

D. C. Allison rightly suggests that this correlates with Jewish thought, which could envision the final events—the judgment of evil and the arrival of the kingdom of God—as extending over a time and as a process or series of events that could involve the present. When Jesus announced that the kingdom of God *has* come and *is* coming, this means that the last act has begun but has not yet reached its climax; the last things have come and will come.[42]

THE KINGDOM IN THE REDEMPTIVE STORY

To many thinkers, the kingdom is one of the key ways of understanding the whole Bible story. The creation account is the account of the establishment of a world completely submitted to the reign of God. Humanity is created in God's image, which in the ancient Near East had royal significance, with rulers considered the sons of the gods or their representatives (cf. 2 Sam 7:13-16; Ps 2:7). As such, "Mankind is appointed as God's royal representatives (i.e., sonship) to rule the earth in his place."[43] However, at the fall (Gen 3), due to human disobedience, the authority of God was usurped by Satan and sinful humanity, and evil and sin entered God's creation. Thus, humanity opted for another king and, while God remained King, his realm was violated, and a new ruler emerged.

The story of Israel is the story of God as King calling to himself a people and walking with them. The treaty at Sinai between God and Israel (Exod 20) was a treaty whereby God saved Israel and was established as her King, the law giving the terms of the covenant. The story continues with Israel falling in and out of relationship with God, a cycle of obedience and disobedience. The monarchy was in many ways a rejection of God as King, and it accelerated the idolatry of the nation as it opted for other gods and rejected the one true God. The call of the prophets was a call to honor God as King. They foretold his coming to establish his reign and to restore his world.

The coming of Christ is the decisive moment culminating God's redemption and Israel's story. Jesus came as Messiah (anointed King) to take back God's world from those who usurped his kingdom and so establish the reign of God. Jesus came to call a people to himself, to save them through

---

42. D. C. Allison, *The End of the Ages Has Come: An Early Interpretation of the Passion and Resurrection of Jesus* (Philadelphia: Fortress, 1987), 105-106.

43. K. A. Mathews, *Genesis 1-11:26*, NAC 1A (Nashville: Broadman & Holman Publishers, 1996), 164.

his death and resurrection, and then to work in and through them for the restoration of God's world. This work is being done by the Spirit through God's people amid a world still broken with the enemies of God working against him and his purposes. Ultimately, Christ will return when the work of God through his people is complete to his satisfaction, and all will be well.

The mission of the kingdom then is a great mission of the restoration of the whole cosmos. As N. T. Wright puts it: "The world is God's great project. Just as a bride and bridegroom plan their wedding day, and work to make it perfect, God is working at bringing his world to perfection and doing what is necessary to make it complete."[44] This may be termed the "Great Cosmission"[45] of God in which God is on a mission to transform his cosmos, removing evil's taint, so that goodness, love, and *shalom* are established.[46]

At the heart of this glorious project, or Great Cosmission, is the transformation of the apex of creation—humanity—restored to right relationship with the King so that it will be the *Imago Dei* as God intended it to be. Evangelism, personal conversion, transformation, and discipleship are at the center of the kingdom (the Great Commission). Yet, the mission will always be greater than these central concerns. Those who heed the call of the King and experience conversion and transformation are thrust out into every part of God's world, whether it be politics, justice, education, health, economics, sport, the arts, science, or business, and seek to reflect God's ideals and be transforming agents in these spheres. There is nothing in life that stands outside the notion of the kingdom and the work of the King. Central to this, too, is local gatherings of Christians—the church. Each church in its local community is to embody the faith and ethic of the kingdom and bring Christ to the people among whom they are established.

---

44. See N. T. Wright, *Hebrews for Everyone* (London: SPCK, 2003, 2004), 75.

45. A play on the Great Commission, which I still hold as a critical and central aspect of the Great "Cosmission." The Cosmission is the overall plan for the restoration of the cosmos. Indeed, it began before the fall as God commissioned his image-bearers to use the resources of the world to build human society, but in obedience to God. Now, this Cosmission goes on. We are called to work for God for the redemption of his cosmos.

46. See Mark J. Keown, *What's God Up to On Planet Earth? A No-Strings Attached Explanation of the Christian Message* (Tauranga; Eugene, Or.: Castle; Wipf & Stock, 2010), 66.

THE CENTRALITY OF CHRIST TO THE KINGDOM OF GOD

The idea of the kingdom of God is rooted in the person of Christ. Just as in Daniel, where one like a son of man is the agent of the kingdom (Dan 7), so it is in the Gospels. Indeed, the coming of the Christ is coterminous with the coming of the kingdom.

Regarding the Old Testament and Judaism, Jesus is the long-awaited Messiah, through whom God establishes his kingdom. Jesus is both the proclaimer and the proclaimed of the kingdom.[47] The present and future dimensions of the kingdom also center on the person of Christ—the kingdom inaugurated in his first coming as a child, the kingdom consummated at his second coming as triumphant King. He continues to exercise his reign through the Spirit from heaven, where he is enthroned as Lord at the right hand of the Father.

The utterly surprising and unforeseen dimension is that he first came, not as the all-conquering Davidic cosmic Son of Man, or Messiah, but as a baby, a carpenter, and then as a caring, healing servant to the masses who died the most humiliating of deaths. He renounced all direct political and military action. He is the servant found in the Servant Songs of Isaiah (Isa 42:1-7; 49:1-6; 50:4-9; 52:13–53:12; 61:1-3). While he is the Davidic Messiah, and as John and Paul would say, the divine pre-existent God (John 1:1; Phil 2:6), he came encased in the form of a slave rather than the expected triumphant Davidic figure.

Finally, it is important to recognize the significance of the cross, resurrection, and Pentecost events to the kingdom. In these events, the kingdom is fully revealed in suffering and death and God's power to overcome death, and its extension, was set in place as his power was released to draw all humanity into his realm (Pentecost). This act not only saves the world, but demonstrates the nature of true power. It is found not at the end of a sword, but in love and embrace, seen in the pattern of the cross: selflessness, servanthood, sacrifice, and suffering.

---

47. C. D. Marshall, *Kingdom Come*, 59-61.

THE SUBVERSIVE NATURE OF
THE KINGDOM'S COMING

The kingdom did not arrive as the Jews expected. Most Jews expected the Messiah and the kingdom to arrive at the climax of history, the end of the age. Instead, the kingdom arrived in the middle of time.

It was inaugurated in an unexpected way. The Gospels tell of a King who comes as a baby and not as a triumphant military and political ruler. This is made even more significant in that the womb of a woman in the ancient world was a place of extraordinary danger due to mortality rates.

The King established his rule in an unexpected way. Jesus renounced the use of coercive and political force or violence. Rather, he opted to identify himself with the servant of Isaiah, ministering as a servant and suffering and dying on the cross.

The death and resurrection of the King were unexpected. The vicarious death of the Messiah was not anticipated in Judaism. Christians tend to read passages like Isaiah 53 and find it incomprehensible that Jews did not see this and understand Jesus. However, political and militaristic notions of a victorious messiah, or another figure who ended suffering, dominated Jewish thought. Jesus suffered and died at the hands of the gentiles, those he was expected to destroy. The manner of his death by crucifixion was also a great surprise; Jews considered anyone hung on a tree (or cross) cursed (cf. Deut 21:22; Gal 3:13). While there was a hope of the resurrection of the dead, the idea of a messiah dying and rising was too much for many Jews. Further, the notion of incarnation was problematic as it challenged the exclusivity of Yahweh.

It was also a surprise that the kingdom did not come for Israel alone and that its goal was not the subjugation of the gentiles to Yahweh and Yahwism. The Jews expected the messiah would establish Israel as supreme and Judaism would be the door to relationship with God. However, Jesus came with an adapted agenda. He certainly sought to restore Israel spiritually. But he called *all* people to repentance and faith in him, Jews included. He called for a breaking down of the barriers that divided humanity and a bringing together of the whole world into relationship with God. The basis of this was not the Jewish law, but love and unity around his person.

The mission of the kingdom was also a surprise. It was expected that God would subdue his enemies with power, and they would flock to

Jerusalem to hear the law and bring the wealth of the nations. Anyone who wished to be saved needed to become a Jew. This meant submitting to the boundary markers of Judaism—exclusive belief in Yahweh, circumcision, Sabbath and other calendric rituals, ritual purity, kosher food, and synagogue attendance. They did not expect that Jew and gentile alike would be justified purely by repentance, faith, and following Jesus. Mission was primarily centripetal, or attraction. Now, mission is also centrifugal: believers are radiating out into all society serving, sharing the message, and giving themselves in service for the world.

The kingdom's coming was a reversal of many of Israel's expectations. It is a veiled kingdom, a subversive kingdom, an upside-down kingdom—a kingdom of love, service, suffering, humility, and sacrifice retaining the element of human volition as the kingdom is proclaimed.

THE CENTRALITY OF THE KINGDOM IN JESUS' MINISTRY

In the Synoptics, the kingdom is mentioned 112 times. Clearly, the kingdom is the basis and essential content of Jesus' preaching, teaching, and actions, which are signs of the kingdom. Mark begins his account of Jesus' ministry in 1:14-15: Jesus came into Galilee, proclaiming the gospel of God, and saying, "The time is fulfilled, and *the kingdom of God is at hand*; repent and believe in the gospel" (Mark 1:15). Matthew begins with similar words. In Matthew, both John the Baptist and Jesus' ministries begin with the declaration, "Repent, for *the kingdom of heaven* is at hand" (Matt 3:2; 4:17). When the people of Capernaum want Jesus to remain in the town, Luke narrates that Jesus "said to them, 'I must *preach the good news of the kingdom of God* to the other towns as well; for I was sent for this purpose'" (Luke 4:43). Thus, Jesus was declaring the kingdom of God was near and the King was among them, and hence, the eschatological reign of God had begun. The Synoptics say in several places that Jesus went around preaching the good news of the kingdom (Matt 4:23; 9:35; Mark 1:15; Luke 4:43). His parables were "the message about the kingdom" (Matt 13:19 NIV). Many begin with something like, "The kingdom of God/heaven is like ..." or, "To what can we compare the kingdom?"[48] Jesus used simple similitudes to explain the kingdom.

Similarly, in Luke 9:11, Jesus "spoke ... about the kingdom of God" (NIV). Jesus also exhorted his disciples to go and preach the same message (Luke 8:1; Matt 10:7; Luke 9:2, 60; 10:9-11). Hence, it is apparent that "the kingdom of God is at hand" is a summary of the essential proclamation of Jesus and his disciples.

DIMENSIONS OF THE KINGDOM

SALVATION AND THE KINGDOM

Salvation is making people whole. It has a central spiritual dimension: restoring people to relationship with God. It also has material and social dimensions: people restored to physical wholeness, to relationship with God's people, and to creation.

The concept of salvation is linked directly to the kingdom. The coming of the kingdom is the invasion of God's reign into a world dominated by evil. It began the progressive defeat of evil and the release of humanity from evil's thralldom. At the heart of Jesus' ministry is the salvation of those under the powers of darkness. This is seen first when, after being anointed and empowered as the Christ, and before beginning his ministry proper, Jesus is led by the Spirit into the wilderness where he faces God's ultimate antagonist—Satan. When tempted by Satan, he defeats him three times and then goes out to set people free from Satan's spiritual and material tyranny (see Luke 3-4). Jesus' ministry is summarized in Luke 4:18-20 where he sets people free from spiritual and material poverty, blindness, and oppression; he brings Jubilee to the world (Lev 25). Jesus' exorcisms and healings make people whole and release them from the powers of darkness, sickness, and social marginalization (e.g., Luke 7:50: "your faith has saved you"). The purpose of Jesus' preaching ministry was to achieve the salvation of people (Luke 8:12; 19:10).

Salvation is gained through repentance and faith (Mark 1:15; John 10:9), followed by a commitment to a life of sacrifice for the kingdom and the

---

48. See especially in Matthew: Matt 13:24, 31, 33, 44, 45, 47, 52; 18:23; 20:1; 22:2; 25:1. See also Mark 4:26, 30 and Luke 13:18, 20.

gospel (Matt 16:25; Mark 8:35; Luke 13:23-24). Salvation is a problem for the rich who must renounce their love of money and acquisition of wealth to gain salvation (Matt 19:16-30; Mark 10:17-28; Luke 18:18-29). The needs of the kingdom, the restoration of God's ideal for his world, and the amelioration of human suffering must be put ahead of the accumulation of personal wealth.

Salvation is fully experienced by those who hold firm, persevering to the end despite great suffering for the kingdom (Matt 24:13; Mark 13:13). In John, salvation is integral to the ministry of Christ; the true purpose of his ministry is to achieve the salvation of the lost (John 3:17; 12:47).

THE PRIORITY OF THE KINGDOM

The call to enter the kingdom is not a soft option; it is a call for complete submission. The idea of total submission is inherent in a first-century understanding of "kings and kingdom." A king was all-powerful and demanded full allegiance. Anything less could be severely punished. This summons is explicit in the appeal of Matt 6:33: "But seek *first* his kingdom and his righteousness" (Matt 6:33 NIV; see also Luke 12:31). Jesus places allegiance to the kingdom above meeting personal, material need (food and clothing, Matt 6:19-32). However, for those who do seek his kingdom first, he will provide. The subject of the kingdom is to radically trust the King for his provision in the present and into the future.

Jesus also teaches full engagement in the parables of the treasure and pearl in which people give up all they possess to gain the kingdom (Matt 13:44-46). It is also seen in the choice of some to renounce marriage in service of the kingdom (Matt 19:12). Jesus' teaching on the radical cost of discipleship also points to the priority of the kingdom. In Luke 9, Jesus speaks of following him and being homeless, placing allegiance to the kingdom above family, and refusing to turn back once one has set out in ministry (Luke 9:57-62). One who seeks to be a disciple must leave behind false excuses—even family allegiance—and count the cost, giving up all for the sake of the King and kingdom (Luke 14:26-33).

THE PROVISION OF THE KINGDOM

Matthew 6:25-34 points to the promise of the provision of God for those who pursue the kingdom as their priority. Jesus assures his disciples that he will provide for them because they have given up their hopes, dreams, livelihood, and even lives for him (cf. Matt 19:27; Mark 10:28; Luke 18:28). This is not a prosperity doctrine, promising riches. It refers to basic needs. This does not mean that disciples of the kingdom will never face poverty; there are plenty of promises of suffering. However, God does provide for his workers. Ultimately, all will be materially blessed in the coming kingdom.

THE VEILED NATURE OF THE KINGDOM

As noted earlier, the kingdom did not come as expected at the time. Rather than the triumphant arrival of the Messiah to establish the kingdom of God militarily and politically, the kingdom arrived in quiet. This is seen in parables comparing the arrival of the kingdom to the planting of a seed that grows imperceptibly among the weeds until it is the largest of all garden plants (Matt 13:24-26, 31-32; Mark 4:26-32; Luke 13:18-19). It is also seen more generally in Jesus' persistent use of parables. They are stories with double meanings that require discernment and openness on the part of the hearer to understand (Matt 13:11-13; Mark 4:11; Luke 8:10). This quiet and veiled coming of the kingdom is seen in the coming of Christ as a baby, then in his life of suffering and rejection, and ultimately, in his death. Even after his resurrection, Jesus appears to a select few of his followers who are charged to tell the world, rather than to the powerful. The kingdom's call is implicitly veiled in ambiguity, without coercion, allowing people to respond.

THE COMPLETE PENETRATION OF THE KINGDOM

The kingdom of God is also sometimes explained using domestic metaphors (i.e., the women's domain in that culture). For example, it is likened to a tiny portion of yeast that is mixed into the dough and causes it to rise (Matt 13:33; Luke 13:20-21). The kingdom, thus, begins in insignificance, but will permeate every dimension of society. The metaphor of "salt" points in a similar direction as the kingdom works flavor and healing into every part of the world through the efforts of its subjects (Matt 5:13). Similarly, just as light drives out the darkness each day as the earth turns on its axis, the kingdom is like light penetrating darkness—Jesus is the light of the world as are his followers (John 8:12; Matt 5:16). While evangelism, personal conversion, and salvation are central to the kingdom, it cannot be limited to this. The kingdom is about the transformation of God's world. It is seeing creation, society, and humanity reflecting God's dream for his world.

THE INEVITABLE AND UNSTOPPABLE GROWTH OF THE KINGDOM

From its quiet "insignificant" beginnings, Jesus taught that the kingdom would grow imperceptibly and inevitably, like a seed in a field (Matt 13:24; Mark 4:26). In Mark 4:28, the Greek term used is *automatos* to describe this growth (i.e., just as earth produces plants imperceptibly, so the kingdom will grow "automatically"). Thus, while the kingdom will be challenged by "weeds" planted by the enemy, the growth of the kingdom is remarkable and unstoppable. The parable of the mustard seed teaches that the kingdom will grow from the smallest of beginnings to be the largest and most influential entity in God's world (Matt 13:31; Mark 4:30; Luke 13:18).

THE INESTIMABLE VALUE OF THE KINGDOM

Two parables especially point to the fathomless value of the kingdom. The first, the parable of the buried treasure, suggests that the kingdom is of such value that it is worth giving up everything one has to pursue it (Matt 13:44). Rather than walk away sad, as did the rich ruler, believers should respond as the disciples and "leave everything" to follow Jesus, because his kingdom is truly a "buried treasure."

In the second, the parable of the pearl of great value, a pearl merchant discovers an amazing pearl and sells everything he owns to gain it. This no doubt includes every other pearl and precious gem in his possession (Matt 13:45-46). The kingdom then is likened to the most wonderful of pearls, a stone (*margaritēs*) highly valued in antiquity (e.g., *T. Jud.* 13.5; 1 Tim 2:9; Rev 17:4; 18:12, 16; 21:21), drawn from the Red Sea, the Persian Gulf, and the Indian Ocean.[49] This indicates that the kingdom is of such worth that it is worth sacrificing everything in its pursuit. The story of Zacchaeus is a great example of what is required (Luke 19:1-10).

---

49. See F. Hauck, "μαργαρίτης," in *TDNT* 4:472.

THE KINGDOM OF GOD

THE KINGDOM AND THE PRESENT (PARTIAL) AND FUTURE (ULTIMATE) DEFEAT OF EVIL

While this is difficult for some modern thinkers to handle, rejecting it as a remnant of an ancient worldview, Jesus clearly taught that he was engaged in a spiritual war. This is seen first in the temptation in the wilderness where he resists Satan, who apparently has control over the nations of the world (Matt 4:1-11, esp. 4:9). Again, in the parable of the sower, it is the devil who seeks to snatch away the meaning of the message of the kingdom (Matt 13:38-39).

Jesus' miracle ministry points to the progressive defeat of Satan, and evil and its consequences (see esp. Matt 12:25-28; Mark 3:24; Luke 11:17-20). This is directly seen in Jesus' temptation and in exorcisms, which show Jesus' complete authority over Satan and his demon forces. The healings point to the healing of all creation, the overthrow of sickness, and the ultimate physical wholeness of the kingdom of God. Evil has worked through every part of God's creation and its structures, corrupting it and warping it. The kingdom is to work through all of the creation and the structures of the world, restoring it and healing it through the work of the Spirit in the King's subjects. They are his healing and restorative agents. This restoration will never be fully achieved in this age, for Satan and his minions will resist. However, Jesus will ultimately return, restore, and re-create God's world. In the meantime, the kingdom's work is the restoration of a world corrupted by evil.

The miracles that demonstrate Jesus' power over natural forces point to the healing of the corruption of nature (see Rom 8:19-23). The feeding miracles point to the righting of economic oppression and the full provision of God in the age to come. The resurrections point to the defeat of the ultimate consequence of evil and death, and so point to eternal life. The miracles over nature indicate the power of God to restore all of the creation, which groans awaiting its redemption (cf. Rom 8:19-23).

THE PRESENT AND FUTURE REWARD AND PUNISHMENT OF THE KINGDOM

Reward

Jesus promises reward to the subjects of the kingdom who adhere to the radical principle of placing the needs of the kingdom and others above themselves. This is seen powerfully in Luke 12:32-34, where Jesus appeals for fearless, radical giving along with the promise of treasure in heaven:

> Do not be afraid, little flock, for your Father has been pleased to give you the kingdom. Sell your possessions and give to the poor. Provide purses for yourselves that will not wear out, *a treasure in heaven* that will never fail, where no thief comes near and no moth destroys. For where your treasure is, there your heart will be also. (Luke 12:32-34 NIV, emphasis added)

The notion of treasure in heaven is an exclusively Synoptic idea found elsewhere in Jesus' teaching. It recurs throughout Matthew 6 for those who pray, fast, and refuse to be led astray by the idolatry of wealth (Matt 6:19-21). Similarly, Jesus assures the disciples and others who give their life to the service of the gospel that they will receive eternal life (Mark 10:28-30; and parr.).

This dimension of reward and punishment is strong in the account of the sheep and the goats (Matt 25:31-46). The righteous and unrighteous are separated before God—the Judge—based on their actions toward their needy "brothers" (i.e., believers within the Christian community).[50] The righteous who care for God's people and missionaries are rewarded with eternal life in the kingdom prepared for the righteous from the creation of the world. Those who have not cared for the needy are punished (Matt

---

50. It is common to read the sheep and goats in regard to judgment on humanity for its action on behalf of the poor and needy. Thus "the least of these my brothers" in Matthew 25:40 and "the least of these" in Matthew 25:45 are read as "all other people." However, aside from literal use of blood brothers, "brothers" and especially "my brothers" is limited to fellow disciples in Matthew (Matt 5:22-24, 47; 7:3-5; 12:48-50; 18:15, 21, 35; 23:8; 28:10). Further, "least" is used of disciples (Matt 5:19). As such, humanity is judged on its treatment of Jesus' people and especially the least. It thus parallels Matthew 10:42: "And whoever gives one of these little ones even a cup of cold water because he is a disciple, truly, I say to you, he will by no means lose his reward." See also Blomberg, *Matthew*, 378.

25:34, 46). Jesus also speaks of conferring on the disciples a kingdom in which they will eat and drink with Christ and will judge the tribes of Israel (Luke 22:29-30). The granting of the prayer of the thief on the cross also points to the future reward of the kingdom (Luke 23:42-43).

The question is: What is the reward, and when is it received? The reward can be understood purely spiritually (that is, the presence of relationship with God and his glory is reward enough). However, there is clearly a material element to blessing as seen in Matthew 6:33 ("and all these things will be added to you") and in Mark 10:30 ("receive a hundredfold now in this time, houses and brothers and sisters and mothers and children and lands").

There are clear indications that there is reward both in the present and in the future. Matthew 6:33 and Mark 10:30 indicate there is blessing in the present for believers, both in terms of the Spirit and relationship with God, and in terms of material gain. In Luke 6:38, the generous will receive something in return (reciprocity): "Give, and it will be given to you. Good measure, pressed down, shaken together, running over, will be put into your lap. For with the measure you use it will be measured back to you." However, there is no indication of when this will occur. There is the usual now-not-yet tension associated with this. Interestingly, Jesus notes that alongside blessing there will be persecution for those who give to the kingdom (Mark 10:30).

If there is present-day material blessing in mind, it does not need to lead believers to the prosperity gospel. First, there is no absolute equation: "give generously and receive generously *in this present age.*" The experiences of Christ, Paul, and many others in the New Testament indicate that at times there was present-day blessing, but often there was struggle, suffering, and even poverty (e.g., Rom 8:35; 15:26; 1 Cor 4:11; 2 Cor 6:5; 8:2, 9; 11:27; Phil 4:11-12; Jas 2:2-6). Second, there is no sense that believers should be motivated by the promise of material blessing so that they give to receive more, a carrot often used by contemporary preachers. Promises of God's blessings are there for sure, but the authentic motivation for giving is not to receive, but to bless others as one has been blessed by God. This is being motivated for the gain of others and the kingdom and not for oneself. Paramount is 1 Corinthians 13:3, where Paul makes it clear that there is no reward for those who give without love (i.e., selfishly, or with wrong motives). For Paul, giving should reflect the pattern of giving laid down by Christ, who voluntarily became poor to make humanity rich (2 Cor 8:9; Phil 2:5-8). Finally, it is clear in the Gospels that any material blessing is not for gain or accumulation (Luke 12:13-21), but so believers can live according to their needs and give lavishly (e.g., Mark 10:21). Excess wealth is to be reinvested for the kingdom, and there are terrible warnings for those who do not do so (e.g., Luke 16:19-31). Followers of Jesus are stewards and not owners of what they have been given.

Another point of contention is whether believers will receive varying rewards in heaven based on their works (i.e., not salvation by works, but degrees of *blessing* by works). Scholars are split on this. Some posit that 1 Corinthians 3:12-15 suggests believers are rewarded differently based on works (cf. Rom 2:6). Passages urging effort for "treasure in heaven," and Luke 6:38, can lead to the same conclusion. However, it is possible that this is an over-reading of these texts, which do not define the nature of the reward and that in eternity all will receive the same reward. This is certainly suggested by the parable of the workers in the vineyard (Matt 20:1-16).[51]

Punishment

Matthew, in particular, emphasizes eschatological punishment. Matthew's Jesus says that those who are from Israel but reject his teaching will be thrown outside the consummated kingdom and will suffer greatly, cast "into the darkness, where there will be weeping and gnashing of teeth" (Matt 8:12). Similarly, in the parable of the seed (weeds), the King (Jesus) leaves the good plants (his subjects) among the weeds (those who reject his kingship) until the end of the age, at which time there is a harvest and those who are outside the kingdom experience great suffering—they will "throw them into the fiery furnace. In that place there will be weeping and gnashing of teeth" (Matt 13:42), while "the righteous will shine like the sun in the kingdom of their Father" (Matt 13:43). This reference echoes Daniel 12:1-4, which speaks of eternal life for the righteous and everlasting

---

51. At the same time, however, this may be over-reading the parable of the workers in the vineyard. The parable may point to the general principle that the gentiles will receive the same reward of eternal life as the Jews. However, see Craig L. Blomberg, *Interpreting the Parables* (Downers Grove, IL: InterVarsity Press, 1990), 222-25, who argues persuasively that this parable suggests all receive the same reward.

contempt for the evil. Again, in the parable of the net, a net is cast until it is full of both good and bad fish. At a set point, the "bad fish" experience great suffering—"throw them into the blazing furnace, where there will be weeping and gnashing of teeth" (Matt 13:47–50 NIV). In the sheep-and-the-goats account, the unrighteous are thrown into the "eternal fire prepared for the devil and his angels" (Matt 25:41, 46). There is a warning to so-called believers that some who claim to be Christians will not experience eternal life, in such texts as Matthew 7:21–23. Those who minister powerfully in the name of Christ but do not live in relationship and obedience to Christ will experience eternal separation (Matt 25:46).

The terrible extent of suffering is found in the warning to avoid sin at all costs because of the terrible nature of hell (Mark 9:47–48). The exact nature of this destruction is unclear, with literal eternal "burning," eternal separation from God, and utter annihilation for eternity among the possibilities vigorously defended by scholars. What matters is not the exact nature of hell, but the horror of separation from God forever in whatever form.

It is clear, then, that the coming of the kingdom will divide humanity. Some will volitionally accept the reign of Christ and experience eternal life and blessing. Those who do not will experience destruction and be separated from God eternally. The question of those who have not heard the gospel is not resolved in the Synoptics.

THE COMMUNITY OF THE KINGDOM

While the kingdom of God is in a sense the whole world, Jesus spoke of a kingdom composed of a community, the people of God on earth. These people are the subjects of God their King who live in submission to him. This people stands in continuity with historical Israel and includes those in Israel, such as the disciples, who respond to the message of Christ with faith, as well as people of all nations as the gospel is preached and some yield to Jesus the King. Jesus' teaching on the kingdom broaches many dimensions of this community.

Entry into the community of the kingdom

In Judaism, it is assumed that one is born into the covenant community under God's kingship. This is signified for a male by circumcision. For a woman, this is automatic based on the father's Jewishness. A gentile had to convert to become a Jew, a proselyte. For a male, this involved circumcision, integration into the community, and a commitment "to complete observance of the traditional Jewish law and cult" (Josephus, *Ant.* 20.38-48).[52] For a woman, the process was less clear, but may have included immersion (baptism), marriage to a Jewish man, and on occasion, an elaborate penitential process (e.g., *Jos. Asen.* 10.10-13).[53] For a Roman, if one's parents were citizens, Roman citizenship was automatic.

In Jesus' preaching in the Synoptics, the key responses required to enter the kingdom are "to repent and believe the gospel" (Mark 1:15; Matt 4:17) or to "follow me" (Mark 1:17; 2:14; 8:34; 10:21; and parr.). In Matthew, Jesus tells his hearers that entry into the kingdom of heaven depends on surpassing the righteousness of the Pharisees and the teachers of the law (Matt 5:19-20). In the Sermon on the Mount, Jesus interprets the law in a new way, which calls believers to a life of radical trust, ethical integrity, material generosity, humility, and intention to please God by living in accordance with Christ's teaching. This probably means kingdom people should go beyond the Pharisees' legalism, which forbade such things as healing on the Sabbath, to a radical ethic especially expressed faith, love, and self-sacrifice for others.

Jesus also surprises his hearers in the Sermon on the Mount by telling them that not everyone who professes allegiance to the kingdom will enter into the kingdom (Matt 7:22). Rather, entry is afforded those who follow up their profession of his Lordship with obedience to the will of the Father and who are in a relationship with Christ (Matt 7:21-23).

Jesus shocked his Jewish hearers by telling them that many will come from areas beyond Israel ("from the east and the west") and will dine at the eschatological feast of the kingdom of heaven (Isa 55:1-5) with the Patriarchs of Israel ("Abraham, Isaac and Jacob"), whilst those who are subjects of the kingdom by their Jewish heritage ("the subjects of the kingdom") will not enter (Matt 8:11-12, cf. Luke 13:28-29). Jesus also likens the kingdom to a wedding banquet and points out that many who have been invited (Jews [Matt 22:2-3]) have refused to come. Rather, gentiles "from east and west, and from north and south" will accept and enter the kingdom

---

52. J. E. Burns, "Conversion and Proselytism," in *EDEJ* 484.
53. Burns, "Conversion," 484.

(Luke 13:28-30). Thus, many gentiles will enter this kingdom and many Jews will not.

Jesus similarly challenges his Jewish hearers by telling them that they have to emulate a child to enter the kingdom of God (Matt 18:1-4; Mark 10:14-15; Luke 18:16-17). While Jesus does not specify what attributes of a child are required, apart from humility, one can postulate innocence, trust, honesty, joy, and dependence. At that time, children were at the bottom of the pecking order, and yet they are the prime examples of the last being first.

In the same way, his hearers would have been stunned when Jesus says to them that "the tax collectors and the prostitutes go into the kingdom of God ahead of you" (Matt 21:31). Tax collectors were repudiated as sell-outs to the unclean Romans and utterly sinful. Prostitutes, too, were repudiated as vile sinners and enemies of Jewish concern for sexual purity. Consequently, Jesus' words were inconceivable and highly charged.

Against the cultural understandings of wealth and blessing, Jesus points to great difficulty (if not impossibility) of the rich in entering the kingdom of God. Their entry appears to rely on a radical renunciation of the love of money demonstrated by selling one's possessions and putting those earnings to work for the poor (Matt 19:23-24; Mark 10:23-25; Luke 18:24-25; 19:1-10). Converting people from greed to generosity is something only God can do.

Jesus also directly tells those Jewish leaders who reject him and his message that they will not enter the kingdom and that their ministry effectively shuts others out (Matt 23:13). Those who can enter, however, are identified in: Jesus' interaction with Nicodemus (John 3:3-5); his encouragement of the teacher of the law concerning his nearness to the kingdom (Mark 12:34); Joseph of Arimathea (Mark 15:43; Luke 23:51); and Jesus' statement of the richness of the knowledge of a teacher of the law who finds the kingdom (Matt 13:52). In John, anyone who wishes to see or enter the kingdom, whether Jew or gentile, must be reborn. The Greek *anōthen* has a dual meaning, "again" or "from above" (i.e., spiritually reborn through the Spirit). To see and enter the kingdom, one must experience spiritual regeneration, which can only come from God based on faith (John 3:3, 5, 16-18).

The Subjects of the Kingdom: The Kingdom Community

All kingdoms have subjects. Some are willing; some come through coercion. In Judaism, one becomes a member of the covenant community through conversion. In any kingdom, true subjects are those who are loyal to the kingdom and live by its ethical code. In most kingdom contexts, it is the wealthy and powerful who are welcomed to be a part of the kingdom and who willingly accept its call.

Jesus, too, made many statements indicating who the true subjects of the kingdom are. However, rather than the wealthy and powerful, they include the poor in spirit (Matt 5:3), the literal poor (Luke 6:20), children (Matt 19:14), tax collectors, prostitutes, gentiles (Luke 13:28-30), and those who are persecuted because of righteousness (Matt 5:10). These are the people who will openhandedly accept the kingdom. The kingdom brings eschatological reversal whereby the poor are cared for and blessed, while the rich are marginalized, the opposite of views of wealth and poverty at the time.

On the other hand, those who are rich find it difficult indeed to enter the kingdom (Matt 19:23-24; Mark 10:23-25; Luke 18:24-25). Entry requires a radical heart change (repentance) that causes them to turn from their greed to generosity; such a change is only possible with God. It requires a new focus and trust in God, and not self or riches. Thus, it is difficult for the Pharisees and other Jewish leaders to enter the kingdom. They need a complete reorientation of their understanding of God and Christ to enter the kingdom (see Matt 5:20; 23:13; John 3:3-8).

At its core, the kingdom of God is the gathering of a new humanity under the authority and kingship of God and his agent, Jesus. The whole thrust of Jesus' ministry was to draw people to salvation, healing, deliverance, resurrection, and teaching on human response and behavior. The kingdom completely reverses worldly understandings of status and blessing; those who appear to the world to be of the highest honor and rank are, in fact, the least in the kingdom.

Greatness in the kingdom community

Usually, in response to false understandings of honor held by his disciples, Jesus spoke often of greatness within the kingdom. In a sense, all who enter the kingdom of God are of a new order to those who lived before Christ. One factor that diminishes one's standing within the kingdom is breaking the law of God (in the sense of the Sermon on the Mount) and teaching others to do the same (Matt 5:19). When Jesus is directly asked, "Who is the greatest in the kingdom of heaven?" he replies it is those who are humble like a child, not the rich and powerful (Matt 18:1-4; Mark 10:14-15). The supreme evidence of greatness in the kingdom is willing servanthood (Matt 20:26; Mark 10:43). The role models of greatness are not the rulers of the gentile world, but the servant-king who has come not to be served but to serve through his sacrifice on the cross (Mark 10:42-45). The path of life for the subject of the King is selflessness, service, self-sacrifice, and suffering for the sake of the kingdom and the needs of others (cf. Mark 8:34-38).

Suffering in the kingdom community

Even though there is blessing for those in the kingdom, Jesus at no stage paints a picture of the kingdom in this age as a utopian bliss. He is no prosperity-gospel preacher. Rather, he is (at times brutally) honest that life in the kingdom will involve not only general human suffering (Matt 6:34; John 16:33), but also suffering for Christ in his service (Matt 5:10-12, 44; 10:23; 13:21; 20:21-23; 24:9; Mark 10:30; Luke 11:49; 21:12). The ongoing mission is within a hostile world where Satan, particularly through those holding power, continues to usurp the true King—God—and his Son, Jesus. The evil forces will resist through the corruption of sin and evil. In addition, as Paul teaches, sin and death still hold sway in the present age (Rom 8:19-23; 1 Cor 15:55-57). The work of the kingdom within this fallen world will bring conflict and Christian suffering. This reflects the reality of Christ's experience as the suffering Messiah.

HUMAN AUTHORITY AND THE KINGDOM

All authority abides with God through Christ. However, within the kingdom, there is delegated authority. Just as at the time of Christ when kings appointed leaders over regions, cities, and spheres, Jesus was commissioned and authorized by God as his Messiah-King over the whole world. Jesus willingly submitted, fully and unconditionally, to his Father's will. Jesus extended this authority to his delegated leaders. For example, Jesus calls and grants authority to the apostles and the seventy-two, empowering them to overcome evil (Matt 10:1; 28:18; Mark 3:15; 6:7; Luke 9:1; 10:19). He confers authority on Peter: "I will give you the keys of the kingdom of heaven; whatever you bind on earth will be bound in heaven, and whatever you loose on earth will be loosed in heaven" (Matt 16:19 NIV, see also John 20:23). However, this authority must not be used in an autocratic manner or through force, but in servanthood and humility, out of love and grace (Mark 10:39-45). Jesus is the primary example of this kind of authority; he refused to use his power to coerce and manipulate others. Indeed, he preferred to go to the cross rather than do this. Christian leadership is servanthood, from below and not above, not through coercion, but by love and grace. The function of leadership is the making of disciples and equipping them to grow in their ministry.

THE GRACE AND FORGIVENESS OF THE KINGDOM

A cursory reading of the Gospels can easily take one into a theology of works. Certainly, Jesus powerfully stressed the importance of obedience and of works as a demonstration of true life in the kingdom. However, on closer examination, grace is found in much of Jesus' teaching and in his parables.

One good example is the parable of the Pharisee and the tax collector, where it is the sinful tax collector who is justified based on his appeal, "be merciful to me, a sinner" rather than the highly religious and self-righteous Pharisee (Luke 18:11-13). The granting of eternal life at the very last minute to the rebel on the cross also points to the grace of God—he can hardly have been saved because of his works, but on his repentance and faith (Luke 23:42-43).[54] The parable of the workers in the vineyard also points to grace, the last hired being granted the same reward as the first. Similarly, in the parable of the unforgiving servant, the king forgives his servant a prodigious debt that the servant could never have repaid. This

---

54. The Greek *lēstēs* (Mark 15:26) suggests this man is likely a rebel (BDAG, 594) who worked with the insurrectionist Barabbas (Mark 15:7) whose cross Jesus filled. Yet, he is the first to recognize Jesus as a suffering Messiah. Whereas the Jewish observers ridiculed Jesus, the disciples deserted him, and the women watched from afar, the rebel on the cross recognized that despite being crucified, Jesus would enter a kingdom ("your kingdom"). The second to understand this concept would be a Roman centurion (Mark 15:39; and parr.). Again, the stunning reversal of expectations is seen in the Gospel accounts.

emphasizes the grace of God in forgiving human sin. When the forgiven servant fails to forgive a smaller debt, he is condemned for his failure to demonstrate grace. Put plainly, subjects of the kingdom must forgive others as God has forgiven them (Matt 18:23-35, cf. Matt 6:12; Luke 6:37; Col 3:13). The parable of the prodigal son also speaks of a God who yearns to receive back the penitent sinner, even to the extent of breaking cultural protocol and shaming himself to receive back his son (Luke 15:11-32).[55] The parables of the lost sheep and coin conclude with celebrations because the sinner has repented and turned to God. These endings indicate God's deep desire to impart grace, and they anticipate the great eschatological feast (Luke 15:7, 10, cf. Isa 25:6-8). The great banquet speaks of grace as all are invited, even those at the margins (Luke 14:12-24).

Grace is seen in the Lord's Prayer: "and forgive us our debts, as we also have forgiven our debtors" (Matt 6:12, cf. 6:14-15). God's grace is reflected in his forgiveness, and believers should reciprocate with forgiveness toward others. This prayer is important as it lies in the center of the Sermon on the Mount, in which Christ preaches the ethics of the kingdom. This prayer for forgiveness removes any thought that Jesus is preaching perfectionism. Rather, he knows people will fail, but grace is there for them as they earnestly seek to live up to the ideals of the kingdom.

THE WORK OF THE KINGDOM

Jesus' teaching clearly assumes that those who enter the kingdom will work for the King as their priority. As such, while there is much unemployment in the world, the disciple is never unemployed—there is always work, even if material payment is lacking. While the Jewish leaders work passionately, their works fall short of the deeds expected of those in the kingdom (Matt 23:5; Luke 11:48; John 3:19).

This call to work is seen in Christ's example (e.g., Matt 11:2, 19; Luke 24:19; John 3:21; 4:34; 17:4), in his calling of his disciples, his appeals for selfless living on behalf of the gospel and Christ, his statements concerning the good work(s) of disciples (e.g., Matt 5:16; 26:10), his parables involving

---

55. The son's behavior was deeply shaming, effectively wanting his father dead. He deserved punishment and rejection. By accepting him back with such lavishness, the father opened himself up to social shame. Further, by running to him, the father acted in a manner that was culturally inappropriate.

work (e.g., yeast, net, and seed parables; the workers in the vineyard parable; the parable of the two sons; the parable of the servants; see Matt 20:12; 21:28; 25:16; Mark 13:34; John 14:12), and the work of mission (John 4:38). The call to discipleship is the call to put one's hand to the plow without looking back (Luke 9:62). The parables of the minas (Luke 19:11-13) and talents (Matt 25:14-28) indicate his subjects are to invest what he has entrusted to them on his behalf. They also carry a direct threat for those who refuse to do so.

The work of the kingdom is to labor so that God can extend his reign as his subjects live in obedience to their King. This will involve disciples living out the calling they receive from their King (esp. Mark 13:34: "each with his work"). Traditionally, this has been limited to "spiritual" work, such as ministry within the church and/or evangelism. However, the work of the kingdom is bigger. It also involves a believer's vocation (e.g., a teacher, an accountant, a waiter, or a laborer). This is the fulfillment of the initial commission of God to his image bearers, who have a responsibility to rule over the earth, utilizing its resources for good, and building human society while caring for the world (Gen 1-2). If properly understood, to "go to work" is to serve God. Whereas an unbeliever may do the same for selfish purposes such as personal gain and prestige, the believer does this for God, recognizing that they are living out their creation mandate. Even where first-century slaves are concerned, they are to work for God as they serve their masters (Eph 6:7; Col 3:23). In a fallen world, as believers go about this work, they also carry the Great Commission imperative to give witness to God—with right attitudes; by good deeds; and with careful, gracious words (Col 4:5). All believers, wherever their vocation is situated, have a dual vocation within the world—to use their gifts to build up the church (esp. 1 Cor 12:7; Eph 4:11-12), and to work to build God's world, the human imperative. They are to work out the Great Commission, and the Great Cosmission. So, it is that believers are God's agents to work in all parts of his world, bringing his reconciliation and restoration as they are called and led by the Spirit.

THE ETHICS OF THE KINGDOM

Every kingdom in the ancient world had an ethical system that formed its basis. For the Greeks, this was found in its religious and philosophical traditions. The Romans effectively took over the Greek mindset, and people lived by the Roman way, the constitutional understanding of the Empire. The Jews' ethical system was found in the law.

Jesus, too, has an ethical system that forms the constitutional basis for the kingdom. Its ethics are the attitudes and the resulting actions that King Jesus expects from his subjects. These are found in the Synoptics and John, and include a wide range of attitudes and actions including love, humility, the renunciation of a love of wealth and radical generosity to the poor and needy, radical dependence on God, egalitarianism, inclusion of all including sinners (except where false gospels are propounded), non-judgmentalism, humility, sexual purity, marital fidelity, honesty, the renunciation of violence and hatred, and forgiveness, among other virtues. Kingdom ethics are summarized in the Sermon on the Mount (Matt 5-7) and the Plain (Luke 6:17-49), in which the evangelists gather together Jesus' teaching in clumps.[56] These commands stand in continuity to the Old Testament, but Jesus radically redefines them in terms of the spirit rather than the letter of the law. The ethics of the kingdom are summarized in the two greatest commandments. First, to love God with everything one has; second, to love one's neighbor as one would like to be loved (Mark 12:29-31; cf. Matt 7:12). Jesus taught that his subjects should love their enemies. This was revolutionary at the time, when love was reserved for family, kith, and kin. Ultimately Jesus' subjects should emulate Jesus, for he is the focal point of the kingdom.

THE MISSION OF THE KINGDOM

Finally, it is important not to neglect the heart of the mission of the kingdom—its extension. The kingdom in the New Testament usually has the sense of God as coming king, coming to deal with his enemies, and resolve the problem of human rebellion through the death and resurrection of his Son. The kingdom then extends as people yield willingly to the King as they hear

---

56. It is unclear whether either is an actual sermon recalled by the disciples or typical sermons that Jesus may have preached through Israel, or collections of Jesus' sayings gathered by Matthew and Luke for teaching purposes. See the brief discussion in Blomberg, *Matthew*, 96.

the good news of the kingdom. It also extends as people do the work of the kingdom and the value system of the kingdom penetrates and transforms (heals) the broken structures of human life, from the family to whole nations, even where people do not necessarily yield to the king (seen in western civilization as we speak). At the heart of the mission is individual people bowing their knee to their sovereign. From this, the work of the kingdom flows through his people empowered by the Spirit of the King.

That the kingdom is pervasive is seen in parables involving growth, infiltration, and extension. The essential way the kingdom is to be extended is seen in the mission of Jesus to call people to him, to preach, heal, deliver, and provide for the needy. The mission is thus comprehensive. It includes spiritual conversion and transformation, along with the establishment of a new community of inclusiveness and the restoration of the whole person and community. Jesus' mission is not a one-man solo adventure. It is a team mission; people are saved into the kingdom and commissioned to join him in his mission. Within that team are people with differing roles.

Jesus' commission is first extended to the Twelve who are called to do what he is doing (Mark 3:13-19; 6:7-13; Matt 9:36-10:23; Luke 9:1-6) and then to the seventy-two (Luke 10:1-12). Aside from Mark (except for the longer ending, which is likely not original), all the Gospels and Acts record some form of commission to continue this mission after the ascension and exaltation of Christ (the Great Commission; see Matt 28:18-20; Luke 24:46-49; Acts 1:8, cf. John 20:21; Mark 16:15-20). The commission is variously described as "making disciples" in Matthew, "preaching repentance and forgiveness" in Luke, "sending" in John, and "witnessing" in Luke and Acts. The making of disciples is marked by baptism into the people of God (Matthew, and the long ending of Mark). Matthew emphasizes teaching based on the person and message of Christ. Luke in Acts emphasizes the power of the Spirit. It is significant that Matthew and Luke end with a mention of this commission in some form or another (i.e., Jesus' last words are recalled in terms of mission, cf. John 20:21; Acts 1:8). The addition to Mark's Gospel of the differing endings, which emphasize mission indicates that the church retained this passion as it developed.

In Acts, the essential point of empowerment is the experience at Pentecost where the primary mark of the Spirit is not tongues, which occurs in most but not all contexts,[57] but empowerment for mission (Acts 1:8). This is anticipated in Luke 24:9 and in John's account of Jesus breathing on the disciples (John 20:21). Acts 1:8 points to the whole world ("all nations," "all creation," and "the end of the earth") as the extent of mission. Throughout Acts, there are five other significant moments of Spirit-empowerment: (1) On the Jerusalem community, stimulating a wave of evangelism, signs and wonders, radical generosity, and persecution (Acts 4:29–5:42); (2) When the Spirit pours out on Samaritans (Acts 8:14–24); (3) When the Spirit falls on Paul and he is propelled into mission (Acts 9:1–18); (4) When the Spirit falls on gentiles (Acts 10:34—48); and (5) When the Spirit falls on the Ephesians, sparking the evangelization of Ephesus, Asia Minor, and further persecution (Acts 19:1–41).

The post-Pentecost story of Acts and the letters of Paul point to the continuation of the mission, beginning in Jerusalem and extending to "the end of the earth." The consummation of the kingdom appears to be intimately linked to the fulfillment of this mission, the end coming when the gospel has been preached to all nations (Mark 13:10; Matt 24:14). Through the mission, Christ extends the kingdom through the agency of his Spirit working through disciples (Acts 1:8). Through the acceptance of the message of salvation, people become subjects of the kingdom.

THE CHURCH AND THE KINGDOM

It is easy to equate the church and the kingdom (i.e., the kingdom is the church). In one sense this makes sense; the genuine people of the kingdom are the genuine people of the invisible church (made up of all true believers). However, this does not exist in an absolute sense. There exists a series of visible churches scattered over the world. These are mixed multitudes, including genuine believers and others who are not. As such, the kingdom of God extends well beyond the church. The kingdom is found where the people of God are and the work of God by his Spirit across all of creation.

If the church is the gathered people of God, then its believing core could be argued to be at the center of the kingdom on earth. The church is

---

57. Tongues occurs at Pentecost (Acts 2:4), with Cornelius (Acts 10:46), and in Ephesus (Acts 19:6). They are not mentioned in Samaria in Acts 8, or in Paul's conversion in Acts 9, 22, and 26. See further below on Acts and the Spirit's role in the Jerusalem church.

the gathering point where the people of God's new creation come together. However, there is more to the kingdom than the church. The whole of creation is God's. This means that every nation, human institution, the natural order, and all parts of society are, in one sense at least, a part of God's kingdom. It is just that God's authority has been usurped. Where God by his Spirit and through his people has penetrated these institutions and creation itself, one could say the kingdom is found.

Christ is in the business of establishing his reign in what is rightfully his: creation. The full picture of God's salvation hope in the kingdom is *shalom* across creation. This means all dimensions of human society, and creation itself, are to be restored. The church clearly has a primary role in this; the people of God will radiate out from local churches each week to be God's agents to transform his world. The church is vital to the restoration of the cosmos, God's Great Commission, his "great project." The church ideally is to be a community that reflects the kingdom and shows the world what it looks like: a community of love and unity where God is honored, and people living as he intended. As such, each church should seek to live according to the ethics of the kingdom so that people who come into it experience the full life of the kingdom. It is from the base of the church that God's people will go out and do the work of the kingdom throughout creation seeking to see all people come to realize God is King, and submit to him, and to see his world transformed into his ideal.

QUESTIONS TO CONSIDER

- How do you define the kingdom of God?
- In what sense does the kingdom already exist?
- What is the relationship between the Spirit and the kingdom?
- How is the kingdom extended?
- How would you define the relationship between the kingdom and the church?
- In a nation where ideas of monarchies, kings, and queens have lost their power, should believers continue to use the language of the kingdom? Should they return to making the notion of the kingdom of God central as Jesus did?

THE POWER OF THE KINGDOM

CHAPTER 12

This chapter continues the theme of the kingdom of God that is at the heart of Jesus' teaching. The miracles of Jesus and their implications will be considered. It will be argued that while Jesus' miracles testify to a God who is immanent and intervenes in human life, more importantly, they speak of the fulfillment of the hope of God's intervention to restore, and are snippets of the future consummated kingdom. They are "signs of the kingdom."

WHAT IS A MIRACLE?

The term "miracle" comes from the Latin *mīrārī*, "to wonder at," and *mīrāculum*, "miracle." The technical term for "miracle worker" is *thaumaturge*, which derives from the Greek *thauma*, which means "to wonder," or "to marvel" (e.g., 2 Cor 11:14; Rev 17:6).[1] From a Greek point of view, Jesus is a *thaumaturge*.

In the New Testament, there are a few terms that are connected to the concept. These include:

1. *Dynamis* and the plural *dynameis*: "mighty work(s)," "miracle(s)," or "wonder(s)" (e.g., Mark 6:5; Matt 7:22; Acts 2:22)

2. *Teras*: "wonder," or "portent" (e.g., Acts 2:22; 2 Cor 12:12)

3. *Sēmeion*: "sign" (e.g., John 2:11, 23; 20:30)

---

1. The verb *thaumazō*, "astonished, amazed," is also frequent in the New Testament (forty-three times, e.g., Matt 8:10, 27).

4. *Paradoxon*: "strange thing" (Luke 5:26)

5. Combinations: *sēmeia* and *dynameis*, "signs and miracles" (Acts 8:13); *sēmeia* and *terata*, "signs and wonders" (Mark 13:22; Matt 24:24; John 4:48; Acts 2:43; Heb 2:4; cf. Deut 13:1–2; 34:11; Ps 135:9); *dynamis (-meis)*, *sēmeia*, and *terata*, "miracles, signs, and wonders" (Acts 2:22; Rom 15:19; 2 Cor 12:12).

In the Synoptic Gospels, Jesus' miracles are predominately called "deeds of power" (*dynameis*), whereas in John they are called "signs" (*sēmeia*). In Acts, Luke speaks of Jesus performing "signs and wonders," suggesting that the distinction may be overplayed in some people's minds (e.g., Acts 2:22, 43).

In biblical scholarship, a *miracle* normally denotes a supernatural event, or an event that "so transcends ordinary happenings that it is viewed as a direct result of supernatural power."[2] Aside from false signs, which have their source in Satan (e.g., 2 Thess 2:9; 2 Cor 12:11–12; Rev 13:13), the agency for these events is God, whether directly, through Christ, through the Spirit, or through human agency. Miracles, then, are "supernatural events in the space-time world."[3] Writers differ as to whether predictive prophecy falls under this definition. Clearly, they do, as prophecy indicates Jesus' ability to know something across time and space.

A miracle story is a self-contained account or narrative that focuses on a miracle event. Apart from angelophanies (angelic appearances), Jesus is the subject of all such stories in the Gospels. However, there are references to the disciples doing miracles on occasions (e.g., Mark 6:13; Luke 9:6; 10:17). There is also an example of their failure (Mark 9:14–29).

MIRACLES IN THE VARIOUS GOSPELS

MARK

Miracles feature prominently in all the Gospels. Nevertheless, Mark presents Jesus as a miracle worker with the highest percentage of miracle material—eighteen miracles. Jesus himself is the object of three (baptism, transfiguration, and resurrection). There is also a set of summaries

---

2. B. L. Blackburn, "Miracles and Miracle Stories," *DJG*, 549.
3. Blackburn, "Miracles," 549.

of Jesus doing miraculous things—each signifies any number of miracles (Mark 1:32-34, 39; 3:10-12; 6:5, 54-56). Another feature of Mark is the link between Jesus' miracles and his identity. Four are found in the first half of Mark, leading to Peter's confession of Jesus' identity (Mark 8:29). After performing each of these four miracles, Jesus commands silence (Mark 1:44; 5:43; 7:36; 8:26). There are also frequent deliverance miracles, with the demons commanded to be silent (e.g., Mark 1:25, 34; 3:12). Mark records that Jesus acted in compassion (Mark 1:41;[4] 6:34; 8:2). Jesus' concern to keep the miracles quiet is strategic; he did not want people to identify him as a political, military Messiah and prevail upon him to attack the Romans. Rather, he came as a servant Messiah. The secrecy also enabled him to move about freely. Mark emphasizes the need for faith where the miracles are concerned (see esp. Mark 2:5; 5:34; 6:6; 10:52). They serve mainly to reveal that Jesus is Messiah. They show Jesus' utter supremacy over negative forces whether demons, chaos, the elements, hunger, sickness, or death. They beg the question, "Who then is this?" (Mark 4:41).

MATTHEW

Matthew includes almost all the Markan miracle stories except three,[5] while he abbreviates some. He retains Mark's reference to Jesus' compassion and at other points emphasizes his mercy and grace (Matt 9:36; 14:14; 15:32; 20:34). He also includes a range of other miracles from Q, and L. Of note is the cluster of angelophanies in the infancy narrative and events surrounding the passion-resurrection.[6] Matthew emphasizes faith using the phrase "according to your faith be it done to you" (Matt 9:29, cf. 8:13; 15:28). He notes dramatic instant healing with the phrase, "was

---

4. The TNIV and NIV have "indignant," preferring the reading *orgizō*, meaning "angry." However, Metzger, *Textual Commentary*, 65, prefers "compassion," giving it a B rating, suggesting it is reasonably certain and so preferred by a number of translations (ESV, NET, NAB, NIV, NKJV).

5. The first deliverance at Capernaum (Mark 1:23-28), the healing of the deaf man (Mark 7:31-37), the healing of the blind man at Bethsaida (Mark 8:22-26).

6. These include: the angelophanies, star and virgin conception of the birth narrative (see Matt 1:18, 20; 2:2, 12, 13, 19, 22); the centurion's servant (Matt 8:5-13, cf. Luke 7:1-10); the blind and mute demoniac (Matt 12:22, cf. Luke 11:14, i.e., Q); the mute man healed (Matt 9:32-33, unique, i.e., M); the healing of two blind men (Matt 9:27-31); Peter walking on the water (Matt 14:28-33); the coin in the fish's mouth (Matt 17:24-27); the passion/resurrection miracles, including an earthquake and resurrected saints (Matt 27:51-53); the angelic rolling of the stone (Matt 28:2); and a final christophany (Matt 28:16).

healed at that very moment" (Matt 8:13, cf. 9:22; 15:28; 17:18). Matthew also has doublets of healings (e.g., Matt 9:32-34/12:22-24; 9:27-31/20:29-34; 12:38-39/16:1-4).

Miracles are associated with Jesus' divine nature and with Jesus at miracles (usually healings). He is often addressed as "Lord," or *kyrie* (Matt 8:2, 6, 8, 25; 9:28; 15:22, 25; 17:4; 20:31, 33), or worshiped, *proskyneō*, meaning "bow down" (Matt 8:2; 9:18; 14:33; 15:25). Matthew also emphasizes the complete power of Jesus to heal "all" (Matt 4:23-24; 8:16; 12:15; 14:35; 15:37).

Matthew also emphasizes how Jesus fulfills prophecies of the long-awaited Messiah and that he will perform miracles (Matt 11:5, cf. Isa 29:18, 35:5, 42:7). For example, he sees the virginal conception as a fulfillment of Isaiah 7:14 (Matt 1:22-23). Similarly, Jesus' exorcisms and healings fulfill Isaiah 53:4 (Matt 8:17), i.e., he is the Servant Messiah who heals (Matt 12:18-21, cf. Isa 42:1-4). Jesus' miracles described in Matthew 11:5 correspond to Isaianic prophecies, i.e., he is the Messiah. Matthew builds on Mark's presentation of Jesus as Messiah. Matthew demonstrates that indeed Jesus is the Messiah and that he is imbued with the power of the divine. Matthew emphasizes Jesus' fulfillment of messianic prophecy in his presentation of Jesus for his Jewish readership.

LUKE

Luke's presentation of Jesus' miracles aligns reasonably with Mark and Matthew, but there are some differences, such as the angelophanies in the Lukan infancy narrative.[7] While Luke includes most of Mark's stories, he does exclude some miracles (the "Great Omission," Mark 6:46-8:26) including Jesus' walking on water; the healings of the Syrophoenician woman, a deaf-mute man, and a blind man; and the feeding of the four thousand.[8] He also excludes the cursing of the fig tree (Mark 11:14-25), perhaps because it doubles with Luke 13:6-9. He includes the Q healings of the centurion's

---

7. See Matt 1:18, 20; 2:2, 12-13, 19, 22.

8. As noted above on the composition of Luke (Chapter 7), this is probably due to a desire to avoid repetition and to avoid the use of "dog" for gentiles, which would not have gone down well with a primarily gentile audience.

servant (Luke 7:1-10, cf. Matt 8:5-13) and a blind and deaf demoniac (Luke 11:14-22, cf. Matt 12:22). He includes seven unique miracles.[9]

Intriguingly, Luke eliminates all note of Jesus' compassion from the Markan and Q accounts, although he does mention Jesus' compassion at the raising of the widow's son (Luke 7:13, see also 10:33; 15:20). Rather, he stresses that the miracles are a result of the *dynamis*, "power" (Luke 4:36; 5:17; 6:19; 8:46), which Jesus shares with his disciples (Luke 9:1), and which overcomes the enemy (Luke 10:19). For example, Luke 5:17 says, "And the Lord's healing power was strongly with Jesus" (NLT). Luke links power and miracles to the Spirit (e.g., Luke 4:14-20; Acts 1:8). Prayer is quite often associated with miracle and power in Luke. This is seen on three occasions where Jesus prayed shortly before he moved in power (Luke 5:16; 6:12-16; 9:29). This suggests that Luke wants to first emphasize the Spirit's role in miracles, and then the link between prayer and the release of God's miraculous power through the Spirit. These links are found throughout Acts in particular (e.g., Acts 4:29-31 and what follows, esp. 5:12-16). Thus, Luke stresses that Jesus is Messiah empowered by the Spirit who is bringing restoration and *shalom*. He can do what no Caesar can—that is, bring miracle power to save and transform the cosmos.

JOHN

Miracles also play a key role in John. Rather than the virgin conception and birth, John's Gospel begins with the miracle of incarnation (John 1:14). John includes seven main miracles, the so-called seven signs of John (see Chapter 9). These include two that have parallels in the Synoptics: (1) the feeding of the five thousand (John 6:1-15, see also Matt 14:13-21; Mark 6:32-44; Luke 9:10-17); and (2) Walking on the sea (John 6:16-21, see also Matt 14:22-33; Mark 6:47-51). Five are unique: (1) The healing of the

---

9. For example: (1) Luke 5:1-11, the miraculous catch of fish at the call of the first disciples; (2) Luke 7:11-17, the resurrection of the widow of Nain's son; (3) Luke 8:2, the exorcism of seven demons from Mary Magdalene, which is mentioned in passing; (4) Luke 13:10-17, the healing of the disabled woman in the synagogue; (5) Luke 14:1-6, the healing of a man with dropsy on the Sabbath in the home of a Pharisee; (6) Luke 17:11-19, the cleansing of ten lepers, when only the Samaritan returns to express gratitude; and (7) Luke 22:51, the report of the healing of the high priest's ear. At the resurrection, he includes: the appearance of the two men wearing dazzling clothes (Luke 24:4) and Christophanies (appearances of Christ), including one on the road to Emmaus (Luke 24:13-35), one to Peter (Luke 24:34), and an evening appearance before the eleven and others (Luke 24:36-49).

nobleman's son (John 4:46-54);[10] (2) Changing water to wine (John 2:1-12); (3) The healing of the paralytic at the pool (John 5:1-15); (4) The healing of the blind man (John 9:1-7); and (5) The raising of Lazarus (John 11:1-44). John culminates with the ultimate miracle of Jesus' resurrection.

There are some distinctive aspects to John's miracles when compared to the miracles in the Synoptic Gospels:

1. **The language:** In John, they are called "signs" (*sēmeia*) rather than "mighty deeds" or "miracles" (*dynameis*). While the signs still stress the power of Jesus, calling them signs highlights the function of the miracle; namely, their parabolic and sign character—they signify who Jesus is; they point the way to Jesus' identity. The right response to the sign is faith. Faith in miracle is not sufficient. However, it must go further to faith in Jesus Christ for eternal life (John 2:23-25; 6:60-65).

2. **The relationship of the signs to faith:** Whereas in the Synoptics the miracles are in many instances a result of the faith of the inquirers, in John, the signs are not the result of faith but serve to evoke faith in Jesus the Christ, the Son of God (John 20:30-31). This reinforces that they are signs pointing to the identity of Christ. Jesus does miracles, and they lead to faith (e.g., John 4:53). Jesus also takes the initiative (John 5:6-8).

3. **The absence of deliverance miracles:** Interestingly, there are no exorcisms in John. This is possibly because John sees the lifting up of Christ at his death and resurrection as the point of Satan's demise (see John 12:31-32; 13:2, 27; 14:30). Interestingly, there is a similar lack of reference to exorcism in Paul's writings; although Luke records that Paul cast out demons (e.g., Acts 16:16-18; 19:12).

4. **Signs linked to debate and discourse:** John uses "signs" theologically, i.e., they lead to or follow debates with the Jews

---

10. While there are similarities to the Roman Centurion's Servant healing, the differences are too great for it to be the same event (see earlier on John's Gospel). See Köstenberger, *John*, 168, who lists the differences such as a different setting (Cana and Capernaum) and the nature of the person healed (a royal official and a servant of a centurion).

and long discourses through which John explicates the identity of Jesus. So, the feeding of the 5000 leads to the bread-of-life discourse (John 6), and the healing of the blind man follows the light-of-the-world discourse (e.g., John 9; 11).

Markan Miracles				
	Mark	Matthew	Luke	John
Possessed Man in Synagogue	1:23-26		4:33-35	
Peter's Mother-in-Law	1:30-31	8:14-15	4:38-39	
Man with Leprosy	1:40-42	8:2-4	5:12-13	
Paralyzed Man	2:3-12	9:2-7	5:18-25	
Man with Shriveled Hand	3:1-5	12:10-13	6:6-10	
Calming the Storm	4:37-41	8:23-27	8:22-25	
Gerasene Demoniac(s)	5:1-15	8:28-34	8:27-35	
Raising Jairus' Daughter	5:22-24, 38-42	9:18-19, 23-25	8:41-42, 49-56	
Hemorrhaging Woman	5:25-29	9:20-22	8:43-48	
Feeding of Five Thousand	6:35-44	14:15-21	9:12-17	6:5-13
Walking on Water	6:48-51	14:25-32		6:19-21
Canaanite Woman's Daughter	7:24-30	15:21-28		
Deaf-Mute	7:31-37			
Feeding of Four Thousand	8:1-9	15:32-38		
Blind Man at Bethsaida	8:22-26			
Demon-Possessed Boy	9:17-19	17:14-18	9:38-43	
Two Blind Men	10:46-52	20:29-34	18:35-43	
Fig Tree Withered	11:12-14, 20-25	21:18-22		
Miracles Found Only in Matthew and Luke (Q)				
Roman Centurion's Servant		8:5-13	7:1-10	
Blind, Mute, and Possessed Man		12:22	11:14	

	Mark	Matthew	Luke	John
Miracles Found Only in Matthew (M)				
Two Blind Men		9:27-31		
Mute and Possessed Man		9:32-33		
Coin in Fish's Mouth		17:24-27		
Miracles Found Only in Luke (L)				
First Catch of Fish, Call of Disciples			5:1-11	
Deliverance of Mary Magdalene			8:2	
Raising Widow's Son at Nain			7:11-15	
Crippled Woman			13:11-13	
Man with Dropsy			14:1-4	
Ten Men with Leprosy			17:11-19	
High Priest's Servant's Ear			22:50-51	
Miracles Found Only in John				
Water to Wine				2:1-11
Official's Son at Capernaum				4:46-54
Sick Man at Pool of Bethesda				5:1-9
Healing of the Blind Man				9:1-41
Raising Lazarus				11:1-44
Second Catch of Fish				21:1-11

FIGURE 24: THE MIRACLES OF JESUS

CATEGORIES OF MIRACLES

It can be argued that there are five types of miracles in Jesus' ministry, all of which point to his messianic status and divine nature, and which overcome problems humanity faces, caused by the fall. The miracles all point to the nature of the kingdom and God's intentions for humanity.

1. **Miracles of healing:** the physical healing of illness and/or deliverance of demons.

2. **Miracles of provision:** feeding miracles and the provision of wine.

3. **Miracles over nature:** miracles that defy the "laws" of nature. Some call these "rescue miracles"; however, not all the miracles over nature are rescues.

4. **Miracles over death:** miracles of resurrection, of raising the dead.[11]

5. **Miracles of divine knowledge:** miracles that indicate supernaturally gained knowledge (i.e., predictive prophecy).

BREAKDOWN OF MIRACLES IN THE GOSPELS

Aside from predictive prophecy, miracles in which Jesus is the object of the miraculous,[12] and angelophanies,[13] there are thirty-four specific miracles performed by Jesus in the New Testament. There are also fifteen that are summary statements speaking of an unspecified number of Jesus' miracles, including healing and deliverance encounters.[14] In addition, there are references to disciples' miracles.[15] The table below shows the miracles of Jesus, classified across the Gospel.

Only one miracle features in all four Gospels, the 5000. Eleven are found in three, six in two, and seventeen are found in only one Gospel. The mention of twelve miracles in three to four Gospels suggests that the historical tradition that Jesus performed miracles is sound (see further below).

---

11. Some argue the word "resurrection" should only be used for "the resurrection" of the dead to eternal life. Those reanimated in the New Testament, aside from Christ and the believer at the final day, die again. Some words chosen include reanimation, revivication, or resuscitation. However, these suggest that the recipient was not completely dead and was reanimated, revived, or resuscitated. On the contrary, they were raised, albeit not to eternal physical life but to ongoing present life, until death.

12. Where God is the agent (e.g., the virginal conception, Jesus' baptism, the transfiguration, the resurrection and the ascension, and resurrection appearances).

13. Appearances of angels, e.g., Matt 1:20, 24; 2:13, 19; 4:11; 28:2, 5; Luke 1:11-19, 26-38; 2:9-10, 13-15; 22:43; 24:23; John 20:12; Acts 5:19; 8:26; 10:4, 7, 22; 11:13; 12:7-11; 12:23; 27:23; Rev 1:1; 22:1, 6, 8.

14. See Matt 4:24; 8:16; 12:15; 14:14; 15:30; 19:2; 21:14; Mark 1:34; 3:10; 6:5; Luke 4:40; 5:15; 6:18-19; 7:21; 8:2.

15. See Mark 6:13 (deliverance and healing); Luke 9:6 (healing); Luke 10:17 (deliverance implied [the seventy-two]). See also Mark 9:38-41; and parr. where some "non-disciples" do miracles of deliverance in Jesus' name.

MIRACLES OF HEALING, DELIVERANCE, AND REANIMATION

THE FULL NOTION OF HEALING

God's kingdom project is a mission to heal the world and everything in it, to transform it into what it was intended to be. Creation remains subject to the final enemy to be defeated—death (1 Cor 15:26)—as creation groans in pain awaiting full restoration (Rom 8:19-23). This can only come at the consummation. God's plan of healing extends to all of creation, including all of nature, every dimension of society, families, marriages, and to humans in all that they are. God has placed within creation the power for healing, as seen in the amazing capacity of humans and animals to restore themselves, and in medicine. The greatest healing is the restoration of the breach between humankind and God, the reconciliation of God and people through individual salvation. This happens in the present. Forgiveness and finding freedom from guilt, shame, and psychological torment are essential to healing (being made whole). Miracles of healing are always happening as people come to Christ. Though complete healing will be experienced in eternity, it is experienced spiritually in this present day. The healing of broken human relationships also lies at the heart of God's purposes, whether with others or with creation itself. Physical healing in the Gospels and the wider New Testament is one dimension of this holistic view. Every miracle of Jesus and by God within history, aside from the resurrection and the eschatological miracles to come, is a temporary alleviation of suffering. When Jesus fed the poor, raised the dead, and healed the sick and suffering, the recipients ultimately weakened and died. Only when the final state is experienced is God's miraculous action permanent.

THE CONTEXT

The world of the New Testament is prior to the advent of modern medicine and social welfare. While medicine was widely practiced among the Greek and Roman aristocratic classes with comparatively limited success, most people were poor and did not have access to medical assistance. Life expectancy was short, 30-45 years.[16] In contrast to today's world, women lived shorter lives than men, particularly because of death in childbirth. Medical knowledge was limited, with a blend of the spiritual and material (e.g., the god Asclepius, the god of healing). Sin and illness were often linked; people believed that ongoing sickness was a demonstration of a spiritual problem (see John 9:1-2).

Interestingly, in the Jewish apocryphal book Sirach 38 (200-170 BC), readers are urged to honor doctors as God-ordained professionals. The text refers to healing herbs, anesthetics, and drugs. It affirms the use of prayer in medical healing and attributes sickness to sin (Sir 38:15). Kee notes that this perhaps shows a Greek influence. Since the fifth century, the Greeks (e.g., Hippocrates, the Hippocratic Oath) had a strong medical tradition (especially the Stoics), holding that a physician could draw on natural law in healing, finding the healing power of natural objects. The Essenes also sought to heal through the natural world (Josephus, *J.W.* 2.136).

In addition, many illnesses created purity issues for the Jews; subsequently, the sufferer was marginalized from religious and general life (e.g., lepers because of Lev 13-14, and especially fear of contagion). This marginalization often meant a person lost their capacity to provide for themselves.

Not only was sickness associated with sin; it was also linked to the demonic. In the story of Tobit, Tobit is blinded by sparrow droppings, and healing is prescribed with fish guts, which also purportedly expelled demons (see Tob 2:10; 6:7; 8:1-3; 11:8). In 1 *Enoch* 6-11, fallen angels cause human illness. In the Jubilees, cures are both found in medicinal herbs (*Jub.* 10:12). Josephus states that a wise man is one who knows the natural world and the incantations and formulas to stave off demons (Josephus, *Ant.* 8.44-46). In the Qumran community, the demonic and illness are directly linked (1QapGen 20:12-29).[17]

So, when Jesus arrives on the scene, he encounters a world in which spiritual healing, superstition, magic, and medicine are all part of the scene.

---

16. Richard N. Jones, "Paleopathology" in *ABD* 5:67 notes that "while there are always some long-lived individuals in every society, life expectancy in the ancient biblical world was short by modern standards, averaging in the range of thirty to forty-five years, depending on the place and time. The advances of Greek society alone are credited by some with the extension of average longevity about five years to roughly forty to forty-five years of age, and it appears that at turn-of-the-era Jericho, one-fourth of the population survived beyond age fifty."

17. H. C. Kee, "Medicine and Healing," *ABD* 4:661.

FEATURES OF JESUS' HEALING MIRACLES

The Extent of Jesus' Healing

There are twenty-four healing encounters in the Gospels and fifteen healing summaries. John the apostle testifies that there were many others, which are unrecorded (John 20:30). Jesus performed a huge number of healing miracles, unsurpassed in human history. The healing summaries indicate that: (1) the sick were brought to Jesus in droves; (2) there was a wide range of diseases; (3) Jesus' healing was amazingly effective with only one instance given of any limitation—in his hometown—and this only in Mark's version of the event ("he *could do* no mighty work there"). Matthew's version clarifies that it was not Jesus' inability to heal, but his unwillingness because of the lack of faith that was at stake ("and he *did not* do many mighty works there," Matt 13:54-58; Mark 6:1-4).

The Variety of Healings

Jesus healed a wide variety of diseases including demonic possession, paralysis, leprosy, muteness, deafness and blindness, fever, bleeding, a shriveled hand, and dropsy. He also performed three resurrections. Most were extreme conditions that, in many cases, marginalized a person economically, socially, and religiously.

The Demography of Those Healed

Of the specific healings recorded, most were men (twenty), and four were women (Mark 1:30-31; 5:38-42; 7:24-30; Luke 13:11-13); most were Jews (twenty-one), with one a Samaritan (Luke 17:11-19) and two or three gentiles (Mark 7:24-30; Matt 8:5-13; John 4:46-50);[18] twenty-one were adults, while at least two or three were children (Mark 5:38-42; 7:24-30; 9:17-20);[19] twenty-two were unknown to Jesus, while one was his friend's mother-in-law (Peter, Mark 1:30-31) and was one was a friend (John 11). Most of

---

18. Assuming the royal official is a gentile, he could be from Herod's retinue and a Jew; assuming the centurion's servant is a gentile, and assuming the others healed are Jews, although this is not always stated.

19. The age of the royal official's child in John 4 is unclear, as is the widow of Nain's son in Luke 7. There were also children blessed by Jesus, and many could have been healed. Similarly, some in the crowds brought for healing may have been children.

the crowds were poor, while most of the other recipients were likely poor or had low-level incomes. Some, like the royal official (John 4:46-50), and perhaps others like the Roman centurion[20] and Jairus, the synagogue ruler, were wealthy.

The Contexts for Healing

Three of Jesus' healings were performed in synagogues, and some in homes: a Pharisee's home (Luke 14:1-6), Simon Peter's home (Mark 1:29-34; and parr.), and the synagogue ruler's home whose daughter was raised (Mark 5:21-42; and parr.). While Jesus made himself available, in the Synoptics, almost all healings were initiated by people who came for healing for themselves (seven times) or on behalf of others (twelve times). Jesus appears to have initiated healing on five occasions.

The Mode of Healing

Jesus usually healed through a simple word of healing (twelve times) and sometimes with touch as well (word and touch seven times). He used saliva for healing twice (Mark 8:23; John 9:6). On one occasion, a woman reached out to touch Jesus (Mark 5:28-30). It appears his main modus operandi was a statement of healing and the laying on of his hands.

The Speed of the Healings

His miracles were *usually instant* (twenty-three times). The only time it took two healings was in Mark 8:22-26 with the two saliva healings of the blind man. However, that appears to have been intentional on Jesus' part; the double healings mirror the two feeding miracles, and are symbolic representations of the spiritual healing of the disciples (see Peter's confession of Jesus' messiahship at 8:29). There was almost always a total success with those brought for healing. However, Jesus did not perform many miracles apart from a few healings in his home town due to the people's lack of faith.

---

20. The Roman centurion during Augustus' reign was paid 15,000 sestertii a year, with four sestertii worth one denarius, which was a day's wages.

The Success of Healings

Jesus refused to perform signs on request (Mark 8:11-12; Matt 12:38-39; 16:1-4; Luke 11:16, 29-30). However, he never once turned a person away who genuinely needed and sought healing. The difference is that those seeking a sign wanted to control Jesus and demanded proof that he was the Messiah. They wanted signs like those demonstrated by Moses when he came to Israel as their deliverer in Exodus (Exod 4:1-17). Where a genuine request for healing was concerned, Jesus had a "never refuse" policy; he never rejected anyone. This demonstrates a complete welcome: *all* are invited to find healing and wholeness in the kingdom. Indeed, he was even prepared to heal those in Jewish leaders' homes if their request was genuine, as in the case of Jairus, the synagogue ruler (Mark 5:22) and with the high priest's servant's ear—although this was not requested but initiated by Jesus (Luke 22:50-51). However, in some situations, Jesus did not heal many people (Mark 6:1-6). Healing is found in the present for anyone in a spiritual sense (i.e., eternal salvation). There are situations in which Jesus did not heal every sick person present. For example, in John 5:1-9, Jesus healed one disabled man amidst a multitude of the unwell. Further, even where he does intervene, these are temporary, for death is inevitable.

On a few occasions, Jesus felt *compassion* for the crowds that came to him for healing. This indicates Jesus was motivated by love, mercy, and grace in his healing ministry. For example, Matt 9:35-36: "Jesus went through all the towns and villages, teaching in their synagogues, proclaiming the good news of the kingdom and healing every disease and sickness. When he saw the crowds, *he had compassion on them*, because they were harassed and helpless, like sheep without a shepherd," (cf. Mark 6:34. Other examples include Matt 14:14; 15:32; 20:34; Mark 1:41; 8:2). The only example in Luke is for the widow before he raised her son (Luke 7:13).

The Greek for "compassion" (*splanchnizomai*),[21] literally connoting "to be moved in one's gut or bowels," suggests Jesus was moved deeply in his internal being for the plight of those who were suffering. His compassion was not mere sentiment; it moved him to act on behalf of others to

---

21. The verb is *splanchnizomai* ("feel compassion for, have pity on, have one's heart go out to someone"; see Matt 9:36; 14:14; 15:32; 18:27; 20:34; Mark 1:41; 6:34; 8:2; 9:22; Luke 7:13; 10:33; 15:20). The noun is *splanchnon* ("compassion, tender mercies, affection"; see Luke 1:78).

relieve their suffering. Believers are to respond to the needs of humanity in the same way, moved not only in their inner being, but moved to act. It is not enough to feel sympathy; followers of Jesus must respond with action. This is the basis of all ministry and work on behalf of others.

THE ISSUE OF FAITH

A common question within the church is: "Is faith required to experience healing?" This leads to the next question: "If faith is required to experience healing, what sort of faith?" Such questions are important, as some streams of the church argue that where sufficient faith is found, healing will result. Conversely, where healing does not occur, there is a lack of faith.

"Faith" is mentioned many times in the miracle accounts. Sometimes it refers to the patient's faith (Mark 5:34; 10:52; Matt 9:22, 29; 15:28; Luke 7:50; 8:48; 17:19; 18:42), while at other times it was the enquirer's faith (Matt 8:10; 9:2; Luke 5:20; 7:9). Twice Jesus made summary statements on the power of faith (Mark 11:22-24; Matt 17:20; 21:21-22; Luke 17:5-6, cf. Luke 18:8) and he rebuked people for their lack of faith (Matt 6:30; 8:26; 14:31; 16:8; 17:20; Mark 4:40; Luke 8:25; 12:28). Jesus also inquired directly of the recipient's faith on occasion (Matt 9:28). He directly commanded one recipient, Jairus, to believe (Mark 5:36; Luke 8:50). There are also a few global statements of faith. The clearest is Mark 9:23: "Everything is possible for one who believes" (NIV).

It seems indisputable that faith is required for healing, whether from the ill person, or those bringing them to Jesus. However, there are also many miracle events in which there is no mention of faith.[22] This poses an interesting question: Is faith always required? One could argue that,

---

22. Examples where faith (or belief) is *not mentioned* include: The possessed man in the synagogue (Mark 1:23-26); Peter's mother-in-law (Mark 1:30-31; and parr.); the leper (Mark 1:40-42; and parr.); the Gerasene demoniac (Mark 5:1-15; and parr.); Mark's version of the Syrophoenician woman (Mark 7:24-30); the deaf-mute man (Mark 7:31-37); the blind man at Bethsaida (Mark 8:22-26); the man with the withered hand (Matt 12:10); Matthew's version of the two blind men in Jericho (Matt 20:29-34); Luke's version of the demon-possessed boy (Luke 9:38-43); the casting out of a demon (Luke 11:14); the deliverance of Mary Magdalene (Luke 8:2); the raising of the widow of Nain's son (Luke 7:11-15); the crippled woman (Luke 13:11-13); the man with dropsy (Luke 14:1-4); the healing of the nine lepers, other than the Samaritan (Luke 17:11-19); the healing of the high priest's servant's ear (Luke 22:50-51); and the healing of the disabled man at the pool of Bethsaida (John 5:1-9). These form a substantial corpus of miracles where faith is not mentioned. It cannot simply be assumed.

because these thirteen texts have no mention of faith, faith is *not* always required. On the other hand, the expectation of faith may be read into these thirteen based on other situations where faith is clearly implied. However, this is surely flawed and assumptive. Certainly, faith seems to be a factor on occasion, and Jesus responds to it. On other occasions, Jesus simply chooses to act sovereignly as he is free to do as Lord.

With that said, faith certainly on occasion led Jesus to act. What kind of faith is in mind? One common thought is that the faith required must be specific to the sickness—absolute belief that God will heal the problem. For some, it is not enough to think God can heal, or that he could heal in a particular situation. One must *believe* specifically. Further, some contend that conditional prayers like, "If it is your will God, please heal ..." are inadequate as they show a lack of faith.

Even though it isn't a healing situation, it is helpful to consider Jesus' experience in the Garden of Gethsemane. On the eve of his death, Jesus prays for deliverance from what he is about to face, knowing he is about to go to the cross. In his humanness, understandably, he does not want to go through the physical agony that awaited him. While this is not healing, it is parallel; he wants to be released from the pain that is to come. It is clear Jesus knows he is heading to suffering and death, as the three Passion predictions indicate (Mark 8:31; 9:31; 10:32-33). Yet, despite knowing that he *must* die as a ransom for many (Mark 10:45), Jesus does not hold back but pleads with God, with all his might, for release from the path of suffering three times. He prays based on faith in God, not for the specific answer to the specific request, but on the basis that he knows God could do so *if* he willed. Jesus had faith in God, not necessarily to do what he himself wanted, but that God would do what is best for Jesus, for the world, and for his (God's) purposes. In other words, Jesus asked for what he wanted and asked with passion. But he did so because of his faith in God to act for the best, whatever God deemed so. Faith, then, is not faith for a *specific outcome* that the person decides beforehand (e.g., a healing from cancer, deliverance from the cross), but with absolute *trust in God*, whatever the outcome. Such a faith believes that God can and will act if he deems it his will, but recognizes that God is God and allows him to be God.²³ It gives God the freedom and honors his sovereignty deserved while expressing absolute trust in him.

Jesus expresses all this in these clauses:

1. **Abba, Father:** "Abba" is a transliteration of the Aramaic for "father," which is "a nursery word, part of the speech of children (not the determinative form of the noun 'father'), with the meaning approximating, 'Daddy.' "²⁴ He is the obedient, trusting child (cf. Exod 20:12; Deut 5:16; Eph 6:2).

2. **Everything is possible for you:** Another expression of trust, this time a statement of total confidence in God's infinite capability to do good. He can deliver and heal if he *chooses* to.

3. **Yet not what I will, but what you will:** Another expression of trust in God, a trust that transcends Jesus' own desire: "I want one thing desperately, but I submit it to your will because you know what is best. If you need me to go through this and its outcome is not what I desire, I still believe and trust."

This trust is also expressed in his acceptance of his fate and then living out God's will for his life, even though God's will is terrible torment. This is because God needed Jesus to suffer and die. The path to the world's salvation was Jesus' suffering. Jesus demonstrates living according to the tenets of the Lord's Prayer: "Our Father, who is in heaven ... Your will be done on earth as it is in heaven" (Matt 6:9-10).

Paul exhibits this kind of trust in 2 Corinthians 12:7-9 when he is tormented by a thorn in the flesh, a "messenger of Satan." This is some unknown affliction.²⁵ He pleads three times with God "that it should leave

---

23. It is faith in Jesus as King. It is faith in his absolute authority and will. It is trust in his sovereignty that he is divine and he knows best. It is trust that in a fallen world sometimes God's purposes require him to allow suffering in this age to achieve his great goal of seeing as many people as possible come to Christ. Ultimate healing will come in the eschaton.

24. H.-W, Kuhn, "ἀββά," in *EDNT* 1.1.

25. On the thorn, see Murray J. Harris, *The Second Epistle to the Corinthians: A Commentary on the Greek Text*, NIGTC (Grand Rapids, MI; Milton Keynes, UK: Eerdmans; Paternoster Press, 2005), 858-59, who notes that there are three basic possibilities: 1) Spiritual or psychological anxiety, e.g., conscience over his earlier persecution, anguish over Israel's unbelief; 2) Opposition to Paul, e.g., opposition in general, a single opponent, opposition in Corinth;

me," but he received a word from God: "My grace is sufficient for you, for my power is made perfect in weakness." Paul sees his thorn as something positive to keep him humble after his amazing revelations (2 Cor 12:1-4). God thus says no, despite Paul's pleading with him, with faith.

True faith is not naming an outcome and demanding it by faith (i.e., "name it and claim it"; e.g., "heal me from this disease"), then naively clinging to the claim knowing what is best, or desperately trying to drive away doubt. Rather, it is an absolute trust in God (he knows what is best and is in control), his ability (he can do it), and his purposes (he decides the outcome). It is placing one's life in his hands in total trust, asking him for what is desired, but allowing him to determine the outcome and trusting that, whatever the result, it is for the best. Both Jesus and Paul continued with their ministries—Jesus to the cross, and Paul his mission. They accepted what God chose and continued to trust in him, even when he said no. This is the faith Jesus delights in.[26]

God heals according to his will. People don't control him. Faith doesn't heal a person; only his power does. If it were faith, then people would be the prime agent. This is poor theology. It is God who is the healer, not man. Man's role is to trust him no matter what. When someone is sick, believers should do as Jesus and Paul did, and pray earnestly for what they want and desire—no holds barred. They should pray knowing that he can heal if he chooses to, and that "all things are possible" with God (Matt 19:26). Believers should do so allowing for his will to be done. He knows what is best. Pray persistently. However, when things don't go as expected, accept God's will and continue to walk in relationship with him, serving him. In this way, followers of Jesus will find the balance between passionate prayer expressing desire and knowing that not all prayers end with a "yes." Assuredly, God hears his people's prayer, and acts. He gives strength to carry on, and works for his people, for "we are more than conquerors through him who loved us" (Rom 8:37).

---

3) A physical problem (e.g., something unspecified, malarial fever, Malta fever, defective vision, migraines).

26. On the material in this section see Mark J. Keown, "The Gethsemane Prayer: A Pattern for Believers," in *Journeying into Prayer*, ed. N. Darragh (Auckland: Accent Publications, 2012), 235-42.

INDICATIONS THAT NOT ALL WOULD BE HEALED

While it could be argued from some proof texts that all will be healed with prayer and faith, Scripture provides important examples of Jesus' teaching that could be[27] read to anticipate situations where Christians will *care for the sick rather than heal them.*

Care for the Sick (Matt 25:36)

In the sheep-and-goats passage, Jesus says to those who have pleased him and will receive eternal life, "I was sick, and you *visited me.*" He does not say, "*you healed me.*" This suggests that the righteous will visit the sick without necessarily healing them. In fact, the Greek *episkeptomai* can even connote the stronger notion of not just "visit," but "care for" or "look after."[28] In other words, Jesus is granting eternal life because the righteous have a faith demonstrated through caring for the sick. This anticipates some not being healed and Christians providing medical care for those suffering in a fallen world.

The Example of the Samaritan (Luke 10:34)

In the parable of the good Samaritan, the Samaritan is commended for caring for the injured man's medical needs ("he went to him and bandaged his wounds, pouring on oil and wine"), not for healing the injured man on the road (Luke 10:34 NIV). In addition, he provides lavishly for the injured man's ongoing care.

Invite the Sick (Luke 14:13, 21)

In the great banquet parable, the servant invites a range of people. While Jesus is clearly in mind, the parable speaks to those he sends and to future Christian missionaries, whose role is to issue the invitation of God to the great eschatological feast. As such, believers are exhorted by the parable to *invite* the poor, the crippled, the lame, and the blind. There is no reference to healing in the parable. This implies the inclusion of the disabled and sick *despite* their illnesses, which would have seen them excluded from

---

27. "Could be," because none are direct and explicit and some are found in parables. However, the weight of these verses supports the idea.

28. BDAG 378.

the people of God due to uncleanness (Luke 14:13, 21). This does not rule out God healing on occasion; whether they are healed or not, believers are to care for them as God's people.

God Sometimes Says "No"

While it is not directly related to healing, Jesus' prayer for deliverance from the cross was not answered positively despite pleading with God three times (Mark 14:32–42). Similarly, in 2 Corinthians 12:7, Paul writes of the thorn in his side, which was not healed after three prayers. This indicates God declined to heal him to keep him humble and dependent. As such, believers must understand healing in the broader scheme of God's purposes in their lives and on earth. Sometimes, God chooses not to heal to achieve those purposes; often, those purposes cannot be seen or known.

The Ongoing Problem of Death and Decay

Passages such as the temptation narrative and Ephesians 6:10–17 indicate that Christ and his people are engaged in a legitimate spiritual battle where sickness and suffering are part of the "not yet" of life on earth. Ultimately, death and decay are caused by the fall (even if not by personal sin, in most cases). Although Christ has come and the victory is in one sense won, the whole of creation groans under sin and death (Rom 8:19–23). Death is the final enemy to be defeated. Until then, sickness, decay, and death permeate the world and are inevitable (1 Cor 15:26). As such, it is theologically naïve to argue that all will be healed if people have enough faith. Even the most faithful will eventually die, their bodies giving out on them through weakness. God intervenes on occasion to do miracles and can heal in any situation if he so chooses. However, he does so for his own purposes in a world where death has not yet been defeated. Ultimately, every illness will be completely healed (Rev 21:1–4), but in this present age, sometimes a person will not be healed physically. Bodies remain corruptible and perishable, but believers await their transformation when they will be imperishable (see 1 Cor 15:50–54; Phil 3:21). However, spiritual healing continues in Christ as believers are reconciled to God through the cross.[29]

---

29. In one sense, it is already complete; in another, people are being renewed progressively.

False Theology Challenged through Healing

Jesus healed in the context of clashes with Jewish leaders over their understanding of God, the law, and healing. Despite these situations, they were unimpressed, locked in their prioritizing of boundary markers over the heart of the law. There are at least three such false ideas Jesus confronted:

Misunderstanding of the Sabbath

The main theological issue with Jesus' healings is his preparedness to heal on the Sabbath. In Israel's story, the Sabbath was sacred, and work strictly forbidden. The Sabbath was a "sign" of the covenant (e.g., Exod 31:13-17), and the penalty for breaking it, death (Exod 31:15; 35:2; Num 15:32-36). In the Old Testament, a range of work activities is rejected.[30] At the time of Jesus, with circumcision and food laws, the Sabbath was a most important boundary marker that set Israel apart from the nations. It was a day of worship (e.g., Philo, *Moses* 2.215; Josephus, *Ag. Ap.* 1.209) as seen in the New Testament (Luke 4:16-17; Acts 13:14-15). Within Judaism, effort was made to define the law to ensure its maintenance. In Jubilees (c. 150 BC) and the Damascus Document in Qumran (CD 10:14-11:18), strict laws are in place.[31] Falk notes that in Qumran, "It is not permissible to profane the Sabbath for the sake of property or gain, nor assist an animal giving birth or rescue an animal from a pit. One may rescue a person from a pit, but one must not use a tool (cf. 4Q265 frg. 6 lines 6-8)."[32]

Not surprisingly, for someone who ministered frequently in synagogues, Jesus quite often healed on the Sabbath, provoking strong reactions from the Pharisees and scribes (Matt 12:1-12; Mark 3:2-4; Luke 6:1-9;

---

30. See Daniel K. Falk, "Sabbath," in *EDEJ* 1174-76. He notes the gathering wood and kindling fire (Exod 35:3; Num 15:32-36), plowing and harvesting (Exod 34:21), food preparation (Exod 16:5, 22-30), business or selling (Amos 8:5; Isa 58:13-14), bearing burdens (Jer 17:19-27), treading wine presses, and loading and moving produce (Neh 13:15-22).

31. Falk, "Sabbath," 1175. "In addition to prohibitions mentioned or implied in Scripture (pursuing one's own interests, preparing food or drink, carrying items in or out of a city or dwelling, setting out on a journey, selling or buying, tilling, kindling a fire), they prohibit lifting a load, drawing water, eating or drinking anything not prepared the preceding day, riding an animal, sexual intercourse, talking about work, traveling by ship, striking or killing, slaughtering or trapping an animal, fasting, and making war." At Qumran, breaking the Sabbath led to seven years' probation. Some things forbidden include: planning work, handling stones or earth, a nurse carrying a child from one domain to another, and carrying a bottle of perfume.

32. Falk, "Sabbath," 1175.

13:10-16; 14:3-5; John 5:9-18; 7:22-24; 9:1-34). Their reaction to Jesus was that healing was "work" and unlawful and a violation of the Sabbath, on which no work should be done (esp. Matt 12:2; Mark 2:24). In these encounters, Jesus strongly rebukes their failure to understand the law correctly (i.e., through the lens of the great commandment "love your neighbor"). Jesus replies that Israel's own tradition sees their leaders "break" the Sabbath through priestly duty (Matt 12:5) and circumcision (John 7:22-23). If a boy can be circumcised (a physical operation) on the Sabbath, and recognized as being part of Israel—God's covenant people in relationship with God)—Jesus declares that surely a person can be physically restored on the Sabbath (John 7:23).

Controversially, Jesus declares his lordship over the Sabbath (Matt 12:8). This is not only a blatant challenge to the Jewish leaders by an untrained "rabbi," but a violation of monotheism, for God alone is "Lord of the Sabbath."[33] For Jews, this is blasphemous, and they react accordingly (Mark 2:28; Luke 6:5). Jesus quotes Old Testament law demonstrating that a sensible Jew will save a dying animal on the Sabbath (Matt 12:11; Luke 13:15; 14:5). He uses this as a logical basis for what he does with a "lesser to greater" argument (i.e., humans are more valuable than animals; if one will save an animal, healing on the Sabbath is justified [Matt 12:12; Luke 13:16]. In Luke, Jesus declares the leaders are hypocrites for their inconsistency in this regard (Luke 13:15). He tells them that the purpose of the Sabbath is the good of people, not that the Sabbath should rule people to the extent that they would refuse to heal or help another in need (Mark 2:27). This inverts the intention of the Sabbath law. He demonstrates that what is lawful on the Sabbath is not adherence to oral or written specific injunctions, but doing good and saving lives, including physical and spiritual healing (Mark 3:4). By implication, to fail to heal on the Sabbath is to do evil and to destroy (Luke 6:9). The Sabbath is about freedom and release from the tyranny of the fall and from Satan. To forbid someone healing on *any day* is a disgrace (Luke 13:16). Jesus demonstrates there is a far greater law at work—that is, "love your neighbor." Love heals! The Pharisees misunderstood the nature of the law and its center: love for God and love for others.

---

33. As Edwards, *Mark*, 97 says, "Once again, Jesus puts himself squarely in the place of God."

Personal or Familial Sin Causes Sickness

On at least two occasions Jesus implicitly rejects the notion of a direct link between personal sin and sickness. In John 9:1-12, he is asked whether a man's congenital blindness was caused by his sin or his parents'. The question indicates that the disciples assume the man's blindness is due to personal or family sin. This is logical, as the Scriptures affirm that sometimes sin causes sickness (e.g., Gen 12:17; Num 12:10-16; 2 Kgs 20:1-7; Ps 38:3-4), and at times, states the principle that the consequences of sin are passed on to the third or fourth generation (e.g., Gen 15:16; Exod 20:5; 34:7; Num 14:18; Deut 5:9). Indeed, the Talmud states, "No one gets up from his sickbed until all his sins are forgiven" (b. Ned. 41a).[34] However, this thinking is also challenged in the Old Testament in such stories as that of Job, whose sin is not the cause of his suffering, and in Ezekiel 18 where the prophet argues that the sins of a father have no bearing on a righteous son. Jesus replies to the disciples that the man's blindness was not caused by sin at all, but existed so that God would be glorified.

The assumed connection between sin and sickness is also the key to unlocking the meaning of the healing of the paralytic (Mark 2:1-12; Matt 9:2-8; Luke 5:18-26). Jesus forgives the sick man, and this offends the Jewish leaders who, no doubt, believe the man was not forgiven because he remained paralyzed (i.e., his paralysis is evidence of his sin; see the above Talmudic reference). This is because they link physical infirmity with personal sin. Jesus then demonstrates that the man is forgiven by healing him, which is "harder" because to heal him requires him to be forgiven. His healing visually demonstrates the man's forgiveness and indicates that Jesus is not wrong to claim the power to heal. It is suggestive that Jesus is more than a prophet and man. He is the Son of God.

In Luke 13:1-5, Jesus more directly severs the link between sin and suffering, asking whether people who were killed by Pilate or in the fall of a tower were worse sinners than others. His answer is clearly, "no"—all are sinners and need to repent or they will perish.

Such accounts demonstrate that Jesus overthrew the idea that all sickness and suffering is the result of *personal sin* or that earthquakes and such

---

34. Morna D. Hooker, *The Gospel According to Saint Mark*, BNTC (London: Continuum, 1991), 85.

things are the result of a city's sin. Jesus points out that there are deeper things at work in sickness and suffering than personal sin. This is important today where some link the two. Certainly, it may be possible that a person's problem is linked to personal sin (e.g., Acts 5:1–11; 1 Cor 11:28), and this may be explored in prayer and counseling. However, it cannot be assumed.

Demonic Causation of Sickness

At times, there is no doubt that the cause of the illness Jesus heals is demonic, as in the cases of the demon-possessed man who was mute (Matt 9:32) and the demon-possessed boy who had seizures (Luke 9:37–43, cf. 12:22; 15:22; Luke 11:14; 13:11). However, in most healings, demons are not mentioned. The Gospel writers clearly distinguish between the demon-possessed and the sick (e.g., Matt 8:16; 10:1–2; Luke 7:21; 8:2; 9:1). This indicates there is no certain link between demon possession or oppression, and sickness. In ministry, demonic possession can be explored in prayer and counseling as a possibility, but not assumed. Great damage can be done by assuming that something is demonic, especially with a long-term mental illness. If something is demonic, it requires clear guidance that is confirmed through wise Christians.

THE LINK BETWEEN HEALING, FEEDING, AND EVANGELISM

Jesus' ministry of healing attracted huge crowds. The accounts suggest that people came largely to experience healing and deliverance. At these healing meetings, Jesus both preached and healed, and the two remained intimately connected throughout his ministry. For example, Scripture says:

> Jesus went throughout Galilee, *teaching* in their synagogues, *proclaiming the good news of the kingdom*, and *healing* every disease and sickness among the people. News about him spread all over Syria, and people brought to him all who were ill with various diseases, those suffering severe pain, the demon-possessed, those having seizures, and the paralyzed; and *he healed them.*" (Matt 4:23–24 NIV, emphasis added; see also Matt 9:35)

This typical example indicates evangelism and healing are intimately entwined in Jesus' approach to mission.

This link is found throughout the remainder of the New Testament, including Acts (Acts 5:12-16; 19:11-12) and Paul (Rom 15:19). In addition, at times when the crowd was far from options for food,[35] Jesus fed them (Mark 6:30-44; 8:1-13). This demonstrates that authentic Christian ministry can never be limited merely to proclamation, but is concerned for wholeness; the *shalom* of the kingdom. This suggests that healing (both prayer and medical assistance), deliverance ministry where God guides in this regard, and material help for those in need should be natural parts of Christian ministry today. Mission is holistic. Evangelism and teaching should be accompanied by the offer of prayer for healing and meeting the needs of others. Always, it should stem from an attitude of love and humble service.

HEALING IN THE LIFE OF BELIEVERS

Without doubt, Jesus envisaged his followers continuing his ministry of healing and deliverance through the power and authority he bestowed upon them by his Spirit. The mission of the apostles and the seventy-two included healing, deliverance, and even raising the dead (Mark 6:12-13; Matt 10:1, 8; Luke 9:6, see also Mark 16:18). This is evident in the remainder of the New Testament where healings, sometimes quite dramatic, are scattered through Acts.[36] There are prayers for God to do signs and wonders that have dramatic results (Acts 4:30; 5:12-16).[37] There are summaries of extraordinary occasions of healing (Acts 5:12-16; 19:11).[38]

Although Paul does not sensationalize miracles, he notes several times in his letters that miracles were a natural part of his ministry (Romans 15:19; 2 Cor 12:12; Gal 3:5). In the face of the triumphalist "super apostles" who demean his theology of suffering, he states in 2 Corinthians 12:12 that

---

35. Jesus did not feed every crowd, but only two (unless there were other situations not recorded). In both, the events happened "in a remote place" (lit. deserted, isolated, desolate place or a desert, wilderness). In such places, finding food was difficult (Mark 6:35; 8:4).

36. See Acts 3:1-10 (a paralytic man); 8:5-7 (paralytics and crippled); 9:32-35 (a paralytic), 36 (a resurrection), 14:8 (a lame man); 16:16-18 (exorcism); and 20:9 (a second resurrection—probably, although Luke's words are a little ambiguous).

37. This is a particularly interesting account where the believers pray for boldness to preach and for God to do signs and wonders among them. The result, in Acts 5:12-16, is astonishing with the apostles doing many miracles so that people brought their sick into the streets for healing from Peter's shadow.

38. Healing through cloths, possibly some sweat bands used in Paul's tent making (Witherington, *Acts*, 579).

signs and wonders authenticate his ministry. However, he generally does not make a feature of them, preferring to focus on the power of God seen in weakness and suffering, emulating the pattern of the cross. Yet, unique to the New Testament, he also refers to the spiritual gift of healings[39] (1 Cor 12:9, 30). The latter text is couched as a question expecting the answer "no," and suggests that some believers—but not all—have a special gift from the Spirit to heal, just as some are apostles (not all), some are prophets (not all), and some speak in tongues (not all). James 5:14-16 also refers to elders who pray, and the sick requesting the laying on of hands when they are ill.

It is conclusive, then, that Jesus called for his people to continue the healing ministry he had begun and that at times, God moves in healing. For James, it should be a ministry of the elders. For Paul, it is the ministry of the apostles and others so spiritually gifted. Thus, the opportunity for prayer for healing should be a natural part of church life today, especially from elders and those with a spiritual gift of healing. It should be seen alongside evangelistic proclamation ministry and social justice for the needy. Part of the role of elders is prayer for healing. Those with the gift of healing should be released to function in their gift. The church should possess a theology that embraces the possibility of healing, and times when God does not heal.

The Eschatological Function of Miracles

The miracles of Christ do not function primarily to reveal that, if people pray, God will fix everything. Rather, miracles function as John describes them: as signs of the kingdom. They point to the nature of the kingdom and especially to the complete physical restoration of all people, and the world, at the end of history.

THE SIGNIFICANCE OF THE MIRACLES

There are many ways Jesus' miracles can be understood.

---

39. The word "healings" in the Greek is plural. This leads to questions of whether the gift is given to the healer, the person(s) healed, whether the gift is permanent or granted on each occasion, or whether it refers to various kinds of healing (see Gordon D. Fee, *The First Epistle to the Corinthians*, NICNT [Grand Rapids, MI: Eerdmans, 1987], 594; Roy E. Ciampa and Brian S. Rosner, *The First Letter to the Corinthians*, PNTC [Grand Rapids, MI; Cambridge, U.K.: Eerdmans, 2010], 578-90).

THE MIRACLES AS FICTION

Many people over the centuries, especially in western philosophic tradition, have denied that the miracles are genuine. They see Jesus' miracles as leftovers from an archaic worldview, constructs of the early church, or false claims to make Jesus seem divine. *The Da Vinci Code*, for example, argues that the miracles were made up to validate the divinity of Christ. Since David Hume (mid-eighteenth century), many philosophers have rejected the possibility of miracles by limiting reality to the natural (i.e., that which can be rationally assessed and experienced). They reject any claim to a miracle on the basis that "miracles cannot happen."[40] Where they exist in the Scriptures, they are either completely fictitious, or embellishments of something much more basic. So, some liberal thinkers have sought alternative explanations for the miracles. For example, Jesus did not walk on water; he walked "beside" the water (i.e., at the water's edge),[41] or on a sand bar, on rocks,[42] or even on ice.[43] Others argue that the miracles are not part of the earliest tradition about Jesus and are the creation of the early church to make Jesus seem more divine or messianic. In this line, "form critics" believe that the early church took stories about the virgin birth, baptism, the transfiguration, and the resurrection, which were part of the culture of the Greco-Roman world, and attached them to Jesus so that Jesus looked more like a "divine man" (*theios anēr*) and the Gospels like an aretalogy.[44] In this sense, the Gospels are religious propaganda telling the story of a divine man who has miraculous powers.[45]

---

40. David Hume, *An Enquiry Concerning Human Understanding* (New York: Bobbs-Merill, 1955), 114. Hume writes, "A miracle is a violation of the laws of nature; and as a firm and unalterable experience has established these laws, the proof against a miracle, from the very nature of the fact, is as entire as any argument from experience can possibly be imagined."

41. E.g., Albert Schweitzer, *The Quest of the Historical Jesus: A Critical Study of its Progress from Reimarus to Wrede*, 2nd ed. (London: Adam and Charles Black, 1926), 378.

42. See Edwards, *Mark*, 196, who notes Schweitzer's *Quest of the Historical Jesus* (1906) has many examples of people who argue that it was an optical illusion and Jesus walked on a sandbar.

43. See Libby Fairhurst, "Jesus Walked on Ice, Study Says," (April 4, 2006); Sara Goudarzi, "Did Jesus walk on water?" (April 4, 2006).

44. The recitation of the *aretai* (Greek, "virtues," "mighty deeds") of a god, hero, or charismatic figure.

45. For example, Philostratus' *Life of Apollonius of Tyana* from the second century presented a synthesized portrait of the wonder-working Pythagorean philosopher. See the discussion in C. A. Evans' work, "Apollonius of Tyana," in *DNTB*, 80–81. Understanding of

Others suggest that Jesus used magic to heal and that he was essentially a magician. Some, such as Rudolph Bultmann (1884–1976), believe that the miracles are to be rejected as unhistorical along with all remnants of an ancient worldview. This process, called demythologization, involves the removal of all aspects of the supernatural including the devil, the demonic, angels, heaven, hell, a three-storied universe, miracles, resurrection, and even the concept of God.

On the one hand, it is impossible to successfully and completely prove the authenticity of the miracle accounts. They are exceptional events, and there are no records other than the Gospels and a few summary statements elsewhere. There are no criteria by which theologians can completely and confidently assess their validity. However, a few comments can lend support to the idea that these are authentic accounts.

Miracle Stories in the Surrounding World Do Not Prove Borrowing

The existence of other accounts of healings from the time does not prove correspondence. Such stories of healing, divine or otherwise, are common to many cultures and prove little. Further, close studies of these stories have shown that the accounts of Jesus are distinct to what are myths. Jesus' accounts occur in physical space and time and amid actual people who can be verified historically.[46]

Apollonius is found in Philostratus, *Vita Apollonii*. A comparison between Jesus and Apollonius was made by Hierocles (*Lover of Truth*) arguing that Christian claims to Jesus' divinity were flawed as Apollonius did much the same things. Eusebius wrote a response *Against the Life of Apollonius of Tyana* showing the differences with Jesus. Form critics (e.g., Dibelius, Bultmann) have argued that Jesus' life was embellished with stories from such workers. Several scholars (e.g., Twelftree, Koskenniemi, and Evans) have responded and rejected this, seeing better parallels in Jewish tradition (Old Testament, Pseudepigrapha). Rabbi Apollonius' miracles include: (1) Healing a lame man with massage (Philostratus, *Vit. Apoll.* 3.39); (2) Healing a blind man (*Vit. Apoll.* 3.39); (3) Healing a paralytic (*Vit. Apoll.* 3.39); (4) Healing a woman through releasing a hare (*Vit. Apoll.* 3.39); (5) Exorcism of a young boy who then became a philosopher (*Vit. Apoll.* 4.20); (6) Raising a dead girl during a funeral, although it is unclear whether she was actually dead (*Vit. Apoll.* 4.45); (7) Miraculous translations (*Vit. Apoll.* 4.10; 8.12); (8) Apollonius' ascension (*Vit. Apoll.* 8.30); and (9) a Post-mortem appearance (*Vit. Apoll.* 8.31). Evans notes that while there is a superficial similarity with Jesus, Jesus does not use the same fanciful trickery as attributed to Apollonius. The credibility of the sources is also uncertain. Finally, the date of Apollonius' work is generally agreed to be between AD 217 and 238; if there is dependence, it is far more likely it is from Christianity to Philostratus' work, as the Gospels were completed by *the end of the first century*.

46. See especially R. Nash, *The Gospel and the Greeks: Did the New Testament Borrow from Pagan Thought?* The Student Library (Phillipsburg, NJ: P & R Publishers, 2003); J. P. Moreland,

Magic or Psychosomatic Explanations Are Unsatisfactory

It is also unlikely that magic or psychosomatic suggestion is an adequate explanation for Jesus' healings. Jesus does not use any aids, incantations, or tricks to heal. His healings are simple and straightforward, and performed through word and touch. Howard C. Kee has helpfully delineated the differences in ancient thought concerning medicine (building on the foundation of the natural order), miracle (based on belief in divine intervention), and magic (manipulating mysterious forces for personal benefit). Kee demonstrates that Jesus' healings normally belong to the second of these three categories: miracle.[47] The only times Jesus uses anything other than word or touch are when the bleeding woman touches the hem of his robe and power flows from him spontaneously, or when he uses saliva (on one occasion mixed with mud). The hem of his robe is not magic as if the healing is active, nor did Jesus "use" his robe in any way; rather, the healing is passive, indicating that healing power radiates from Jesus' presence, even through his clothing. This is an extension of touch. Similarly, the use of saliva is an extension of touch. Jesus' body is infused with God's power by the Holy Spirit.

Alternative Explanations are Supposition

The process of rationalization of Jesus' miracles through finding alternative explanations is pure supposition. The texts clearly explain things as they were seen.

The Claims of the Gospels to Authenticity

Richard Bauckham has made a solid claim that the Gospels are eyewitness accounts (Matthew, John) or accounts of those in direct contact with eyewitnesses (Mark/Peter; Luke/Paul, and those encountered in Luke's trips, including Jerusalem). As such, they have as reasonable a claim to authenticity as any ancient document. Indeed, if their historicity is rejected, the historicity of other ancient writers such as those who recorded the details of the Roman Empire—Tacitus, Suetonius, and Cassius Dio—should be rejected as well.

Scaling the Secular City: A Defense of Christianity (Grand Rapids, MI: Baker, 1987), 159–84.
   47. See Blackburn, "Divine Man/*Theois Anēr*," 189.

The Absence of Evidence for "Demythologization"

The process of so-called demythologization is also fraught with difficulties. It assumes naivety on the part of those living at the time. It also evacuates the whole Gospel account and the Christian message of anything but the nice ethical teaching of Christ. There are sound historical reasons for accepting the authenticity of the resurrection in terms of the remarkable development of Christianity. "Myth" is so fused into the story there is little left when it is demythologized. Neither is there evidence of the process of this occurring in the early church.

The "Divine Man" Hypothesis is Unlikely

The concept of *theios anēr* is highly disputed by New Testament scholars. There is no evidence that Jewish thinkers couched their message in these terms.[48]

The a priori *Rejection of Miracles is a Weak Argument*

The philosophical rejection of miracles based on science and experience is also weak. There is no *a priori*[49] reason to reject miracles on rational grounds. If there is a God who is all supreme and who created nature and its "laws," then miracles are possible. It becomes a matter of faith for both parties. One has faith in natural processes and creation by "chance" or some unknown agent. The other has faith in a supernatural God who creates and does miracles in the time-space continuum. However, the Christian faith is not based on foolishness. Within the Scriptures themselves and in the history of the Christian church, there are many testimonies of healings and other miracles that cannot be discounted rationally. In addition, miracles and creation are feasible philosophical explanations of reality.

---

48. See Blackburn, "Divine Man/*Theios Anēr*," 190.

49. Lewis Sperry Chafer, *Systematic Theology* (Grand Rapids, MI: Kregel Publications, 1993), 1.142 defines an *a priori* argument in this way: "The *a priori* argument is one which is based on something which has gone before as an assumed reality, an innate belief, or intuitive impression."

*The Form-Critical Criteria of Authenticity
Supports Their Authenticity*

Importantly, there is now little debate among New Testament scholars of all persuasions concerning the healings and exorcisms of Jesus. This is because, even according to the criteria of authenticity applied by form critics, these miracles appear authentic and are from the earliest traditions.[50] Jesus' healing and deliverance ministry is attested in every stratum of Gospel material (Q, Mark, M, L, John) and across all literary forms (sayings, miracle stories, summaries, controversy stories, the so-called legends, and the passion narratives [Mark 15:31 parr.]). As such, somewhat surprisingly, there is convincing evidence that Jesus performed miracles, even using criteria that reject other aspects of his ministry.

Jesus as a Miracle Worker Is Supported in Extra-Biblical Sources

Interestingly, Jesus was also known as a healer/exorcist outside of early Christianity in non-Christian sources. These include the magical papyri (PGM 4.3019-30)[51] and within later Jewish circles (e.g., *Topsepta Hul. Hullin* 2:22-23),[52] as well as the Qur'an.[53] From a form-critical perspective, the evidence that Jesus raised the dead is also reasonably strong. There is a saying in Q that states that in Jesus' ministry "the dead are raised" (Matt 11:4-5). In addition, there are resurrection accounts in Matthew, Luke, and John, meaning that the resurrection is found in all traditions (Mark, Q, L, M,

---

50. See Blackburn, "Miracles and Miracle Tradition," in *DJG*, 550.

51. On the magical papyri, see Clinton E. Arnold, "Magical Papyri," in *DNTB*, 668-70. They are a collection of 230 papyri documents from the Greco-Roman context, found mainly in Egypt, dated from before the first century to the fourth century AD, which include "incantations, rituals, formulas, spells, hymns and a variety of magical symbols, characters and names" in Greek and other ancient languages, including Aramaic. Many are recipes to make amulets and curse tablets—which pronounce curses on enemies. They include formulas, spells, rituals, protective charms, how to cast out spirits and sickness, and love spells. They help understand popular understandings of magic, superstition, and the supernatural, which were widespread. Magic was important to coerce the spirits and gods to do one's bidding. Despite negative attitudes toward magic, such magical ideas flourished in Israel. They give background to Jesus' exorcism and healing ministry.

52. Blackburn, "Miracles," 556.

53. In the Qur'an, Jesus did miracles including: (1) Speaking while in the cradle (19:30); (2) Breathing life into clay models of birds (perhaps indicating knowledge of the Gospel of Thomas [3:43]); (3) Curing a leper and a blind man (5:110); (4) Raising the dead (5:110); and (5) Requesting a table descend from heaven with a feast in answer to the prayers of his disciples (5:110-14). None of these are in the New Testament or reliable.

John), making it unlikely that the Markan stories are inauthentic. As such, there is good reason to accept that Jesus performed miracles and even raised the dead.

THE MIRACLES AS EVIDENCES OF JESUS' MESSIAHSHIP AND DIVINITY

In the past, some thought that the miracles were proofs of Jesus' divinity. That is, they *prove* that Jesus is God's divine Son and Messiah. However, it is generally agreed now that it is going too far to say they are proofs that Jesus is divine. First, although a good case can be made for their validity, they are unable to be authenticated absolutely in historical and scientific terms. This means they fall short of *proof* in a historical or scientific sense. Second, even if they are accepted as authentic, they do not establish Jesus as anything more than a prophet or a *thaumaturge* ("miracle worker"). However, what distinguishes Jesus from other miracle workers of the ancient world is the phenomenal extent and impact of his miracles. At best, his miracles point to his amazing access to divine power, but they do not prove his divinity. Other people in Israel's story performed miracles, notably Moses, Joshua, Elijah, and Elisha. Further, there is no thought in Israel that these people were divine because of miracles; rather, they were recognized as spiritual, imbued prophets sent from God. In the case of Jesus, it is uncertain how many miracles of Jesus were seen by people. They may have only encountered him once or twice. Only those who traveled with him possessed the full picture. Gospel readers are able to read of his phenomenal miracle ministry.

As such, it makes perfect sense that Jesus was seen as one sent by the divine as an amazingly endowed prophet as evidenced by his miracles (e.g., Mark 6:15; 8:28). There is no reason for Jews to see him as their messiah or divine because of miracles. However, his arrival is exciting as was John's; the silence of the prophets was broken. As such, he may precede the messiah like John and is not necessarily *the* messiah. They are, at best, highly suggestive of his messiahship, and raise the possibility he is Messiah and divine.

From the perspective of a resurrected Jesus, they have greater evidential strength—but only if Jesus did rise and only if people believe it. Assuming they happened, they strongly suggest that Jesus was sent from

God and was a prophet in the Jewish tradition. After all, the Jews had no idea that God would come as a man.[54]

The argument for Jesus' divinity is cumulative. It is the sum total of the miracles, the way he fulfilled prophecy (e.g., Isa 9:6), his claims to divinity found in his teaching and that of the disciples, his resurrection, his ascension, and his impact on humanity and the world. The miracles of Jesus point *parabolically* to his identity as, along with his resurrection, evidence of his messiahship. His miracles beg the question, "Who is this man?"

MIRACLES AS ACTS OF COMPASSION
CHRISTIANS ARE TO CONTINUE

In the past, some scholars saw the primary significance of the miracles as acts of compassion. This view was particularly favored by those who saw Jesus' ministry in liberal this-worldly terms (e.g., the social gospel). Having removed all supernatural elements, only a loving Jesus who teaches compassion is left. So, the miracles had to be reinterpreted naturalistically; from this "actual" event grew the miracles as understood within the early church.

For example, they interpreted the feeding of the five thousand and four thousand as people sharing their food together. The story teaches that people should share what they have. The miracles are examples of loving your neighbor and teach the importance of showing compassion for the needy and working for their healing and deliverance from suffering.

It is critical that believers affirm that Jesus' miracles are most certainly acts of compassion, with the language of compassion used regularly of Jesus' miracle ministry of feeding and healing (Matt 9:36–10:1; 14:14; 15:32; 20:34; Mark 6:34; 8:2; 9:22; Luke 7:13). Jesus was deeply moved to help others in need, and so should his people. The desire of Christians to alleviate poverty and heal the sick, whether supernaturally or through medicine (not that the two are mutually exclusive), is noble, right, and a part of Jesus'

---

54. It is interesting to compare Isaiah 9:6 in the Masoretic Text on which the English Bible is translated and the LXX, the Greek translation. Isaiah 9:6 appears to say that the messiah will be called "Almighty God," and "everlasting Father." When the translators came to this passage, to protect God's absoluteness, they translated it thus: "Because a child was born to us; a son was given to us whose leadership came upon his shoulder; and his name is called 'Messenger of the Great Council,' for I will bring peace upon the rulers and health to him" (LES). Two-and-a-half centuries before Christ, there could be no way that the messiah was God.

call to mission. Indeed, one dimension of the call of the kingdom is restoration, and compassion should underpin mission efforts. However, while the miracles are certainly acts of compassion, there is general agreement among New Testament scholars today that there is much more at stake in Jesus' miracles.

MIRACLES AS INDICATORS OF THE POWER OF GOD TO HEAL TODAY

Some, particularly in the contemporary charismatic and Pentecostal movements, see the miracles primarily as indicators of what Jesus can do in this day through his people. Heaven has come to earth and his followers, infused with the Spirit, have total authority over sickness and demons and continue the ministry of Jesus. Some of Jesus' teaching is taken literally (e.g., Mark 11:22–24), while other elements and a deeper understanding of Jesus and the kingdom are downplayed. Extreme views, such as hyper-faith thinking, attest that believers can heal all disease with sufficient faith. This is not possible, considering this world contains the graves of many hyper-faith healers.

A favorite proof text is John 14:12: "Truly, truly, I say to you, whoever believes in me will also do the works that I do; and greater works than these will he do, because I am going to the Father." Views differ on the meaning of this text. Earlier thinkers tended to interpret it as pointing to the missionary successes in Acts, whereby the disciples did "greater things" than Jesus in leading thousands to faith and performing signs and wonders. Most today read it eschatologically. They note that the key is Jesus "going to the Father," and so, post-Easter, his people will not do *more* miracles (quantitative), but because Jesus is risen and the Paraclete has come, "greater things" has a qualitative sense. Also, in John, the customary word for miracles is "signs," but he did not use this word in John 14:12. Rather, he used *ergon*, works. While *ergon* in John is sometimes used of miracles (John 7:21; 9:3), it is in John a term mostly used generically of all Jesus' works, which are God's work in and through him.[55] It implies far more than

---

55. Specifically, Jesus' "works that the Father has given me to accomplish" (John 5:36), "works you [Jesus] are doing" (John 7:3), "works of him who sent me" (John 9:4), "works that I do in my Father's name" (John 10:25), "many good works from the Father" (John 10:32, 33), "works of my Father" (John 10:37), "the works" (John 10:38), "the Father in me does his works"

miracles. The three ideas brought together here do not suggest that an individual believer can do *more* miracles than Jesus. Rather, it encompasses all three ideas. First, it speaks of the era of the Spirit in which people of faith will do wonderful things in the name of Jesus. Second, while many contemporary scholars reject the missional interpretation, it is possible that "greater works" includes early church missional work evidenced as the church spread from its small beginnings in Israel to the world (cf. John 4:34). The spread of Christianity to the present vindicates Jesus' prophetic statement. Third, "greater works" are as diverse as God's work on earth. Christians have been decisive in ending institutional slavery; pioneering the vote to women; "Christianizing" nations; dying for their faith; leading countries; composing glorious music in Jesus' name; feeding multitudes of the poor; building universities, schools, and hospitals; and much more. Jesus knew that when he rose, and his Spirit was liberated, the capacity of his people would be released, and they would do the most marvelous things in his name. To limit this to miracles is an insipid reading.

However, there is some truth in the idea that the function of miracles is to encourage Christians to believe that God will intervene. His Spirit is present, and God's capacities in Christ by his Spirit are limitless. Evidence of healings in the New Testament span Luke's edited highlights of the first thirty years of the church and elsewhere (e.g., Phil 2:27). Paul believed in the gifts of healings, and James urged the sick to go to the elders for healing. It is central of church life to lay hands on the sick. So, when a person needs healing or a miracle of provision or some other grave need, believers should not hold back. They should come to God, *Abba* Father, state their trust that he can do anything if he wills, and pray in the name of Jesus for their need. Then, it is up to God, for man does not control him. When believers pray, something happens—and God decides what he will do. Sometimes he heals, or he directly provides. At other times, he heals

---

(John 14:10), "believe on account of the works themselves" (John 14:11), "the works" (John 15:24), and "the work that you gave me to do" (John 17:4). Also used of greater deeds by God indicating resurrection (John 5:20), the work of God that is faith (John 6:28-29), the deeds of Abraham (John 8:39). Also, God's works in believers (John 3:21) and God's missional work in a general sense (John 4:34). It can be negative of the deeds of Satan (John 8:41) and people's evil actions (John 3:19, 20; 7:7).

through the wonderful world of medicine. He always meets his people in their need through prayer, and he strengthens, encourages, and comforts.

There are two equal and opposite dangers. One is to go in the direction of the hyper-faith movement and believe that with enough faith, what is prayed for will materialize. The other is what is called cessationism, a feature of classical dispensationalism,[56] whereby on a false reading of 1 Corinthians 13:8–9,[57] the miracles ended at the age of the apostles. Both extremes are heretical and both dangers must be avoided.

THE MIRACLES FROM THREE POINTS OF
REFERENCE: PAST, PRESENT, AND FUTURE

Thinking in salvation historical and theological terms, the miracles have three points of reference (temporal):

1. **Fulfilment:** First, the miracles of Jesus look *backward* to the hopes and expectations of Israel for wholeness (*shalom*), including healing.

2. **The presence of the kingdom:** Second, the miracles of Jesus speak into both the *present* at the time of Jesus' ministry and into *this present age*, suggesting that the power of God, and thus his kingdom, is present in the ministry of Christ. In that, the kingdom has come, and the Spirit of God has been released to his people; by the Spirit, the ministry of signs and wonders will continue in the present age as part of the mission of the church.

---

56. See "Dispensationalism," in Grenz et al., *PDTT* 40. It is a theological system that originated in the early to mid-1800s by John Nelson Darby (18 November 1800–29 April 1882) and was popularized, especially in America, by the *Scofield Reference Bible*. It breaks salvation history into dispensations (eras) with distinct plans for Israel and the church, a so-called literal reading of Scripture (although with some strange results like the so-called rapture in Matthew 24 and cessationism in 1 Corinthians 13), a secret rapture before Christ's return, and a literal millennium in which Christ will rule with Israel. It has morphed over the years with progressive dispensationalism modifying this substantially.

57. It is argued that the cessation of tongues and prophecy speaks of the end of the period of spiritual gifts. However, (1) the contrast is between this age and the eschaton, not the age of the apostles and church, and (2) the whole context is about the spiritual gifts God has given his church, not their cessation.

3. **The future consummation:** Third, and arguably most importantly, the miracles *point forward* to the future consummation of the kingdom, at which time all suffering will cease. They provide a glimpse into what the kingdom coming means (i.e., they demonstrate the nature of the kingdom). They also reveal the nature of the King—he is a compassionate healer, not a violent destroyer.

The Miracles as Fulfillment (Past)

The first temporal point of reference is the way in which the miracles throw a spotlight on the past. This indicates the hopes expressed in the Old Testament and other Jewish literature are coming to pass in the life and ministry of Jesus. The King and kingdom are here.

God the miracle worker. In the Old Testament, God is a healer and miracle worker (e.g., Gen 1–2; Exod 13–14; Josh 10:12–13; 2 Kings 20:1–11). There are also the many miracles of Moses, Joshua, Elijah, and Elisha, which were seen as God's work. There are specific examples of healing. These include:

1. **The God who heals:** After Moses had thrown a piece of wood into bitter waters to make them drinkable, he brings a message from the Lord: "If you listen carefully to the Lord your God and do what is right in his eyes, if you pay attention to his commands and keep all his decrees, I will not bring on you any of the diseases I brought on the Egyptians, *for I am the Lord, who heals you*" (Exod 15:26 NIV, emphasis added). Jesus is thus the new Moses, fulfilling and transcending God's healing in the torah, through whom God is healing.

2. **The God who wounds and heals:** God declares, "There is no god besides me; I put to death and I bring to life; *I have wounded and I will heal*" (Deut 32:39 NIV, emphasis added). Similarly, in Job, Scriptures says, "For he wounds, but he also binds up; he injures, but *his hands also heal*" (Job 5:18 NIV, emphasis added).

Jesus, then, is the fulfillment and expression of God's healing character.

The conquest, judges, prophets, and miracles. One of the distinctive features of the Old Testament prophets was the performing of miracles. Moses was seen as the first great prophet in the line of Deuteronomy 18:15. He was instrumental in many miracles, including judgment, deliverance, provision, revelation, and guidance.[58] Joshua was also a miracle worker, manifested through military victories, the conquest of Canaan, the giving of the law, and prophecy.[59] The history of Israel from Moses to the rise of the ninth-century prophets included miracles, usually in relation to the exodus-conquest (seen as one great miracle), the defeat of armies, judgment, and momentous cosmic events.[60] In the history of the pre-monarchy and monarchy, there are a number of deliverance miracles interpreted by the Deuteronomic historian as God's intervention.[61]

The ninth-century prophets Elijah and Elisha performed great miracles, including miracles of provision (1 Kgs 17:7-16; 2 Kgs 4:1-7, 38-44), healing (2 Kgs 5:1-14), reanimation (1 Kgs 17:17-24; 2 Kgs 4:18-36), judgment (2 Kgs 6:8-23), and miracles over nature (1 Kgs 18:22-39; 2 Kgs 2:19-22; 6:1-7).

Jesus' miracles, then, declared him to be a prophet in the line of Moses, Elijah, and Elisha. Hence, he was seen by many as a prophet (Mark 6:15; 8:28; Luke 24:19). However, he transcended these miracle workers in the nature, number, and extent of his miracles, which indicated he was more than merely a prophet. Theologically, as Messiah, he fulfilled the prophetic ministries of the Old Testament.

Eschatological expectation of healing (messianic age). The hope of the Messiah and the kingdom of God included the hope of physical wholeness (and indeed cosmic wholeness) — *shalom*. This is reflected in how John the

---

58. *Judgment*: the plagues of judgment on Egypt (see Exod 7:14-12:30); judgment for rebellion (Exod 32:1-25; Num 11:1-3; 12:9-11; 14:1-45; 15:32-36; 16:1-50; 21:4-9; 25:1-9); *deliverance*: the parting of the Red Sea (Exod 13:17-14:41); defeat of enemy armies (Exod 17:8-16; Num 21:1-3, 21-35; 31:1-24); *provision*: water and food (see Exod 15:22-17:7; Num 11:4-35; 20:1-13); *revelation*: the bringing of the law (Exod 20); *guidance*: (Exod 23:20-33; Num 10:11-13, 33-34).

59. Joshua's military victories (Exod 17:8-13; Josh 5:13-27; 10:1-14); the giving of the law (Exod 24:13; 32:17); prophecy (Josh 6:6-26).

60. This includes the stopping of the river Jordan for Israel's crossing into the land (Josh 3:9-17), the fall of Jericho (Josh 5:13-6:27), the punishment on Achan (Josh 7:1-26), and the stilling of the sun for a day (Josh 10:1-15).

61. For example, Gideon (Judg 6-8), Samson (Judg 13-16), and David's defeat of Goliath (1 Sam 17).

Baptist's disciples questioned Jesus' identity (Matt 11:4-5). John, who initially recognized Jesus as Messiah, wanted assurance that Jesus is the one who is to come and not another forerunner like John himself. Perhaps he was surprised that Jesus was non-militaristic. Jesus' response reflects this expectation: "Go back and report to John what you hear and see: The blind receive sight, the lame walk, those who have leprosy are cleansed, the deaf hear, the dead are raised, and the good news is proclaimed to the poor" (NIV). Clearly, these miracles showed that Jesus was Messiah more than any expected military victory.

These words recall a series of passages in Isaiah, such as Isaiah 29:18, which reads, "In that day the deaf will hear the words of the scroll, and out of gloom and darkness the eyes of the blind will see" (NIV). Similarly, Isaiah 35:5-6 says, "Then will the eyes of the blind be opened and the ears of the deaf unstopped. Then will the lame leap like a deer, and the mute tongue shout for joy" (NIV). Again, in Isaiah 61:1, which Jesus cites in the Nazareth synagogue (Luke 4:18-20), the prophet declares, "The LORD has anointed me to proclaim good news to the poor ... to bind up the brokenhearted" (NIV).[62]

The coming servant is also a healer. Isaiah 42:6-7 says this servant will "be a covenant for the people and a light for the Gentiles, to *open eyes that are blind*" (NIV, emphasis added). Isaiah predicts of the servant:

> Surely he took up our pain and bore our suffering, yet we considered him punished by God, stricken by him, and afflicted. But he was pierced for our transgressions, he was crushed for our iniquities; the punishment that brought us peace was on him, and by his wounds we are healed. (Isaiah 53:4-5 NIV)

Thus, by his vicarious sacrifice, the servant will bring healing and *shalom*.

Through his many miracles Jesus is declaring, for those with eyes to see, that he is God's agent of this healing—the servant-Messiah. In his ministry, God had come to redeem his people and world (i.e., his kingdom is here). This note of fulfillment is explicit in Matthew 8:17 where Matthew states that Jesus' ministry is "to fulfill" the words of Isaiah 53:4. In the Prophets,

---

62. Interestingly, when Jesus quotes this text in Nazareth (Luke 4:18-19), he deletes the reference to binding up the brokenhearted.

this restoration is also cosmic—the healings are but one dimension of the whole of creation restored to what God intends it to be. These are signs of the bigger picture of cosmic healing.

The Kingdom and God's Power Are Present Now in the Messiah King (Present)

The texts of fulfillment from the Old Testament point to the miracles being a physical demonstration of the presence of the power of God (i.e., the reign of God is expressed in the miracles). Jesus' miracles are then one expression of God's royal power in Christ. The connection to the kingdom is found throughout the Synoptics. Each miracle points to the nature of the kingdom and the ultimate outcome in the consummated future.

His healings point to the healing power of God to make the broken whole and the future kingdom free of illness and suffering. Jewish tradition expected miracles in the eschaton. After Christ's resurrection, healings are found in the New Testament (Acts 3:1–10; 5:12–16; 8:7; 14:8–11; 19:11; 28:7–10). There are also rare instances of God acting in judgment causing people illness or death (Acts 5:1–11; 13:8–11; 1 Cor 11:28). While it is disputed, they still happen today.[63]

Jesus' exorcisms are pointers to his victory over the powers of darkness and the ultimate defeat of evil (Luke 11:20; Matt 12:28 NRSV). While the Old Testament does not say much about demons or deliverance ministry, some apocalyptic writers expected the advent of the kingdom to spell doom for Satan and his demonic minions[64] (Acts 5:16; 8:7; 16:16–18; 19:12). Interestingly, outside of Acts, there is no mention of the specific issue of casting out demons or evil spirits. It is probably seen as an aspect of miracles and healing. Although a complex issue, demonic deliverance remains a vital ministry in the church.

The resurrections demonstrate victory over death, even if a temporary reprieve. They look forward to the glorious resurrection of Christ. Ultimately, they look to the final resurrection of the dead and the gift of eternal life. Old Testament texts point to the hope of resurrection in the

---

63. See Young, "Miracles in Church History"; Wimber and Springer, "Signs and Wonders in Church History."

64. See for example: 1 *En* 10:11–15; 54–55; 11QMelch; *T. Levi* 18:12; *T. Mos.* 10:1–2, cf. Matt 12:28; Luke 11:20.

"age to come" (i.e., at the culmination of the age; Isa 26:19; Dan 12:1-3, see also Chapter 15). While they are rare and disputed by skeptics, there are examples of the resurrection of dead people in the post-resurrection New Testament, and in the history of the church.

The provision miracles actualize and foreshadow the dream of a future messianic feast for all nations where the finest food and wine is consumed in peace (Isa 25:6-9).[65] The abundance of bread points to the eschatological equivalent of the provision of manna in the wilderness (2 *Bar.* 29:7-8, cf. John 6:4-5, 14, 30-31; Rev. 2:17). Many Christians lay claim to personal experiences of provision.

The two nature or rescue miracles—Jesus' calming of and walking on the sea—point to "Yahweh's assertion of his sovereignty over the sea in creation (Job 26:12-13; Ps 74:12-15), the exodus (Ps 77:16-20), and the eschaton (Isa 27:1, cf. Rev 21:1)."[66] They declare Christ's power as Creator (John 1:3; Col 1:16; Heb 1:2) and a new creation in which the forces of nature will no longer threaten immortal humanity (Matt 19:28; Rom 8:19-23; 2 Cor 5:17; Gal 6:15; Rev 21-22). Nature miracles today are more difficult to verify.

The disciples and the early church continued in healings and miracles, supporting the view that there was no cessation of miracles in New Testament writers' minds. The Spirit's power is present in the disciples, and it is the same power used by God and Christ to perform miracles. As the disciples minister in the power of the same Spirit, they are used by God and Christ to perform miracles, and the powers of darkness are forced back. However, the "already, not yet" eschatological tension continues in the present age with death and decay still strongly present and dominant. Indeed, in each person's case, these forces always "win" at a physical level; all people face aging and death. However, God is present to intervene as he wills. He is also present in and through suffering and will bring his people healing on the other side. Death is not the final word!

The Nature of the Future Consummation of the Kingdom (Future)

The miracles also point to the character of the kingdom and the future final state. The kingdom in its fullness is a place of *shalom* ("peace") and

---

65. See also 2 *Bar.* 29:4; Matt 8:11; Luke 13:29; 14:15.
66. Blackburn, "Miracles," 559.

wholeness in which there will be no illness, pain, evil, death, or suffering (cf. Rev 21:1-4). The deliverance miracles announce the defeat of Satan and evil. The healings declare the end of decay and physical suffering. The miracles over nature proclaim that the laws of nature may be transcended in the new creation. The miracles of resurrection point to Christ's resurrection and that of all believers (1 Cor 15:50-55; Phil 3:12). The provision miracles speak of humanity without poverty. The miracles, then, are signs of the kingdom—windows into the nature of the kingdom to come.

HEALING MIRACLES AS SIGNS OF THE
COSMIC HEALING OF THE KINGDOM

The miracles of healing reveal that the reign of God is about total human and cosmic physical and spiritual restoration. They show that humanity, the apex of God's creation (Gen 1:26-27), is being restored through the work of Christ. They affirm that God is deeply concerned about the body. There is no dualism, no belief in the body as evil or inferior. Rather, the kingdom brings restoration to the whole person, including the physical (and society, and ultimately, creation itself). The healing miracles speak of a restored creation as the effects of sin are reversed in the removal of physical suffering and pain (Rev 21:4).

The exorcisms point to the overthrow of evil, the defeat of Satan, and the deliverance of humanity from him and his physical, psychological, and social effects. Satan's defeat was achieved at the cross and will be completed at the end. At the second coming, disease, suffering, pain, and evil will end. Followers of Jesus live in the "not yet," not the "already." In the present, death, decay, and disease are still the believer's experience (even when miracles occur). They long for the end and must live with decay, suffering, pain, illness, and evil in the meantime; like all of creation, believers groan for redemption (Rom 8:22). True healing comes amongst suffering as God's people are inwardly restored despite the suffering of their bodies.

Deliverance Miracles

The exorcisms of Jesus cannot be removed from his ministry as a remnant of some ancient worldview; they are etched into each source and are an inexorable part of his ministry. The exorcisms are a visible expression of the war between God's kingdom and the dominion of Satan and evil (cf. Eph

6:11–17). They show the power of God plundering Satan's realm. This is indicated in the statement by Jesus at the Beelzebub controversy in Matthew 12:28: "But if it is by the Spirit of God that I drive out demons, *then the kingdom of God has come upon you*" (NIV, emphasis added). Jesus challenges the Pharisaic doubters—who believe he is an emissary of Satan—to recognize that his ministry of deliverance is the defeat of Satan. This part of the drama begins at Jesus' temptation, where he resists Satan's attempts to deceive him, warding him off. This was something the first Adam failed to do in the garden, and Israel was unable to achieve in the wilderness (Matt 4:1–11; Luke 4:1–13). After he defeats Satan, Jesus goes out into the world Satan thinks he owns, which he had the temerity to offer to Jesus (as if it was his to give), and begins work. He works for the salvation of every person and the entire world, not through submission to Satan's false reign, but through defeating him with compassion, word, touch, and the Spirit's power. He works within human volition through servanthood and grace.

His most "violent" acts are to drive out demons who have gripped people's souls and from whom they must be released. The deliverance ministry, then, is the invasion of Satan's dominion, the progressive release of the oppressed by the power and reign of God. Jesus brings complete deliverance from Satan's hold for individuals who willingly submit to the reign of God. This is why, at the return of the seventy-two, Jesus cries out, "I saw Satan fall like lightning from heaven." As the disciples laid hands on the sick and oppressed, they saw demons submit to the name of Christ (Luke 10:18). This not then a pre-Adamic fall of Satan, but Satan's fall brought about by the kingdom invading "his" domain. The world's rightful King—Jesus—is taking back what was, is, and will be God's world. The disciples are given the same authority as Jesus so they, too, can participate as "warriors" of God in the deliverance of God's humanity from evil. However, they must do so without the weapons of the world or violent coercion, but with compassion, love, and servanthood (cf. 2 Cor 6:4–10; 10:1–4; Eph 6:11–17). Eschatologically, the exorcisms point to the kingdom to come, in which there will be no evil or demonic possession. God's people will be freed completely from the grip of evil. Satan and his minions will be completely cut off and thrown into destruction for all eternity (cf. Matt 25:41;[67] Rev 20:10).

---

67. Note the fire is not prepared for humanity, but for "the devil and his angels."

Miracles of Provision

Jesus taught radical trust in God to provide for the needs of his people. He essentially told his disciples that if they were prepared to renounce a love of money and self-reliance and place their full trust in God, living in dependence and pursuing God's kingdom and his righteousness as their first priority, they would experience God's ongoing provision for their need.[68] Jesus likened God's provision for those who seek first his kingdom to the provision of God for the natural world: food for birds of the air and beautiful adornment of flowers (Matt 6:19-34). His provision flows as naturally.

He also called for the disciples to continue his work in caring for the poor, distributing what he gives them for the needs of others (Luke 12:33; Matt 6:1-4). Wealth is a gift from God. But where it is given, it is not to be hoarded for a rainy day (Luke 12:13-21) but redistributed for the needs of the marginalized and God's mission. Jesus demonstrates this radical trust and concern for the poor in two miraculous provisions of food: the feeding of the five thousand (Matt 14:13-21; Mark 6:30-44; Luke 9:10-17; John 6:1-14) and the four thousand (Matt 15:28-39; Mark 8:1-9). Both are set in the context of his preaching and healing ministry. The crowds are hungry, and the disciples want to send them away, but Jesus has compassion (Matt 14:14) for them in their plight. On both occasions, Jesus goes through the same process and orders the disciples to feed the people (Mark 6:37; and parr.). With almost no food, the disciples are understandably lost and seek logical solutions. So, Jesus takes what little they have and miraculously distributes the small amounts of food to huge crowds. He makes the natural "supernatural," so to speak. Remarkably, the crowds are completely satisfied (*chortazō*). Both miracles emphasize the bountiful provision of God—the people are filled, and there is plenty left over. These miracles anticipate the eschatological complete provision of God and the satisfaction of God's people.

Jesus' transformation of water into wine (John 2:1-11) also radically defies the laws of nature. Jesus likely wants to spare the host shame for running out of wine. He turns water from six water jars, each containing 2 to

---

68. Not "their want." Food and clothing are promised (cf. 1 Tim 6:8). This speaks of provision of basics for survival, not luxuries.

3 *metrētēs* (seventy-five to 115 liters, twenty to thirty gallons), into wine—a total of approximately 600 liters (or 200 gallons) of wine. It is also of the best quality (John 2:10). This also demonstrates the abundant provision of the kingdom. The miracle both provided wine and relieved the host's social shame; it was socially dishonorable to run out of wine.[69]

The provision miracles function primarily as windows into the nature of a kingdom in which all oppression, famine, poverty, and material privation will be resolved. There will be no haves and have-nots in God's consummated kingdom. An eschatological reversal will have taken place whereby the rich will mourn, and the poor will rejoice (Luke 6:20-21, 24-25). The poor will not only be blessed because of what the kingdom will do for them; it will be done. The hope of a poverty-free people will be realized (Deut 15:4). In the "not yet" present experience, believers do not fully experience the kingdom, but see glimpses of the future in the miracles. This full provision and distribution will be realized at the feast of the kingdom. The provision of wine points to the eschatological feast at which Jesus will again drink of the fruit of the vine (cf. Luke 22:16). It will be a party to end all parties, a wedding feast where Jesus and his bride—the church—are reunited.

Miracles over Nature

There are four other miracles that demonstrate Jesus' power over the natural order. These are: the calming of the storm (Matt 8:23-27; Mark 4:35-41; Luke 8:22-25), walking on the water (Mark 6:47-51; Matt 14:22-33; John 6:16-21), turning water to wine (John 2:1-11, also above), and the coin in the fish's mouth (Matt 17:27). Some consider these to be "rescue" miracles in that they are examples of Jesus saving his disciples, or others. Certainly, this is true of the calming of the storm. However, in the water-walking miracle, although the disciples are struggling against the wind, there is no evidence that they are facing real danger or death. Jesus' motive seems to be to reach the other side as soon as possible. In the transformation of the wine, Jesus delivers the host from the social shame of failing to provide enough wine. The coin in the fish's mouth demonstrates Jesus' sovereignty

---

69. Keener, *John*, 502: "The groom was facing a potential social stigma that could make him the talk of his guests for years to come. Wine was indispensable to any properly hosted public celebration, and wedding guests sometimes drank late into the night."

over the natural order, or at least his providential knowledge. It is likely that it does not have a rescue dimension, as it was supposedly not imposed on those who lived off charity.[70] All the healings and resurrections, in a sense, demonstrate Jesus' power over nature, too.

These miracles demonstrate Jesus' power and lordship over nature. They recall the power of God to create (Gen 1:1). They recall Old Testament episodes where God controlled the natural order to save Israel, such as the exodus through the Red Sea (Exod 13:17-14:31), the crossing of the Jordan (Josh 3:1-17), and the hailstones and the stopping of the sun (Josh 10:11-14). They call to mind the miracles of Elijah and Elisha that cause a suspension of the laws of nature, such as the raising of the axe head (2 Kgs 6:1-7). The New Testament testifies that Jesus was actively involved in this creation as Creator (John 1:3; Col 1:16; Heb 1:3) and so his miracles anticipate the new creation—the new heaven and the new earth at the culmination of history (Rev 21; Isa 65-66). God will resolve the issue of a broken world, in ecological shambles; chaos will be ordered. Jesus' miracles reassure believers that God is in control and that he will bring about a new creation.

Miracles over Death

On three recorded occasions Jesus raised the dead. In a sense, these are healing miracles, the restoration of life to a corpse. However, they are of a far more dynamic category, involving the greatest enemy known to humanity: death. The first is the raising of a synagogue ruler's twelve-year-old daughter (Matt 9:18-26; Mark 5:21-43; Luke 8:40-56). On the second occasion, moved with compassion for a grieving widow in the town of Nain, Jesus raises her son (Luke 7:11-17). This resurrection also has a rescue dynamic, motivated not only by Jesus' concern for the boy who has died, but for the welfare of the widow who would be without financial support with the loss of her son.[71] The third resurrection is that of Lazarus after four

---

70. See Craig S. Keener, *The Gospel of Matthew: A Socio-Rhetorical Commentary* (Grand Rapids, MI; Cambridge, U.K.: Eerdmans, 2009), 443-44, who notes that the annual two-drachma tax, although voluntary, was demanded by the Romans, yielding enormous wealth. Some Jewish groups did not pay it (Sadducees, Essenes, and nationalists). Although it was not compulsory, however, it could be that it was demanded and if so, there may be a rescue element to the miracle.

71. I. H. Marshall, *Luke*, 283, writes, "... at the same time the stress on the helplessness of the widow, deprived of the support of both her husband and her son, draws attention to

days in the tomb (John 11:1-43). It is the context of the "I am" saying, "I am the resurrection and the life" (John 11:25). This miracle anticipates Jesus' resurrection, and in John, catalyzes the authorities to move against him.

These miracles recall the resurrections by Elijah and Elisha and signal that Jesus is, at the least, prophet (cf. 1 Kgs 17:17-24; 2 Kgs 4:8-27). Further, they indicate Jesus' dramatic power in the present. Ultimately, they point to the resurrection itself when Jesus will triumph over death, humankind's final enemy (cf. 1 Cor 15:26, 50-57). They point to the believer's hope of resurrection and being raised from death to life, a reality guaranteed by the first fruit of the resurrection harvest, Jesus Christ the Lord (1 Cor 15:23). They also point to the ultimate defeat of death and evil. Thus, they are windows into the nature of the kingdom, the place where the God of life reigns with those who wish to live forever with him in eternity.

MIRACLES AS VISUAL PARABLES

As John rightly demonstrates in calling them "signs," the miracles of Jesus function as signs or *visual parables* which, like spoken parables, have various levels of meaning. They are open to interpretation.

The Jewish leaders see the miracles, but instead of rationalizing them with naturalism, they do so spiritually—Jesus has a demon! Then, they demand more signs, which Jesus refuses (Matt 12:38-39; 16:1-4; Mark 8:11-13; Luke 11:16, 29-30; John 2:18; 4:48; 6:30).

Interestingly, these demands for signs *all* occur in the context of Jesus performing his regular signs.[72] The problem for the Jewish leaders was the nature of the signs. They were not the sort of powerful, transcendent demonstrations of divine power that they expected from God's Messiah to vindicate himself to them and draw them to his cause. After all, they were the guardians of Israel, and any true messiah would embrace them. But first, he had to prove himself to them as did Moses in Egypt (Exod 4). They were, unfortunately, trapped in a false mindset, a worldview that precluded them from seeing what God was really doing. They had misread

---

the gracious compassion of Jesus in caring for those in distress."

72. In Matt 12 and Luke 11, Jesus has just cast out a demon for all to see. In Matt 16 and Mark 8 he has *just* performed an amazing feeding miracle. In John, he has performed healing and feeding miracles.

their Bibles and were trapped in a false theology. The servant Messiah's ministry was not in line with their false expectations of conquest; rather, it was an invasion of grace, mercy, and love and the meeting of genuine human need. Jesus never did miracles for his own status or acceptance or for self-aggrandizement. Rather, his miracles were genuine acts of service to heal and help those who sincerely sought his help. If they had really understood their God, they would have recognized him. Some did, but did not follow through.

For others, the signs generate faith, as in John (e.g., John 2:23-3:1). This faith must grow from inquiry to a saving faith.

Miracles, then and now, are parabolic, open to interpretation. Jesus' opponents should have seen what was happening reflected on the Old Testament passages prophesying a servant messiah (cf. Isa 29:18; 35:5; 42:7; 61:1 [LXX]), and believed. However, they demanded more and more and were never satisfied (cf. 1 Cor 1:22).

For those who accept miracles as realities, the miracles speak at three levels. First, they stand in continuity with the heart and power of God in creation and the history of redemption, showing that God's salvation and reign has come. Second, they speak of the power of God to do miracles today and give present-day hope of healing, deliverance, provision, and life in abundance (within the broader framework of a world and human race subject to decay and death). Third, they speak of the future nature of the kingdom and the end to all oppression, suffering, pain, and death. They are parabolic in that they suggest these things rather than prove them, and so they must be "read." The question for believers today is how they will read them.

CONCLUSION

The following conclusions may be drawn regarding miracles in the Gospels:

MIRACLES ARE INTEGRAL TO CHRISTIAN LIFE AND MINISTRY

Miracles are central to Christ's ministry and were an important part of the disciples' ministry, and should be integral to the continuing ministry of the church. It is not possible to evacuate miracles from Christianity without depriving faith of its power. Christianity is a supernatural faith, based on the first miracle (creation), and seen in the history of Israel, and in the life of Christ (incarnation, virgin birth, miracles, resurrection, ascension, Pentecost). Its hope is equally miraculous: believers will be resurrected after death, and the universe transformed. To believe in Christianity is to base one's life on the existence of miracles. Christianity doesn't exist without them; without miracles, it becomes the tragic story of a prophetic claimant who taught some good things, but is dead. All that awaits people who don't believe after death is nothingness (1 Cor 15:12–19). Hope is limited to this life, and people may as well "eat and drink, for tomorrow we die" (1 Cor 15:32; Isa 22:13; see also Isa 56:12; Luke 12:19).

HEALING IS INTEGRALLY LINKED TO PREACHING AND FEEDING THE POOR

There is no separation of the miracle ministry of Christ in healing and feeding from his ministry of preaching. In fact, the ministry of preaching is also healing; the word of God functions to heal people spiritually and restore shattered relationships with God. Hence, healing, preaching, and feeding those in need should function together in the life and ministry of the local church.

FAITH IN THE MATTER OF HEALING

The connection of faith to miracles should not be overstated, nor should it be denied. In the Synoptics, faith, in the sense of trust in Jesus and God, is important. However, this should not lead to hyper-faith thinking as God is not limited by faith, with Christ healing on many instances despite a lack of faith or where faith is not mentioned. Further, death and decay remain realities, and there are indications in the New Testament that people will not always be healed and that ministry to the sick involves more than just healing. In John, miracles are signs that should cause people to recognize who Jesus is and place their trust in him. However, often this faith was not complete, or was shallow. It must grow to a saving faith.

MIRACLES, SCIENCE, AND MEDICINE

There are two extremes when considering the relationship of miracles and medicine. On the one hand, people can reject medicine as second-rate and rely purely on "miracles" for healing. This is found in situations where people rely purely on prayer and reject medicine. On the other hand, people can reject miracles and deal with problems purely from the point of view of rationalism, science, and medicine. This is found among people who claim to be Christian, but do not consider prayer for illness worthwhile. They go to a doctor but not for prayer. Both perspectives are dualistic and flawed. Medicine should be understood as the exploration of the created order and discovery of the "natural" healing placed in it by the Creator. It is an aspect of healing theology, recognized as such in Sirach 38. There is room for a holistic view of healing, involving the spiritual, the scientific, and the "natural." Setting up a hospital in which people are healed is sacred business and God's work. Praying for the sick is always appropriate. Finding natural remedies that bring relief should be respected. Visiting a doctor is equally appropriate, for it may be through this that God heals. A kingdom perspective on medicine is critical, not a narrow hyper-spiritual naivety.

THE KEY POINT OF REFERENCE TO UNDERSTANDING THE MIRACLES IS THE KINGDOM OF GOD

The miracles point to the power of the kingdom in the present, and the future *shalom* of the consummated kingdom.

THE BIG PICTURE AND HEALING

Healing, deliverance, and even resurrections are tiny glimpses of the bigger picture of God healing his world. Ultimately, healing will be cosmic, God's people raised and transformed, and the cosmos healed.

QUESTIONS TO CONSIDER

- How would you define a miracle?
- How would you classify the miracles?
- Do miracles happen today?
- Why do miracles not occur as often as in New Testament times? Or do they?
- How can people in the West, amid skepticism, keep faith in the miraculous?
- How should believers exercise this ministry today?

THE TEACHING OF THE KINGDOM: PARABLES

CHAPTER 13

WHAT IS A PARABLE?

Whereas in John, Jesus teaches the crowds in long dialogues with metaphor (e.g., bread, light, shepherd, and vineyard), in the Synoptic Gospels, Jesus' primary mode of communication to the crowds is through parables.

The classic definition of a parable is "an earthly story with a heavenly meaning." At another level, a parable is a form of teaching. Telling a story is a timeless means of conveying truth (e.g., Aesop's Fables). In Jesus' ministry, it is no different. Snodgrass defines parables generally as "stories with two levels of meaning."[1] The story is about events grounded in the everyday, providing a lens through which a deeper reality can be interpreted; in Jesus' case, parables point to the kingdom of God. A parable is a saying or story told by Jesus that challenges the hearer (or reader) to discern and act upon a second deeper spiritual level of meaning.

The Greek term is *parabolē*. The term carries the sense of "comparison." It has a range of meanings that is broader than the English word "parable." The meaning derives from the Hebrew *māšal* (Aramaic = *mathla*), translated as *parabolē* in the LXX (twenty-eight out of thirty-nine times). At times, its use anticipates Jesus. Matthew cites Psalm 78:2, which anticipates the psalmist speaking in parables hidden from creation (Matt 13:35).

---

1. Klyne R. Snodgrass, "Parable," in *DJG* 594.

It is used in a New Testament sense in Ezekiel 17:2, where God tells the "son of man," Ezekiel, to utter a parable against the house of Israel, followed by a parable of two great eagles that planted two twigs that grew into vines symbolizing Israel and Babylon. This resembles the mustard-seed parable (see Ezek 24:3; Philo, *Conf.* 99).[2]

In the New Testament, a parable is a figurative saying or story with a variety of nuances and can include proverbs (the usual Old Testament meaning; e.g., Luke 4:23),[3] riddles (e.g., Matt 3:23),[4] comparisons (e.g., Matt 13:33),[5] contrasts (e.g., Luke 18:1-8),[6] simple stories (e.g., Luke 13:6-9),[7] and complex longer stories (e.g., Matt 22:1-14).[8]

It is generally agreed among scholars of all persuasions that the parables are to be trusted as authentic and reliable (although some reject the framing or explanations). This is because: (1) they are consistent with Jesus' teaching and his conflict with authorities; (2) they reflect knowledge of daily life in Israel at the time; (3) such extensive use is unique to Jesus; apart from a few examples (e.g., Ezek 17; 2 Sam 12:1-4), there is little evidence that parables were used frequently before Jesus; (4) there is also little suggestion that the early church used parables or created new ones, which counts against them creating the ones in the New Testament account; and (5) they are found in all strands of the Synoptic tradition, Mark, Q, M, and L. As such, the Jesus Seminar, in its edition of the Parables of Jesus,[9] considers only the parables of the tower builder and the warring king in Luke 14:28-32, and the fishnet parable in Matthew 13:47-50, to be inauthentic (black). Only four are rated as parables Jesus did not use, but he expressed

---

2. *Māšal* can also mean "a taunt, a prophetic oracle, or a byword." *Parabolē* is used in the LXX of a prophetic oracle (e.g., Num 23:7), but most commonly, of a proverb (e.g., 1 Sam 10:12; 24:14; Prov 1:6; Ezek 18:2, see also Josephus, *Ant.* 8.44).
3. "Physician, heal yourself!"
4. "How can Satan drive out Satan?"
5. "The kingdom of heaven is like yeast ..."
6. "In a certain town there was a judge ... a widow ..."
7. "A man had a fig tree, planted in a vineyard ..."
8. "The kingdom of heaven is like a king who prepared a wedding banquet for his son. He sent his servants ..."
9. They use a color scale reflecting varying degrees of authenticity: (1) Red = Jesus said the words; (2) Pink = Jesus said something like these words; (3) Grey = Jesus did not say the words but expressed similar ideas; (4) Black = Jesus did not say them and they were added in later.

similar ideas. The remainder they consider authentic.[10] On the basis that the others are considered authentic, there is no reason to view these four as inauthentic.

THE USE OF PARABLES PRIOR TO JESUS

Although his extensive use of parables is unique, Jesus was not the first person to use parables. There are some in the Old Testament. Aside from Ezekiel 17 above, an example is the parable Nathan used to expose David's sin with Bathsheba (see 2 Sam 12:1-4).[11] However, while there are Greek and Semitic parables, "there is no evidence of anyone prior to Jesus using parables as consistently, creatively and effectively as he did."[12] There are many rabbinic parables, and this has led some to argue that Jesus used popular stories from his time. However, the evidence from rabbinic literature *post-dates* Jesus, and it is unclear whether such a pool of stories existed at the time. Beyond this, there is sparing evidence of teaching in parables before Jesus, and he could have been innovative in his use of them. So, for example, there are no parables from Qumran, the Apocrypha, or the Pseudepigrapha. Jesus, then, is unique in the extent to which he based his public ministry on parables.

CLASSIFICATION OF PARABLES

One popular way of classifying parables is to distinguish between four essential forms:

---

10. The problem with the conclusions of the Jesus Seminar is that they try to create out of the Gospel tradition a Jesus who fits contemporary assumptions and modern expectations. They give far too much preference to Q, which does not actually exist, and to the *Gospel of Thomas*, which is likely a later writing than the canonical Gospels. The rejection of introductions, conclusions, and allegory is out of kilter with Jewish tradition. Without doubt the writers of the Gospels edited Jesus' parables according to their purposes. However, it is futile to seek to discern out of the final text Jesus' exact words (*ipsissima verba*). The Gospels present the "very voice" of Jesus (*ipsissima vox*).

11. For others that are parabolic, see 2 Sam 14:5-20; 1 Kgs 20:35-40; Isa 5:1-7; Ezek 17:2-10; 19:2-9, 10-14; Judg 9:7-15; 2 Kgs 14:9.

12. Snodgrass, "Parable," 594.

SIMILITUDE[13]

Many of the parables are extended similes with an explicit comparison using "like" or "as." They relate a typical or recurring event in real life and often occur in the present tense. One example is the parable of the mustard seed, which begins, "the kingdom of heaven is *like* a mustard seed," (see Matt 13:31). There are many of these kingdom comparison parables in Jesus' teaching, especially in Matthew (see also Matt 13:33, 44-45, 47, 52; 20:1; Mark 4:26; Luke 7:28, cf. Mark 4:31).

EXAMPLE STORY

These parables present characters, positive or negative, given as examples to be imitated or avoided. Many of Jesus' parables fall into this category. An example is the good Samaritan, which ends with "go and do likewise," urging the lawyer to be like the Samaritan and not like the priest and Levite (Luke 10:25-37). Other example stories include: the parables of the wise and foolish builders (Matt 7:24-27; Luke 6:47-49), the two debtors (Luke 7:41-50), the hidden treasure and pearl of great price (Matt 13:44-46), the householder (Matt 13:52), the rich fool (Luke 12:13-21), the great banquet and wedding banquet (Luke 14:15-24; Matt 22:1-14), the tower builder and warring king (Luke 14:28-33), the lost sheep and coin (Luke 15:1-10), the rich man and Lazarus (Luke 16:19-31), the persistent widow (Luke 18:1-8), the Pharisee and the tax collector (Luke 18:9-14), the unmerciful servant (Matt 18:23-25), the laborers in the vineyard (Matt 20:1-16), the two sons (Matt 21:28-32), faithful and unfaithful stewards (Matt 24:45-51; Luke 12:42-46), the wise and foolish maidens (Matt 25:1-13), and the talents and pounds (Matt 25:14-30; Luke 19:11-27).

ALLEGORY

An allegory is a series of related metaphors where each aspect, other than a character, has a correlating reference point. The best example is the parable of the sower, which Jesus tells and then explains (Mark 4:1-20; and parr.). As Jesus explains the parable's meaning to the disciples, this is clearly an allegory, unless taking the form-critical view that the explanation is

---

13. A similitude is "a comparison between two things" (*Concise Oxford Dictionary*) or "an imaginative comparison" (*Merriam-Webster's Collegiate Dictionary*).

non-authentic, which is without warrant. Similarly, the parable of the weeds is explained by Jesus in allegorical terms (Matt 13:24–30, 36–43). Many other parables have allegorical aspects.[14] Allegorization is a major area of debate among parable scholars—primarily the distinction between a parable and an allegory.

CHARACTERISTICS OF THE PARABLES OF JESUS

The parables of Jesus have certain features. These include:

BREVITY

The parables of Jesus vary in length from the longest, the prodigal son (392 words in the Greek), to the shortest, "Physician, heal yourself," (Luke 4:23), just three Greek words. So, assuming a speaking rate of around 150 words a minute, the longest of Jesus' stories would take just over two-and-a-half minutes. Though Jesus' parables are short, they have had a profound effect on the world.

SIMPLICITY

Even the most complex of Jesus' parables only have a few characters and relatively simple plotlines. They are brief, to the point, and simple. Unnecessary descriptions, characterization, and motives are left out, and questions left unanswered. For example: Why are the priest and Levite traveling down the road from Jerusalem to Jericho? Does the story of the rich man and Lazarus provide descriptions of heaven and hell? Where are other characters unimportant to the parable, such as the wife of the father in the prodigal? Where are the goats burned up in the sheep and goats?

---

14. See the parables of the wedding guests (Mark 2:19–20; and parr.), the unshrunk cloth and wineskins (Mark 2:21–22; and parr.), the strong man (Mark 3:22–27; and parr.), savorless salt (Matt 5:13; and parr.), the mustard seed (Mark 4:30–32 and parr.), the wicked tenants (Mark 12:1–12 and parr.), the budding fig tree (Mark 13:28–32; and parr.), the watchman (Matt 13:34–36), the two ways/doors (Matt 7:13–14; Luke 13:23–27), the lost sheep (Matt 18:12–14; Luke 15:1–7), the sheep and gates (Matt 25:31–46), and the barren fig tree (Luke 13:6–9). Allegorization is found within the context (e.g., sinful Israel).

SYMMETRY

The parables often have a symmetrical structure based around contrasts, characters, and moments. For example, in the parable of the weeds, the weeds are thrown in the furnace, while the plants grow and are harvested (Matt 13:24–30). Similarly, in the parable of the net, there are good and bad fish, which are harvested at the end of the fishing (Matt 13:47–50). This symmetry is ethical, good contrasted with bad. Others have a symmetry based on three main characters or, as in the case of the parable of the sower, four types of soil (responses to the gospel; see Mark 4:1–20; and parr.).

CONTRAST

Linked to parables' symmetry, and especially in the longer parables, there are contrasting characters (antithetical symmetry). Sometimes there are two, such as the older and younger sons in the prodigal son (Luke 15:11–32), the rich man and Lazarus (Luke 16:19–31), the virgins who are ready and those not prepared (Matt 25:1–13), the sheep and the goats (Matt 25:31–46), or the Pharisee and the tax collector (Luke 18:9–14). Sometimes there are three.

TRIPLETS

In longer parables, some have three key players (e.g., the priest, the Levite, and the Samaritan in the good Samaritan [Luke 10:25–37]; the father and the two sons in the prodigal son [Luke 15:11–32]; or Abraham, Lazarus, and the rich man in the rich man and Lazarus [Luke 16:19–31]). There are also three servants in the parable of the talents (Matt 25:14–30). These are often antithetical, as in the parable of the good Samaritan; the two Jewish leaders neglect the injured man, contrasting the Samaritan's response, which adds emphasis to their lack of compassion.

CONTEXTUAL

The parables are set in the context of first-century life. Frequently, the context is first-century middle-eastern farming (e.g., parable of the lost sheep, Luke 15:1–7). Other common situations from contemporary life include: domestic work (e.g., parable of the lost coin, Luke 15:8–10), fishing (e.g., parable of the net, Matt 13:47–50), pearl harvesting (e.g., parable of the pearl, Matt 13:45-46), and the enmity between Jews and Samaritans (the parable of the good Samaritan, Luke 10:25-37). They connect to the lives of real people and have a cultural cutting edge often lost on modern people reading them from a post-industrial and electronic world.

THE ELEMENT OF SURPRISE

While they are rooted in the life of first-century Israel, they are not always realistic and often contain hyperbole that adds shock value. Among many examples is the ten-thousand-talent debt in the parable of the unforgiving servant, which the master grants (Matt 18:23-27). The extent of the debt is highly unlikely (Matt 18:23-35). The father who runs to and accepts his son back in the parable of the prodigal son is also most unlikely; the father would not sit and wait for his son who effectively wanted him dead, nor run to him (Luke 15:11-40). The 100-fold yield is surprising in the parable of the sower (Mark 4:8). The pearl in Matthew 13:46 is also unlikely. The tax collector who is declared justified, while the Pharisee is not, is a shock (Luke 18:9-14). One of the keys to interpreting the parables is connecting this surprise and shock to the point Jesus is making.

THOUGHT-PROVOKING AND PARTICIPATIVE

Aside from the material that draws people in to consider where they are in the story, twenty-two parables begin with a question such as: "Who from you ... ?" or, "What do you think?" Jesus is inviting people to think and participate in the parable, to consider their own place in the narrative.

REVERSAL

Linked to shock is the unexpected reversal found in some of the parables. One of the best examples is in the parable of the good Samaritan where the ideal neighbor is the Samaritan rather than Jewish religious leaders. The wicked younger son who takes his inheritance and spends it, but becomes the "hero," while the older son who is faithful becomes the "villain" in the prodigal (Luke 15:11-40). The tax collector is considered righteous, and not the Pharisee (Luke 18:9-14). Lazarus, not the rich man, ends up in paradise (Luke 16:19-31). Readers are challenged to emulate those who demonstrate the values of the kingdom, even if that person is most surprising.

THE END OFTEN DEFINES THE MEANING

Scholars often speak of "the rule of end stress," whereby the primary emphasis of the parable is drawn out at the end of the parable. For example, in the parable of the tenants, the stress falls on the killed son and the judgment (e.g., Mark 12:1–12). "Go and do likewise" climaxes the good Samaritan, where Jesus challenges hearers to emulate the compassionate action of the enemy of Israel rather than their own religious leaders. "For everyone who exalts himself ..." climaxes the Pharisee and the tax collector, calling hearers to reject the arrogance and self-righteousness of the Pharisee and emulate the supposed traitor's humility before God.

KINGDOM AND DISCIPLESHIP ORIENTATED

All parables focus on God, his kingdom, and Jesus' expectations for his disciples in terms of behavior and discipleship.

DISTRIBUTION OF THE PARABLES IN THE GOSPELS

About one-third of Jesus' teaching in the Synoptic Gospels is in parables. The term *parabolē* occurs fifty times in the New Testament. All are in the Synoptic Gospels, other than Hebrews 9:9 and 11:19, where the term is used of figurative or symbolic thought. Parables make up 16 percent of Mark, 29 percent of the common material in Luke and Matthew (Q), 43 percent of Matthew's special material (M), and 52 percent of Luke's unique material (L). In John, while Jesus does not teach in "story parables," there are many comparisons that are used to describe Jesus that are parabolic—especially in the "I am" sayings. These fall within the broad sense of *parabolē* and *māšal* (e.g., John 10 [the good shepherd]; John 15 [the true vine]).[15]

The parables are thematically arranged. A brief analysis of Mark's parables indicates how they are etched into Mark's picture of Jesus. Mark has a whole chapter devoted to essential kingdom parables including the sower, lamp, growing seed, and mustard seed (Mark 4). He also includes other simple sayings like his disciples will "become fishers of men" (Mark 1:16). He compares his ministry to that of a doctor (Mark 2:17). He includes riddles like, "Which is easier, to say to the paralytic, 'Your sins are forgiven,' or

---

15. See Snodgrass, "Parable," 594.

to say, 'Rise, take your bed and walk'?" (Mark 2:9, cf. 11:30; 12:16-17, 35). He includes the cloth and wineskin parables in Mark 2:18-22, which compare the kingdom fitting into Judaism to sewing new cloth on old, or pouring new wine into old wineskins. He compares the clash of Satan to a strong man plundering a home (Mark 3:23-29). He describes his disciples as his family (Mark 3:33-35) and being a disciple as being a child (Mark 10:13-15).

He includes *five story parables*, including the sower (Mark 4:1-20), the lamp (Mark 4:21-25), the secretly growing seed (Mark 4:26-29), the mustard seed (Mark 4:30-32), and later the tenants. The command to take up one's cross is parabolic, and only properly understood after the resurrection (as are all the parables). Similarly, being thrown into the sea with a millstone around one's neck parabolically describes the fate of those teaching others to sin (Mark 9:42). Another parable is the image of squeezing a camel through the eye of a needle to describe the difficulty of the rich entering the kingdom (Mark 10:25). Suffering is parabolically described as a baptism (drenched in suffering) and a "cup" (Mark 10:38-39; 14:36, cf. 14:22-25). The power of prayer is illustrated by the parable of sending mountains into the sea (Mark 11:23). Mark also includes the parable of the wicked tenants (Mark 12:1-12), a vital parable that describes the failure of Jewish leadership and antagonizes them. The greedy Jewish leaders are likened to devouring beasts (Mark 12:40). Drawing on Daniel, Jesus speaks of an abomination that will violate the temple (Mark 13:14). The Olivet Discourse (Mark 13) includes parables of the fig tree and prepared servants, urging watchfulness and preparedness for Jesus' return (Mark 13:28-37). The Last Supper is parabolic, the bread and wine symbolizing Jesus' body and blood (Mark 14:22-25). Even the miracles are parabolic. It is clear parabolic discourse is worked into the fabric of Mark.

Matthew and Luke include all the major parables of Jesus except the secretly growing seed, and they include the "lost" parables (Luke 15; Matt 18:10-14). They also include parables about guests who reject invitations to a feast (Matt 22:1-14; Luke 14:16-24) and servants who are entrusted with money to invest (Matt 25:14-30; Luke 19:11-27). It is unclear whether they are the same parables because of the different wording. It is possible they are accounts of the same parable told on different occasions, as Jesus probably told the same parables at different times across Israel. Matthew places most of his parables in Chapters 13, 18, and 20-25. He has at least twelve unique parables. Luke arranges most of his parables in the travel narrative in Luke 10-19, and incorporates many unique parables (at least fifteen). In addition, fourteen parables occur among the sayings of the *Gospel of Thomas*, three of which are not recorded in the canonical Gospels. The *Apocryphon of James* also has three parables not recorded in the canonical Gospels.

It is difficult to assess the actual number of parables because there is disagreement as to what constitutes a parable. There are somewhere between forty and sixty-five, depending on the definition.

Markan Parables			
	Mark	Matthew	Luke
Wedding Guests	2:19-20	9:15	5:33-39
Unshrunk Cloth	2:21	9:16	5:36
Wineskins	2:22	9:17	5:37-39
Divided Kingdom	3:24	12:25	11:17
Divided Home	3:25	12:25	11:17
Strong Man Bound	3:22-27	12:29-30	11:21-23
Sower	4:1-9, 13-20	13:1-9, 18-23	8:4-8, 11-15
Lamp and Measure	4:21-25		8:16-18
Seed Growing Secretly	4:26-29		
Savorless Salt	9:50	5:13	14:34
Mustard Seed	4:30-32	13:31-32	13:18-19
Wicked Tenants	12:1-12	21:33-46	20:9-19
Budding Fig Tree	13:28-32	24:32-36	21:29-33
Watchman	13:34-36		12:35-38
Parables Shared by Matthew and Luke (Q)			
Blind Leading the Blind		15:14	6:39
Sawdust and Plank in Eye		7:3-5	6:41
Good and Bad Fruit		7:16-20	6:43-45
Wise and Foolish Builders		7:24-27	6:47-49
Playing Children		11:16-17	7:31-32
Harvest and Laborers		9:37	10:2
Father and Children's Requests		7:9-11	11:11-13

TEACHING OF THE KINGDOM: PARABLES

	Mark	**Matthew**	**Luke**
The Lamp of the Body		6:22	11:34–36
Two Ways/Doors		7:13–14	13:23–27
Leaven		13:33–34	13:20–21
Lost Sheep		18:12–14	15:1–7
Wedding Banquet		22:1–14	14:15–24
Thief in the Night		24:42–44	12:39–40
Faithful and Unfaithful Steward		24:45–51	12:42–46
Talents and Pounds		25:14–30	19:11–27
Parables Found Only in Matthew			
City on a Hill		5:14	
Divided City		12:25	
Wheat and Tares		13:24–30, 36–43	
Treasure		13:44	
Pearl		13:45–46	
Fishnet		13:47–50	
Householder		13:52	
Unmerciful Servant		18:23–35	
Laborers in the Vineyard		20:1–16	
Two Sons		21:28–32	
Wise and Foolish Maidens		25:1–13	
Sheep and Goats		25:31–46	
Parables Found Only in Luke			
Physician, Heal Yourself			4:23
Two Debtors			7:41–50
Good Samaritan			10:25–37
Friend at Midnight			11:5–8
Rich Fool			12:13–21
Weather Signs			12:54–56
Barren Fig Tree			13:6–9
Tower Builder			14:28–30
Warring King			14:31–33
Lost Coin			15:8–10
Prodigal Son			15:11–32

	Mark	Matthew	Luke
Unjust Steward			16:1-8
Rich Man and Lazarus			16:19-31
Faithful Servant			17:7-10
Persistent Widow			18:1-8
Pharisee and the Tax Collector			18:9-14
Parabolic Material Found Only in John			
Good Shepherd (John 10:1-18, cf. Matt 18:12-14; Luke 15:1-7)			
The Seed in the Ground (John 12:23-25)			
True Vine (John 15:1-8)			

FIGURE 25: THE PARABLES OF JESUS[16]

ALLEGORY OR NOT?

THE DEBATE

Up until the late nineteenth century, the main approach to interpreting the parables was to allegorize them.[17] In this approach, parts of the parable are seen to correspond with realities (e.g., the servants killed in the parable of the talents correspond to the prophets, while the son corresponds to Jesus; see Mark 12:2-8). Approaching the parables this way meant people would read *into* the parables elements of the life and theology of contemporary

---

16. This list is based on the list in Snodgrass, "Parable," 596, with some amendments.

17. An allegory is a story in which the component parts correspond with aspects of truth that the story is designed to teach (e.g., *A Pilgrim's Progress*, see also the biblical example in Mark 4:1-20: the sower = Christ/God/preachers; seed = God's word; soil = people with different responses to the word; shallow soil on the path = people who don't understand; the birds = Satan and demons; rocky soil = initial believers who fall away through persecution and trouble; the withering sun = persecution and trouble; thorny soil = believers who are unfruitful; thorns = worries, wealth, desire; good soil = true fruitful believers; crop = good works or other believers).

churches, which had little if anything to do with the parable's original context or Jesus' intention in telling the story.

The best-known example is Augustine's (AD 354-430) interpretation of the parable of the good Samaritan (Luke 10:30-37)[18] in which he assigned to every aspect of the parable some dimension of his understanding of the gospel: (1) The injured man = Adam (humanity); (2) Jerusalem to Jericho = The movement from the heavenly city of peace to the fall; (3) The robbers = The devil and his angels who strip humanity of immortality and persuade them to sin, leaving them lost in sin; (4) The priest and Levite = the priesthood and the ministry of the Old Testament, which profit nothing for salvation; (5) The good Samaritan = Christ, who brings restraint of sin (bandages), the comfort of good hope (oil), and encouragement to work fervently (wine); (6) The donkey = the incarnation; (7) The inn = the church; (8) The next day = after the resurrection of Christ; (9) The innkeeper = the apostle Paul; and (10) The two denarii = the two great commandments, or the promise of this life and eternal life. One can see that although Augustine's understanding is consistent with the gospel and sound theologically, he has made several basic mistakes. First, he has read back into the parable his own theology, what is called "eisegesis." Second, to do so, he has illegitimately allegorized aspects that are merely details, most especially aligning the donkey with the incarnation, and the innkeeper with Paul. Third, he has read it out of context and stripped away the parable's subversive power whereby an enemy is the hero and to be emulated. While the message of the parable reinforces the gospel, its powerful call to compassionate care is reduced.

While there were a few exceptions—such as John Chrysostom, Thomas Aquinas, and John Calvin[19]—who did not always allegorize the parables, almost all interpreters allegorized not only those parables that appear to have an allegorical component, but *all* parables, reading them eisegetically through the context of their age.[20]

---

18. See Dodd, *The Parables*, 13-14.

19. Calvin called earlier allegorization "idle fooleries" and was much more sensible in his approach.

20. Blomberg, *Interpreting the Parables*, 31, notes the example of Archbishop Trench, who believed every aspect of the parable should be allegorized (Richard Chenevix, *Notes on the Miracles of Our Lord* [New York: D. Appleton and company, 1873], 37).

It was the German scholar A. Jülicher (1888-1889) who caused a seismic shift in parable studies.[21] Jülicher completely rejected an allegorical approach, even where Jesus is recorded allegorizing his own parable as in the parable of the sower (Mark 4:13-19). Jülicher argued that this was a creation of the Gospel writer and not a part of the original teaching of Jesus. He contended that the parables were simple, straightforward comparisons and that they have only *one point of comparison* between the image and the idea expressed. This key point is usually a general religious principle, a "timeless moral truth," as in Aesop's Fables. For example, the parable of the talents teaches that "a reward is only earned by performance."[22] The parable of the unjust servant teaches "wise use of the present is the condition of a happy future."[23] Jülicher's parable interpretation reduces the power of the parables into moral truths that align with Protestant liberal moralization.

Since Jülicher, most have used his work as a point of reference arguing against allegorization and for one meaning for a parable. Two leading New Testament scholars in the twentieth century, C. H. Dodd and J. Jeremias, are examples, contending that parables have one meaning and must be understood in their original historical and eschatological context. Dodd argued that the parables teach the kingdom is here, rejecting a futuristic interpretation ("a realized eschatology"). Jeremias "reconstructed" the "original form" by stripping away any introductions and conclusions around the parables[24] and removing any allegorical features.[25] He differed from Dodd in that, like those who uphold an inaugurated eschatology view, he saw Jesus' life and ministry bringing the kingdom, which is growing toward a final eschatological climax. Jesus used parables to present people with a moment of decision and an invitation to respond to God's mercy. Jülicher,

---

21. A. Jülicher, *Die Gleichnisreden Jesu* (2 vols. Tübingen: J. C. B. Mohr [Paul Siebeck]) 1888-89.

22. Richard Lischer, *Reading the Parables*, Interpretation (Louisville: Westminster John Knox Press, 2014), 7.

23. Lischer, *Reading*, 7.

24. E.g., Mark 12:10-12, where Jesus quotes Ps 118:22, 23; and Luke 16:10-12 and explains the parable of the shrewd manager. Jeremias believed both are creations of the Gospel writers.

25. Both Dodd and Jeremias were heavily influenced by source and form criticism, which argued that the introductions, conclusions, and interpretative aspects (including allegorization) of the parables were added in by the early church and are not to be considered as authentic or critical for interpretation.

Dodd, and Jeremias, then, assert that there is only one real meaning to a parable and reject *any* allegorization.

RESPONSE: MODERATE ALLEGORIZATION WHERE APPROPRIATE

Dodd and Jeremias rightly argue that the parables must *first* be understood against their Jewish historical setting. However, while it is good to find the main point of a parable, boiling the parables down to one theme is not always appropriate. For example, the parable of the prodigal son has strong themes associated with all three characters: (1) The love of the father—which speaks of God's love; (2) The repentance and restoration of the lost son—which speaks of people responding to God with repentance and returning to him; and (3) The rejection of the return of the younger son by the older son—which refers to the faithful who despise those who return to God (e.g., some Jewish attitudes to gentile conversion).

To fully understand the parables, both the historical setting and the various kingdom themes they raise need to be understood. Further, some parables are clearly allegorical with the comparisons found on the lips of Jesus. One example is Jesus' interpretation of the parable of the sower; there is no reason to reject it as inauthentic (Mark 4:13-20). Another is the parable of the tenants, where the son is clearly Jesus, the servants the prophets, and those who kill the son are the leaders of Israel (Mark 12:1-12). Similarly, in the mustard-seed parable, the seed is Jesus, the tree the kingdom, and the birds the enemies of God or the nations (Mark 4:30-32). Further, in the prodigal son, the father speaks of God; the younger son rebellious Jews, Samaritans, or gentiles; and the older son Jews who reject Jesus. Yet another is the parable of the banquet where the banquet master speaks of God, the servants are Jesus and/or the apostles, the disabled perhaps the marginalized of Israel, and those on the roads and byways likely the gentiles (see Luke 14:15-24).

In some parables, there is no need to allegorize because the key players are clearly identified in the story. For example, in the parable of the good Samaritan, the priest, Levite, and Samaritan are identified (Luke 10:25-37). Similarly, in the parable of the Pharisee and the tax collector, both characters are clearly identified (Luke 18:9-14). However, in each of these parables and others, readers are intended to apply the story to themselves and their context. They will find parallels that can be used to draw out and apply the meaning of the parable.

Hence, allegorization must not be ruled out, but readers must also consider each parable in its original context(s) and in relation to Jesus' wider teaching on the kingdom. The key interpretative key is to read the parable in this initial setting and then apply it to today. This will guard against ludicrous constructions. What is needed is a *moderate contextual allegorization* approach to the parables. That is, to consider the core elements of the parable against their setting without excessive speculation. Not every element means something; however, many elements are allegorical. There is also no absolute meaning in every situation, as there is a range of possible comparisons. This is seen in the parable of the banquet, where the one who gives the invitation can be God, Jesus, the apostles, or all missional Christians. Jesus' parables are multivalent, and good interpreters recognize multiple possibilities.

ADDITIONAL APPROACHES TO PARABLES

There is a range of other approaches to parables with many attempting to move beyond the skeptical historical approach of the early to mid-twentieth century. Some of these attempts are of dubious value. These include *existential approaches* where the parables are not constrained by context or historical setting; rather, through them Jesus invites people into a fresh understanding of existence. Some in the 1970s and 1980s took *structuralist approaches,* looking at the surface and deeper structures of the text of the parables.[26] These approaches are of little value for serious biblical students. Also, radical and of limited value are *reader-response approaches* whereby the meaning of the text is drawn from the interaction of the contemporary reader and the text, rather than the author and the original context. It is true that readers bring themselves to the text and ultimately apply the text to their lives. However, without the anchor of the historical first reading, this leads to extraordinary subjectivity whereby the contemporary interpreter can read anything they like into the text.

Literary approaches, such as narrative criticism, move beyond the purposes of the evangelists to examining the text itself. Such approaches take

---

26. On different methods of interpretation, see Blomberg, *Interpreting the Parables,* 132-64.

the text as read and seek to discern its plot, characterization, and patterns. They also consider the function of the parable in the Gospel narrative. Narrative and other literary approaches can be greatly helpful for contemporary interpretation.

Also useful are *comparative Jewish parable approaches*, whereby Jesus' parables are compared to rabbinic parables. Approximately two thousand rabbinic parables have been collected. The problem with this is that the rabbinic material postdates the New Testament period and it is unclear which of the parables are authentic to Jesus' time and whether a pool of such stories existed. Today, there is a return to a more balanced reading of parables in the work of many scholars.[27]

THE TRIPLE HORIZON OF PARABLES

Interpreting parables is not simply about reading the parable in its context and applying it. Interpretation is complicated because, within the Gospel itself, there are two contexts: the historical moment when Jesus first spoke the parable, and the Gospel writer's situation. In fact, every parable, from the perspective of the modern interpreter, has three points of reference.

THE ORIGINAL HISTORICAL SETTING

The cultural and social context of Jesus must be considered to make sense of the parables. It is also essential to consider how the parables were originally spoken and heard. How did the first audience hear the parables? Did they initially understand what Jesus meant?

THE EVANGELIST'S HISTORICAL SETTING

The second point of reference is the situation of the evangelist retelling the story in the Gospel. For Matthew, his focus is Jewish and gentile readers, perhaps in the Antioch area in the 70s–80s AD. For Mark, he likely has Roman gentile Christians in the later 50s–60s AD in mind. For Luke, his target is people like Theophilus—well-to-do gentiles in the Greco-Roman world. So, for example, in the parable of the prodigal son, for Luke, the son

---

27. E.g., Blomberg, *Interpreting the Parables*; Arland J. Hultgren, *The Parables of Jesus: A Commentary* (Grand Rapids, MI: Eerdmans, 2000); Klyne R. Snodgrass, *Stories with Intent: A Comprehensive Guide to the Parables of Jesus* (Grand Rapids, MI: Eerdmans, 2008).

might not only refer to wayward Jews but to gentiles who are hearing and responding to the gospel. Or, the son might be the gentiles per se who are coming back to their Creator God. Similarly, in the parable of the tenants, the rejected son may point to rejected Christians who are persecuted by gentile authorities. When examining a parable in Matthew and Luke that is also found in Mark, this is further complicated as this setting is, in fact, two-fold. First, there is Mark's setting. Secondly, there is Matthew's context as he uses Mark. Similarly, there is Luke's situation in which he writes. There is Mark's setting as well as the way that Matthew and Luke have used Mark. An example is the parable of the sower, where it is clear Matthew and Luke have adapted Mark for their audiences. So, the triple horizon becomes a quadruple horizon.

THE SETTING OF THE PRESENT READER

The final point of reference is the contemporary reader's situation. What does the parable say to believers now? After diligently working out what the parable initially meant on the lips of Jesus and how it is used by the evangelists, readers can *apply the parable carefully* to their context. Hence, the prodigal becomes the wayward sinner wallowing in sin who is called back and accepted graciously by God.

When pulling the three horizons together, one can say that the first setting has priority for interpretation and the second builds on it and provides a lead on how it can be applied. From such consideration, the principles from the first two may be applied to the reader's setting.

THE PURPOSE OF THE PARABLES

THE OVERALL PURPOSE: TO EXPLAIN THE KINGDOM OF GOD

The primary purpose of the parables is not merely to teach and instruct at a moral or personal level, but to instruct people concerning the kingdom of God—what it is, what the King is like, and how his people should live as subjects of the King in his kingdom. Hence, they are not merely stories to enjoy with a moral truth or truths, but they need a kingdom interpretation to explain their full significance. Jesus told parables "to confront people with the character of God's kingdom and to invite them to participate in it and to live in accordance with it."[28]

One of the features of Jesus' coming was the subversive and veiled nature of his advent, rather than the cosmic, militaristic political kingdom expected. The kingdom came imperceptibly in the person of a king born in obscurity who refused to use his power to bring the kingdom by force. The parables fit this type of kingdom. They are simple, short stories a child can understand. Yet, they declare the kingdom in a veiled and indirect way, challenging without forcing the hearer to "hear" the parable and discern the kingdom in and through it.

THE PURPOSE OF PARABLES AND THE KINGDOM IN MARK 4:10–12

The difficult text Mark 4:11-12 needs to be understood in this light. It reads:

> And he said to them, "To you has been given the secret of the kingdom of God, but for those outside, everything comes in parables; in order that [*hina*] 'they may indeed look, but not perceive, and may indeed listen, but not understand; so that they may not turn again and be forgiven.'" (NRSV)

After teaching on the various responses to God's word sown in his ministry, Jesus explains to the disciples that his use of parables is intentional. Through them he communicates to believers (disciples) the secrets of the kingdom that God is inaugurating through his ministry. However, for others "everything is in parables." What did Jesus mean?

The meaning of the small Greek conjunction *hina* is key to understanding this passage. There is a range of understandings of this text that can apply to the parables, or to Jesus' ministry generally.

Unlikely Textual or Grammatical Solutions

There have been several attempts to resolve the problem of interpreting Jesus in this passage through far-fetched grammatical and other solutions. Dodd argues that these verses are an *interpolation*, added from the Pauline part of the church because of their strong determinism.[29] However, there is

---

28. Snodgrass, "Parable," 596.
29. C.H. Dodd, *The Parables*, 13-15.

little external evidence of this. Some take *hina* as "who," basing this interpretation on an obscure Targum version of the Masoretic Text of Isaiah 6:10 that has *hina* in place of the Aramaic *de* meaning "who." This requires readers to believe that Jesus used the Targum version, which is unlikely.[30] Some take the *hina* as "because" based on Revelation 14:13, noting that the parallel in Matthew 13:13 has *hoti* ("because"). This is possible, but unlikely, as this is a rare use of the term. Jeremias argued that *hina* was shorthand for *hina plerothē* ("in order that it might be fulfilled").[31] Again, this is stretching the Greek and is based purely on assumption. There are other possibilities that accept *hina* as original and seek to interpret Jesus with reference to its usual range of meanings.

A Purposive (or Final) Hina: *Jesus Purposefully Sought to Harden His Hearers*

First, some take *hina* in its most common sense (i.e., "with the purpose that"). Some of these hold a *harsh, literal view,* arguing that Jesus intentionally sought to preach in a way to ensure some would not be saved and would receive eternal destruction. Others take it purposively, but in a *softer, literal way,* arguing that Jesus spoke in parables to ensure his rejection so his death and ultimately salvation would be achieved. Thus, this approach is a part of the veiling of Jesus to Israel for the salvation of the world. This view is not necessarily wrong, but it stands in contrast to the apparent openness of Jesus' invitation to all people throughout the Gospels. Another literal view argues that Jesus intentionally taught in this way to veil his proclamation so that those with true faith would understand, and those who remained blind and unbelieving would continue to be blind.[32] The veiling of the kingdom is part of the answer. However, God's appeal for human forgiveness and repentance is always genuine, so a better answer is needed.

---

30. See especially T. W. Manson, *The Teaching of Jesus* (Cambridge: University Press, 1939), 78–80.

31. J. Jeremias, *The Parables of Jesus* (London: SCM, 1972), 17.

32. C. E. B. Cranfield, *The Gospel According to Saint Mark* (Cambridge: University Press, 1974), 157–58.

TEACHING OF THE KINGDOM: PARABLES

The Hardening Is Not Jesus' Intention, but Is a Consequence or Result of Jesus' Parables

A range of other approaches soften the purposive aspect of Jesus' parables. They see the hardening as a consequence of his parabolic teaching, rather than his direct intent.

A Causal *Hina*: Jesus' Approach Caused His Hearers to Harden. Lohmeyer contends that the *hina* is causal, so the reason Jesus taught in parables to the crowd was because of their hardness. As such, the emphasis falls on Israel's hardness, rather than on Jesus' intent.[33] This is a possibility, as it removes the problem of Jesus going out of his way to harden the crowds.

An Epexegetical (Explanatory) *Hina*: The Hardening Explains the Use of Parables. Lampe argues that the *hina* is epexegetical,[34] explaining "everything" (i.e., "to them all is imparted in parables, namely that they ..."). He argues that the Isaiah citation gives the content of the parable of the seed.[35] This view, however, does not resolve the issue.

A Consecutive *Hina*: The Hardening is a Logical Consequence of Parables. Peisker argues that the *hina* is consecutive in meaning, whereby it introduces the logical consequence of what precedes. Thus, the hardening and rejection follow from the choice of Jesus, not necessarily by intention, but as a consequence of his approach.[36] However, this retains the problem of Jesus intentionally choosing an approach that led to their hardening.

A Result *Hina*: The Hardening is a Result of Jesus Using Parables. The most likely interpretation is that the *hina* clause does not express Jesus' *purpose* in using parables, but the *result* of his using them. The conjunction

---

33. E. Lohmeyer, *Mark* (KEK), as referenced by P. Lampe, "ἵνα," in *EDNT* 2.188.
34. The term "epexegetical" is used of something that is explanatory, which draws out the meaning of something. Other parallel terms include "explanatory," or "explicative." It is commonly used for conjunctions, or genitives. See DeMoss, *PDSNTG*, 52.
35. Lampe, 141, as referenced in Lampe, "ἵνα," in *EDNT* 2.188.
36. C. H. Peisker, "Konsecutives *hina* in Markus 4.12," *ZNW* 59 (1968): 126–27.

hina often invokes a result rather than a purpose. As such, the *purpose* of parables is *not* to blind, but *the result of teaching in parables* is that the people are blind to their deeper meaning.[37] Thus, Jesus intentionally preached in a veiled way, preserving people's freedom, and inviting them to hear and understand his message. The disciples are those people who discern through the parables the "secrets of the kingdom." However, he did so knowing that his teaching would result in most rejecting the message. This plays out through his ministry and culminates in his death. Such an interpretation aligns nicely with Isaiah and broader theology. In Isaiah 6, the prophet's appeal to Israel was genuine in his call for repentance, but God in his omniscience knew the outcome: they would reject the message. Similarly, although Jesus longed for people to hear his message, repent, and believe (Mark 1:14-15), he knew that the outcome of his teaching for many would be even greater hardening. As the Markan narrative develops, it becomes clear Jesus knew this would lead to his rejection and death. In broader theological terms, this interpretation keeps open the genuineness of God's desire for human response, but the inevitability of human rejection. So, Jesus preached in parables knowing that they would call people to the kingdom, but also that they would harden many.

THE GENIUS OF PARABLES

Aside from the above issues, there are a few reasons Jesus preached in parables:

PARABLES RETAIN THE VEILED NATURE OF THE KINGDOM

Parables are indirect and noncoercive. As fictional stories relevant to culture and context with generic characters, they do not directly challenge, but are invitational and nonconfrontational. One must interpret them and find one's place in the story, and this place is open to the choice of the hearer. As such, they invite but do not impose. They cause a person to reflect on the meaning and make a choice. They function in the subversive manner of the coming of the kingdom.

---

37. Lampe, "ἵνα," 2:188, notes that out of sixty-four uses of *hina* in Mark, only thirty-three are purposive.

TEACHING OF THE KINGDOM: PARABLES

PARABLES PRESERVE VOLITION

Parables are not coercive. They allow people to choose their own interpretation, thus preserving their volition. For those with ears to hear, a parable is an invitation into the kingdom and instructs on what the kingdom means. For those who are hardened and cannot hear, it is a story that deepens their rejection. A person can hear a parable and be unaffected. Alternatively, a person can be excited to want to know more from Jesus. Or, they may be angered and seek to kill him, as with the Jewish leaders after the tenants parable (e.g., Mark 12:12).

PARABLES CHALLENGE THOSE WHO HEAR THEM

Although they are non-confrontational and invitational, parables do challenge the hearer or reader to ponder their deeper meaning. If they recognize Jesus and perceive the kingdom, they understand and experience the challenge. They are also challenged to act on their understanding (e.g., in the parable of the good Samaritan, where they are challenged to love their enemies). The prodigal son challenges the Jew to receive the gentile and wayward sinner (e.g., the prostitute and tax collector).

PARABLES ARE MEMORABLE

Parables are truly memorable as evidenced by their preservation through the centuries. Many of the parables have become part of everyday life, such as a "good Samaritan," or "a prodigal." They disarm and communicate truth in a manner that is interesting, memorable, and provocative. Thus, they are ideal teaching devices, able to be remembered and retold by people of all ages and educational standards.

PARABLES ARE UNIVERSALLY RELEVANT

Jesus spoke in stories that are relevant to all cultures because they take aspects of popular culture and use them to draw out spiritual insights. Anyone can understand them. In this regard, they are timeless, which means that they remain some of the most powerful means of communicating God's truth. They are capable of being applied in every context. While Augustine and others' allegorization may appear puzzling, many contemporary preachers do the same thing. This is appropriate because of the power of story (if the theology is sound and it is consistent with the parable's original meaning). Jesus chose material from his world that his hearers would have understood. A.M. Hunter suggests that the stories may have involved characters and events drawn directly from his life. So, for example, the parable of the leaven may have been drawn from Jesus watching his mother, Mary, making bread. The ten virgins may reflect a real situation known to his hearers.[38] Parables, then, are timeless pieces that transcend culture, gender, and social status.

GUIDELINES FOR INTERPRETATION

Following are some key ideas to bear in mind when reading and interpreting the parables:

1. **Think the kingdom:** Always remember that the parables are windows into the kingdom. Consider what they are saying about the King, God, and his Messiah Son, Jesus; the nature of God's reign; and what it means to live as a subject of the King.

2. **Think the big story:** Remember that the parables are set in the context of a redemptive historical narrative. Reach back to creation, the fall, and Israel's story, and forward to the church, mission, Spirit, justice, gospel, and consummation. What does the parable say in the context of the whole of God's story? There are often Old Testament antecedents. For example, the birds in the tree in the parable of the mustard seed are probably the nations (cf. Ezek 17:23; 31:6). Similarly, the great banquet recalls the great eschatological feast of Isaiah 25:6. The parable of the sower speaks of the power of God's word to bring creation (Gen 1) and to achieve God's purposes (Isa 55:10-11). What does it say about mission? For example, the banquet parable speaks of evangelism that is invitational. The Samaritan and the rich-man-and-Lazarus parables call God's people to social justice for those the believer meets on the journey of life who are in need.

---

38. See Hunter, *The Gospel*, 15-16.

3. **Think the whole ministry of Christ:** A parable is set in the context of the whole Gospel, and should not be interpreted in isolation. Most of the parables illustrate a point made by Jesus somewhere else in his ethical teaching and dialogue. For example, in Matthew, the mustard-seed and yeast parables speak of the kingdom growing from smallness to greatness, penetrating the world (Matt 13:31-32). This concept looks back to the Sermon on the Mount and the call for believers to be the "salt of the earth," but also looks forward to the Great Commission, whereby disciples are made in all nations (Matt 5:13; 28:18-20). In Matthew and Luke, it is especially important to link Jesus' parables to the Sermon on the Mount and the Sermon on the Plain material (Matt 5-7; Luke 6:20-49). In Luke too, each parable can be linked to the programmatic statement in Luke 4:18-19 and understood in terms of his overall purpose in writing the Gospel.

4. **Think context:** Each parable is placed in the story by the evangelist in relation to its surrounding matter, and often, the key to understanding is found in its immediate context. For example, the good Samaritan should be interpreted against the two questions and the second great commandment: "What must I do to be saved?," "Who is my neighbor?," and "Love your neighbor as yourself." These provide the hermeneutical keys for interpretation. The parable of the wicked tenants (Matt 21:33-44 and parr.) must be considered in light of the question about Jesus' authority (Matt 21:23-27). The parables of Matthew 24-25 flow out of the eschatological discourse of Matthew 24 and must be understood in regard to eschatology and being ready for the return of Christ.

5. **Think the triple horizon:** Parables have a triple horizon of interpretation. What did the parable mean in the initial Jewish, historical context? What is the point Mark, Matthew, or Luke is making in the flow of his Gospel and purposes? Further, how do Matthew and Luke reshape Mark's initial version? For example, Matthew places the parable of the lost sheep in

a chapter about the church and shapes it in the direction of the pastoral care of the wayward believer. On the other hand, Luke places it in a chapter about the lost, beside the lost-coin story, and its thrust is evangelistic (cf. Luke 15:1-7; Matt 18:10-14). He also balances the story with the lost coin, in a patriarchal context, giving a gender balance in the two stories. This shows that the same story of Jesus has multiple applications.

6. **Think the main point(s):** While most parables resist being constrained by one point, consider what the main point is, or what the *points* of the story are. There are often multiple points based on the characters.

7. **Allegorize moderately and contextually:** Be careful in applying the parables. It is not necessary to identify how parables relate to personal situations, but only in a way consistent with the original context in Jesus' teaching, and the evangelist's use of the parable.

8. **Avoid over-interpretation:** Not everything in the parables has another meaning. For example, the donkey in the good Samaritan is probably incidental to the story. The ring in the prodigal son speaks of honoring the son, but doesn't necessarily mean anything specific. Read parables moderately, building on the obvious meanings, but not creating hermeneutical fiction.

9. **Think characterization:** Often, the characters reflect something Jesus wishes to convey. In the prodigal, the father represents God and the two sons represent different responses to the new work in Christ. Similarly, in the banquet parable, the servants, invitees, disabled, and others are representative of preachers of the gospel, the invitation to Jews to dine in the kingdom Jesus is inaugurating. The disabled represent those at the margins of Jewish culture, and those from further afield are likely the gentiles. Carefully and judiciously make the connections appropriate to the context.

10. **Think culture:** Most parables cannot be fully understood without some knowledge of the Jewish or Greco-Roman culture. For example, in the good Samaritan, one must understand Jewish-Samaritan relationships to comprehend the story. In the parable of the sower, one must have a grasp of the Jewish understanding of the word of God (Isa 55:10-11) and know something about Jewish farming techniques and typical yields to understand the story. In the parable of the rich man and Lazarus, understanding Jewish and Greco-Roman attitudes toward wealth and poverty is critical to perceive the irony in the story—the wrong person is in heaven and the wrong person in Hades! In the parable of the banquet, it is important to understand Jewish and Greco-Roman meal etiquette and social norms. In the Pharisee and the tax collector, understanding the religious and social status of the two men illuminates the parable's meaning. There is usually a shock in the parable that needs uncovering.

11. **Think the narrative:** Read parables as stories, noting the plot, flow, contrasts, structure, characterization, and devices. They are literature and should be treated as such. For example, the contrast between the priest/Levite and Samaritan is what makes the good Samaritan work (Luke 10:25-37). Similarly, the contrast between the Pharisee and tax collector gives meaning to that parable (Luke 18:10-14).

12. **Think the climax of the parable:** Some scholars highlight the "rule of end stress" whereby the end of the parable unlocks a key to its understanding (although not all parables fit this model). For example, at the conclusion to the parable of the wicked tenants (Matt 21:33-44) is a quotation from Psalm 118:22 that, via wordplay, forces the religious authorities to realize that they, the "builders" of the Jewish nation, have rejected God's Son. Whatever else may be true in the parable of the lost sheep, the focus is on the joy at recovering that which was lost (Luke 15:7). If applied to the prodigal son,

the emphasis falls more on the older son's rejection than the younger son's return. Similarly, the Samaritan is the focus of the good Samaritan.

THE TEACHING OF THE PARABLES

The heart of the parables is the nature of the King, the coming of the kingdom of God, and the resulting discipleship that the kingdom requires. When Jesus preaches the kingdom, he means that the new era of God's reign is now inaugurated on the earth through his ministry. Hence, it involves the coming of the grace of God and a radical call to discipleship. Some of the parables anticipate a future consummation of the kingdom, but the main emphasis is that the kingdom is present and available to those who hear Jesus' message. The parables also embody an invitation to enter the kingdom and to live according to its standards. Following are some of the core elements of Jesus' teaching in the parables:

THE KINGDOM AS PRESENT BUT VEILED

Some of the parables speak of the *presence* of the kingdom. This is evident in Matthew 13, where each parable gives a different insight into the kingdom. The recurring metaphor of the "seed" points to the secret and almost imperceptible beginning of the kingdom in the present. The similarly recurring concept of growth indicates that the kingdom will grow from the point of its initial beginnings and become dominant through the work of God. However, the parables point to opposition and challenge in this growth. They also point to the consummation of the kingdom and the gathering of the righteous and unrighteous. The "strong man" parable (Matt 12:29) points to Jesus' ministry of overcoming Satan's work and, not unlike a person coming to rob a house, binding the security guard on the way.

There are other parables that indicate the kingdom is here now and available, such as the parables of the banquet (Luke 14:15-24) and of the wedding (Matt 22:1-14). These parables also point to the refusal of some to accept Jesus' message and the celebratory dimension of the kingdom (cf. prodigal son).

The notion of "grace" is strong in these parables. While Jesus did not use the term, it is strong in his invitation to outcasts in the banquet parables, the parables of the two debtors (Luke 7:41-43), the "lost" parables in Luke 15, the unmerciful servant (Matt 18:23-35), the laborers in the vineyard (Matt 20:1-16), and the Pharisee and the tax collector (Luke 18:9-14).

THE KINGDOM AS FUTURE

There is a tendency among some scholars to downplay this dimension in the parables and in Jesus' teaching in general (e.g., C. H. Dodd). Yet, it is clear from the parables that there is a future unconsummated dimension to the kingdom. This is evidenced in the parables of growth (e.g., weeds and net, see Matt 13:24-30, 47-50), which speak of a future harvest, judgment, or of a master who returns to settle accounts. That is, there will be a point of separation between the obedient, faithful, and merciful who will enter the kingdom and those who will not. This judgment involves punishment and destruction.

The purpose of this future dimension is to cause a change in attitude and life *in the present* (i.e., to produce faithfulness, mercy, and obedience in the listeners). This is particularly demonstrated in the parables of the ten virgins and the talents in Matthew 25:1-30 (cf. parable of the ten minas, Luke 19:11-27).

THE NATURE OF THE KINGDOM

Some parables give insight into the nature of the kingdom. It is veiled, coming in hiddenness and insignificance, and yet will grow to be a vast kingdom into which all nations will come. It will be a mixed multitude of authentic believers (good plants/good fish/sheep) and nonbelievers (weeds/bad fish/goats), which will be sorted at the culmination of the age. It is of inestimable value, a treasure worth giving everything up for—the greatest of pearls that the pearl merchant will give everything up to gain. It will be a place of great celebration and satisfaction as seen in the parables of the wedding feast and the great banquet. The miracles have a parabolic dimension as well. They are living demonstrations symbolizing that the kingdom will be a place of complete physical and emotional wholeness (physical healings and deliverance), of good and not evil (deliverance), of satisfaction and not poverty (feeding), of peace and not chaos (calming storm), and of life and not death (resurrection).

ISRAEL'S REJECTION AND THE KINGDOM FOR THE MARGINALIZED, THE SAMARITANS, AND THE GENTILES

Some parables have their first point of reference in Israel's rejection of Jesus and the kingdom. A clear example is the parable of the tenants in which the leaders of Israel reject the prophets of old (servants) and then the son, killing him. This is, in effect, a prediction of the passion and the rejection of Jesus by the leaders of the nation. They clearly understood Jesus' teaching and wished to kill him (Matt 21:33-46). Similarly, the parable of the wedding feast in Matthew's Gospel (with that Gospel's emphasis on Jesus as the Jewish Messiah) highlights the refusal of most of Israel to come to the feast of the kingdom and the resultant invitation for those from the streets to enter (Matt 22:1-14).

The parables of the wineskins and cloth are also best understood as referring to the failure of Israel to receive the new wine of the kingdom. These parables refer to the truth that some would receive the new wine and others would not, leading to a schism among Jews at the coming of the kingdom. Judaism itself had to be renewed to accept the new wine (Mark 2:19-22).

One probable interpretation of the lost son (Luke 15:11-32) is based around Israel and the gentiles. The younger son arguably represents the gentiles who come back to the Father through the work of Jesus. The Father accepts them while the older son (Israel) will not accept the Father's acceptance of these unclean sinners (cf. Luke 4:23-30; Acts 21:21). The good Samaritan challenges Jewish attitudes to Samaritans and anticipates the Samaritans' reception of the Gospel in Acts 8 (cf. John 4). The banquet speaks of inviting the disabled to the feast, and their acceptance; the kingdom is a kingdom for the margins.

FORGIVENESS FOR THE REPENTANT SINNER

The parable of the lost son illustrates the nature of God (Luke 15:11-32) in the attitude of the father who quite remarkably forgives the returning son completely, despite his squandering all he has given him. He accepts him completely, providing him with lavish gifts of clothing, a ring, and the best meal possible. His attitude is contrasted with the older brother who will not accept his brother, feeling he deserves punishment for his sin. Other parables, such as the parable of the unmerciful servant (Matt 18:21-35) and the Pharisee and the tax collector (Luke 18:10-14), also speak of God's great forgiveness.

THE MISSION OF THE KINGDOM

There are many parables that point to the mission of the church and individuals in church and society. The parabolic images of salt and light indicate the Christian's role in society is to work to bring God's reign and the establishment of righteousness (Matt 5:13-16). These parables suggest God's overall goal of transforming all creation through his people infiltrating every avenue of society, incarnating the love and light of God. The metaphor of salt speaks of the function of believers to preserve, to flavor, and to influence society with the grace and justice of the gospel.[39] The parable of the yeast (Luke 13:21) has the same sense; just as yeast penetrates dough and causes it to rise, the Christian's influence penetrates human society and causes it to rise.[40] The mustard-seed parable has a missionary sense in that the kingdom grows from hidden insignificance to a great size (Matt 13:31-33). This will happen as each individual Christian, as well as the church, acts as God's seeds, bringing life wherever they go, seeing humanity and the world transformed. The parable of the lamp also has a missiological emphasis; the believer must not hide their light but bring it out so that others will see it and be drawn to the right path (Luke 8:16-17).

---

39. Salt in Jewish writing functioned positively in many ways including: to flavor (Job 6:6), to preserve food (Philo, *Opif.* 66; *Spec.* 1.175) and bodies (Philo, *Spec.* 1.289), to season offerings (Lev 2:13; *T. Levi* 9.14; Josephus, *Ant.* 3.227; Philo, *Spec.* 1.289), to heal (*T. Sol.* 18.34), to purify (Exod 30:35; 2 Kgs 2:20-21), to clean (Ezek 16:4), and as a symbol of hospitality and table fellowship (Philo, *Somn.* 2.210; *Ios.* 196). It was also a negative idea, a symbol of judgment (Deut 29:23), death (as in the Salt Sea [Dead Sea], Deut 3:17; Lot's wife, Gen 19:26), and to render barren (Ps 107:34; Judg 9:45; Josephus, *Ant.* 5.248). Just as Christians as the aroma of Christ can be the fragrance of life, and the aroma of death (a rotting corpse, cf. Jesus), so being salty has positive and negative connotations to "the world" (cf. 2 Cor 2:15). Light can also repel (cf. John 3:18).

40. Yeast or leaven causes fermentation. This was also viewed negatively, as leaven caused decay and corruption (e.g., Mark 8:15; Matt 16:6, 11-12; Luke 12:1; 1 Cor 5:6-8; Gal 5:9). On leaven, see further "Leaven," in *BEB*, 2.1320. The feast of unleavened bread reminded Israel of Passover and called her people to purity (Exod 12:15, 19), as did unleavened bread at sacrifices (Lev 2:11; 6:17).

The parable of the sower (Matt 13:1-23) is a parable about evangelism, whether by Jesus or his disciples. The proclaimed word is likened to a seed, which, when it is scattered, either grows or dies, depending on the type of soil it lands on. When the word is preached, people respond to it in different ways. Some respond with complete incomprehension and rejection (cf. 2 Cor 4:4; Eph 2:1-3). Some receive the word with gladness, but give up quickly because of troubles and persecutions (cf. Demas in 2 Tim 4:10; Judas). Others receive the word of God and appear to be fully converted, but fail to grow to maturity and become full disciples because of the anxieties of life, and the love of money and pleasure. It is unclear whether these are believers who are unfruitful or pseudo-believers whose fruitlessness reveals their real state. Such judgments must be left to God. Finally, there are the ideal respondents who hear the word, are completely converted, and become seed-bearing and fruitful Christians (cf. the disciples). Fruit in the New Testament is usually ethical, such as "the fruit of the Spirit" in Galatians 5:22-24 (cf. Matt 7:17-19; 12:33; Eph 5:9; Phil 1:11). This may be so here. However, in the context of the parable of the sower, fruit is likely the fruit of evangelism, further missional engagement, and even converts. They, too, will experience the same range of responses, but in their faithfulness, will achieve differing levels of fruitfulness.

The power of the gospel to generate life is also seen in Mark's version of the growing seed, where the word of God planted grows "by itself" (*automaton*), not dependent on the preacher, but the gospel's latent power to cause its own growth (Mark 4:28). As Brooks says, "The success of the Christian message similarly does not depend upon human effort or understanding—though Christians certainly need to scatter the seed—but upon divine power."[41]

The universal nature of the mission to the gentiles is hinted at in some parables such as the wedding feast/great banquet where, after the rejection of the servants of God by Israel, those from the streets are invited to the banquet (Matt 22:1-14; Luke 14:15-24). The concept of "invitation" suggests evangelism and is a wonderful motif for understanding what sharing the gospel means: inviting people to dine at the banquet of God for eternity (Luke 14:16).

---

41. Brooks, *Mark*, 85.

The first two of the three "lost" parables of Luke 15 (sheep and coin) are missiological; the believers, male (lost sheep) and female (lost coin), seek the lost so that they will repent. These give priority to seeking the one lost sheep over the ninety-nine who are not lost, and the one lost coin. These imply a powerful call to both men and women to seek and save the lost as Jesus did through the proclamation of the word (Luke 15:1-10, see also 19:10; 4:43). Interestingly, all three parables end with a celebration—God and his angels rejoice when *one* turns to God! This is eschatological—the salvation of the lost in the present anticipating the final joy experienced at the consummation.

The third of the "lost" parables concerns the son who becomes a horrendous sinner, effectively wishing his father dead, demanding and then squandering his inheritance on loose living. This son finds himself working a job feeding unclean pigs—anathema for a Jew. Yet he is accepted back by his father, who runs to embrace him. There is no mission focus to this story, and perhaps again this is a condemnation of the older son, who should have gone looking for the lost brother (see esp. 15:16: "no one gave him anything to eat"). As such, it is an implicit appeal for evangelism and mission to sinners, gentiles, and the lost sheep of humanity.

DISCIPLESHIP

Discipleship is a central theme of Jesus' teaching, and his parables involve a call to radical discipleship at many levels. Through the parables comes a clarion call to complete submission to the reign of God for the kingdom's subjects. The cost of discipleship is mentioned in the parables of the tower builder and the warring king—one must count the cost and give up all to be a disciple (Luke 14:28-32). Complete obedience is reflected in the parable of the owner and his servant (Luke 17:7). Building one's life on the foundation of Jesus' teaching is the theme of the parable of the two builders (Matt 7:24-27). The parable of the two sons (Matt 21:28-32) stresses the importance of carried-out obedience while condemning good intentions with no follow-through. A strong emphasis is found on the importance of doing acts of mercy in the parables of the unforgiving servant (Matt 18:33), the sheep and the goats (Matt 25:32-46), and the good Samaritan (Luke 10:25-37).

This discipleship is to be wholehearted. Quite often, the parables indicate that the believer is to be fully devoted, above all other allegiances, to God and his kingdom. In the parables of the hidden treasure and buried pearl, those who find the treasure and pearl sell *everything* they own to gain the kingdom because of its inestimable value (Matt 13:44-46). The parables of the talents and the minas stress that the believer is to take what God has given them in material and spiritual terms and invest it for his purposes and so receive a reward in kind (Matt 25:14-30; Luke 19:11-27). The parable of the shrewd manager should probably be understood in this regard. Just as business people of this world are shrewd in their management of worldly wealth and so commended by the world, subjects of the kingdom should be much more trustworthy and shrewd in their management of the resources of the kingdom. It is not an encouragement to be dishonest, but rather the opposite; Christians should invest the resources of the kingdom with integrity to bring gain for the kingdom (Luke 16:1-15).

THE RIGHT USE OF WEALTH

The right use of wealth is a dominant theme in Jesus' teaching, particularly in Luke, who emphasizes this dimension to challenge the elite of the Roman world. There are many parables that warn against greed and its consequences. In the parable of the rich fool, Jesus rebukes the greedy who store up their wealth for personal aggrandizement at the expense of the poor (Luke 12:16-21). In the rich man and Lazarus, there is a strong warning to those who fail to respond to those in need (Luke 16:19-31).[42] It is possible that Jesus commends shrewdness with the use of wealth while remaining subservient to kingdom economic principles (the parable of the shrewd manager, Luke 16:8-9, cf. 12:33). The practice of pedantic tithing without justice and mercy is critiqued in the parable of the Pharisee and the tax collector. The Pharisee tithes regularly, but in a pompous and self-righteous fashion, and so is not justified before God (Luke 18:10-14). The good Samaritan's generosity is a living example of the radical generosity of the kingdom. Note that Jesus enlivens this parable by making the

---

42. Note the rich man knows his name is Lazarus, indicating he knew the beggar on earth but failed to care for him.

character who shows such generosity one of the despised Samaritans (cf. Luke 10:33-35).[43]

BOLDNESS, PERSISTENCE, AND CONFIDENCE IN PRAYER

A concern for prayer is also emphasized in the parables in Luke. Two parables illustrate the need for audacity, boldness, persistence, perseverance, and confidence in prayer (Luke 11:5-8; 18:1-8). The parable of the Pharisee and the tax collector urges humility in prayer as believers stand before God crying, "have mercy on me, a sinner" (Luke 18:13 NIV). The many parables of Jesus concerning servitude and obedience to the master implicitly remind believers that they must be connected to their Lord and carry out his commands faithfully (e.g., Matt 20:1-16; 25:14-30). Bowing in prayer and reading Scripture with open spiritual ears are vital for hearing God's voice.

REPENTANCE AND HUMILITY

The parable of the lost son gives a paradigm of right response to sin as the son turns from his life of sin and debauchery among the pigs and returns to the father in repentance (Luke 15:21). This is even more emphatic in the parable of the Pharisee and the tax collector where the tax collector, though a terrible sinner, is declared righteous due to his penitent humility before God (Luke 18:9-14).

JUDGMENT

A few parables speak strongly of the coming judgment for those who reject the King and his kingdom. Matthew, in particular, has a harsh tone to some of his parables, such as the weeds, which are pulled up and thrown "into the blazing furnace, where there will be weeping and gnashing of teeth" (Matt 13:42 NIV). Similarly, in the parable of the net, the bad fish are separated from the good and thrown "into the blazing furnace, where there will be weeping and gnashing of teeth" (Matt 13:50 NIV). In the parables of the wedding feast and talents, those who try to enter the kingdom illegitimately suffer the same fate (Matt 22:13; 25:30). In the parable of the

---

43. The two denarii would give twenty-four days' board, a day's board being 1/12th of a denarius. See I. H. Marshall, *Luke*, 449. This is a very generous contribution. The Samaritan offers to pay *even more* if there is a shortfall on his return.

virgins, those who are not ready for the return of Christ are shut out of the wedding banquet (Matt 25:10). On the other hand, "the righteous will shine like the sun" (Matt 13:43, cf. Dan 12:1-3).

The strongest warning probably comes in the parable of the rich man and Lazarus where the rich man neglects the cries of the poor and ends up in eternal torment from which there is no escape (Luke 16:19-31). True faith is expressed in concern for the needy. Similarly, in the sheep and the goats, many are condemned to eternal punishment for failing to put their faith to work in caring for the needy among God's people. Those who fail to do so reject Jesus himself. He identifies himself with his people who are in need (Matt 25:31-46).

PARABLES AND THEOLOGY

It is disagreed whether theological premises can be derived from these stories. Some argue believers should not and cannot, as parables are stories set in a given context and, therefore, cannot be confidently applied to other times and places. Others treat the parables like all Scripture and do not allow for genre, symbolism, and context, drawing theology from the parables directly and literally. What is needed is a careful balance between these two extremes. On the one hand, interpreters must be able to draw principles and concepts from the parables as they clearly refer to truth, are based on truth, and seek to convey truth. On the other hand, believers can over-interpret parables and fail to account for ambiguity in the text. An example is the rich man and Lazarus. In this story, the rich man is in Hades, and the poor man is in paradise with Abraham. This inverts the expectations of the first hearers, who would expect the converse, as wealth was associated with righteousness and blessing, while poverty was associated with sin and cursedness. That much appears clear. Beyond this, it is questionable how much of this parable should be applied to theology. For example: (1) What is paradise? Is it an intermediate state? Is it metaphorical and not to be taken seriously at all? Is it effectively the equivalent of eternal life after judgment? (2) Should readers take the picture of hell literally? Is Hades a place of everlasting thirst and literal pain? Or is this some intermediate state awaiting judgment? Is hell visible from heaven? Such questions may push beyond Jesus' intention in telling the story.

However, theological principles can be drawn from parables, but must be done judiciously. The first principle is to interpret the parable within its book and initial settings (i.e., the moment of first telling), and its book (e.g., Luke). Readers must beware reading later theological questions or ideas developed in church history into a parable that is not really concerned with them. An example is the topic of the intermediate state; it is questionable that Luke had even thought of this concept. Most importantly, readers should develop their theology with careful concern for the wider teaching of the Scriptures, Christ, and the New Testament, with regard for genre. The parables usually make a point(s) that supports or develops ideas that are found in the more direct teaching of Jesus and the apostles. So, rather than making the parables the basis for theology, they add to the picture already painted.

PREACHING AND PARABLES TODAY

Much can be gleaned from Jesus' approach to preaching. He chose to use stories to express the truth. Stories have a timeless, disarming power. Actually, stepping back from the text of Scripture, the whole of Scripture is a story. Acts is a story. The Gospels are stories or narratives, the accounts of the life of Jesus, each with a different emphasis. The letters are glimpses into a story that must be told to explain it (i.e., the narrative *behind* the text). Parables are short, effective stories that make a point(s) in a creative and winsome manner.

Believers must reclaim the power of story in their preaching. They need to find stories and narratives of others and from their own lives that speak into the lives of others. Framing whole sermons in this genre can be powerful. Unpacking the letters of Paul, for example, through story, can bring these old letters alive. Philemon comes alive when the living situations of Paul, Philemon, and Onesimus—a runaway slave worthy of extreme punishment—are considered in a first-century setting. There is a story behind every biblical book that needs exploring.

Sermon material may be drawn from parables, but first they must be understood in their first contexts—that is, Jesus and the evangelist's time—so that their principles are translated well to the world. Look for intersecting stories. It is good to retell parables; however, Jesus' teaching about the kingdom of God must be preserved.

QUESTIONS TO CONSIDER

- How might the three (or four) horizons affect interpretation of the parables of the good Samaritan and the great banquet?

- What do you think Jesus meant in Mark 4:10-11?

- Take the prodigal son or another parable and work through the rules of interpretation outlined in this chapter. What do you discover?

- What is the one main idea Jesus wants people to hear in the following parables? Or are there multiple core ideas?

    a. the prodigal son

    b. the good Samaritan

    c. the parable of the sower

    d. the parable of the great banquet

    e. the parable of the mustard seed

    f. the parable of the Pharisee and the tax collector

- What is your favorite parable, and why?

- Should believers preach in parables today?

- What would it mean to preach through story?

- Try writing a modern parable and try it out on others. Was it easy or hard? What did you learn?

BIBLIOGRAPHY

Achtemeier, Paul J. "Gospel of Mark." *ABD* 4:541–557.
"Acropolis." *TBD* 10.
Aeschylus. *Aeschylus, with an English Translation by Herbert Weir Smyth, Ph. D. in Two Volumes. 2. Eumenides* (ed. Herbert Weir Smyth; Medford, MA: Harvard University Press, 1926).
Aland, Kurt, and Barbara Aland. *The Text of the New Testament: An Introduction to the Critical Editions and to the Theory and Practice of Modern Textual Criticism*. Translated by Erroll F. Rhodes; 2nd ed. Leiden: Brill, 1989.
Allison, D. C. *The End of the Ages Has Come: An Early Interpretation of the Passion and Resurrection of Jesus*. Philadelphia: Fortress, 1987.
Algie, Brian. "Caesarea Philippi." *LBD*.
Arndt, William, Frederick W. Danker, and Walter Bauer. *A Greek-English Lexicon of the New Testament and Other Early Christian Literature*. Chicago: University of Chicago Press, 2000.
Arnold, Clinton E. "Magical Papyri." *DNTB* 666–70.
Aune, D. E. "Religions, Greco-Roman." *DPL* 786–95.
———. "Religion, Greco-Roman." *DNTB* 917–26.
Bacon, B. W. "The 'Five Books' of Matthew against the Jews." *Exp* 15 (1918): 56–66.
Barrett, C. K. *The Gospel According to St. John*. 2nd ed. Philadelphia: Westminster, 1978.
Bauckham, Richard J. "Gospels (Apocryphal)." *DJG* 286–91.

———. *Jesus and the Eyewitnesses: The Gospels as Eyewitness Testimony.* Grand Rapids, MI: Eerdmans, 2006.
Baum, A. D. "Synoptic Problem." *DJG2* 911–19.
Beasley-Murray, George R. *Baptism in the New Testament.* Exeter: Paternoster, 1972.
———. *Jesus and the Kingdom of God.* Grand Rapids, MI: Eerdmans, 1986.
———. *John.* WBC 36. Dallas: Word, Incorporated, 2002.
Bellinzoni Jr, A. *The Two-Source Hypothesis: A Critical Appraisal.* Macon: Mercer University, 1985.
Berkouwer, G. C. *Holy Scripture*, ed., Jack Bartlett Rogers, "Studies in Dogmatics." Grand Rapids, MI: Eerdmans, 1975.
Black, David Alan. "New Testament Semitisms." *The Bible Translator* 39.2 (April 1988): 215–23.
Blackburn, B. L. "Divine Man/*Theios Anēr*." *DJG* 189–91.
———. "Miracles and Miracle Stories." *DJG* 549–59.
Blomberg, Craig L. *Interpreting the Parables.* Downers Grove, IL: InterVarsity Press, 1990.
———. "Form Criticism." *DJG* 243–49.
———. *Jesus and the Gospels: An Introduction and Survey.* Leicester: Apollos, 1997.
———. *Matthew.* NAC 22. Nashville: Broadman & Holman Publishers, 1992.
Bock, Darrell L. *Acts I.* BECNT. Grand Rapids, MI: Baker Academic, 2007.
———. *Luke: 1:1–9:50.* Vol 1. Grand Rapids, MI: Baker Academic, 1994.
———. *Luke: 9:51–24:53.* Vol. 2. BECNT. Grand Rapids, MI: Baker Academic, 1996.
———. "Luke, Gospel of." Pages 495–509 in *DJG*.
Borchert, Gerald L. *John 1–11.* NAC 25A. Nashville: Broadman & Holman Publishers, 1996.
———. *John 12–21.* NAC 25B. Nashville: Broadman & Holman Publishers, 2002.
Bowden, Andrew M. "New Testament Semitisms." *LBD*.
Bowley, J. E. "Pax Romana." *DNTB* 770–75.
Bowman, J. "The Identity and Date of the Unnamed Feast of John 5:1." In *Near Eastern Studies in Honor of William Foxwell Albright*, 43–56. Edited by H. Goedicke. Baltimore: Johns Hopkins Press, 1971.

Brand, Chad, et al., eds. *Holman Illustrated Bible Dictionary*. Nashville, TN: Holman Bible Publishers, 2003.
Braun, F. *L'Evangile selon Saint Jean*. Paris: du Cerf, 1946.
Breneman, Mervin. *Ezra, Nehemiah, Esther*. NAC 10. Nashville: Broadman & Holman Publishers, 1993.
Brisco, Thomas V. *Holman Bible Atlas*. Holman Reference. Nashville, TN: Broadman & Holman Publishers, 1998.
Brooks, James A. *Mark*. NAC 23. Nashville: Broadman & Holman Publishers, 1991.
Brown, C. "Historical Jesus, Quest of." *DJG* 326-341.
Brown, Derek. "Docetism." *LBD*.
Brown, Raymond E. *The Gospel According to John: John I-XII*. AB. Garden City, NY: Doubleday, 1966.
Bruce, F. F. "Is the Paul of Acts the Real Paul?" *BJRL* 58 (1976): 282-305.
———. *The Acts of the Apostles*. NICNT. 3rd ed. Grand Rapids, MI: Eerdmans, 1990.
———. *The Acts of the Apostles: The Greek Text with Introduction and Commentary*. London: Tyndale, 1962.
Bruns, J. E. "The Confusion between John and John Mark in Antiquity." *Scripture* 17 (1965): 23-26.
Burge, Gary M. *John*. NIVAC. Grand Rapids, MI: Zondervan Publishing House, 2000.
Burns, J. E. "Conversion and Proselytism." *EDEJ* 484-86.
Burridge, R. A. "Biography, Ancient." *DNTB* 167-70.
Butler, B. C. *The Originality of St. Matthew: A Critique of the Two-Document Hypothesis*. Cambridge: Cambridge University Press, 1951.
Caragounis, C. C. "Kingdom of God." *DJG* 417-30.
———. *Peter and the Rock*. Berlin: de Gruyter, 1990.
Carson, D. A. *The Gospel According to John*. PNTC; Leicester, England; Grand Rapids, MI: Inter-Varsity Press; Eerdmans, 1991.
Chafer, Lewis Sperry. *Systematic Theology*. Grand Rapids, MI: Kregel Publications, 1993.
Chapman, D. J. *Matthew, Mark and Luke: A Study in the Order and Interrelation of the Synoptic Gospels*. London: Longmans, Green, 1937.
Chenevix, Richard. *Notes on the Miracles of Our Lord*. New York: D. Appleton and Company, 1873

Chilton, B., and E. Yamauchi. "Synagogues." *DNTB* 1145-53.

"Christmas." *EBD* 210.

Ciampa, Roy E., and Brian S. Rosner. *The First Letter to the Corinthians*. PNTC; Grand Rapids, MI; Cambridge, U.K.: Eerdmans, 2010.

Cole, Susan Guettel. "Festivals, Greco-Roman." *ABD* 2:793-94.

Collins, John J., and Daniel C. Harlow, eds. *The Eerdmans Dictionary of Early Judaism*. Grand Rapids, MI; Cambridge, U.K.: William B. Eerdmans Publishing Company, 2010.

"Consul." *TBD* 311.

"Consul." *ISBE* 1:766.

Corley, Bruce, Steve W. Lemke, and Grant I. Lovejoy. *Biblical Hermeneutics: A Comprehensive Introduction to Interpreting Scripture*, 2nd ed. Nashville, TN: Broadman & Holman, 2002.

Cranfield, C. E. B. *The Gospel According to Saint Mark*. Cambridge: University Press, 1974.

Crossan, J. Dominic. *The Historical Jesus: The Life of a Mediterranean Jewish Peasant*. San Francisco: HarperCollins; Edinburgh: T. & T. Clark, 1991.

Culpepper, R. *John, the Son of Zebedee: The Life of a Legend*. Minneapolis: Fortress, 2002.

DeMoss, Matthew S. *Pocket Dictionary for the Study of New Testament Greek*. Downers Grove, IL: InterVarsity Press, 2001.

Dicken, Frank E. "Herod Philip." *LBD*.

———. "Luke." *LBD*.

Dionysius of Halicarnassus. *Thucydides*. Translated by Charles Forster Smith. 4 Vol. LCL. Cambridge: Harvard University Press, 1956.

Dockery, D. S. "Baptism." *DJG* 55-58.

Dodd, C. H. *Historical Tradition in the Fourth Gospel*. Cambridge: Cambridge University Press, 1963.

———. *The Apostolic Preaching and Its Developments*. London: Hodder and Stoughton, 1936 [1963 edn.].

———. "The Framework of the Gospel Narrative." *ExpTim* 43 (1932): 396-400.

———. *The Parables of the Kingdom*. Glasgow: Collins, 1961 [orig. 1935].

Downing, F. Gerald. *Cynics and Christian Origins*. Edinburgh: T. & T. Clark, 1992.

Dunn, J. D. G. *The Epistles to the Colossians and to Philemon: A Commentary on the Greek Text.* NICNT. Grand Rapids, MI; Carlisle: Eerdmans; Paternoster, 1996.

Eades, K. L. "Testament." *ISBE* 4:796-97.

"Earthquake." *BEB* 1:647.

"Ἑβραΐς." *EDNT* 1:370.

Edwards, J. R. *The Gospel According to Mark.* PNTC. Grand Rapids, MI; Leicester, England: Eerdmans; Apollos, 2002.

Eichhorn, G. *Einleitung in das Neue Testament.* Vol 1. Leipzig: Weidmann, 1804.

Elwell, Walter A., and Philip Wesley Comfort. *Tyndale Bible Dictionary.* Tyndale reference library. Wheaton, IL: Tyndale House Publishers, 2001.

Ellis, Earle E. *The Gospel of Luke.* 2nd ed. NCBC; Grand Rapids, MI; London: Eerdmans; Marshall, Morgan & Scott, 1974.

Eusebius. *The Ecclesiastic History.* Translated by Kirsopp Lake and J. E. L. Oulton. 2 Vols. LCL. London; New York: William Heinemanna; G. P. Putnam's Sons, 1926-1965.

Evans, Craig A. "Apollonius of Tyana." *DNTB* 80-81.

———. *Mark 8:27-16:20.* WBC 34B. Dallas: Word, Incorporated, 2001.

Everts, J. M. "Financial Support." *DPL* 295-300.

Falk, Daniel K. "Sabbath." *EDEJ* 1174-76.

Farmer, W. *New Synoptic Studies: The Cambridge Gospel Conference and Beyond.* Macon: Mercer University, 1983.

———. *The Synoptic Problem: A Critical Analysis.* New York: Macmillan, 1964.

Farrer, A. M. "On Dispensing with Q." In *Studies in the Gospels: Essays in Memory of R. H. Lightfoot,* 55-88. Edited by D. E. Nineham. Oxford: Blackwell, 1955.

Fee, Gordon D. *The First Epistle to the Corinthians.* NICNT. Grand Rapids, MI: Eerdmans, 1987.

Fernandes, P. *The Atheist Delusion: A Christian Response to Christopher Hitchens and Richard Dawkins.* Brentwood, TN; Xulon, 2009.

"Filioque." *ODCC* 614-15.

Filson, F. "Who Was the Beloved Disciple?" *JBL* 48 (1949): 83-88.

Fitzmyer, Joseph A. *The Gospel According to Luke (i–ix)*. AB 28. Garden City, NY: Doubleday, 1981.
France, R. T. *The Gospel of Mark: A Commentary on the Greek Text*. NIGTC. Grand Rapids, MI; Carlisle: Eerdmans; Paternoster Press, 2002.
———. *Matthew*. TNTC. Grand Rapids, MI; Leicester: Eerdmans; IVP, 1985.
Gaertner, Dennis. *Acts*. The College Press NIV Commentary. Joplin, MO: College Press, 1995.
Galli, Mark, and Ted Olsen. *131 Christians Everyone Should Know*. Nashville, TN: Broadman & Holman Publishers, 2000.
Gamble, H. Y. "Canon (New Testament)." *ABD* 1:837–61.
Gangel, K. O. *Acts*. HNTC 5. Nashville, TN: Broadman & Holman Publishers, 1998.
Gardner-Smith, P. *St John and the Synoptic Gospels*. Cambridge: Cambridge University Press, 1938.
Garland, David E. *Mark*. NIVAC. Grand Rapids, MI: Zondervan, 1996.
Gaventa, Beverly Roberts. "Ethiopian Eunuch." *ABD* 2:667.
Gieseler, C. L. *Historisch-kritischer Versuch über die Entstehung und die frühesten Schicksale der schriftlichen Evangelien*. Leipzig: Engelmann, 1818.
Gill, D. W. J. "Erastus the Aedile." *TynBul* 40 (1989): 293–310.
Goodacre, Mark S. *The Case Against Q: Studies in Markan Priority and the Synoptic Problem*. Harrisburg, PA: Trinity Press International, 2002.
———. *Goulder and the Gospels: An Examination of a New Paradigm*. JSNTSup 133. Sheffield: Sheffield Academic Press, 1996.
Gorman, Michael J. *Abortion in the Early Church: Christian, Jewish & Pagan Attitudes in the Greco-Roman World*. Eugene, OR: Wipf and Stock, 1982.
Goulder, Michael D. *Midrash and Lection in Matthew*. London: SPCK, 1974.
Green, Joel B., Jeannine K. Brown, and Nicholas Perrin, eds. *Dictionary of Jesus and the Gospels, Second Edition*. Downers Grove, IL; Nottingham, England: IVP Academic; IVP, 2013.
Green, Joel B. *The Gospel of Luke*. NICNT. Grand Rapids, MI: Eerdmans, 1997.
Grenz, Stanley, David Guretzki, and Cherith Fee Nordling. *Pocket*

Dictionary of Theological Terms. Downers Grove, IL: InterVarsity Press, 1999.

Griesbach, J. J. "Commentatio qua Marci Evangelium totum e Matthaei et Lucae commentariis decerptum esse monstratur." In *J. J. Griesbachii Opuscala Academica II*, 358-425. Edited by J. P. Gabler and J. C. G. Goepferdt. Jena: Frommanni, 1825.

Griffin, B. G. "The Disciple Whom Jesus Loved." *ExpTim* 32 (1920-21): 379-81.

Guelich, Robert A. *Mark 1-8:26*. WBC 34A. Dallas: Word, 1998.

Gutbrod, Walter. "ἑβραΐς." *TDNT* 3:88-89.

Haacker, Klaus. "Gallio." *ABD* 2:901.

Hadjiantoniou, G. *Learning the Basics of New Testament Greek*. Chattanooga, TN: AMG Publishers, 1998.

Hagner, Donald A. "Matthew." *ISBE* 3:280-88.

———. *Matthew 1-13*. WBC 33A. Dallas: Word, 2002.

———. *Matthew 14-28*. WBC 33B. Dallas: Word, 1998.

Hansen, G. W. "Rhetorical Criticism." *DPL* 822-25.

Harris, Murray J. *The Second Epistle to the Corinthians: A Commentary on the Greek Text*. NIGTC. Grand Rapids, MI; Milton Keynes, UK: Eerdmans; Paternoster Press, 2005.

Harrison, R. K. "Physician." *ISBE* 3:865.

Hauck, F. "μαργαρίτης." *TDNT* 4:472.

Hawthorne, G. F. "Marriage and Divorce, Adultery and Incest." *DPL* 594-600.

Hemer, Colin J. *The Book of Acts in the Setting of Hellenistic History*. Tübingen: Mohr-Siebeck, 1989.

Hengel, Martin. *Acts and the History of Earliest Christianity*. London: SCM, 1979.

———. "Literary, Theological and Historical Problems in the Gospel of Mark." In *The Gospel and the Gospels*, 209-51. Edited by Peter Stuhlmacher. Grand Rapids, MI: Eerdmans, 1991.

———. *Studies in the Gospel of Mark*. Philadelphia: Fortress, 1985.

———. *The Four Gospels and the One Gospel of Jesus Christ: An Investigation of the Collection and Origin of the Canonical Gospels*. Harrisburg, PA: Trinity Press International, 2000.

Herder, J. G. "Vom Erlöser der Menschen." *Herder Werke: Theologische Schriften* 9/1. Frangurt: Deuscher Klassker, 1994: 671-87.

Heyink, Brenda. "Kidron, Brook of." *LBD*.

Hixon, Elijah. *Diatessaron*. *LBD*.

Hock, R. *The Social Context of Paul's Ministry: Tentmaking and Apostleship*. Philadelphia: Fortress Press, 1980.

Holmes, M. W. *The Apostolic Fathers: Greek Texts and English Translations*. Updated edition. Grand Rapids, MI: Baker Books, 1999.

Hooker, Morna D. *The Gospel According to Saint Mark*. BNTC. London: Continuum, 1991.

Houston, J. M. "Palestine." *NBD* 855-61.

Horsley, Richard A. "Early Christian Movements: Jesus Movements and the Renewal of Israel." *HTS* 62.4 (2006): 1201-25.

Huffman, D. S. "Genealogy." *DJG* 253-58.

Hultgren, Arland J. *The Parables of Jesus: A Commentary*. Grand Rapids, MI: Eerdmans, 2000.

Hume, David. *An Enquiry Concerning Human Understanding*. New York: Bobbs-Merill, 1955.

Hunter, A. M. *Christ and the Kingdom*. Edinburgh: Saint Andrew Press, 1980.

———. *The Gospel of the Kingdom: Popular Expositions on the Kingdom of God*. Grand Rapids, MI: Eerdmans, 1959.

Hurtado, Larry W. *Mark*. UBCS. Grand Rapids, MI: Baker Books, 2011.

Irenaeus of Lyons. "Irenæus Against Heresies." In *The Apostolic Fathers with Justin Martyr and Irenaeus*, 315-57. Edited by Alexander Roberts, James Donaldson, and A. Cleveland Coxe. Vol. 1. The Ante-Nicene Fathers. Buffalo, NY: Christian Literature Company, 1885.

Isaacs, E. D., and J. B. Payne. "Feasts." *ISBE* 2:293.

Jeffers, James S. *The Greco-Roman World of the New Testament Era: Exploring the Background of Early Christianity*. Downers Grove: IVP, 1000.

Jeremias, J. *Infant Baptism in the First Four Centuries*. London: SCM, 1960.

———. *The Parables of Jesus*. London: SCM, 1972.

Johnson, Luke T. "Gospel of Luke." *DPL* 502.

Jones, D. W., and R. S. Woodbridge. *Health, Wealth & Happiness: Has the Prosperity Gospel Overshadowed the Gospel of Christ?* Grand Rapids, MI: Kregel Publications, 2011.

Jones, Donald L. "Roman Imperial Cult." *ABD* 5:806-809.

Jones, Richard N. "Paleopathology." *ABD* 5:60-69.

Josephus. *Josephus*. Translated by Henry St. J. Thackeray et al. 10 vols. LCL. Cambridge: Harvard University Press, 1929-1965.

Jülicher, A. *Die Gleichnisreden Jesu*. 2 vols. Tübingen: J. C. B. Mohr [Paul Siebeck], 1888-89.

Kähler, M. *The So-Called Historical Jesus and the Historic Biblical Christ.* Philadelphia: Fortress, 1964 [orig. 1892].

Kee, Howard Clark. "Medicine and Healing." *ABD* 4:659-61.

Keener, Craig S. *The Gospel of John: A Commentary*. 2 vols. Grand Rapids, MI: Baker Academic, 2012.

———. *The Gospel of Matthew: A Socio-Rhetorical Commentary*. Grand Rapids, MI; Cambridge, U.K.: Eerdmans, 2009.

Keown, Mark J. "An Imminent Parousia and Christian Mission: Did the New Testament Writers Expect Jesus' Imminent Return?" In *Christian Origins and the Establishment of the Early Jesus Movement*. Edited by Stanley E. Porter and Andrew W. Pitts. TENTS; ECHC 4; Leiden: Brill, accepted for volume, forthcoming.

———. "Congregational Evangelism in Paul: The Paul of Acts." *Colloquium* 42.2 (2010): 231-51.

———. *Jesus in a World of Colliding Empires*. Forthcoming, Lexham.

———. "The Gethsemane Prayer: A Pattern for Believers." In *Journeying into Prayer*, 235-42. Edited by N. Darragh. Auckland: Accent Publications, 2012.

———. *What's God Up to On Planet Earth?: A No-Strings Attached Explanation of the Christian Message*. Tauranga; Eugene, OR.: Castle; Wipf and Stock, 2010.

Kimelman, R. "Birkat Ha-Minim and the Lack of Evidence for an Anti-Christian Jewish Prayer" In *Jewish and Christian Self-Definition*. Vol. 2. *Aspects of Judaism in Greco-Roman Period*, 391-403. Edited by E. P. Sanders, Albert I. Baumgarten, and Alan Mendelson. Philadelphia: Fortress, 1981.

King, Philip J. "Jerusalem." *ABD* 3:747-66.
Klein, W. W., C. Blomberg, and R. L. Hubbard, Jr. *Introduction to Biblical Interpretation*. Rev ed. Nashville: Nelson, 1993, 2004.
Köstenberger, Andreas J. *John*. BECNT. Grand Rapids, MI: Baker Academic, 2004.
Krahmalkov, Charles R. "Phoenicia." *EDB* 1053-56.
Kreitzer, L. J. "Travel in the Roman World." *DPL* 945-46.
Kuhn, H. -W. "ἀββά." *EDNT* 1:1-2.
Laird, Benjamin. "Muratorian Fragment." *LBD*.
Lea, Thomas D., and Hayne P. Griffin. *1, 2 Timothy, Titus*. Vol. 34. The New American Commentary. Nashville: Broadman & Holman Publishers, 1992.
Lessing, G. E. "Neue Hypothese über die Evangelisten als blos menschliche Geschichtschreiber betrachtet." In *Theologiekritische Schriften I und II*. Gotthold Ephraim Lessing, Werke 7, 614-36. Edited by H. G. Göpfert. München: Hanser, 1976.
Lewis, C. S. *The Lion, the Witch and the Wardrobe*. London: Geoffrey Bliss, 1950.
Liddell, Henry George, Robert Scott, Henry Stuart Jones, and Roderick McKenzie. *A Greek-English Lexicon*. Oxford: Clarendon Press, 1996.
Lischer, Richard. *Reading the Parables*. Interpretation. Louisville: Westminster John Knox Press, 2014.
Long, V. P., T. Longman III, R. A. Muller, V. S. Poythress, and M. Silva. *Foundations of Contemporary Interpretation: Six Volumes in One*. Leicester: IVP, 1996.
MacDonald, Dennis R. *Two Shipwrecked Gospels: The "Logoi of Jesus" and Papias's "Exposition of Logia about the Lord."* Atlanta: Society of Biblical Literature, 2012.
McBirnie, William Stuart. *The Search for the Twelve Apostles*. Revised Edition. Carol Stream: Tyndale House, 1973.
McDonald, Lee Martin. "Anti-Marcionite (Gospel) Prologues." *ABD* 1:262-63.
McKnight, S. "Matthew, Gospel of." *DJG* 526-41.
Mack, Burton L. *A Myth of Innocence: Mark and Christian Origins*. Philadelphia: Fortress, 1988.

Malherbe, A. J. *Paul and the Popular Philosophers*. Minneapolis: Fortress, 1989.
Manson, T. W. *The Teaching of Jesus*. Cambridge: University Press, 1939.
Marcus, Joel. *Mark 8–16: A New Translation with Introduction and Commentary*. AYB 27A. New Haven; London: Yale University Press, 2009.
Marshall, Christopher D. *Kingdom Come: The Kingdom of God in the Teaching of Jesus*. Auckland: Impetus, 1993.
Marshall, I. Howard. *Acts*. TNTC. Grand Rapids, MI; Leicester, Eng.: Eerdmans; IVP, 1984.
———. *The Gospel of Luke: A Commentary on the Greek Text*. NIGTC. Exeter: Paternoster, 1978.
———. "Lord's Supper." *DPL* 569–75.
Martin, Ralph P., and Peter H. Davids, eds. *Dictionary of the Later New Testament and Its Developments*. Downers Grove, IL: InterVarsity Press, 1997.
Martin, Thomas W. "Nicolaus." *ABD* 4:1107–1108.
Martyn, J. *History and Theology in the Fourth Gospel*. Rev. ed. Nashville: Abingdon, 1979.
Mathews, K. A. *Genesis 1–11:26*. NAC 1A. Nashville: Broadman & Holman Publishers, 1996.
Maynard-Reid, P. U. "Samaria." *DLNTD* 1075–77.
Mbiti, John. *African Religions and Philosophies*. New York: Doubleday and Company, 1970.
Metzger, Bruce Manning, and United Bible Societies. *A Textual Commentary on the Greek New Testament*. 4th Rev. Ed. London; New York: United Bible Societies, 1994.
Metzger, Bruce Manning, and Bart Ehrman. *The Text of the New Testament: Its Transmission, Corruption, and Restoration*. 4th Edition. New York: Oxford University Press, 2005. Kindle Edition.
Miller, Jeffrey E. "I Am Sayings." *LBD*.
Michaels, Ramsay J. *The Gospel of John*. NICNT. Grand Rapids, MI; Cambridge, UK: Eerdmans, 2010.
Moo, Douglas J. *The Epistle to the Romans*. NICNT. Grand Rapids, MI: Eerdmans, 1996.

Morgenthaler, R. *Statistische Synopse.* Zürich: Gotthelf-Verlag, 1971.

Moreland, J. P. *The Scaling of the Secular City: A Defense of Christianity.* Grand Rapids, MI: Baker, 1987.

Nash, R. *The Gospel and the Greeks: Did the New Testament Borrow from Pagan Thought?* The Student Library; Phillipsburg, NJ: P & R Publishers, 2003.

Newton, J. "Augustine of Hippo." In *Who's Who in Christian History,* 47-52. Edited by J. D. Douglas and Philip W. Comfort. Wheaton, IL: Tyndale House, 1992.

Nolland, John. *Luke 1:1-9:20.* WBC 35A. Dallas: Word, Incorporated, 2002.

———. *Luke 9:21-18:34.* WBC 35B. Dallas: Word, Incorporated, 1998.

———. *Luke 18:35-24:53.* WBC 35C. Dallas: Word, Incorporated, 1998.

———. *The Gospel of Matthew: A Commentary on the Greek Text.* NIGTC. Grand Rapids, MI; Carlisle: Eerdmans; Paternoster, 2005.

Novak, R. M. *Christianity and the Roman Empire: Background Texts.* Harrisburg, PA: Trinity Press International, 2001.

Oakman, D. E. "Economics of Palestine." *DNTB* 303-308.

Odor, Judith A. "Lystra." *LBD.*

Omanson, Roger L., and Bruce Manning Metzger. *A Textual Guide to the Greek New Testament: An Adaptation of Bruce M. Metzger's Textual Commentary for the Needs of Translators.* Stuttgart: Deutsche Bibelgesellschaft, 2006.

Osborne, Grant R. "Hermeneutics." *DLNTD* 482-84.

———. *The Hermeneutical Spiral: A Comprehensive Introduction to Biblical Interpretation.* Downers Grove: IVP Academic, 2006.

Overman, J. Andrew, and William Scott Green. "Judaism." *ABD* 3:1037-54.

Packer, J. I. *Evangelism and the Sovereignty of God.* Downers Grove: IVP, 1961.

Paige, T. "Philosophy." *DPL* 713-18.

Parker, P. "John and John Mark." *JBL* 79 (1960): 97-110.

Paterson, J. H. "Galilee, Sea of." *NBD* 395.

Patzia, Arthur G., and Anthony J. Petrotta. *Pocket Dictionary of Biblical Studies.* Downers Grove, IL: InterVarsity Press, 2002.

Paulien, Jon. "Parmenas." *ABD* 5:165.

———. "Prochorus." *ABD* 5:473.

———. "Timon." *ABD* 6:558.

Peisker, C. H. "Konsecutives *hina* in Markus 4.12." *ZNW* 59 (1968): 126-27.

Philo. *Philo.* Translated by F. H. Colson, G. H. Whitaker, and J. W. Earp. 10 Vols. LCL. London; England; Cambridge, MA: William Heinemann Ltd; Harvard University Press, 1929-1962.

Polhill, John B. *Acts.* Vol. 26. The New American Commentary. Nashville: Broadman & Holman Publishers, 1992.

Polybius. *Histories.* Medford, MA: Macmillan, 1889.

Porter, Stanley E. "Textual Criticism." *DNTB* 1210-1214.

Prosper, J. M. *The Prosperity Gospel, Truth or Lie? Reviewing the "Wealth Gospel."* Bloomington, IN.: WestBow Press, 2012.

Ramsay, W. M. *St. Paul the Traveler and the Roman Citizen.* London: Hodder & Stoughton, 1907.

Rapske, B. M. "Travel and Trade." *DNTB* 1245-50.

Reasoner, M. "Imperial Cult." *DLNTD* 321-25.

Reicke, B. *The Roots of the Synoptic Gospels.* Philadelphia: Fortress, 1986.

Riesner, R. "Galilee." *DJG* 252-53.

Rist, John M. *On the Independence of Matthew and Mark.* SNTSMS 32. Cambridge: Cambridge University Press, 1978.

Roberts, Roberts, et al. *The Apostolic Fathers with Justin Martyr and Irenaeus.* 9 Vols. Edition. The Ante-Nicene Fathers. Buffalo, NY: Christian Literature Company, 1885.

Sanders, E. P. "Law." *ABD* 2:242-65.

Schleiermacher, F. D. E. *Ueber die Schriften des Lukas, ein kritischer Versuch: Erster Theil.* Berlin: Reimer, 1817.

Schnabel, Eckhart J. *Acts.* ZECNT. Grand Rapids, MI: Zondervan, 2012.

———. *Early Christian Mission: Jesus and the Twelve.* Vol 1. Downers Grove; Leicester, Eng.: IVP; Apollos, 2004.

———. *Early Christian Mission: Paul and the Early Church.* Vol 2. Downers Grove; Leicester, Eng.: IVP; Apollos, 2004.

Schweitzer, Albert. *The Quest for the Historical Jesus: A Critical Study of Its Progress from Reimarus to Wrede.* 2nd ed. London: Adam and Charles Black, 1926.

Sell, Henry Thorne. *Studies in Early Church History.* Willow Grove, PA: Woodlawn Electronic Publishing, 1998.

Skene, B. "Medicine." *LBD.*

Sievers, J. "Hasmoneans." *DNTB* 438-42.

Silverman, Jason M. "Daniel, Book of." *LBD.*

Smith, Billy K., and Franklin S. Page. *Amos, Obadiah, Jonah*. NAC 19B. Nashville: Broadman & Holman Publishers, 1995.
Smith, Zachary G. "Proselyte." *LBD*.
———. "Gnosticism." *LBD*.
Snodgrass, Klyne R. "Parable." *DJG* 591–601.
———. *Stories with Intent: A Comprehensive Guide to the Parables of Jesus*. Grand Rapids, MI: Eerdmans, 2008.
Sherwin-White, A. N. *Roman Society and Roman Law in the New Testament*. London: Oxford, 1963.
Simmons, William. "Taxation." *LBD*.
Spencer, F. S. "Philip the Evangelist." *DLNTD* 929–31.
Stählin, Gustav. "περίψημα." *TDNT* 6:84–93.
Stein, Robert H. *Mark*. BECNT. Grand Rapids, MI: Baker Academic, 2008.
———. "The Synoptic Problem." *DJG* 784–92.
Sterling, G. E. "Philo." *DNTB* 789–793.
Stoldt, H. *History and Criticism of the Marcan Hypothesis*. Macon: Mercer University, 1980.
Stoops Jr., R. F. "Passion of Peter and Paul." *ABD* 5:264.
———. "Simon (Person)." *ABD* 6:28–31.
Streeter, Burnett Hillman. *The Four Gospels: A Study of Origins Treating of the Manuscript Tradition, Sources, Authorship, Date*. London: MacMillan & Co, 1930.
Swan, John T. "Feasts and Festivals of Israel." *LBD*.
Torrey, C. C. *The Four Gospels*. New York: Harper, 1933.
Thiselton, Anthony C. *The First Epistle to the Corinthians: A Commentary on the Greek Text*. NIGTC. Grand Rapids, MI: W.B. Eerdmans, 2000.
Thomas Nelson Publishers. *Nelson's Complete Book of Bible Maps & Charts: Old and New Testaments*. Rev. and Updated ed. Nashville, TN: Thomas Nelson, 1996.
Thompson, M. M. "John, Gospel of." *DJG* 368–83.
Tidball, D. J. "The Social Setting of Mission Churches." *DPL* 883–91.
Utley, Robert James. *Luke the Historian: The Book of Acts*. Study Guide Commentary Series Vol 3B. Marshall, TX: Bible Lessons International, 2003.
Watson, D. F. "Cities, Greco-Roman." *DNTB* 212–14.

Wedderburn, A. J. M. *Baptism and Resurrection: Studies in Pauline Theology Against Its Graeco-Roman Background*. WUNT I.44. Tübingen: J. C. B. Mohr, 1987.

Wenham, J. W. "Did Peter go to Rome in A.D. 42?" *TynB* 23 (1972): 97-102.

Witherington III, Ben. *Conflict and Community in Corinth: A Socio-Rhetorical Commentary on 1 and 2 Corinthians*. Grand Rapids, MI: Eerdmans, 1995.

―――. *The Acts of the Apostles: A Socio-Rhetorical Commentary*. Grand Rapids, MI: Eerdmans, 1998.

―――. *The Gospel of Mark: A Socio-Rhetorical Commentary*. Grand Rapids, MI: Eerdmans, 2001.

White, L. Michael. "Christianity (Early Social Life and Organization)." *ABD* 1:926-35.

Wimber, John, and Kevin Springer. *Power Evangelism*. London: Hodder and Stoughton, 1995.

Wilke, C. G. *Der Urevangelist oder exegetisch kritische Untersuchung über das Verwandtschafts-verhältniss der drei ersten Evangelien*. Dresden: Fleischer, 1838.

Williamson, H. G. M. "Samaritans." *DJG* 724-28.

Wright, Christopher J. H. "Sabbatical Year." Edited by David Noel Freedman. The Anchor Yale Bible Dictionary. New York: Doubleday, 1992. 861.

Wright, N. T. *Hebrews for Everyone*. London: SPCK, 2003, 2004.

―――. *Jesus and the Victory of God*. Christian Origins and the Question of God. London: SPCK, 1996.

―――. "Quest for the Historical Jesus." *ABD* 3:796-802.

―――. *The New Testament and the People of God*. Minneapolis: Fortress, 1992.

―――. *The Resurrection of the Son of God*. Christian Origins and the Question of God. London: SPCK, 2003.

Yamauchi, E. M. "Hellenism." *DPL* 383-87.

SUBJECT INDEX

Aaron 257
Abraham 34, 36, 42, 201, 203, 238, 248, 281, 291-93, 303, 312, 378-79, 393, 405, 419, 448, 516, 546
Abomination (Desolation) 22, 137, 519
Acts
 Title 319-20
 Authorship 320-21
 Date 321-22
 Recipients 322
 Historicity 322-29
 Emphases 329-31
 Text 331-32
 Structure and Purpose 332-35
 Jerusalem Church 335-408
 To the Ends of the Earth (Acts 13-28) 408-15
Adultery 97
Africa (African) 14, 20, 53, 345, **397-99**, 406
Alexander the Great 9, **15, 18-19, 21**, 50, 141, 356, 394, 395, 419
Alexandria 50, 73, 136, 140, 270-71
Allegorization (Parables) **514-15, 520-526**, 533
Agabus 407, 414
Agrippa I **28-29**, 31, 384, **407-409**, 414
Agrippa II **28-29**, 327, 362, 365, **414**
Ananias
 Of Damascus 344, 346-47, 375, 397, 399-400
 (and Sapphira) 346, 381, 383-87, 390, 409
Andrew 8, 260, 263, 266-67, 269, 279, 296, 307
Angel (also angelology) 28, **35**, 36, 44, 144, 148, 163, 173-74, 178, 206, 242, 244, 248, 258, 288, 327, 337, 341-42, 364, 366, 370, 390, 398, 403-405, 408-409, 429, 447, 461-63, 468, 470, 487, 523, 543
Antioch (Pisidia) 59, 88, 327, 343-44, **348**, 349, 358, 361-2, 364, 367, 400
Antioch (Syria) 59, 133, 136, 140, 191-5, 220, 224, 230, 270-71, 322, 330-31, 335, 346, 359, 361, 391, **405-7**, 409, 527
Antiochian missions – see Paul
Antiochus IV Epiphanes **22**, 40, 49, 301, 395
Antisemitism (Anti-Semitic) 30, 190, 212, 255, 311
Antonia (Fortress) 37, 158
Apocalyptic (Apocalypticism) 4, 8, **35**, 42, 43, 47-8, 169, 179, 423-5, 429, **430-31**, 499
Apocrypha 5, 15, **41-42**, 470, 513

Aramaic 5, **18-19**, 41, 130, 132, 134, 136, 137, 142, 182-83, 186, 193, 233, 275-76, 281, 307, 327, 418, 425, 476, 511, 530
Aramaic Proto-Gospel **112-13**, 143, 183-84
Aramaism(s) 5, 123, 142, 281
Aristotle 105
Assyria **21**, 49, 394, 419
Athens 65, 67-68, 76, 79, 87, 222, 327, 360, 362, 364, 412
Augustus 25, 73, 78-79, 85, 87, 91, 141, 395
Augustinian Hypothesis **114-15**

Babylon (Babylonian) 14, **21**, 36, 37, 131, 419, 512
Baptism 62, 77-78, 154, 166-67, 234, 238-39, 247, 254, 276, 309, 338, 341-45, 347-50, 352-53, 363, 368, **373-77**, 396, 398, 404, 448, 456, 461, 486, 519
  Christian 62, 77-78, 338, 374-77
  Jesus (by John) 154, 166-67, 234, 238-39, 247, 254, 276, 309, 368, 461, 486
  John the Baptist (his ministry) 309, 373-4
Barabbas 164, 170, 177
Barnabas 8, 66, 79, 126, **133-34**, 136, 231, 252, 325, 342, 348, 354-55, 357, 359, 361, 364, 369, 380-81, 383, 385, 400, 406-407, 409-11
Bartimaeus 157
Beelzebub (Beelzebul) 165, 502
Believe (belief) 5-6, 9, 23, 30, 33, 35, 42-48, 53, 61, 63, 77, 79-81, 83-85, 97-100, 107-108, 114, 119, 123, 128, 130-32, 134-36, 138, 140, 142, 146, 148-49, 155, 163, 166-67, 169-70, 172, 175, 178, 182, 186, 189-90, 195, 207, 215-16, 218, 220, 228, 241, 261, 268-69, 278, 282-83, 286-87, 291, 293, 295-300, 304-307, 309-13, 316-17, 321-23, 326, 337, 339, 345, 347, 349-351, 357-58, 361, 366, 375, 392-96, 406, 408, 411, 415, 417, 422, 425-30, 432-33, 438, 448, 457, 470, 474-76, 482, 486-88, 491, 493-95, 501-502, 507-508, 530, 532

Beloved Disciple **264-67**, **269-70**, 276
Bethesda (Pool) 271, 280, **294-96**, 300, 465, 467
Bethsaida 15, 152, 162, 168, 201, 466
Bethlehem 27, 206, 307
Blind (Blindness) 155, 157, 162, 201, 211, 235, 247, 280-82, 292, 294-95, 297-98, 301, 303-304, 306, 347, 384, 399, 410, 439, 463-67, 470-72, 478, 482, 498, 520, 530, 532

Caesar 27-28, 46, 73-74, 78, 85, 91, 141, 155-6, 159-61, 169-70, 187, 221, 243, 339, 391, 395, 412, 419, 426, 464
  Augustus 24, 25, 73, 78-79, 85, 87, 91, 141, 395
Caesarea Maritima 27-28, 52, 87-88, 193, 222, 325, 327, 362, 401-402, 404, 408, 410, **413-14**
Caesarea Philippi 128, 154-55, 168
Cana 280, 294-5
Canon (Canonical) **7-8**, 41-42, 113, 275, 279, 320, 521
Capernaum 15, 52, 168, 187, 201, 295, 403, 438, 467
Children (child, childhood) 25, 27, 33, 48, 53, 59, 65, 81, 90-91, 111, 128, 157, 164, 166, 172, 209, 212, **252**, 255, 257, 304, 306, 314, 375, 376-7, 388, 405, 436, 445, 449-51, (470 - childbirth), 471, 476, 519-20, 529
Christ (New Testament Centre) **1**, 4-5, 9, 14-17, 19, 33, 35, 37-38, 40-43, 52-54, 62, 67, 76-77, 79, 97-99, 106-109, 122, 126, 141-42, 148,

SUBJECT INDEX 567

166, 170-75, 177-81, 187, 190,
200-203, 208-209, 213, 218-19,
223, 227, 229, 231, 242, 246, 248,
254-55, 264, 279, 287-88, 290,
292-94, 298, 306, **307**, 310, 314,
316-18, 320, 322, **331**, 333-41, 346,
349, 352-53, 357-59, 364, 366,
374-75, 377, 379, 388-93, 395-96,
402-403, 406, 411, 413, 415, 417,
422, 426, **427**, 428-36, 439-41,
445-48, 450-51, 453, 456-58,
461, 465, 469, 479, 485-86, 489,
494-95, 499-502, 506-508, 523,
535-36, 546-47
Ascension 242, 508
Birth 4-5, 77, 441, 508
Death 4, 43, 67, 109, 126, 141, 148, 178,
374, 379, 388, 403, 441, 508
Resurrection 40, 122, 126, 141, 179,
294, 338, 379, 441, 499, 501, 508,
523
Return (Parousia) 178-79, 200-202,
213, 334, 430-31, **433-34**, 435,
535, 546
Church 1, 3-4, 6-8, 10-1, 33, 39, 41, 47,
54, 58-63, 68-69, 86, 92-94, 101,
103-104, 113, 123, 126, 129-31,
133—37, 139-42, 145, 148-49,
182-84, 186-87, 189-92, 196-97,
201, **204-205**, 207, 216, 222-24,
230-31, 241-42, 247, 252, 256,
258, 260-61, 263, 265, 268-69,
272, 274, 276, 278, 283, 312,
319-20, 322-27, 330, **331-32**,
333-34, 335, **336-416**, 432, 435,
454, 456-59, 474, 485-86, 489,
492, 494-95, 499-500, 504,
507-508, 512, 523, 529, 534, 536,
541, 547
Evangelistic Church 358-367
Circumcision (circumcised) 35, 41,
47-49, 141, 219, 223, 347, 350, 354,
366-67, 374, 380, 398, 403-406,
411-12, 414, 427, 438, 447-78,
480-81

City (the) 16, 27, 37, 50-52, **58-60**, 65,
65-66, 68, 79, 81, 92-93, 95, 156,
180, 194, 222, 234, 291, 346, 357,
361, 391, 393-96, 399, 410, 412,
521, 523
Claudius 25, **73-4**, 87, 133, 137, 141, 383,
397, 407-8, 412
Edict of Claudius (expulsion) 412
Clement of Alexandria 136, 139-40, 189,
263, 269, 271, 282-83, 285
"Common People" (also people of the
land) 32, 37, 45, **47-9**
Codex (Codices) 41, 147, 241, 333
Alexandrinus (A) 41
Bezae, (Dea 05) 241, 333
Claromontanus (Dp 06) 241
Sinaiticus, (333 ,241 ,147 ,41 (□
Vaticanus, (B) 41, 147, 241, 333
Compassion (compassionate) 155, 253,
296, 462, 464, 473, **492-93**, 496,
502-3, 505, 516, 518, 523
Context (contextual) 7, 10-12, 45, 53,
57, 60-1, 67, 70, 77, 80, 88, 94-5,
100-2, 124, 132, 134, 138, 142, 149,
162, 187, 193, 203, 206, 213, 237,
251, 258, 266, 298-301, 312, 320,
327, 352, 353, 358, 364, 366, 373,
383, 403, 419, 433, 450, 457, 469,
472, 480, 503, 506, 516, 523-4,
526-8, 532-6, 542, 546, 547
of Jewish 14-55
of Greco-Roman 56-97
of Mark see Mark
of Miracle of healing 469-70
Contextualization 364
Convert(s) (conversion) 38, 49-50,
61-62, 68, 80, 141, 181, 218, 222-
23, 252, 322, 334, 337, 340-41,
343-7, 355-56, 365-67, 374-76,
391, 397-98, 401, 405-406,
410-12, 448-49, 542
Corporate Mindset (lifestyle?) **52-3**,
55, 62
Cornelius 35, 61, 327, 330, 342, 344, **347**,
349-50, 357, 362-64, 366-67, 371,

373, 375, 397-98, 401, **403-405**, 408, 411
Covenant 2, **34**, 39, **48**, 158-59, 165-66, 176-77, 314, 382, 419-20, 422, 427, 434, 447, 450, 480-81, 498
  Abraham 34
  Davidic 34
  Mosaic (Sinai) 34, 159
  New Covenant 158, 177, 382
  Old Covenant 165
  Creation 1, 37, 40, 64, 69, 83, 85, 146, 149, 167, 169, 181, 203, 207-208, 258, 279, 302, 306, 363-64, 403, 418, 421-22, 424, 428-30, 434-35, 439, 442-44, 454-5, 457-58, 469, 479, 486, 489, 499-501, 505, 507-508, 512, 524, 534, 541
  (new creation?) 40, 430, 458, 500-501, 505
Curtain (Temple) 177
Cynics 81, **85-86**, 93
Cyril of Jerusalem 183
Cyrus 21
Cyprus 134, 381, 406, 410-401, 415

David (Davidic) 1, 34, 36, 47, 49, 141, 155, 157, 169, 177, 199, 201, 203, 209, 211, 277, 238, 243, 291, 308, 342, 379, 419-23, 425-6, 436, 486, 513
Dating **4-9**, 43, 138, 191, 226, 271, 284, 322
  Acts 322-23
  John 271-72
  Luke 225-31
  Mark 136-39
  Matthew 189-193
  New Testament 4-9
Dead Sea - see Sea
Dead Sea Scrolls 15, **43**
Deaf (deafness) 235, 463-64, 466, 471, 498
Deliberative Rhetoric **105**
Demon (demons, demonology, also evil or unclean spirits) 4, 34, **35**, 44, 64, 79, 80, 146, 155, 161,

163-64, 173, 206, 210, 238, 281, 291, 294, 299, 306, 308, 346, 386-87, 392, 412-13, 418, 424, 425, 428-431, 433-34, 439, 443, 447, 451-2, 462, 465-67, 470-71, 481, **483**, 487, 493, 499, 501-2, 506, 523, 539
Destruction 14, 23, 25, 27, 37, 43, 48, 66, 138, 159, 190, 193, 199-200, 205, 212-13, 230, 251, 256, 271-72, 305, 309, 396, 421, 447, 502, 530, 539
Corinth (old) 66
Eternal 199-200, 205, 213, 230, 305, 421, 447, 502, 530, 539
Jerusalem (fall of) 25, 27, 138, 158, 190, 193, 212, 256, 271
Temple 14, 23, 37, 43, 213, 27-72
Rome 48
Diaspora 3, 16, 19, 37, **50**, 60, 193
Disability (disabled) 79, 251, 295-96, 338, 351, 359-60, 380, 387, 389, 473, 478, 525, 536, 540
Disciple(s) 1, 16, 20, 46-47, 56, 61, 87, 107, 111, 128-29, 138, 144, 146-48, 152-64, 168-74, 176-79, 181, 187-88, 202-203, 205-207, 209-12, 238-39, 245-47, 252-55, 258, 260, 262-67, 269-70, 275-77, 279-80, 284-85, 289-90, 292-97, 299, 309, 311-15, 317, 319-21, 331, 335, 337-38, 341, 343-44, 346-49, 351, 355, 358-61, 365-66, 368, 370, 377-78, 380, 384, 386, 393, 397, 399-403, 406, 409, 433, 439-42, 444-45, 447, 450, 452-4, 4565-7, 461, 464, 467-68, 472, 482, 492-93, 498, 500, 502-504, 507, 514, 518-19, 529, 532, 535, 538, 542-43
Discipleship 157, 166-67, 170-71, 173, 197, 200, 235, 245, 435, 440, 454, 518, 538, 543-44
Markan Theology 170-3
Matthean Theology 205
Lukan Theology 255

SUBJECT INDEX

Parables 543-4
Divine man 102, 276, 486, 489
Divorce 53, 56, 166, 175, 376
Domitian 25, **74-75**, 267, 272, 303

Election **33-34, 48**, 378-79
Eleusinian Mystery(-ies) 63, 76
Elijah 161-62, 166-67, 209, 420, **423**, 491, 496-97, 505-506
Elisha 491, 496-97, 505-506
Elizabeth 238, 246, 251, 254, 257
Ends of the Earth 3, 7, 174, 211, 237-38, 322, 332, 335, 365
Epicureans (Epicureanism) 81, **82-83**
Epideictic Rhetoric 105
Ephesus 59, 65, 68, 73-74, 79, 167, 219, 226, 241, 262-64, 270-72, 284, 333, 343-44, 348-51, 358, 375, 385, 413, 457
Essenes 20, 31, 43, **47**, 49, 187, 381, 425, 470
Eternal Destruction see Destruction
Eternal life 213, 248, 280, 287, 291-93, 296-7, 301, 305-306, 309, 312-13, 317, 353, 429, 443-44, 446-47, 452, 465, 468, 478, 499, 523, 546
Ethics 84-5, 166, **203**, 239, 312, 453, **454-55**, 458
Ethiopia 189, 230
Ethiopian Eunuch 341-42, 357, 375, **397-99**
Evangelical 104-105
Evangelism (Evangelistic) 188, 200, 342, 344, 346, 349, 358-60, 362, 364-66, 370, 372, 390, 392, 401, 409, 412, 435, 441, 454, 457, 483-84, 534, 542-43, 358-366
Exegesis 83, **100**
Exile 14, 21, 23, 34-37, 40, 49-50, 78, 203, 212, 394-95, 424
 Assyrian 21, 49
 Babylonian 14, 21, 37
Exorcism(s) (also deliverance, drive out, cast out) 52, 146, 155, 160-61, 164-65, 171, 175, 201, 211, 250, 291, 360, 386, 395, 412, 430-31, 439, 443, 450, 462-3, 465, 468-69, 483-84, 490, 492, 497, 499, **501-502**, 507, 509, 539
 Blind, Mute, and Possessed Man 466
 Deliverance of Mary Magdalene 146, 251, 467
 Demon-Possessed boy 463, 466
 Fortune-telling slave girl 412
 Gerasene Demoniac(s) 171, 466
 Mute and Possessed Man 467
 Possessed man in synagogue 201, 462, 466
Exodus 33, 38, 158, 209, 297-98, 300, 378-79, 473, 497, 500, 505

Faith 3, 12, 35, 41, 47, 58-9, 62, 67, 80, 93, 99, 106-7, 108, 123, 141, 146, 153, 156, 159-60, 172-3, 176-8, 189, 203, 206, 213, 218, 227, 232, 240, 244-5, 250, 255, 260, 262, 282, 286-8, 293-8, 310-1, 313, **316-7**, 319, 328, 331-2, 334, 340, 343-5, 347-8, 350, 353, 357-8, 361, 364-5, 370, 372, 375-6, 392, 394-6, 402, 404-7, 409-11, 427-9, 435, 437-9, 447-9, 452, 462, 465, 471-2, **474-7**, 478-9, 489, 493-5, 507, 508, 510, 530, 546
Family (Kinship, Fictive) 18, 29, 38, 49, 51, **53-54**, 55, 59, 61-62, 65, 89, 94-96, 168, 171, 205, 252, 261, 295, 335, 344, 347, 349, 358, 375-76, 381, 384, 386, 403-405, 411, 440, 455-56, 482, 519
Fall (the) 1, 166, 169, 434, 467, 479, 481, 502, 523, 534
 Pre-adamic fall 502
Fall of Jerusalem 25, 109, 138-39, 158, **178-79**, 201, 212-13, 226, **228**, 246, 322
Farrar (Goulder) Hypothesis **117-18**, 124
Fasting 39, 168, 257, 347, 369, **371**, 372

Feeding Miracles 38, 48, 52, 154-5, 162, 164-5, 173-4, 235, 279, 281, 283, 294, 296-7, 300, 417, 443, 463, 464, 466, 468, 472, 483, 492, 503
Feeding 4000 154-55, 162, 173-74, 235, 463, 466, 472
Feeding 5000 38, 154-55, 162, 164, 165, 279, 281, 283, 294, 296-97, 300, 464, 466, 472, 492, 503
Feast(s)(festival) 16, 36, **37-40**, 41, 49, 52, 63, **67-68**, 69, 93, 158, 168, 188, 255, 257, 259, 280, 286, **299-301**, 303, 305-307, 313, 427, 448, 453, 478, 500, 504, 519, 534, 539, 540, 542, 545
  Day of Atonement **39**, 371
  Eschatological Feast 255, 257, 259, 448, 453, 478, 500, 504, 519, 534
  Hanukkah (Dedication) 22, **40**, 301, 303
  Herod Antipas 168
  Nicanor **40**
  Passover 36, **38**, 39-40, 158, 177, 209, 295, **299-301**, 395
  Pentecost **39**, 40, 126, 189, 191, 205, 247-8, 300, 319, 330, 334, 341, 343-47, 349-51, 357, 360, 362-64, 369-71, 396, 433, 436, 456-57, 508
  Parables (wedding) 539, 540, 542, 545
  Purim **40**
  Tabernacles (Booths) 38, **39-40**, 280, 300-1, 307, 313
  Trumpets **39**
  Unleavened Bread **38-39**, 299
Food 48, 51, 69, 93, 165, 173, 175, 257, 291, 296, 355, 365-66, 379, 381, 403, 405, 411, 427, 438, 440, 480, 484, 492, 500, 503
  Early Church (also Table Fellowship, distribution of) 355, 365, 379, 381
  Law (Kosher) 48, 165, 173, 366, 405, 427, 438, 480
Forensic Rhetoric **105**

Form Criticism **103-104**, 108, 275, 324
Forgiveness (forgive) 33, 160-1, 163, 201, 204, 243, 245, 251, 257, 281, 334, 339, 375, 386, 396, **452-3**, 455-6, 469, 482, 518, 529-30, **540-1**
Four Source Hypothesis **115-17**, 124, 126, 229

Galilee (place) **15-6**, 21, 27-8, 46, 58, 140, 144, 149, 154, 156, 159, 163, 168, 178, 195, 202, 234, 237-8, 247, 260, 275, 277, 283, 295, 307, 331, 361, 393, 401, 406, 408, 438, 483
Galilee (Sea) See Sea
Gennesaret (Lake) 15, 153
Genealogy 53, 66, 71, 201, 203, 234-5, **238**, 248
Grace 156, 160, 274, 328, 334, 337, 340, 353, 357, 366, 386, 411, **452-3**, 462, 473, 477, 481, 502, 507, 538-9, 541
Great Commission 143, 174, 202, **207**, 211, 366, 393, 435, 454, 456, 458, 535
Greek Philosophy 20, 58, **80-86**, 302
Greek Religion **63-69**
  Divination 69
  Domestic Cults **69**
  Festivals **67**
  Gods and goddesses **63-67**, 71
  Prayer 67
  Rituals **67**
  Sacrifice **67**
  Temples **68-69**
Griesbach Hypothesis 114-15

Hades 64-5, 67, 76, 98, 537, 546
Hasmonean Empire (Dynasty) 15, **23**
Healings (heal, healer) 48, 52, 63, 65, 79, 141, 154-55, 157, 161-64, 169, 171-73, 175, 201, 206, 211, 220, 235-36, 245, 247, 250-51, 254, 258, 280-82, 292-98, 300-301,

SUBJECT INDEX

303–304, 306, 309, 312, 316, 338–39, 341, 344, 346–47, 349, 351, 353, 359–60, 365, 369–71, 374, 380, 385–86, 389, 396, 399, 401–403, 410, 415, 430, 436, 439, 441, 443, 448, 450, 456, 462–68, **469–85**, 487–90, 492, 494–501, 503, 505, 507–509, 515, 521, 539

Bartimaeus (plus one) 154, 157, 466

Blind Man of Bethsaida 154, 155, 162, 201, 235, 466

Blind, mute, possessed man 235, 463, 466

Blind Man from birth 280–2, 292, 294, **297–8**, 301, 303–4, 306, 312, 465–7, 470

Crippled Woman 235, 251, 467

Man with Dropsy 467

Mute and possessed man 463, 467

Deaf and Mute Man 235, 466

Hemorrhaging Woman 173, 463, 466

High Priest's Servant's Ear 467

Leper 254, 466

Paralyzed Man in Synagogue 258, 466

Peter's Mother-in-Law 466

Royal Official's Son 280, 282, 293, 295, 300, 464, 467

Roman Centurion's servant 201, 251, 295, 403, 463, 466

Shrivelled hand 175, 466

Sick man by Pool of Bethesda 280, 294–5, 309, 312, 465, 467

Syrophoenician (Canaanite) woman 173, 206, 235, 236, 463, 466

Two blind men 211, 235, 463, 467

Ten Lepers 235, 251, 396, 467

Heaven 78, 97, 111, 146, 158, 162, 166, 168, 174, 207–8, 210–11, 247, 281, 302, 305, 317, 386, 417, 418, 420, 423, 430–32, 436, 438–39, 444, 446, 448, 451–52, 476, 487, 493, 502, 505, 514, 515, 537, 546

Kingdom of Heaven 111, 207–208, 281, 317, 417, 431, 438–39, 448, 451, 514

New Heaven 78, 97, 505

Hell 65, 204, 447, 487, 515, 546

Hellenism 19–20, 22, 42, 51, **57**, 102, 108

Hermeneutics 99, **100**

Herodian(s) 18, 31, 36, 155–6, 243

Herod the Great 26, **27**, 28–9, 31, 36, 46, 156, 169, 209, 393, 395, 407

Herod Antipas **27**, 29, 31, 162, 167–8, 187–8, 236, 295, 312, 369, 409

Historical Criticism **101–102**, 103, 106–7

Honor-Shame **55**, **96–97**, 233

Hospitality 53, 94–5, **256–57**, **379**, 387, 404

Household(s) 52–3, **61–62**, 69, 91, 358, 375–6, 385, 404, 514, 521

"I am" sayings 260, 281, **290–2**, 296–7, 301, 303, 305, 308, 506, 518

Ignatius (Bishop of Antioch) 189, 194–95, 271

Imperial cult see Roman Religion

Infancy Narrative 160, 197, 211, 233, 237, 238, 242, 246–47, 257, 325, 462–63

Matthew 211, 462

Luke 233, 237–38, 246–47, 257, 325, 463

Intertestamental Period (Second Temple Judaism) 10, **14–5**, 34–5, 41, 108

Israel 1, 9–10, 14–23, 26–28, 31, 33–40, 42–43, 45, 47–52, 56, 125, 128, 134, 136, 141, 153, 155–56, 158–59, 162, 164–67, 169–70, 173, 177, 181, 187, 193, 199, 203–207, 209, 212, 238, 242–46, 248, 255–58, 270, 278, 285, 292, 298, 301, 303, 305, 310, 315, 319, 331, 343, 364, 367–68, 377–79, 384, 393–94, 396–97, 404, 408–409, 418–22, 424–28, 434, 437–38, 445–48, 473, 480–81, 491, 494–95, 497, 502, 505–506,

508, 512, 517-19, 525, 530-32, 534, 540, 542
Cultural Influences 19-55
Division of Kingdom 21
Geography 15-16
Languages 16
Population 16

Jairus 61, 402, 466, 472-4
James (brother of John) 28, 38, 46, 133, 157, 162, 188, 226, 251, 260-61, 264-67, 270, 332, 334, 356, 357, 364, 370, 374, 391, 396, 407-408, 414
James (brother of Jesus) 3,5,8, 43, 225, 269(?), 325, 332, 334, 357, 388, 411, 414-15, 485, 494, 520
   Apocryphon 520
   Letter 3, 5, 8, 388, 485
James (son of Alphaeus) 139, 186, 266, 485, 494
Jericho 16, 168, 266, 515, 523
Jeroboam **21**, 396
Jerusalem 3, 14, 15-16, 19, 21, 25, 27-28, 31, 36-40, 43, 46, 49, 52, 73, 81, 87, 109, 121, 126, 128, 132-34, 137-39, 154-58, 160, 164-66, 168, 175-76, 178, 189-93, 195-96, 199, 201, 212-13, 217, 219, 222, 226, 228-29, 233-34, 236-39, 245-46, 256, 258, 260-61, 265-66, 271, 275, 279, 285, 289, 295, 297, 299-301, 305, 319-22, 325-28, 330-32, 334-411, 413-14, 416, 423-34, 438, 457, 488, 515, 523
   Church 3, 126, 133, 319-20, 325, 330-32, 336-409, 411, 413, 416
   Collection 382, 388, 413-14
   Community 189, 457
   Council 45, 141, 219, 222, 230, 349, 366, 393, 401, 405, 410-11, 412
   Fall of - see Destruction
   Temple See Temple
Jesus 1-3, 6-7, 9-10, 15-16, 18-19, 23, 25-27, 32-34, 36-41, 43-48, 50-55, 58, 65-66, 73-75, 78, 85, 87, 93-94, 100, 102-104, 107-109, 111-12, 115, 120-21, 123-26, 128-32, 134, 136, 138-42, 144, 146-49, 152-59, **160-66**, 167-79, 181-83, 185-88, 191, 195-97, 199-216, 222, 226-27, 229, 234-61, 264-67, 269, 274-322, 327, 331, 334, 336-54, 356-60, 362-68, 370-75, 377-80, 382-84, 386-90, 392, 394-97, 399-405, 411, 415, 417, 420, 426-434, 436-53, 455-57, 459, 460-88, 490-508, 511-15, 517-19, 522-36, 538-40, 542-48
   Baptism 15, 154, 166, 199, **238-39**, 247, 368
   Birth 25-27, 160, 199, 209, 242, 258
   Death 2, 4-5, 26-27, 39, 46, 108, 154, 159, 161, 163, 166, **175-78**, 199, 226, 240, 285, 289, 312, 314, 335, 363, 377, 388-89, 396, 404, 476
   Resurrection 4-5, 136, 146, 148, 154, 159-60, 172, 175, **178**, 199, 240, 242, 285, 239, 299, 305, 307, 319, 335-36, 363, 377-79, 396, 404, 450, 465, 491, 493, 506
Jewish Setting for NT **14-56**
Jewish War (with Rome) 25, 31, 42
Jewish Mission **35**, 205, 219
Joy 247, 258, 259, 280, 299, 305, 333, 344, 346, 347-49, 351, 353, 361-62, 380, 396, 410, 449, 498, 537, 543
John the Baptist 25, 27, 47, 50, 128, 153-54, 161-62, 166, **167**, 168, 170, 173, 181, 187, 199, 209, 211-13, 234, 238, 242-43, 246-47, 257-58, 308, 309, 340, 352, 373-74, 405, 413, 431-32, 491, 498
John the Apostle 5, 28, 46, 103, 129, 130, 157, 188, 251, 260-70, 332, 338, 341, 346, 351, 354, 357, 359, 367, 374-75, 389-90, 396-97, 407, 414, 438, 471
John the Elder 129, 130, 140, 260, 269-70

SUBJECT INDEX

John's Gospel 2-4, 11, 57, 101, 103, 110, 149, 169, 174, 204, 209-10, 212, 216, 246, 250, **260-318**, 353, 394, 432, 436, 440, 449, 456-57, 461, **464-67**, 485, 488, 490-91, 493, 506-508, 511, 518, 522
  Authorship 260-70
  Date 271-72
  Historicity 284-86
  Johannine Community 275-79
  Key Dimensions 289-318
  Provenance 270-71
  Purpose 287-88
  Recipients 272-74
  Relationship to the Synoptics 279-84
  Sources 274-78
  Structure 288-89
  Text 274-75
Joppa 402-404
Jordan River 15
Joseph (Father of Jesus) 163, 238, 252
Josephus (Flavius) 15-16, 36, **42-43**, 47, 143, 224-25, 248, 394, 407, 470
Joshua 170, 491, 496-97
Judgment 35, 44-45, 66-67, 197, 206, 208, 211, **213-14**, 245, 298, 346, 384-86, 398, 409, 422-23, 434, 455, 497, 499, 518, 539, 542, **545-6**
Judas (Iscariot, Sicarii) 46, 107, 158, 163, 171, 188, 190, 246, 261, 264-66, 285, 294, 306, 314, 319, 338, 342, 368, 378, 386-87
Judea 3, 15-16, 25-28, 31, 41, 47, 149, 154, 166, 229, 237, 265, 270, 277, 283, 285, 295, 325, 331-32, 334-35, 361, 390-91, 393, 401-402, 406-8
Justification 218, 328

Koine Greek 9, 19, 57, 59
Kingdom of God/Heaven 111, 128, 137, 153, 161, 165, 167, **169-70**, 175, 178, 181, 187, 199-200, 203, 205-208, 211, 213, 227, 239, 241, 244-45, 251, 253, 255, 257-58, 281, 305, 309, 313, 317, 321, 337-38, 353, 383, 402, 405, 415, **417-459**, 460, 467, 469, 473, 483-485, 493, 495-97, 499-504, 506-507, 509, 511, 514, 517-19, 524-26, 528-30, 532-36, 538-41, 543-45, 547
  Heaven (specific usage) - see Heaven
  In OT **418-22**
  In Judaism 422-26
  In Matthew 207-8

Last Supper 126, 131, 176, 261, 264-66, 280, 285, 306, 312-15, 519
Latin (Latinism) 2, 9, 19-20, 41, 59, 76, 91, 132, 135, 139, 142, 144, 185, 241, 406, 460
Law 1-2, 19, 22, 27-28, 32-34, 38, 43-45, 47, **48**, 49, 52, 60, 70-71, 83, 91, 106, 161-62, 175, 203, 208-209, 218-19, 236, 243, 245, 256, 291, 300, 366, 404-405, 411, 425, 427, 432, 434, 437-38, 449, 451, 455, 468, 470, 480-81, 489, 497, 501, 503, 505
  Torah (the law) 2, 33-34, 37, 43-45, **48**, 49, 60, 83, 106, 161-62, 175, 203, 208, 212, 218-19, 243, 256, 300, 308, 403, 405, 423, 425, 427, 432, 434, 438, 448-49, 451, 455, 480-81, 496-97
Lazarus (and Rich Man) 235, 253, 256-57, 514-17, 522, 534, 537, 544, 546
Lazarus (brother Mary and Martha) 261, 264, 269, 270, 279-80, 290, 292, 294, 298, 305, 307, 312, 465, 467, 505
Leper (Leprosy) 158, 164, 168, 235, 251, 254, 374, 396-97, 466-67, 470-71, 498
Life after Death **97-98**
Lord (lordship) 10, 28, 33-34, 46, 48, 64, 73-75, 78, 93, 129, 142, 146, 161, 166, 181, 202, 208, 210, **211**, 230, 236, 240-43, 247, 249-50, 254,

262–63, 269, 281, 291, 298, 303, 308, 331–32, 336–40, 342, 347, 349, 358–59, 361, 363, 368–69, 373, 375, 378, 391, 396, 398, 402–403, 415, 418–20, 427–28, 436, 448, 453, 463–64, 475–76, 481, 496, 498, 505–506, 545

Lord's Supper (also Eucharist, Communion, breaking of bread) 2, 54, 77, 158, 261, 265, 276, 283, 368, 373, **379–80**, 384

Love 9, 33, 50, 65, 97, 109, 128, 137, 141, 155, 160, 165, 177, 206, 231, 239–40, 244–45, 251, 253, 257, 260, 280, 286, 315, **317–18**, 358, 384, 386–88, 391–93, 428–29, 435–38, 440, 445, 448–49, 452, 455, 458, 473, 481, 484, 502–03, 507, 525, 533, 535, 541–42

Luke (person, Gospel) 2–4, 7, 11, 57, 96, 103, 107, 111, 113–26, 129, 131, 138–39, 147, 149, 165–66, 168–69, 172–74, 179, 182, 186, 195, 200, 203–205, 209–13, **214-259**, 262, 266, 270, 274, 283–85, 290, 294, 306, 308, 312, 314, 319, 320–21, **322**, 323–36, 338, 340–41, 345, 347–48, 350–57, 359, 361–62, 364–75, 377, 380–81, 384, 386–89, 391, 393–94, 396–403, 408–10, 412–15, 431–32, 438–40, 444–45, 456–57, 461, **463-64**, 465–67, 473, 481–82, 488, 490, 494, 512, 518–22, 527–28, 535–36, 539, 543–45, 547
- Authorship 216–24
- Composition 233–37
- Date 225–31
- Key Emphases 241–59
- Provenance 224–25
- Recipients 231–33
- Structure 237–40
- Text 241

LXX (see Septuagint, Greek Old Testament) See Septuagint

Lydia 56, 61–62, 92, 252, 356, 375–76, 412

Lydda 401–402

Macedonia 19, 87, 189, 217, 222, 342, 401, 412–13

Macedonian Empire (Greek) 15, 19, 21, 57, 419

Maccabean Revolt and Period 15, 19, **22-23**, 40, 43, 46, 48–49, 301

Magdala 15, 52

Mark (Person, John Mark) 103, 128–32, **133-34**, 135–36, 138, 261, 325–26, 357, 370, 379–80, 408–11

Markan Priority 107, **115-17**, 126, 131, 190, 228

Mark's Gospel 2–5, 22, 36, 57, 74, 101, 103, 107, 109, 111, 113–127, **128-180**, 181–87, 189–92, 198, 200–206, 208–13, 216–17, 223–24, 228–29, 231–37, 241, 244, 246, 252, 254–56, 261–62, 265–66, 283–85, 297, 314, 316, 322, 326, 354, 366, 374, 403, 438, 442, 445, 456, 461–464, 466, 471–72, 490–91, 512, 518–20, 527–29, 532, 535, 542
- Arrangement 152–59
- Audience 140–41
- Authorship 127–34
- Chronology 152–53
- Context 148–51
- Date 135–38, 228–29
- Ending 144–49
- Provenance 138–39
- Setting 139–40
- Sources 141–42
- Structure 153–60
- Textual Issues 142–43
- Theological Themes 159–78

Marriage 64, 71, 88, 90, 97, 157, 166, 212, 245, 440, 448, 469

Martha 235, 241, 264, 269, 282–83, 298, 307, 311

SUBJECT INDEX

Mary Magdalene 146, 257, 290, 299, 467, 534
Mary (mother of Jesus) 238, 243, 246, 248, 251–52, 258, 368
Mary (mother of John Mark) 133, 325, 370, 379, 408
Mary (sister of Martha) 235, 264, 269, 283, 311
Matthew (Person) 103, **181–89**, 190–93, 266, 269
Matthew's gospel (Matthean) 2–4, 11, 27, 103, 107, 111, 113–126, 129–31, 133–35, 138, 140, 142, 165–66, 168–69, 174, 179, **181–214**, 216, **229**, 233–36, 238–39, 241, 246, 249, 254–55, 262, 283–84, 290, 294, 297, 305, 310–11, 314, 326, 354, 366, 374, 403, 418, 431, 433, 438, 440, 444–48, 456, **462–63**, 466–67, 471, 473, 488, 490, 498, 502, 511–12, 514, 517–21, 527–28, 530, 535, 538–40, 545
  Authorship 181–86
  Date 189–93
  Provenance 193–95
  Purpose 199–200
  Similarities and Differences to Mark 200–214
  Structure 195–99
Matthias 8, 319, 354, 368
Medo-Persian Empire 15, 18, 21, 419
Mercy 51, 56, 109, 155, 203, 211, 239, 244, 258, 296, 462, 473, 507, 524, 539, 543, 544–45
Messiah (messianic, messiahship) 1, 23, 30, 32, 34–35, 44, 47, **49**, 50, 107–109, 128, 140–41, 148, 153–64, 166–67, 169–70, 172, 176, 181, 187, 199–200, 204, 208–11, 239, 242–44, 260, 277–78, 281, 284, 287–88, 293–97, 299, 301, **307**, 310–13, 315, 338–41, 345, 350, 359, 363–64, 369, 373, 377–79, 395–96, 400, 418, 420–26, 429–31, 436–37, 441, 451, 462–64, 467, 472–73, 486, 491–92, 497–500, 506–507, 534, 540
Messianic Secret 164
Miracle(s) 3, 48, 102–103, 107–108, 123, 141, 155, 160–64, 167, 169, 209, 235, 241, 243–44, 260, 263, 275–76, 280, 286, 288, 293–98, 307, 312, 316, 338–40, 351, 359, 363, 371, 389, 402, 417, 429, 432, 443, **460–510**, 519, 539
Mission(al) 3, 7, 9, 57–60, 62, 79–80, 134, 136, 143, 149, 156–58, 161, 164, 168–69, **173–75**, 181, 185, 194, 196–201, **205–207**, 212, 217–19, 226, 236–40, 242, 244–47, **249–50**, 251, 254, 259, 278, 282, 286, 308, 312–13, 320, 322, 326, 330–31, **332–33**, 334–40, **341**, 342–49, 351–53, 355–61, 364–66, 369, 371–72, 382, 386, 390–91, 393, 395, 399–403, 405–406, 409–13, 415, 421, 432, 435, 437–38, 451, 454, **455–57**, 469, 477, 483–84, 493–95, 503, 526, 534, **541–43**
Missionary 45, 86–87, 133–34, 136, 174, 221, 227, 331, 343, 348, 401, 409, 412, 493, 541
Mithras 77
Monotheism 28, 33, 35, 48, 63, 67, 481
Moses 42, 45, 48–49, 161, 170–71, 196, 208–209, 218, 244, 277, 296, 298, 300, 308, 378, 395, 401, 418, 423–24, 473, 480, 491, 496–97, 506
Mount of Olives 168, 174, 274, 314
Muratorian Canon (fragment) 216, 223, 263, 321
Mystery Religions 63, **76–77**

Nathan 420, 513
Nathanael 266–67, 279, 303
Nation(s) 10, 15–16, 20–23, 25, 28, 33–35, 37, 39, 45, 47, 49–50, 125, 128, 141, 149, 155–56, 158–61, 167,

170, 174, 179, 181, 199-200, 202, 205-207, 212, 214, 245, 252, 257, 301, 334-35, 345, 350, 357-58, 366, 378, 394, 404-405, 407, 409, 419-22, 428, 434, 438, 443, 447, 456-59, 480, 494, 500, 525, 534-35, 537, 539-40

Nationalism 22, 32, **33**, 46, 48

Narrative Criticism **106-107**, 127, 526

Nature Miracles
Calming the Storm 161, 211, 466, 500, 504, 540
Coin in Fish's Mouth 467, 504
Fig Tree Withered 165, 236, 463, 466
Miraculous Catch of Fish (John) 266, 280, 283, 306, 467
Miraculous Catch of Fish (Luke) 467
Walking on Water 155, 161, 164, 235, 279, 283, 294, 297, 463-64, 466, 500, 504
Water to wine 280, 293-94, 309, 465, 467-68, 503-504

Nazareth 52, 234-35, **239**, 244, 249, 256, 498

Nero 25, 61, **74**, 130, 138-40, 142, 148, 191, 221, 225-27, 284, 322, 335, 414-15
  Persecution 148, 191, 225-27, 284, 322

Nerva (Emperor) 25

Noah 203

Oral Transmission(tradition) **5-6**, 44, 103, 112-13, 142, 324

Olivet Discourse 179, 194, 197, 201, 212-13, 519

Otho (Emperor) 25

Papias 120-21, 123, 129-30, 133-34, 136, 152, 182-84, 186, 188-89, 193, 263, 266, 269, 274

Papyri (papyrus) 73, 101, 216, 271, 321, 490
  P^{52} 101
  P^{66} (Bodmer) 216, 271, 274
  P^{75} 271, 274

Paul (Saul, the Apostle) 2-5, 8, 11, 19, 25, 27-28, 33, 35, 38-40, 42, 45, 50-51, 53-54, 57-61, 66, 68-69, 74-75, **77-80**, 81, 83, 85-89, 93-94, 124, 131, 133-34, 136-40, 142, 171, 175, 183, 187, 191-92, 194, 208, 216-29, **230**, 231-33, 241-42, 251, 256, 260, 262, 284, 286, 293, 302, 310, 312, 314, 317, 322-23, 325-27, **328**, 330, 332-35, 337-39, 341-44, **347**, 348-57, 359-362, 364-66, 369, 371-72, 375-76, 379-80, 382, 384, 386, **387-88**, 390-91, 393, 397, 399-403, 405-407, 409-15, 432, 436, 445, 451, 457, 465, 476-77, 479, 484-85, 488, 494, 523, 529, 547

Parables 18, 103, 155, 158, 160, 165, 168-69, 174, 176-77, 182, 185, 188, 191, 196-97, 199, , 201, 207, 213-14, 235-36, 240, 251, 253-58, 260, 285-86, 426, 430, 432-33, 438, 440-43, 446-47, 452-54, 456, 478, 506, **511-548**
Barren Fig Tree 235, 521
Blind leading Blind 520
Budding Fig Tree 519-520
City on a Hill 521
Divided City 521
Divided Kingdom 520
Divided Home 520
Faithful and Unfaithful Steward 201, 514, 521
Faithful Servant 522
Father and Children's Requests 520
Fishnet (dragnet) 512, 521
Friend at Midnight 521
Good and Bad Fruit 520
Good Samaritan 235, 248, 251, 478, 514, 516-18, 521, 523, 525, 533, 535-38, 540, 543-45, 548
Good Shepherd 280, 286, 291, 308-309, 518, 522

SUBJECT INDEX

Great Banquet 201, 251, 255, 257, 426, 448, 453, 478-79, 514, 521, 525-26, 534, 536-40, 542, 546, 548
Harvesters and Laborers 520
Householder 514, 521
Laborers in Vineyard 201, 446, 452, 454, 514, 521, 539
Lamp and Body 521, 541
Lamp and Measure 174, 518-20
Leaven (Yeast) 251, 521, 534
Lost Coin 235, 240, 251, 453, 514, 516, 519, 522, 536, 539, 543
Lost Sheep 240, 251, 308, 453, 514, 516, 519, 521, 535, 537, 539, 543
Mustard Seed 174, 251, 432-33, 442, 512, 514, 518-20, 525, 534, 535, 541, 548
Playing Children 520
Persistent Widow 235, 514, 522
Pearl 440, 442, 514, 516-17, 521, 539, 544
Pharisee and Tax-Collector 253, 522
Physician Heal Yourself 515, 521
Pounds (minas) 258, 454, 514, 521, 539, 544
Prodigal (Lost) Son 235, 240, 256, 453, 515-17, 522, 525, 527-28, 533, 536-38, 540, 545, 548
Rich Fool 235, 253, 514, 521, 544
Rich Man and Lazarus 235, 253, 256, 514-17, 522, 534, 537, 544, 546
Savorless Salt 203, 206, 441, 520, 535, 541
Sawdust and Plank 520
Seed (growing secretly) 433, 441, 454, 518-20, 542
Seed in the ground (John) 442, 454, 516, 522, 542
Sheep and Goats 201, 213-14, 444, 447, 478, 515-16, 521, 543, 546
Sower 236, 433, 443, 514, 516-20, 524-25, 528, 534, 537, 542, 548
Strong Man Bound 519-20, 538
Talents 176, 201, 214, 454, 514, 516, 521-22, 524, 539, 544-45
Ten Minas 539
Tenants 176-77, 285, 518-20, 525, 528, 533, 535, 537, 540
Thief in the Night 521
Tower Builder 512, 514, 521, 543
Treasure 440, 442, 514, 521, 539, 544
True Vine 280, 286, 518, 522
Two Debtors 514, 521, 539
Two Doors 521
Two Sons 201, 454, 514, 521, 543
Two Ways 521
Unjust Steward 514, 522
Unmerciful Servant 452-53, 514, 517, 521, 524, 539, 541, 543
Unshrunk Cloth 520
Warring King 512, 514, 521, 543
Watchman 520
Weather Signs 521
Wedding Banquet 201, 426, 448, 514, 521, 538-40, 542, 545-46
Wedding Guests 420
Wheat and Tares 521
Wineskins 165, 309, 519-20, 540
Wise and Foolish Builders 514, 520, 543
Wise and Foolish Maidens 514, 521
Paraclete (*Paraklētos*) 278, 280, 313, 432, 493
Patriarchy **56**, 233
Patronage **54-55, 92-96**, 233, 253
  Personal Patronage 95-96
  Public Patronage **95**
Paul (person, also Saul)
  Paul's Missions
    First Antiochian Mission 405, 410-11
    Second Antiochian Mission 217, 410, 411-13
    Third Antiochian Mission 217, 410, 413-14
    To Rome 414-15
Peasant life **51-52**
Persecution (Persecute) 4, 25, 61, 76, 138-40, 148, 159, 191-92, 200, 204, 225-27, 255, 277, 284, 287,

322, 330-32, 334-35, 350-51, 356-57, 359, 362, 364-66, 370-71, **389-92**, 393, 399, 401, 405, 407, 409-10, 413, 415, 445, 450, 457, 528, 542

Peter (Apostle, also Simon, Simon Peter) 3, 5, 28, 38, 74, 103, 125-26, 128-40, 142-44, 148, 152, 155-57, 160-63, 165, 172-73, 183, 185, 187, 192, 204, 210-11, 223, 225-27, 230-31, 254, 258, 260-62, 264-67, 269-71, 283, 299, 306-309, 314, 318, 322-23, 326, 330, 332, 335, 338-39, 341-42, 344-47, 349-51, 354, 357, 359-60, 362-67, 370-71, 373-76, 383, 385, 389-92, 396-97, 401-405, 407-409, 411, 452, 462, 466, 471-72, 488

Pharisee(s) 19, 23, 32, 34, 43, **44-45**, 60, 165, 168, 175, 188, 197-98, 205, 208, 212, 235, 253, 256-57, 281, 297, 306, 311, 355, 390, 408, 411, 414, 425, 448, 450, 452, 472, 480-81, 514, 516-18, 522, 525, 537, 539, 541, 544-45, 548

Philip
  Apostle 260, 265-67, 269, 279, 296
  Evangelist 27, 222, 251, 332, 335, 338, 341-42, 346, 355, 357-58, 360, 365, 375, 393-98, 401, 408-409, 414

Philo 19, **42**, 83, 270, 308, 381, 480, 512

Philo-Alexandrian exegesis 83

Philippi 37, 39, 50, 59, 73, 87, 94, 222, 226, 367, 412

Poor (poverty) **18**, 32, 60-61, 89, 91-92, 96, 133, 164-65, 175, 231, 239, 244, 247, 249, **252-53**, 285, 296, 332, 354, 380-82, 388, 392, 403, 429, 439, 441, 444-46, 449-50, 455, 469, 472, 477-78, 492, 494, 498, 501, 503-4, 508, 537, 540, 544, 546

Platonism (Plato, Platonist) 42, 81, 232, 352

Middle Platonism 81-82, **83-84**

Plutarch (232?), 329

Praise 105, 258, 337, 334, 347, 349, 353, **380**, 409

Prayer 28, 37, 41-42, 63, **67**, 69-70, **72**, 75, 133, 172, 176, 236, 238, 241, 245, **254**, 258, 280, 312, 315-16, 337-39, 344, 346, 349, 351, 355, 360, 365, **367-72**, 373, 380, 389, 402-03, 408, 433, 445, 453, 464, 470, 475-79, 483-85, 495, 509, 519, 545

Prescript(s) (Gospel) **182**

Priest(s)(-ess) 6, 9, 18, 22, 26-27, 30-31, 37, 39-40, 43-45, 47, 56, 69, 71-72, 78, 169, 210, 257, 261, 265, 270, 361, 365, 370, 394-95, 467, 473, 514-16, 523, 525, 537

Prophet (The, Eschatological Figure) 6, 69, 108, 128, 155-56, 161-62, 164, 166-67, 171, 173, 176, 201-202, 209, 212, 239, 244, 256, 277, 295-96, 298, 304, 308, 337, 349, 378, 385, 393, 395-96, 407, 420-21, 423, 434, 482, 485, 491-92, 497-98, 506, 522, 525, 532, 540

Prophets (the, OT) 44, 162, 379, 432, 498

Proselyte(s)(God worshiper, God fearer) 35, 50, 61, 221, 231-32, 355-56, 367, 374, 398, 403, 406, 448
  Cornelius - see Cornelius
  Lydia - see Lydia
  Titus Justus 219, 221, 413

Pseudepigrapha 15, **42**, 418, 513

Ptolomies (Ptolemy)
  Ptolemy I 308
  Ptolemy III 22

Purity 39, 41, 45, 48, 55, 175, 203, 219, 235-36, 331, 374, 405, 414, 427, 438, 449, 455, 470

SUBJECT INDEX

Q (Quelle) 103-4, 107, **115-17**, 120-21, 123-26, 142, 182-83, 186, 200, 224, 229, 233-37, 244, 283, 326, 463-64, 466-7, 490, 512, 518, 520-21
Quest for the Historical Jesus 106-108
Qumran 43, **47**, 308, 381, 419, 425, 470, 480, 513

Reciprocity **54**, 93, 96, 253, 445
Religionsgeschichte 77, **102-3**
Repentance (repent) 39, 50, 128, 153, 156, 160, 165-66, 169, 172, 177-78, 260, 281, 316, 334, 338, 363, 373-76, 386, 396, 405, 424, 427, 437-39, 448, 450, 452-53, 456, 482, 525, 530, 532, 540-41, 543, 545
Resurrection 1, 4-5, 9, 34, 40, 43-44, 77, 97-98, 102, 106, 126, 136, 143-44, 154, 157, 160, 162-64, 166, 172, 175, 178-79, 195, 197, 199-200, 202, 207, 215-16, 234-36, 240, 243, 251, 259, 276, 279, 283, 289-92, 294, 298-99, 303, 305, 307, 326, 331, 338, 340, 363, 365, 377-79, 396, 402, 404, 414, 417, 428-29, 433, 435-37, 441, 443, 450, 455, 461-62, 465, 468-69, 471, 486-87, 489-90, 492, 499-501, 505-506, 508-509, 519, 523, 540
   Greek Perspective 97-98
Jesus' Resurrection see Christ and Jesus
Jairus' Daughter 173-4, 402, 466
Lazarus 279-80, 290, 292, 294, 298, 305, 307, 312, 465, 467, 505
Widow of Nain's Son 235, 251, 402, 464, 467, 473, 505
Roman Centurion 201, 206, 226, 251, 259, 295, 403, 414, 463, 466, 472
Redaction Criticism 102, **104-105**, 324
Rich(es) (wealth(y)) 18, 32, 51, 55, 58-59, 61-62, 84, 89-90-92, 93-97, 157, 164-66, 171, 188, 221, 232-33, 235, 245, 252-53, 256-57, 269, 296, 354, 379, 380, 383, 385, 388, 392, 438, 440-42, 444, 446, 449-51, 455, 472, 503-4, 514-17, 519, 521-22, 534, 537, 544-46
Righteousness 106, 203, 205, 420, 422, 440, 448, 450, 503, 518, 541, 546
Roman (Greco-) Religion 67, **70-80**
   Gods and goddesses 70-71
   Pax Deorum 70, 79
   Priests 71-72
   Practices 72
   Prayer 72
   Sacrifice 72
   Temples 72
   Imperial Cult 28, 30, 63, 73-6, 78
Rome (Roman Empire/rule) 7, 9, 14-15, 18-20, 23, **25-32**, 35-37, 42, 44-47, 50-51, 55, 57, 59, 62, 73, 76, 86-88, 92, 94, 96, 126, 128, 131, 133-42, 145, 155, 157, 159, 161, 170, 174, 179-80, 183, 187-88, 190-91, 216-17, 221-23, 225-29, 231-33, 244-46, 259, 284, 319, 322, 325-26, 330, 332, 335, 337, 345, 354, 359, 391, 397, 399, 403, 407, 410, 412, 414-15, 419, 488
Roman Emperors 25
Roman governance 26-28
Roman privileges 28-30
Roman Empire Unity 30

Sabbath(s) 9, 28, 33, **37-38**, 40-41, 45, 47-49, 153, 161, 165, 168, 175, 203, 235, 256, 296-97, 299-301, 312, 368, 373, 405, 410, 427, 438, 448, **480-81**
Sadducees 26, 31, 34-35, 40, **43-44**, 49, 212, 272, 281, 311, 378, 395, 414, 426
Salome 29
Salvation 1, 7, 9, 40, 52, 76-78, 80, 145, 158-61, 169, 172, 216, 230, 232, 239-40, 242, **243-46, 248-49,**

250–52, 257, 262, 284, 291, 304–305, 310, 313, **316–17**, 318–19, 331, 336–38, 358, 361, 364, 366, 393, 402, 405, 422, 427–28, 439–41, 446, 450, 457–58, 469, 473, 476, 495, 502, 507, 523, 530, 543
Salvation History **248–49**, 319, 364, 393, 405
Samaria 3, 15, 21, 27–28, 149, 229, 237–38, 249, 319, 331–32, 334–35, 338, 344, **346–7**, 349–51, 355, 357, 360–61, 371, 375, 390–91, 393–94, 396–97, 401, 406, 408
Samaritan(s) 21, 23, **49–50**, 235, 248, 251, 270, 285, 308, 312, 332, 343–44, 349–50, 366, 394–97, 406, 457, 471, 478, 514, 516–18, 521, 523, 525, 533–38, 540, 543–45, 548
Samaritan Woman 280, 282, 307
Sanhedrin (also Council, Jewish Council) 26, 31, 37, **40–41**, 43, 177, 192, 311, 327, 338–39, 341, 345, 359, 362, 364, 369, 378, 389, 414
Sapphira 346, 381, **383–87**, 390, 409
Satan (Devil) 35, 44, 157, 161–62, 165, 169, 204, 210, 238–39, 244, 247, 294, 299, 308–309, 386–87, 418, 425, 430, 434, 439, 443, 447, 451, 461, 465, 476, 481, 487, 499, 501–502, 519, 523, 538
Savior (soter) 73–75, 78, **307–308**, 339, 358, 363, 375
Scribes 37, 45, 165, 168, 197, 205, 212, 217, 274, 281, 311, 480
Sea 15–16, 20, 27, 47, 52, 59, 64, 77, 86–88, 149, 152, 168, 222, 266, 309, 319, 381, 442, 464, 500, 505, 519
  Aegean 222, 413
  Adriatic 87
  Chinnereth (also Chinneroth) 15
  Dead Sea 15–6, 27, 47, 381
  Galilee 15, 52, 149, 152, 290
    Mediterranean 14–15, 87, 319, 406
    Red Sea 442, 505

Sea of Tiberias 15
Seleucid(s) 15, 19, **22**, 23, 395
Semitism **132**, 139, 276
Septuagint (also LXX, Greek Old Testament) 5, **41**, 42, 79, 112, 184, 193, 202, 204, 224, 230, 232, 238, 242, 292, 308, 319, 418, 507, 511
Sermon on the Mount 122, 125–26, 169, 174, 194, 196–77, 199, 201, **203**, 205–6, 208, 213, 234, 236, 371, 448, 451, 453, 455, 535
Servant(s) 81, 83, 128, 141, 153–54, 157, 159–61, 166, 173, 176, 201, 208, 240, 247–48, 251, 258, 289, 295, 303, 369–70, 378–79, 403, 408, 432, 436–37, 451–54, 462–64, 466–67, 473, 478, 498, 507, 514, 516–17, 519, 521–22, 524–25, 536, 539–43
Seventy-two (or Seventy) 41, 174, 236, 245, 247, 386, 452, 456, 484, 502
Sexual Immorality 66, **97**, 411
Silas 134, 222, 355, 357, 364, 376, 411–12
Sharon (place) 402
Shema 33, **48**
Simeon 247–48, 254, 258
Simon the Zealot 46, 188, 266
Slavery (Slaves) 38, 53, 58–62, 64–65, 68, 77, 79, 90, **91**, 92, 159, 170, 376, 406, 411–12, 436, 454, 494, 547
Social Stratification 88–92
  Equestrian Class 26, 89–90, 91–92, 96
  Free People 91
  Lower Classes **90–91**, 95
  Senatorial Class 26, 89, 90, 92
  Slavery 91
  Women 91
Socio-economic conditions NT **18**
Solomon 8, 21, 36, 42, 177, 211, 271, 275, 420
Son of God 63, 66, 73, 75, 78, 101, 153, 159–61, 166, 169–70, 177, 190, 199, 208–11, 243–44, 287, 293–97, 299,

SUBJECT INDEX

301, 304, 307, 339-41, 400, 427, 465, 482
Son of Man 156-58, 160-61, 169, 199, 208, 210, 240, 244, 249-51, 298, **304**, 421, 423-24, 427, 433, 436, 512
Source Criticism **103**, 104, 107
Sovereignty of God 45, **330**, 365-66, 389-90, 401, 414, 415, 421, 455, 476, 500
Spirit 3, 7, 35, 39, 65, 76, 78-79, 84, 102, 159, 166-67, 173, 210, 229, 237-40, 242-44, 246-50, 254, 262-63, 280, 283, 286, 309, 312-15, 319, 321, 330-43, 345-54, 356-61, 363-66, 369-71, 373-75, 381, 383-87, 389-90, 393, 396-400, 404-407, 409, 411-13, 417, 426-29, 431-33, 435-36, 439, 443, 445, 449-50, 454-59, 461, 464, 484-85, 488, 493-95, 499-500, 502, 534, 542
  Holy Spirit (the) 3, 7, 39, 78, 84, 102, 159, 166-67, 173, 210, 229, 237, 238-40, 242-44, 246-48, 249-50, 254, 262-63, 280, 283, 286, 309, 312-14, 315, 319, 321, 330, 331-32, 333, 334, 335-43, 345-54, 356-61, 363, 364-66, 369-71, 373-75, 378, 381, 383-87, 389-90, 393, 396-400, 405-407, 409, 411-13, 417, 426-28, 431-33, 435-36, 439, 443, 445, 449, 454, 456-59, 461, 464, 484-85, 488, 493-95, 500, 502, 534, 542
Spiritual gifts (charismata) 175, 262, 312, 353, 373, 432, 454, 494
Stephen 192, 226, 326, 332, 334, 337, 341, 346, 351, 355-58, 362, 364-65, 378-79, 390, 399, 401
Stoicism (Stoics) 81-82, **84-85**, 302, 360, 470
Suffering 4, 9, 106, 139-42, 148, 157, 159-62, 170-71, 173, 175-76, 239, 245, 250, 255, 289, 318, 338, 364,

374, 378, 390-91, 403, 414, 417, 425, 436-38, 440-41, 445-47, 451, 469, 473-76, 478-79, 482-85, 492, 496, 498-501, 507, 519
Synagogue(s) **37**, 41, 44, 49-50, **60-61**, 73, 94, 168, 190, 212, 219, 221, 234-35, 239, 244, 247, 251, 272, 277-78, 310-11, 327, 341, 347, 359, 362, 368, 391, 400, 410, 412, 438, 466, 472-73, 480, 483, 498, 505
Syncretism 20, 22, 63, 67
Synoptic Problem **110-127**
Syrophoenician (Canaanite) Woman 164, 173, 206, 236, 463, 466

Taheb 395
Targums **41, 425**
Tax-Collector(s) 20, 22, 171, 181, 183-85, 186-88, 204, 235, 253, 256, 281, 449-50, 452, 514, 516-18, 522, 525, 533, 537, 539, 541, 544-45, 548
Taxes (taxation) 18, 20, 22, 28, 30, 32, 37, 46, 52, 90, 166, 187-88, (385?)
Teaching (Teach) 5-7, 10, 18, 33, 39, 53, 70, 93, 99, 128-29, 152, 157, 161, 163-65, 167-69, 171, 175, 188, 194, 200-201, 203, 207-208, 227, 234-35, 239, 244-45, 247-48, 251-52, 254, 256, 258, 263, 274, 277, 279, 285-88, 292, 300, 312-13, 315, 319, 321, 337, 339-40, 349, 353, 355-56, 364, 368, 373, 377, 403, 406, 415, 417, 429, 438, 440, 442, 444, 446-48, 450-53, 455-56, 460, 473, 478, 483-84, 489, 492-93, **511-548**
Temple 9, 14, 16, 18-19, 21-23, 27, 31, **36-37**, 40, 43-44, 47-49, 52, 58-60, 63, 66, **68-69, 72**, 73-74, 79-80, 93, 97, 109, 137, 158-59, 164-66, 173, 175-77, 179, 192, 208, 212-13, 219, 236, 247, 252, 258-59, 271-72, 277, 279, 283, 285, 291, 294, 299-301, **305**, 311-12, 315, 339, 344, 362, 364, 367, 373, 378,

389-90, 394-96, 414-15, 420, 423, 519
Destruction see Destruction Jerusalem (the) 14, 16, 21, 23, 27, 36-37, 40, 43, 109, 137, 158-59, 164-66, 173, 175-77, 179, 192, 208, 212-13, 219, 236, 247, 252, 258-59, 271-72, 277, 279, 283, 285, 294, 299-301, 305, 311, 315, 339, 344, 362, 364, 367, 373, 389-90, 394-95, 414-15
Textual Criticism **100-101**
"The Jews" 212, 260, 281, **310-312**, 316
Tiberias (city) 52
Tiberias (sea) see Sea
Tiberius (Emperor) 25, 73
Tithe (Tithing) 18, 36, 381-82, 388, 544
Titus 3, 25, 74, 217, 219, 221, 413, 415
   Disciple 217, 219, 221, 413
   Emperor 25, **74**
      Theophilus 7, 96, 138, 215, 224, **227**, 231-32, 261, 321, 323, 338, 377, 399, 403, 410, 527
Theophilus of Antioch 261
Thessalonica 59, 87, 222, 226, 412, 414
Timothy 88, 131, 217, 219-22, 357, 376, 412
Tomb 66, 69, 128, 144, 148, 159, 163, 173, 178, 201-202, 241, 265, 299, 506
Trajan 25, **75-6**
Transfiguration 161-62, 178-79, 209, 243, 254, 367, 433, 461, 486
Travel in the Roman World 86-88
   Roads 87
   Sea 87-88
   Postal Service 88
Travel Narrative (Luke) 195, 234-35, 237, 239, **240**, 520
Treasure(s) 72, 440, 442, 444, 446, 514, 521, 539, 544
Triple Horizon **527-48**
Trinity 338, 340
Troas 217, 221-24, 413
Two Source Hypothesis 115-17

Urban life **51-52**
Ur-Gospel **112-13**

Vespasian 25, **74**
Virtue 58, 78, 84, 95, 137, 455
Vitellius 25
Voluntary Associations (also Collegia) **62-63**

Walking on water (Jesus) 155, 161, 235, 279, 283, 294, 297, 463, 466
Washing feet 280, 314
Water to Wine (Jesus) 465, 467, 504
"We passages" **217-18**, 221-22, 228, 332, 399
Western Text 217, 241, 322, **333**
Wilke Hypothesis **118-19**, 124
Witness(es) 100-1, 149, 165, 167, 173-74, 185, 188, 200, 204, 206, 229, 237, 267, 269, 306, 319, 321, 333, **334-35**, 336, 338, 341, 353, 358-59, 365, 371, 377, 454, 456
Wisdom 8, 65, 71, 84, 108, 161, 177, 210-11, 230, 257, 302, 356, 418
Women 53, 56, 61-62, 64, 68-69, 71, 77, 90, **91**, 92, 94, 96, 128, 144, 148, 159, 172-73, 202, 240, 245, **251-52**, 265, 274, 332, 345, 350, 354-56, 358, 361, 368, 380, 390, 402, 427, 441, 470-71, 494, 543
Word (of God/Lord, His) 9-12, 99, 161, 165, 243, 250, 302, 304, 306, 337, 339, 342, 351, 361, 365, 370, 477, 508, 529, 534, 537, 542
Work(s) 3, 9, 11-12, 37, 41-43, 48, 50, 55, 58-59, 92, 103-104, 107, 123, 126, 132, 134, 145, 158, 163, 167, 173, 188, 207, 215-17, 223-25, 232, 237, 240, 242-48, 258-59, 261, 264, 268, 270, 279-80, 284, 293, 296, 298-99, 301, 305, 309, 316, 320-24, 330-31, 338, 340-42, 345, 351, 353, 357, 360, 363, 372-73, 378, 399, 402, 404, 409, 423, 427-28, 430-32, 435, 443, 446,

449, 451-52, **453-54**, 456-58, 460, 471, 477, 480-81, 483, 493-94, 496, 501-503, 509, 516, 524, 527, 536-38, 540

Worship(-ed) 19, 28, 33, 37-38, 40-41, 44, 49, 61, 63, 68, 72, 75, 77, 79, 93, 97, 181, 200, 206, **211**, 212, **257-59**, 298, 299, 301, 303-304, 339, 353, 355, 371, **372-73**, 380, 398, 404, 463, 480

Yam Kinneret 15

Zacchaeus 188, 235, 248, 250, 252-53, 442

Zechariah
  Old Testament Prophet 21, 157, 176
  Priest 247-48, 254, 257-58

Zealots (also Nationalists) 20, 31-32, 45, **46-47, 426**

Zeus 22, 49, 64-66, 68, 71, 73, 76, 79, 308, 359

Zion 423, 425

AUTHOR INDEX

Achtemeier, Paul J. 135
Aeschylus. 98, 308
Aland, Barbara xv, 218
Aland, Kurt xv, 218
Allison, D. C. 433-34
Algie, Brian 156
Arndt, William xiii.
Arnold, Clinton E. 490
Aune, D. E. 63, 67, 68, 77, 80

Bacon, B. W. 196-97
Balz, Robert Horst xv
Barrett, C. K. 310
Bauckham, Richard J. 2, 6, 130, 132, 152, 153, 325, 329, 488
Bauer, Walter xiii.
Baum, A. D. 111
Beasley-Murray, George R. 40, 287, 288, 300, 301, 315, 377, 422, 431, 432
Beck, Astrid B. xiii
Beitzel, Barry J. xiii
Bellinzoni Jr, A. 114
Black, David Alan 132
Blackburn, B. L. 276, 461, 488, 489, 490, 500
Blomberg, Craig L. 12, 22, 104, 195, 196, 198, 207, 237, 382, 444, 446, 455, 523, 526, 527

Bock, Darrell L. 223, 225, 228, 242, 243, 249, 266, 322, 406, 407
Bond, Steve xv.
Borchert, Gerald L. 264, 268, 270, 274, 275, 276, 279, 287, 303, 311, 315
Bowden, Andrew M. 132
Bowley, J. E. 32
Bowman, J. 299
Brand, Chad xv.
Braun, F. 299
Breneman, Mervin 40
Bromiley, Geoffrey W. xvi
Brisco, Thomas V. 24, 272
Bromiley, Geoffrey W. xv
Brooks, James A. 133, 542
Brown, Derek 287
Brown, Jeannine K. xiv
Brown, Raymond E. 268, 276, 277, 311, 315
Bruce, F. F. 83, 104, 217, 219, 222, 233, 322, 323, 328, 355, 368, 379, 384, 387, 390
Bruns, J. E. 264
Burge, Gary M. 288, 309
Burns, J. E. 448
Burridge, R. A. 2
Butler, B. C. 114
Butler, Trent C. xv

Caragounis, C. C. 204, 431

Carson, D. A. 198, 268, 269, 270, 287, 288, 293, 294, 299, 300, 301, 302, 303, 353
Chafer, Lewis Sperry 489
Chapman, D. J. 114
Chenevix, Richard 523
Chilton B. 356
Ciampa Roy E. 485
Clendenen, E. Ray xv.
Cole, Susan Guettel 68
Collins, John J. xiv,
Comfort, Philip Wesley xvii, 114
Corley, Bruce 102
Coxe, A. Cleveland 262, 392
Cranfield, C. E. B. 530
Cross, F. L. xvi
Culpepper, R. 263, 264, 268

Danker, Frederick W. xiii
Davids, Peter H. xiv
DeMoss, Matthew S. xvi, 144, 145, 152, 239, 290, 531
Dionysius of Halicarnassus 329, 360, 390
Dodd, C. H. 132, 283, 362, 428, 429, 430, 431, 523, 524, 525, 529, 539
Donaldson, James 262, 392
Draper, Charles xv.
Dunn, J. D. G. 219, 220, 350

Eades, K. L. 2
Edwards, J. R. 46, 142, 153, 179, 481, 486
Eichhorn, G. 113
Ehrman, Bart 217, 241
Elwell, Walter A. xii, xvi
England, Archie xv.
Ellis, Earle E. 223, 328
Eusebius 8, 120, 129, 130, 137, 139, 147, 152, 182, 183, 184, 189, 216, 223, 224, 262, 263, 269, 271, 283, 320, 487
Evans, Craig A. xiv, 48, 78, 148, 486, 487
Everts, J. M. 93

Falk, Daniel K. 480
Farmer, W. 114
Farrar, A. M. viii, xii, 117, 118, 124
Fee, Gordon D. 485
Filson, F. 264
Fitzmyer, Joseph A. 223, 228
France, R. T. 196, 235
Freedman, David Noel xiii
Friedrich, Gerhard xvi

Gaertner, Dennis 369, 406
Gamble, H. Y. 8
Gangel, K. O. 70
Gardner-Smith, P. 283
Garland, David E. 133, 135, 140
Gaventa, Beverly Roberts 398
Gieseler, C. L. 112
Gill, D. W. J. 92
Goedicke, H. 299
Goodacre, Mark S. 117
Gorman, Michael J. 53
Goulder, Michael viii, 117, 124
Graf, David F. xiii
Green, Joel B. xiv, 431,
Grenz, Stanley xvi, 7, 190, 246, 314, 495
Griesbach, J. J. vii, xii, 114, 115, 138, 142, 192
Griffin, B. G. 264
Griffen, Hayne P. 8, 221
Guelich, Robert A. 46, 130, 153
Guretzki, David xvi.
Gutbrod, Walter 183

Haacker, Klaus 89
Hadjiantoniou, G. 9
Hagner, Donald A. 38, 187, 188, 189, 190, 191, 192, 204, 382, 431
Hansen, G. W. 105
Harlow, Daniel C. xiv.
Harris, Murray J. 476
Harrison, R. K. 220
Hauck, F. 442
Hawthorne, Gerald F. xiv, 97
Hemer, Colin J. 139, 323, 324

AUTHOR INDEX

Hengel, Martin 119, 131, 132, 182, 217, 324
Herder, J. G. 112
Herion, Gary A. xiii
Heyink, Brenda 315
Hixon, Elijah 145
Hock, R. 86
Holmes, M. W. 194
Hooker, Morna D. 485
Houston, J. M. 16
Horsley, Richard A. 50
Hubbard, Jr. R.L. 12
Huffman, D. S. 235
Hultgren, Arland J. 527
Hume, David 486
Hunter, A. M. 427, 428, 431, 534
Hurtado, Larry W. 132

Irenaeus 7, 129, 130, 139, 145, 182, 183, 186, 216, 225, 261, 262, 263, 268, 269, 270, 271, 299, 397
Isaacs, E. D. 38

Jeffers, James S. 90
Jeremias, J. 108, 376, 431, 524, 525, 530
Jones, Donald L. 73, 75
Jones D. W. 70
Jones, Henry Stuart xv.
Jones, Richard N. 470
Josephus 15, 16, 36, 42, 43, 44, 47, 51, 61, 65, 73, 143, 156, 194, 224, 225, 232, 248, 315, 334, 369, 383, 390, 394, 395, 398, 406, 407, 419, 422, 448, 470, 480, 512, 541
Jülicher, A. 524

Kähler, M. 175
Karavidopolous, Johannes xiv
Kee, Howard Clark 470
Keener, Craig S. 130, 504, 505
Keown, Mark J. 38, 179, 358, 435, 477
Kimelman, R. 310
King, Philip J. 16
Kittel, Gerhard xvi
Klein, W. W. 12

Köstenberger, Andreas J. 274, 287, 288, 296, 300, 303, 313, 315, 465
Krahmalkov, Charles R. 406
Kreitzer, L. J. 86
Kuhn, H. -W. 476

Laird, Benjamin 8
Latta, Bill xv
Lea, Thomas D. 8, 221
Lemke, Steve W. 102
Lessing, G. E. 113
Liddell, Henry George xv.
Lischer, Richard 524.
Livingstone, A. xvi
Lovejoy, Grant I. 102

MacDonald, Dennis R. 120
McBirnie, William Stuart 192
McDonald, Lee Martin 139.
McKenzie, Roderick xv.
McKnight, S. xiv, 183.
Mack, Burton L. 108
Malherbe, A. J. 86
Manson, T. W. 429, 530
Marcus, Joel 135
Marshall, Christopher D. 418, 421, 422, 425, 426, 427, 430, 431, 436
Marshall, I. Howard xiv, xv, 93, 104, 220. 223, 224, 322, 323, 324, 327, 328, 330, 381, 382, 505, 545
Martin, Ralph P. xiv.
Martin, Thomas W. 355.
Martini, Carlo M. xv
Martyn, J. L. 268, 276, 278, 310
Mathews, K. A. 434
Maynard-Reid, P. U. 393
Mbiti, John 53
Metzger, Bruce Manning xv, 101, 145, 153, 174, 217, 241, 303, 462.
Miller, Jeffrey E. 292
Michaels, Ramsay J. 287, 288
Moo, Douglas J. 220
Morgenthaler, R. 119
Moreland, J. P. 487
Myers, Allen C. xiv

Nash, R. 487
Nelson, Thomas 17, 18, 149, 151 (Maybe delete)
Newton, J. 114
Nolland, John 198, 205, 231, 256, 266
Nordling, Cherith Fee xvi
Novak, R. M. 311

Oakman, D. E. 54.
Omanson Roger L. 101
Osborne, Grant R. 12, 84
Overman J. 50

Packer, J. I. 365
Page, Franklin S. 51
Paige, T. 80, 86
Parker, P. 264
Paterson, J. H. 15
Patzia, Arthur G. xvi, 3, 6, 102, 106, 274
Payne. J. B. 38
Perrin, Nicholas xiv, 123
Petrotta, Anthony J. xvi, 3, 6, 102, 106, 274
Paulien, Jon 355
Peisker, C. H. 531
Philo 19, 50, 63, 65, 308, 368, 381, 424, 480, 512, 541
Pleins, John David xiii
Polhill, John B. 345, 359, 369, 407, 408
Polybius 22
Pritchard, James Benett xiii
Porter, Stanley E. xiv
Prosper, J. M. 70.

Ramsay, W. M. 323
Rapske, B. M. 88,
Reasoner, M. 28
Reicke, B. 112
Reid, Daniel G. xiv
Riesner, R. 16
Rist, John M. 112
Roberts, Alexander 262, 392
Rosner, Brian S. 485
Robertson, A. T. 320

Sanders, E. P. 34, 109, 270, 310
Schleiermacher, F. D. E. 113, 123
Schnabel, Eckhart J. 86, 219, 229, 230
Schneider, Gerhard Xv
Schweitzer, Albert 107, 108, 430, 486
Scott, Robert xv
Sievers, J. 23
Silverman, Jason M. 14
Smith, Billy K. 51
Smith, Zachary G. 7, 35
Snodgrass, Klyne R. 511, 513, 518, 522, 527, 529
Sherwin-White, A. N. 323, 324
Simmons, William 32
Spencer, F. S. 398
Springer, Kevin 499
Stählin, Gustav 68
Stanton, G. N. xiv, 124
Stein, Robert H. 111, 112, 233, 382
Sterling, G. E. 19
Stoldt, H. 114
Stoops, Jr. R. F. 130, 397
Streeter, Burnett Hillman 115
Swan, John T. 40
Swanson, James xiv

Tidball, D. J. 58, 61
Torrey, C. C. 113, 137
Thiselton, Anthony C. 349
Thompson, M. M. 268
Trebilco, Paul R. 48

Utley, Robert James 321

Watson, D. F. 58
Wedderburn, A. J. M. 77
Wenham, J. W. 137
Witherington III, Ben 46, 69, 79, 105, 152, 215, 217, 220, 224, 264, 321, 323, 355, 356, 360, 368, 374, 379, 382, 383, 384, 385, 390, 395, 484
White, L. Michael 94
Wimber, John 499
Wilke, C. G. viii, xii, 118, 119, 124

Williamson, H. G. M. 393
Wood, D. R. W. xv
Woodbridge, R. S. 70
Wright, Christopher J. H. 239
Wright, N. T. 23, 36, 86, 109, 179, 311, 408, 430, 435

Yamauchi, E. M. 20, 356

ANCIENT TEXTS INDEX

Old Testament

Genesis
1 534
1–2 .... 454, 496
1:1 505
1:4 306
1:26–27 501
1:27 202
2:1–3 .... 37, 48
2:15 403
2:24 202
3 434
3:6 384
3:15 420
9:3 403
10:10 419
12:1–3 .... 393, 405
12:10 51
12:17 482
14:1–3 419
15 34
15:16 482
17 .... 34, 48
19:26 541
22:18 .... 363, 378, 379
26:1 51
26:4 .... 363, 378, 379
36:37 399
37:5 65

41:27 51
46–47 209
46:10 399
49:10 .... 420, 424

Exodus
1:15–22 209
2 209
3 171
3:6 202
3:14 .... 292, 303
4 506
4:1–17 473
4:18–31 298
5–12 209
7:14–12:30 497
11–12 209
12–14 209
12:15 541
12:19 541
12:21–31 .... 38, 56
13:17–14:31 .... 497, 505
13–14 496
15:22–17:7 497
15:26 496
16 .... 162, 296
16:5 480
16:22–30 480

16:31–35 297
17:8–16 497
19:5–6 33
19:6 420
19:18 51
20 .... 34, 420, 434, 497
20–23 209
20:2 33
20:3 46
20:5 482
20:9–11 48
20:11 369
20:12 476
22:29 377
23:11 38
23:20–33 ....
24:13 .... 170, 497
24:18 209
30:35 541
31:13–17 480
31:15 480
32:1–25 497
32:2 377
32:13–16 377
34:7 482
34:21 480
34:26 39
34:28 209

35:2 480	26:55-56 368	7:1 384
35:3 480	28:11-15 38	7:1-26 497
	32:33 419	10:1-14 497
Leviticus	34:11 15	10:1-15 497
2:11 541		10:11-14 505
2:13 541	**Deuteronomy**	10:12-13 496
6:17 541	3:4 419	12:3 15
10:1 384	3:17 541	13:12 419
10:10 403	5:9 482	15:25 46
12:8 252	5:16 476	18:8-19:49 368
13-14 470	6:4 48	
13-17 374	6:4-6 33	**Judges**
16 39	6:5 202	6-8 497
16:8-10 368	6:13 202	9:7-15 513
19:18 202	6:16 202	9:45 541
20:25 403	8:3 202	13-16 497
23 38	9:26 419	13:5 202
23:3 38	10:9 381	20:26 371
23:4-8 39	131-2 461	
23:10 39	15:1 38	**Ruth**
23:10-14 39	15:4 .... 381, 504	1:1 51
23:23-25 299	16:11 39	
25 439	16:14 38	**1 Samuel**
25:1-7 38	18:15 .... 209, 296, 308, 363,	2:6 65
25:8-18 38	378, 379, 423, 497	7:6 371
25:8-55 250	18:18 .... 363, 379	8 170
	18:18-19 378	8:4-5 420
Numbers	18:19 379	8:5 419
3:12 377	21:22 437	8:6-8 420
6:1-21 219	21:23 170	9:2 399
10:10 38	23:1 398	10:2 512
10:11-13 497	25:5 202	10:18 419
10:33-34 497	28:56-57 51	12:12 419
11:1-3 497	32:15 308	13:14 363
11:4-35 487	32:17 79	14:15 51
12:10-16 482	32:22 65	16:14 35
14:18 482	32:39 496	17 497
15:32-36 480	34:11 461	24:4 512
16:30 65		31:13 371
16:31 51	**Joshua**	
18:20 381	3:1-17 505	**2 Samuel**
19 374	3:9-17 497	1:12 371
20:1-13 497	5:13-27 497	7 34
21:1-3 497	6:6-26 497	7:12-16 420
23:7 512	7 384	7:13-16 434

8:17 43	19:22 308	6:6 541
12:1-4 .... 512, 513	20:1-7 482	7:9 65
12:16 371	20:1-11 496	26:12-13 ....
14:5-20 513	24-25 21	41:34 419
21:11 51	25 36	
	25:3 .... 516:24-2551	**Psalms**
1 Kings		2 244
4:24 419	**1 Chronicles**	2:1-2 .... 369, 378, 379
6-9 36	6:24 399	2:1-3 424
8:11 36	21:1 35	2:7 .... 210, 339, 363, 378,
8:37 51	25:8 369	379, 434
11:1-13 420	26:13-14 368	5:2 419
12 .... 21, 396, 420	28:5 418	6:6 65
16:24 394	29:11 418	7:11 422
17:7-16 497		8:2 202
17:17-24 .... 497, 506	**2 Chronicles**	8:4 156
18:2 51	5:14 36	8:4-5 304
18:22-39 497	7:1-3 36	8:4-6 304
19:11 51	13:8 418	9:4 419
20:35-40	30 395	10:16 .... 419, 420
21:9 371	34:6 395	16:8-11 .... 363, 378, 379
21:12 371		16:10 .... 378, 379
	Ezra	18:50 422
2 Kings	3:7-6:18 36	21:19 369
2 162	3:12 36	22 .... 1, 176
2:19-22 497	8:21 371	22:1 202
2:20-21 541	8:23 371	23:1 .... 291, 308
4:1-7 497		24:7 419
4:8-27 506	**Nehemiah**	29:10 419
4:18-36 497	1:4 371	35:13 371
4:38 51	5:3 51	44:4 419
4:38-44 497	9:1 371	45:6 419
5 374	9:6 369	45:7 422
5:1-14 497	13:15-22 480	47:2-9 419
5:8 384		47:8 419
6:1-7 .... 497, 505	**Esther**	50:6 422
6:8-23 497	1:2 419	51:2 374
6:25 51	3:7 369	51:7 374
7:4 51	4:3 371	55:17 367
8:1 51	4:16 371	68:24 419
14:9 513	9:31 371	69:25 .... 378, 379
17 .... 21, 394		74:12 419
17:24-41 394	**Job**	74:12-15 500
17:29 394	1:6-12 35	77:16-20 500
17:41 394	5:18 496	78:2 .... 202, 511

84:3 419	6 532	42:1 350
95:3 419	6:1 419	42:1-4 .... 202, 463
95:5 79	6:5 419	42:1-6 157
98:6 419	6:1-14 171	42:1-7 436
103:19 418	6:9-10 ... 165, 193, 202, 415	42:5 369
105:37 79	6:10 530	42:7 ....463, 507
107:34 541	7:14 .... 202, 463	42:6-7 498
109:8 .... 378, 379	8:21 419	43:10 292
110:1 ..... 153, 166, 202, 240, 243, 378, 379	9:1-2 202	43:13 303
	9:1-7 157	43:15 419
118:22 ....378, 379, 537	9:6 492	43:25 292
118:22-23 ....202, 524	9:7 421	44:3 ....309, 350
118:25-26 164	11:1 202	44:6 419
118:26 ....202, 258	11:1-9 157	44:28 .... 21, 363
135:9 461	11:1-3 350	45:1 21
145:1 419	11:6-9 422	45:18 292
146:6 369	13:10 202	46:4 292
146:10 420	16:5 421	49:1-6 ....157, 436
149:2 419	22:13 508	49:6 .... 378, 379, 422
	24:23 420	50:4-9 ....156, 436
Proverbs	25:6 534	51:12 292
1:6 512	25:6-8 .... 257, 453, 500	52-53 202
1:12 65	25:9 422	52:6 292
8-9 210	26:19 500	52:7 153
8:22-31 161	27:1 500	52:10 422
16:33 369	29:13 202	52:13-52:12 ....157, 436
	29:18 .... 463, 498, 507	53 ..... 1, 160, 176, 303, 341, 376, 398, 437
Ecclesiastes	32:15-20 309	
3:17 422	33:22 ....419, 421	53:4 .... 202, 463, 498
9:10 65	34:4 202	53:4-5 498
	35:5 507	53:7-8 ...342, 378, 379, 398
Isaiah	35:5-6 .... 463, 498	53:12 289
1:1-2 250	37:16 418	55:1-5 448
1:46 ....47, 248	37:16-20 369	55:3 ....363, 378
1:67-71 248	40-55 292	55:10-11 ....534, 537
1:77 248	40-66 78	56:7 .... 176, 202, 258
2:10 248	40:2 193	56:12 508
2:25-30 248	40:3 ...... 153, 166, 202, 289	58 371
3:6 248	40:3-5 .... 242, 248, 373	58:13-14 480
4:4 374	40:9 153	60:6 153
4:5 36	40:9-11 421	61:1 .... 153, 422, 498, 507
5 .... 292, 310, 315	41:4 303	61:1-2 ....157, 239, 244, 247, 249, 350
5:1-7 513	41:21 419	
5:14 65	41:27 153	61:1-3 436
5:24-25 191	42 244	65-66 505

65:8 390
65:25 390
66:1 419

Jeremiah

1:4-10 171
3:18 396
3:22 422
7:11 .... 176, 202
8:19 419
10:7 419
10:10 419
14:1-6 51
14:12 371
17:19-27 480
19:9 51
23:1-8 ....
23:5-6 421
23:6 396
31:15 202
30:3 396
31:31 34
31:1-37 396
31:27 396
31:31 396
31:31-33 .... 158, 422
31:31-34 2
33:15 421
36:6 371
37:7-12 381
40:1-5 395
41:5 65
48:24 46

Lamentations

2:20 51
4:9 51
4:10 51

Ezekiel

1:26 419
2:1 156
2:1-6 304
4:14 403
5:10 51

11:19 350
16:4 541
17 512
17:2 512
17:2-10 513
17:23 534
18 482
18:2 512
19:2-9 513
19:10-14 513
24:3 512
31:6 534
31:16-17 65
34 .... 291, 308
34:23-24 421
36 157
36:25-27 309
37:15-28 396
37:24 421

Daniel

1 48
1:8-12 403
3:88 65
6:12 367
6:26 418
7 .... 421, 424, 436
7:13 304
7:13-14 .... 1, 156, 157, 161,
                   169, 244, 424
9:3 371
9:25-26 422
9:27 22
11:31 22
12:1-4 446
12:11 22
12:1-3 .... 500, 546

Hosea

1:10-11 396
2:2 396
6:6 202
11:1 .... 202, 209
11:1-4 396
11:10-12 396

13:12 65

Joel

1:14 371
2:12 371
2:20 338
2:28 309
2:28-32 .... 326, 345, 350,
                   363, 378, 379
3:3 369

Amos

1:1 51
2:16 135
8:5 480
9:2 65
9:11 .... 21, 421
9:11-12 411

Obadiah

11 269

Jonah

1:7 369
2:3 65
3:5 371

Micah

5:2 202
7:6 202

Nahum

1:15 153

Habakkuk

1:5 .... 378, 379
2:5 65
3:13 422

Zephaniah

3:15 419

Zechariah

3:1-2 35
7:3 371

7:5 371
8:19 371
9:9 .... 157, 164, 202
10-11 308
12:10 350
13:7 .... 176, 178, 202

14:5 51
14:9 419
14:16-17 .... 301, 419

Malachi

1:14 419

New Testament

Matthew

1 235
1:1-2 209
1:1-16 10
1:1-17 .... 201, 202, 234
1:1-2:23 .... 197, 199
1:1-4:11 195
1:1-4:16 196
1:2 248
1:18 .... 203, 210, 463
1:18-22 210
1:18-2:23 201
1:20 .... 210, 462, 463, 468
1:21-22 202
1:22 201
1:22-23 463
1:23 .... 184, 210
1:24 468
2 27
2:1 27
2:1-11 209
2:1-12 206
2:2 .... 211, 462, 463
2:6 202
2:8 211
2:11 211
2:12-13 463
2:12 462
2:13 .... 462, 468
2:13-15 209
2:15 .... 201, 202, 210
2:16-18 209
2:18 202
2:19 .... 462, 463, 468
2:22 .... 28, 462, 463
2:23 202

3-4 197
3:1-4:25 199
3:1-7:29 197
3:2 438
3:3 .... 112, 193, 202
3:7 212
3:9 203
3:9-12 213
3:11 166
3:15 201
3:23 512
4:1-11 ... 169, 209, 443, 502
4:4 .... 202, 306, 371
4:3 210
4:6 210
4:7 .... 202, 210
4:8 426
4:10 202
4:11 268
4:12-15:20 195
4:15 193
4:15-16 202
4:17 .... 196, 198, 448
4:17-16:20 196
4:18-22 267
4:23 .... 207, 208, 212, 359, 438
4:23-24 .... 463, 483
4:24 468
4:30-32 515
5 123
5-7 .... 124, 125, 126, 165,
      169, 194, 196, 197, 201,
      209, 234, 236, 455, 535
5:1-7:29 199
5:2 193
5:3 450

3:1 .... 153, 166
3:1-2 .... 243, 289, 324
4:5 .... 166, 289, 324
4:5-6 162

5:5 194
5:10 444
5:10-12 451
5:13 .... 249, 441, 520,
                               515, 535
5:13-16 .... 206, 541
5:14 521
5:16 .... 249, 441, 453
5:17 201
5:17-20 .... 203, 212
5:19 .... 444, 451
5:19-20 448
5:20 .... 205, 213, 317, 444
5:22 .... 193, 213
5:22-23 444
5:23-24 192
5:29-30 213
5:41 194
5:43-47 206
5:44 .... 254, 451
5:44-47 194
5:45 253
5:46 188
5:47 444
5:48 .... 194, 205
6 444
6:1-4 .... 96, 503
6:4 213
6:5-7 254
6:6 213
6:9 254
6:9-10 476
6:9-13 .... 194, 236, 254
6:10 .... 207, 433
6:12 453
6:14-15 453

6:16 184	8:14–15 466	9:37 520
6:16–18 371	8:16 .... 463, 468, 483	9:38 .... 211, 254
6:18 213	8:17 ..... 201, 202, 463, 498	10 .... 174, 196, 197, 201,
6:19–32 440	8:18–22 .... 205, 255	206, 236, 481
6:19–34 503	8:19 .... 171, 208	10:1 452
6:22 520	8:22 356	10:1–42 .... 199, 205
6:24 193	8:23–27 .... 466, 504	10:1–2 483
6:25–34 440	8:25 317	10:3 .... 182, 184, 186
6:30 474	8:26 474	10:5 ....50, 394
6:33 .... 205, 440, 445	8:27 460	10:5–15 236
6:34 451	8:28–34 466	10:6 205
7 194	9:2 .... 316, 474	10:7 439
7:3–5 ....444, 520	9:2–7 466	10:8 481
7:6 194	9:2–8 482	10:15 .... 203, 213
7:9–11 520	9:6 112	10:16 189
7:12 ....333, 455	9:9 .... 181, 182, 184	10:17 212
7:13 .... 213, 317	9:9–13 .... 184, 185, 186	10:22 316
7:13–14 .... 213, 291, 310,	9:10–11 188	10:23 451
515, 520	9:11 188	10:26 124
7:14 213	9:14 371	10:35 202
7:16–20 520	9:15 520	10:38 ....255, 356
7:17–19 542	9:16 520	10:42 444
7:21 ....211, 317	9:17 520	10:44 451
7:21–23 .... 213, 447, 448	9:18 463	11 311
7:22 .... 448, 460	9:18–19 466	11–12 197
7:24–27 .... 204, 514,	9:18–26 505	11:1 196
520, 543	9:20–22 466	11:1–12:50 199
7:28 196	9:22 .... 316, 463, 474	11:1–13:58 197
7:29 208	9:22–23 462	11:2 ....209, 453
8–9 ....194, 197	9:23–25 466	11:2–6 161
8:1–4 271	9:27–31 ....462, 463	11:2–19 234
8:1–9:38 199	9:28 .... 463, 474	11:3 202
8:1–10:42 197	9:28–29 316	11:4–5 .... 490, 498
8:2 463	9:27–31 467	11:5 463
8:2–4 466	9:29 ....293, 462, 474	11:7 346
8:5–13 ... 201, 206, 234, 271,	9:32 483	11:10 184
466, 462, 464, 471	9:32–33 467	11:11 167
8:6 423	9:32–34 463	11:11–14 432
8:8 423	9:35 ....207, 208, 319,	11:12 ....398, 432
8:10 .... 316, 460, 474	438, 483	11:16–17 520
8:10–12 213	9:35–36 473	11:19 .... 188, 211, 453
8:11 .... 203, 500	9:36 ....462, 473	11:21–24 .... 203, 213
8:11–12 448	9:36–10 249	11:23 65
8:12 ....207, 213, 356	9:36–10:1 492	11:25 210
8:13 .... 316, 462, 463	9:36–10:23 456	11:25–30 211

12 506	13:21 451	14:13–21 ....464, 503
12:1–2 480	13:22 194	14:14 .... 462, 468, 473,
12:1–23:39 199	13:24 ....439, 442	492, 503
12:2 481	13:24–26 441	14:15–21 466
12:5 481	13:24–30 .... 515, 516,	14:22–33 504
12:5–7 192	521, 539	14:22–32 .... 235, 464
12:7 202	13:29–30 213	14:23 254
12:8 481	13:31 .... 439, 442, 514	14:25–32 466
12:9 212	13:31–32 .... 205, 441,	14:27 297
12:10 474	520, 535	14:28–29 354
12:10–13 466	13:31–33 541	14:28–33 462
12:11 481	13:33 ....39, 439, 441,	14:30 317
12:12 481	512, 514	14:31 ....316, 474
12:15 .... 463, 468	13:33–34 521	14:33 .... 210, 211, 463
12:17 202	13:35 ....202, 511	14:35 463
12:18–21 463	13:36–43 .... 514, 521	15 ....366, 403
12:22 .... 462, 463, 466	13:38 219	15:1–20 235
12:22–24 463	13:38–39 443	15:9 112
12:25 ....520, 521	13:40–43 213	15:8–9 202
12:25–28 443	13:41 207	15:11 403
12:28 .... 431, 499, 502	13:42 .... 446, 545	15:14 520
12:28–29 426	13:43 .... 207, 546	15:21–28 .... 206, 235, 466
12:29 ....398, 538	13:44 ..... 207, 439, 442, 521	15:21–18:35 195
12:29–30 520	13:44–45 514	15:22 463
12:31 194	13:44–46 .... 440, 514, 544	15:24 .... 205, 212
12:31–32 213	13:45–46 ....442, 517	15:25 463
12:33 .... 189, 542	13:45–47 521	15:28 ..... 316, 462, 463, 474
12:35–37 213	13:45 .... 207, 439	15:28–39 503
12:38 293	13:46 517	15:30 468
12:38–39 ......463, 473, 506	13:47 .... 205, 439, 514	15:32 ....462, 473, 492
12:40–41 203	13:47–50 .... 447, 512, 516,	15:32–38 466
12:42 211	521, 539	15:32–16:12 235
12:46–13:58 111	13:49 213	15:33–58 234
12:48–50 444	13:50 543	15:34–36 515
13 ....196, 197, 519, 538	13:52 ....207, 439, 449,	15:37 463
13:1–9 520	514, 521	15:38 293
13:1–23 542	13:53 196	16 506
13:1–31 207	13:54 .... 211, 219	16:1 .... 212, 238
13:1–52 199	13:54–58 471	16:1–4 ....463, 473, 506
13:11–12 441	13:58 .... 123, 316	16:4 ....238, 294
13:13 .... 207, 530	14–17 197	16:6 ....39, 212, 541
13:13–15 202	14:1 ....202, 295	16:8 ....316, 474
13:14–15 193	14:1–12 27	16:11 .... 39, 212
13:18–23 520	14:1–20:34 199	16:11–12 541
13:19 .... 208, 319, 438	14:1–18:35 197	16:12 .... 39, 212

16:13–20:34 111	19:1–25:46 197	21:28–32 .... 201, 514,
16:16 .... 190, 210	19:1–20:34 195	521, 543
16:18 .... 189, 204	19:2 464	21:31 .... 188, 317, 449
16:19 452	19:4–5 .... 202, 203	21:31–32 .... 188, 213
16:21 .... 196, 198	19:12 .... 189, 446	21:32 .... 187, 188
16:21–28:20 196	19:13 254	21:33–34 .... 535, 537
16:22 211	19:13–15 111	21:33–46 540
16:23–27 433	19:14 450	21:42 202
16:24 255	19:16–30 440	21:43 206
16:25 431	19:17 319	22:1–13 545
16:28 .... 207, 433	19:23–24 .... 317, 449, 450	22:1–14 .... 201, 426, 512,
17:1–13 433	19:24 213	514, 519, 521,
17:4 .... 211, 463	19:25 316	538, 540, 542
17:10 423	19:26 477	22:2 439
17:14–18 466	19:27 441	22:2–3 448
17:18 463	19:28 .... 85, 208, 500	22:7 .... 138, 190, 191
17:20 .... 316, 474	20–25 519	22:11–14 213
17:24–27 .... 184, 462, 467	20:1 .... 207, 439, 454, 514	22:15–22 271
17:27 504	20:1–16 .... 184, 201,	22:23 35
18 .... 196, 197, 204, 519	213, 446, 514,	22:23–24 212
18:1–4 .... 449, 451	521, 539, 545	22:23–38 44
18:3 317	20:20–28 266	22:24 202
18:6 316	20:21 207	22:32 203
18:7–9 213	20:21–23 451	22:37 .... 194, 210
18:8–9 317	20:26 451	22:32 202
18:10–14 .... 519, 536	20:29–34 ..... 463, 466, 474	22:37 202
18:10–35 201	20:30 211	22:37–39 202
18:12–14 .... 308, 515,	20:31 463	22:39 .... 194, 202
521, 522	20:33 463	22:44 202
18:15 444	20:34 .... 462, 473, 492	23 .... 212, 256
18:17 .... 188, 189, 204	21:1–23:39 199	23–25 197
18:20 204	21:1–25:46 195	23:1–39 45
18:21 .... 202, 211, 444	21:3 210	23:5 453
18:21–35 541	21:4 202	23:8 444
18:23 439	21:5 202	23:10 208
18:23–25 .... 184, 201, 453,	21:9 210	23:13 .... 213, 317, 449, 450
514, 521	21:13 .... 202, 254	23:15 35
18:23–35 .... 517, 539	21:14 468	23:16 192
18:27 473	21:16 202	23:23 382
18:30–35 213	21:18–22 466	24 .... 25, 179, 212, 213,
18:33 543	21:21–22 .... 316, 474	236, 495, 535
18:34 185	21:22 254	24–25 .... 433, 535
18:35 444	21:23–27 535	24:1–25:46 199
19–22 197	21:23–22:46 208	24:2 212
19:1 193	21:28 454	24:3 213

Reference	Pages
24:7	426
24:7–12	423
24:9	451
24:10	194
24:10–12	194
24:13	194, 316, 440
24:14	205, 206, 207, 457
24:15	112
24:20	254
24:24	461
24:29	202
24:30	194
24:31	194, 206
24:32–36	520
24:37–38	203
24:42	211
24:42–44	521
24:42–25:46	201
24:44	202
24:45–51	201, 514, 521
24:49	346
24:51	213
25:1	439
25:1–13	194, 201, 214, 514, 516, 521
25:10	213, 546
25:14–28	454
25:14–30	201, 214, 514, 516, 519, 521, 544, 545
25:16	454
25:19–23	213
25:31–46	201, 206, 213, 214, 424, 426, 444, 515, 516, 521, 546
25:32–46	543
25:34	208
25:34–40	213
25:36	478
25:37	211
25:40	444
25:41	447, 502
25:41–46	213
25:44	211
25:45	444
25:46	447
26–28	197
26:1–28:20	195
26:1–27:66	199
26:2	38
26:6–13	205
26:10	453
26:13	206
26:17	38, 39
26:20	265
26:25	184
26:29	207, 433
26:31	202
26:36	254
26:41	254
26:63–64	210
27:6	193
27:8	190
27:3–5	163
27:3–10	184
27:25	212
27:40	317
27:46	202
27:49	317
27:51–53	462
27:54	51, 206
27:62–64	408
27:62–66	201
28:1	40
28:1–20	199
28:2	51, 468, 462
28:5	468
28:9	290
28:10	444
28:11–15	184
24:14	249
28:15	190
28:16	462
28:16–20	290
28:17	211
28:18	452
28:18–20	10, 320, 374, 432, 456, 535
28:19	185, 190, 207, 374

Mark

Reference	Pages
1–8:26	
1:1	101, 153, 160, 178, 208
1:2	112
1:2–3	166
1:2–13	153
1:3	208
1:7–8	161
1:8	174
1:9	167
1:9–11	254
1:11	153, 208
1:12–13	165, 169
1:13	168
1:14	168
1:14–15	128, 153, 160, 169, 438, 532
1:14–8:29	155
1:15	172, 178, 316, 438, 439, 448
1:16	132, 162, 168, 518
1:16–20	161, 162, 164, 169, 171, 267
1:16–8:29	163
1:17	171, 356, 448
1:21–28	164, 201
1:21–34	168
1:22	161, 163, 175
1:23–24	161
1:23–26	466, 474
1:23–28	462
1:24	308
1:25	462
1:27	163
1:28	175
1:29–34	472
1:30–31	173, 466, 471, 474
1:32–33	164
1:32–34	462
1:34	163, 164, 462, 468
1:35–37	164
1:35–39	168
1:38–39	164
1:38–40	169

1:39 462	3:1-6 168	4:11-12 .... 165, 529
1:40 168	3:1 359	4:13-19 524
1:41 473	3:2-4 480	4:13-20 .... 520, 525
1:40-42 .... 466, 474	3:4 .... 317, 481	4:21-23 ....166, 174
1:40-44 254	3:6 175	4:21-25 .... 519, 520
1:40-45 271	3:7 163	4:22 124
1:41 462	3:7-12 168	4:23 143
1:44 .... 164, 462	3:9 163	4:24-25 166
1:45 ....164, 175	3:10 468	4:26 .... 439, 442, 514
2:1 168	3:10-12 462	4:26-29 .... 519, 520
2:1-12 481	3:11 ....153, 161, 208	4:26-32 441
2:2 163	3:12 ....164, 462	4:26-34 169
2:3-12 466	3:13 168	4:28 .... 442, 542
2:4 163	3:13-19 456	4:29 213
2:5 .... 112, 172, 293,	3:14 173	4:30 .... 439, 442
316, 462	3:15 452	4:30-32 .... 174, 234, 432,
2:5-7 175	3:16 .... 162, 354	519, 520, 525
2:6 163	3:16-19 .... 164, 254	4:31 514
2:9 519	3:17 46	4:35 .... 152, 153
2:9-10 161	3:18 ....46, 181, 182, 186	4:35-41 .... 161, 504
2:10 208	3:20 ....163, 168	4:36 163
2:12 161	3:21 .... 161, 168	4:37-41 466
2:13 ....163, 168, 169, 171	3:22 .... 163, 168, 175	4:38 161
2:13-14 ....164, 184, 185	3:22-27 ....515, 520	4:39 167
2:13-16 171	3:22-30 165	4:40 .... 172, 316, 474
2:13-17 ....161, 171, 186	3:23-27 234	4:41 462
2:14 ....171, 181, 182,	3:23-29 519	5:1 ....152, 168
186, 188, 356, 448	3:24 .... 443, 520	5:1-15 ....466, 474
2:15-16 188	3:25 520	5:1-20 171
2:16 .... 163, 175	3:31 168	5:7 153
2:17 ....164, 518	3:31-34 171	5:8 112
2:18 .... 168, 171	3:31-6:6 111	5:19 208
2:18-22 519	3:32 163	5:20 164
2:19-20 ....515, 520	3:33-35 519	5:21 .... 152, 163, 168
2:19-22 .... 165, 540	4 .... 155, 168, 518	5:21-43 ....173, 505
2:21 520	4:1 ....163, 168	5:22 .... 61, 473
2:21-22 515	4:1-9 520	5:22-24 466
2:22 ....309, 520	4:1-20 .... 165, 514, 516,	5:24 163
2:23 .... 167, 175	519, 522	5:25-29 466
2:23-28 168	4:1-34 164	5:27 163
2:23-3:6 ....165, 256	4:4 167	5:28-30 472
2:24 481	4:8 .... 163, 517	5:30 163
2:27 481	4:10-11 548	5:31 163
2:28 ....208, 481	4:10-12 529-32	5:34 ...... 172, 293, 462, 474
3:1-5 466	4:11 441	5:35 161

5:36 .... 172, 316, 474	6:47-51 .... 464, 504	8:22-26 .... 155, 162, 201,
5:37 .... 162, 354, 402	6:48-51 466	235, 462, 466,
5:38-42 .... 466, 471	6:48-52 162	472, 474
5:41 136	6:50 297	8:23 472
5:41-42 472	6:51 161	8:26 462
5:42 .... 161, 164	6:54-56 462	8:27 168
5:43 .... 164, 462	7 366	8:27-28 155
6 206	7:1 168	8:27-29 .... 162, 254
6:1 168	7:1-15 175	8:27-30 155
6:1-4 471	7:1-8:9 174	8:27-10:52 111
6:1-6 ..... 163, 234, 316, 473	7:1-23 .... 163, 165, 235	8:28 .... 162, 164, 308,
6:2 153	7:2-4 136	491, 497
6:5 .... 123, 460, 462, 468	7:4 374	8:29 .... 155, 156, 162, 190,
6:6 .... 168, 172, 462	7:7 112	208, 308, 462
6:6-13 236	7:14 163	8:29-33 354
6:7 .... 168, 452	7:15 143	8:30 .... 156, 164
6:7-11 174	7:16 143	8:31 .... 163, 178, 198,
6:7-13 ... 168, 205, 430, 456	7:17 163	289, 474
6:12-13 .... 174, 484	7:21 237	8:31-32 .... 156, 176
6:13 .... 461, 468	7:24 168	8:31-37 162
6:14 .... 162, 167, 295	7:24-30 ...... 173, 235, 466,	8:32-33 162
6:14-15 162	471, 474	8:33 165
6:14-16 155	7:24-8:9 173	8:34 .... 163, 171, 356, 448
6:14-29 .... 167, 261	7:31 .... 136, 168	8:34-36 171
6:14-44 168	7:31-37 .... 235, 462,	8:34-38 451
6:14-13:37 202	466, 474	8:35 .... 316, 440
6:15 .... 162, 164, 308,	7:33 163	8:38 174
491, 497	7:34 .... 5, 136	9-10 157
6:16 295	7:36 462	9:1 .... 179, 354, 433
6:17 27	8 506	9:1-13 .... 161, 178
6:23 426	8:1 163	9:2 168
6:30 168	8:1-9 .... 466, 503	9:2-8 254
6:30-34 .... 484, 503	8:1-13 484	9:5 .... 162, 233, 354
6:31 163	8:1-21 235	9:7 .... 153, 167, 208
6:32-34 464	8:2 .... 163, 462, 473, 492	9:9 .... 168, 176
6:34 .... 163, 462, 473, 492	8:4 484	9:13 167
6:35 484	8:5 39	9:14 .... 163, 168
6:35-44 466	8:6 163	9:14-29 461
6:37 .... 132, 165, 503	8:11 168	9:15 163
6:45 .... 152, 163	8:11-12 .... 293, 473	9:17 .... 161, 163
6:45-51 235	8:11-13 506	9:17-19 466
6:45-52 168	8:14 168	9:17-20 471
6:45-8:26 235	8:15 541	9:20 161
6:46 254	8:21 162	9:22 .... 473, 492
6:46-8:26 463	8:22 168	9:23 .... 172, 474

9:23-24 316	10:33 .... 163, 289	11:32 163
9:24 172	10:33-34 157	12 168
9:25 163	10:34 178	12:1-12 .... 177, 515, 518,
9:26 167	10:33-34 176	519, 520
9:29 254	10:35-45 .... 166, 266, 314	12:2-8 522
9:30 168	10:37-39 46	12:6 .... 153, 208
9:31 .... 176, 178, 289, 475	10:37-40 213	12:6-8 176
9:31-32 157	10:38-39 519	12:10-12 524
9:33 168	10:39 374	12:12 .... 163, 176, 177, 533
9:33-35 166	10:39-45 452	12:13-17 .... 46, 166, 271
9:36-37 166	10:41-45 266	12:14 .... 161, 163
9:38 161	10:42-45 451	12:15 132
9:38-41 468	10:43 451	12:16-17 519
9:41 208	10:43-45 208	12:18 212
9:42 .... 172, 316, 519	10:45 ....176, 475	12:18-27 ....166, 213
9:44 143	10:46 ....163, 168	12:19 ....161, 163
9:46 143	10:46-52 466	12:24-27 44
9:47-48 447	10:52 ..... 172, 293, 462, 474	12:28-34 166
9:47-50 166	11 37	12:28 163
9:49-50 234	11-12 165	12:29-30 33
9:50 520	11:1 168	12:29-31 .... 317, 382, 455
10 206	11:1-11 .... 157, 164	12:32 161
10:1 ....163, 168	11:8 163	12:34 449
10:1-12 .... 97, 166, 175	11:11 168	12:35-519
10:13-15 519	11:12 168	12:36-37 208
10:13-16 ....111, 166	11:12-14 466	12:37 .... 153, 163
10:14-15 .... 449, 451	11:12-19 164	12:39 266
10:16 377	11:12-25 165	12:40 ....254, 519
10:17 161	11:14-25 463	12:41 163
10:17-22 171	11:15 168	12:41-44. 165, 166, 173, 201
10:17-28 440	11:17 254	13 .... 25, 109, 138,
10:17-31 ....165, 166	11:18 ....163, 175	166, 168, 179, 201,
10:18 206	11:19 168	213, 236, 407, 519
10:19 171	11:20 168	13:1 ....36, 161
10:20 161	11:20-25 466	13:1-25 158
10:21 ....171, 269, 356,	11:21 .... 131, 162, 354	13:1-36 213
446, 448	11:22-24 ....172, 316,	13:2 138
10:23-25 ....449, 450	472, 493	13:2-4 179
10:25 519	11:23 519	13:3 .... 162, 354
10:28 ......162, 171, 354, 441	11:24-25 ....176, 254	13:4 213
10:28-30 444	11:26 143	13:5-8 179
10:29-31 .... 166, 171	11:27 ....163, 168	13:8 426
10:30 .... 213, 445, 451	11:27-12:34 176	13:10 .... 158, 173, 174, 179,
10:32 168	11:27-12:39 176	205, 206, 320, 457
10:32-33 475	11:30 519	13:11 174

13:12-23 179	14:28 159	15:26 .... 170, 452
13:13 .... 179, 440	14:29 162	15:28 143
13:14 .... 22, 112, 137, 519	14:29-31 158	15:29 .... 138, 305
13:18 254	14:29-37 354	15:31 ....163, 490
13:21 172	14:31 162	15:31-32 170
13:22 461	14:32 .... 168, 254	15:32 172
13:24-27 179	14:32-42 .... 159, 177,	15:34 .... 5, 136
13:25 346	254, 479	15:38 177
13:25-27 158	14:33 162	15:39 .... 132, 153, 170,
13:27 .... 174, 179	14:36 .... 5, 160, 172,	178, 208, 452
13:28-27 519	213, 519	15:40-16:8 173
13:28-30 179	14:37 163	15:41 251
13:28-32 .... 515, 520	14:38 254	15:43 .... 45, 449
13:30 179	14:43 .... 163, 177	15:44 132
13:32-34 179	14:43-45 177	15:45 132
13:33-37 234	14:47 177	15:46 135
13:34 .... 179, 454	14:48-50 177	16 178
13:34-36 520	14:51 126	16:1-4 178
13:35-37 179	14:51-52 132,177	16:2 40
14:1 .... 38, 39, 163, 177	14:53 163	16:5 135
14:1-9 .... 158, 177	14:53-59 177	16:6-8 .... 144, 178
14:3 168	14:54 162	16:7 .... 132, 147, 159,
14:5 132	14:58 .... 138, 305	162, 289
14:9 .... 173, 174, 179	14:60-64 177	16:7-8 163
14:10-11 .... 158, 177	14:61 .... 153, 208	16:8 .... 143, 144, 147, 148
14:12 .... 38, 39	14:61-62 169	16:9-20 ... 143, 145-46, 149
14:12-16 314	14:62 213	16:11-17 172
14:12-26 177	14:65 177	16:15-18 146
14:13 168	14:69 173	16:15-20 .... 310, 432, 456
14:14 161	14:72 131	16:16 316
14:17 168	14:66-72 .... 162, 177	16:16-17 316
14:17-18 265	15:1 163	16:18 484
14:17-21 314	15:1-15 .... 177, 179	
14:18-20 177	15:2 170	**Luke**
14:20-21 158	15:7 .... 170, 452	1-2 .... 224, 233, 238, 251
14:22-25 .... 177, 314, 519	15:8 163	1:1 .... 6, 115, 124, 223, 229
14:23-25 158	15:11 163	1:1-4 ..... 145, 232, 238, 248
14:24 176	15:12 170	1:2 .... 325, 326
14:25 433	15:13 170	1:2-3 377
14:26 168	15:15 163	1:3 .... 96, 215, 231, 321, 326
14:26-31 254	15:16-20 177	1:3-4 227
14:26-42 314	15:17-20 170	1:4 .... 96, 224
14:27 .... 158, 176, 289	15:21 177	1:5 .... 27, 237, 257, 258
14:27-28 178	15:22-37 177	1:6 258
14:27-31 177	15:24 369	1:8-10 257

1:10 258	2:29 369	4:15-16 247
1:11-19 468	2:29-32 258	4:15-30 359
1:11-21 242	2:32 232	4:16 258
1:14 259	2:36-37 371	4:16-17 480
1:15 246	2:38 258	4:16-20 256
1:17 246	2:41 38	4:16-30 244
1:21 246	2:41-49 243	4:18 .... 238, 247, 252, 340
1:23 257	3 .... 224, 374	4:18-19 .... 249, 312, 333,
1:26-38 .... 242, 468	3-4 .... 234, 238, 439	387, 498, 535
1:32 .... 243, 244	3:1 .... 27, 28, 237, 244	4:18-20 .... 239, 240, 249,
1:35 .... 244, 247	3:1-9:50 .... 234, 237	316, 439, 498
1:41 247	3:2 243	4:18-21 350
1:44 .... 246, 259	3:3 373	4:20-30 256
1:46-47 248	3:4 112	4:21 250
1:46-55 .... 243, 372	3:4-6 242	4:22-24 240
1:46-56 258	3:6 248	4:23 .... 512, 515, 521
1:47 .... 246, 259	3:8 405	4:23-30 540
1:56-66 242	3:12-13 187	4:25-27 248
1:58 258	3:15-22 397	4:27 374
1:64 258	3:16 .... 238, 247, 340,	4:31-32 244
1:66 258	350, 352, 373, 405	4:31 258
1:67 247	3:17 373	4:33 246
1:67-71 248	3:18 439	4:33-35 466
1:67-78 247	3:19 27	4:33-37 244
1:67-79 .... 258, 372	3:20 .... 27, 439	4:34 308
1:77 248	3:21 .... 254, 367	4:36 .... 246, 386, 464
1:78 473	3:22 .... 245, 247, 240	4:38-39 466
1:80 246	3:23-28 .... 10, 234	4:38-40 244
2:1 .... 237, 244	3:38 248	4:40 468
2:1-7 242	4 .... 246, 306, 312	4:41 245
2:2 89	4:1 .... 238, 247, 340	4:43 .... 243, 244, 438, 543
2:8-10 253	4:1-13 .... 169, 244, 502	4:44 258
2:9 244	4:2-3 386	5 .... 169, 266, 283
2:9-10 468	4:3 .... 243, 245	5:1 .... 15, 243
2:10 248	4:5 .... 386, 426	5:1-11 .... 267, 464, 467
2:13-14 .... 244, 372	4:5-13 239	5:8 258
2:13-15 468	4:7-8 372	5:11 245
2:14 258	4:9 .... 243, 245	5:12-13 466
2:20 .... 258, 259, 372	4:12 386	5:12-16 .... 254, 271
2:22-24 377	4:13 386	5:15 468
2:23-24 48	4:14 .... 238, 246, 247,	5:16 .... 254, 312, 367, 464
2:24 252	258, 312, 340	5:17 464
2:25-27 .... 247, 258	4:14-20 464	5:18-25 466
2:25-30 248	4:14-30 .... 234, 235, 239	5:18-26 482
2:28-32 372	4:14-9:50 234	5:20 474

5:21 243	6:37 453	8:2 .... 147, 251, 386, 464,
5:24 112	6:37-42 245	467, 468, 474, 483
5:25 258	6:38 .... 96, 346, 445, 446	8:2-3 251
5:26 .... 372, 461	6:39 520	8:3 295
5:27 .... 181, 245	6:41 520	8:4-8 520
5:27-32 .... 186, 245	6:43-45 .... 236, 520	8:10 441
5:28 187	6:43-45 520	8:11 243
5:29 .... 181, 182, 256	6:43-49 245	8:11-15 520
5:29-30 188	6:47-49 .... 514, 520	8:12 .... 248, 317, 387, 439
5:30 .... 245, 253, 256	6:48 346	8:16-17 541
5:30-32 249	7 .... 234, 235, 237, 468	8:16-18 520
5:33-39 520	7:1-10 .... 232, 234, 251,	8:17 124
5:36 520	295, 403, 404,	8:19-56 111
5:37-39 520	462, 464, 466	8:21 243
6 .... 123, 165, 234	7:9 474	8:22-25 .... 466, 504
6:1-3 243	7:11-15 .... 251, 467, 474	8:25 474
6:1-9 480	7:11-17 .... 234, 235,	8:27-35 466
6:1-11 256	402, 464, 505	8:28 245
6:5 481	7:12 252	8:29 112
6:6-10 466	7:13 .... 231, 464, 473, 492	8:40-56 .... 244, 504
6:9 481	7:16 .... 258, 259, 372	8:41 325
6:12 .... 254, 258, 367	7:18-23 161	8:41-42 466
6:12-16 .... 245, 464	7:18-35 234	8:42 252
6:14 186	7:21 .... 244, 386, 468, 483	8:43-48 466
6:15 .... 181, 182, 186	7:22 252	8:46 464
6:17-36 258	7:22-25 244	8:48 474
6:17-49 .... 234, 245, 455	7:24 346	8:49-56 466
6:18 386	7:28 514	8:50 474
6:18-19 468	7:29 188	9 440
6:19 464	7:29-30 187	9:1 .... 452, 464, 483
6:19-49 .... 125, 126, 169	7:33-35 256	9:1-6 .... 174, 236, 456
6:20 450	7:34 .... 188, 253	9:2 439
6:20-21 .... 252, 504	7:35 257	9:6 .... 461, 468, 484
6:20-26 245	7:36-38 258	9:7 295
6:20-36 .... 387, 388	7:36-50 .... 234, 245,	9:10-17 .... 235, 244,
6:20-49 ....239, 535	251, 256, 257	464, 503
6:21 259	7:37-50 253	9:11 439
6:22 244	7:41-43 539	9:12-17 466
6:22-23 389	7:41-50 .... 514, 521	9:13 387
6:24 253	7:44-48 258	9:18 .... 258, 367
6:24-25 504	7:48 243	9:18-20 254
6:28-29 367	7:50 .... 293, 316, 439, 474	9:18-51 111
6:28 .... 367, 390	8:1-3 ...... 94, 356, 380, 402	9:21-26 245
6:29-30 96	8:1-15 .... 244, 439	9:21-27 245
6:35 96		9:22 .... 242, 244

9:23 255	10:25-37 ....50, 235, 244,	12:7............................ 245
9:24 248	245, 251, 387, 396,	12:12 .... 247, 340
9:27 433	397, 514, 516, 517,	12:13-21 ....235, 244, 446,
9:28-29 254	521, 525, 537, 543	503, 514, 521
9:29 464	10:27............................ 372	12:13-34 .... 245, 387
9:35 .... 243, 245	10:30-37 ...... 248, 258, 523	12:16-21 .... 253, 544
9:36-48 245	10:33....................464, 473	12:19 508
9:37-42 244	10:33-35..................... 545	12:22............................483
9:37-43 483	10:34 478	12:28............................ 474
9:38-43 474	10:38-39 325	12:31............................440
9:38 252	10:38-42 .... 235, 245,	12:32-34......................444
9:38-43 466	251, 283	12:33............380, 503, 544
9:43 258	10:41-42 241	12:35-28.......................520
9:44 242	10:42 382	12:35-48....... 234, 245, 257
9:47 252	11................................506	12:39-40 521
9:51............. 239, 241, 246	11:1-4............... 236, 254	12:42-46 .... 514, 521
9:51-55 .... 248, 251	11:1-13.......... 245, 254, 367	12:54-56.......................521
9:51-56 .... 235, 396	11:2-4....................241, 433	12:50.................... 374
9:51-18:27 235	11:5-8 ....521, 545	13:1-2............................50
9:51-19:27 .... 195, 234, 240	11:6-13 254	13:1-5............................482
9:52 ....50, 237, 394	11:11-13 520	13:6-9...........235, 463, 512,
9:52-56......................397	11:13.................... 247, 340	515, 521
9:54 .... 46, 270	11:14............ 235, 462, 466,	13:10 258
9:57 171	474, 483	13:10-16 481
9:57-62............... 245, 255,	11:14-22 464	13:10-17 .... 235, 243,
388, 440	11:14-26 234	244, 251
9:59 356	11:14-27 244	13:11......................251, 483
9:60 439	11:16..............293, 473, 506	13:11-13 ....467, 468, 474
9:62 454	11:17............................520	13:11-15 467
10-19 520	11:17-20 443	13:13 .... 259, 372
10:1.............................355	11:18............................ 387	13:14 61
10:1-12....................... 456	11:20............................499	13:15............................. 481
10:1-24 ....174, 236	11:21-23 520	13:16 ....243, 387, 481
10:2 520	11:29............................294	13:18 442
10:9-11........................439	11:29-30 ......293, 473, 506	13:18-19 .... 441, 520
10:15 65	11:29-32 244	13:18-20 244
10:16 243	11:34-36 521	13:18-21 ....234, 251
10:17............244, 461, 468	11:37-52 45	13:20-21.................... 441
10:18..................386, 502	11:37-54 256	13:21 .... 39, 541
10:19............ 147, 452, 464	11:41............................ 258	13:22-30 259
10:20 386	11:48............................ 453	13:22-30 245
10:21..... 247, 252, 259, 340	11:49............................451	13:23 .... 248, 317
10:22 243	12:1........................ 39, 541	13:23-24......................440
10:25-31.......................317	12:2 124	13:23-27............... 515, 521
	12:4-6...................... 245	13:28............................405

13:28-29 448	15:10 453	18:8 474
13:28-30 .... 449, 450	15:11-32 .... 235, 256, 453,	18:9-14 .... 235, 245, 253,
13:29 500	516, 516, 521, 540	514, 516, 517, 521,
13:31-35 245	15:11-40 517	525, 539, 545
14 257	15:20 .... 464, 473	18:10-11 367
14:1-4 .... 467, 474	15:21 545	18:10-13 .... 188, 254
14:1-6 .... 464, 468	15:22 483	18:10-14 .... 537, 541, 544
14:3-5 481	15:23 259	18:11 253
14:5 481	15:32 259	18:11-13 452
14:8-11 266	16:1-12 244	18:12 .... 371, 382
14:8-20 255	16:1-15 544	18:13 545
14:12-24 .... 259, 453	16:1-31 387	18:13-18 328
14:13 .... 478, 479	16:1-8 521	18:15 377
14:13-24 387	16:10-11 253	18:15-17 .... 111, 252
14:15 500	16:10-12 524	18:15-43 111
14:16 542	16:13 372	18:15-24:53 234
14:15-24 .... 514, 521,	16:16 432	18:16 252
525, 538, 542	16:18 245	18:16-17 449
14:15-35 245	16:19-31 .... 235, 244,	18:18-27 253
14:16-24 519	253, 256, 257, 446,	18:18-29 440
14:21 .... 478, 479	514, 516, 516, 517,	18:18-30 .... 245, 387
14:23 251	521, 544, 546	18:21-33 245
14:24-30 235	16:8-9 544	18:22 .... 237, 380
14:25-33 255	16:22-30 405	18:24-25 .... 449, 450
14:26 255	16:23 65	18:26 248
14:26-33 440	17:2 252	18:28 441
14:26-34 388	17:2-3 145	18:31-33 242
14:28-30 521	17:5-6 .... 245, 474	18:35 237
14:28-32 .... 512, 543	17:7 543	18:35-43 .... 235, 466
14:28-33 514	17:7-10 521	18:42 474
14:31 426	17:10-19 397	18:43 .... 258, 372
14:31-33 521	17:11 .... 237, 394	19 239
14:33 .... 255, 380	17:11-14 271	19:1 237
14:34 520	17:11-15 467	19:1-10 .... 188, 234, 235,
14:34-35 234	17:11-17 244	252, 253, 387,
15 .... 240, 244, 253,	17:11-19 .... 235, 251, 396,	442, 449
519, 539, 543	464, 467, 468, 474	19:6 259
15:1 188	17:15 372	19:8-10 248
15:1-7 ..... 308, 516, 521, 536	17:16 .... 50, 248	19:9 405
15:1-10 .... 514, 543	17:19 .... 293, 474	19:9-10 317
15:3-10 251	17:20-37 245	19:10 .... 238, 240, 244, 249,
15:6-7 259	17:21 431	250, 253, 439, 543
15:7 .... 453, 537	17:25 242	19:11 231
15:8-10 .... 235, 516, 521	18:1-8 ... 235, 245, 254, 367,	19:11-13 454
15:9-10 259	512, 514, 521, 545	

19:11-27 .... 234, 245, 258, 514, 519, 521, 529, 544	22:51 464	1-14 271
19:28 231	22:54-62 403	1:1 .... 157, 280, 302, 436
19:28-39 258	22:69 244	1:1-5 .... 145, 288
19:37 380	22:70 243	1:1-18 .... 279, 288
19:37-39 372	23-24 335	1:2 291
19:40 258	23:8-12 .... 234, 236	1:2-3 294
19:43 138	23:24 243	1:3 .... 500, 505
19:43-44 228	23:26-43 234	1:3-4 .... 297, 306
19:45 258	23:47 .... 259, 372, 403	1:4 .... 305, 306
20-21 274	23:51 449	1:4-5 306
20:9-20 520	23:53 241	1:5 .... 281, 306
20:20-26 271	24 .... 236, 238, 319	1:6 .... 267, 279
20:27 212	24:1 40	1:6-9 289
20:37-38 243	24:1-49 246	1:6-3:36 288
20:45-21:4 245	24:4 464	1:7 316
21 .... 25, 179, 228, 246	24:7 242	1:7-8 306
21:1-4 253	24:9 457	1:9 306
21:10 426	24:10 251	1:12 .... 304, 316
21:12 451	24:13-32 .... 147, 234	1:14 .... 36, 302, 303, 305, 464
21:20-21 228	24:13-35 464	1:15 .... 267, 279
21:24 .... 228, 256	24:23 468	1:18 ...... 100, 280, 302, 303
21:26 340	24:18 325	1:19 311
21:29-33 520	24:19 .... 453, 497	1:19-20 289
21:38 274	24:21 245	1:19-28 50
22:1 .... 38, 39	24:25-27 243	1:19-42 279
22:1-5 246	24:26-27 377	1:19-51 .... 276, 279
22:3 .... 386, 387	24:32 .... 242, 377	1:21 .... 308, 423
22:7 .... 38, 39	24:34 .... 234, 464	1:25 308
22:14 265	24:36-49 464	1:26 309
22:16 504	24:44-45 243	1:29 .... 38, 303
22:16-18 433	24:44-47 377	1:29-35 289
22:22 242	24:44-53 .... 240, 327	1:29-38 289
22:24-27 266	24:46-49 ...... 147, 320, 321, 345, 366, 432, 456	1:31 309
22:24-30 ...... 258, 266, 314	24:49 .... 247, 334, 338, 340, 350, 351, 357	1:32-33 313
22:29-30 445	24:50-53 ....147, 234, 246	1:33 .... 309, 313
22:31 387	24:51 242	1:34 303
22:32 254	24:52 .... 259, 372	1:35-40 .... 270, 279
22:35-38 234	24:53 259	1:35-42 267
22:39-46 254		1:35-51 289
22:42 172	**John**	1:41 .... 281, 307
22:42-43 .... 445, 452	1 ... 169, 250, 267, 275, 288	1:42 267
22:43 468	1-11 271	1:43-45 279
22:50-51 ...... 467, 473, 474	1-12 288	1:43-51 267
		1:44 279

1:45-49 279	3:8 .... 313, 353	4:34 494
1:49 303	3:12-18 316	4:38 454
1:50 316	3:13 302	4:39-42 316
1:51 304	3:13-14 304	4:41-42 .... 307, 308
2 .... 285, 288, 299,	3:15-18 316	4:43-54 .... 280, 295
305, 309	3:15-19 307	4:46-50 .... 471, 472
2-11 275	3:16 .... 303, 317, 318	4:46-54 ...... 276, 282, 293,
2:1-11 .... 276, 280, 467,	3:16-18 449	465, 466
503, 504	3:17 .... 317, 440	4:48 .... 293, 461, 506
2:1-12 .... 293, 465	3:18 .... 303, 541	4:48-50 295
2:4 288	3:19 .... 281, 453, 494	4:53 .... 295, 316, 465
2:6 311	3:19-20 304	4:54 293
2:10 504	3:20 494	5 .... 275, 299, 300
2:11 ...... 293, 294, 316, 460	3:21 .... 306, 453, 494	5:1 .... 40, 299, 311
2:12 268	3:22 .... 299, 309, 311	5:1-4 295
2:12-25 279	3:22-24 268	5:1-9 .... 466, 473, 474
2:13 .... 38, 311	3:23-24 353	5:1-15 .... 280, 465
2:14-19 276	3:23-27 279	5:1-18 299
2:13-25 .... 37, 268	3:24 261	5:1-47 294
2:18 .... 293, 311, 506	3:28 307	5:2 271
2:18-20 382	3:30 289	5:2-9 276
2:18-22 165	3:31-36 277	5:3 274
2:18-22 294	3:34 .... 304, 313	5:6-8 465
2:19 .... 271, 305	3:35 317	5:7 309
2:19-22 305	3:35-36 307	5:9-10 312
2:20 .... 27, 36	3:36 316	5:9-18 481
2:22-23 316	4 .... 270, 282, 471, 540	5:10 311
2:23 .... 38, 293, 295,	4:1 279	5:15-16 311
316, 460	4:1-42 .... 280, 289	5:16 311
2:24 295	4:4-5 394	5:16-30 305
2:23-25 .... 293, 465	4:5 394	5:16-47 280
2:23-3:1 507	4:7 394	5:18 .... 281, 292, 302, 311
3:1 311	4:7-42 50	5:18-24 278
3:1-7 295	4:1-12:23 288	5:19-20 317
3:1-8 .... 45, 313	4:9 311	5:20 .... 293, 296, 317, 494
3:1-9 282	4:10-11 281	5:21 305
3:1-12 312	4:10-15 .... 282, 309	5:21-22 305
3:1-15 289	4:14 309	5:24 316
3:1-21 280	4:19 308	5:24-25 275
3:2 .... 293, 306	4:22 311	5:24-30 305
3:3 .... 281, 305, 353, 449	4:23-24 353	5:28-29 275
3:3-5 449	4:25 .... 281, 395	5:31-36 289
3:3-8 .... 282, 450	4:25-26 .... 307, 395	5:34 .... 281, 317
3:5 .... 281, 305, 449	4:26 .... 290, 292	5:35 306
3:5-6 353	4:32-45 268	5:36 .... 296, 493

5:38-47 316	6:51-58 .... 275, 277	7:50-51 282
5:39 311	6:52 311	7:53-8:11 .... 145, 274
5:39-47 271	6:53 304	8-9 .... 281, 292
5:42 317	6:53-58 305	8:1 274
6 .... 275, 281, 282, 292, 296, 300, 466	6:54-58 300	8:2 274
	6:60-65 .... 282, 465	8:3 274
6:1-4 294	6:60-66 289	8:4 274
6:1-13 296	6:61-70 296	8:6 274
6:1-14 .... 279, 503	6:62 304	8:7 274
6:1-15 464	6:63 353	8:8 274
6:1-20 260	6:67-69 294	8:9 274
6:1-25 276	6:68-69 289	8:10 274
6:2 293	6:69 .... 308, 316	8:10-11 274
6:4 .... 38, 300, 311	6:70-71 294	8:12 .... 281, 290, 297, 306, 312, 441
6:4-5 500	7 39	
6:5 279	7:1 311	8:12-58 280
6:5-13 466	7:1-51 280	8:16 304
6:8 279	7:1-10:21 300	8:18 .... 291, 292
6:14 .... 293, 308, 500	7:2 .... 39, 311	8:20 288
6:14-15 294	7:3 .... 293, 493	8:22 311
6:14-65 293	7:5 316	8:23 281
6:15 .... 155, 164, 398	7:7 494	8:24 .... 291, 292, 315
6:16-21 .... 235, 294, 464, 504	7:8-10 300	8:26 304
	7:11 311	8:28 .... 291, 304
6:16-24 .... 279, 297	7:13 311	8:30 316
6:19 309	7:15 311	8:31 316
6:19-21 466	7:20 299	8:31-59 312
6:20 .... 290, 292	7:21 .... 296, 297, 493	8:39 494
6:25-71 280	7:22-23 .... 312, 481	8:41 .... 293, 494
6:26 293	7:22-24 481	8:42 .... 304, 317
6:26-58 282	7:23 481	8:44 312
6:27 304	7:25-31 .... 297, 307	8:45-46 316
6:28-29 494	7:28 304	8:48 .... 50, 311, 312
6:29 .... 305, 316	7:30 288	8:48-52 299
6:30 .... 293, 506	7:30-49 312	8:51 281
6:30-31 .... 297, 305, 500	7:31 .... 293, 297, 307, 316	8:52 311
6:33-40 305	7:35 311	8:57 311
6:35 .... 281, 290, 305	7:37 313	8:58 .... 281, 291, 303
6:35-40 297	7:38 .... 281, 309, 313, 353	8:59 292
6:35-70 311	7:38-39 316	9 .... 282, 297, 301, 306, 466
6:41 .... 290, 311	7:39 313	
6:41-58 309	7:40 308	9-10:21 40
6:44 305	7:41 307	9:1-2 470
6:48 .... 281, 290	7:42 307	9:1-7 465
6:51 290	7:50 .... 45, 289, 295	9:1-8 276

9:1-12 482	10:33 .... 292, 302, 303, 311, 493	12:23 .... 289, 304
9:1-41 .... 278, 280, 294, 299	10:37 .... 304, 493	12:23-25 522
9:1-34 481	10:37-38 .... 293, 316	12:25 318
9:3 .... 297, 394, 493	10:38 .... 316, 493	12:27-28 289
9:5 .... 290, 297, 306	10:42 316	12:31-32 465
9:6 472	11 .... 282, 288, 292, 298, 466, 471	12:32-33 289
9:14-16 312	11-12 .... 277, 279	12:34 304
9:16 .... 293, 297	11:1-43 506	12:35 306
9:17 298	11:1-44 .... 280, 465, 466	12:36 306
9:18 311	11:1-45 .... 276, 298	12:37 .... 293, 316
9:19 306	11:1-57 294	12:38 289
9:22 .... 272, 310, 311	11:3 .... 264, 269	12:42 .... 272, 310
9:31-32 298	11:5 .... 264, 269, 317	12:42-46 316
9:35 304	11:10 304	12:44-50 277
9:35-38 .... 298, 304, 316	11:15 316	12:46 306
9:38 .... 289, 298, 303	11:16 279	12:47 .... 319, 440
9:40-41 298	11:19 311	12:49 304
10 .... 288, 292, 298, 518	11:25 .... 290, 298, 305, 506	13-14 315
10:1-18 .... 286, 308, 522	11:27 .... 289, 307	13-17 315
10:1-42 280	11:31 311	13-20 289
10:7 290	11:33 311	13:1 .... 289, 317
10:7-9 310	11:36 .... 269, 311, 317	13:1-2 317
10:9 .... 290, 317, 439	11:45 311	13:1-7 .... 280, 289
10:10 .... 305, 308	11:46 311	13:1-20 .... 276, 314
10:11 .... 290, 308	11:47 293	13:1-16:33 288
10:14 .... 290, 309	11:47-53 276	13:2 .... 265, 294, 465
10:15 304	11:54 311	13:6 265
10:17 317	11:54-12:9 312	13:8-10 309
10:19 311	11:55 311	13:15 312
10:20-21 299	12 289	13:18-38 279
10:22 .... 22, 301	12-15 271	13:19 .... 291, 292, 316
10:23-33 312	12:1-8 .... 276, 289	13:23 .... 261, 265, 317
10:24 .... 307, 311	12:1-11 279	13:23-24 267
10:25 .... 293, 298, 493	12:4 294	13:27 465
10:25-26 .... 307, 316	12:9-11 289	13:29 380
10:25-30 304	12:11 311	13:30 306
10:30 303	12:12-15 276	13:31 304
10:31 311	12:12-19 279	13:34-35 317
10:31-32 293	12:18 293	14 .... 275, 292, 298, 315
10:31-39 271	12:20-22 289	14-16 .... 313, 432
10:32-33 293	12:20-26 280	14-17 280
10:32-38 298	12:21-22 279	14:1-8 315
10:32 .... 304, 493	12:22 279	14:1-14 280
		14:5 .... 265, 279
		14:6 .... 65, 290, 310

14:8-9 279	16:14 .... 313, 353	19:31-34 289
14:9 265	16:15 314	19:32-35 265
14:9-10 310	16:17-33 .... 280, 315	19:34 309
14:9-14 315	16:27-31 316	19:35 .... 267, 316
14:10 494	16:33 451	19:38-42 289
14:10-12 316	17 .... 312, 316	19:39 ...... 45, 282, 289, 295
14:10-17:10 304	17:1 .... 289, 312	19:40 311
14:11 .... 298, 494	17:1-26 280	19:42 311
14:11-12 293	17:3 305	20:1 40
14:12 .... 298, 453, 493	17:4 494	20:1-21:23 279
14:15 317	17:8 316	20:1-18 289
14:15-31 .... 280, 315	17:11-12 312	20:2 ..... 265, 266, 267, 299
14:16 353	17:15 312	20:4-6 267
14:17 353	17:17 312	20:4-10 299
14:17-20 313	17:18 312	20:8 .... 265, 316
14:21 .... 317, 318	17:20-21 316	20:11-18 .... 147, 299
14:23-24 .... 317, 318	17:21-22 312	20:12 468
14:26 .... 313, 353	17:23 .... 317, 318	20:19 .... 40, 311
14:27 313	17:23-24 317	20:19-20 299
14:29 .... 315, 316	17:26 .... 274, 317	20:20 267
14:30 465	18 271	20:21 ..... 174, 320, 456, 457
14:31 .... 274, 315, 317	18-20 276	20:22 432
15 .... 292, 518	18:1 315	20:23 452
15-17 .... 277, 315	18:1-19:42 279	20:24-28 .... 279, 289, 299
15:1 290	18:1-21:25 288	20:24-29 282
15:5 290	18:5 291	20:25-31 316
15:1-7 286	18:6 292	20:28 .... 74, 281, 303
15:1-8 .... 280, 315, 522	18:8 291	20:30 .... 293, 460, 471
15:8-25 315	18:10 289	20:30-31 .... 275, 293,
15:9 317	18:14 .... 311, 312	299, 465
15:9-10 317	18:15 .... 261, 265	20:31 .... 287, 307, 317
15:9-16:4 280	18:19-24 289	21 .... 261, 266, 275,
15:11-12 317	18:28 312	277, 289, 357
15:13 318	18:31 .... 27, 41	21:1 15
15:17 317	18:36 .... 281, 305, 312	21:1-7 309
15:19 318	18:38 .... 291, 311	21:1-11 466
15:24 .... 293, 298, 494	19:6 289	21:1-14 .... 276, 289
15:26 .... 313, 353	19:7 .... 311, 312	21:1-23 280
16 275	19:12 .... 311, 312	21:2 279
16:2 .... 272, 310	19:14 38	21:3-4 306
16:5-15 315	19:17 289	21:7 265
16:5-16 280	19:20 289	21:15 261
16:7 351	19:25-27 289	21:15-18 401
16:8-11 .... 313, 353	19:26 265	21:15-19 403
16:13 .... 313, 353	19:31 312	21:16 261

21:16-19 318	1:16 .... 342, 378, 398	2:38 .... 351, 362, 363, 376
21:17 261	1:20 378	2:38-39 .... 334, 351, 374
21:19 271	1:21-22 377	2:38-41 375
21:20 .... 261, 264, 265	1:21-23 338	2:39 350
21:23 271	1:22 373	2:39-41 375
21:23-25 268	1:24-26 368	2:41 .... 361, 363, 375, 376
21:24 .... 264, 268, 269	1:26 354	2:42 .... 368, 373, 377, 379
21:24-25 270	2 .... 50, 246, 343, 349,	2:42-47 .... 331, 373
21:25 .... 145, 285	364, 402, 432	2:43 .... 373, 389, 461
Acts	2-3 401	2:44-45 380
	2:1 371	2:46 373
1 .... 238, 325	2:1-4 .... 39, 147, 247, 254,	2:47 .... 337, 351, 380, 389
1-7 237	334, 341, 343, 344,	3 .... 364, 389
1-8 33	350, 373, 397, 404	3:1 .... 354, 367
1-8:4 3	2:1-41 .... 313, 359	3:1-4 267
1-12 325	2:4 .... 352, 358, 457	3:1-6 354
1:1 .... 7, 96, 215, 231,	2:5 337	3:1-10 ... 147, 401, 484, 499
232, 321	2:10 398	3:6 338
1:1-2 321	2:11 337	3:8-9 .... 337, 380
1:1-8 335	2:11-41 354	3:11 267
1:1-11 ..... 236, 319, 321, 327	2:13 389	3:11-12 359
1:1-8:3 335	2:14-41 362	3:12 354
1:2 233	2:16 362	3:12-16 362
1:3 .... 336, 337, 338	2:17-20 326	3:12-26 338
1:4 341	2:17-21 .... 363, 378	3:13 .... 362, 363
1:4-5 338	2:20 337	3:13-14 362
1:5 .... 338, 352, 374	2:22 .... 337, 362, 363,	3:13-15 .... 337, 389
1:6 245	460, 461	3:14 363
1:8 .... 3, 173, 229,	2:22-39 .... 337, 338	3:15 .... 334, 362, 363
237, 238, 246, 249,	2:23 .... 243, 362, 363	3:17-18 389
308, 316, 322, 330,	2:24-31 362	3:18-26 .... 337, 362
332, 333, 334, 336,	2:25 .... 240, 346	3:19 363
341, 345, 357, 358,	2:25-28 .... 363, 378	3:20 363
366, 391, 393, 394,	2:27 65	3:21 362
397, 401, 407, 409,	2:30 327	3:22 362
432, 456, 457, 464	2:30-31 362	3:22-23 378
1:9 242	2:31 .... 65, 363	3:23 .... 363, 389
1:9-11 147	2:32 .... 334, 363	3:24 362
1:12 .... 338, 341	2:32-34 240	3:24-25 363
1:13 .... 182, 186, 189, 267	2:33 ...... 331, 350, 362, 363	3:25-26 378
1:13-26 354	2:33-36 362	3:26 .... 363, 389
1:14 .254, 250, 368, 371, 372	2:34 363	4 .... 325, 350, 360, 362,
1:14-16 345	2:34-35 278	381, 382, 402
1:15-19 163	2:36 363	4-5 .... 192, 256, 358
1:15-26 354	2:37 361	4:1 354

4:1-3 359	4:37 381	6:7 .... 327, 337, 361,
4:1-20 351	5 ...325, 346, 349, 362, 388	365, 370
4:2-3 390	5:1-2 386	6:8 337
4:4 .... 345, 361, 385	5:1-10 370	6:9 401
4:5-22 345	5:1-11 ... 346, 409, 483, 499	6:10 341
4:8 .... 247, 341, 342,	5:3 .... 383, 386, 407	7 .... 337, 356, 364, 378
352, 354	5:5 383	7-8 .... 192, 368
4:8-12 .... 338, 354	5:8 386	7:1-8:4 256
4:10 .... 337, 338, 362	5:9 331	7:2-50 363
4:11 .... 362, 378	5:11 .... 204, 331, 385	7:2-53 .... 362, 378
4:13 .... 267, 270, 341, 354	5:12 313	7:16 394
4:13-14 389	5:12-16 .... 346, 351, 370,	7:35 337
4:15-17 327	464, 484, 499	7:37 363
4:17-20 339	5:13 389	7:38 .... 204, 337
4:19 .... 267, 354	5:14 .... 361, 370	7:51 .... 352, 363
4:19-20 .... 335, 364, 405	5:15 .... 385, 401	7:52 363
4:19-30 389	5:16 .... 386, 499	7:54-60 .... 226, 334
4:20 .... 364, 365	5:17-40 351	7:54-8:1 364
4:21 337	5:17-42 370	7:54-8:3 390
4:23-30 369	5:18-19 370	7:55 240
4:23-5:16 371	5:18-21 360	7:55-56 337
4:24 .... 336, 337, 339	5:19 .... 337, 468	7:56 .... 240, 304
4:24-31 .... 337, 341	5:19-21 364	8 .... 246, 248, 308, 342,
4:25 .... 378, 398	5:29 .... 335, 339, 354,	375, 391, 454, 540
4:25-26 378	364, 405	8-11 346
4:26-5:16 408	5:29-32 337	8-12 .... 3, 237, 393, 409
4:27-28 243	5:31 .... 240, 331, 362, 363	8:1 204, 331, 390, 394, 405
4:29-30 .... 346, 370	5:32 .... 334, 350	8:1-4 ...... 351, 357, 358, 399
4:29-31 .... 335, 373, 464	5:34-40 327	8:1-17 .... 344, 366
4:29-5:16 254	5:37 50	8:3 .... 204, 331, 390
4:29-5:42 457	5:29-32 360	8:4 .... 332, 335, 365, 393
4:30 .... 339, 351, 364,	5:41 390	8:4-7 360
369, 484	5:42 .... 339, 358, 360,	8:4-25 .... 50, 359, 393
4:31 .... 247, 313, 334, 337,	364, 373, 390	8:4-40 .... 355, 358
341, 343, 349, 350,	6 .... 356, 358, 370	8:4-12:25 335
351, 352, 360, 404	6-7 .... 346, 355	8:5 .... 338, 394
4:32 370	6:1 .... 356, 373	8:5-7 484
4:32-37 .... 346, 381	6:1-2 380	8:5-25 .... 241, 391
4:32-5:11 351	6:1-4 381	8:6 394
4:32-5:16 351	6:1-7 369	8:6-12 396
4:33 .... 338, 370	6:1-8:4 325	8:7 .... 386, 396, 499
4:34-35 381	6:2 .... 337, 365, 381	8:7-8 346
4:34-37 370	6:3 618	8:8 .... 361, 394
4:36 .... 37, 252, 385	6:4 .... 355, 365, 369	8:9 69
4:36-37 400	6:5 358	8:9-11 396

8:9-24 351	9:17-19 .... 346, 347, 400	10:9 .... 367, 371
8:12 .... 337, 338, 347	9:18 .... 347, 375, 376	10:9-16 403
8:12-13 .... 375, 376, 396	9:19-21 399	10:17-23 404
8:14 .... 267, 337, 375, 394	9:19-22 349	10:19 .... 342, 360
8:14-17 .... 397, 406	9:20 .... 337, 339, 347	10:22 .... 327, 337, 468
8:14-24 457	9:20-22 341	10:24-29 404
8:16 .... 339, 352	9:20-30 351	10:30-31 .... 327, 367
8:17 .... 247, 334, 343, 346,	9:22 339	10:30-33 404
350, 352, 371,	9:22-30 325	10:31 337
375, 404, 461	9:23-25 400	10:34-42 362
8:18 .... 346, 349	9:26 .... 328, 400	10:34-43 .... 338, 404
8:18-24 396	9:27 400	10:34-46 337
8:22-23 378	9:27-30 349	10:34-48 457
8:25 394	9:28-29 401	10:36 331
8:26 .... 337, 398, 468	9:29 400	10:37 373
8:26-40 .... 391, 397	9:29-30 401	10:38 .... 247, 249, 340,
8:27 398	9:30 .... 359, 361, 401	350, 363, 386
8:29 .... 313, 341, 360, 398	9:30-11:19 391	10:39 334
8:36 .... 375, 376	9:31 .... 204, 331, 394, 401	10:40-41 363
8:36-38 .... 375, 398	9:32 401	10:41 334
8:38 375	9:32-35 484	10:44 .... 334, 338, 352,
8:39 331	9:32-42 401	397, 404
8:39-40 .... 360, 398	9:33-35 402	10:44-46 347
9 .... 246, 251, 346,	9:34 .... 339, 402	10:44-48 .... 247, 344, 375
366, 399, 454	9:35 402	10:45 .... 343, 352, 404
9-12 335	9:39 402	10:45-48 376
9-28 336	9:40 371	10:46 .... 404, 456
9:1-2 399	9:41-42 402	10:46-47 350
9:1-16 339	10 .... 236, 246, 327,	10:47 .... 352, 363, 373, 404
9:1-18 457	350, 364, 366,	10:47-48 .... 375, 376
9:1-27 376	397, 402, 405	10:48 .... 339, 363
9:1-22 344	10-11 .... 251, 357, 366,	10:49 363
9:1-28 325	373, 398	11 .... 366, 382, 413
9:1-31 .... 335, 399	10:1-2 .... 61, 403	11-15 355
9:2 .... 240, 310	10:1-48 366	11-28 339
9:3-4 399	10:1-11:18 .... 335, 402	11:1 337
9:7-9 399	10:2 367	11:1-3 405
9:8 399	10:2-4 337	11:4-11 405
9:10 383	10:2-7 403	11:5 371
9:10-16 400	10:3-4 342	11:8 339
9:11 371	10:3-7 337	11:12-13 495
9:13 400	10:3-23 254	11:12-14 405
9:15-17 313	10:4 .... 367, 468	11:13-14 327
9:17 .... 274, 350, 371, 397	10:4-5 217	11:13 468
9:17-18 .... 334, 343, 404	10:7 468	11:14 358

11:15 .... 343, 347	12:11–12 408	13:23 .... 339, 363
11:15–16 405	12:12 ...... 126, 133, 261, 370	13:23–24 339
11:15–17 347	12:12–13 379	13:24 .... 362, 373
11:16 .... 339, 350, 352, 373, 374	12:15–17 408	13:27 339
11:17 .... 339, 405	12:19–23 324	13:29 363
11:17–19 337	12:20 .... 23, 28	13:31 334
11:18 405	12:20–23 .... 384, 409	13:32 379
11:19 .... 332, 335, 406	12:23 .... 337, 468	13:32–39 243
11:19–20 398	12:24 .... 337, 361	13:33 .... 339, 363, 378
11:19–21 .... 357, 359, 391	12:24–25 409	13:34 .... 363, 378
11:19–22 194	12:25 .... 126, 133, 261	13:34–35 391
11:19–23 366	12:25–15:35 325	13:35 .... 363, 378, 379
11:19–26 195	13 .... 37, 364, 412	13:38 .... 339, 363
11:19–30 ...... 195, 325, 335	13–21 373	13:47 378
11:20 339	13–28 .... 3, 237, 349, 366, 393, 409, 416	13:38–39 .... 218, 328
11:20–21 136	13:1 ...... 194, 204, 220, 398	13:41 .... 378, 379
11:21 .... 339, 361, 406	13:1–2 .... 331, 373	13:43 337
11:21–22 406	13:1–3 .... 59, 194, 369, 371	13:44 339
11:22 .... 204, 331	13:1–12 410	13:44–45 362
11:23 337	13:1–14:28 410	13:46 337
11:23–24 ....339, 406	13:1–28:31 335	13:46–47 391
11:24 406	13:2 .... 339, 342, 369	13:47 .... 340, 379
11:25–26 406	13:2–3 371	13:48–49 339
11:26 .... 204, 331, 406	13:3 369	13:49 .... 59, 358, 361, 365, 391
11:26–30 .... 382, 411	13:5 .... 133, 261, 337, 359	13:49–51 391
11:27–30 .... 133, 324, 328, 407	13:6–37 337	13:50–52 362
11:28 .... 25, 51, 333, 383	13:6–41 359	13:52 ..... 247, 343, 348, 350
11:30 .... 325, 328	13:7 337	14 364
12 .... 28, 354, 362, 370, 401	13:7–12 89	14:1 .... 358, 359
12:1 .... 204, 331, 364, 413	13:8–10 .... 387, 499	14:3 340
12:1–2 ... 226, 334, 356, 407	13:8–11 384	14:5–6 362
12:1–10 391	13:9 .... 342, 352	14:8 484
12:1–19 354	13:9–11 409	14:8–11 499
12:2–10 373	13:11 339	14:8–18 358
12:3–4 38	13:12 339	14:11–13 79
12:3–5 408	13:13 .... 134, 261, 411	14:12 .... 64, 66
12:5 .... 204, 331, 337, 370	13:14 400	14:13 68
12:6–9 408	13:14–15 480	14:14 354
12:7 337	13:14–43 359	14:15 363
12:7–11 .... 337, 468	13:15 61	14:15–18 .... 360, 362
12:10 408	13:16–41 .... 327, 362	14:19 .... 37, 362, 391
12:11 337	13:16–23 363	14:22 337
	13:17–22 378	14:23 .... 204, 331, 340, 369, 371
	13:22 363	

14:26 .... 194, 337	16:5 .... 204, 331	17:18 .... 83, 358
14:26-27 59	16:6-7 313	17:22-31 .... 327, 362
14:27 .... 204, 331, 337	16:6-9 .... 342, 360	17:23 79
15 .... 230, 328, 335, 366, 401, 405, 407, 411	16:7 .... 331, 339	17:23-31 337
	16:10 337	17:24 .... 336, 337, 363
15:1-35 410	16:10-17 .... 217, 221, 222, 322	17:28 .... 85, 363
15:4 331		17:29-30 363
15:1-2 194	16:11-14 61	17:30 .... 362, 363
15:1-5 357	16:11-15 .... 56, 252	17:31 363
15:1-12 219	16:13 .... 37, 356	17:31-32 340
15:1-19 325	16:14 .... 61, 92, 337, 340, 356, 367	17:34 .... 356, 360
15:3 204		18 94
15:4 .... 204, 328, 331, 337	16:14-15 376	18:1 337
15:5 45	16:15 .... 62, 219, 340, 358, 375, 376	18:2 .... 25, 141, 324, 355
15:7 323		18:4 .... 358, 359
15:7-11 354	16:16 .... 65, 367	18:4-6 391
15:7-14 337	16:16-18 ....79, 465, 484, 499	18:5 339
15:7-8 349		18:6 .... 362, 391
15:8 347	16:16-39 391	18:7 ....61, 219, 337
15:10 386	16:16-40 362	18:7-8 ....359, 391
15:11 340	16:17 64	18:8 .... 61, 62, 340, 358, 375, 376
15:13-21 226	16:18 340	
15:16-17 378	16:19-40 226	18:9 339
15:18 405	16:25 .... 337, 346	18:11-17 227
15:20 333	16:25-26 358	18:12-17 391
15:22 204	16:29-33 376	18:12 89
15:22-23 194	16:31 .... 328, 340, 358	18:12-17 362
15:22-35 222	16:31-34 62	18:13 337
15:26 340	16:32 339	18:17 61
15:30 194	16:33 .... 375, 376	18:18 .... 219, 355
15:35 194	16:33-34 337	18:18-19 355
15:35-36 339	17 364	18:19 .... 219, 359
15:36-40 231	17:1 222	18:22 .... 194, 204, 328, 331, 401
15:36-41 ....357, 401	17:1-2 359	
15:36-18:22 .... 410, 411	17:2-3 359	18:23-20:16 .... 410, 413
15:37 .... 133, 261	17:3 339	18:24 398
15:38 134	17:4 .... 337, 356	18:24-19:1 65
15:39 .... 133, 134	17:5-8 391	18:25 .... 167, 240, 339, 340, 373
15:40 340	17:5-9 .... 226, 362, 391	
15:41 .... 204, 331	17:7 339	18:26 ....61, 252, 337, 355, 359, 374
16 342	17:10 359	
16:1 37	17:12 356	18:28 339
16:2-3 37	17:13 ....337, 346	19 .... 284, 350
16:3 .... 219, 359	17:17 359	19:1-5 289
16:4 .... 376, 411	17:17-31 360	19:1-10 376

19:1-20 .... 344, 361	20:17-26:32 .... 410, 414	23:12 400
19:1-41 457	20:19 340	23:15 400
19:3 167	20:20 337	23:23-24 87
19:3-4 373	20:21 .... 339, 340	23:23-27:1 401
19:5 .... 340, 348, 375, 376	20:23 342	23:30 400
19:5-6 374	20:24 .... 337, 340	24:3 232
19:6 ...... 246, 334, 343, 348, 350, 397, 454	20:27 337	24:14 .... 243, 337
	20:28 .... 204, 331, 337	24:23 403
19:7 339	20:35 340	24:24 339
19:8 .... 337, 359	21 27	25:3 400
19:8-9 391	21-28 227	25:12 391
19:9 .... 310, 333, 391	21:1-18 .... 217, 221, 322	25:13-22 327
19:10 .... 59, 241, 339, 348, 365, 391	21:4 342	25:14-26:32 28
	21:8 .... 226, 365	25:19 340
19:10-20 .... 349, 358	21:8-16 401	26 .... 364, 365, 454
19:11 .... 484, 499	21:10 167	26:1-23 362
19:11-19 346	21:10-11 407	26:7-8 337
19:12 .... 386, 465, 499	21:13 340	26:10 .... 390, 399
19:14 340	21:16 398	26:14 183
19:17 340	21:17 328	26:14-18 400
19:18-19 79	21:17-18 325	26:16 334
19:20 .... 339, 365, 391	21:19 .... 222, 337	26:18 .... 337, 386
19:21-40 .... 352, 362	21:20 337	26:20 337
19:21-41 226	21:21 540	26:21 400
19:23 240	21:31 400	26:22-23 243
19:32-41 391	21:38 50	26:23 .... 28, 340, 363
19:23-41 79	21:40 183	26:25 232
19:24-25 65	22 .... 233, 364, 365, 454	26:29 337
19:27 68	22:1-21 362	26:30-32 327
19:32 204	22:2 183	27 .... 88, 228, 325
19:35 68	22:3-21 23	27:1 222
19:39 204	22:4 390	27:1-2 398
19:41 204	22:5 399	27:1-28:16 .... 88, 217, 221, 222, 321
20:1-3 87	22:8 340	
20:3 400	22:8-21 339	27:1-43 493
20:4 .... 37, 413	22:12-16 400	27:1-28:31 .... 410, 414
20:5 222	22:14 .... 337, 363	27:2 222
20:5-16 .... 217, 221, 322	22:14-16 400	27:9 371
20:6 39	22:15 334	27:23 .... 337, 468
20:7 .... 40, 373	22:20 334	27:25 337
20:9 484	22:26 403	27:35 337
20:9-10 402	23-26 27	28 233
20:13 .... 87, 217, 241, 322	23:8 44	28:1-6 147
20:16 39	23:10 398	28:7-10 499
20:17 .... 204, 331	23:11 .... 339, 391	28:14-16 87

28:15 337	15:24-26 51	4:17 220
28:23 .... 337, 339	15:24-31 388	5:6 385
28:28 337	15:25 328	5:6-8 .... 39, 541
28:28-31 232	15:26 445	5:7 38
28:30-31 .... 124, 227, 335, 337	15:26-28 382	6:1-8 97
28:31 .... 225, 339, 415	15:31 382	6:19 .... 69, 312, 382
	16 .... 141, 413	7 97
Romans	16:1 .... 88, 92	7:5 386
1-8 328	16:1-2 .... 94, 402	7:13-16 62
1:8 174	16:3 .... 92, 94, 221, 355	7:17 358
1:16 391	16:3-5 61	8 72
2 85	16:5 .... 94, 220	8-10 69
2:6 446	16:8 .... 147, 220	8:4 33
3:29 404	16:9 .... 220, 221	8:5 77
3:30 33	16:12 220	8:6 33
4 177	16:13 139	9 93
5:8 317	16:14 .... 61, 66	9:1-5 93
6 77	16:15 61	9:5 .... 137, 401
6:23 384	16:21 221	9:19-22 .... 218, 219
8:1-17 353	16:23 61	10:14-22 93
8:1-27 312	16:20 .... 220, 223	10:20 79
8:9 432	16:21 220	10:24-11:1 392
8:16 349	16:22 3	10:28 79
8:22 501	16:23 .... 92, 94	11 72
8:19-23 .... 208, 443, 451, 469, 479, 500		11:1 356
	1 Corinthians	11:28 .... 483, 499
8:26 349	1:1 3	11:29-30 384
8:35 445	1:10 323	11:30 409
8:37 477	1:10-17 62	12-14 .... 312, 349, 432
9-11 .... 141, 256	1:10-11 .... 941:1161	12:1-3 349
10:9 349	1:12 .... 65, 137, 354	12:1-31 353
11 310	1:12-17 376	12:3 349
12 432	1:22 .... 293, 507	12:7 454
12:3-8 353	1:26 92	12:9 485
12:4-8 312	1:30 161	12:10 100
12:13 387	3:2-15 446	12:28 349
12:20 387	3:4-6 65	12:28-29 167
13:8-10 317	3:11 340	12:30 485
14-15 94	3:16 .... 69, 312, 382	12:31-13:13 349
14:5 40	3:22 65	13 .... 317, 495
15:4 11	4:6 65	13:1 343
15:19 .... 59, 87, 484, 222, 461, 484	4:11 445	13:3 445
	4:13 68	13:8-9 495
15:24 328	4:16 356	14 .... 69, 343, 349
		14:1 343

14:2 343	11:14 460	4 432
14:3 343	11:7–9 94	4:5 374
14:4 343	11:25 88	4:6 33
14:5 .... 343, 349	11:32–33 400	4:11 312
14:7–10 343	12:1–4 477	4:11–12 454
14:14 343	12:2 398	4:11–16 ....353, 358
14:16 343	12:4 398	4:27 387
14:18 .... 347, 349	12:7 479	5:5 417
14:23 343	12:7–9 476	5:9 542
14:26 100	12:11–12 461	5:18 352
14:29–32 167	12:12 .... 460, 461, 484	5:21–6:9 53
15 ....77, 98	13:14 191	6:2 476
15:7–8 368		6:7 454
15:12–19 508	**Galatians**	6:10–17 479
15:23 506	1:18 .... 328, 354	6:11–17 502
15:26 .... 469, 479, 506	1:18–2:10 325	6:12 238
15:32 508	2–3 328	6:21 220
15:50–54 479	2:1 328	
15:50–57 506	2:1–10 382	**Philippians**
15:55–57 451	2:3 .... 219, 407, 411	1 .... 141, 142, 227
16 413	2:7–8 401	1:11 491
16:1–3 382	2:7–14 354	1:12–13 .... 358, 365
16:1–4 388	2:10 388	1:12–14 ....227, 391
16:2 .... 40, 51, 373	2:11 .... 59, 140, 194	1:19–26 227
16:8 39	2:11–14 .... 230, 323, 357	2:1–11 172
16:12 65	2:11–15 323	2:3 385
16:16 62	3 177	2:5–8 446
16:19 355	3:5 484	2:5–11 191
	3:13 .... 170, 437	2:6 436
2 Corinthians	3:20 33	2:25 .... 66, 88, 221
1:1 3	3:27–28 411	2:25–30 221
1:21–22 312	4–5 312	2:27 494
2:11 386	4:10 .... 38, 40	3:4–6 44
2:12 222	5:9 .... 39, 385, 541	3:8–10 106
2:15 541	5:14–25 317	3:10 390
4:4 542	5:22–23 542	3:12 501
5:17 500	5:22–25 353	3:17 356
6:3–10 70	6:15 500	3:21 479
6:4–10 502		4:2–3 ....94, 252
6:5 445	**Ephesians**	4:3 221
6:16 69	1:13 350	4:9 356
8–9 .... 51, 96, 382, 388, 413	1:13–14 312	4:10–20 .... 94, 96
8:9 446	2:1–3 542	4:11–12 445
8:23 221	2:20 167	4:14–19 94
9:7 47	2:21 .... 69, 382	4:22 ....88, 91

Colossians

1:6 .... 174, 361, 365, 413
1:7 .... 220, 348
1:13 417
1:15–29 191
1:16 .... 302, 500, 505
1:24 390
2:9 191
2:16 .... 38, 40
2:23 40
3:13 453
3:18–4:1 53
3:23 454
4 .... 217, 228
4:5 454
4:6 358
4:7 .... 88, 220
4:10 .... 131, 134, 139, 126, 133, 223, 357
4:11 223
4:14 .... 220, 222, 325, 126, 219, 223, 230, 322
4:15 .... 56, 61, 92, 94, 358

1 Thessalonians

1:8 59
3:2 .... 88, 221
4:17 398

2 Thessalonians

2:1–10 74
2:2 346
2:9 461

1 Timothy

2:9 442
3:16–17 11
5 388
5:15 386
6:8 503

2 Timothy

1:2 220
2:9 365

2:15 10
2:20 7
2:26 386
3:11 37
4:5 365
4:10 542
4:11 .... 133, 134, 219, 221, 223, 322, 357
4:19 355

Philemon

1 .... 92, 94, 220, 221
2 61
10–16 220
22 .... 61, 94
24 .... 126, 131, 133, 134, 139, 219, 221, 222, 223, 229, 322, 325, 357
25 230

Hebrews

1:1–3 157
1:2 .... 302, 500
1:3 505
2:4 461
7:1–10 382
9:9 518
9:20 374
10:1–18 382
11:19 518
11:28 38
12:26–27 346
12:29 386

James

1:27 388
2:2–6 445
2:19 33
4:7 387
5:14–16 485
5:16 371

1 Peter

1 345

1:1 .... 348, 354, 361
2:9 382
3:1–2 .... 62, 392
3:15 358
4:12–16 .... 390, 391
4:16 406
4:17 385
5:8 387
5:13 .... 131, 133, 134, 139, 223, 354

2 Peter

3 231
3:15–16 .... 230, 323

1 John

1:1–3 310
3–4 317
3:16–17 317
3:16–18 388
4:2–3 278
4:8 318

Jude

23 398

Revelation

1:1 468
1:10 .... 40, 373
1:13 304
1:18 65
2 7
2–3 .... 348, 361, 413
2:6 355
2:13 335
2:15 355
2:17 500
6:8 65
6:10 369
10:7 167
11:15 417
12:5 398
12:10 417
13 28
13:13 461

Reference	Page
14:13	530
14:14	304
17:4	442
17:6	460
18:12	442
18:16	442
20:1–6	424
20:10	502
20:13	65
20:14	65
21	505
21–22	208, 291, 315, 500
21:1–4	479, 500, 501
21:4	510
21:21	442
21:22	69
22:1	468
22:6	468
22:8	468

Apocrypha

Tobit

Reference	Page
1:10–11	403
2:10	470
3:10	65
6:7	470
8:1–3	470
11:8	470

Judith

Reference	Page
10:5	403
12:2	403

The Wisdom of Solomon

Reference	Page
1:14	65
3:8	420
10:10	418

Sirach

Reference	Page
1:8	419
9:12	65
28:23	390
38	470
38:15	470
48:10–11	423
50:26	394

Baruch

Reference	Page
2:17	65
4:7	79
4:36–37	424
5:5–9	424

1 Maccabees

Reference	Page
1:62–63	48
4:46	166
4:52–59	40
9:27	166
14:41	166

2 Maccabees

Reference	Page
5:22–23	394
5:27	403
6:2	394
6:18–25	403
6:23	65

3 Maccabees

Reference	Page
4:8	65
5:13	422
6:13	422
6:15	422

Pseudepigrapha

Apocalypse of Daniel

Reference	Page
2.15	406
8.6	406
12.8	406
13.7	406
14.4	406
14.6	406
14.8	406
14.9	406
14.13	406

Assumption of Moses

Reference	Page
10.1	418

2 Baruch

Reference	Page
27–30	424
29.4	500
29.7–8	500
36–40	323
39.7–40.2	424
53–74	424
70.2–8	423
73	418

1 Enoch

Reference	Page
1.2	308
6–11	470
10.11–15	499
37–71	156, 161, 244, 304, 423
45.3	424
46.4–6	425
46.1–6	424
46.4–6	424
48.2–6	424
52.4–9	424
53.6	424
54–55	499
55.4	424
61.8–10	424
62.3–12	425
62.5–7	424
62.3–12	424

62.12-16 425	**Joseph and Aseneth**	3.652-56 .... 423, 424
63.4 425	10.10-13 448	3.663-68 424
69.27-29 .... 424, 425	**Jubilees**	3.704-706 424
71.15-17 425	1.29 424	3.796-808 423
90.16 424	10.12 470	7.139 369
90.16-38 424	23.26-30 424	**Testament of Judah**
90.18-19 424	**Letter of Aristeas**	13.5 442
4 Ezra	49 232	**Testament of Levi**
6.23 423	**Odes of Solomon**	4.1 65
7.26 424	18.3 418	8.12 369
7.28-29 425	23.12 418	9.14 541
9.1-12 423	**Psalms of Solomon**	18.12 499
12.32 424	8.6 65	**Testament of Reuben**
12.32-33 424	12.7 422	4.6 65
12.32-38 424	15.10 65	**Testament of Abraham**
13.29-31 423	17 49	17.5 490
13.33-43 424	17.1-4 424	19.7 490
13.39-47 424	17.4 418	**Testament of Moses**
14 42	17.4-41 424	1.18 424
Greek Apocalypse of Ezra	17.5 423	9.6-7 424
1.6 406	17.22 422	10.1 424
2.7 406	17.23-32 423	10.1-2 499
5.1 406	17.25 424	10.2-7 424
4.32 65	17.36 422	10.7-10 424
History of the Rechabites	**Sibylline Oracles**	**Testament of Solomon**
12.9 318	1.81 65	18.34 541
	3.49 423	
	3.423 424	

Dead Sea Scrolls

1QapGEn	19.1-2 423	**4Q40**
20.12-29 470	**1QS**	I.2.2 419
1QM	1 381	**4Q200**
12.7 425	3.5 419	6.5 419
12.9 423	5.3 369	**4Q265**
15-19 424	6.16 369	VI.6-8 480
19.1 424	9.11 423	

ANCIENT TEXTS INDEX

4QTestim
5–8 .... 308, 423

11QMelch 499

CD
10.14–11:18 480

Rabbinic Sources

b. Ned.
41a 482

b. Sanh.
98b 423

m. Ber.
2.2 419
2.5 419

m. Mid.
3.8 315

y. Ber.
4a 419
7b 419

Josephus

Against Apion
1 42
1.1 224
1.1–5 248
1.217 232
1.209 480

Jewish Antiquities
3.227 541
3.320–21 407
4.290–91 398
5.43 369
5.248 541
6.61 369
6.332 65
7.396 369

8.44 512
8.44–46 470
11.340–47 394
12.10 394
12.256 390
13.297 43
15.120–21 51
15.395 315
18:11–15 44
18.16–17 44
18.29–30 395
18.63 .... 43, 422
18.64 406
20.38–48 448
20.51–53 383
20.118 395
20.195 61

20.199 43
20.200 ...... 43, 225, 335–36
20.214 156

Jewish War
1.370 51
2.119–35 47
2.136 470
2.156 65
2.184–203 73
2.278 390
3.388–91 369
3.443–44 156
5.210 315
7.23–24 156
7.43 194

Philo

Creation (Opif.)
66 541

Confusion (Conf.)
99 512

Dreams (Somn.)
1.254 308
2.210 541

Embassy (Legat.)
235 65
353 63

Flaccus (Flacc.)
43 50

Heir (Her.)
179 368

Joseph (Ios.)
196 541

Moses (Mos.)
1.195 65
2.215 480

Good Person (Prob.)
85–88 381

Posterity (Post.)	*Rewards (Praem.)*	**Spec. Laws (Spec.)**
31 65	28 424	1.175 541
		1.289 541

Apostolic Fathers

1 Clement

13:2 216	48:4 216

2 Clement

13:4 217

Didache

1:1 194	3:7 194	16:4 194
1:2 194	8:2 194	16:5 194
1:3 194	9:5 194	16:6 194
1:4 194	11:7 194	16:7–8 194
1:8 194	16:1 194	

Diognetus

2.6 406	5 392
2.10 406	6.6 406

Ignatius

Ephesians

14.2 189

Magnesians

4.1 406

Smyrna

6.1 189

Polycarp

2.2 189

Martyrdom of Polycarp

12.1 406

Apostolic Constitution (Const. Ap.)

Other Greek Texts

Aeschylus

Agamemnon (Ag.)
512..............................308

Callimachus

Hymnnus in Delum
166 308

Cicero

De Republica (Rep.)
6.13............................. 98

Clement of Alexandria

Hypotyposes 130

Paedagogus (Paed.)
2.1.............................. 189

Stromata (Strom.)
4.9 ....189, 192

Codex justinianus
9.4.............................. 408

Constitiones apostolicae (Const. Ap.)
8.6.8 406

Dionysius of Halicarnassus

Antiquitates romanae (Ant. rom)
3.25.3.........................390

De Thucydide (Thuc.)
1.22 329

Eusebius

Historia ecclesiastica (Ecclesiastical History) (Hist. eccl.)

2.14.6 137	3.39.15 .... 129, 152	6.14.5–7 130
3.4.2 .... 216, 223	3.39.14–16 182	6.14.6–7 139
3.4.6 224	3.39.14–17 120	6.14.7 263
3.24.6 189	5.8.2 183	6.15.5 130
3.36.1 263	5.20.5–6 .... 262, 271	6.25.4 183
3.39.4–5 269	6.14 283	

Herodotus

Historiae (Hist.)

3.17–20 398

Hesiod

Theogony 64

Hippolytus

Refutio omnium haeresium (Philosophoumena) (Haer.)

6.2 397	6.4–15 397

Homer

Iliad (Il.)

23.99–107 98

Odyssea (Od.)

1.22–23 398

Irenaeus

Adversus haeresis (Elenchos) (Haer.)

1.23–27 397	3.1.2 .... 130, 139	3.15.1 225
2.22.3 299	3.13.1–3 216	3.15.30–35 216
3.1.1 .... 183, 216, 262, 271	3.13.3 225	15.30–35 216

Jerome

De viris illustribus (Ver. ill.)

3 183

Commentariorum in Matthaeum libri IV (Comm. Matt.)
Prologue 183

John Chrysostom

Homiliae in Matthaeum (Hom. Matt)
1.3 140

Justin

Apologia I (1 Apol.)
1.26 397

Dialogus cum Tryphone (Dial.)
8 423   103.19 223
103.9 216   106 130

Lucian

Alexander (Pseudomantis) (Alexander the False Prophet) (Alex.)
25 406   *Bis accusatus (Bis acc.)*
38 406   29 94

De Morte Peregrini (The Passing of Perigini) (Pereg.)
11 406   13 406
12 406   16 406

Origen

Commentarium in evangelium Matthaei (Commentary on Matthew) (Comm. Matt.) 130
1 183

Ovid

Metamorphoses (Metam.)
8.626 360

Philostratus

Vita Apollonii (Life of Apollonius of Tyana) (Vit. Apoll.)
3.39 487   4.45 487   8.31 487
4.10 487   8.12 487
4.20 487   8.30 487

Pindar

Olympionikai (Olympian Odes) (Ol.)
5.17............................308

Plato

Cratylus (Crat.)
394e..........................232

Symposium (Symp.)
176b 352

Pliny the Younger

Epistulae ad Trajanum (Ep. Tra.)
10.96–97............... 75, 406

Plutarch

Alexander (Alex.)
32.5............................ 232   33.3............................390

Suetonius

Claudius
18 383   25.4 141

Domitianus (Domitian) (Dom.)
13 ....74, 303   13.2..............................63

Tiberius (Tib.)
26.1 73

Vespasianus (Vespasian) (Vesp.)
23.4 74

Tacitus

Annales (Ann.)
4.37–38 73   13.8.1 74   15.44 .... 140, 226, 406

Historiae (Hist.)
5.5 315

Tertullian

Adversus Marcionem (Marc.)
4.2.2. 216   4.5 130   4.5.3 .... 139, 216

Apologeticus (Apol.)
50 392

Theophilus

Ad Autolycum (Autol.)
2.22 261

Xenophon

Cyropaedia (Cyr.)
1.14.21 390